FINANCING URBAN SHELTER

FINANCING URBAN SHELTER

GLOBAL REPORT ON HUMAN SETTLEMENTS 2005

United Nations Human Settlements Programme

UN-HABITAT

EARTHSCAN

London and Sterling, VA

First published in the UK and USA in 2005 by Earthscan

United Nations Human Settlements Programme (UN-Habitat)
PO Box 30030, Nairobi, Kenya
Tel: +254 2 621 234
Fax: +254 2 624 266
Web: www.unhabitat.org

HS/752/05E

ISBN: 1-84407-211-8 paperback
1-84407-210-X hardback
92-1-131739-8 (UN-Habitat paperback)
92-1-131740-1 (UN-Habitat hardback)

Typesetting by MapSet Ltd, Gateshead, UK
Printed and bound in Malta by Gutenberg Press
Cover design by Susanne Harris
Index by Indexing Specialists (UK) Ltd

For a full list of publications please contact:

Earthscan
8–12 Camden High Street
London, NW1 0JH, UK
Tel: +44 (0)20 7387 8558
Fax: +44 (0)20 7387 8998
Email: earthinfo@earthscan.co.uk
Web: **www.earthscan.co.uk**

22883 Quicksilver Drive, Sterling, VA 20166-2012, USA

Earthscan is an imprint of James and James (Science Publishers) Ltd and publishes in association with the International Institute for Environment and Development

A catalogue record for this book is available from the British Library

Library of Congress Cataloging-in-Publication Data has been applied for

Printed on elemental chlorine-free paper

FOREWORD

Reaching the objectives of the Millennium Declaration agreed by all governments will require us to achieve significant improvement in the lives of slum dwellers. That, in turn, cannot be done without sound and sustainable economic development policies conducive to the establishment of a strong shelter sector. As emphasized in *Financing Urban Shelter: Global Report on Human Settlements 2005*, one of the key challenges in meeting the Millennium Declaration objective on slums is mobilizing the financial resources necessary for both slum upgrading and slum prevention by supplying new housing affordable to lower income groups on a large scale.

In response to the Millennium Declaration objective of achieving a 'significant improvement in the lives of at least 100 million slum dwellers by 2020', *The Challenge of Slums: Global Report on Human Settlements 2003* presented the results of the first global slums assessment by the United Nations. It revealed a staggering number of slum dwellers – about 924 million in 2001. The current projection is that, without concerted action by governments and their partners, the slum population will increase by slightly more than one billion in the next 25 years, to about two billion in 2030. Providing better shelter for all these will require better, more effective and sustainable financing mechanisms that truly benefit the poor.

Financing Urban Shelter: Global Report on Human Settlements 2005 provides a timely assessment of current trends in the financing of urban shelter. It examines the characteristics and performance of conventional mortgage finance, highlighting its strengths and limitations. It further looks at the financing of social and rental housing, especially through subsidies, as well as emerging trends in meeting the specific shelter finance needs of urban poor households.

The report shows that small housing loans, disbursed through housing microfinance institutions, are among the most promising developments in housing finance of the past decade. It also highlights the increasing popularity of shelter community funds for upgrading informal and slum neighbourhoods. The growth of both financing mechanisms is a highly encouraging response to the shelter needs of the urban poor, many of whom develop their housing incrementally in progressive stages.

The report also emphasizes the need for robust and efficient conventional mortgage finance institutions, especially for the middle- and upper-income groups that can afford the housing loans offered by such institutions. Experience has shown that, without sustainable mortgage financing, higher income groups often resort to appropriating for themselves shelter opportunities developed for the poor.

It is my hope that, by highlighting the impacts of current shelter financing systems on low-income households, and by identifying the types of financing mechanisms that appear to have worked for them, this report will contribute to the efforts of the wide range of actors involved in improving the lives of slum dwellers – including governments at the central and local levels, as well as non-governmental and international organizations.

Kofi A. Annan
Secretary-General
United Nations

INTRODUCTION

Financing Urban Shelter: Global Report on Human Settlements 2005 examines the challenges of financing urban shelter development, focusing on the shelter needs of the poor and within the overall context of the United Nations Millennium Development target on slums. Recent estimates indicate that more than 2 billion people will be added to the number of urban dwellers in the developing countries over the next 25 years. If adequate financial resources are not invested in the development of urban shelter and requisite services, this additional population will also be trapped in urban poverty, deplorable housing conditions, poor health and low productivity, thus further compounding the enormous slum challenge that exists today.

In many developing countries, it is unlikely that conventional sources of funds will be available for investment on the scale needed to meet the projected demand for urban infrastructure and housing. Most poorly-performing countries continue to face deficits in public budgets and weak financial sectors, and the contribution of official development assistance to the shelter sector is generally insignificant. While city authorities have started to seek finance in national and global markets, this practice is only in its infancy. The report concludes that countries and cities will have to rely mainly on the savings of their citizens.

The report shows that mortgage finance has been expanding during the last decade and is increasingly available in many countries, which was not the case 20 years ago. New mortgage providers have emerged, including commercial financial institutions and mortgage companies. However, the report emphasizes that only the middle and upper income households have access to such finance while the poor are generally excluded.

The report further highlights the continuing and necessary contribution of the public sector towards financing shelter for the urban poor, as many households, even in developed countries, cannot afford home-ownership or market rents. While social housing is becoming less important in Europe and in countries with economies in transition, the need to provide shelter that is affordable to low-income households still exists, including in developing countries.

Complete houses available through mortgage finance are well beyond the reach of the lower income groups, because they are unable to meet the deposit and income criteria set by conventional mortgage institutions. In this situation, the majority of urban poor households can only afford to build incrementally in stages, as and when financial resources become available. In response to this, microfinance institutions have started lending for low-income shelter development and have become very important in the last decade or so. The report also shows that guarantee schemes can, by providing credit enhancement, go a long way in broadening the appeal of microfinance institutions to lenders.

Another important trend in the last decade has been increasing interest in shelter community funds, which are often linked to housing cooperatives as well as rotating savings and credit societies. Community-based financing of housing and services has been used for both settlement upgrading and for building new housing on serviced sites. It has also been used to enhance the access of poor households to housing subsidies by providing bridge financing. The report concludes that, in light of the general success of small loans and the increasing urbanization of poverty, community funds have many advantages for low-income households.

Constraints to mobilizing financial resources for investment in shelter development are both financial and non-financial in nature. Non-financial constraints include land legislation that makes it difficult to use real estate as effective collateral, as well as inappropriate national and local regulatory frameworks governing land use, occupancy and ownership. In light of this, the report analyses the role of secure tenure in housing finance and highlights the need for legal and institutional reform designed to protect the rights of both lenders and borrowers as well as to enhance access to credit.

Finally, *Financing Urban Shelter: Global Report on Human Settlements 2005* emphasizes the fact that finance is only one dimension of securing sustainable solutions that can fill the gap between the two extreme outcomes of current systems and processes: affordable shelter that is inadequate; and adequate shelter that is unaffordable. The report therefore concludes that the locus of policy attention should be on both the cost of housing (the supply side) and the level of payment received by workers (the demand side). I believe that this report will help governments, local authorities and all Habitat Agenda Partners to identify opportunities for addressing the shelter affordability gap and to put in place financing mechanisms that are more able to meet the shelter needs of the urban poor.

Anna Kajumulo Tibaijuka
Under-Secretary-General and Executive Director
United Nations Human Settlements Programme (UN-Habitat)

ACKNOWLEDGEMENTS

Preparation of the Global Report series would not be possible without the dedicated assistance of eminent urban researchers, practitioners and policy-makers, whose knowledge and expertise have always been helpful in the production of this series. The current volume, departing from the findings and recommendations of the 2003 Global Report, deals with issues of the financing of urban shelter development. With the selection of this topic, the Global Report series reflects UN-Habitat's strong commitment to the goals of sustainable human settlements development, as outlined in the Habitat Agenda and Agenda 21. The Report is also guided by further decisions adopted by the Governing Council of the United Nations Human Settlements Programme and by the General Assembly of the United Nations. The Millennium Development Goals and the tasks ahead determine the overall motif and tone of this issue of the Global Report.

Financing Urban Shelter: Global Report on Human Settlements 2005 was prepared under the general guidance of Donatus Okpala, Acting Director of the Monitoring and Research Division. Naison Mutizwa-Mangiza, Chief of the Policy Analysis, Synthesis and Dialogue Branch, supervised the preparation and editing of the report, with Iouri Moisseev managing its preparation.

Members of the UN-Habitat Senior Management Board provided strategic advice in the areas of their respective responsibility at different stages in the preparation of the report. These included: Alioune Badiane, Nefise Bazoglu, Daniel Biau, Axumite Gebre-Egziabher, Jorge Gavidia, Lucia Kiwala, Madhab Mathema, Joseph Mungai, Jane Nyakairu, Lars Reutersward, Sharad Shankardass, Anathakrishnan Subramonia, Paul Taylor, Farouk Tebbal and Rolf Wichmann.

The Report benefited from a number of international meetings. Firstly, it should be mentioned that, during 2004, the Global Research Network on Human Settlements (HS-Net) was established to provide guidance in the preparation of the Global Report series. HS-Net focuses on sharing policy-orientated research results and its meetings are organized by UN-Habitat's Policy Analysis, Synthesis and Dialogue Branch. At its meeting in November 2004, HS-Net reviewed and discussed the outline and contents of the 2005 Global Report. The meeting was attended by the following experts: Marisa Carmona, Department of Urban Renewal and Management, Faculty of Architecture, Delft University of Technology, Netherlands; Suocheng Dong, Institute of Geographic Sciences and Natural Resources Research, Chinese Academy of Sciences, China; Alain Durand-Lasserve, Sociétés en Développement dans l'Espace et dans le Temps, Universite Denis Diderot, France; Jozsef Hegedüs, Metropolitan Research Institute, Varoskutatas Kft, Hungary; Paola Jiron, Housing Institute, University of Chile, Chile; Vinay Lall, Society for Development Studies, Indian Habitat Centre, India; Om Prakash Mathur, National Institute of Public Finance and Policy (IDFC), India; Diana Mitlin, Institute for Development Policy and Management (IDPM), University of Manchester, UK; Winnie Mitullah, Institute of Development Studies (IDS), University of Nairobi, Kenya; James G. Mutero, Human Settelements Consultant, Kenya; Peter Ngau, Department of Urban and Regional Planning, University of Nairobi, Kenya; Tumsifu Jonas Nnkya, Institute of Housing Studies and Building Research, University College of Lands and Architectural Studies, University of Dar es Salaam,Tanzania; Gustavo Riofrio, Centro de Estudios y Promoción del Desarrollo (DESCO), Peru; Nelson Saule, Instituto de Estudios Formacao e Assessoria em Politicas Sociais (POLIS), Brazil; Mona Serageldin, Centre for Urban Development Studies, Harvard University Graduate School of Design, US; Dina K. Shehayeb, Housing and Building Research Centre, Egypt; Richard Stren, Centre of Urban and Community Studies, University of Toronto, Canada; Riad Tabbarah, Centre for Development Studies and Projects, Lebanon; A. Graham Tipple, School of Architecture, Planning and Landscape, University of Newcastle upon Tyne, UK; Luidmila Tkachenko, Institute of Moscow City Master Plan, Russian Federation; Jose Luis Lezama de la Torre, Center for Demographic, Urban and Environmental Studies, Mexico; Vladimer Vardosanidze, Institute of Architecture, Georgia; Patrick Wakely, University College of London, Development Planning Unit, UK; Mutapha Zubairu, Centre for Human Settlements and Urban Development, Federal University of Technology, Nigeria.

The outcomes of the expert group meetings organized by UN-Habitat's Urban Economy and Finance Branch provided valuable ideas towards the conceptualization and preparation of the report. The expert group meetings were concerned with assessing the impacts of macroeconomic factors on urban growth as well as the role of microfinance in human settlements development. Some insights were also provided by the meeting of the International Union of Economists that took place in Nairobi in February 2005. The theme of the meeting was financing shelter and urban development. In particular, a major background paper prepared by V. Ivanter, O. Ptchelintsev, N. Nozdrina, M. Minchenko and E. Shcherbakova was very helpful.

Background papers and drafts of sections of the report were prepared by a number of expert urban researchers and scholars, including: Gabriella Carolini, Columbia University, US; Michael Cohen, New School University, New York, US; Pietro Garau, University of Rome, Italy; David Jones, Harvard University Graduate School of Design, US; Diana Mitlin, IDPM,

University of Manchester, UK; Elliott Sclar, Columbia University, US; Mona Serageldin, Harvard University Graduate School of Design, US; Elda Solloso, Harvard University Graduate School of Design, US; Graham Tipple, University of Newcastle upon Tyne, UK; and François Vigier, Harvard University Graduate School of Design, US. Research assistance for preparation of background papers and data analysis was provided by Shannon Bassett, Harvard University Graduate School of Design, US; Deanna Fowler, New School University, New York, US; Balakrishna Menon, Harvard University Graduate School of Design, US; and Luis Valenzuela, Harvard University Graduate School of Design, US.

The following staff members of UN-Habitat were involved in the preparation of the Statistical Annex: Iouri Moisseev, Guenter Karl, Gora Mboup and Markandey Rai. Eduardo Moreno and the staff of the Global Urban Observatory Section assisted with data analysis and checking. Philomena Fernandes assisted in data processing and preparation of the camera-ready copy of the Annex, while Phillip Mukungu provided technical assistance in data checking. Several professionals of UN-Habitat made other valued contributions. In particular, the following staff kindly gave their time amidst competing demands: Clarissa Augustinus, Selman Erguden, Yejin Ha, Inge Jensen, Uwe Lohse, Tatiana Roskoshnaya, Ananda Weliwita and Christopher Williams.

In addition, many other people, whose names are not listed here, were helpful in reviewing and commenting on drafts, making valuable contributions to the report, compiling data, preparing graphs, contributing information and in a variety of other ways. The report also benefited from consultations with colleagues in many international organizations. Finalization of the Report, its structural organization and substantive editing was carried out by Iouri Moisseev and Naison Mutizwa-Mangiza, under the overall direction of Donatus Okpala and with editorial support from Pamela Murage.

Karina Rossi and Antoine King, of UN-Habitat, as well as Josie Villamin, of the United Nations Office at Nairobi (UNON), provided administrative support during the preparation of the report. Design support was provided by Pouran Ghaffaroup and Jinita Shah. Secretarial and general administrative support was provided by Mary Kariuki, Mary Dibo, Josephine Gichuhi, Ramadhan M. Indiya, Pamela Murage, Stella Otieno and Florence Bunei of UN-Habitat.

Special thanks are due to the Governments of Germany, Italy and The Netherlands for their earmarked contributions to the United Nations Habitat and Human Settlements Foundation in support of research inputs to the Global Report series. Special thanks are also due to the staff at James & James/Earthscan, in particular Jonathan Sinclair Wilson, Publishing Director; Victoria Brown, Editor; Hamish Ironside, Production Editor; and Andrea Service, who copy-edited the report.

CONTENTS

PART I
ECONOMIC AND URBAN DEVELOPMENT CONTEXT

PART II
SHELTER FINANCE: ASSESSMENT OF TRENDS

PART III
TOWARDS SUSTAINABLE SHELTER FINANCE SYSTEMS

PART IV
STATISTICAL ANNEX

LIST OF FIGURES, BOXES AND TABLES

FIGURES

BOXES

Sources for text in boxes are attributed in notes beneath each box unless the material was originally written for this report, in which case no source is listed.

TABLES

LIST OF ACRONYMS AND ABBREVIATIONS

ABO	area-based organization
ABSA	Amalgamated Banks of South Africa
ACHR	Asian Coalition for Housing Rights
ACODEP	Asociación de Consultores para el Desarrollo de la Pequeña, Mediana y Microempresa
ADB	Asian Development Bank
ADEMI	Associación para el Desarollo de Microempresas (Dominican Republic)
AHS	American Housing Survey
AIDS	acquired immune deficiency syndrome
AIT	Asian Institute of Technology
ANC	African National Congress
ANZRSA	Australia and New Zealand Regional Science Association
APHRC	African Population and Health Research Centre
ASA	Association for Social Advancement (Bangladesh)
ASB	Anjuman Samaji Behbood (Faisalabad)
ASCUD	Asociación para la Cooperación con el Sur
ASDB	Asian Development Bank
ASDE	Alternativas Sostenibles de Desarrollo, España
ASEAN	Association of Southeast Asian Nations
AU	African Union
AusAID	Austrian Agency for International Development
BANANA	build absolutely nothing anywhere near anyone
BANSEFI	Banco del Ahorro Nacional y Servicios Financieros
BHS	Banque de l'Habitat du Sénégal
BIT	bilateral investment treaty
BOOT	build–own–operate–transfer
BOT	build–operate–transfer
BRI	Bank Rayat Indonesia
BRRI	Building and Road Research Institute (Ghana)
CBO	community-based organization
CBRI	Central Building Research Institute (India)
CDC	community development committee (Sri Lanka)
CDS	city development strategy
CER	collection efficiency rate
CGAP	Consultative Group to Assist the Poor
CIDA	Canadian International Development Agency
CIP	capital investment programme
CIS	Commonwealth of Independent States
CIUDAD	Centro de Investigaciones (Ecuador)
CLIFF	Community-led Infrastructure Financing Facility (India)
CMHC	Canada Mortgage and Housing Corporation
CMP	Community Mortgage Programme (the Philippines)
CODATU	cooperation for the continuing development of urban and suburban transportation
CODI	Community Organization Development Institute (Thailand)
COHRE	Centre on Housing Rights and Evictions (Switzerland)
Comecon	Council for Mutual Economic Aids
COPE	Community Organization of the Philippines Enterprise
CPF	Central Provident Fund (Singapore)

CPRC	Chronic Poverty Research Centre
CRESEM	Comisión para la Regulación del Uso del Suelo del Estado de México
CUDS	Center for Urban Development Studies
DAC	Development Assistance Committee (OECD)
DANIDA	Danish International Development Agency
DAU	general purpose grant (Indonesia)
DAWN	Development Alternative for Women in a New Era
DBSA	Development Bank of Southern Africa
DESCO	Centro de Escudios y Promoción del Desarrollo (centre for study and promotion of urban development, Peru)
DFI	development finance institution
DFID	Department for International Development (UK)
DGI	Direction Générale des Impots (Ministry of Finance, Côte d'Ivoire)
DHS	Demographic and Health Survey (Nairobi)
DIM	Dual Index Mortgage (Mexico)
DINKY	double income no kids yet
EBRD	European Bank for Reconstruction and Development
EC	European Commission
ECA	Economic Commission for Africa
ECE	Economic Commission for Europe
ECLAC	Economic Commission for Latin America and the Caribbean
EDSA	Epifanio de los Santos avenue (Manila)
EGM	Expert Group Meeting
EHLP	Expanded Home Lending Programme
ENHR	The European Network for Housing Research
ESCAP	Economic and Social Commission for Asia and the Pacific
ESCWA	Economic and Social Commission for Western Asia
EU	European Union
EWS	economically weaker sections (India)
Fannie Mae	Federal National Mortgage Association (US)
FAO	Food and Agriculture Organization of the United Nations
FDI	foreign direct investment
FDLG	Local Development Trust Fund (Guatemala)
FGTS	Severance Indemnity Fund for Employees (Brazil)
FHA	Federal Housing Administration (US)
FHOS	First Home Owners Scheme (Australia)
FIABCI	International Real Estate Association
FIE	Centro de Fermento a Iniciativas Economicas (Bolivian microfinance agency)
FIG	International Federation of Surveyors
FINDETER	Financiera de Desarrollo Territorial (Colombia)
FINNIDA	Finnish International Development Agency
FMCU	World Federation of United Cities
FONHAPO	Fondo Nacional de Habitaciones (Mexican National Popular Housing Fund)
FOVISSTE	Fondo de la Vivienda del Instituto de Seguridad y Servicios Sociales de los Trabajadores del Estado (Mexico)
Freddie Mac	Federal Home Loan Mortgage Corporation (US)
FUCVAM	Federación Unificadora de Cooperativas de Vivienda por Ayuda Mutua (Chile)
FUNDEVI	Urban and Rural Social Housing Development Foundation (Honduras)
FUNHAVI	Fundación Habitat y Vivienda A.C (Mexico)
FUPROVI	Foundation for Housing Promotion (Costa Rica)
FUSAI	Salvadoran Integral Assistance Foundation
GATT	General Agreement on Tariffs and Trade
GCST	Global Campaign for Secure Tenure
GCUG	Global Campaign for Urban Governance
GDI	Gender-related Development Index
GDP	gross domestic product
Ginnie Mae	Government National Mortgage Association (US)
GIS	geographical information systems
GLAD	Group Land Acquisition Support Programme (the Philippines)
GNI	gross national income
GNP	gross national product
GPI	genuine progress indicator
GSS	Global Strategy for Shelter to the Year 2000
GTZ	Gesellschaft für Technische Zusammenarbeit (German Development Agency)

GUO	Global Urban Observatory
HABRI	Housing and Building Research Institute (Kenya)
HBFC	House Building Finance Corporation (Bangladesh)
HDA	housing development authority
HDB	Housing Development Board (Singapore)
HDFC	Housing Development and Finance Corporation (India)
HDI	Human Development Index
HDMF	Home Development Mutual Fund (the Philippines)
HDR	Human Development Report
HFCK	Housing Finance Corporation of Kenya
HIPC	Heavily Indebted Poor Countries (debt initiative)
HLGC	Home Loan Guarantee Company (South Africa)
HMFI	housing microfinance institution
HRDU	Housing Research Development Unit (now HABRI)
HSD	Human Settlements Development
HUDCO	Housing and Urban Development Corporation (India)
IADB	Inter-American Development Bank
IADF	International Association of Development Funds
IDA	international development agency
IDA	International Development Association
IDP	internally displaced person
IDRC	International Development Research Centre
IEPALA	Instituto de Estudios Políticos para América Latina y Africa
IFC	International Finance Corporation
IFI	international financial institution
IFPRI	International Food Policy Research Institute
IIED	International Institute for Environment and Development
ILO	International Labour Office
ILO	International Labour Organization
IMF	International Monetary Fund
INFONAVIT	Instituto del Fondo Nacional de la Vivienda para los Trabajadores (Mexico)
IRGLUS	International Research Group on Law and Urban Space
ISD	informal subdivisions of state land (Pakistan)
ISIC	International Standard Industrial Classification
ISSC	International Social Science Council
ITDG	Intermediate Technology Development Group
IULA	International Union of Local Authorities
KATE	Centre for Ecology and Development
KERN	Knowledge and Expertise Resource Network
KIP	(Comprehensive) Kampung Improvement Programme (Indonesia)
LAC	Latin America and the Caribbean
LDA	land development agency
LDC	least developed country
LDR	less developed region
LEARN	Link Environmental and Academic Research Network
LLDC	landlocked developing country
LMI	low and moderate income
LTAP	Land Tenurial Assistance Programme (the Philippines)
LTV	loan-to-value ratio
MBS	mortgage-backed security
MDA	Millennium Development Agenda
MDF	municipal development fund
MDG	Millennium Development Goal
MDP	Municipal Development Programme
MDR	more developed region
MELISSA	Managing the Environment Locally in Sub-Saharan Africa
MFI	microfinance institution
MFRC	Microfinance Regulatory Council
MHT	Gujarat Mahila Housing SEWA Trust (India)
MI	mortgage insurance
MOST	Management of Social Transformations (UNESCO)
MPP	Municipality of Phnom Penh

MSE	micro- and small-scale enterprise
N-AERUS	Network Association of European Researchers on Urbanization in the South
NACHU	National Housing Co-operative Union (Kenya)
NAFTA	North American Free Trade Agreement
NAHECO	Nakuru Housing and Environment Co-operative (Kenya)
NATO	North Atlantic Treaty Organization
NAVIKU	Nairobi Vikundi vya Kujisaidia (self-help group, Kenya)
NCC	Nairobi City Council
NESDB	National Economic and Social Development Board (Thailand)
NGC	National Government Centre (the Philippines)
NGCHC	National Government Centre Housing Committee (the Philippines)
NGO	non-governmental organization
NHA	National Housing Authority (Zambia)
NHDA	National Housing Development Authority (Sri Lanka)
NHFC	National Housing Finance Corporation (South Africa)
NIC	newly industrialized country
NIMBY	not in my backyard
NMV	non-motorized vehicle
NORAD	Norwegian Agency for International Development
NSDF	National Slum Dwellers Federation (India)
NSS	National Statistical Survey (India)
NURCHA	National Urban Reconstruction and Housing Agency (South Africa)
NUREC	Network on Urban Research in the European Union
NYCHA	New York City Housing Authority
NZ	New Zealand
OA	official aid
ODA	official development assistance
OECD	Organisation for Economic Co-operation and Development
OHCHR	Office of the United Nations High Commissioner for Human Rights
OPIC	Overseas Private Investment Corporation (South Africa)
OUP	Office of University Partnerships
PAAC	Programa de Auto Ajuda e sistenciana Casa (programme of self-help for housing, Brazil)
PANA	participatory appraisal and needs assessment
PB	participatory budgeting
PHASE	People's Housing Alternative for Social Empowerment (the Philippines)
PHI	Presidential Housing Initiative (Zambia)
PKSF	Palli Karma-Sahayak Foundation (Bangladesh)
PPP	purchasing power parity
PPPUE	Public–Private Partnerships for the Urban Environment (UNDP)
PRODEL	Programa de Desarollo Local (Local Development Programme, Nicaragua)
PROSAVI	Programa Especial de Crédito y Subsidios a la Vivienda (the special programme for housing loans and subsidies, Mexico)
PROSPECT	Programme of Support for Poverty Elimination and Community Transformation
PRS	poverty reduction strategy
PRSP	poverty reduction strategy paper
PSH	Programme for Social Housing (Brazil)
PUSH	Project Urban Self-help (Zambia)
RDC	residential development committee (PUSH)
RDP	Reconstruction and Development Programme (South Africa)
RHLF	Rural Housing Loan Fund (South Africa)
ROSCA	rotating savings and credit association
SAP	structural adjustment programme
SDC	Swiss Development Cooperation
SDI	Shack/Slum Dwellers International
SELAVIP	Servicio Latinoamericano y Asiatico de Vivienda Popular (Latin American and Asian low income housing service)
SEWA	Self-employed Women's Association (India)
SFNV	National Housing Financing System (Costa Rica)
SHF	Federal Mortgage Bank (Sociedad Hipotecaria Federal, Mexico)
SHI	Sustainable Homes Initiative
SIDA	Swedish International Development Agency
SIDS	small island developing states

SIV	Housing Incentive System (Ecuador)
SNA	System of National Accounts
SODECI	Société de Distribution d'Eau de Côte d'Ivoire
SOFOLES	Sociedad Finaciera de Objeto Limitado (Mexico)
SPARC	Society for the Promotion of Area Resource Centres (Mumbai)
SPV	special purpose vehicle (China)
SSE	small-scale enterprise
STDP	Small Town Development Programme
SUPF	Squatter and Urban Poor Federation (Cambodia)
TFYR	The former Yugoslav Republic
TNC	transnational corporations
TNUDF	Tamil Nadu Urban Development Fund (India)
TUHF	Trust for Urban Housing Finance (South Africa)
UCSF	Urban Community Support Fund (Nepal)
UCDF	Urban Community Development Fund (Thailand)
UCDO	Urban Community Development Office (Thailand; now CODI)
UCLG	United Cities and Local Governments
UDIC	Shanghai Urban Development Investment Corporation
UEMOA	West African Economic and Monetary Union
UHLP	Unified Home Lending Programme (the Philippines)
UK	United Kingdom
UMP	Urban Management Programme (UN-Habitat, World Bank and UNDP)
UNCED	United Nations Conference on Environment and Development
UNCHR	United Nations Commission on Human Rights
UNCHS	United Nations Centre for Human Settlements (Habitat) (now UN-Habitat)
UNCTAD	United Nations Conference on Trade and Development
UNDG	United Nations Development Group
UNDP	United Nations Development Programme
UNEP	United Nations Environment Programme
UNESCO	United Nations Educational, Scientific and Cultural Organization
UNFPA	United Nations Population Fund
UNGA	United Nations General Assembly
UN-Habitat	United Nations Human Settlements Programme (formerly UNCHS (Habitat))
UNHCR	United Nations High Commissioner for Refugees
UNHRP	United Nations Housing Rights Programme
UNICEF	United Nations International Children's Fund
UNIFEM	United Nations Development Fund for Women
UNON	United Nations Office at Nairobi
UNRISD	United Nations Research Institute for Social Development
US	United States
USAID	US Agency for International Development
UTO	United Towns Organization
UVA	Union of African Towns
VA	Veterans Administration
VAMBAY	Valmiki Ambedkar Yojna (subsidy scheme for housing the urban poor in India)
VAT	value added tax
VHC	Viviendas Hogar de Cristo (Chile)
WACLAC	World Assembly of Cities and Local Authorities Coordinators
WCED	World Commission for Environment and Development
WEOG	Western European and Other States Group
WMO	World Meteorological Organization
WOCSOC	World Civil Society Conference
WTO	World Trade Organization
ZNBS	Zambia National Building Society
ZNPF	Zambia National Provident Fund
ZSIC	Zambia State Insurance Corporation

KEY ISSUES, FINDINGS AND MESSAGES

Financing shelter is an important component within development policy frameworks intended to secure environmental sustainability, economic prosperity, cultural diversity and social equality. *Financing Urban Shelter: Global Report on Human Settlements 2005* examines recent shelter finance trends and driving forces. It also explores policies and strategies that hold the promise of making shelter development truly sustainable, in the process filling the gap between the two extreme outcomes of current shelter systems that are being witnessed today: affordable shelter that is inadequate, and adequate shelter that is unaffordable.

In the next 20 years, there is little likelihood that in many developing countries conventional sources of funds will be available for investment on the scale needed to meet the projected demand for urban infrastructure and housing. Many countries around the world continue to face deficits in public budgets and weak financial sectors. Local governments have started to seek finance in national and global markets, but this is only in its initial phase. Countries and cities, therefore, will have to rely on the savings of their citizens.

With the exception of East Asia, most developing country regions have not experienced sustained, positive growth over the past two decades. Africa has continued to suffer the most, with at best uneven growth in a few countries. Most sub-Saharan states have continued to deteriorate, thus failing to provide needed urban employment and incomes. Latin America has also been quite disappointing, as the promised neo-liberal reforms have failed to deliver the promised patterns of sustained growth. In general, the upper end of the income distribution has benefited from the new patterns of economic growth in the age of globalization. While in some countries there is evidence of a new middle class, particularly in China and India, the middle class has actually disappeared in other countries, joining the poor in the absence of 'living wages'.

Despite considerable effort to encourage urban and infrastructure policy reform and capacity-building in the developing countries, there is little evidence of any sustained large-scale impact. In general, national economic authorities have been preoccupied with macrostability, debt and trade and have tended to neglect implementation of needed policy and institutional reforms in the urban sector, with a few exceptions such as India, China, and richer developing countries such as the Republic of Korea, Thailand and Mexico.

Against this background, the key issues and messages emerging from this report are presented below, starting with broader contextual issues, followed by those issues more specific to shelter finance, including: conventional mortgage finance; subsidies and financing of social housing; shelter microfinance; and shelter community funds.

BROADER CONTEXTUAL ISSUES

The problem in many developing and even in some developed countries is not that housing is too expensive, but that incomes are too low. It is clear that an efficient housing finance system is a necessary but not a sufficient condition for the development of sustainable urban shelter and that improving the access of poor households to adequate shelter has two further requirements: reducing housing production and delivery costs and increasing income levels. The locus of attention should therefore be on both the cost of housing and the level of payment received by workers. This demand-side focus is in line with current trends in subsidies and concentrates attention on the systemic problem of poverty, which is the underlying source of poor shelter conditions.

In processing housing loans, lenders should take into account future income generated, directly and indirectly, from house improvement. There is a well-documented link between finance for income generation and improvements in housing. Many homeowners operate one or more home-based enterprises from the structure on which they raise housing finance. The same goes for rental income. One of the most important sources of low-cost rental property, which is becoming more important as the years pass, is the extra room built on to a home and rented out to a stranger for rent, or to a co-villager or relative for no rent but some other benefit (if only to satisfy family obligations). It is obvious that improvements in housing can benefit home-based income generation, including room rentals. Thus, lenders should take account of the likelihood of income improvements in the application procedure, through a process which factors in future income generated by the housing goods to be provided under the loan.

The cost of urban housing can be reduced by the adoption of more appropriate standards. In many countries in the South, the cost of urban housing is increased significantly by the high standards to which it must comply. The introduction of lower standards that are more appropriate to the local context could potentially make housing more affordable to a far greater proportion of the urban population. Lower standards would still, however, have to safeguard the health and safety of the occupants and protect the public interest.

There is much to be gained from encouraging multi-occupied housing development where it fits in with local norms. Most national shelter policies, some of them supported by official development assistance, are based on the provision of independently serviced, single household dwellings, owned by their occupants. However, this is by no means the main form of occupation by households living in poverty. Instead, large numbers of households live in buildings occupied by many households.

Financing schemes to assist small-scale landlords, in the context of informal settlement upgrading, are necessary. Small-scale landlords in informal settlements are a major source of affordable housing for a growing majority of households living in poverty in the towns and cities of developing countries, but there are few initiatives to assist them. It is imperative, therefore, to understand how best to assist the informal rental sector within informal settlement and slum upgrading programmes, and at the same time preserve affordability so as to preclude gentrification.

Finance to provide healthy liquidity among small-scale contractors and single artisans is an essential prerequisite to effective housing supply to scale. In the spirit of the Habitat Agenda, and if the current massive housing backlog is to be cleared at all, it is vital that all actors in the housing process are involved in the role in which they are most efficient. The most important suppliers of dwellings for urban low-income communities, and their ancillary services, are the millions of small-scale building contractors, the single artisans or small groups of skilled people and the labourers who service their needs. However much demand there is for housing, it can only be supplied as quickly as the construction industry can build it.

In developing countries, large-scale developers of both private rental housing and housing for sale to owner occupiers need financing systems capable of providing bridging loans. In countries where the housing supply system is efficient and speculative of what the market demands, developers are often an important part of the process. Some mechanism for recognizing their contribution with financial assistance, especially for bridging loans, may be very beneficial for the housing supply process in developing countries and could institute the efficient speculative building of housing which is common in developed economies.

Domestic savings play a crucial role in the development of robust and effective shelter finance systems. The countries in which most of the urban growth will take place in the next 20 years have very low domestic savings measured as both per capita and as a percentage of gross domestic product (GDP). As savings are the foundations for investment, this does not auger well for urban shelter development. It is important that developing countries maintain as much of the investment and savings arising from local economic activity within their borders, or benefit from net inflows from investments overseas. The importance of reliable banks and low inflation in discouraging capital flight cannot be overemphasized

CONVENTIONAL MORTGAGE FINANCE

In recent decades, governments have generally sought to encourage homeownership and have, in many cases, provided preferential financing to influence consumer choice. There has been a general shift towards market-based mechanisms for the provision of housing, with attempts to reduce subsidies and deregulate markets. In part, this is due to the past ineffectiveness of housing strategies that depended on direct provision by the state. This trend is also consistent with the overall direction of macroeconomic strategies in recent decades.

Mortgage finance has been expanding during the last decade and is increasingly available in many countries. Many developing countries now have access to market rate housing finance, which was not the case 20 years ago. New mortgage providers include commercial financial institutions, or in some cases, mortgage companies. However, only the middle- and upper-income households have access to such finance while the poor, especially in developing countries and countries with economies in transition, are largely excluded.

It is in the interest of governments to extend mortgage markets down the income scale, as homeownership is beneficial economically, socially and politically. Measures that have been adopted by some countries, and could be emulated by others, include: reducing the cost of lending, especially through reduction of interest rates; supporting the system of mortgage financing, especially through extension of secondary markets and reduction of risk; and providing direct capital grants to reduce the size of the households' mortgage in comparison with the dwelling cost.

Loan periods and loan-to-value ratios are vital components of mortgage loans that have important access implications, especially for the urban poor. These are determined by the lender rather than the global macro-economic environment. Decisions about them can be the difference between success and failure of the mortgage company and determine who can afford to borrow, at least at the margins. Low loan-to-value ratios (and, therefore, high initial deposits) reduce risk but increase the need for upfront capital. The level of repayments can be varied to help households meet their obligations. Adoption of variable-interest loans allows low payments at the beginning, increasing as income improves to repay the loan on time.

Well-run mortgage facilities are undoubtedly important to the health of the housing supply systems, although they generally fail to reach the poor. Conventional mortgage facilities constitute the dominant means of shelter financing in developed countries and may be a major contributor to housing improvement in countries with economies in transition. They are also important in providing upper- and middle-income groups in developing country cities with housing finance, without which they would claim the shelter opportunities provided for those lower down the income scale. However, as mortgage finance is unlikely to assist the majority of the people, it must not be allowed to divert attention from financing helpful to lower-income groups, or to drain resources away from low-income households towards those in the middle- or upper-income groups.

SUBSIDIES AND FINANCING OF SOCIAL HOUSING

Three specific trends with respect to social housing that are consistent with privatization and deregulation are well established in a number of countries:

1. governments have shifted away from the direct construction and management of public housing and have used several strategies to reduce their stocks, with large-scale transfers to occupiers in some cases;
2. there is increasing assistance for homeownership through direct demand (capital) subsidies; and
3. consistent with the two trends above is the greater use of housing allowances (rather than direct provision) to assist low-income families renting accommodation in the private or non-profit sectors. Despite their focus on lower income households, direct subsidies are often smaller in scale than interest rate subsidies when the full costs of the latter over the life of the loan are considered.

Those who cannot afford homeownership or market rents in the private market need shelter through public rental housing. Social housing is, almost by definition, subsidized housing. The subsidy element is a financial credit to the occupier and, thus, often constitutes an important element in a nation's housing finance system. Although social housing is becoming residual in Europe and in countries with economies in transition, the need to provide more housing that is affordable to low-income households is still present.

While subsidies are necessary for deserving low-income groups, the need for them can be reduced by adopting effective shelter-financing systems. At present, subsidies come in many guises, including: direct interest rate reductions; allowing mortgage interest payments to be deducted from income tax; supporting housing-related savings; supporting insurance of mortgages; supporting the secondary mortgage markets; and direct grants for shelter (or capital grant subsidies). If appropriate housing finance is in place, the proportion of households requiring subsidy should be minimized, i.e. to only those too poor to afford the real cost of the shelter available. The need for subsidy can, thus, be reduced by adopting effective financing systems. The work of some non-governmental organizations in providing funding to help individual households attract a subsidy is very helpful. In some countries, revolving funds that provide the down payment necessary to obtain a national housing subsidy grant have been very effective.

SHELTER MICROFINANCE

The majority of urban poor households can only afford to build incrementally in stages as financial resources become available. These stages may be separated by many months, or even years. In new building, this is usually implemented a room or a few rooms at a time but it may, less commonly, occur in construction stages, i.e., all the foundations, followed by all the walls, etc. Complete houses available through mortgage finance are far too expensive for the poor and they are unable to meet the deposit and income criteria set by mortgage institutions. It is therefore imperative that national and international institutions recognize that low-income people build incrementally and provide microfinance suitable for that process. This may also call for reform of building regulations that often do not allow incremental building of formally recognized dwellings.

Short-term, small-scale loans of one to eight years and in amounts of US$500 to 5000, are more useful for incremental development than the long term, large value loans favoured by the mortgage markets. Improvements and efficiency gains possible through incremental building with small loans, rather than with savings, include: greater likelihood of building well (though small) immediately and avoiding high annual maintenance costs arising from poor construction; avoidance of the wasteful process of improvising a dwelling in temporary materials and then discarding them as they are replaced with permanent materials; and reducing the age at which a householder can afford to be an owner, as stages do not have to await money being saved but can be paid for in arrears.

Small housing loans, disbursed through housing microfinance institutions, are some of the most promising developments in housing finance during the last decade. They are suitable for extending existing dwellings, building on already serviced land, adding rooms (often for renting out), adding facilities such as toilets and house improvements within *in situ* neighbourhood or slum upgrading. They tend to reach much further down the income scale than mortgage financing, but not to the households close to or below poverty lines. Experience shows that there is great demand for microfinance even if interest rates are high.

In the context of large numbers of new low-income households in cities over the next two decades, it is important to increase the number of lenders in the housing microfinance sector rather than concentrate only on mortgage finance. Mortgage finance inevitably serves the middle- and upper-income groups, while generally excluding the poor. However, there is a serious issue of funding for on-lending by microfinance institutions. Many have received concessionary funds and their lending reflects the low price of the capital. If they are to expand their operations, they may have to borrow at international market rates and reflect this in their loans.

Guarantees are important in broadening the appeal of microfinance institutions to lenders. Microfinance institutions continually look for ways of reducing their risks, even though the lowest-income groups tend to be assiduous at repayment. The establishment of formal guarantee organizations is an important prerequisite to lending in many circumstances. Governments have much to gain from setting up guarantee funds to allow microfinance institutions to lend to low-income households at reduced risk. In addition, development assistance should be directed towards guarantee funds in order to capture their full value as catalysts for shelter development for the urban low-income groups.

COMMUNITY-BASED SHELTER FUNDS

Another significant trend in the last decade has been increasing interest in shelter community funds group loans. The growth of these funds has partly arisen from a general acknowledgement that small-scale lending has been somewhat successful and that the urbanization of poverty is a growing challenge. Two further current trends related to the development of shelter community funds are: first, the growing interest by local government in the possibility of using such funds to extend essential infrastructure; and, second, the expansion of Shack or Slum Dwellers International (SDI), a community/NGO network whose strategies incorporate savings and lending activities for shelter improvements.

Community-based financing of housing and services has been used for both settlement upgrading and for building on greenfield sites, and, in a context where small loans are evidently successful and where there is an increase in poverty, it has many advantages for low-income and otherwise disempowered households. It provides the benefits of scale – strength in lobbying, ability to affect neighbourhoods comprehensively rather than just single dwellings, ability to raise capital funding – and it builds the cohesion of the community because its members act together. It takes strength from the willingness of people to work together as communities through a variety of self-help cooperation traditions. The experience of the affiliates of the Shack or Slum Dwellers' Federation (SDI) has demonstrated that there is great potential for community-based organizations to manage development finance to the benefit of large numbers of relatively poor households. The evident success of community funds has attracted some governments to take part in their financing. However, there are issues about how far non-members of such community groups are excluded by the activities of groups who so successfully lay claim to limited resources.

MDG SPECIAL FEATURE: FINANCING THE TARGET ON SLUMS[1]

MILLENNIUM DEVELOPMENT GOALS AND THE TARGET ON SLUMS

The history of cities is the history of civilization. For centuries, migrants have sought improved lives for themselves and their families in increasingly dense urban landscapes. Cities represent the greatest hopes of every age. The hope widens, falls and re-emerges in new form through the social interactions that define the fabric of urban society. In 2007, and for the first time in human history, the world's urban population will exceed its rural population. Are the world's urban centres ready for this monumental shift?

The *Global Report on Human Settlements 2005* focuses on broadening our understanding of the complex financial foundation lying at the heart of this growing urban challenge. The report critically asks and answers, with examples, the question of how the costs of growing demographic pressures across different regions of the world will be met. It is known that roughly one out of every six people live in what can be characterized as 'slums' in small and large cities alike. Thus far, it has been relatively easy to ignore the woefully inadequate living conditions which this statistic implies by assuming that city life necessarily equates with improved life. Although the aspirations of urban dwellers flow in that direction, the reality on the ground has often proven quite different. Ill-conceived and mismanaged policies and beliefs have too often translated into the pricing-out of affordable and humanely adequate housing in accessible urban areas. Worse yet, in misdirected efforts to erase this market failure, forced evictions dominated policy responses for decades. This was done despite the fact that the population of the urban poor never disappeared. Instead, the population of the urban poor and their informal settlements continued to grow in depth and scale.

In the face of such adversities, the urban poor have emerged with creative solutions. 'Slums' are often a solution in progress – a gradual realization of the abiding hope to make a home in the city and create a better life. This has been recognized by international organizations in declarations and policy agendas over the past two decades. And, increasingly, both local and national governments have awakened to the promise of building better cities and nations through partnerships with the urban poor.

It was in this context that the United Nations Millennium Assembly of 2000 highlighted the need to improve the lives of the urban poor through the inclusion of a 'slums target' in the Millennium Declaration. This goal – 'by 2020, to have achieved a significant improvement in the lives of at least 100 million slum dwellers, as proposed in the Cities without Slums Initiative' – was later subsumed as Target 11 of Millennium Development Goal (MDG) 7, that of environmental sustainability. The United Nations Millennium Project, commissioned by Secretary-General Kofi Annan, was charged with establishing groups of experts and practitioners from around the world, organized in ten thematic task forces, to make recommendations on how to achieve the MDGs and their targets. The work of Task Force 8 was to address the 'slum' target.

From the beginning, it was evident to the task force that addressing Target 11, as the slum target is described in the MDGs, in essence meant not only improving the lives of an existing 100 million slum dwellers, but also creating alternatives to slums for the future urban poor. Furthermore, it became apparent that the key to achieving Target 11 and leveraging the development potential of cities to the benefit of all was the networking and coordination of the activities of interested actors and relevant parties, placing the urban poor at the centre of this process.

It is not surprising, then, that the task force's report highlights an investment model for upgrading today's slums and planning alternatives for tomorrow that assumes the active participation and commitment of the urban poor themselves, in partnership with the more usual actors: local and national governments, as well as international organizations. Too often, the Millennium Project's central message is misinterpreted as merely securing more foreign aid alone. In fact, the Millennium Project's main message and central theme is quite different – it is that the Millennium Development Goals are *achievable*, that even as one reads this report, a diversity of activities undertaken by the poor themselves are moving forward towards the realization of the MDGs, and that what is needed is acknowledgement, support for and coordination of this work – at every level. This reality of achievement is evident in slums, as is amply documented in *A Home in the City*, Task Force 8's report.[2] The urban poor, often in partnership with local authorities and with the support of international organizations and donors, are improving their own living conditions every day. But these successes remain relatively piecemeal. The challenge at present is to elevate such successes to scale and in a sustainable fashion.

Realigning Target 11

Task Force 8's report, *A Home in the City*, highlights two distinct and necessarily related routes to achieving the scale and sustainability of Target 11 – that of slum upgrading today and urban planning for tomorrow. These dual tasks reflect the original intention of the Cities without Slums Action Plan, which informed the United Nations Secretary-General's 2000 report *We, the Peoples*.[3] The action plan itself specifically called on governments to:

- Start with the mobilization of political and financial commitment to slum upgrading and gear up the capacity to support large-scale actions.
- Initiate 20 citywide and nationwide programmes in five regions to change the lives of 5 million urban poor.
- Upscale the approach over the 2006–2020 period with 50 national programmes, with slum improvement as a central element of urban development strategies in most countries, resulting in the provision of basic services to 100 million slum dwellers *and slum formation stopped* (emphasis added).

Part of this last phase – the move to provide basic services to 100 million slum dwellers – was incorporated by the United Nations General Assembly (UNGA) as a target under the MDGs, given its quantifiable nature. However, the Millennium Declaration's language leaves no doubt that the target was to incorporate all phases of the Cities without Slums Action Plan, including putting an end to new slum formation. Consequently, Task Force 8 realigned this quantifiable target with its original partner – that of 'slum formation stopped' – in its approach to effectively address the intent of Target 11. In the task force's interpretation, Target 11 is properly understood as: 'By 2020, improving substantially the lives of at least 100 million slum dwellers, while providing adequate alternatives to new slum formation'.[4]

In this interpretation, the task force refrained from the use of 'stopping slum formation' to avoid any confusion regarding its position against forced evictions. This interpretation is also fully consistent with the other targets of the MDGs, which call for a halving of identified poverty challenges. Using recent estimated and projected slum population figures, Task Force 8's interpretation of Target 11 calls for halving the number of the slum population to be expected in the world by 2020 if no remedial action is taken.[5] A calculation exercise shows that the currently projected number of slum dwellers in 2020 (1.6 billion people), if no action is taken, would be halved through both the improvement of 100 million current slum dwellers' lives, as well as the projected creation of alternatives for future urban poor residents, thus aligning Target 11 with other MDG targets.

Why is this realignment of Target 11 necessary? As mentioned earlier, by 2007 the world's urban residents will, for the first time, represent the majority of the world's population. Roughly 80 per cent of urban residents in the lowest-income countries already live in slum conditions. Given the projected demographic trends, this population of slum dwellers is expected to double by 2030 if alternatives to slums are not developed today.[6] In short, improving the lives of 100 million slum dwellers alone is not ambitious enough to sustainably and significantly alleviate poverty in urban centres. In realigning Target 11 with the original intention of its foundation in the Cities without Slums Action Plan, Task Force 8 recognizes that Target 11 is a *moving target*, and that achieving the MDGs at the city level – and, most specifically, where the urban poor are concerned – will require an equally dynamic solution. This latter call is one for effectively planning accessible, affordable and adequate housing and urban services for the low-income urban residents of tomorrow.

The proposed path takes a relatively innovative, yet obvious, approach to urban development – one which embraces the historic reality of the urbanization trend. In short, it is a strategy to recognize the great macro- and micro-potentials of urbanization, while also ensuring that its challenges are adequately addressed. It is important to emphasize that urbanization at scale is a positive, and not a negative, reality, although some policy-makers continue to believe that stemming this trend ought to be the focus of global economic development. However, history has already shown that attempts to curtail urbanization are always both unsuccessful and undesirable. The struggle between misconceived development policies and well-established migration patterns has proven destructive and disruptive, both in physical and non-physical terms, at the household, local, regional and national levels. The most prosperous nations in the world are the most urbanized ones. Moreover, urbanization brings with it significant development benefits for both urban centres and rural areas. These synergistic linkages between urban and rural are important and acknowledged in Task Force 8's report. In fact, there is a

Figure P.1

Urbanization and income levels

Source: UN Millennium Project, 2005a, p14.

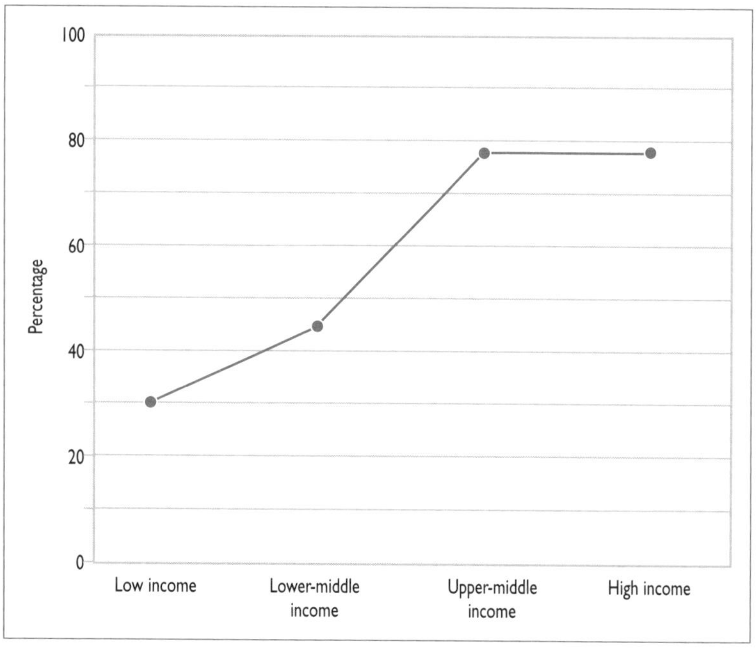

clear correlation between levels of urbanization and national income levels, as Figure P.1 shows.

The real challenge is not the trade-off between urban and rural development; rather, it is channelling the benefits of development in a socially equitable fashion. This is the reason why meeting Target 11 is so critical. But is meeting Target 11 in Task Force 8's interpretation realizable – financially *and* politically? The answer is yes. To answer in any other way would mean ignoring the reality of what is now taking place at the urban level, as well as the political momentum building in support of the MDGs worldwide. While it is crucial that Target 11's financial outlook is seen within the greater context of financing the MDGs overall, the specific components of the investment model developed by Task Force 8 to achieve Target 11 is revealing of how movement towards this target is already under way. Most notably, while achieving the MDGs overall will require significant contributions from donors – contributions which, in fact, have already been promised – it is of interest that the Target 11 component of the overall financing of the MDGs is largely based on domestic capital. This is the case both in upgrading slums today and in planning alternatives for tomorrow.

MODELLING INVESTMENT IN SLUM UPGRADING AND PROVIDING ADEQUATE ALTERNATIVES

As already acknowledged, residents in informal settlements and slums are already making significant investments to upgrade their housing and communities – particularly when tenure is secure. Therefore, in preparing its model of upgrading and planning, Task Force 8 considered known examples of existing upgrading programmes across regions, and focused particularly on three successful large-scale programmes in Central America for which detailed data was available over a period of more than ten years.

In addition, the task force's model was built on the working estimates of upgrading costs and identifying interventions in the most recent authoritative studies. These studies included the Cities without Slums Initiative of the Cities Alliance, the 2003 *Global Report on Human Settlements*,[7] the need-assessment studies of Ghana, Tanzania and Uganda prepared by the United Nations Millennium Project, as well as a special investment modelling report requested by the task force and commissioned by UN-Habitat (United Nations Human Settlements Programme). In addition, the task force referred to a number of sector-specific studies to estimate the costs of interventions, such as those required for community schooling and health services.

The task force combined estimations of demand for regularization and upgrading based on UN-Habitat's 2001 estimation of slum dwellers, with programme examples and expert studies to derive its own estimations regarding which interventions to include and which to exclude from its model. The Task Force 8 investment model included five overall components:

1. land;
2. physical improvements to the housing stock;
3. basic physical infrastructure (water, sanitation, drainage, road paving, electricity);
4. basic community services (schools and clinics); and
5. security of tenure.

The five components of the model all require human, infrastructural and financial resources which clearly vary with context. For this reason, the aim of the task force was not to treat the model as an exact estimation, but as an opportunity to demonstrate – using data from existing programmes – the range of investment costs required to upgrade slums and to plan for alternatives. The resulting estimates show the significance of cost ranges across regions, largely due to differences in the cost of labour and land.

Upgrading

More specifically, within the five overall components, the task force identified and estimated the investments required for the following eight interventions in its upgrading-specific model:

1. construction of basic housing;
2. purchase of land or transfer;
3. relocation (if necessary);
4. provision of networked infrastructure;
5. provision of bulk infrastructure (calculated as 30 per cent of the value of networked infrastructure);
6. construction of schools and clinics;
7. construction of community facilities; and
8. planning and oversight.

In addition, recognizing the importance of human resources available to manage the above interventions, the task force also included a final component in its upgrading model – that of capacity-building, which was calculated as 10 per cent of the overall costs of the eight components identified above. The estimates are presented in Table P.1.

In total, the estimates below translate into US$4.2 billion per year, or roughly US$42 per beneficiary per year, given the target to improve the lives of an existing 100 million slum dwellers between 2005 and 2020. These figures were partially based on the costing estimates for interventions proposed in the report commissioned for Task Force 8,[8] and were further adjusted by the task force on the basis of the estimated costs of each intervention component identified in the studies of three Central American programmes mentioned earlier.

Table P.1

Per capita investment requirements (US$) to upgrade slums between 2005 and 2020 (provisional estimates by region)

Arab States, Turkey and Iran	Asia (including East China) and Oceania	Latin America and the Caribbean	South-central Asia	Southeast Asia	Sub-Saharan Africa, Egypt and Sudan
1328	619	1200	612	643	528

Source: UN Millennium Project, 2005a, p128.

East Asia	Latin America and the Caribbean	North Africa	Oceania	South-central Asia	Southeast Asia	Sub-Saharan Africa	Western Asia
334	780	829	334	285	363	352	829

Source: UN Millennium Project, 2005a, p138.

Table P.2

Per capita investment requirements (US$) for alternatives to slum formation (provisional estimates by region)

Adequate alternatives to new slum formation

In order to develop a model of investment required to create alternatives to the formation of new slums between 2005 and 2020, Task Force 8 first estimated the costs of the five aforementioned components (land, housing, physical infrastructure, community services and tenure) across the three large-scale Central American examples. The examples, drawn from El Salvador, Honduras and Nicaragua, indicated that an investment of roughly US$600 per person is needed to provide alternatives to slums for future low-income urban residents.[9] By using this overall average estimate (and its component costs) from the Central American experience and the assumption that different housing options could be developed based on residents' capacities, the global estimates for a typical new settlement were calculated, also based on an adjustment of regional figures and interventions proposed in the report commissioned by UN-Habitat for Task Force 8.[10] The new settlement model was assumed to be for approximately 2500 new low-income residents, or 500 households, and as in the case of upgrading, the task force's model demonstrated significant regional variance in investments required, as shown in Table P.2.

Table P.3

Envisaged sources of funding for slum upgrading, 2005–2020 (US$ billion, by region)

Funding Source	Sub-Saharan Africa, Egypt and Sudan	Arab States, Turkey and Iran	South-central Asia	Southeast Asia	China, rest of East Asia and Oceania	Latin America and the Caribbean	Total
Subsidies	9.8	3.2	11.0	2.7	7.4	5.8	39.9
Loans	4.9	1.6	5.5	1.4	3.7	2.9	20.0
Savings and self-help	1.6	0.5	1.8	0.5	1.2	1.0	6.7
Total cost	16.4	5.3	18.3	4.5	12.4	9.6	66.5

Source: UN Millennium Project, 2005a, p129.

The average regional estimates of resources required for alternatives to slum formation presented in Table P.2 were based on the conservative demand assumption of another 570 million people between 2005 and 2020, reflecting UN-Habitat's slum population projections.[11] In aggregate form, the global total required amounts of roughly US$14 billion per year from 2005–2020, or roughly US$25 per person per year to provide adequate alternatives to new slum formation. This estimate is lower than the one calculated for slum upgrading. Furthermore, it confirms empirical observations suggesting that it is less costly to plan new affordable housing solutions than to regularize and upgrade existing slums – one more argument in favour of planning ahead of informal urban development.

Table P.4

Assessment of funding sources for adequate alternatives to new slum formation, 2005–2020 (US$ billion, by region)

Funding Source	North Africa	Sub-Saharan Africa	Latin America and the Caribbean	East Asia	South-central Asia	South-east Asia	Western Asia	Oceania	Total
Subsidies	8.58	33.6	21.6	22.8	29.46	8.22	11.52	0.1	135.9
Loans	4.29	16.8	10.8	11.4	14.73	4.11	5.76	0.05	67.9
Savings and self-help	1.43	5.6	3.6	3.8	4.91	1.37	1.92	0.02	22.7
Total cost	14.3	56	36	38	49.1	13.7	19.2	0.17	226.5

Source: UN Millennium Project, 2005a, p141.

MOBILIZING FINANCIAL RESOURCES

The upgrading and planning models highlighted in the previous section indicate that Target 11, in its full original intent, can be achieved with an average investment of approximately US$294 billion or US$440 per person over the period of 2005–2020. Such an investment would touch the lives of roughly 670 million poor residents of urban centres. This is not an unrealizable amount. It is already known that the urban poor significantly contribute to housing and settlement upgrading. Thus, the call here is to mobilize national, international and private-sector financial support for such efforts that are already under way and for scaling up the example of urban poor-led upgrading. Tables P.3 and P.4 project across regions the types of funding Task Force 8 envisioned as the resource base for its upgrading and planning models – namely, via subsidies, loans and savings/self-help financing.

In considering the subsidies, loans and personal household contributions necessary for both upgrading and planning alternatives, Task Force 8 formulated the following distribution model of responsibility:

- 30 per cent of investment needs could be secured through small loans to participating households.
- 10 per cent of required funds would be contributed by beneficiaries themselves.
- 60 per cent of resources would be provided in the form of subsidies from national and local governments, through a mix of domestic and international resources.

Of course, the model of responsibility here also varies according to income-level context, as well as the overall needs assessment of the locale and the country in question. This principle also holds wider meaning with regard to the role of international actors and donor assistance. More specifically, donor contributions are necessary to enable local and national governments to provide required subsidies for upgrading and planning. As highlighted in Task Force 8's report, *A Home in the City*, international financial assistance could also be a key facilitator of loans to participating households and communities, as demonstrated by the role of international donors in the examples of the Community-led Infrastructure Financing Facility (CLIFF) in India and the Local Development Programme (PRODEL) in Nicaragua (see Chapters 2, 3 and 6).[12] Donor guarantees can also facilitate the involvement of the private banking sector, as again demonstrated by the PRODEL example, thus ensuring that small loans are accessible when required and appropriate. Furthermore, donor financial assistance will be of special importance in low-income countries where resources to address the overall package of Millennium Declaration targets are severely lacking. There is also a need for donors to reconsider their contribution to development in middle-income countries. Most importantly, Task Force 8 has called on donors to re-evaluate their implicit and explicit macro-economic guidelines for middle-income countries in order to liberalize government access to domestic resources for social investment.

In sum, responsibilities for achieving Target 11 exist for every interested actor (see Table P.5). Together, these actors are already achieving Target 11 – in isolated cases. The challenge remains to expand the reach of achievement through a network of coordinated action.

	Investment requirements			Source of funding		
	Target Population (millions)	Average cost per person (US$)	Total cost (US$ billion)	Donors (US$ billion)	Government (US$ billion)	Slum dwellers and future low-income urban dwellers (US$ billion)
Upgrading slums	100	670	67	23	37	7
Providing adequate alternatives to slums formation	570	400	227	78	126	22
Total	670	440	294	101	163	29

Source: UN Millennium Project, 2005a, p143.

Table P.5

Investment requirements and envisaged sources of funding to meet Target 11

NOTES

1 This prologue was prepared by Pietro Garau, University of Rome, Italy; Elliott Sclar, Columbia University, US; and Gabriella Carolini, Columbia University, US.
2 UN Millennium Project, 2005a.
3 UN Millennium Report, 2000
4 UN Millennium Project, 2005a, p21.
5 UN-Habitat, 2003b.
6 UN-Habitat, 2003a, b
7 UN-Habitat, 2003a.
8 Flood, 2004.
9 UN Millennium Project, 2005a, p132.
10 Flood, 2004.
11 UN-Habitat, 2003b.
12 See UN Millennium Project, 2005a, Chapter 5.

SYNOPSIS

More than 2 billion people will be added to the number of urban dwellers in the developing countries over the next 25 years. This implies an unprecedented growth in the demand for housing, water supply, sanitation and other urban infrastructure services. This new challenge exists in a context of already widespread poverty and inequality in cities, with millions of people living in slums without adequate basic services. Providing these services to new residents will be essential if this additional population is not to be trapped in urban poverty, poor health and low productivity. It is an urban problem with significant macroeconomic consequences. This Global Report examines the urgent challenge of financing urban shelter development over the next generation. The report is divided into four parts. Part I presents the macroeconomic, shelter policy and urban finance contexts of financing urban shelter development. Part II describes and assesses recent global trends in shelter finance, including mortgage finance, financing for social housing, shelter microfinance and shelter community funds. Part III provides an overall assessment of the shelter financing systems analysed in Part II and examines policy directions towards sustainable shelter finance systems. The Epilogue in Part III examines the implications of the report's findings on sustainable urban shelter policy. In Part IV, the Statistical Annex comprises 16 tables covering three broad categories: demographic indicators and households data; housing and housing infrastructure indicators; and economic and social indicators. These tables are divided into three sections presenting data at the regional, country and city levels.

PART I: ECONOMIC AND URBAN DEVELOPMENT CONTEXT

Chapter 1 – Challenges of Sustainable Shelter Development in Macroeconomic Context

By presenting the latest global demographic projections, Chapter 1 highlights the major social and economic challenges of urban shelter provision in the next 25 years. The chapter also presents a macroeconomic framework within which to situate the problem of financing urban shelter and to understand its broader implications. While most of the urban population growth will occur in East and South Asia, particularly China and India, many places around the world will experience the urbanization of poverty and inequality between rich and poor.

Understanding urban shelter development challenges

The current global backlog of slum dwellers is about 925 million people. When this figure is combined with the projected 1.9 billion additional urban population, it is apparent that 2.825 billion people will need housing and urban services by 2030. The demand for housing – just to accommodate the increase in the number of households over the next 25 years – is estimated to be 877 million housing units.

This challenge is not just about the quantity of population, but also its composition. Cities are changing rapidly, especially in terms of both the scale and rate of demographic, social and economic transformation. This pattern of growth will also place additional strains on environmental resources needed for cities, such as clean water and clean air. Growing demand for infrastructure services places immediate pressures on natural resources. Environmental studies show that cities have important impacts upon the natural environments in which they are located, what is known as their 'ecological footprint'. Consumption of natural resources by urban residents – for example, firewood in Africa – is frequently growing faster than nature is able to reproduce those resources. This pressure on natural resources is most dramatically shown by the increasing cost of potable water in almost every city in the world.

With this backdrop, it is clear that the capacity of developing countries to finance their needs depends largely upon their level of future economic growth and development. If countries are able to generate employment and incomes for growing populations at an accelerated rate, they will be able to generate and mobilize the savings and investment to finance housing and infrastructure services. Two key factors are needed to translate macroeconomic growth into finance for urban development. The first is governance – how public, private and non-governmental institutions work together to plan and manage cities. These institutional challenges range from establishing the laws and regulations governing life in the city, to developing new residential areas for the growing population, to decentralized problem-solving at the community level. The growing trend towards decentralization in most national governments in developing countries has transformed the roles and responsibilities of these institutions over the last two decades. However, this process is also insufficient to provide the needed housing and infrastructure services for growing populations. The second factor, finance, is essential for this process. While the financial challenges are introduced in Part I, they are the subject of the body of this report.

The macroeconomic context of urban shelter development

The second part of Chapter 1 examines the macroeconomic context for urban development. It addresses the following factors: patterns of economic growth; sectoral performance and productivity; income distribution and inequality; poverty and employment; savings; external debt; patterns of investment (public, private and foreign); impacts of external factors upon macroeconomic performance; and the urbanization of national economies.

2004–2005 has been a period of unprecedented economic growth at the global level. All developing regions grew at a pace faster than their growth rates of the 1980s and 1990s. Global trade also expanded considerably, with China's demand for imported raw materials and food spurring exports from other developing countries. The most striking feature of economic growth has been the high rate of growth for the developing countries, going above 6 per cent for the first time. However, the distribution patterns are worrying because they continue the trend towards greater disparity in income levels between the regions, as well as between developing and developed countries. Global inequality between rich and poor countries, therefore, continues to worsen, even when there have been extraordinarily high rates of economic growth. The most questionable aspect of this growth in 2005, however, is whether it is likely to be sustained in the future.

The growing importance of world trade means that 'tradeables', whether manufacturing products or commodities, have become increasingly central to the economic growth of all countries, whether developed or developing. While this places great emphasis on agriculture and production of raw materials, it also requires improvements in the efficiency of infrastructure in telecommunications, transport and key services such as electricity and water supply needed for manufacturing and other industries.

Despite the impressive economic growth of the past few years, the enduring problem of massive poverty in the developing countries remains the top priority problem facing the world today. The incidence of poverty at the national level is highly correlated with low levels of education and poor health status, as well as lack of access to basic infrastructure services such as clean water supply, sanitation and electricity.

The most direct and important factor contributing to urban poverty is the shortage of well-paid employment in cities. The challenge here is both the creation of jobs and the level of wages. The generation of employment depends generally upon savings and investment within the macro-economy and local economies, as well. One problem that is associated with high levels of poverty is a lack of domestic savings within national economies. Low levels of domestic savings – both public and private – contribute to low levels of capitalization of the financial institutions in poor countries. They are also reflected in low levels of tax revenue collection and therefore place great limitations on public expenditures and public budgets. The issue of savings is particularly important to the financing of urban infrastructure and housing.

The legacy of external borrowing for diverse purposes has left many countries with unsustainable levels of external debt service. In some countries, particularly in Africa, the debt service to gross domestic product (GDP) ratio has reached over 400 per cent. These levels of debt immediately reduce available domestic capital for investment. Given the above, the patterns of investment in the developing countries have changed markedly over the past decade. At the same time, there has also been an important segmentation in the global financial markets, with some countries – particularly the East Asian countries – being able to attract high levels of foreign direct investment (FDI). Public investment as a share of GDP is also low in most developing countries. They have relatively large deficits in their public budgets, with items such as the maintenance of infrastructure being a low priority in most countries.

The lack of resources for public investment in the poorest countries poses a serious dilemma. Many of these countries do not qualify for FDI. They are dependent upon official development assistance (ODA) as the major source of financial support for economic development. Yet, ODA is also severely limited. Even with promises of additional finance, the actual levels of official development aid are constrained by lack of domestic political support in the developed countries, or by the restrictions of macro-economic agreements with the international financial institutions.

Here, urban development must compete with other priorities in the fund allocation at international and national levels, which are clearly politically determined within individual governments. Many governments increasingly assign responsibility for housing and urban development to the provincial, state and local levels, rather than to the national level. The weaknesses of the public sector and its inability to mobilize substantial resources for urban development therefore point to the need to give greater attention to private sources of finance, including the role of privatization of infrastructure services.

A final characteristic of the macroeconomic context for urban development is the urbanization of national economies themselves. Abundant evidence exists to demonstrate the growing importance of cities in the overall productivity of countries. The increasing share of national GDP produced in cities has been well documented. Despite historically rapid rates of economic growth, there is little likelihood that conventional sources of funds will be available for investment on the scale needed to meet the projected demand for urban shelter and related infrastructure.

Chapter 2 – Shelter Policy and Finance: Retrospective Overview

Discussing the general trends in housing and urban development policy, this chapter highlights the paradigm shifts that have occurred – particularly in the policy context of urban shelter finance.

Between 1972 and 1982: Habitat I

By the early 1970s, the concept of intermediate technology had been developed and became popular, with the recognition that different technologies were appropriate in different contexts. Between 1972 and 1982, the focus of financing was on low-interest loans, loan guarantees and subsidies as a means of making housing affordable to low-income people. Interventions in this period concentrated on demonstration projects of limited size, with regard to a city or region, and were usually confined to a particular neighbourhood or group of neighbourhoods.

Projects tended to be outside of municipal control, to have different standards from elsewhere, different means of implementation and to have little effect 'outside the fence'. Projects generally focused on self-help, providing a context in which the spare time and energy of low-income people could be devoted to house construction or infrastructure provision. They were broadly of two types: sites-and-services projects for new housing provision; and settlement upgrading for bringing squatter and other informal settlements up to an acceptable standard of servicing and public space provision.

The concept of adding value through physical work, referred to as 'sweat equity', was strongly ingrained in the projects of the 1970s. Participants in sites-and-services schemes were helped in their construction efforts by project staff who provided a range of services. However, evaluations have shown that many participants used professional building workers in lieu of sweat equity.

In addition to finance by sweat equity, there were many subsidies. Some were declared in the project (on-budget) and others were hidden (off-budget). The participants in sites-and-services schemes tended to have rather higher incomes than the rhetoric and intention implied. Dwelling owners in upgrading schemes, on the other hand, tended to be among the low-income groups and their tenants were probably in even lower income echelons.

Many beneficiaries found themselves unsuited to the project and bought their way out by selling to richer households, ignored some of the project requirements to better suit it to their needs, or defaulted on payments to make it affordable. Tenants did not benefit much as their rents would rise and tended to move out to other non-upgraded settlements where rents were still affordable.

The projects were often too complex for the municipal authority to implement. The great majority of citizens – those outside the project 'fence' in the cities affected and those not finding work in the project – benefited hardly at all.

The 1980s to the 1990s: Towards financial sustainability

For all the efforts aimed at improving housing, the un-serviced informal settlements appeared to be expanding rather than in decline. The limitations of this approach sequenced a low impact upon overall urban economic development, restrained institutional reforms and the funds were restricted to 'retail' rather than 'wholesale' roles.

The 1980s saw 'step-by-step moves towards a more comprehensive whole housing-sector approach'. There was a perceived need to incorporate housing within the wider economic environment. It was recognized that the individual sites-and-services and slum upgrading projects alone could not affect the growing housing need and that a well-functioning finance system for housing for the majority was necessary.

This generated a paradigm shift from multi-sectoral but quite localized projects, affecting a fortunate few, to an emphasis on creating a sustainable capability for housing supply and urban development affecting most residents and congruent with the overall policy and economic environment. The locus of borrowing changed from almost exclusively public-sector institutions to financial intermediaries. In parallel, attention shifted from the physical asset financed to the institutional structure of the implementing agency and its ability to mobilize the development required.

Reviews of housing policy transition have shown that there was a fulcrum of policy change during 1985 to 1987, a mid point between the two United Nations world conferences on human settlements. By the end of this short period, the enabling approach had been put together and launched on the international agenda, at the same time as macroeconomic structural adjustment programme (SAP) initiatives designed to enable governments to recover from years of decline were being implemented.

The enabling approach treated housing and urban development as a multi-sectoral issue, affected just as much by efficiencies and inefficiencies in finance as in the construction industry or land tenure systems or the regulatory framework. The task of the state was seen as creating the legal, institutional and economic framework for economic productivity and social effectiveness, in which efficient settlement development could then flourish.

The mid 1980s also saw the birth of sustainability as an overarching rubric for development activity. From that time on, no agency could ignore the need to consider environmental impact alongside social and economic benefits from its projects. Chapter 7 of Agenda 21 reiterated the overall objective of improving the social, economic and environmental quality of human settlements and the living and working environments of all people, particularly the poor. At the same time, there was a realignment of emphasis from 'ability to pay' to 'willingness to pay' as a result of economic analysis which found that the latter produced much more accurate estimates in shelter-related cost-recovery calculations.

By 1988, the Global Strategy for Shelter to the Year 2000 (GSS) had been formulated. It recognized that governments had an obligation to ensure that an appropriate environment was created for the mobilization of finance for housing. The objectives of such an effort were seen as promoting and mobilizing savings, reducing costs, improving the efficiency of financial intermediation, and assisting the free movement of capital through the national economy. Housing finance reform, which is a key component of a shelter strategy, was seen as part of a broad effort to reform and develop the financial sector.

The GSS had a laudable but over-optimistic objective of 'decent housing' for all by 2000. Later in the decade, this term was replaced by 'adequate housing'. The need for adequate housing has also been included in many United Nations summit recommendations and closing declarations. The new paradigm encouraged institutional reform and development. This coincided with the spread of decentralization of power from the centre to regions and municipalities and the growth of a local sense of responsibility for urban conditions.

Reflecting the globalization beginning during the early 1990s, the need for housing finance institutions to be able to compete for deposits and investments on equal terms with other financial institutions was emphasized. Thus, lending had to be at positive, real interest rates and deposits had to be of sufficient term to support long-term lending.

During the 1990s, some developing countries developed proactive and well-integrated housing finance policies and institutions. There was a recognition that purely government-managed finance institutions had failed in their laudable aims and become bureaucratic, inefficient and prey to exploitation by insiders.

Mortgage finance is now available in most countries, but its limitations are obviously militating against its being the solution for most low-income households. In filling this gap, microfinancing has progressed from being only enterprise focused to being an important feature of the housing finance system.

Strategy for the new millennium

Just before the turn of the millennium, the Habitat Agenda was adopted at the United Nations Conference on Human Settlements in Istanbul in 1996. The agenda provides a basis for international and national housing and urban development policy for the 21st century. With regard to finance, the member states agreed to strengthen existing financial mechanisms. The importance of developing innovative approaches for financing the implementation of the Habitat Agenda was also underlined.

In addition, the United Nations Conference on Human Settlements reinforced the commitment of states to the full and progressive realization of the *right to adequate housing*, as provided for in international instruments. Any retrogressive measures, such as forced evictions, are regarded as violations of the right to housing. Indeed, states are seen as having a duty to respect, protect and fulfil housing rights. However, none of this is considered to entail a state obligation to provide everyone with free housing but, rather, to set up the legal, social and economic environment in which households have adequate chance to fulfil their needs.

Chapter 3 – Financing Urban Development

Highlighting the key issues of municipal finance systems, this chapter analyses the main sources of municipal finance, municipal spending patterns and privatization of municipal services. The chapter emphasizes the relevance of urban development finance for shelter development. The comparative review of the approaches developed all over the world reveals the emergence of several new trends: the broadening of locally generated revenue sources; the strengthening of local financial management; partnerships in the financing of capital investments; and the enhancement of access to long-term credit for municipalities.

Sources of municipal finance

The sources of municipal finance – such as central government transfers, taxes on property and businesses, user fees, betterment taxes, development exactions, borrowing and income-generating enterprises – vary within the regions and from one municipality to the other. The main revenue sources at present are from central government transfers; locally generated revenues which include taxes on property and on economic activities; user fees for the delivery of services and the improvement of infrastructure; and loans borrowed to finance long-term investments.

Municipal spending patterns

Municipal budgets, which reflect the policies and strategies for the delivery of mandatory and locally approved public services, should be capable of demonstrating the extent to which the financial results have been realized, the intended activities performed and the anticipated outcomes achieved. The analysis of municipal spending patterns in relation to the local government budgeting, which includes participatory budgeting and multi-year capital budgeting, shows that these are rarely achieved.

With regard to local government budgeting, problems arise from the lack of financial management skills at the local levels. Reliance on central government transfers also results in a number of constraints. The controls meant to improve efficiency and collection, or equity in distribution, sometimes also stifle local initiative and negate some advantages of decentralization and democratic governance. Most local capital budgets reflect immediate needs or political expediency rather than a long-term development strategy, and most municipalities in developing countries are unable to borrow long-term funds from capital markets.

Participatory budgeting has emerged from the growing demands for accountability and transparency in municipal budgets and financial management, especially in the allocation of scarce local resources and their utilization. Most developing countries lack funding for maintaining existing assets. Thus, 'preventive maintenance' has to increasingly become 'crisis management'. The undue importance laid on operating expenditures often leads to the deferment of expenditures on maintaining existing assets.

The experience in many countries has shown that decentralization policies do not necessarily lead to responsible financial management, as demonstrated by budget deficits, accumulated debts and the inability to repay loans. Accountability for performance is a cornerstone of good governance and a major tool in financial management. It places as much emphasis upon transparency as upon financial management. Demands for greater accountability and transparency by voting and taxpaying constituencies have combined with the constraints on the financial resources available to the public sector to exert political pressures for improving municipal financial management. Indeed, increasingly, mayors, councils and city managers are held accountable for financial outcomes, as well as for the qualities of the services they deliver and the projects they implement. Reforms of existing systems and the introduction of newer concepts and techniques have provided useful alternatives in financing and operating public services.

Privatization of municipal services

In both developing and advanced economies, privatization has resulted in revenue-producing services, including water supply and solid waste management, being gradually taken over in the larger urban centres by specialized multinational firms serving many local government units. Formal privatization in many cities has not benefited lower income communities, which underscores the need for the public sector to have a role in the delivery of essential services.

In the effort to deliver services effectively and efficiently, public–private partnerships have been used under joint-funding ventures. Such partnerships range from the granting of concessions, to joint venture agreements, to build–operate–transfer (BOT) or build–own–operate–transfer (BOOT) schemes. Of special interest to poorer countries are solutions based on partnerships between municipalities, non-governmental organizations (NGOs) and community-based organizations (CBOs). In these countries, integrating poorer communities into the city fabric and giving the poor access to basic services is hampered by the spread of chaotic urbanization, the mounting densities in the central zones, the obsolescence of existing conventional systems and the lack of resources to maintain and upgrade existing systems.

Municipalities are particularly reluctant to delegate authority or share revenue with their peer entities. This reluctance is attributed to the difficulties encountered in getting municipalities to collaborate in joint initiatives. Moreover, formalizing collaboration through negotiated agreements and inter-municipal compacts is an even more challenging task since there are no institutional incentives fostering such strategic associations.

Decentralization and the privatization of services are facing a number of constraints in developing countries, as opposed to advanced and transitional economies. Developing economies have not been able to enact and implement successful decentralization policies that redistribute resources effectively. While privatization has forced governments to examine entrenched practices and to consider alternatives for their modification or replacement with considerable success, it is not a panacea.

The major challenges that must be addressed include the large numbers of smaller, financially weak municipalities; asymmetrical decentralization; retrenchment of central transfers; weakness of local revenue sources; lack of strong domestic capital markets; impediments to the development of municipal credit institutions; inadequate capacity and rules for sound financial management at the local level; lack of mechanisms to finance urban investments; and lack of funds for maintaining existing assets.

In conclusion, the following recent trends in municipal finance may be highlighted:

- Financial discipline and the commercial outlook of competing private enterprise have, in some countries, forced public administrators to lower costs, achieve greater efficiency and improve the quality of outputs.
- Opening up of public services to market participation has created more opportunities for competition in the delivery of these services than previously.
- A growing demand for accountability and transparency in municipal budgeting has accompanied political and fiscal decentralization. There is a marked trend for more rigorous financial management, clear procedures for the allocation of resources, and the participation of residents in decisions that affect their communities.
- Public–private partnerships, which require significant delegation of authority and can be very productive, have been on the increase. Some locally based partnerships involving CBOs and microenterprises have been found to provide successful means for empowerment and social inclusion, especially in the developing countries.

PART II: SHELTER FINANCE – ASSESSMENT OF TRENDS

Chapter 4 – Mortgage Finance: Institutions and Mechanisms

The cost of a complete dwelling could be between 2.5 to 6 times the average annual salary. To purchase property, it is very difficult to finance such costs without a loan and, generally, such loans will need to be long term. When the repayment period is to stretch for such a considerable period, a legal framework is required for lenders to be confident about the security of their finance – hence the significance of mortgage finance in which the loan is secured on property.

Chapter 4 first considers emerging trends in the provision of mortgage finance and summarizes the current terms and conditions of such finance. Second, it looks particularly at the situation with regard to lower income households who might be seeking mortgage finance and the affordability of such options for these households. Third, it examines emerging tensions and opportunities in current mortgage finance and assesses its potential *contribution* to addressing household needs for housing finance.

Providing mortgage finance

In general, governments have sought to encourage homeownership and have, in many cases, provided preferential financing to influence consumer choice. There has been a general shift towards market-based mechanisms for providing housing, with attempts to reduce subsidies and deregulate markets. In part, this is due to the past ineffectiveness of housing strategies that have depended upon direct provision by the state. This trend is also consistent with the overall direction of macroeconomic strategies during recent decades.

The importance of deposits to the bank system is widely acknowledged. Deposits account for 62 per cent of the funding of all mortgage loans within the European Union (EU) countries, and this percentage is even higher in the transition countries. However, if the only source of finance available to the mortgage lenders is deposits, then even if they can secure sufficient funds, lenders face a risk when committing long-term loans with short-term finance. As an alternative to short-term deposits, there are several sources of longer-term finance. One source is the state itself and the direct contributions that it might make. A second source is private funds institutionalized for housing finance through specialist saving schemes. A third source is private commercial investment. Despite these multiple sources, the availability of long-term finance is limited in many countries.

The secondary market in mortgage finance developed in order to cope with the risks associated with short-term deposits and longer-term loans. The US has led developments in secondary markets, which have become notably significant from the mid 1980s onwards. For the last 25 years, there have been significant changes in mortgage finance with the growth of the involvement of capital markets; this began in the US and spread to Europe and, more recently, is being explored in Latin America and Asia.

A number of measures have been taken in Africa to strengthen secondary markets and, specifically, securitization. In Kenya, a recent draft national housing policy aims to create a secondary market to ensure additional capital from overseas and a reduction in the costs of borrowing.

A further and remaining source of finance, despite frequent criticisms on the grounds of economic efficiency and ineffectual targeting, is the state. Governments have over many decades intervened in housing markets with the intention of widening access to housing finance, and they continue to have a major role in housing finance through the continued use of subsidies.

There are several motivations for state involvement. With respect to the welfare of households, motivations are, notably, to promote homeownership as a whole and to specifically address the needs of those with inadequate housing. The state may also have systemic interests to ensure that the financial markets for housing are stable.

The common strategies to increase homeownership through the enhanced provision of finance are:

- mortgage interest relief;
- interest subsidies;
- housing savings schemes;
- guarantees;
- subsidies for 'key' public-sector workers; and
- intermediate tenures.

A more recent shift has been subsidies designed to augment the payment capacity of the poor (direct-demand subsidies).

One of the most far-reaching systems of state intervention through direct construction has been used in the case of Singapore, where 96 per cent of the households are living in homeownership apartments. The strategy has been based on the provision of subsidized mortgage finance (primarily through the interest rate), combined with a dedicated supply of funds through already existing provident/pension funds. However, there are many examples of failed public housing policies. One example is the National Housing Corporation in Kenya, whose production was well below need, with only several thousand units a year. Two parastatals in Côte d'Ivoire together constructed 41,000 units between 1960 and the 1980s before being wound up.

Taxation-related incentives

In many West European countries, mortgage interest payments are, to some extent, tax deductible. Interest rate subsidies have been a popular way of enhancing housing finance affordability. Occasionally this policy has been criticized as acting as a substitute for prudent macroeconomic management. Interest rate subsidies may be associated with savings schemes for housing investments.

However, the case against interest rate subsidies has been strongly made. It has been argued that direct subsidies are a preferred way of offering assistance with housing costs as they can be more precisely targeted on those in need. Interest rate subsidies inevitably favour those who can afford loans and larger subsidies go to those who are able to afford larger loans. In spite of this, interest rate subsidies appear to continue to be used.

In addition to direct assistance to households to increase the affordability of housing finance, governments have sought to ensure the stability of the system and to reduce the risks for lending institutions when they extend services to lower income households. As the greater availability of finance has been reflected in growing levels of owner occupation, risks have increased.

Regional highlights

Homeownership is now the majority tenure across Western Europe, with exceptions – notably in Germany. Nevertheless, levels of owner occupation vary considerably, being highest among some of the Southern European countries (Spain and Italy) where homeownership can be described as being 'dominant'. Homeownership is relatively high in several other countries, notably the UK, at around 70 per cent. In countries, such as France, the Netherlands, Denmark and Sweden, homeownership has been established as the 'majority' tenure without being especially high or dominant. There is little evidence of convergence in homeownership levels, either in the sense that they are moving in the same *direction*, or that they are converging towards similar *levels*.

In 2003, the European market as a whole continued to grow, with the total value of residential mortgage debt increasing by 7.4 per cent, a little below the ten-year average of 8 per cent. The total volume of mortgage loans in Europe at the end of 2003 was US$3.4 trillion. This figure has grown rapidly and it now accounts for 42 per cent of EU GDP. This rapid expansion in lending has been encouraged by lower interest rates. However, it should be remembered that the rise in the volume of lending is not necessarily associated with increasing access, as one further trend has been rising house prices, with capital gains for current homeowners and increasing difficulties for those seeking to become homeowners for the first time. In the US, homeownership grew on average, as did income, throughout the largely prosperous 1990s and now stands at a record high.

The transition countries face a particular problem in that commercial housing finance markets were previously non-existent. There has been state support to the development of housing finance systems, with the expectation that the commercial sector will become an increasingly significant provider. Unfortunately, much of this support has been to the benefit of higher income groups who are the only ones able to afford such finance.

Volumes of housing loans are low in the transition countries. However, there are indications that housing loan markets are growing rapidly; for example, in Estonia the scale of housing loans doubled between 1997 and 2000, and in the Czech Republic the scale of loans grew more than sixfold during the same period. During 2002 and 2003, mortgage lending grew particularly strongly in Hungary, Poland and Latvia (by more than 85 per cent).

The privatization process that took place resulted in the transfer of significant numbers of dwellings into private hands. Owner occupation is now close to or above 90 per cent in Hungary, Bulgaria, Estonia and Romania, while in Poland, Slovakia and Slovenia it is above 70 per cent. However, despite this increase in homeownership, the financial systems needed for such ownership have not developed.

The problems of affordability in the South are considerable. The supply of mortgages in Southern countries has been limited by a large number of factors, including low incomes that barely cover subsistence needs for a considerable proportion of the population, a lack of formal financial institutions that can capture people's savings, as well as macroeconomic instability. The recent financial crises have had negative impacts upon the formal housing finance systems in a number of countries and have particularly deterred commercial provision of mortgage finance. However, there are signs of a recovery in lending in both Asian and Latin American countries.

In China, the system of housing finance has been significantly redeveloped. The previous system was one in which dwellings were primarily provided through work units that housed employees in return for a nominal rent. In 1995, the government introduced two major programmes to encourage home purchase, the National Comfortable Housing Project and the Housing Provident Fund.

In Latin America, less than 30 per cent of dwellings are produced by the formal housing market. Residential debt is in general a fairly low percentage of GDP, indicating that mortgage lending is not extensive. Significant difficulties of foreclosure, with long foreclosure periods taking over one year, are just one set of the problems that has reduced the attractiveness of mortgage finance in this region. During the last decade, the core issues facing governments in Latin America appear to be the longstanding problems of macro-economic performance and, notably, inflation, the specific economic difficulties of the late 1990s and the need to extend finance to those with lower incomes. The related strategies have been titling, direct-demand subsidies, the use of specially defined units for housing investment and the expansion of capital into the system through strengthening of the secondary market.

While there are continuing problems of underdeveloped housing finance systems, in part as a result of the economic difficulties of recent decades, there are some positive trends in Chile, Costa Rica, Panama, Mexico and Peru, with uneven progress in Colombia, Bolivia and Ecuador. These improvements include financial-sector reforms to facilitate the expansion of mortgage financing, judiciary reform to facilitate the recovery of collateral and increases in housing production/finance in the private sector. They also involve attempts to have public housing agencies working more effectively with the treasuries, private banks and developers to address the housing needs of beneficiaries.

The situation in sub-Saharan Africa divides between South Africa (and, to a lesser extent, Namibia and, until recently, Zimbabwe), where the commercial banking sector is significantly involved in mortgage lending, and the rest of the continent. South Africa's mortgage market is about 198 billion rand (US$30.7 billion). Most of its housing finance is provided through bank mortgages. Despite this scale of finance, there is evidence to suggest that the lower income households remain excluded from the market. While those who are in formal employment can use their provident funds to guarantee housing loans, many work in the informal sector. Moreover, mortgage finance is unaffordable to many.

Although state housing finance institutions have continued in some cases, the greater emphasis on cost recovery and operating efficiency during the 1990s has given them considerable problems in securing finance. Generally, those that do exist have been heavily regulated and have also been seen as social instruments, rather than financial mechanisms. More recently, the state has withdrawn from this area and some housing finance institutions have withdrawn as well. A particular and continuing problem faced in Africa has been a lack of effective institutions and instruments to mobilize savings and to channel them into housing investment. For the most part, housing finance institutions have remained dependent upon deposits and have not been able to secure long-term finance.

Terms and conditions

Mortgage lending is associated with a standard package of terms and conditions which specify the contribution of deposits, in some cases the period of savings, the interest rate to be charged on the loan (and if it is fixed or variable), the period of the loan (potentially with penalties for early and late repayment), and loan-to-value ratios (the maximum percentage of the loan against a verified value of the dwelling). A further important factor is the amount that the loan institution is willing to lend in relation to the borrowers' income(s).

The increased diversification of housing loan suppliers has reduced the general significance of savings activities that are specifically linked to housing; but some form of saving remains essential if mortgage loans are offered for less than the full cost of the property.

Considerable effort has been made to extend opportunities to secure housing finance during recent years. This is the product of two related factors. On the one hand, the housing finance market has become more competitive as new providers have been encouraged to enter the market. Such providers have been seeking new customers to extend their activities. On the other hand, the state has been looking to the market to address housing need. Faced with considerable housing problems and seeking to reduce public expenditure, governments have sought to encourage the market to address needs where possible.

As noted earlier, affordability is not just about access to and the cost of housing finance, it is also critically about the price of housing. One of the most important trends in housing finance in Western Europe has been the widening 'gap' between incomes and house prices, House prices have risen since 1997, notably in Australia, Ireland, Spain and the UK. In 2003, the European Mortgage Federation noted strong price increases in Latvia, Portugal, Spain, the UK and Ireland.

In a number of countries, housing supply appears to be inelastic, responding only slowly to increases in housing demand expressed through rising prices. Research has shown that local regulations that prevent housing construction are a significant cause of high house prices in the US and UK, as well as in Malaysia, Republic of Korea, Tanzania and New Zealand.

In a context of rising house prices, housing finance systems have a greater job to do in bridging the gap between incomes and prices. Young people have particular difficulties in purchasing dwellings as they have had less time to save for a down payment (deposit) and earnings are lower for those who have recently entered the labour market.

Turning to more general problems of affordability, US data for 2004 indicates that there are some 6 million households living in owner-occupied dwellings who fall below the poverty line. This is not that much less than the 7.9 million households below the poverty line who are living in rental accommodation. In the transition countries, there are real problems with affordability due to generally low levels of income. For example, only 10 to 20 per cent of the population in Estonia and Latvia are considered to be eligible for housing loans. In the South, the numbers of people able to afford formal housing with the associated financing costs are limited. As indicated earlier, the clear emerging trend in a number of countries is that of the extension of mortgage finance. However, it is very difficult to assess how successful this has been.

Chapter 5 – Financing for Rental and Social Housing

While a narrow definition of housing finance may focus only on the provision of credit, the scale and significance of housing finance subsidies primarily through rental housing, subsidized loan finance and direct-demand (capital) subsidies makes this component difficult to ignore. An understanding of how the financing of social housing can fit within a broader system of housing financing is needed. This chapter looks specifically at some strategies that have recently been used to provide financial subsidies.

Financial subsidies seek to provide incentives to enable and persuade a certain class of producers or consumers to do something they would not otherwise do by lowering the opportunity cost or otherwise increasing the potential benefit of doing so. Some argue that such financial subsidies are best avoided and should be a policy of last resort. Such concerns focus on the potential distortion of markets and are often accomplished by recommendations on institutional and regulatory reforms. In addition, subsidies, especially those offered on interest rates, may have a huge hidden cost.

While subsidies tend to be criticized by economists seeking to encourage a greater realization of the potential effectiveness of markets, they remain popular with governments. The interest in subsidies has resulted in multiple approaches to their delivery, which notably include direct interest rates reductions; allowing mortgage interest to be deducted from income taxes; support for housing savings; support for insurance in the primary market; support for insurance in secondary markets; and direct grants. However, concerns remain, notably that such subsidies rarely reach the poor. Governments in the North and the South have primarily used two financing strategies to assist families to obtain housing: assistance for ownership and/or the assistance to afford adequate rental accommodation.

Three specific trends are well established in a number of countries:

1. Governments have shifted away from the direct construction and management of public housing. They have used several strategies to reduce their stocks, with large-scale transfers to occupiers in some cases.
2. There is increasing assistance for homeownership through direct-demand (capital) subsidies.
3. Consistent with the two trends above is the greater use of housing allowances (rather than direct provision) to assist low-income families renting accommodation in the private or non-profit sectors.

Despite their focus on lower income households, funding for direct subsidies is often smaller in scale than interest rate subsidies when the full costs of the latter over the life of the loan are considered.

Rental housing in the North

Although in the North the state is generally playing a less direct role in economic intervention, this is not necessarily the case in housing. Despite the shift to income-related support, the social rented sector (defined as housing let at below-market prices and allocated administratively on the basis of housing need, rather than on the ability to pay) remains a significant tenure in several states. However, there have been significant changes in policy and the nature of housing support has shifted in Western Europe. Support systems with large, general interest subsidies for new construction and rehabilitation have been phased out. Targeted income-related subsidies have become relatively more important, as have subsidies to depressed housing areas.

There has been a general marked decline in the levels of new housing units in this sector. As the numbers of designated social housing and/or public properties fall, there are concerns that the scale of social disadvantage associated with such accommodation will rise. It is feared that this will result in a high concentration of social disadvantage, thereby exacerbating social exclusion, reducing mobility and creating greater marginalization for tenants. One further concern is that the growth of means-tested housing allowances (also encouraged by the use of private finance) has resulted in higher rents. However, means-tested housing allowances are considered to offer better incentives in terms of labour mobility and to enable more effective targeting.

One of the most significant developments in social rented housing has been the increased use of private finance for rented housing in much of Western Europe. Despite this use, there has been limited private equity investment. Another key trend during recent years has been the emergence of surpluses in the social rented sector, as a whole, in many countries. Declining debt burdens arising from lower levels of construction and the repayment of older debt have coincided with rising rents to create these surpluses. Several countries have attempted to establish 'revolving-door' systems of finance whereby surpluses are reinvested in the sector. However, it seems that revolving-door finance alone does not stimulate increased construction, either because funds are inadequate or incentives are absent.

Rental housing in transition countries

Prior to transition, in most Eastern European countries housing was provided by state institutions (workplace, local government and/or housing co-operatives). Essentially, the system was one in which state-provided social rental systems dominated, with low rents and administrative allocation systems.

The transition phase included the transfer of some of these dwellings to their occupants under privatization programmes. In some countries, more than 90 per cent of the stock was sold, while in others the percentage was as low as 6 per cent. However, housing markets were very limited. Even where people own their dwellings, it appears to have been difficult to trade them.

By the end of the 1990s, there was some interest in reinvestment in rental housing – for example in Poland, Slovakia, the Czech Republic and Hungary. A significant scale is planned – between 10 and 30 per cent of new construction in Poland, Romania and Hungary. However, a considerable problem remains, which is that the institutional strategies for addressing the housing needs of the poorest have collapsed, with no alternative being developed.

Rental housing in the South

Large-scale public housing has not been that significant in the South despite exceptions such as Hong Kong. While many countries have experimented on a minor scale, in general the scale of provision reflects the limited funds available to invest in public housing initiatives and the high standards that are required. In general, public rental housing has not been allocated to the poor, nor would it necessarily have been affordable even if it had been allocated. In some cases, these properties have now been privatized following the increased emphasis on market provision. As with the transition countries in Europe, China has relatively recently begun a policy to transfer to homeownership dwellings that had previously been rented from state-owned enterprises and from other state housing providers.

Despite a general trend against direct provision in the South as well as the North, there is some continuing support for rental housing in a number of countries. In Hong Kong, the Housing Authority actually increased its stock by 18,000 units between 1991 and 2001. In the Republic of Korea, there has been (since 1989) a growing interest in a permanent rental dwelling programme for those on low incomes. In South Africa, there has also been a policy (albeit as a secondary strategy subsidiary to the main emphasis on homeownership) to support the development of a social housing sector and, more specifically, to encourage the development of housing associations to manage low-income estates and rental accommodation.

Social housing and homeownership

In practice, the high costs of construction of rental public housing and the ongoing costs of maintenance, often in a context in which rents remain very low and national housing budgets very limited, has resulted in large-scale rental programmes being considered impossible in many Southern countries. Despite these problems, there are some governments that have sought to introduce subsidy programmes of a significant scale.

In a number of cases, they have chosen to use limited funds to support small loan programmes that enhance the process of incremental housing development. In other cases, governments have chosen to subsidize a minimum complete dwelling. In yet other cases, effective subsidies have been given through low-interest loans. The limited resources that exist for housing finance mean that allocations may be made as political favours rather than as universal entitlements.

Despite the initial political commitments and significant programmes, the Chilean, Colombian and South African governments have not put large-scale funding into capital subsidies. The percentage of state expenditure for these three countries does not exceed 1.25 per cent, while 2 per cent has been considered typical in the South.

Chapter 6 – Small Loans: Shelter Microfinance

For individuals or households with limited incomes, the only possibility of homeownership (even in an illegal settlement) is through shelter investment made in several stages. Land purchase, service installation and upgrading, and housing construction, consolidation and expansion are all made at separate times. An estimated 70 per cent of housing investment in developing countries occurs through such progressive building. Such incremental shelters, often initially built of temporary materials, frequently require repairs because of damage (for example, from natural forces).

In the vast majority of cases these households are ineligible for commercial mortgage finance. Households seeking to invest in their shelter (land, infrastructure and housing) have been forced to use their own limited income, seek additional resources from family and friends, and borrow on informal credit markets or, in some cases, from groups like credit unions. There have been several institutional efforts to assist these households secure access to some kind of loan finance. In particular, shelter microfinance and community finance mechanisms have grown considerably during recent decades. This chapter discusses the use of microfinance approaches to shelter lending. The loans are almost universally to individuals, generally those with some security of tenure, for investment (construction, improvement and extension) in housing rather than land and infrastructure.

The growth of microfinance for shelter

The growth of microfinance agencies since their inception during the 1980s has been considerable and there are now many such organizations. To exemplify the situation in one country, in India the number of such grassroots-level organizations engaged in mobilizing savings and providing micro-loan services to the poor is estimated to be in the range of 400 to 500 organizations. Evaluations of microfinance organizations have demonstrated that, whatever the loans were taken for, a proportion as large as 25 per cent could be diverted for shelter investments. Findings such as these have encouraged the exploration of microfinance lending specifically for shelter.

There are a considerable number of NGOs who have been working with housing issues, generally for lower income groups, and who have been drawn into loan financing in order to scale up their activities and/or to provide assistance to residents who have been successful in acquiring land. Shelter NGOs looked to the examples of microfinance agencies seeking to bring financial markets to those who traditionally had been excluded from opportunities for savings and credit. There are two distinct groups of such NGOs working in housing finance. The first group is professional urban development NGOs who have primarily been drawn into finance programmes to influence state policies and the demands of low-income communities. The second group are humanitarian agencies who have worked to improve housing conditions in low-income areas. Recognizing that families are able and willing to invest in their own dwellings, they have directly developed small loan programmes at scale.

In addition to NGO initiatives, there has been considerable interest in housing lending shown by the microfinance sector. Microfinance agencies appear to be diversifying rapidly into housing microcredit in at least some regions. One study funded by the International Finance Corporation (IFC) identifies 141 institutions providing shelter-finance loan products to the poor. The speed with which housing loans have been integrated within such agencies appears to have been facilitated by the similarity of lending practice.

One reason for the diversification of microfinance agencies into housing is commercial advantages. Such diversification may increase the financial stability of their loan portfolio and enable them to take advantage of opportunities for growth, as well as avoid losing clients to other microfinance agencies that provide housing loans. A further notable advantage is that the longer repayment period associated with housing loans helps to draw the borrowers into a longer-term relationship with the lending agency and increases the likelihood that further loans will be taken.

Neighbourhood improvement (slum upgrading)

A further potential role for shelter microfinance is within more comprehensive slum upgrading programmes. There appears to be a growing interest in using microfinance agencies to provide specialist financial services within more comprehensive neighbourhood improvement and poverty reduction programmes. Within this strategy, the development agency, central government and/or municipality finances a process to upgrade the low-income area with components to regularize tenure and provide and/or upgrade infrastructure and services. The upgrading programme then contracts with an organization to offer small-scale housing loans for those who wish to upgrade their homes.

A good example is the Local Development Programme (PRODEL) in Nicaragua that was set up to enhance development in smaller towns and cities with a number of components, including infrastructure improvements, housing loans and loans for microenterprises. A more focused (and smaller-scale approach) is illustrated in Ahmedabad, India, where the Slum Networking Project (undertaken within the municipality) wished to include a credit component to help households afford to contribute to infrastructure improvements.

While most slum upgrading initiatives have been led by the state, an alternative approach is that developed from an Indian alliance of the Society for the Promotion of Area

Resource Centres (SPARC) – an NGO – the National Slum Dwellers Federation and *Mahila Milan* (a network of women's collectives). Their strategy is to develop the capacity of local communities to manage a comprehensive upgrading and redevelopment process that is financed primarily by the state (through subsidies), with additional monies through loans taken by communities and repaid by individual members. Through a not-for-profit company, *Samudhaya Nirman Sahayak*, communities draw down the funds they need to pre-finance land, infrastructure and housing development. The scale of activities has resulted in additional donor finance being drawn into the process through the Community-led Infrastructure Financing Facility (CLIFF).

A further model offering a more comprehensive development strategy than shelter microfinance is the strategy of combining small loans for housing improvement with land development. One illustration is the case of El Salvador where low-cost subdivision regulations established during the early 1990s have helped to stimulate a low-income land development industry of 200 firms. After developing the area and selling the household a serviced plot, many of these developers offer a small loan (often around US$1000) to build an initial core unit. It appears that this strategy has resulted in affordable secure tenure over the last decade and – with greater supply – has lowered real estate prices in real terms.

The neighbourhood development (slum upgrading), together with the servicing of greenfield sites, approaches suggest a number of distinct neighbourhood and housing strategies that include a role for small-scale housing loans:

- improvements of existing housing units (this is the dominant approach today within shelter microfinance);
- linked land purchase and housing loan developments;
- linked land development and/or upgrading paid for with a capital subsidy and housing loan developments; and
- linked settlement upgrading and housing loan.

Sources of capital finance

How do microfinance agencies secure capital for their lending? Some providers draw on their own capital, notably the private sector and, for the most part, the small-scale voluntary organizations such as credit unions.

In general, microfinance agencies have four sources of capital finance: deposits, development assistance, governments and the private sector. The problem of lack of capital remains even in countries with a well-developed microfinance sector.

There is a difference of opinion between microfinance agencies about the need for housing subsidies. On the one hand, there is a belief that subsidies are needed both because of the traditional association between subsidies and low-income housing and because of the larger size of housing loans. On the other hand, it is widely accepted that microfinance needs to perform without subsidy finance in order to be able to expand as market conditions permit.

In situations in which there is no state support, there appears to be an effective cross-subsidy from enterprise to shelter lending, as the interest rates are lower in the latter. In some countries, particularly in Asia, subsidies are available through reduced interest rates, and microfinance agencies have become a conduit to deliver state support to the poor. In some cases, the subsidy is provided in the form of an interest rate reduction. Grameen Bank in Bangladesh and the Self-employed Women's Association (SEWA) in India have both accessed low-interest sources of funds and pass on this subsidy.

Savings and collateral

The link between housing investment and savings extends well beyond the microfinance sector. In the North, families have traditionally saved for several years simply to access conventional mortgage finance. Similarly, many microfinance programmes for housing, particularly in Asia and Africa, have savings requirements. Savings has a place in microfinance for many reasons. It is a strategy to assist with repayments in which borrowers have to demonstrate a capacity to make regular payments and accumulate sufficient funds for the required down payment or deposit.

Collateral is an asset pledged to a lender until the borrower pays back the debt. Its major role is in reducing lender risk and it is widely recognized that a key challenge for shelter microfinance is that of loan security. Many microfinance agencies seek to minimize the need for collateral by using existing client history (enterprise lending). A further strategy used when lending for income generation is small repeat loans as a way of building up repayment skills and capacities and providing an incentive for repayment. However, the larger size of shelter microfinance makes this strategy more difficult to follow.

Another strategy used by microenterprise lenders is that of group guarantees. However, this strategy has been found to be problematic for housing loans, again because of the bigger loans and longer loan period. In the absence of such strategies, a wide range of collaterals are used, including mortgages, personal guarantees, group guarantees, fixed assets and/or pension/provident fund guarantees. Pension fund collateral is used particularly in South Africa and Bangladesh and, more recently, in Namibia, but is not significant elsewhere.

Foreseen challenges

While shelter microfinance might not be effective in every context, there is now widespread experience and understanding of the process and considerable appreciation of the approach in many countries. There are two notable challenges facing the shelter microfinance sector. The first is the nature of the beneficiary group and the difficulties faced by very poor households due to problems of affordability and lack of secure tenure. The second is sources of funding.

Shelter microfinance programmes appear, in general, to reach the income groups served by microfinance agencies lending for enterprise development and families with similar incomes in the formal sector. Many shelter microfinance programmes appear to be targeted at the higher income urban poor, sometimes those with formal employment (at least one member of the family) and often those with diversified household livelihood strategies. This bias reflects the need of the agencies to secure high levels of repayments and give out larger loans (with the administration costs therefore being a smaller proportion of the loan).

Lack of capital emerges as being a very significant constraint on expansion. Banco ADEMI (in the Dominican Republic) cited lack of capital as the principal challenge that the organization faces in providing housing credit, for which there has been substantial demand. These difficulties reflect a general constraint on the microfinance sector and, in general, do not appear to be specifically related to housing lending. In addition, microfinance agencies face an issue of scale. To be profitable they have to increase the quantity of lending. There is evidence that this is driving their expansion into shelter microfinance; but for the smaller agencies, lack of capital to expand operations appears to be a significant constraint. Longer-term loan repayment periods are also common in shelter microfinance agencies despite the small size of the loans. Raising funds for shelter microfinance may be more complicated than for enterprise lending because of these longer loan periods. Donor support has placed emphasis on building the institutional capacity of lending agencies and assisting in the accumulation of their capital base. There has been a resistance to providing concessional funds for on-lending.

Chapter 7 – Community Funds

Community funds are of growing significance in assisting the poor to address their shelter needs. As the role of the state has diminished, increased emphasis has been placed on alternative strategies to support secure tenure, access to basic services and improved dwellings. Community funds offer small loans to households but route these loans through community organizations. The emphasis on collective loans is for many reasons, but one is that the loans support investments in land and infrastructure which are necessarily made by a group working together. This chapter describes community funds, identifying their key characteristics, and discusses trends within this sector. It looks specifically at a number of key challenges, notably the affordability of their strategies and sources of funds.

Community funds are financial mechanisms that encourage savings through establishing and strengthening local savings groups that provide collective finance for shelter improvement. This may include any one or more of the following activities: land purchase; land preparation; infrastructure installation; service provision and housing construction; and extension and improvement. Their most distinguishing characteristic is the way in which funding is perceived – rather than the mechanisms of the financing process. Community funds use savings and loans to trigger a development process – not simply to increase the access of the poor to financial markets. They seek to strengthen the social bonds between community members (building social capital) so that existing finance within the community can be used more effectively and external finance can be integrated within community development strategies. Community funds are targeted at group borrowing and therefore may include those with lower incomes.

Generally, there has been increasing interest in community funds during the last decade. The growth is supported by a general acknowledgement that small-scale lending has been somewhat successful and that urban poverty is growing. Two further current trends related to the development of such funds are worth noting: first, the growing interest by local government in these approaches, in part related to the use of such funds to extend essential infrastructure; and, second, the expansion of Shack or Slum Dwellers International (SDI), a community/NGO network whose strategies incorporate savings and lending activities for shelter improvements.

With respect to the latter trend, over the last 15 years, SDI has evolved into an international movement with affiliates in more than 12 countries. SDI groups have spawned a host of local community-owned and NGO-administered funds. In Cambodia, the Philippines, South Africa, Nepal, Sri Lanka, Zimbabwe and Kenya, federation groups have established their own funds, which they lend to savings schemes. State contributions have been obtained in South Africa, Namibia and, more recently, Nepal.

Funding sources

The importance of mixed funding sources is evident. In some cases, funds have been established by government and located within a state agency with access to subsidies. In other cases, the fund has been set up by civil society organizations and financed through a combination of state funds, NGO monies, community contributions and, generally, international development assistance agencies. In both cases, the communities may make direct contributions to the fund through deposits to secure loans.

An important and common characteristic of community funds is that some subsidy is provided – either through state funds or international development assistance. This is a further significant difference from conventional microfinance and its individualized housing loans. While conventional microfinance programmes may offer a subsidy, in general there is an understanding that this should be avoided. Within community funds, greater priority is placed on achieving poverty reduction goals and neighbourhood improvement. Subsidies may be needed for institutional survival if interest rates are below the level required to maintain the real value of the fund. Equally or alternatively, subsidies may be required to reach everyone in a community or to reach very low-income communities.

There are several routes through which subsidies are delivered. The primary routes are direct subsidies, interest rate subsidies, additional support (for example, community development and technical assistance) and unintended subsidies when delayed payment and/or default occurs.

A further source of finance is that of commercial financial institutions. A number of groups managing community funds have sought to draw in commercial banks. At a minimal level, loan funds are released through banks, thereby encouraging the poor to see such institutions as something that they might use. In CLIFF, a donor-financed programme working with SPARC, the National Slum Dwellers Federation and *Mahila Milan* in India, there is an expectation that the urban poor groups will become strong enough to be able to borrow from the banks.

Terms and conditions

Savings plays a central role in community funds. However, the programmes may differ in the speed and the intensity of savings. This difference reflects both the orientation of the programme itself and the possibilities within different countries. For example, in a large number of countries (including those with experience of informal savings and loan mechanisms), communities have been sceptical about the value of savings for shelter investment, and loan finance has been provided rapidly once the savings commitment was fulfilled. This is particularly true of countries that have experienced rapid inflation and/or where the state has confiscated or temporarily frozen savings.

Interest rates are generally subsidized, especially for land purchase and infrastructure, but often also for housing investment. Three major reasons emerge for this policy: practical, political and social. On the practical side, many of these early programmes evolved with an interest rate subsidy because the relatively large size of the loan made affordability difficult if market rates were used. Politically, the policies may have been influenced by communities who were familiar with state support for housing through a reduced interest rate. This appears to be particularly strong in Asia where, for example, the Bangladeshi, Indian, Thai and Philippine governments all have programmes with interest rate subsidies for low- (and low-medium) income households. From a social development perspective, inclusion of the poorest and affordability are critical.

There are two distinctive characteristics of the collateral strategies used by community funds. First, there is reliance on community systems and community collateral rather than claims over the individual borrowers. Second, in cases of land purchase, legal title deeds may be used. However, the difficulties of loan security are considerable because of the different attitude towards non-repayment.

Loan periods appear to be longer than those used for shelter microfinance with, for example, rates of 25 years in the Philippines and 10 years in Thailand. To a certain extent, this is because of the large size of the loan relative to family incomes. It is also an acknowledgement of the fact that land purchase, for example, may be only a part of the investments that the family needs to make. NGO loan periods are lower and are generally less than five years. While some appear longer, such as those of the *uTshani* Fund in South Africa, the design reflects the fact that funds are primarily released as bridge finance for the state subsidy.

Challenges

Community funds face challenges that are very similar to those faced by agencies supporting shelter microfinance initiatives. How can they secure the funding they need for long-term viability and how can they be effective in reaching out to those in need of shelter investment?

A particularly different challenge faces community funds as they develop – what should their strategy be with respect to the state? Fundamentally, this is about strategies that maximize possibilities for scaling up funds while retaining a process that can be controlled by local communities. Links to the state are almost certainly essential if funding on the required scale is to be available. However, there is a concern that funds will be bureaucratized.

Community fund programmes are designed for relatively stable communities who are in need of finance to secure land tenure and to upgrade their neighbourhood. With regard to the challenge of inclusion, community funds may struggle to include all residents living within the settlement. They may also find it difficult to assist those who do not live permanently in areas of the city.

Throughout Asia, Latin America and Africa, conventional development processes have failed to deal with many groups of poor people. In some cases, these are the poorest; but this is not always the case. There are particular groups who are vulnerable, such as illegal migrants. For example, Nicaraguans living in Costa Rica, Peruvians in Ecuador or West Africans in South Africa are often treated as non-citizens. The practice of daily saving in India helps to ensure that even the poorest can participate. The livelihoods of the poor are generally managed daily (or in three- to five-day cycles), not monthly. Groups who save monthly exclude the poor. At the same time, richer households may not be interested in a process that requires them to save daily.

A group who may also face exclusion is tenants. It may be difficult to ensure that tenants are granted equal rights as tenure is secured and development takes place. A further aspect of inclusion is that of gender. There is a widespread understanding that the centrality of women is important. In part, this is because women are concerned about their neighbours, about who is sick and who needs what; it is also related to the level of poverty and vulnerability experienced by women. Women's community role means that if women are central to managing the savings process, then it is likely that there will be fewer problems with exclusion within the community. However, this requires that the process is orientated towards women taking up a leadership role. While this seems prevalent in the case of savings and loans, in some contexts, the shift to construction encourages higher levels of involvement by men.

PART III: TOWARDS SUSTAINABLE SHELTER FINANCE SYSTEMS

Chapter 8 – Assessing Shelter Finance Systems

The analysis in Chapter 7 highlights a number of specific issues that have policy implications with regard to the value of shelter finance in addressing urban shelter needs. This chapter discusses these issues across the different approaches to shelter finance addressed in the Global Report. The issues considered are affordability and the difficulties of reaching the poor; access to capital and the lack of loan finance; the move to markets and what the market cannot manage – including the issues of maintaining financial viability; connections and diversity within globalization; and risk management within the market.

Affordability and the difficulties of reaching the poor

Rising house prices have made affordability more difficult in the North, as well as in the South. There have been very considerable attempts supported by government to extend homeownership to lower income groups – for example, through the more extensive use of mortgage insurance. There are some indications of success (higher homeownership rates) and some areas of concern as households may find it difficult to manage the associated risks.

In the South, the percentage of those who cannot afford mortgage loans is significantly higher in many countries, reflecting high levels of poverty. The estimates suggest that these numbers may be over 70 per cent in sub-Saharan Africa and the lower income countries of Asia, and at or above 40 per cent in the higher income countries of Asia and Latin America.

Opportunities to acquire small loans for land acquisition, infrastructure and housing do appear to have grown significantly during the last two decades, particularly during the last ten years. However, provision still appears very small given potential demand (and in the context of estimated housing deficits).

The growth of microfinance agencies for enterprise development pre-dates the specific rise of shelter microfinance. These agencies have been encouraged to move into this sector due, in part, to the scale of enterprise loans that were 'misdirected' at housing investment. In other cases, they have extended their loan services to respond to explicit needs and requests, and because of their own commercial needs to expand their markets. The major problem faced by these agencies appears to be a lack of capital for expansion.

The tradition of community funds has grown up to respond to the needs of urban poor groups to invest in land purchase and to develop infrastructure on such land. While many loans are for secure tenure and infrastructure, the financial systems are also used for more individualized lending, both for housing and income generation.

Once more, there are indications that the poorest find it difficult to participate. Such problems are evident in assessments of the Community Mortgage Programme (CMP), a group-lending scheme in the Philippines that has provided almost 150,000 households with secure tenure, but which finds it difficult to include the poorest households. However, it has to be recognized that the use of loans carries inherent risks for those who are too poor to manage repayment risk, and greater emphasis may need to be placed on savings and grant combinations. Although there have been some attempts to develop micro-insurance schemes with microfinance initiatives, relatively little attention has been given to such strategies in the context of shelter microfinance.

The role of mortgage finance: Access to capital and the lack of loan finance

Mortgage finance is unaffordable for many of those living in the South and a significant minority in the North. Despite this, great emphasis has been placed by both governments and development agencies on mortgage finance, and state subsidies for mortgage finance still appear to be at a considerable scale in more than a few countries.

Different housing markets are not distinct and if no other arrangements are made the higher income groups could take up those opportunities that are being offered to the poor.

In both Latin America and Asia, there have been initiatives at the government and multilateral agency level to support the development of secondary markets to increase wholesale finance to mortgage lenders. While it is possible that it is a shortage of capital that is preventing the expansion of mortgage finance, many other reasons have been identified in this report. What appears to be of most significance is the scale of informality in property and labour markets. It seems that much emphasis has been placed on formalizing land titles; but, as seen in Peru, this has not necessarily increased the take-up of either mortgages or enterprise loans. This suggests that access to loans may be limited in ways that cannot be addressed by reforms to property titles, increasing the ease of foreclosure or the scale of finance and competition in the sector.

Despite these problems, mortgage lending does appear to have expanded in a number of countries. This appears to be associated with economic growth and with increasing affluence. Competition has intensified and the market for mortgage finance is moving beyond a small number of lenders in several countries.

There are risks for individual households in taking on mortgage loans, and some of these risks have been evident when housing prices have fallen, notably in the UK and Japan. While mortgage insurance has been extended, it appears that much emphasis has been placed on protecting the lender rather than the borrower. Mortgage finance has survived difficult circumstances in Asia and Latin America during the last decade.

The bigger picture and what the market cannot manage

Despite a general emphasis on the expansion of market-orientated mortgage finance and housing support, more generally, the analysis in this report does point to a number of areas in which markets alone appear to be struggling, including institutional failings related to necessarily collective rather than individual investments in shelter, and issues related to urban planning and land-use management.

The housing finance market is strongly orientated towards providing loans to individual households. In two of the situations discussed in this report, there is a need for collective investment: to maintain multi-family dwellings in transition countries and to invest in land and infrastructure for those without tenure in the South. In both cases, it appears that the market is unable to make an adequate response, in part due to reasons of affordability, but also because local institutions that can manage the finance are missing. While the suggestion proposed by government agencies is often the establishment of formal management committees, care needs to be given that these do not discriminate against the poor. To address the housing needs of the poor, housing finance systems need to provide for loans for such collective purposes, and appropriate local structures must be in place for this to happen.

The market also seems to struggle with ensuring the quality of the urban environment (in a physical and social sense). The greater emphasis on targeting and reduced social provision in the North appears to have resulted in a greater concentration of low-income households in specific areas. This applies both in the case of the transition countries and for the richer countries of Western Europe.

Another important issue is the nature of the developments that are being supported by the direct-demand subsidies – for example, in South Africa and Chile. A consequence in both countries is that low-income housing has been located on low-cost sites, often a considerable distance from jobs, services and other facilities, with little consideration of the social cost that results from such physical exclusion. This suggests that the market is unable to respond to the needs of the poor without greater interventions from the state – either the funding agency and/or the local authority. This further suggests that a key task for government is to ensure adequate supplies of well-located and well-serviced land.

Connections and diversity within globalization

The broad context within which the analysis in this report is situated is one in which financial markets are deregulating and the state is withdrawing from direct involvement in the economy. Despite this financial deregulation, there is relatively little evidence that financial globalization is taking place in the housing sector. Markets for housing finance have internationalized rather than globalized. Hence, at present, while money can flow across borders and assets are sold offshore as well as domestically, there is no globalized market in which there is a continuous flow of funds into assets whose risks and returns are independent of national regulatory and banking structures, and where prices are identical across national borders (for areas with similar risks).

Internationalization has occurred in place of globalization because, although the state has withdrawn to some extent, it remains involved and housing finance markets are still particular, depending upon their specific historical and structural contexts. As a result, rather than there being a single market, many national markets exist.

Chapter 9 – Pollicy Directions Towards Sustainable Urban Shelter Finance Systems

Chapter 9 discusses the ways in which shelter finance systems could be strengthened, in terms of both performance and sustainability, on the basis of the experiences reviewed in the preceding chapters. Its main purpose is to point the way forward, highlighting best policies and practices. The chapter starts by identifying policy directions in improving urban development finance, which is necessary for citywide infrastructure development. It then proceeds to identify policy directions in shelter finance.

The essential basis of the municipal side of the compact between households and the public realm is a system of financing public goods so that they can be provided across the city, in appropriate quality and quantity, and at affordable cost, and so that the city can be managed effectively. Unless urban areas can produce more income at the same rate that they absorb more people, the resources to develop infrastructure and build shelter will not be available.

It is vital that powers, duties and revenues are congruent. If the municipal authority is responsible for social housing, it should have the power to take policy decisions on how it will act and receive the required revenue, or be able to raise the finance.

Towards inclusive urban infrastructure and services

Municipalities should be able to raise at least part of their revenue from local taxation, at levels which reflect local conditions. As a consequence, municipalities and governments need to build the institutional capacity to levy and collect these taxes, and to spend them responsibly. Indeed, legislation may be necessary to guide the responsible use of municipal revenues.

It is vital that there is some source of loans for capital projects to which municipalities can apply in order to allow them to develop major projects that cannot be financed out of annual budgets. There are many models. Funds may be made available through loans from central government or an agency thereof, a mortgage bank, a finance company, a provincial-level institution, or a group of municipalities working cooperatively.

Just as protecting endangered environments can be funded through debt swaps, so such exercises can be used to fund housing and urban services, as shown in the case of Bolivia (described in Chapter 3). As in many other financing arrangements, having a poverty reduction strategy paper (PRSP) in place which influences urban policy enables debt swapping in that it gives the parties confidence that the money will be spent within a strategy for poverty reduction rather than *ad hoc*.

The rising value of urban land is a significant potential source of finance for cities. Extracting public value out of the development process has been practised in many countries, some with great success. The US linkage process, in which city authorities leverage funds from the profits derived by developers of real estate to fund social projects, might be effective in cities in the South.

The level of accuracy required in land records for the collection of property taxes is lower than that for avoidance or resolution of land disputes. Thus, such systems as half cadastres and the use of regular low-resolution aerial photography can provide a level of accuracy well able to support property taxation systems at relatively low cost, compared with an expensive, high-resolution land survey.

It is also important that municipalities are paid economic charges for their services. Thus, functions such as land registry, building regulation and planning control should be subject to a charge that covers the cost. Similarly, user fees for municipal services (markets, abattoirs, car parks, transport interchanges, bus services, assembly halls, etc.) should cover life-cycle costs and, where appropriate, generate revenue.

In many cities, there is a culture of replacing regular maintenance with irregular capital projects. It is better practice to cost infrastructure over its whole life (life-cycle costing) and put aside money for periodic maintenance over a long life. The savings are considerable compared with rebuilding at the end of a short life.

The ability of the small-scale private sector to run local supplies of water, waste collection and other services in partnership with the public authorities is well documented and should be explored by municipalities not already using such partnerships.

Wherever it occurs, corruption saps the ability of central and municipal governments to meet the needs of their constituents through diverting money away from the development and maintenance of services. Only when real progress is made on making corruption simply unacceptable in business and government, and involving people in eradicating it wherever it is found, will cities function efficiently and with trust from all partners.

It is likely that government funding can have the greatest effect if it is directed towards infrastructure and services for low-income neighbourhoods and welfare services for the poorest. In the provision of land, basic infrastructure and social services to the poor and poorest, subsidy is likely to be required unless the cost of services is low indeed.

Unless urban areas can produce more income at the same rate that they absorb more people, per capita incomes will fall and urban poverty will deepen. Thus, employment and income are central to the financing of urban development. The potential of shelter provision to generate employment for low-income workers should be utilized to generate income to improve people's ability to pay for housing. The income multipliers are very high for construction and even higher for low-technology, labour-intensive construction. In parallel, the provision of efficient infrastructure and appropriate shelter is critical in ensuring the economic productivity of the work force in urban areas and countries as a whole.

Local governments should reduce the costs of economic activity by streamlining land allocation, development control and other regulatory activities, while retaining appropriate ability to act in the public good. One-stop shops allowing planning and building control to be streamlined are capable of radically reducing the transaction costs of development and encourage more people to take the formal development route.

Strengthening the sustainability and performance of the shelter finance system

Turning to housing finance, there is both a need and a demand for layers of finance for different sectors of the housing supply process. Mortgage finance, for relatively large sums over a long period of repayment, is essential for those well off enough to buy a complete formal dwelling. However, small loans, taken out over short terms of between one and eight years, loaned at market rates, are growing in importance in the housing sector.

The problem in many developing (and even in some developed) countries is not that housing is too expensive, but that incomes are too low. The locus of attention should not be on the minimum quality and cost of housing, but on the level of payment received by workers. This demand-side focus is in line with current trends in subsidies and concentrates attention on the systemic problem of poverty, which generates poor housing consequences.

In many countries in the South, the cost of urban housing is increased significantly by the high standards to which it must comply. The introduction of lower standards that are more appropriate to the local context could potentially make housing more affordable to a far greater proportion of the urban population. Lower standards would still, however, have to safeguard the health and safety of the occupants and protect the public interest.

Most policies behind official development assistance and national policies are based on the provision of independently serviced single-household dwellings, owned by their occupants. However, this is by no means the main form of occupation by households living in poverty. Instead, large numbers of households live in buildings occupied by many households. There is much to be gained from encouraging multi-occupied housing development where it fits in with local norms.

Small-scale landlords in informal settlements are a major source of affordable housing for a growing majority of households living in poverty in the urban South; but there are few initiatives to assist them. It is imperative, therefore, to understand how best to assist the informal rental sector and, at the same time, to preserve affordability in order to preclude gentrification.

In the spirit of the Habitat Agenda, and if the housing backlog is to be cleared at all, it is vital that all actors in the housing process are involved in the role in which they are most efficient. The most important suppliers of the dwellings themselves, and their ancillary services, are the millions of small-scale building contractors, the single artisans or small groups of skilled people and the labourers who service their needs. However much demand there is for housing, it can only be supplied as quickly as the construction industry can build it. Finance to provide healthy liquidity among small-scale contractors and single artisans is an essential prerequisite to effective housing supply to scale.

In countries where the housing supply system is efficient and speculative of what the market demands, developers are often an important part of the process. Some mechanism for recognizing their contribution with financial assistance, especially for bridging loans, may be very beneficial for the housing supply process and could institute the efficient speculative building of housing, which is common in industrialized economies.

Recent research into regulatory frameworks for urban upgrading and new housing development has recommended the removal of constraints that prevent the poor from borrowing from financial institutions or accessing credit through other formal channels. In particular, administrative procedures that delay investments and/or increase risks should be reviewed as they add to the cost and deter the poor from conforming.

The countries in which most of the urban growth will take place during the next 25 years have very low domestic savings measured as both per capita and as a percentage of GDP. As savings are the foundations for investment, this does not auger well for urban development. It is important that developing countries maintain as much as possible the investment and savings arising from local economic activity within their borders, or benefit from net inflows from investments overseas. It is difficult to overstress the importance of reliable banks and low inflation in discouraging capital flight.

It is in governments' interests to extend mortgage markets down the income scale, as homeownership is seen to be beneficial economically and politically. Measures that could be adopted include reducing the cost of lending, especially through reducing interest rates; supporting the system of mortgage financing, especially through extending secondary markets and reducing risks; and providing direct capital grants to reduce the size of a household's mortgage in comparison with the dwelling cost.

Well-run mortgage facilities are undoubtedly important to the health of the housing supply system in the North and may be a major contributor to housing improvement in transitional countries. They are also important in providing upper- and middle-income groups with housing finance, without which they would claim the shelter opportunities provided for those lower down the income scale.

As mortgage finance is unlikely to assist the majority of the people, it must not be allowed to divert attention from financing that is helpful to lower income groups or to drain resources away from low-income households towards those in the middle- or upper-income groups.

Loan periods and loan-to-value ratios (LTVs) are vital components of mortgage loans, which are determined by the lender rather than the global macroeconomic environment. Decisions about them can be the difference between the success and failure of the mortgage company and can determine who can afford to borrow, at least at the margins. Low LTVs (and, therefore, high initial deposits) reduce risk but increase the need for upfront capital. The level of repayments can be varied in order to help households meet their obligations. Variable-interest loans allow low payments at the beginning, increasing as income improves to repay the loan on time.

There is a well-documented link between finance for income generation and improvements in housing. Many homeowners operate one or more home-based enterprises from the structure on which they raise housing finance. The same goes for rental income. One of the most important sources of low-cost rental property, which is becoming more important as the years pass, is the extra room built on to a home and rented out to a stranger for rent, or to a co-villager or relative for no rent but some other benefit (if only to satisfy family obligations).

It is obvious that improvements in housing can benefit home-based income generation, including room rentals. Thus, lenders should take account of the likelihood of income improvements in the application procedure through a process which factors in future income generated by the housing goods, to be provided under the loan. It is also important that financiers recognize that the poor are more concerned about access to credit than its cost. Experience shows that there is great demand for microfinance even if interest rates are high.

Subsidies come in many guises, including direct interest-rate reductions; allowing mortgage interest payments to be deducted from income tax; supporting housing-related savings; supporting insurance of mortgages; supporting the secondary mortgage markets; and direct grants for shelter.

If appropriate housing finance is in place, the proportion of households requiring subsidy should be minimized to only those too poor to afford the real cost of the shelter available. The need for subsidy can, thus, be reduced by adopting effective financing systems. The work of some NGOs to provide funding to assist individuals in accessing subsidies is very helpful to many households. In Ecuador, a revolving fund provides the down payment necessary to obtain a national housing subsidy grant.

Social housing is, almost by definition, subsidized housing. The subsidy element is a financial credit to the occupier and, thus, often constitutes an important element in a nation's housing finance system. Although social housing is becoming residual in Europe and transitional countries, the need to provide more housing that is affordable to the low-income households is still present. Those who cannot afford homeownership or market rents in the private market need shelter through public rental housing. In the South, however, few countries have been successful in large-scale public rental housing.

Small housing loans, disbursed through housing microfinance institutions (HMFIs), are some of the most promising developments in housing finance during the last decade. They are suitable for extending existing dwellings, building on already serviced land, adding rooms (often for renting out), adding services such as toilets, and housing improvements within *in situ* neighbourhood upgrading. They tend to reach much further down the income scale than mortgage financing, but not to the households close to or below poverty lines.

In the context of large numbers of new low-income households in cities over the next two decades, it is important to increase the number of lenders in the housing microfinance sector, rather than to concentrate only on mortgage finance which, inevitably, serves the middle- and upper-income groups.

There is a serious issue of funding for on-lending by HMFIs. Many have received concessionary funds, and their lending reflects the low price of the capital. If they are to expand their operations, they will need to cope with borrowing at international market rates and reflect this in their loans.

In comparison to enterprise microfinance, shelter microfinance lending involves long-term and large loans and generates a need for group security or some security of tenure backed by documentation. In the context of group lending, mandatory savings periods before loans not only build up an understanding of finance, but also strengthen community ties among savers through regular group meetings. Then the group becomes the collateral, as the members will support each other in times of difficulty and take away from the lender the complication of following up defaulters.

Throughout the days of sites-and-services projects and other aided self-help, efforts have been made to reduce the financial burden of low-income homeowners by allowing materials to be drawn from dedicated warehouses or to be supplied on credit through local commercial suppliers. Recent experience in Mexico and elsewhere has shown how there may be great potential for this to expand alongside housing microfinance and the downscaling of mortgages to lower income households using the longstanding credit culture operated by furniture and household goods retailers.

Remittances from overseas residents of local nationality are an important part of housing finance in many countries. Many people can remit enough to build a house in a few years overseas in quite lowly employment that would be impossible if they stayed at home in higher-level employment. But there is a danger that tastes, standards and ability to pay from a different context may take over the local markets and drive other residents into poorer housing than they would otherwise have.

Many charities give large amounts of money towards housing improvement and shelter for the poorest. There is a place in funding shelter for the poor for that which arises from altruistic humanitarian support.

Community-based financing of housing and services has been used for both settlement upgrading and for building on greenfield sites. In a context where small loans are evidently successful, and where there is an increase in poverty, it has many advantages for low-income and otherwise disempowered households. The experience of the affiliates of the Shack or Slum Dwellers' Federation has demonstrated that there is great potential for community-based organizations to manage development finance to the benefit of large numbers of relatively poor households. The evident success of community funds has attracted some governments to take part in their financing.

Epilogue: Towards Sustainable Urban Shelter

The shelter issue has become one of a global nature after the concept of 'human settlements' found its place in the international development agenda. Until recently, the classical response to the shelter problems of the urban poor was social housing, both in developed and developing countries. However, the massive demand for affordable housing in developing countries, coupled with the limited resources of the public sector, would have made this solution inapplicable, even in the presence of a well-organized and transparent public-housing delivery sector. Notable exceptions are states such as Singapore, which implemented huge and very successful public housing programmes, as well as successful policies in other larger countries such as Tunisia and isolated exemplary projects in many others.

The notion of 'financing shelter for the poor' corresponds, in a way, to the abandonment of the traditional concept of public responsibility embedded in the 'social role of the state'. With the commodification of the economy, where housing is but another good to be produced, sold and bought, the solution to the shelter dilemma is based on the notion that 'the poor' will always exist, and that their access to a fundamental human need – adequate shelter – will always require special measures and special solutions.

This Epilogue starts from the premise that 'special approaches' and *ad hoc* solutions, however ingenious, will never work at the scale required. Three points are made. First, the percentage of the urban poor in the cities of the developing world is far too high to be considered a residual issue. Second, the demand for affordable shelter is increasing at an extremely fast pace, notably in the rapidly growing cities of the developing world. Third, the standards and costs that city life requires are high and complex. Shelter is only one, albeit the central, requirement of all citizens. Given the rapid spatial growth of cities in the developing countries, transport, for example, becomes a crucial necessity for survival. The living, working and spatial circumstances of city life require standards and services for all that are far superior in quality and sophistication to those usually associated with minimal shelter – a roof over one's head.

Given these considerations, the issue is not simply financing shelter for the poor. The issue is making adequate shelter affordable to the poor. This approach may be called 'sustainable shelter': shelter that is environmentally, socially and economically sustainable because it satisfies the Habitat Agenda requirements of adequacy. Its acquisition, retention and maintenance are affordable by those who enjoy it. It does not overburden the community with unaffordable costs. Finally, it is located in areas that do not constitute a threat to people or to the environment.

There is no single magic formula to achieve this. Individual self-help can only produce solutions that are admirably suited to the harsh circumstances of urban migration, but are also the most fragile of all. Community-based funding has proven a valuable and indispensable asset, particularly for improving services and, in some cases, infrastructure in informal settlements; but it is not likely to reach the scale required, at least in the short term. It must also be noted that the admirable solidarity mechanisms found in poor urban communities stem from the common will to stave off a common threat, often rooted in a state of illegality and a risk of eviction. They also depend upon the cultural and ethnic composition of the informal settlement. Strongly desirable and supported outcomes such as regularization, infrastructure upgrading and the improvement of economic circumstances can also bring the attenuation of community solidarity and mutual self-help mechanisms. Therefore, they cannot be assumed to work in all cases and for indefinite periods of time.

Abating housing costs

Housing is becoming an increasingly expensive commodity in all countries. Between 1997 and 2004, according to a very recent survey, average housing prices grew by 131 per cent in Spain, 147 per cent in the UK, 179 per cent in Ireland, 113 per cent in Australia, 90 per cent in France and 65 per cent in the US. The only developing country listed in the survey is South Africa, which registered the highest growth in the sampled countries: 195 per cent.

Of course, these sharp increases in housing prices can, in many cases, be due mainly to speculative bubbles. But there is little that policies can do to prevent or control these phenomena. On the other hand, while average housing prices are lower in the developing countries, they are also influenced by steeply rising costs of land, building materials and other cost components.

Affordability, therefore, rests to a large extent upon policies capable of bringing down housing production costs. Housing production cost components are known: capital, land, infrastructure, building materials, standards, design, location and modes of production. To be affordable, all of these elements will require a substantive element of subsidy; but in some cases they will only need intelligent policy changes.

Increasing purchasing power

In the developed world, a household with two sources of income, wife and husband, however humble the occupation or the source of income may be, normally can gain access to decent shelter on the market, however modest. In the developing world, this is virtually impossible – hence, the virtual necessity of finding affordable inadequate shelter in a slum. People who live in slums are known as 'slum dwellers'. In reality, they are 'working poor': people who work for a living, but whose income cannot guarantee them access to the basic needs that everybody in developed countries take for granted – adequate shelter, proper nourishment, health, education and decent and non-threatening living environments.

There is something terribly wrong about the inability of vast numbers of the working poor in developing countries to gain access to adequate housing. Part of the problem is the rising costs of conventional housing addressed above; but an equally important issue is the extremely low wages in the formal sector and income from other income-earning activities, particularly in the informal sector. This is why making shelter affordable to the poor also depends upon increasing the poor's income.

The issue, of course, is not simply that of higher wages. A regular income is also a standard prerequisite for accessing mortgage or shelter microfinance markets. Continuity in income earning is important once one enters a mortgage agreement in order to avoid the risk of losing all of one's investment through the painful process of repossession. But a decent income is the minimum basis for accessing decent shelter, particularly in the situations of virtually all developing countries where workers' benefits and pensions are virtually non-existent and where the prices of basic necessities rise as rapidly as those of housing.

Lower housing prices and higher incomes

Increasing both wages and income opportunities for the working poor augments the saving potential of the same earning group. The urban poor show a marked propensity and ability to pool part of their incomes into community funds and other forms of saving arrangements. This triggers virtuous circles: the more capital is saved, the more is available for improving shelter conditions, productivity, skills formation and income-earning activities. With upgrading and adequate shelter solutions, more disposable income can become available to contribute to basic infrastructure and services, thus making public capital investment in this area more sustainable.

Financing shelter is only a component of the broader goal of securing solutions that can make shelter truly sustainable and that can fill the gap between the two extreme outcomes which are being witnessed today: affordable shelter that is inadequate and adequate shelter that is unaffordable. One starting point is to look at the inhabitants of informal settlements not simply as 'slum dwellers', but as 'working poor'. Important opportunities exist for addressing the affordability gap by acting on both ends of the sustainable shelter equation – reducing housing production costs and increasing the incomes of the working poor.

Given the urgency and growing significance of the 'urbanization of poverty' challenge, it is difficult to think of other areas of development that deserve more attention and investment on the part of the local, national and international institutions committed to reaching the Millennium Development Goals (MDGs), including the target of improving the lives of at least 100 million slum dwellers by 2020 and, more generally, to find practical and sustainable solutions to the global fight against poverty. Cities can lead the way, and the MDG targets within them – the urban poor – can become the protagonists, leading actors and living examples of a brighter future for all of humanity.

PART I

ECONOMIC AND URBAN DEVELOPMENT CONTEXT

CHAPTER 1

CHALLENGES OF SUSTAINABLE SHELTER DEVELOPMENT IN MACROECONOMIC CONTEXT[1]

During recent years, there has been a growing recognition of the importance of urbanization in the economic and social futures of nations by the international community, member states of the United Nations and a wide range of civil society organizations. This recognition is based on country experiences, development policies, studies and projects since the first United Nations Conference on Human Settlements held in Vancouver, Canada, during 1976.

Urbanization – and its many dimensions – has been important in all countries. The first and most evident dimension is demographic, as most developing countries have urbanized considerably since the 1950s and are projected to continue this process through the middle of the 21st century (see Figure 1.1). This increasing share of total population living in cities is similar to the historic patterns of Europe and North America, with increasing urbanization accompanying rising levels of gross domestic product (GDP). The key differences lie in the faster pace of urban growth in developing countries during this period and the absolute levels of urban population as represented both in the concentration of people living in mega-cities (urban agglomerations of over 10 million residents) and the increasing numbers of medium-sized cities of up to 3 million.

These facts of contemporary life in the 21st century have themselves transformed the world, with higher levels of individual and household incomes resulting from unparalleled levels of economic productivity benefiting from economies of agglomeration and scale. The concentration of economic activity and power in cities has, in turn, attracted footloose capital from the global economy, transforming the world itself in what is now understood as a process of 'globalization'.

These processes, however, have also created many problems and contributed to growing patterns of difference within countries and people. Urbanization, for example, has been accompanied by continued out-migration from rural areas in many countries. The mechanization of agriculture and the globalization of agricultural production have reduced both the local control of the rural sector and the demand for rural labour. When placed into a national and international context, what might be called 'a geography of difference' can be easily seen.

Together, these processes set the stage for the fundamental issue that this Global Report addresses: how can housing and infrastructure services be financed for growing numbers of urban residents during the 21st century? The first part of this chapter presents the building blocks of a conceptual framework for answering this question, while the second part presents, as a background, the macroeconomic context of financing urban shelter development.

The fundamental issue is: how can housing and infrastructure services be financed for growing numbers of urban residents during the 21st century?

UNDERSTANDING URBAN SHELTER DEVELOPMENT CHALLENGES

As mentioned in the preceding section, this first part of the chapter presents the building blocks of a conceptual framework for understanding the global challenge of financing the development of urban shelter, as well as related infrastructure and services. Individually, these building blocks are not controversial. They reflect the current knowledge and the collective thinking of observers and participants in the world's urbanization experience. However, when linked together, they demonstrate that the world is facing an urgent and dramatic problem, with significant consequences for individual cities, countries, regions and the world itself.

Demographic framework

The starting point of this analysis is the process of demographic transformation. United Nations projections and recent assessments of expected demographic growth in developing countries (see Statistical Annex, Tables B.1 and B.2) indicate that the *developing countries will add approximately 2 billion new urban residents during the next*

Table 1.1

Demographic highlights (China and India)

	China	India
Urbanization level in 2000, estimate (%)	35.8	27.7
Urbanization level in 2030, projection (%)	60.5	41.4
Urban population in 2000, estimate (000)	456,247	281,255
Urban population in 2030, projection (000)	877,623	586,052
Increase in urban population, 2000–2030 (000)	421,376	304,797
Increase in number of total households, 2000–2030 (000)	284,040	129,358
Average quinquennial increment, 2000–2030 (000)	47,840	21,560
Average annual increment, 2000–2030 (000)	9.568	4,311

Source: UN Population Division, 2004. UN-Habitat, 2003a.

25 years.[2] This robust finding, added to the existing numbers of 1 billion people currently living in slums, frames the 'demand side' for the need for housing and infrastructure services in developing countries.

Looking more closely, approximately 90 per cent of this demand will occur in 48 countries, with most of the growth occurring in East and South Asia. The concentration of this demand reflects both the overall population sizes of China and India, but also other large Asian countries such as Bangladesh and Pakistan in South Asia, and Indonesia, the Philippines and Viet Nam in East Asia. During 1950, these countries were largely rural; today they continue to experience rapid urban growth, with many of their urban concentrations reaching over the 1 million population level. Much of this growth has been fuelled by economic growth itself, with higher urban incomes attracting rural migrants. The enormous growth of urban populations of China and India are shown in Table 1.1, demonstrating that these countries have both experienced large-scale shifts in their populations towards urban centres while continuing to grow at aggregate levels.

Developing countries will add approximately 2 billion new urban residents during the next 25 years

It is predicted that the scenario of a decreasing rural population and increasing urban population, with the only possible exception of the African continent, will be exacerbated by expected universal reductions in fertility levels. Indeed, the prediction is that by 2020, the rural population growth rate will turn negative for the first time.[3]

Africa will also continue to experience rapid urban demographic growth, reflecting continued rural-to-urban migration, with push factors from the lack of productivity of agriculture and the inability to feed and provide incomes for rural populations. The slow growth of rural productivity in African countries has many causes: environmental pressures in the Sahel and East Africa, with severe water shortages, loss of topsoil and lack of rural infrastructure; overpopulation in some parts of the Great Lakes Region of Central Africa; or armed conflicts destabilizing cultivation patterns. These internal problems have been exacerbated by the global trading system, with subsidies by developed countries – for example for cotton – which displace cotton produced in Burkina Faso or Mali from world markets.

Even though Africa's cities have not generated the jobs needed to sustain growing urban populations, they have, nonetheless, attracted large numbers of people fleeing rural poverty. While studies during the 1970s showed that these migrants were largely attracted by the prospects of higher wages from urban employment,[4] this motivation has been strengthened by the lack of food security in rural areas, as well as by the need for physical security from armed conflict and environmental risks. This 'urbanization of rural poverty' is reflected in the increasingly large urban slums in most African countries.

In contrast, the Latin American countries experienced urbanization at an earlier period in which economic growth generated the financial resources needed for the construction of housing and urban infrastructure. Cities such as Buenos Aires, São Paulo or Mexico City demonstrated spectacular growth during the mid 20th century. Even during these periods of economic boom, however, this growth did not keep up with the growing demand for housing and urban infrastructure, such as water supply, sanitation and electricity. Public-sector institutions were unable to provide these services at a rate faster than the proliferation of *favelas* in Rio de Janeiro, *barriadas* in Lima or *tugurios* in Quito.

Nevertheless, Latin American cities have become the loci of economic productivity and employment growth. At the same time, they are also the loci of growing urban poverty and inequality between the rich and poor. How to bridge this gap will be discussed in later chapters of this Global Report.

In contrast to the developing countries, transition economies and developed countries face different challenges in the financing of urban development. Previous public patterns of provision of housing and infrastructure in the transition countries have been disrupted by the political and economic changes following the collapse of the Soviet Union. These systems had provided a very minimum quality of housing and infrastructure in most countries, with long waiting periods for new households. Whether these cities will become productive engines for the growth of their new reformed economies remains to be seen.

Cities in developed countries have occupied an increasingly important place in their respective national economies. As economies shift towards financial services and the knowledge economy, these activities tend to be located in large cities. How well the cities perform with these functions depends upon the reliability of their infrastructure and the quality of urban life as factors in attracting new investment.

Each of these regions and individual countries have always had their own set of characteristics that determine their patterns of urban growth and specific development challenges to be faced by their governments and societies at large.[5]

Translating demographic growth into the demand for housing and infrastructure

Recent data and analyses indicate that the current global backlog of slum dwellers is about 925 million people.[6] As shown in Table 1.2, when this figure is combined with the projected 1.9 billion additional urban population, approximately *2.825 billion people will require housing and urban services by 2030*. This projection is the starting point for this Global Report.

In considering this number, precision is not really very important. What is critical, however, is the *order of magnitude*. Close to 3 billion people, or about *40 per cent of the world's population by 2030*, will need to have housing and basic infrastructure services. Table 1.3 demonstrates that in order to accommodate the increments in the number of households over the next 25 years, 35.1 million housing units per year will be required. This estimate, in turn, translates into completing 96,150 housing units per day or 4000 per hour. These figures do not include replacements of deteriorated and substandard housing stocks.

Socio-behavioural framework

The challenges raised are not, however, exclusively about the quantity of population, but also about its composition. A recent publication argued that the *processes of social differentiation in cities are also accelerating*[7] because they are interacting with the scale and rate of demographic change. There are not only more people in cities, but they eat, work, play, educate, dress and express themselves differently. The richness and, indeed, the tolerance of the culture and diversity of urban behaviour is a major factor in explaining why there is not more violence and conflict than exists in cities. One could easily make the argument that Mumbai and Bangkok are surprisingly peaceful, given their scale and complexity. These processes of urban social and cultural differentiation require much more documentation and research because they are an important factor in what would actually be 'sustained' in sustainable cities.

Processes of differentiation also have financial implications as diverse populations express their special needs, with more elderly populations requiring special services at the same time that there are school-age children require more schools and teachers. A wider diversity and range of social needs implies a wider and more diverse set of services, whether provided by government or non-governmental organizations (NGOs). Growing ethnically diverse cities can also create the need for ethnically sensitive policies and programmes, as well as the necessity to maintain peaceful relations between communities. For example, one can imagine that ethnically homogeneous neighbourhoods and communities may exclude other people not sharing their particular identity. These conflicts can have direct impacts upon the quality of life in neighbourhoods and on access to infrastructure services.[8]

Economic framework

The capacity of developing countries to *finance* their needs depends largely upon their level of future economic growth and development. If countries are productive and able to generate employment and incomes for growing populations at an accelerated rate, they will be able to generate and mobilize the savings and investment to finance basic needs, such as housing and infrastructure services. Then, with realistic policies supported by effective institutions, they can have a chance at meeting growing needs. If, however, they remain at current growth rates or, as in some cases, are unable to grow economically, there will be little likelihood that these resources will be available. In this sense, *macro-economic growth* is a necessary but not sufficient condition for addressing this problem.

Urban population (2003)	3,043,934,680
Estimated urban population (2030)	4,944,679,063
Additional urban population 2003–2030	1,900,744,383
Population living in slums (2001)	923,986,000
People requiring housing and urban services by 2030	2,824,730,383

Source: Statistical Annex of this report

Table 1.2

People requiring housing and urban services by 2030

This Global Report will examine that relationship and identify each of the possible sources of finance for urban development in order to determine which policies and programmes are likely to assist in this process. The following sections present the differences between the macro-economic conditions of countries, as well as the various sources of macroeconomic growth needed to provide the foundation for urban development, while also demonstrating that this is a two-way process: cities and towns are also important contributors to macroeconomic performance.

Urban development requires the support of urban-based economic activities, including manufacturing, services and construction, among others. It must also alleviate existing constraints to those economic activities, such as reducing infrastructure deficiencies by improving the reliability of water supply, electricity and telecommunications, as well as by addressing the negative health and environmental impacts of human and solid waste, as well as pollution from transportation.

The capacity of developing countries to finance their needs depends largely upon their level of future economic growth and development

Public authorities will also need to strengthen the institutional framework within which private economic activity occurs – for example, the regulatory framework determining how many steps are required to obtain a building permit or a licence to open a small business. Studies during the 1990s showed that some countries required extraordinary numbers of steps to obtain construction permits, such as 55 in Malaysia and 27 in South Africa.[9] These excessive regulatory steps sharply increased the cost of housing through the delays involved, even reaching 3 per cent of GDP in Malaysia, as well as the transaction costs for individual builders and construction enterprises. Local government institutions have a large role to play in reducing the costs of economic activity in cities. Similarly, local financial institutions that provide credit for construction or loans for small enterprises also play a pivotal role in stimulating the local urban economy.[10]

The economic paradox of this situation is that while cities are the loci of productivity, they are also the loci of increasing poverty. This poverty has many causes. Some of it is a result of the overall level of national income of countries: Burkina Faso is poorer than Brazil, which means that, on average, people in Burkina Faso consume less in absolute

Table 1.3

Housing requirements to accommodate increments in the number of households over the next 25 years

Increments in the number of households over a 25-year period	877,364,000
Average size of annual increments	35,094,000
Per day	96,150
Per hour	4,000

Source: Statistical Annex of this report

amounts of goods and services than do their Brazilian counterparts, and also that there is a narrower range of goods and services than are available in Brazil. It can also mean that the social indicators of health and welfare are lower in terms of longevity, health status, literacy and infant mortality, as well as gender equality.

In urban areas, however, much of this poverty is a result of the lack of housing and infrastructure services that are necessary for people's and enterprises' basic needs, consumption and production. It is clear that the lack of these services has an impact upon the productivity of urban economic activities and, therefore, on the city and the nation as a whole. A study of infrastructure services in Lagos, Bangkok and Jakarta during the 1990s demonstrated that enterprises which had to provide their own water supply, electricity and other infrastructure services had lower profits and were therefore constrained in their growth. Infrastructure deficiencies had a direct impact upon how many jobs were being created. These companies in Lagos actually spent up to 35 per cent of their fixed investment in providing their own infrastructure; as a result, they had lower profits and were thus unable to grow.[11]

Varying types of deprivation, such as health, malnutrition and a lack of clean water supply, also have both short- and long-term impacts upon the health status and, thus, the productivity of men, women, and children.[12] Poverty, therefore, becomes intergenerational, as is observed in many large city slums in developing countries, such as the Dharavi slum in Mumbai, which now houses almost 2 million people, or the slum in Mathare Valley, Nairobi.[13]

Cities will have to increase their productivity in order to generate jobs, incomes and financial resources as well as to provide urban services

The key issue, however, is that increased urban population growth – increasing the denominator in the per capita calculation of gross domestic product – will necessarily mean that urban areas will become poorer if they are unable to augment jobs and incomes faster than their populations grow. Because rapid and large-scale urban population growth is expected between 2005 and 2030, cities will have to dramatically increase their productivity in order to, first, generate jobs and incomes and, second, generate the financial resources for housing and urban services. In this sense, the issue of urban employment generation cannot be easily separated from the options for financing future urban development in developing countries.

Employment and income generation will also have a major impact upon what kinds of housing and infrastructure will be affordable to growing urban populations. These issues are both quantitative and qualitative: quantitative because absolute levels of income will be needed to finance specific types of housing and infrastructure, and qualitative because the stability and growth of income over time will permit certain financing options – for example, mortgages – while lower levels of income will not qualify for financing.

The economic condition of cities – how fast job opportunities and incomes increase – is further complicated by the growing impact of *exogenous economic factors* upon cities. Processes of economic globalization and trade have changed patterns of production in cities, leading to deindustrialization in many cities. This means that footloose industries close in cities with higher relative costs and move to new locations with lower costs – for example, from the US to Mexico or, later, from Mexico to China. The pursuit of profit-maximizing locations by private enterprises has led to major economic and social disruption in many countries over the last two decades.

Today, this disruptive behaviour by firms is compounded by new factors in the global economy, including global interest rates, whereby change in one large economy affects the price of money in the global economy as a whole. The Asian financial crisis of 1997–1998, followed by crises in the Russian Federation, Brazil and, later, Argentina, all demonstrated the volatility of the global economy. Changes in the supply and demand for specific products led to changes in the demand for their inputs, as well. In some cases, the analyses of the distribution of risk for foreign investors at a global level increased the cost of borrowing by individual countries, precipitating new crises, as in the case of Argentina during late 2001. The oil price increases of late 2004 have added to the feeling, in many developing countries, that global market forces are beyond the control of individual countries. These processes have even intensified as competition has grown between countries in providing various factors of production. Overall, the impact of the volatility of global economic and financial forces upon cities is manifested in dramatic and socially harmful impacts upon employment and labour markets, more generally, with the frequent flight of investment and jobs to new locations.[14]

Within this new global economic context, the economic roles of cities have become increasingly important for individual countries. If São Paulo is not productive, the economy of Brazil will suffer; similarly, if India is unable to efficiently move its exports through the port of Mumbai, the costs of those exports will be higher and India's overall economic performance will be hurt. Long journeys to work through the traffic congestion of Bangkok reduce worker efficiency. During the mid 1990s, Mexicans working in the *maquiladora* factories in Ciudad Juarez had to spend 29 per cent of their incomes on transportation to work, thereby reducing the possibility of meeting other household needs.[15] In contrast, the modal integration of transportation in the Netherlands facilitates the access of workers to a wide range of employment opportunities.

The key point here is that housing and urban infrastructure is a critical part of the economic production function of cities. Without housing and public services, workers cannot be productive, and whole urban and national economies will feel the impact. Basic services such as water and sanitation have immediate impacts upon the health of the population.

In this context, meeting the financial needs of cities in developing countries, and particularly the financing of infrastructure and housing, should be high national priorities. Yet, too often, national budgets for investment in urban infrastructure are very low, if existent at all. It is interesting to note that official development assistance also contributes few resources for these investment needs.

Because the economic performance of cities is critical to national economic performance and, indeed, to the functioning of the global economy itself, these financial needs should be considered essential international priorities as well. Housing and infrastructure are essential for both production and human welfare. It will be impossible to reduce urban poverty if slum conditions are not improved in many cities throughout the developing world. In this regard, the Millennium Development Goal (MDG) of significantly improving the living conditions of at least 100 million slum dwellers by 2020 is important in bringing some international attention to this problem. It is equally important, however, to note that this MDG only represents about 4 per cent of the projected demand for slum improvement by 2030.

Environmental framework

An additional and important dimension of this problem is the management of natural resources required by the urban population, such as clean water and clean air. Growing demand for infrastructure services places immediate pressures on these natural resources. It is also apparent from most environmental studies that cities have important impacts upon the natural environments in which they are located. Studies during the 1990s demonstrate that the ecological footprint of cities is having enormous consequences for the sustainability of natural resources.[16] Consumption of natural resources by urban residents is frequently growing faster than the environment's ability to reproduce those resources. A clear example of this situation is the deforestation of areas near African cities. Urban residents collect firewood for use in cooking and heating, cutting down trees and scrub bushes, thereby contributing to the erosion of topsoil and the sustainability of local ground cover.

One of the most important environmental issues to be addressed is the increasing cost of potable water in almost every city in the world. High levels of water consumption, with little attention to conservation or conserving behaviour, has had the effect of increasing the distance that cities must go to find potable water. Beijing now collects its water from sources 1290 kilometres from the city. Indeed, there are over 30 Chinese cities that currently have severe water shortages. This problem affects cities in both rich and poor countries: Los Angeles also goes 1290 kilometres for its water and New York is dependent upon distant water resources in New York State. Yet, efforts to conserve and improve the efficiency of water use are minimal in most cities. Some cities have used higher water charges as incentives for conservation and in order to improve the efficiency of water use. Bogotá has worked on this problem by educating its population.[17]

Another critical area is the management of human and solid waste. This problem also becomes increasingly significant as urban populations grow. Water-borne sewerage systems are prohibitively expensive for most cities in developing countries. On-site methods of sanitation and waste treatment are, in some cities, necessary alternatives to so-called conventional solutions. These issues also apply to non-human solid waste, where the quantities of waste quickly outstrip landfill capacity in many cities. The need for collection and recycling programmes to avoid the complete waste of reusable materials is of high priority.

If these urban problems have important local and regional consequences, they also have global impacts. A recent study from China demonstrates how urbanization is contributing to global warming, with carbon dioxide emissions largely coming from cities.[18] Another study also notes that global warming is reducing rice yields in Asia, suggesting that food may prove to be one of the most serious constraints to urban population growth over time.[19] The systemic character of the impacts of urban settlements upon the environment and, in turn, the impact of global climate change and other forms of environmental change need to be better understood. However, it should be noted that cities can also provide positive impacts upon the environment – for example, in concentrating all of the waste in specific locations rather than dispersing it.

One of the most important environmental issues to be addressed is the increasing cost of potable water in almost every city in the world

These environmental externalities, and particularly the likelihood of severe shortages of natural resources and increasing costs of infrastructure services, must be included in any financial and economic framework for cities in developing countries. The notion of 'sustainable development' needs to be made operational, rather than just a normative and rhetorical objective of governments and visionaries. As a result, this is an important component of the challenge posed by this Global Report. The task of mobilizing finance should not simply be intended to have more resources to extend current housing and infrastructure services, but rather to change the production and consumption of those services in the direction of methods, costs and impacts that can enhance the sustainability of cities and their surrounding regions.[20]

Financial framework

The most fundamental financial issue in this Global Report is that cities will require very large investments in order to create infrastructure and services with long-life benefits – yet, they lack the systems to finance these services. For example, it is almost impossible in most developing country cities to obtain mortgages to finance the purchase of housing. And yet it is difficult to imagine that the great majority of cities and their residents can afford to use disposable cash to finance long-life investments.

The following chapters in this Global Report undertake an in-depth examination of potential sources of finance at the international, national and local levels. A preliminary review of these sources suggests, however, that it is unrealistic to expect major additional financing from international donors, the global financial sector, the national level (where most governments are facing serious fiscal deficits) or the municipal level (where local budgets are also severely constrained).

The problem is both an issue of what is actually financed and whether sufficient levels of finance are being mobilized for this sector

International development aid

Current levels of foreign investment, international aid and government financing are clearly not meeting the current demand for housing, as Box 1.1 illustrates. Furthermore, official development assistance (ODA) to Africa and South Asia does not seem to have had any major impact upon the incidence of slums (see Figure 1.1). Individual projects in

Box 1.1 Demonstrating the foreign direct investment and official development assistance paradox: The case of Mali

Mali has one of the highest amounts of foreign direct investment (FDI) as a percentage of gross domestic product (GDP) and a significant amount of official development assistance (ODA); yet, 93.2 per cent of Mali's urban population live in slums. During 2002, FDI in Mali totalled US$102.2 million and ODA was over US$472 million.

However, if US$574.2 million from the combined FDI and ODA were devoted solely to housing the 3.4 million people in slums, it would not suffice. Estimating 7 persons per household and US$5000 to build each housing unit, it would cost US$2.4 billion to house the current population, not taking into account the projected population growth of over 11 million by 2030.

Source: World Bank, 2004d.

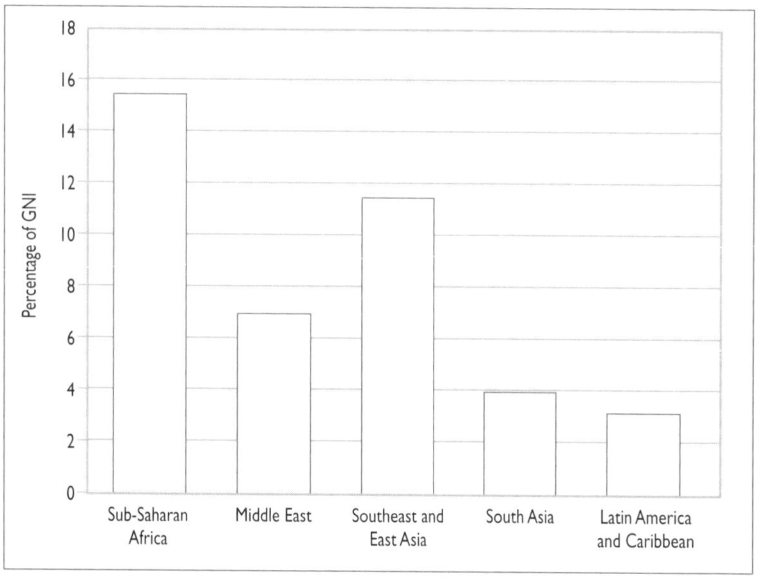

Figure 1.1

Official development assistance (percentage of GNI), 2002

Source: World Bank, 2004e.

Figure 1.2

Gross foreign direct investment (percentage of GDP), 2001

Source: World Bank 2004e.

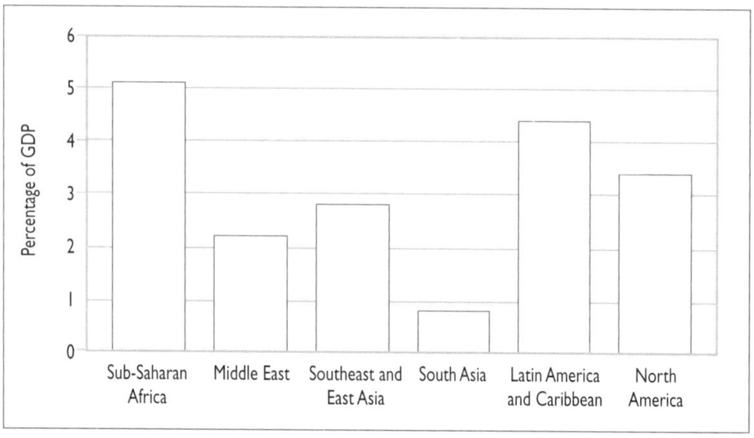

specific cities may have been successful, such as Jakarta, Madras or Nairobi; but their national and even citywide impacts have been limited.

Foreign direct investment

As shown in Figure 1.2, sub-Saharan Africa has the highest levels of foreign direct investment (FDI) as a share of GDP; yet, in absolute terms, this level of FDI is only approximately US$191,329,892, compared to US$535,569,231, which South Asia receives. It is apparent from the data in Figure 1.2 that FDI, even if it were addressed to improving slums, cannot make (and has not made) any appreciable difference.

In any case, only infrequently do private foreign investors place their investment funds in slums, even though there would probably be a high rate of economic return, if not financial return. Exceptions include the Community-led Infrastructure Financing Facility (CLIFF) initiative in India (see Chapter 6, Box 6.9).

National public investment in shelter

A third source of finance for housing and urban infrastructure would be national public investment – that is, publicly allocated funds from national budgets or special funds. With the exception of China and India, very few developing countries have allocated large absolute amounts of financial resources to housing and urban development.

The problem, therefore, is both an issue of what is actually financed: whether public investment in housing and urban infrastructure has been directed towards the needs of the poor and whether sufficient levels of finance are being mobilized for this sector. Both issues are important and are addressed in subsequent chapters of this Global Report.

The question of *what is financed*, however, must be broadened to include a wider range of infrastructure and housing solutions than normally included in international discussions. For example, in lieu of extending the network of urban water supply, it may be necessary to drill boreholes in un-served areas on the urban periphery. This approach would tap aquifers whose water is then distributed by above-ground tubing or pipes. Such a solution is a fraction of the cost of extending the existing water supply network – although, admittedly, it may present other problems, such as the need for later aquifer recharge. This suggests that how housing and urban infrastructure are considered in terms of technology, standards and costs can have very important implications for their financing.

Valuing urban assets

Another related issue to estimating the finance needed for cities is the fact that existing cities have enormous *present asset value*. A rough exercise in the World Bank during the early 1990s attempted to determine the 'financial value of cities'.[21] It concluded that the infrastructure stock of cities in developing countries was worth about US$3 trillion. This compared to an annual investment flow of approximately US$150 billion each year, or 5 per cent of the stock. More than 95 per cent of this annual flow came from domestic resources in countries, both public and private. This is a substantial figure, but woefully inadequate when one observes the large numbers of households worldwide without adequate water supply or sanitation.

Nevertheless, it points to a critical policy problem: it is known that most urban infrastructure in developing countries does not last as long as that in developed countries. Maintenance is neglected, both for financial and technical reasons. If, however, cities were able to obtain, say conservatively, another 5 per cent of benefits from improved maintenance of the stock, this would amount to US$150 billion or roughly current annual investment. Better operations and maintenance could reduce the need for some, though certainly not all, of the new annual investment, thereby reducing environmental and social impacts and avoiding additional debt.[22] Improved initial design of infrastructure will also reduce maintenance costs in the long term.

A key policy conclusion, therefore, is that cities must obtain more benefits from their existing assets, in a financial and economic sense, and that increase can allow their networks to be sustained longer, at lower costs.[23]

This conclusion is of enormous strategic value in assessing the current balance of new investment versus improving the management of current stock. It suggests that a first step in a strategy for sustainable cities would be an intensive examination of *maintenance programmes* to improve infrastructure performance. This might include, for example, various ways of improving information systems about the condition of infrastructure (smart infrastructure), which would alert city managers about the need for maintenance.

When these issues are discussed together, it raises questions about what, indeed, is to be financed. For example, rather than assume that it will be possible to finance large-scale extensions of conventional urban infrastructure, with their heavy upfront investment costs and high maintenance requirements, perhaps an alternative strategy is needed to complement ongoing infrastructure finance. This might involve developing smaller decentralized clusters of infrastructure services that lead to the growth of multi-nucleated urban centres, thus avoiding high downtown densities and mass transit to central points of employment. This spatial alternative is also an engineering and financial alternative.[24]

Governance framework

Such a spatial approach also implies the need for a *decentralized approach* to urban governance. It connects well to the principle of 'subsidiarity', which the European Union (EU) has urged on its members, whereby problems are best resolved at the jurisdictional level at which they occur rather than being referred to high administrative and political levels.

It should also be noted that the participation and voice of urban populations in formulating policy and programmes by the public sector is a critical dimension of urban management. One aspect of participation is the need to shift from the top-down administrative formulation of strategy to including the full range of civil society interests and organizations in governmental processes.[25] This includes thinking about the future and adding broad-based citizen involvement to conventional urban plans. The recent 2050 initiatives in Buenos Aires, New York and, now, Barcelona demonstrate the importance of this issue.[26]

Using these elements of an analytic framework as points of departure, it is important to recognize the value of making virtue from necessity, or rather of using the lack of finance for conventional solutions as an opportunity to refocus the discussion of urban policy towards urban forms and processes that may be able to enhance sustainability. Finance is therefore a critical lever to orient policy and to recognize the growing role of community-based urban processes.

Mobilizing finance: removing constraints and reducing risks

As noted earlier, the conventional forms of finance – national public investment funds; ODA; FDI; national and local private-sector finance; and municipal finance – either do not seem to place high priority on investment in housing and urban infrastructure, or they simply do not have the requisite resources.

While these various forms of finance will be analysed in greater detail in Chapters 4 to 7 of this Global Report, there are three important issues that deserve to be highlighted at the beginning. These are:

1. What forms of housing and urban infrastructure investment are legitimate and deserving of public- or private-sector investment?
2. What are the constraints to mobilizing these types of resources for housing and urban development?
3. What are the risks to providers of finance for these purposes?

Addressing shelter and infrastructure standards

One of the serious issues to be addressed in considering the financing of housing and urban infrastructure is the view that housing and settlements which do not conform to building codes and land-use regulations should necessarily be excluded from consideration. This view, commonly heard during the 1970s, has evolved over recent years; many governments now recognize that millions of people, mostly the poor, are unable to find reasonably priced land for settlement and construction. The drive to evict squatters from land legislated for other purposes, while continuing in some cities, has been reduced substantially as public officials and public opinion have now recognized that the bulldozer and evictions are not effective answers in meeting the demand for shelter. The result of evictions has simply been to move the poor to even more distant locations, increasing their transport costs to places of work. There is now greater willingness for public authorities to upgrade, *in situ*, the settlements of the poor, allowing them at least occupancy permits, if not full ownership of the land.

Public opinion has now recognized that the bulldozer and evictions are not effective answers in meeting the demand for shelter

These upgrading projects have been very successful in many countries, ranging from large-scale efforts such as the Kampung Improvement Programme in Indonesia, begun during the late 1960s and expanded with World Bank support during the 1970s and 1980s, to the Bustee Improvement Programme in Calcutta, to smaller-scale upgrading programmes in African and Latin American cities. These programmes have several key features (see Box 1.2), discussed in more detail in subsequent chapters of this report.[27]

A second aspect of determining what is legitimate for financing is the role of building codes. In many countries, building codes require standards of construction that are prohibitively expensive for the majority of the population.

Box 1.2 Key features of slum upgrading projects

Among the more than 200 donor-assisted projects for slum upgrading, the following features are found in most of them:

- *in situ* introduction of infrastructure services, such as water supply, sanitation and electricity;
- minimal demolition of existing housing structures;
- provision of minimal guarantee of legal occupancy, if not tenure;
- provision of accompanying social services, such as education and public health;
- expectation of community participation in the design, construction and/or maintenance of new community services; and
- some degree of cost recovery through periodic household payments to the implementing public authority.

A sharply declining percentage of the population in many cities in developing countries is actually able to afford living in 'legal buildings' – that is, those buildings which conform to existing codes. This problem, originally a legacy of former colonial rule in many countries in Anglophone or Francophone Africa, or in South Asia, can no longer be simply attributed to the past. Codes which insist on high standards in the name of 'being modern' or ensuring public health standards are very much a product of post-independence governments as well.

Constraints to mobilizing resources

This Global Report will demonstrate that the constraints to mobilizing financial resources are both financial and non-financial. The second part of this chapter explains how macroeconomic circumstances affect national and sub-national systems of public finance and limit the availability of financial resources. However, there are also important non-financial constraints, such as building codes. These include national and local regulatory frameworks governing land use, land occupancy and landownership. In many cities, low-income people are caught in a cycle in which they lack formal permission to occupy land and therefore are not eligible to receive essential infrastructure services, such as water supply or public transport. As a result, they remain without services, which undermines their health and access to employment. This keeps them poor and unable to rent shelter in so-called 'legal' land subdivisions.

During 2004, the global GDP grew by 4 per cent

For example, pavement dwellers in India, who have been frequently subjected to evictions and the demolition of their self-constructed homes, become accustomed to rebuilding using temporary materials that must be replaced annually. It is estimated that over a 20-year period, these investments are equal to those of a household making annual instalments on a 40,000 rupee house.[28] The difference is that one household will have secure tenure and improved access to services and the other will still face periodic demolition and no infrastructure. While one household must use scarce funds to go further and will often pay more for water and cooking fuel, the household with legal tenure frequently has access to these resources more efficiently and cheaply and can use freed-up funds to invest in a better business or better education.

Risks to providers of finance for low-income households

The factors mentioned above also contribute to the risks perceived by lending institutions in providing finance to low-income households. If potential clients live on land without the legal recognition of municipal authorities, these clients are potentially subject to eviction from their homes, regardless of the level of financial investment which has been made. Providing finance for these households is therefore risky business from the lender's perspective. Similarly, if the major assets of these families, their house and the land they occupy are not recognized as collateral, it is unlikely that other smaller and less fixed assets will be more secure forms of collateral.

These issues form part of a vicious circle which millions of poor households have faced for generations. The circle has begun to break down in some countries where its obvious negative results do not benefit anyone – neither governments, nor lending institutions, nor infrastructure providers, nor households. However, this process is slow and filled with institutional impediments, reflecting different perspectives and interests.

What is needed is an acceptance of new categories of risk by the providers of finance, and an understanding that these clients form a majority and growing share of potential consumers for the future. The issues around this risk will be discussed in Parts II and III of this Global Report.

THE MACROECONOMIC CONTEXT OF URBAN SHELTER DEVELOPMENT

The second part of this chapter presents the macro-economic context that influences many of the issues discussed in this report. While much has been written about the global economy and the impacts of globalization, this picture needs to be disaggregated into data and analyses at the regional level in order to distinguish the specific challenges facing particular regions and countries. This section addresses the following factors: patterns of economic growth; sectoral performance and productivity; income distribution and inequality; poverty and employment; savings; external debt; patterns of investment (public, private and foreign); impacts of external factors upon macroeconomic performance; and the urbanization of national economies.

Patterns of economic growth

The publication of this Global Report coincides with a period of unprecedented economic growth at the global level. During 2004, the global GDP grew by 4 per cent. All developing regions grew at a pace faster than their growth rates during the 1980s and 1990s.[29] This is surprising, given the combination of the downturn following 11 September 2001 and the large increase in oil prices during 2004, reaching over US$50 a barrel. Global trade also expanded considerably, with China's demand for imported raw materials and food spurring exports from other developing countries, particularly in Latin America where Brazil exported steel and Argentina provided soy beans and meat to the growing Chinese market. The continued high demand for imports by the US economy supported the growth of global trade.

The most striking feature of economic growth has been the high rate of growth for developing countries, exceeding 6 per cent for the first time. This was heavily fuelled by China at 8.8 per cent. Table 1.4 presents the regional breakdown of economic growth, showing the sharp contrasts between regions.[30] While East Asia and the developing countries in Europe and Central Asia were above 7 per cent, sub-Saharan Africa was below half of that rate, at 3.2 per cent. Latin America and the Middle East grew at 4.7 per cent each, certainly a respectable rate for Latin America after the stagnation of 2002–2003.

From a distribution perspective, these patterns are worrying because they continue the trend towards greater disparity in income levels between the regions, as well as between developing and developed countries. Global inequality between rich and poor countries, therefore, continues to worsen, even when there have been extraordinarily high rates of economic growth.

The most questionable aspect of this growth in 2004, however, is whether it is likely to be sustained in the future. This depends upon many factors, including the changing position of the US dollar in global currencies and, hence, the power of the US economy; how China will cope with the danger of inflation; and whether global interest rates will affect debt payments by developing countries and their ability to finance needed investments for growth. These exogenous factors are clearly important influences on national macro-economic performance.

As Table 1.4 demonstrates, robust growth is expected in all regions, even though the high growth rate in China is expected to decline during 2005–2006, thereby reducing the demand for goods and services from East Asian and other developing economies. In contrast, South Asian countries are expected to sustain their growth through the liberalization of their economies, generating more trade. Latin America is expected to continue to benefit from higher commodity prices and strong trade performance. Africa is expected to improve its performance, but barely, so that its extreme poverty is unlikely to be improved by macro-economic growth in the coming decade.

Sectoral performance and productivity

One of the most startling aspects of the macroeconomic performance of the past few years – and most visible in 2004 – is the growing importance of world trade.[31] This means that 'tradeables', whether manufacturing products or commodities, have become increasingly central to the economic growth of all countries, whether developed or developing. The growth in commodity prices in 2004 suggests that demand has grown, particularly in China and the East Asian countries, for raw materials and specific items such as steel – for example, for automobile and machinery

Percentage GDP change from previous year, except interest rates and oil prices	2002	2003	Estimates 2004	Forecast 2005	2006
Developing countries	3.4	5.2	6.1	5.4	5.1
East Asia and Pacific	6.7	7.9	7.8	7.1	6.6
Europe and Central Asia	4.6	5.9	7.0	5.6	5.0
Latin America and the Caribbean	-0.6	1.6	4.7	3.7	3.7
Middle East and North Africa	3.2	5.7	4.7	4.7	4.5
South Asia	4.6	7.5	6.0	6.3	6.0
Sub-Saharan Africa	3.1	3.0	3.2	3.6	3.7

Source: World Bank, 2005.

Table 1.4

The global outlook in summary

production. While this places great emphasis on agriculture and the production of raw materials, it also requires improvements in the efficiency of infrastructure in telecommunications, transport and key services such as electricity and water supply necessary for manufacturing and other industries.

Another sector demonstrating continued growth is the financial sector, which has benefited from the absence of major crises during 2003 and 2004. Even cases such as the economic collapse and debt default of Argentina in late 2001 proved to have had little impact, or 'contagion', on other than its closest neighbours, thereby reflecting the increased stability of financial markets since that time. While the decline of the US dollar and the growing strength of the Euro are likely to produce some adjustments in 2005 and 2006, there is little likelihood of major changes in the sectoral composition of growth in most countries. Information technology continues to contribute to notable increased efficiencies in industry and services in most countries. Indeed, high returns to industries, such as the financial sector, which rely upon information technologies have contributed to growing inequalities in earnings between sectors within countries.

Income distribution and inequality

One of the consequences of the pattern of economic growth described above is growing inequality. Figure 1.3 depicts the share of income earned by the poorest 10 per cent and richest 10 per cent across the regions. Latin America continues to have the highest rate of inequality, with South Asia the lowest. This extreme inequality in Latin America has been analysed in some depth and has its roots in many historical patterns of landownership, political and institutional development and, more recently, economic policy.[32]

Global inequality between rich and poor countries continues to worsen, even when there have been extraordinarily high rates of economic growth

Inequality has become increasingly recognized not just as a problem to be addressed in its own right, but also because of its substantial impacts upon economic growth, poverty reduction and productive investment strategies for the development of human capital. Studies over the past decade have demonstrated the high correlation between inequality and poor performance in other aspects of development.[33]

While some forms of inequality have been attributed to differences in the level of education between people,[34] and yet others associated with higher returns to capital in

Figure 1.3

Regional income/consumption inequality patterns

Source: UNDP, 2004.

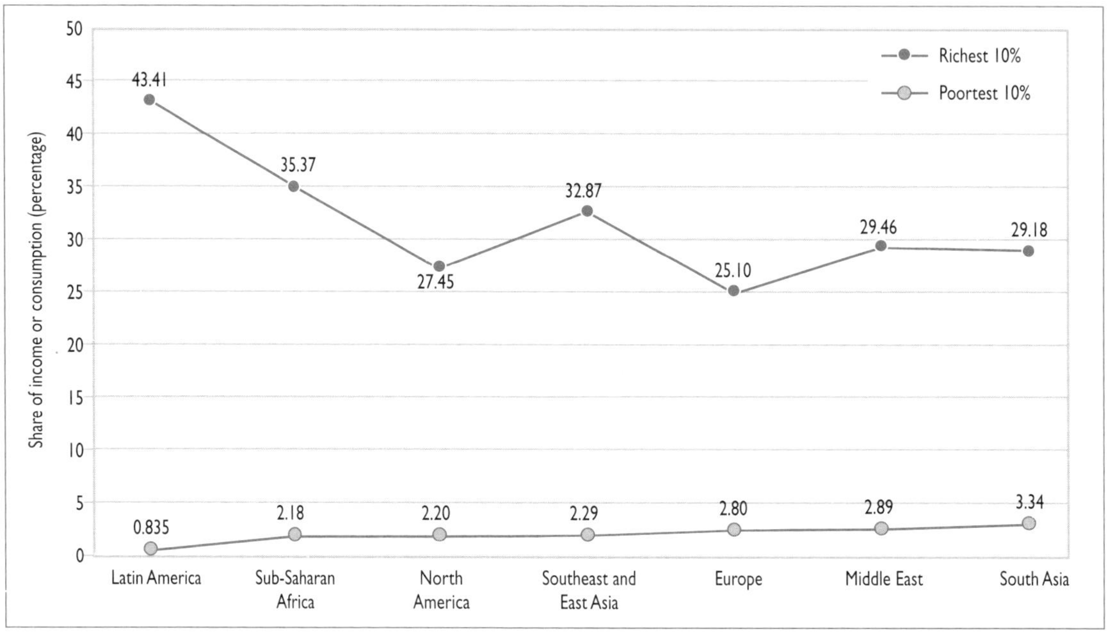

The most direct and important factor contributing to urban poverty is the shortage of well-paid employment in cities

sectors favoured by the global economy, there are also many forms of inequality that can be attributed to the policies of national and local governments in urban areas. A study of public investment in infrastructure among the various neighbourhoods of Buenos Aires from 1991 to 1997 demonstrated that 11.5 per cent of the population received 68 per cent of total investment.[35] Inequality through skewed local public investment can therefore be a local product and cannot always be blamed upon external forces outside the country.

Poverty and employment

Despite the impressive economic growth of the past few years, the enduring problem of massive poverty in the developing countries remains the top priority problem facing the world today. Figure 1.4 depicts the share of the population in the six regions below their respective national poverty lines during the period of 1990–2001, below US$1 per day and below US$2 per day for the period of 1990–2002. These figures are daunting, with approximately 64 per cent of the populations in Africa and South Asia living below the US$2 a day threshold for the period of 1990–2002.

Figure 1.4

Population below income poverty lines in five developing regions

Source: World Bank, 2004e.

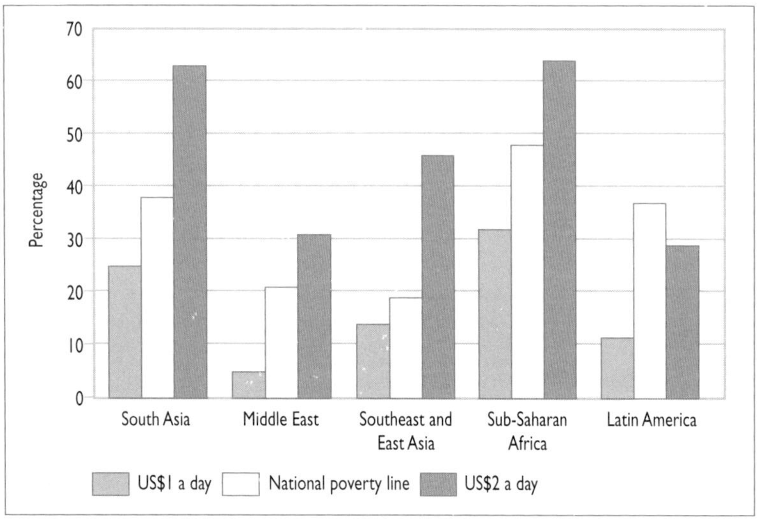

The incidence of poverty at the national level is highly correlated with low levels of education and poor health status, lack of access to basic infrastructure services (such as clean water supply), sanitation and electricity. This vicious circle of poverty is also intergenerational, with families caught in a poverty trap in which income-earning opportunities are frequently tied to educational attainment, location or access to credit.

The poverty problem is also characterized by strong differences between urban and rural residents. If the urban poor lack services and education, they have at least found some 'space' or land to occupy, albeit in squatter settlements in the less desirable areas of the city. In contrast, the rural poor are often landless, working as contract labour and continuously facing the threat of food insecurity. As noted earlier, the rural poor face two major and contradictory threats. High agricultural productivity is most likely to come from increased mechanization of agriculture, thereby reducing the demand for labour. Alternatively, low productivity will keep incomes low for everyone and also push people off the land. Both threats will lead to the same result: rural-to-urban migration. These growing tensions are very much evident in both China and India, but less so in Latin America where the largest share of the population has already moved into urban centres.

The most direct and important factor contributing to urban poverty is the shortage of well-paid employment in cities. The challenge here is both the creation of jobs and the level of wages. The generation of employment depends generally upon savings and investment within the macro-economy and local economies, as well. As noted earlier, much of the growth of economies over the past decade has been in technology industries and financial services, neither of which requires large labour forces to be productive. While many argue that improving education in cities will be sufficient to help young people find jobs, this argument is not always true empirically, especially in the short to medium term because there are growing levels of urban unemployment in cities despite increasing investments in education. Having secondary or even university education may be a necessary, but not a sufficient, condition to find work in environments with growing numbers of job seekers.

With growing global pressures towards profits in manufacturing and service industries, there has also been little incentive for medium- and large-scale enterprises to pay 'living wages' to those lucky people who do find jobs. If cheaper labour is available elsewhere, investors urge the managers of these enterprises to move to sites with lower labour costs. This pattern is found in both developing and developed countries where the so-called 'fast food jobs' pay notoriously low wages. Again, with increasing supplies of labour in local markets, it is not surprising that wage rates are very low.

Box 1.3 Poverty reduction strategy papers

While the dire shortage of affordable housing has been recognized internationally as a deep and pervasive problem, strategies to address this have not been thoroughly addressed in existing mechanisms, such as poverty reduction strategy papers (PRSPs). These are documents that the International Monetary Fund (IMF) and the World Bank require from national governments detailing their plans to reduce poverty in order to qualify for debt relief under the Heavily Indebted Poor Countries (HIPC) initiative. Out of the 54 countries with PRSPs or interim PRSPs, many of them address housing, but with varying degrees of commitment or specificity with regard to resource requirements. Many of the PRSPs discuss housing as a problem and some have conducted surveys to identify housing needs more exactly. Some countries propose building a few hundred or few thousand units, while others propose public–private partnerships and land reform measures. However, it is disappointing that many do not include clear measurable goals or budget information.

Source: www.poverty.worldbank.org/prsp/.

Savings

A strong consequence of high levels of poverty is a lack of domestic savings within national economies. As shown in Table 1.5, national savings rates are closely correlated with levels of GDP, with rates in Africa (14 per cent) and South Asia (13 per cent) less than half of the rate in East Asia (35 per cent). Low levels of domestic savings – both public and private – contribute to low levels of capitalization of the financial institutions in poor countries, including housing finance institutions. They are also reflected in low levels of tax revenue collection and therefore place great limitations on public expenditures and public budgets. Households and families at low incomes are able to find ways to survive, albeit marginally in many cases, with minimal expenditures for food, water and shelter. But paying taxes to institutions that appear to offer little in return is a much lower priority.

The issue of savings is particularly important when considering how to finance urban infrastructure and housing, as is discussed in Part II of this report. As noted earlier, both infrastructure and housing are durables – they are expected to have a long life, at least 50 years in the case of infrastructure; but they require large upfront investments in the expectation that they will provide a long stream of benefits well into the future. Savings is the foundation of investment. Without some surplus, investment in these future benefits is impossible. Therefore, patterns of income generation are critical factors in determining whether households will be able to invest at all in their future.

Table 1.5

Gross domestic savings, 2003

	Percentage of GDP	Current US$
Sub-Saharan Africa	14	1,783,690,767
Middle East	24.5	27,261,325,959
Southeast and East Asia	35	321,936,208,750
South Asia	13	37,536,526,160
Latin America	16	38,121,260,000
North America	19	817,705,450,000
Europe	21	305,467,000,000

Source: World Bank, 2004e.

External debt

Another factor that heavily conditions the macroeconomic environment of developing countries is the significance of external debt for specific countries. Built up over time and frequently connected to the volatility in the world economy during the oil shocks of the 1970s, many national governments borrowed heavily in order to finance increased energy costs during the 1970s, as well as to finance projects in all sectors. Even where these projects were well conceived and 'successful' in meeting their objectives, including contributing important support for economic development such as roads, schools, factories and irrigation canals, the legacy of external borrowing has left many countries with unsustainable levels of external debt service. In some countries, particularly in Africa, the debt service to GDP ratio has reached over 400 per cent.[36] Figure 1.5 depicts the total levels of debt service in various regions.

One of the consequences of these levels of debt is that it immediately reduces available domestic capital for investment. The net transfer out of developing countries to both public and private institutions in the developed countries, as well as to multilateral institutions, underlines the fact that the external community in some countries is not only a source of funds for domestic investment, but is a net drain on available surpluses which individual countries can generate. This negative net transfer has occurred in

Figure 1.5

Debt service, 2002

Source: World Bank, 2004e.

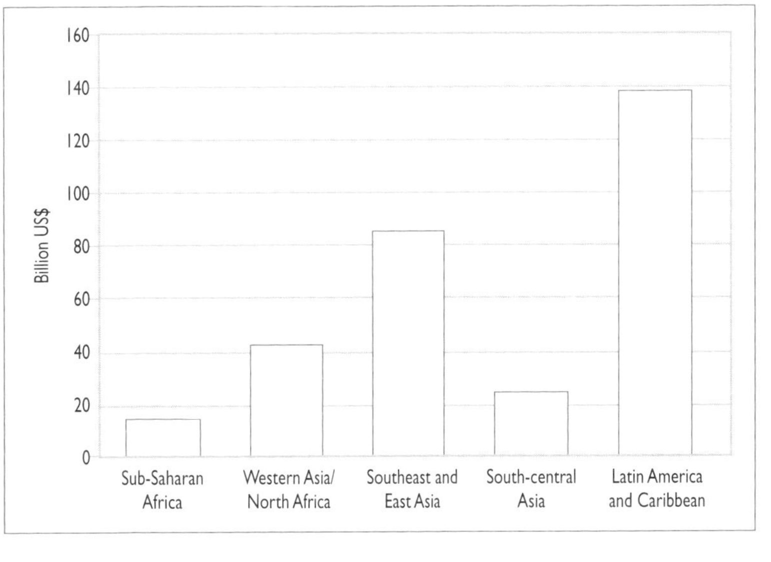

Table 1.6

Size of public budgets relative to GDP (%), selected countries

Argentina	2002	19.54	Lesotho	2003	41.36
Armenia	2003	21.59	Lithuania	2003	30.84
Australia	2003	26.56	Luxembourg	2003	43.37
Austria	2002	40.27	Madagascar	2002	14.26
Bahrain	2002	35.88	Malaysia	2003	28.21
Bangladesh	2003	11.33	Maldives	2003	41.79
Belarus	2002	27.12	Malta	2000	37.03
Belgium	2002	43.18	Mauritius	2003	24.08
Bolivia	2003	31.21	Mexico	2000	15.95
Bulgaria	2003	36.08	Mongolia	2003	42.85
Canada	2003	18.47	Nepal	2003	16.42
Chile	2003	21.85	Netherlands	2003	43.60
Congo, Democratic Republic of	2001	8.95	New Zealand	2003	33.74
Costa Rica	2003	24.34	Nicaragua	2003	26.51
Côte d'Ivoire	2001	16.49	Norway	2003	38.71
Croatia	2001	44.55	Pakistan	2003	22.39
Cyprus	1998	36.81	Panama	2001	24.85
Czech Republic	2003	40.65	Poland	2002	35.29
Denmark	2003	36.06	Portugal	2001	42.11
Dominican Republic	2002	17.64	Romania	2001	30.39
El Salvador	2003	18.00	Russia Federation	2003	25.21
Estonia	2001	28.02	Seychelles	2002	56.73
Finland	2003	36.62	Singapore	2002	18.82
Georgia	2002	12.60	Slovakia	2003	38.63
Germany	2003	32.81	Slovenia	2003	45.56
Hungary	2003	43.68	South Africa	2003	29.70
Iceland	2002	33.69	Spain	2002	32.79
India	2003	16.45	Sweden	2002	37.62
Indonesia	2001	24.77	Switzerland	2001	19.04
Iran	2003	28.50	Thailand	2003	17.49
Israel	2002	52.60	Tunisia	2003	32.10
Italy	2000	38.58	Ukraine	2002	31.24
Jamaica	2003	42.40	US	2003	21.01
Kazakhstan	2003	16.37	Uruguay	2001	31.34
Korea, Republic of	2001	20.16	Vanuatu	1999	23.24
Latvia	2003	28.41	Venezuela	2002	25.38

Source: IMF, 2004

Low levels of domestic savings – both public and private – contribute to low levels of capitalization of the financial institutions

many countries in Latin America, as well as in Africa. However, external debt swaps have begun to be used to finance poverty reduction programmes related to the HIPC initiative, including at the city level, as is shown by the example of Bolivia in Chapter 3.

Patterns of investment

Foreign investment

Given the above, the patterns of investment in developing countries have changed markedly over the past decade. Whereas, during the 1970s and 1980s, many countries relied upon the international institutions to provide needed capital, the transaction costs and conditions of those lenders have reduced their attractiveness for those countries able to enter global financial markets to raise investment capital. Countries such as the Republic of Korea and Thailand have sharply reduced their borrowing from the World Bank and the regional development banks because they are able to obtain necessary funds from private lenders. Other countries, such as Brazil and Mexico, have been able to raise funds from global markets, but by paying a premium to lenders. In contrast, most of the African countries have been unable to enter these markets, despite their offering tax holidays and other benefits, because their economic environments are unable to offer the short- and medium-term financial returns to private capital available elsewhere.

Not surprisingly, there has been an important segmentation in the global financial markets whereby some countries – particularly the East Asian countries and, notably, China – have been able to attract high levels of foreign direct investment.

The reason for this segmentation is, of course, that FDI is now private investment, with no particular public obligation to provide funds to countries where the conditions are not perceived to exist for maximum private financial returns. This logic can be perverse as well, with 'country risk' – the premium that countries must pay to lenders – determined by market perception of the risks of investing in specific countries. This leads to anomalies where risk is not associated with the income levels of countries, or with their levels of education and institutional development, or even with natural resources. Rather, it is determined by a narrow financial and political judgement about whether countries will be able and willing to honour their financial obligations in the short to medium term. This has led, for example, to the declaration that the country risk for Argentina was higher in 2002 than for Nigeria, even though the former has considerably higher social indicators than the latter. These financial market-driven realities have enormous consequences for individual countries, determining both their possible access to the markets themselves as well as the costs of borrowing.

The patterns of FDI also affect the allocation of finance across sectors. A study of FDI in Indonesia from the 1970s to the 1990s found that FDI 'encouraged the growth of a network of large cities but generally neglected rural areas and smaller cities'.[37] In general, there are few cases where FDI was actually devoted to housing projects in developing countries, unless this housing was for upper-class communities. FDI has supported large shopping malls in Latin American and Asian urban and suburban areas, but these investments have not contributed much to financing basic infrastructure for the poor in these communities.

Public investment

Given that there is a paucity of foreign investment in most countries, and that domestic savings rates are low, it should be no surprise that public investment as a share of GDP is low in most developing countries. Developing countries generally have relatively large deficits in their public budgets, straining to meet their recurrent expenditures, such as the salaries of civil servants or operational expenditures in school and health services. Maintaining infrastructure should be a priority in most countries; however, deferred maintenance is often not the exception but the rule. Table 1.6 shows the size of public budgets relative to GDP in selected countries.

The lack of resources for public investment in the poorest countries poses a serious dilemma. If these countries do not qualify for FDI, they are dependent upon official development assistance as the major source of financial support for economic development. Yet, ODA is also severely limited. Even with promises of additional aid from the developed countries at the International Conference on Financing for Development (Financing for Development Summit) held at Monterrey, Mexico, in 2003, the actual levels of official finance for development are constrained by lack of domestic political support in the developed countries, or by the restrictions of macroeconomic agreements with the international financial institutions (IFIs).[38]

It is important to note that the poorest countries have been heavily dependent upon ODA as a source of government revenue. Rwanda, for example, received ODA equivalent to more than 300 per cent of government revenue during the period of 1995–2000. Figure 1.6 shows that a large number of African countries, as well as Central Asian countries such as Tajikistan, Georgia and Kyrgyzstan, are all extremely dependent upon ODA.

It is important to acknowledge that urban development must compete with other priorities in the allocation of ODA for specific countries. The difficulties experienced in raising funds for the Global Fund for HIV-AIDS suggests that it would not be prudent to expect that the international community will be a major source of funds for urban development.

The issue of the composition of public investment also applies within countries. There are two issues here. The first is the sectoral allocation of aid (that is, for housing versus education or urban water supply). These allocations are clearly politically determined within individual governments. Second, there is an issue of the institutional level from which allocations are made. For example, many governments increasingly assign responsibility for housing and urban development to the provincial, state and local levels, rather than to national government. This means that patterns of intergovernmental financial relations and, specifically, financial transfers have a large impact upon what level and type of funds find their way to cities and towns (see Chapter 3).[39]

Public investment as a share of GDP is low in most developing countries

In many cases, the transfer of funds from national to sub-national units is used to cover recurrent priority expenditures. They are often not intended to cover new public investment projects. This process of decentralization has increasingly been both political – in terms of the authority for local issues being transferred to local institutions – and technical, with local officials authorized to make the important design and financial decisions regarding individual projects. What has been missing is authorizing local bodies to be able to enter local, national and global financial markets in pursuit of the funds needed to implement those projects. While there are notable cases of local governments entering financial markets – for example, the Ahmedbad Municipal Corporation during the mid 1990s – this trend has not made as much progress as originally hoped. Financial institutions have tended to be hesitant in buying the municipal bonds of local authorities without clear sources of revenue other than local taxes.

Private investment

The weaknesses of the public sector and its inability to mobilize substantial resources for urban development therefore point to the need to give greater attention to private sources of finance. Here, there is a major policy paradox: on the one hand, it is possible to readily identify the constraints facing private financiers – for example, why should they provide scarce capital to investments with medium- to long-term pay-offs, or why should they orient capital to the urban poor or even to municipalities, who, for different reasons, are equally risky even if they are deserving beneficiaries? Yet, while these questions are posed, it is true that private finance is the foundation for most investment in cities (the private sector finances precisely those infrastructure services and types of shelter for which there is such a large demand). This paradox is clearer when it is acknowledged that in no countries other than China and those of the former Soviet bloc have more than 15 per cent of the demand for housing been financed by the public sector.[40]

While there are notable cases of local governments entering financial markets, this trend has not made as much progress as originally hoped

The answer, therefore, is that the private sector is financing urban development: witness the shopping centre along the highway, the corner store near the market or the houses on the vacant plot across the street. The problem is that this is not keeping up with the pace and magnitude of demographic growth. There are important examples of this finance, as is illustrated in Box 1.4. The promise and limitations of this experience are presented in Chapters 4 and 5 of this Global Report.

Figure 1.6

Official development assistance, selected countries, average during 1995–2000 (percentage of total government revenue, excluding grants)

Source: IMF and IDA, 2004, p8.

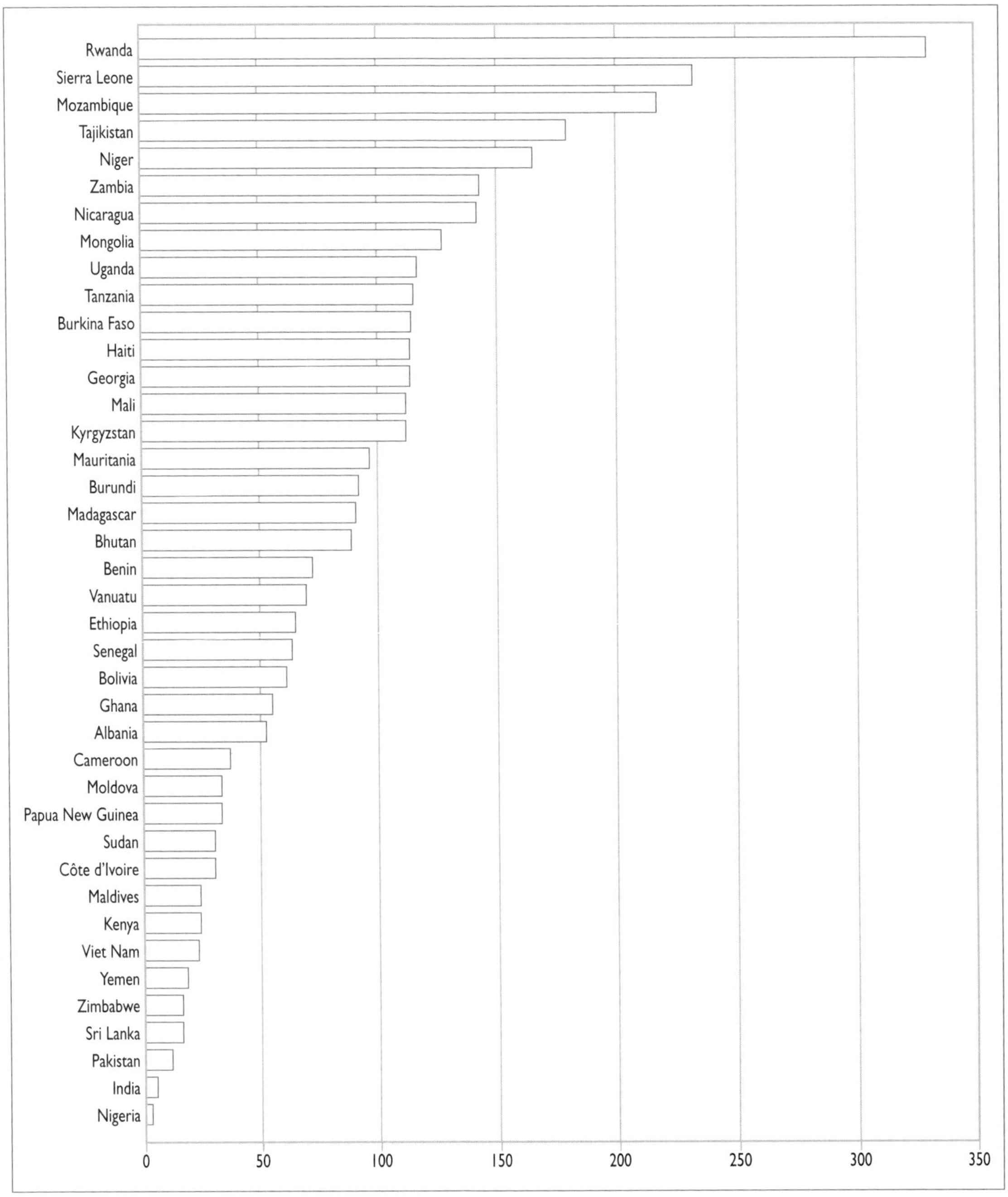

One controversial aspect of private investment was also the trend, during the 1990s, to privatize public services on the grounds that private management was more efficient and cost conscious, and frequently could be counted upon to help mobilize needed capital for investment in the rehabilitation or expansion of infrastructure networks. While some of these privatization experiments resulted in such benefits, many were sharply criticized because private managers often increased the tariffs of previous public services, thereby excluding the poor from needed infrastructure, such as water supply. In addition, many privatized firms were unable to attract new capital for network expansions. This created political problems for public authorities who had justified their decisions to privatize, in part, on the expectation that un-served populations would receive services. While an overall assessment of the privatization experiment remains to be done, it is clear that effective privatization requires effective public regulation, and this factor was often missing (see Chapter 3).

Other dimensions of macroeconomic performance that have affected the availability of private finance for urban development have been the level of interest rates and inflation in the respective developing country economies. While, in general, global interest rates have been low and money has been available for investment in developed countries, this pattern has served to discourage greater exploration of so-called 'emerging markets', where risks are higher and the potential for inflation greater due to uncertainties in macroeconomic management and the impact of the global economy upon local markets and specific investments. The concentration of capital in European and North American markets has tended to attract new investment as well because there are more opportunities to diversify within these markets.

The impact of external factors on macroeconomic performance

As noted earlier, the macroeconomic performance of countries is highly conditioned by the global economic environment. Relative prices of goods and services are determined both by real-sector production costs (land, labour, technology and capital) and by currency values. They are also affected by interest rates, which fluctuate at the global level in relation to the large aggregates of finance – mostly in the US, Japan and Europe – and not very much in relation to regional factors. Countries which have begun to produce specific products for trade – for example, tea in Kenya – find themselves in serious competition with producers in other countries. Countries which followed import substitution strategies during the 1950s and 1960s found themselves at a serious disadvantage during the 1970s as trade expanded and energy prices increased.[41]

These patterns of competition and risk have dramatically increased with the globalization of the economy. Footloose industries which left the US for Mexico under the North American Free Trade Agreement (NAFTA) have, in some cases, moved on to new locations where labour costs are lower, such as China. The notion of 'outsourcing', where parts of industrial and commercial processes are assigned to enterprises in other countries with lower labour costs, has become more than a frequent subject of conversation – it has also become a real threat to the stability of employment in all countries.

While this issue has been largely understood in relation to labour costs, it can also be expected that footloose industries will move some of their production and service functions to locations with more efficient infrastructure services, particularly telecommunications and transport. The most notable example of this process was described in a 2001 book by a leading author on the subject of cities and globalization, which focused on the management functions in the financial sector and how they were located in New York, London and Tokyo.[42] This need for reliable infrastructure has spread well beyond the financial sector in many countries to the creation of industrial or office parks, where special services for particular economic functions are available.[43] Indeed, these spaces are linked within the global economy, creating integrated economic activities through space.[44] While these higher levels of integration have been heralded as offering new levels of productivity and efficiency, they can also lead to new levels of vulnerability to external shocks, where a shock to one economy or activity can affect others.[45]

The urbanization of national economies

A final characteristic of the macroeconomic context for urban development is the urbanization of national economies themselves. Abundant evidence exists to demonstrate the growing importance of cities in the overall productivity of countries. The increasing share of national GDP produced in cities has been well documented.

This is very much related to the 'agglomeration economies' found in urban areas, which results in very large cities having a substantial share of national productivity. For example, São Paulo has 8.6 per cent of Brazil's population, but produces 36.1 per cent of GDP, while Mexico City has 15 per cent of the national population and produces 34 per cent of GDP.[46] These patterns do not only apply to very large metropolitan areas. For example, the five largest cities in Mexico accounted for 53 per cent of national value added in industry, commerce and services, even though they contain only 28 per cent of the Mexican population.[47] A study of 13 industries in India shows that firm output is greater in larger cities.[48]

The phenomenon of increasing concentration of productivity within national economies in cities and towns reflects the absolute advantages of cities resulting from agglomeration economies and localization economies. However, it also reflects the relative advantages of cities vis-à-vis rural areas. This is evident through an examination of the wages earned by workers in cities, even when they are working within the informal sector. A study of labour markets in São Paulo from 1989 to 1999 shows a growth of informal-sector employment from 2.4 million to 3.7 million during this period. There is a noticeable 'casualization of work'.[49] Even if workers do not have the legislated benefits of formal employment, there is, nevertheless, a large increase in informal-sector employment in many cities in developing countries, thereby demonstrating the 'pull' of urban wages.

Patterns of competition and risk have dramatically increased with the globalization of the economy

Box 1.4 Housing Development and Finance Corporation (HDFC) in India

Based in India, the Housing Development and Finance Corporation (HDFC) was incorporated in 1977 to provide the long-term finance that was lacking for housing needs. With offices in over 130 cities in India and abroad, HDFC's loan approvals for 2004 were 152.16 billion rupees while disbursements amounted to 126.87 billion rupees.

While it is common for housing banks to lend to middle- and upper-income households, which are perceived to be less risky, HDFC has made a concerted effort to address the dire shortage of affordable housing for low-income people in India. During 2004, with funds from the German state-owned bank Kreditanstalt für Wideraufbau, HDFC disbursed 1250 million rupees in loans to over 140,000 poor families. It also approved 303 million rupees towards 49 low-income housing projects and 282 million rupees to cover 58 loans under its microfinance facility. HDFC has also released 366 million rupees in grants towards the construction of 10,058 houses for low-income people.

Source: www.hdfc.com, www.kfw.de

CONCLUDING REMARKS

This chapter has presented data suggesting that, despite historically rapid rates of economic growth, there is little likelihood that conventional sources of funds will be available for investment on the scale needed to meet the projected demand for urban infrastructure and housing. Many countries continue to face the combination of significant external debt burdens, deficits in public budgets and weak financial sectors. Local governments have begun to seek finance in national and global markets; but this is only in its initial phase. Countries and cities, therefore, will have to rely upon the savings of their citizens. How those savings are mobilized through diverse mechanisms will be the subject of subsequent chapters of this Global Report.

Key underlying questions that have been addressed in this chapter are summarized and answered as follows:

- *How have macroeconomic trends affected the living conditions of urban households during the last two decades?* With the exception of East Asian countries, most developing country regions have not experienced sustained positive growth over the past two decades. Africa has continued to suffer the most, with at best uneven growth in a few countries; but most sub-Saharan states have continued to deteriorate in providing needed urban employment and incomes. Latin America has also been quite disappointing as the promised neo-liberal reforms have failed to deliver the anticipated patterns of sustained growth. In general, the upper end of the income distribution has benefited from the new patterns of economic growth in the age of globalization. While in some countries there is evidence of a new middle class, particularly in China and India, the middle class has actually disappeared in other countries, joining the poor in the absence of 'living wages'.
- *Have macroeconomic trends and national development policies of the last two decades improved urban- and housing-sector operations?* The answer here is mostly negative. With exceptions in some countries, again in parts of India and China, and in richer developing countries such as the Republic of Korea, Thailand or Mexico, national economic authorities have generally been preoccupied with macrostability, debt and trade, and have tended to neglect implementation of the needed policy and institutional reforms in the urban sector.
- *Has international financial assistance to the municipal and housing sectors made a significant contribution to improving urban infrastructure services and housing within cities in developing countries and countries in transition?* It must be recognized that, despite considerable effort to encourage urban and infrastructure policy reform and capacity-building in the developing countries, there is little evidence of any sustained large-scale impact. One senior government official in a large developing country once replied to this question by suggesting that the question itself was presumptuous in that the level of financial resources and the applicability of the policy advice were both considerably short of what was required.

NOTES

1 This chapter is based on two background papers prepared by Michael Cohen, New School University, New York, US, with assistance from Deanna Fowler.
2 UN Population Division, 2004; National Research Council, 2003.
3 UN Millennium Project, 2003, p4.
4 Harris and Todaro, 1970.
5 George Beier, Anthony Churchill, Michael Cohen and Bertrand Renaud developed this typology of urban growth and the range of challenges facing individual countries. See Beier et al, 1976.
6 UN-Habitat, 2003a.
7 Montgomery et al, 2004. See also UN-Habitat, 2004.
8 Sharma, 2005.
9 Angel, 2002.
10 World Bank, 1991.
11 Lee et al, 1999.
12 National Research Council, 2003.
13 Sharma, 2005.
14 UN-Habitat, 2004.
15 Dillinger et al, 1994.
16 Rees, 1992.
17 Mockus, Antanas, 'Camino a la Igualdad', included in Memorias Encuentro Internacional de Competitividad, 2002.
18 National Academy of Science, 2004.
19 National Academy of Science, 2004.
20 Roberts and Cohen, 2002.
21 World Bank, 1992.
22 According to 1990 World Bank estimates.
23 Cohen, 1998.
24 See Graham and Marvin, 2001.
25 National Research Council, 2003.
26 Margarita Gutman, Presentation on the 2050 Initiatives at the World Urban Forum, Barcelona, September 2004.
27 UN-Habitat, 2003a.
28 Homeless International Dialogue, 'Risk and investment in urban communities around the world', September 2002.
29 World Bank, 2005, p1.
30 World Bank, 2005, p2.
31 UNCTAD, 2004.
32 IADB, 1998.
33 Birdsall, 2001.
34 UNHCS, 2001.
35 Cohen and Debowicz, 2004.
36 For detail see: IMF and IDA, 2004.
37 Douglass, 1997, cited in National Research Council, 2003, p345.
38 United Nations, 'Building on Monterrey' Financing for Development, 2002.
39 See, for example, Bird and Slack, 2003.
40 World Bank, 1993.
41 UNCTAD, 2003.
42 Sassen, 2001.
43 See for example, Graham and Marvin, 2001.
44 Sassen, 2002; UN-Habitat, 2004.
45 Pettis, 2001.
46 Freire and Polese, 2003, p6.
47 National Research Council, 2003, p303.
48 Cited in National Research Council, 2003, p309; see also Shukla, 1996.
49 Buechler, 2000.

CHAPTER 2

SHELTER POLICY AND FINANCE: RETROSPECTIVE OVERVIEW[1]

Housing finance is both the servant and the master of the housing process. The finance available fits into the general policy framework in that it enables the construction of housing within the wider supply context current at the time. It also drives the process: reductions in finance affect the scale of supply and allocation among groups supplying and demanding housing. In times when centralized control is politically dominant, finance is likely to be directed at governments and their agencies. Decentralization directs finance to smaller units, concentrating more on local authorities than on central governments. In times when non-governmental organizations (NGOs) are trusted above governments, shelter finance will be channelled through them. The same occurs when citizen groups gain power and respect.

There have been major shifts in housing policy at the international level during the last six decades or so, and these have tended to drive the agenda, especially when countries rely upon international institutions to support their endeavours. However, at the same time, some countries have been following old agendas, while others have been driving forward innovative ideas.

This chapter discusses the general trends in housing and urban development policy since the end of World War II and highlights the paradigm shifts that have occurred during the last 60 years, and particularly during the last 30 years. From a time when colonial governments, especially in France and the UK, drove policy to supply urgently needed urban improvements and 'homes for heroes', there have been major changes. The recognition that ordinary people could participate in the housing and urban development process gave rise, first, to self-help projects in which people with little income were expected to provide goods and services for themselves that those with high incomes were provided with, often free of charge. This has now developed into community-led urban programmes in which ordinary people drive the process.

The context in which housing is provided has progressed from welfare provision, through an understanding that better conditions result in healthier and more productive people, to housing as a basic human right. In parallel, financing has moved from subsidizing the cost of a few high-quality dwellings in well-serviced neighbourhoods, through enabling the finance markets to provide for most, to the beginnings of a recognition that some subsidized housing is required for households too poor to be catered for by the free market. Table 2.1 depicts the evolution of policies since 1945.

CONTEXT TO INTERNATIONAL THOUGHTS ON FINANCING FOR URBAN DEVELOPMENT

During the early post-World War II years, house building was regarded as a social overhead cost to economic development. This focused on several issues: economic development; the construction industry and construction quality; development of human capital; social development; and subsidies for workers.[2]

It was assumed that good housing assisted economic development; therefore, investments in housing were worth making. As such, it became a suitable case for treatment by international aid organizations and lenders. During the 1960s, the US Agency for International Development (USAID) began loaning substantial sums for housing development in Latin America as a direct contribution to economic development within the context of thrift institutions to finance housing.[3]

It was assumed that good housing assisted economic development; therefore, investments in housing were worth making

During the 1950s and 1960s, the modern movement in architecture generated a branch of interest in tropical architecture.[4] Its concern with climatic comfort and the use of local materials was set within the context of the view that good design and construction were key elements in creating affordable and appropriate towns. At the same time, building research establishments set up in the colonies – such as Central Building Research Institute (CBRI) in Roorkee, India, Housing Research Development Unit (HRDU, now known as Housing and Building Research Institute (HABRI)) in Nairobi and Building and Road Research Institute (BRRI) in Kumasi, Ghana – were at the centre of the housing effort, including experimentation and testing of materials, techniques and designs.

However, the nature of the construction industry, especially the part of it that constructs housing, is so diffuse,

Table 2.1

Milestones of housing policy development

Phase and approximate dates	Focus of attention	Major instruments used	Key documents
Modernization and urban growth: 1945 to early 1970s	Physical planning and production of shelter by public agencies	Blueprint planning: direct construction (apartment blocks, core houses); eradication of informal settlements	
Redistribution with growth/basic needs: mid 1970s to mid 1980s	State support to self-help ownership on a project-by-project basis	Recognition of informal sector; squatter upgrading and sites-and-services projects; subsidies to land and housing	Vancouver Declaration (UNCHS, 1976); *Shelter, Poverty and Basic Needs* (World Bank, 1980); World Bank evaluations of sites-and-services (1981–1983) (e.g. Bamberger et al, 1982; Keare and Parris, 1982; Mayo and Gross, 1987)
The enabling approach/urban management: late 1980s to early 1990s	Securing an enabling framework for action by people, the private sector and markets	Public–private partnership; community participation; land assembly and housing finance; capacity-building	*The Global Shelter Strategy for Shelter to the Year 2000* (UNCHS, 1990a); *Global Report on Human Settlements 1986* (UNCHS, 1987); *Urban Policy and Economic Development* (World Bank, 1991); *Cities, Poverty and People* (UNDP, 1991); *Agenda 21* (UNCED, 1992); *Housing: Enabling Markets to Work* (World Bank, 1993)
Sustainable urban development: mid 1990s onwards	Holistic planning to balance efficiency, equity and sustainability	As above, with more emphasis on environmental management and poverty alleviation	*Sustainable Human Settlements Development: Implementing Agenda 21* (UNCHS, 1994)
Habitat II: 1996	'Adequate shelter for all' and 'sustainable human settlements development'	Culmination and integration of all previous policy improvements	*The Habitat Agenda* (UNCHS, 1996a); *An Urbanising World: Global Report on Human Settlements 1996* (UNCHS, 1996b)
Istanbul+5 2001/the Millennium Declaration and the Millennium Development Goals (MDGs)	Review of the Habitat Agenda process	Renew Habitat Agenda commitments and seek/devise more effective strategies	*Declaration on Cities and other Human Settlements in the New Millennium* (UN, 2001b); *Cities in a Globalising World: Global Report on Human Settlements, 2001* (UNCHS, 2001);

uncontrolled, fluid and complex that many have despaired of its being part of development programmes. Indeed, some even denied that a building industry existed in most developing countries.[5] During the 1950s, there had been several attempts to industrialize building, with success levels varying from reasonable in parts of Europe and America to disastrous in Africa.[6] Their replacement of cheap and abundant labour inputs with expensive and scarce industrial and imported resources was illogical and ran counter to development. However, it is undeniable that there was a lack of trust between governments and local builders, even though they were mutually dependent; the former needed the contracts to be fulfilled, the latter needed the work from a volatile group of politicians and officials. This mistrust was not helped by sometimes poor standards of delivery on the part of the builders, and favouritism, non-transparent and corrupt tendering procedures, and poor payment records on the part of government agencies. Thus, international agencies often favoured large contractors based in the industrialized countries over their local counterparts when they offered contracts to implement aid projects.

However, by the early 1970s, the concept of intermediate technology had been developed and became popular, with the recognition that different technologies were appropriate in different contexts.[7] In the developing world, compromises and hybrid technologies were seen as, perhaps, more suitable than imported 'Western' industrial methods. This coincided with a new interest in the panoply of tiny businesses which were so obvious in developing cities but hardly considered in official documentation. Pioneering work during the early 1970s recognized the presence and contribution of the informal sector in all manner of industrial and commercial sectors, not least construction.[8]

The informality of the construction industry presented a challenge that could only be dealt with positively by the kind of paradigm shift exercised in the acceptance of non-Western technologies. In the same way, informality in land markets and housing credit pointed to the need for lateral thinking about appropriate approaches to assessing urban and shelter development which could embrace their positive aspects while protecting against the negative.

Human capital development has been a concern of economists from the pioneering ideas of Adam Smith, through to the development economists of the 1950s and 1960s, such as Arthur Lewis and Theodore Schultz. Schultz argued that, although housing may have little effect on productivity in affluent countries, better housing may be crucial where health conditions are poor. Thus, investments which improve human capital should be top priorities in development planning.[9]

During the late 1960s and early 1970s, John Turner's writings arising from his experiences in Peru, where squatter invasions were leading housing development, established the important place self-help housing could have in social development.[10] His theories extrapolated an ongoing process of founding and consolidation of neighbourhoods out of observing different settlements in various conditions of development. While this has been criticized, his argument that housing did something for its occupants' welfare and social and economic progress were highly influential and timely, coming as they did when city administrations were being swamped by a pace of development which they had little capacity to control.[11] The ideas that informal suburbs could be the solution rather than the problem, and that improving what was there was the way forward rather than bulldozing it away and starting again, became conventional wisdom in international circles, if not in country policies.[12]

In the formal sector, during the 1950s and 1960s, subsidies were an important part of housing policy. Both before and after the war, housing for urban workers tended to be rented out at less than economic rents, usually related to income. Occasionally, this would be a direct relationship by being a certain percentage of wages extracted at source by employers (typically large manufacturing and extractive industries) who provided housing for their workers. For others, rents were fixed at what was thought to be a realistic amount for the average household to afford. In parallel, during World War II, many countries had sought to control the effect of wartime inflation on urban rents by imposing controls. These were often continued into peacetime and became a feature of many cities' housing. They constitute a subsidy offered (reluctantly) by landlords to tenants.

There was, therefore, little link made between the need to finance housing and its supply. As an example, in the Gold Coast/Ghana, although it was acknowledged in successive development plans during the 1950s and 1960s that the private-sector landlords provided most housing, rents were consistently controlled to levels that affected the profitability of such supply, and rental income was taxed at higher levels than 'earned' income.[13] The costs of such practices, represented by the poor condition of the stock and the lack of new supply, are well known.[14]

TRENDS IN SHELTER AND MUNICIPAL FINANCE DEVELOPMENT: 1972–2004

Between 1972 and 1982: Habitat I

The World Bank began lending for urban development projects during the 1970s. It made an explicit effort to demonstrate that it was financially and economically feasible to provide services and shelter for the lowest income segments of society.[15] However, the focus of financing at that time, as outlined in the report of the first United Nations Conference on Human Settlements, was on low-interest loans, loan guarantees and subsidies as a means of making housing affordable to low-income people.[16] In addition, the active use of pricing policies was seen as the means to enhance equity in service and infrastructure delivery to all. The sources of funding and the implications of under-pricing the services were not discussed.[17]

The project approach

Interventions during this period concentrated on demonstration projects of limited size with respect to a city or region, and usually confined to a particular neighbourhood or group of neighbourhoods. The idea of the projects was to demonstrate the feasibility of providing low-cost housing and services in particular ways thought to be suited to low-income people and capable of replication at a large scale elsewhere in the city/country and in other countries. Replication demanded full-cost recovery as a basic premise. Only in this way could the project benefits be rolled out to the general population living in poor housing conditions through follow-up projects. Unless costs could be recovered, the financing would be used up and the self-perpetuating and limitless growth of subsidies would have to continue.[18] In practice, there was little success in collecting repayments. Project beneficiaries were not pursued when they defaulted and it was politically unacceptable to evict them. Thus, they received further subsidies in forgiven payments and tolerated arrears at the expense of others who could benefit from the replication of the projects. In the event, replication rates were very poor.

During the 1950s and 1960s, subsidies were an important part of housing policy

Projects tended to be outside of municipal control, and to have different standards from elsewhere, different means of implementation (for example, materials procurement through project depots at subsidized prices and soft loans) and little effect 'outside the fence'.

Self-help

Projects during the first period of international financing for urban development focused upon self-help, providing a context in which the spare time and energy of low-income people could be devoted to house construction or infrastructure provision. They were broadly of two types: sites-and-services projects for new housing provision and settlement upgrading for bringing squatter and other informal settlements up to an acceptable standard of servicing and public space provision. Some of the classic projects during the early to mid 1970s, including the World Bank urban development projects in Botswana, El Salvador, Senegal and Tanzania, focused upon new development through sites and services – providing a minimal core house and infrastructure on 'greenfield' sites. This approach was much more cost effective than direct provision of housing. Other classic projects – notably, World Bank projects in Indonesia, Burkina Faso and Zambia – focused upon slum upgrading through improving conditions in un-serviced settlements and providing some serviced sites for overspill. This was more socially and politically acceptable than the alternative of wholesale clearance and relocation. They often ran together, as residents were displaced from the squatter settlements during the rationalization process required to retrofit roads and open up the most congested parts, would be given a serviced plot as recompense for their removal. Both types of development intended to provide occupants with 'acceptable' environments, though they often did not conform to the contemporary legal standards.

Residents of each would be involved in the project through their own physical work, either building the dwellings in sites-and-services schemes, or fitting infrastructure in upgrading. This concept of adding value through physical work, referred to as 'sweat equity', was strongly ingrained in the projects of the 1970s. For a household to engage artisanal help, by employing a builder to construct their home, was felt to be not playing the game by the rules. There was an assumption that, in a reflection of the Protestant ethic, hard work was morally good and, if it was expended building a home or improving the neighbourhood, the occupants would value the dwelling so much that they would look after it well and care for the neighbourhood and its services. In this, the project designers were supported by a then developing literature on the importance of making home as a process, not least by the highly influential work of John Turner.[19] Intuitively, it can be accepted that if someone has been part of constructing a dwelling or a sewer, they will be vigilant with respect to its maintenance and will also be capable of repairing it.

Participants in sites-and-services schemes were helped in their construction efforts by project staff who provided a range of services. They might provide plans of standard dwellings (in first phase and complete forms) including block-by-block guides to construction, help with setting out and laying foundation slabs, and constant encouragement to persevere until the construction was complete. Participants were meant to repay loans taken out to build the dwellings and also to repay the cost of infrastructure and the ongoing services provided. In slum upgrading projects, less repayment was expected; but users were expected to contribute in cash or labour in fitting infrastructure, as well as to pay for the water and other services as they used them. Recipients of upgrading benefits were expected to be among the poorest households in the city.[20]

One analysis of World Bank projects demonstrated that the projects generated greater than expected private investment in housing – in Senegal about eight times as much as the project cost – in addition to considerable benefits in the informal construction industry.[21]

Although land, infrastructure, services and administration were financed from loans, sweat equity became a major housing finance mode; the opportunity cost of leisure time or other economic activity replaced money to pay contractors, just as in pre-industrial societies. Self-help assumed that the opportunity cost of participants' time was near zero when, in fact, most low-income people are not really idle when they are not at their formal work (if they have any). Instead, they work hard as parents or make business to increase their household livelihood portfolio. It was, therefore, difficult for them to fit the sweat equity mould, and many employed artisans to carry out construction tasks.[22] Indeed, evaluations have shown how many participants used professional building workers[23] Only one fifth of households in a Philippines scheme had relied upon their own labour.[24] In Matero, Lusaka, 92 per cent of participants in the World Bank-financed sites-and-services scheme employed construction labour.[25] In the El Salvador World Bank projects, about 72 per cent of labour inputs (by value) were hired – a total of 6.5 work months hired labour per dwelling.[26] As might be expected, households with higher incomes and greater employment opportunities were more likely to contract out their 'sweat equity' contribution to artisans than those with lower incomes.[27]

In addition to finance by sweat equity, there were many subsidies. Some were declared in the project (on-budget) and others were hidden (off-budget). For example, project administrative costs were rarely passed on to the recipients, being absorbed, instead, as a hidden subsidy. Off-budget subsidies were usually many times larger than on-budget.[28]

The participants in sites-and-services schemes tended to have rather higher incomes than the rhetoric and intention implied. As they usually had to apply in writing, often in an international language or an urban *lingua franca*, most successful participants were literate in their second language and, therefore, able to earn more than the minimum wage. It was in the interests of project administrators to allocate plots and the consequent subsidized benefits to households who could well afford to keep up the repayments. Thus, the financial requirements, with respect to upfront payments and ongoing repayments, rendered the projects self-selecting to people who had a likelihood (and some evidence) of long-term stable income. Of course, this undermined the poverty alleviation goal of such projects. It is, therefore, not surprising that, in many projects, low-income households showed themselves able and willing to pay for housing and services in a way that undercut the basic premise of subsidies.[29] In others, poor repayment by occupants undermined any hope of replication. Only in a few countries (notably, Indonesia, Jordan and Tunisia) was substantial replication successful.

Dwelling owners in upgrading schemes, on the other hand, tended to be among the low-income groups and their tenants were probably in even lower income echelons (although their per capita income was probably similar or higher).[30]

Who took part in and benefited from the projects?

The successful project beneficiaries 'won the lottery' by having access to benefits unavailable to the mass population. They undoubtedly benefited with respect to long-term improvements in their housing conditions, the improved security of tenure which went with the schemes, and in terms of the consequent increase in the value of their property. However, they had to accept what was on offer and it may not have been what they had bargained for or what they required the most. Many found themselves unsuited to the project and bought their way out by selling to richer households, ignored some of the project requirements to better suit it to their needs, or defaulted on payments to make it affordable. Tenants tended not to benefit much as their rents would rise to cover any repayments required, often above their willingness to pay. Thus, they tended to move out to another non-upgraded settlement where rents were still affordable. In the process, however, their social and economic networks would probably be seriously dislocated.

Many owners took advantage of demand for the greatly improved housing and sold out to higher income households, who had not enjoyed such secure tenure, and then moved into another un-serviced area. Indeed, it was not uncommon for site-and-service owners to remain in the squatter settlement and rent out the newly built dwelling to another, better-off, household. Where those who sold or rented out achieved a good price for their dwelling, they might be said to have exercised a reasonable market choice to convert housing capital gains into more flexible forms in order to diversify the benefits into other parts of their household livelihoods portfolios.[31] However, anecdotal evidence suggests that few gained a full market price as even a relatively small capital sum represented more money than most had ever contemplated possessing, and they were easily wooed into selling themselves short and moving back into un-serviced squatter areas. This 'raiding', or 'poaching', by middle-income households has been a feature of many such interventions through the decades and is still an issue in South Africa's housing subsidy developments.[32]

Many participants benefited from learning new skills and gaining confidence in, and understanding of, construction and the installation of services, as well as in dealing with authority figures. Some went on to make a living with their new skills. However, it has been argued that the process of teaching lay-people to build their own dwellings is inefficient in that they only really master the process when they have almost finished.[33] The newly learned skills are then usually neglected and forgotten. This is counterproductive as it is more important to have a well-functioning cadre of small-scale contractors than to teach individuals skills that they will only use once.

There was an obvious problem about how far the recipients were being involved in planning and decision-making. Projects tended to include a bundle of services and components chosen by distant decision-makers and imposed upon the recipients, with their involvement sought only in a token participation exercise to gain their cooperation and acquiescence. Thus, in the World Bank's early Lusaka Project in Zambia, residents of squatter settlements went on collective walks to guide the detailed route of roads that had already been roughly marked out in thick felt pen on a diagram of the project.[34] They were not involved in the decisions about how much investment should be devoted to roads and what the general layout should be; their participation was restricted to details of routing and which buildings should be demolished to implement their construction.

The construction industry benefited in contrasting ways. Large formal (sometimes international) contractors had the opportunity to tender for the large contracts and the successful firms undoubtedly benefited. Their workers would also receive regular income and experience. However, much of the construction industry consists of independent artisans who tackle jobs alone or in informal gatherings of tradespeople and labourers. They were often disqualified from tendering because of the conditions about previous experience and the bonds to be deposited. Many, however, benefited from small contracts to provide skilled inputs into so-called self-help housing. However, they were unlikely to have garnered as much work as if the housing had been developed in a manner designed to value the role of local construction firms. The effect of the subsidy element in these self-help projects on small contractors was often conflicting. On the one hand, the reduction in land and other costs allowed clients to spend more on the structure, improving the opportunities for small contractors. On the other hand, the same contractors might also suffer a reduction in the value of their work as subsidized alternative housing goods became available.

The municipalities and utilities agencies took part and benefited in a limited way. The projects were often too complex for the municipal authority to implement. Municipalities provided the land for the projects at subsidized prices. The improvement in the housing stock and the upgrading of some of the worst housing undoubtedly took away some problems and generated potential for improved property tax and utility charges. However, they inherited servicing and maintenance burdens from the new infrastructure and often found that the clients had no intention of repaying the cost of fitting or the ongoing service charges. In addition, collection of taxes and charges is often very poor, so such benefits are minimized. Defaulting behaviour is likely to be particularly serious where some allocations have been made to return political or other favours, or where defaulting has been tolerated in the past or used as a political weapon – for example, apartheid South Africa. More importantly, perhaps, these early projects had almost no positive effect on the ability of the municipalities to manage urban programmes as their staff had been bypassed in the planning, financing and implementation, which were conducted by a specially recruited team only tangentially attached to the municipal councils. However, the negative effect on municipalities was often felt through the 'diversion of scarce talent to a small enclave of public programmes' that were not managed by the municipality in which they took place.[35]

The great majority of citizens – those outside the project 'fence' in the cities affected, those not finding work in the project, and those living elsewhere in the country (including the rural areas) – benefited hardly at all. Indeed, it is likely that they experienced poorer conditions than they could have done if the resources had been used differently, rather than being concentrated on the projects. Most people in the countries affected could, therefore, be excused for feeling it was all a waste of money that could have been better spent helping each qualifying household a little, instead of giving a windfall to a few. Furthermore, large amounts of subsidized dwellings in particular neighbourhoods may well have had a depressing effect on general housing values.[36] The inescapable reality is that most people living in poverty did not benefit from the project-based approach at all. Indeed, its poverty alleviation focus was probably subsumed, in implementation, by the impetus to complete the project on time within budget, and to demonstrate that the approaches worked and could be replicated, even though they did not reach those in the lowest income groups.

The 1980s saw 'step-by-step moves towards a more comprehensive whole-housing sector approach'

Towards financial sustainability: the 1980s

The 1980s were a period of change. The projects of the 1970s were subject to detailed analysis, both within international funding institutions[37] and from outside,[38] and lessons had been learned. For example, for all the efforts aimed at improving housing, the existence of un-serviced informal settlements appeared to be continuing; indeed, they appeared to be expanding rather than in decline. The limitations found in the project approach included the following: that they had a low impact on overall urban economic development; that they encouraged institutional reforms only in those organizations implementing the projects; and that the funder's funds were restricted to 'retail' rather than 'wholesale' roles.[39] The 1980s saw 'step-by-step moves towards a more comprehensive whole-housing sector approach' in which evaluating existing projects was as influential as general changes in policy towards housing and urban development.[40]

There was a perceived need to incorporate housing within the wider economic environment, rather than dealing with it as a special sector requiring attention out of welfare considerations. It was recognized that the individual sites-and-services and slum upgrading projects alone could not affect the growing housing need – a well-functioning finance system for housing for the majority was necessary.

It was recognized that a well-functioning housing finance system for the majority was necessary

This generated a paradigm shift from multi-sectoral, but quite localized, projects, affecting a fortunate few, to an emphasis on creating a sustainable capability for housing supply and urban development affecting most residents and congruent with the overall policy and economic environment. The locus of borrowing changed from almost exclusively public-sector institutions to financial intermediaries. In parallel, attention shifted from the physical asset financed to the institutional structure of the implementing agency and its ability to mobilize the development required.[41]

Quite early in this period, as a way of countering the obvious problem that the components planned were not necessarily the priorities for the recipients, the World Bank developed programmatic projects in which the local municipalities and other institutions could propose side projects within an agreed range. The prototype for these was Brazil's Parana Market Towns Improvement Project, implemented between 1983 and 1988, in which a large number of municipalities could compete for investments according to local priorities. This project demonstrated early success in proliferating urban projects and targeting them to the sectors in which there was local need.

Structural adjustment: towards macroeconomic orthodoxy

During the early 1980s, World Bank loan financing was made available to enable governments to recover from years of decline through structural adjustment programmes (SAPs). Indeed, for many countries, the SAP was imposed as a condition on other loan finance. It consisted of, among other things, a reduction in government and quasi-government agencies, a reduction in public spending, and the introduction of markets in the supply side of housing and urban development. The purpose of SAPs was to:

- introduce economic reforms and reduce balance of payments deficits;
- reduce public expenditure to more manageable levels; and
- carry out medium-term reforms to improve exports and growth.

SAPs were intended to integrate local economies within the international trade and finance systems and to establish balance between state and market roles.[42] The advocates of this approach saw the free market as the means of improving efficiency and injecting dynamism into the economy. The state's role was that of enablement: securing private property rights; reducing regulations in inhibited markets; achieving macroeconomic stability; developing finance capital markets; and providing sector policies and institutional frameworks for effective development.[43]

There was a perceived need to be involved in the promotion of sound financial institutions in the borrowing countries, in which housing finance was seen to be a part.[44] Public institutions were the target provider. At the same time, there was a change in attitudes towards subsidies. It was believed that they should be reduced, effectively targeted and changed from financial (money up front) to fiscal (tax breaks or credits). This occurred in parallel with structural adjustment in the wider economic and financial context.

Structural adjustment has often been seen as ultimately unhelpful to the countries upon which it was imposed. It frequently resulted in a reduction of formal-sector employment without enough alternative employment opportunities, and the social welfare protection introduced in mitigation programmes was often insufficient. It focused upon exports; but Organisation for Economic Co-operation and Development (OECD) countries did not lift tariff and quota restrictions to allow the exports to compete on equal terms in the world market.

Externally supported projects at the time channelled housing and urban loans into housing finance institutions and municipal development funds, where they would be disbursed more widely and quickly than could geographically delineated inputs.[45] A key objective of projects promoted by the World Bank was financial sustainability – creating housing finance systems that fitted into a generally sound and sustainable financial sector.

In the housing sector, the direct results of SAPs were often some or all of the following:

- development of housing finance capital markets, including intermediaries capable of offering mortgages to middle- and low-income households;
- deregulation of interest rates on loans;
- collapse of uncompetitive housing finance institutions;
- curbing of public expenditure, which often cut infrastructure programmes and maintenance;
- taking direct provision away from the state in favour of private developers and NGOs; and
- diversion of investment from construction into other, so-called 'more productive', export-orientated sectors.[46]

The shift from project-orientated lending to lending for housing finance brought about a major shift in the scale of loans. World Bank project averages rose from US$19 million during 1972–1975 to US$211 million during 1985–1990. At the same time, there was an increasing number of loans and a larger share of lending to housing and municipal financing. From 1986–1991, housing and related residential infrastructure (about 70 per cent of urban lending) ranged from 3 to 7 per cent of World Bank lending and averaged US$900 million annually.[47] However, at the same time, the countries assisted by the financial-sector loans tended to be better off than those assisted in the project-based phase.[48]

The birth of the enabling strategy: the mid 1980s

One significant review of housing policy transition argues that there was a fulcrum of policy change during 1985 to 1987, a mid point between the two major United Nations conferences.[49] It was a time when the in-depth reflection on the accumulated experience in the shelter sector was bringing improved understanding and there was discussion of the way forward in several influential documents. There was also advocacy arising out of the 1987 International Year of Shelter for the Homeless.[50] Self-help was then seen as provisional, evolving from sweat equity to contracting of construction professionals.[51] Furthermore, by the end of this short period, the enabling approach had been put together and launched on the international agenda. As mentioned earlier, the 1980s saw 'step-by-step moves towards a more comprehensive whole-housing sector approach' in which evaluating existing projects was as influential as general changes in policy towards housing and urban development.[52]

The Global Report on Human Settlements 1986 introduced the enabling approach as a development from the project-based approach towards settlement-wide, participatory action aimed at reducing the ring-fenced effects of the earlier projects and allowing all to enjoy better housing conditions.[53] It was clear that there was an inescapable need to scale up activities to meet the needs of the very large numbers of people living in poverty. It was also becoming obvious that whole housing sector development depended upon how well the economic, financial, legal and institutional environment supported it.[54]

The enabling approach treats housing and urban development as a multi-sectoral issue, affected just as much by efficiencies and inefficiencies in finance as in the construction industry or land-tenure systems, or the regulatory framework. The task of the state is to create the legal, institutional and economic framework for economic productivity and social effectiveness, in which efficient settlement development can then flourish.

The enabling approach calls for a housing policy environment that oversees and regulates the sector, with the government not supplying housing directly, but leaving actual production and delivery of housing to the housing market, in which all 'actors', ranging from large formal-sector developers through artisans and individual households, to voluntary community organizations, involve themselves at their most effective level in the production process. The enabling approach replaces the interventionist provision of public housing by the state, which presupposes that the government and its agencies are the best actors to supply the kind of housing that society should have.

In the World Bank's 1993 housing sector paper, which reflected many aspects of its urban policy document of 1991, the enabling approach was introduced in some detail in the context of overall financial markets.[55] Both sector papers emphasized enablement approaches, the sectors' contributions to general macroeconomic development, and the acceptance of pro-poor policies, including targeted subsidies.[56] There was also a recognition that most housing and infrastructure loan programmes required a mix of market, state, voluntary sector and household roles, especially in recognizing that each may be most effective at a particular level.

In order to enable housing provision, the six inputs (five markets and one intervention) in the housing supply system should be freed up to operate effectively. The six inputs are: land; finance; construction industry/labour; building materials; infrastructure; and the regulatory framework. The argument is that removing bottlenecks from each of these will enable housing supply at the requisite scale and variety for urban development to effectively accommodate the people. For example, if finance is easily available but construction materials are in short supply, extra financial inputs to end-users might only raise the price of materials. What may be needed more is investment in building materials supply.

The enabling approach treats housing and urban development as a multi-sectoral issue

It is vital for the enabling approach to shelter that a wide range of non-state actors are willing and able to produce and market housing, and to undertake essential support roles in the housing process, such as facilitating the flow of housing inputs, organizing communities and operating services. These non-state actors include the commercial private sector (such as developers/real estate agents and banking/finance institutions) and, more importantly for the urban poor, NGOs, community-based and other socio-civic organizations, as well as small-scale producers in the informal sector. Since each of these actors has distinct comparative advantages in housing, the goal of policy is to develop partnerships that complement their strengths and weaknesses. This will maximize their contributions and minimize costs to particular groups or to the city as a whole. Partnerships are thus fundamental to the enabling approach and to achieving adequate shelter for all.[57]

Sustainability and the brown agenda

The mid 1980s also saw the birth of sustainability as an overarching rubric for development activity. Following the founding of the World Commission for Environment and Development (WCED) in 1983, the Brundtland Report devised the now classic definition of sustainable development as meeting 'the needs of the present without compromising the ability of future generations to meet their own needs'.[58] From that time on, no agency could ignore the need to consider environmental impact alongside the social and economic benefits of its projects. Shortly after, the 1992 United Nations Conference on Environment and Development (UNCED, or the Earth Summit) in Rio de Janeiro agreed on Agenda 21. Its Chapter 7 dealt with human settlements, emphasizing the significance of urban environments and community-based environmental planning and management. Housing, infrastructure and urban governance were firmly rooted into the sustainability agenda. An essential component of sustainability in human settlements is equity in distribution, with particular emphasis on the low-income groups.

The most immediate and critical problems confronting developing country cities are the health hazards deriving from inadequate water, sanitation, drainage and solid waste services; poor urban and industrial waste management; air pollution; accidents linked to congestion and crowding; occupation and degradation of marginal and sensitive lands; and the interrelationships between these problems. This aggregation of problems, which collectively constitute the 'brown agenda', disproportionately affects the urban poor, who are most affected by ill health, lower productivity, reduced incomes and lowered quality of life.

Chapter 7 reiterates the overall objective of improving the social, economic and environmental quality of human settlements and the living and working environments of all people, particularly the poor. Such improvement should be based on technical cooperation activities, partnerships among the public, private and community sectors, and participatory decision-making by community and special interest groups.

At the same time, there was a realignment of emphasis from the 'ability to pay' to 'willingness to pay' as a result of economic analysis which found that the latter produced much more accurate estimates in cost-recovery calculations.[59] Ability to pay depends particularly upon the economic conditions of the potential users and tends to be expressed as a percentage of household income (for example, 20 per cent for housing and 3–5 per cent for water), although this can vary considerably depending upon the nature of the local economy. Willingness to pay, on the other hand, represents perceived utility and benefit of a service. Factors that are likely to affect willingness to pay include household income; the potential of additional income or savings owing to the improved service; the level and value of time saved; and the perceived convenience, reliability and quality of the improved service compared to the old service.

Box 2.1 Seven-point conceptualization of whole-sector development

Sustainable development requires approaches that are integrated, reaching across sectors and touching physical, economic and social activities and institutions. Such integrated approaches have been promoted by major international organizations such as the United Nations system and the European Union (EU).

In its 1993 housing sector paper, *Housing: Enabling Markets to Work*, the World Bank conceptualized whole-sector housing development as comprising seven components, three on the demand side, three on the supply side and one appertaining to managing the sector:

Demand side

1 the development of property rights – for example, in regularizing tenure in squatter settlements and in removing rent controls;
2 the development of housing finance systems, especially mortgage finance;
3 the targeting of subsidies;

Supply side

4 infrastructure provision for residential land development;
5 the regulation of land and housing development, including introducing regulatory audits to remove barriers to development;
6 improved organization and competition in the building industry;

Managing the sector

7 appropriate institutionally loaded reform.

Source: World Bank, 1993; Pugh, 2001.

Whole-sector development: 1987 onwards

The 1990s saw a consolidation of the sector-wide approach that had emerged in the early 1980s in which major donors started giving support in an agreed sector to be coordinated by governments at local or national level (see Box 2.1) This shifted donor interventions from direct programmes, which suited the donor's priorities, to supporting governments to implement their own priorities.

Approaches range from a set of coordinated projects, to simply supporting a sector budget. This often occurred within a context in which governments agreed on core poverty reduction strategy (PRS) principles within which to disburse funding. Assistance was then given to achieve:

- greater government ownership of reform and development programmes;
- increased government accountability;
- development of sustainable capacity;
- transparency and predictability of resource flows; and
- maximum value for money and minimum transaction costs.[60]

The focus moved from physical targets to broad institutional development, including financially sustainable operation of upgrading programmes. In parallel, the lending agencies moved away from a 'retailing role', involved in every detail of the project, to that of a 'wholesaler', with local municipalities or other institutions planning and implementing the details within broad programme parameters and demonstration of administrative capability.[61] As in the Parana Market Towns Improvement Project, finance was awarded to an institution or consortium which then disbursed its components to others. This represented a 'wholesaler' to 'retailer' relationship that promised greater efficiency. Loan conditions required 'sustainable finance', represented in cost recovery, and in the skilled management of receipts and expenditures within a context of operational effectiveness. Members of the consortium (in the Parana case, local governments and their communities) selected their type of sub-projects, costed them, and rationalized community participation in the selection of priorities.[62]

The Global Strategy for Shelter

By 1990, the United Nations Centre for Human Settlements (UNCHS, now UN-Habitat) had formulated its comprehensive ideas of housing reform and released the Global Strategy for Shelter to the year 2000.[63] This had a laudable, but what is now recognized as an over-optimistic, objective of 'decent housing' for all by 2000.[64] Later in the decade, this term was replaced by 'adequate housing'; but this was also defined in some detail in the Habitat Agenda to include the physical conditions of the dwelling, its services, tenure security, location and many other characteristics.[65] The need for adequate housing has also been included in many United Nations summit recommendations and closing declarations, including UNCED in Rio de Janiero,[66] the Social Development Summit in Copenhagen,[67] the Fourth World Conference on Women in Beijing,[68] the United Nations Conference on Human Settlements in Istanbul,[69] as well as the *Durban Declaration on Racism, Racial Discrimination, Xenophobia and Related Intolerance*.[70]

The 1992 UNCED Earth Summit in Rio de Janeiro influenced both UNCHS (Habitat) and the World Bank. As mentioned earlier, it included housing and urban policies within Chapter 7 of Agenda 21, its strategy for the 21st century. Sustainability is seen as a three-pronged approach, joining environmental, social and economic development in housing and urban programmes. Agenda 21 called upon local governments to mobilize their communities for policy formulation and action plans for environmental improvement in Local Agenda 21s.

The Global Strategy for Shelter to the Year 2000 (GSS) recognized that governments have an obligation to ensure that an appropriate environment is created for the mobilization of finance for housing. The objectives of such an effort are to promote and mobilize savings, reduce costs, improve the efficiency of financial intermediation, and assist the free movement of capital through the national economy. Housing finance reform, which is a key component of a shelter strategy, should be seen as part of a broad effort to reform and develop the financial sector.[71]

The GSS encouraged providers to reduce the cost of housing finance to the lowest possible level, but urged that the days of housing subsidies, artificially low interest rates and political interventions to forgive defaults be left behind. Instead, government interventions should be consistent with sound financial and economic principles through prudent interventions in the deposit rate, servicing costs, cost of risk, risks of default, fluctuations in interest rates, liquidity and repayment. Personal savings should still be the cornerstone of housing finance for lower income groups and these had to be mobilized as fully as possible.[72]

The GSS accepted that subsidies were necessary for some groups, but called for ensuring that they provided the greatest benefit to those most in need and treated equally those in equal need. They should be targeted to deliver the greatest possible benefit to their intended beneficiaries at the lowest possible administration cost. In addition, they should not impose unacceptable costs on others, including institutions.[73] Whatever else subsidies are, they should fit into an overall approach to social welfare for people living in poverty.[74]

Focus on building institutional capacity to develop housing and urban services

The new paradigm encouraged institutional reform and development. In contrast to the 1970s approach of bypassing local institutions, sending signals that they were untrustworthy and less than competent, the new approach was to uplift local institutions, affirming their trustworthiness and challenging them to be effective. This coincided with the spread of decentralization of power from the centre to regions and municipalities, and the growth of a local sense of responsibility for urban conditions. It also gave local authorities a financial resource to draw upon in a context where bond and financial securities markets were often undeveloped.[77]

Efforts to improve municipal government led to the setting up of the Urban Management Programme (UMP) as a partnership between UNCHS (Habitat), now UN-Habitat (the executing agency), the World Bank (the associate agency), and the United Nations Development Programme (UNDP) (providing core funding, with various bilateral donors, and monitoring) in 1986 (see Box 2.2)

Box 2.2 Urban Management Programme

The Urban Management Programme (UMP) was set up to strengthen the contribution that towns and cities make towards economic growth, social development, reduction of poverty and the improvement of environmental quality. In its first few years, it was mainly notable for the development of policy frameworks and discussion papers, especially on land and urban environmental management. From 1992 onwards, it focused upon technical cooperation on a demand-driven basis from developing countries, managed through regional offices.[75] It has emphasized participatory urban governance, urban poverty alleviation, urban environmental management and, more recently, the shelter effects of HIV/AIDS, with gender as a cross-cutting issue. Participatory decision-making processes have been institutionalized in participating cities through 120 city consultations. The UMP's way of working directly with cities, both in the city consultations and in its seven city development strategies,[76] is in line with the climate of directly funding existing local institutions.

The focus of the UMP echoes the more holistic, inter-agency approach which grew through the 1980s and the recognition that the future success of development might rest in the cities of the world. The emphasis on assisting municipalities to carry out their functions effectively illustrates the shift from early project-based assistance to addressing the core capabilities of public authorities and their citizens to improve service delivery and sustainability.

GSS recognized that governments have an obligation to ensure that an appropriate environment is created for the mobilization of finance for housing

In 1999, the Cities Alliance was established as a global alliance of cities and their development partners committed to improving the conditions of the urban poor through city development strategies and slum upgrading. Like the Urban Management Programme, it is a partnership between the World Bank and UN-Habitat, with several countries and other agencies involved in funding. It works in partnership with local authorities and national governments to, among other things, scale up solutions promoted by local authorities to address the shelter needs of the urban poor, who are treated as partners, not problems. With respect to finance, it engages potential investment partners to expand the resources available to local authorities and the urban poor, enabling them to build their assets and income.[78]

A holistic approach to settlement upgrading, sometimes called 'the Orangi model' after a successfully upgraded area in Karachi, Pakistan, has been replicated in several countries.[79] The process adopted involves making know-how available to an organized community which has its own leadership for negotiating policy and for mobilizing local people to take part in self-help activities. Choices are made about the selection of affordable technology and resource allocation in water and sanitation services to bring health and economic benefits, including generating investment in housing improvement. Sometimes a community will manage the infrastructure system or contract with private or public sectors.[80] Of course, the model is implemented differently, and has different outcomes, depending upon political, cultural and professional factors in each place. In some projects, for example, the communities expressed their rights and needs in a unified way, and this facilitated better results per unit invested than in cases where political disputes arose among residents when deciding priorities for environmental improvements. Clearly, the 'political' realm can influence the effectiveness of upgrading investments.

It is clear that this is fundamentally different from the 1970s model used in Lusaka and elsewhere, where the only choices offered to the residents were the detailed routes of the already planned service lines, even though they were expected to expend time and energy in fitting the services.

Economic development depends on efficacy of financial systems

The development of mortgage finance became a major focus for the World Bank's interventions and influenced other international lenders. It was recognized that less than 10 to 20 per cent of annual housing investment in developing countries was covered by mortgage finance. Over several decades, national banks and building societies had to cope not only with the age-old problem of mortgage financing (lending over the long term while borrowing over the short term – through deposit and current account balances), but many also had to endure political interference in their business dealings. They were, typically, coerced into lending at fixed rates (often at negative real interest rates) and forgiving loans; as a result, they could not maintain liquidity. Thus, numbers of mortgages were very small and institutions were extremely risk averse, lending only to the most financially secure or politically favoured clients.

Reflecting the globalization beginning during the early 1990s, the World Bank pointed out the need for housing finance institutions to be able to compete for deposits and investments on equal terms with other financial institutions. Thus, lending must be at positive, real interest rates and deposits should be of sufficient term to support long-term lending. Characteristics of lending should include:

- mortgage lending at variable rates and appropriate indexation;
- secure land tenure and property rights; and
- enforceable foreclosure procedures.[81]

All of these are necessary to protect the lenders and to enable them to lend with some confidence.[82]

Finance capital in development

The *World Development Report* of 1989 was devoted to the role of finance capital in development.[83] Its key message was that effective growth and economic development depended upon having financial systems that were effective in linking markets and government agencies with the range of financial institutions and instruments. Gone were the days when it was efficient to have low interest rates in some sectors. It had become clear from research that the formal-sector financial institutions were fragmented, had liquidity problems, could not effectively manage credit and interest rate risks and could not make their capital profitable.[84] Moreover, and probably most importantly, they were involved in only 20 per cent of housing. There was urgent need for reform to generate confidence in finance institutions both among potential customers and among the donor agencies who would channel money through them.

During the 1990s, some developing countries developed proactive and well-integrated housing finance policies and institutions. In this, they responded to the unprecedented rate of urban growth and changes in global finance markets. In addition, there was a recognition that purely government-managed finance institutions had failed in their laudable aims and had become bureaucratic, inefficient and prey to exploitation by insiders.

A 1999 study suggested that there were six broad categories of housing finance systems in place, many of which needed a range of reforms in order to make them more effective (see Box 2.3).[85]

Countries with well-developed housing finance sectors, primarily among middle-income developing countries and some Asian countries, benefited from the international concentration on housing finance. Between 1982 and 1992, the World Bank invested US$715 million in housing finance institutions in Mexico, the Republic of Korea and India. This included a US$250 million loan to the private-sector Housing Development and Finance Corporation (HDFC) of India, with which it was able to take housing credit lower down the distribution of household income. The new policy was an effort to improve the performance of financial institutions by providing guarantees to international investors similar to those of the Housing Loan Guaranty Scheme used by USAID, the US government's bilateral aid agency.[86] Sri Lanka also received significant funds, which were then on-lent to local co-operative societies to boost its 2.5 million small loans programme.

However, some housing finance systems moved from boom to bust, with serious local consequences. One example was the Mexican housing finance system. Despite no lack of interest by private builders, speculative house building was severely limited in scope in Mexico until the end of the 1980s. However, liberalization of mortgage funds from commercial banks and privatization of some investments related to payroll funds boosted the housing development industry so that private developers became active all across the country. During the early 1990s, an influx of investment capital fuelled the mortgage market and increased the impetus of the building boom, especially in condominiums, driving up land prices. This all crashed in December 1994, leaving mortgagees with un-payable debts and negative equity in their homes. A special programme was launched in 1996 to bail out the banks, which continue to loan to middle-income homeowners while the low-income group is left to make its way in the informal sector.[87]

Box 2.3 Housing finance institutions during the 1990s

Housing finance institutions during the 1990s were based on the following systems:

- *Undeveloped housing finance systems*: common in sub-Saharan Africa, with weak financial systems and commercial banks. Priority should be given to improving urban laws, policies and practices affecting housing, beginning with clarifying traditional property rights. Public efforts should concentrate on infrastructure development, the supply of serviced land and titling, all within realistic affordability parameters.
- *Missing housing finance systems in formerly centrally planned economies*: one of the many problems in the former Soviet bloc, China and Viet Nam. Coordinated improvements are needed to establish primary mortgage lenders and secondary market facilities.
- *Fragmented and unstable housing finance systems*: fairly common in Latin America, where housing finance systems are very small with respect to the economy because of macroeconomic mismanagement and/or external shocks, and inflation has been high. In highly unequal societies, most cannot afford mortgage finance, so subsidy distortions are built in, which can help the general economy to implode. It is essential to separate subsidy from finance and to target subsidies at social housing.
- *Segregated but stable housing finance systems*: in the Middle East and East Asia, where a seemingly (but actually not) very stable group of institutions provide housing finance within restrictions and special advantages. They provide poorly targeted subsidies and finance at preferential rates in a context in which numbers of units are important determinants of success. The informal sector has a major role in finance for those missing out, leading to a high implicit cost of capital for housing.
- *Sound and integrated housing finance systems*: some countries in Southeast Asia have developed sound and well-supervised housing finance systems with secondary mortgage markets that manage to reach well down in the income scales. Because the bankers can choose what to fund, building contractors produce better-quality work. In addition, investors seek out innovative technologies from around the world to improve their investments.
- *Advanced housing finance systems*: found in Organisation for Economic Co-operation and Development (OECD) countries, these have grown out of the UK building society tradition and the savings and loans societies in the US. The continental European market tends to use bond market funding; but all of these special mortgage institutions are shrinking as globalized banking provides specialized financing services to take over the mortgaging business.

Source: Renaud, 1999.

GLOBALIZATION OF FINANCE

Globalization of finance has the following theoretical implications with respect to housing finance:

- It appears to force financial institutions to develop to the point where they are integrated within the financial and capital markets of the world. As a result, their capacities to interact locally with communities are eroded.
- It integrates the financial markets of the world so that the homebuyer in the poorest country is competing for finance in the same pool as the richest countries and corporations.[88]

In this way, globalization makes it much more difficult to have special housing loans in which a lending institution lends at below real market rates.[89] Such loans are usually supported by cross-subsidies from other lending activities; but it is very difficult in the globalized financial context as the high-value business simply transfers to any bank in the world to find cheaper rates.[90] Thus, lower income groups miss out on the opportunities to borrow more cheaply and, in turn, become more difficult to reach.[91] The effect of this is lost on most low-income households, however, as very few have access to such loans. Reasons of financial inadequacy are often cited for sluggish housing markets; but in the context of the housing market within South African townships, blame has been placed firmly at the door of legal, institutional and procedural constraints.[92] Householders cannot gain loans from the formal sector because their tenure is inadequate, transactions costs are very high, there is little market information, and loans are not available for the amount they want to borrow over periods that they regard as manageable. Nevertheless, many governments still have privileged circuits for housing finance through direct funding. This is common in Southeast Asia where governments have traditionally funded housing from direct budgets. In addition, regulatory and tax systems vary so much that households are quite removed from the effects of globalization on the funding at the core of their housing finance.

It is worth asking the question: 'Why should a financial institution lend money to low-income people?' This question encapsulates the following problems facing lenders:

- The essential nature of such housing loans, vis-à-vis other commercial lending, is their small size. Loans suitable for households with incomes of US$10 per day (and there are hundreds of millions such households) would be in the region of US$5000–$10,000. They require a similar amount of administration to set up and run as loans of 100 times as much or more, but the fees (charged as a percentage of the loan amount) are miniscule.
- Liquidity can be a problem for the lender. If the lender wishes to sell on the mortgages to another financial institution in order to boost its liquidity, its portfolio of low-income borrowers with doubtful

collateral and poor security is unattractive in financial markets.

It is partly because of these problems that shelter microfinance and community funding solutions have emerged, especially in developing countries (see Chapters 6 and 7).

THE NEW MILLENNIUM: POLICIES AND ORGANIZATIONS IN SHELTER AND URBAN DEVELOPMENT

The new millennium started with a very different climate of shelter and urban finance from that which appertained 20 years ago. During the early 1980s, large formal financial institutions were the main partners for international funders and lending was banker led; secondary mortgage markets were also seen to be the way forward and were thought to be able to reach as far down the income scale as bankers could countenance. Lending to low-income households was too risky a proposition for most banks.

The low-income worker's role in housing finance was often only to contribute to a compulsory savings scheme. However, all but a lucky few of the poor were untouched by the efforts of international and bilateral finance for housing and urban development. Municipalities were beginning to be trusted; but there was little effort to involve elected representatives who actually voted on resource allocation.

In the new millennium, formal bank financing is only one of several players in the field. Mortgage finance is available in most countries, but its limitations are obviously militating against its being the solution for most low-income households. Microfinancing has progressed from being only enterprise focused to being an important feature of the housing finance system. The savings and loans system, which contains within it the tradition of regular meetings of savers, establishing social links, is an important community builder as well as financial resource. Community grassroots activities are now centre stage in at least some countries in setting the agenda and disbursing the funding. They are reaching people at such low-income levels and in such large numbers that other systems can only dream of.

Mortgage finance is available in most countries, but its limitations are obviously militating against its being the solution for low-income households

The Habitat Agenda

Just before the turn of the millennium, the Global Strategy for Shelter to the Year 2000 and Agenda 21, Chapter 7, were consolidated into the Habitat Agenda at the Istanbul Summit in 1996. It reflects the essence of both previous documents and provides a basis for international and national housing and urban development policy for the 21st century (see Box 2.4).

Reaching the lowest income groups: community-based finance

There is no hiding from the unpalatable truth that formal housing finance institutions cannot address the needs of hundreds of millions of households whose incomes are low. Their assets are just too small and too insecurely held for the formal sector to bother with them or to feel secure in handing out funds to them. Even when formal housing financing is deepening and widening, a majority of households still do not meet the assets and collateral conditions of formal-sector lenders. Formally constituted microfinance organizations have been successful in funding many low-income households, especially through group loans; but even they are by no means universally distributed.

Only the most flexible housing finance organizations will directly help some of the poorest people in society, and even they will not reach the many millions of households who find any expense above actual survival difficult. The rise of community-based organizations (CBOs) involved in providing loans to people living in poverty has been an important feature of the last decade. Perhaps equally important has been the setting up of national and international umbrella organizations to enable and assist their operations, such as Shack/Slum Dwellers International (SDI) and the Society for the Promotion of Area Resource Centres (SPARC) in India. These can negotiate directly with the World Bank and bilateral agencies to borrow large amounts of money at favourable rates for onward lending to their member organizations, who can then use it in partnership with their clients, the households living in poorly serviced and ill-constructed housing and places with little security. They can also have access at the highest level to policy-makers in the United Nations system and national governments.[93] Because of the scale of their groups, and the links with major funders and policy-makers, international grassroots networks have become major forces at the international level on behalf of people living in poverty and are changing the way in which funding is offered and how it is disbursed.

This grassroots movement has introduced a new dimension to the financing of housing and urban development. Probably for the first time, the people who are the ultimate beneficiaries of major international loans are in the driving seat, determining how the money should be spent and organizing others to do the same. These more recent shelter financing approaches are discussed in detail in Part II of this Global Report, alongside reviews of the current status of mortgage finance and social housing approaches.

The right to housing

During the 1990s, the need to ensure adequate housing became the right to adequate housing. This had already been on the agenda since it was included in Article 25 of the 1948 Universal Declaration of Human Rights.[94] During the late 1980s, it appeared again in the United Nations General Assembly, which reiterated:

> *... the need to take (at national and international levels) measures to promote the right of all persons to an adequate standard of living for themselves and their families (including adequate housing) (Resolution 42/146).*[95]

It was also reaffirmed in the *Vienna Declaration on Human Rights*, which emphasizes:[96]

> *... the rights of everyone to a standard of living adequate for their health and well-being, including food and medical care, housing and the necessary social services.*

The Istanbul Human Settlements Summit further reinforced the:

> *... commitment to the full and progressive realization of the right to adequate housing as provided for in international instruments. To that end, we shall seek the active participation of our public, private and non-governmental partners at all levels to ensure legal security of tenure, protection from discrimination and equal access to affordable, adequate housing for all persons and their families.*[97]

The 'progressive legal obligation' stance is enshrined in the cornerstone of the International Covenant on Economic, Social and Cultural Rights, which urges all states to make every effort towards 'achieving progressively the full realization' of the rights in the covenant.[98] However, this does not mean that states can wait until economic or financial conditions make fulfilment of housing rights more straightforward. Indeed, all states are expected to provide for at least a minimum essential level of each right such that a state in which 'any significant number of individuals is deprived of basic shelter is *prima facie* failing to perform its obligations under the covenant'.[99]

Any retrogressive measures, such as forced evictions, are violations of the right to housing. Indeed, states have a duty to respect, protect and fulfill housing rights. Respecting obligates the state not to do anything that violates rights; protecting obligates the state to prevent any other agency from violating people's right to housing; and fulfilling incorporates obligations both to facilitate (or enable) through national housing policies and to provide for those for whom housing is impossible within their own resources.[100] The latter is important to the financing of urban shelter development.

None of this embodies a state obligation to provide everyone with free housing, but rather to set up the legal, social and economic environment in which households have an adequate chance to fulfil their needs. An example of the outworking of this can be found in South Africa, where the new state constitution was being drafted at this time.[101] In it, the state must take 'reasonable legislative and other measures, within the available resources, to achieve the progressive realization of the rights'.[102] This has been tested through the legal campaign of displaced people in the celebrated Grootboom versus Oostenberg Municipality case (see Box 2.5).[103]

Box 2.4 Commitments on shelter finance, Habitat Agenda, 1996

On finance, paragraph 47 of the Habitat Agenda commits member states to:

> *... strengthening existing financial mechanisms and, where appropriate, developing innovative approaches for financing the implementation of the Habitat Agenda, which will mobilize additional resources from various sources of finance – public, private, multilateral and bilateral – at the international, regional, national and local levels, and which will promote the efficient, effective and accountable allocation and management of resources, recognizing that local institutions involved in microcredit may hold the most potential for housing the poor.*

Paragraph 48 also commits member states to:

> *(a) [Stimulating] national and local economies through promoting economic development, social development and environmental protection that will attract domestic and international financial resources and private investment, generate employment and increase revenues, providing a stronger financial base to support adequate shelter and sustainable human settlements development.*
>
> *(b) [Strengthening] fiscal and financial management capacity at all levels, so as to fully develop the sources of revenue.*
>
> *(c) [Enhancing] public revenue through the use, as appropriate, of fiscal instruments that are conducive to environmentally sound practices in order to promote direct support for sustainable human settlements development.*
>
> *(d) [Strengthening] regulatory and legal frameworks to enable markets to work, overcome market failure and facilitate independent initiative and creativity, as well as to promote socially and environmentally responsible corporate investment and reinvestment in, and in partnership with, local communities and to encourage a wide range of other partnerships to finance shelter and human settlements development.*
>
> *(e) [Promoting] equal access to credit for all people.*
>
> *(f) [Adopting], where appropriate, transparent, timely, predictable and performance-based mechanisms for the allocation of resources among different levels of government and various actors.*
>
> *(g) [Fostering] the accessibility of the market for those who are less organized and informed or otherwise excluded from participation by providing subsidies, where appropriate, and promoting appropriate credit mechanisms and other instruments to address their needs.*

Source: United Nations, 1996b.

CONCLUDING REMARKS

Despite many changes in emphasis, international and national efforts in housing finance have failed to reach the majority of households. Housing finance from international institutions began by encouraging projects aimed at improving housing in selected areas and for particular groups, primarily to discourage the growth of poor conditions in low-income neighbourhoods. Such finance was narrowly focused but had a catalytic purpose: to spread to other areas and groups until all were assisted. However,

Box 2.5 Housing rights in South Africa

In the final hearing of the Grootboom versus Oostenberg Municipality case, the South African Constitutional Court ruled that it was not for the judiciary to enquire whether better measures could have been adopted to provide adequate housing, but rather to determine whether or not the state had violated the right of access to housing of the people concerned. In determining the 'reasonableness' of the measures taken by the state, it is right to take into account the resources it has at its disposal. The constitution does not expect more than the state can afford and felt that its housing programme was, so far, a major achievement and represented a systematic response to a pressing social need. The overall programme was, indeed, aimed at realizing access to housing for all in the long and medium term. However, the court found that the state had neglected the short-term aspect. It was clear that no real policy existed which could be applied to people in need of housing in crisis situations. Apart from the normal channel of applying for low-cost housing, which normally takes years, there was no relief for Mrs Grootboom, her children and her neighbours. There was no provision in any policy, whether national, provincial or local, that applied to her desperate situation. Thus, they ordered that 'second-best' facilities, falling short of acceptable housing standards, but nevertheless a basic form of shelter, should be provided for the displaced people. However, this was not to be seen as a licence for people to jump the housing queue by squatting and then litigating for their rights.

Source: UN-Habitat, 2002

replicability turned out to be a chimera; projects did not generally provide a way forward for everyone, nor did they change the way in which housing was provided. Indeed, the pace of informal urbanization quickened and was patently untouched by international financing.

Multi-sectoral approaches followed, out of recognition that housing is only one of a group of interlinked sectors affecting the lives of city dwellers. In addition, the importance of the market as a context and a driver of urban development and housing dominated international and many national interventions through the final decade of the 20th century. However, only a few million households have benefited; the majority still have to provide their own housing without assistance from market lenders.

The growth of monitoring tools is probably one of the most important developments in housing finance since it has changed the way in which proposals are viewed. Once, to assist 250 households was sufficient cause for action, no matter what effect it might have on the ability of others to be assisted. With initiatives such as poverty reduction strategy papers (PRSPs) and the Millennium Development Goals (MDGs), targets are visible and can be monitored. Interventions can, therefore, be judged against the larger context, diluting the impressiveness of tightly drawn projects and promoting programmes that are available to a wide spectra of the population.

Similarly, there has been a long-term switch from top-down, imposed projects, in which participation was minimal, to community-led programmes in which people decide how housing finance institutions can help them and lobby for that assistance. This change has been facilitated by the growth of NGOs, through whom large quantities of finance were channelled during the last few years of the 20th century. However, there has also been a recent revival of channelling finance through governments, including local authorities, as an encouragement of, and response to, improvements in transparency and democracy. Chapter 3 turns to a review of recent financing developments at the urban local authority level.

NOTES

1 This chapter is based on a draft prepared by Graham Tipple, University of Newcastle upon Tyne, UK.
2 Harris and Arku, 2004.
3 Harris and Arku, 2004.
4 Fry and Drew, 1964; Koenigsberger, 1973.
5 Abrams, 1964, p60.
6 The Schokbeton scheme in 1950s Gold Coast stands as a farcical waste of resources abandoned following United Nations advice (Abrams, 1964), although the dwellings built still stand.
7 Schumacher, 1973.
8 Hart, 1973; ILO, 1972.
9 Harris and Arku, 2004.
10 Turner, 1968, 1972, 1976.
11 Burgess, 1982; Ward, 1982; Burgess, 1985.
12 For a discussion of the way in which central and local government in Zambia moved from being in the forefront of positive attitudes towards squatter settlements and their upgrading to having a negative view of the informal-sector built environment only a decade later, see Kasongo and Tipple, 1990.
13 Tipple, 1988.
14 Malpezzi et al, 1990; Malpezzi and Ball, 1991.
15 Kessides, 1997.
16 UN, 1976.
17 Kim, 1997.
18 Pugh, 1995.
19 Turner, 1967, 1972.
20 Kessides, 1997.
21 Kessides, 1997.
22 As observed by Martin (1983), one of the main reasons for employing skilled workers was to improve the quality of construction and, therefore, the status of its owner.
23 Keare, 1983.
24 Keare, 1983.
25 Laquian, 1983b.
26 Laquian, 1983b.
27 Jiminez, 1982.
28 Buckley and Mayo, 1989.
29 Kessides, 1997.
30 This is a reasonably consistent finding in work in Ghana over 20 years, and in work on user-initiated extension activities in several countries. See Tipple et al, 1999; Tipple, 2000.
31 Rakodi and Lloyd-Jones, 2002.
32 Gilbert, 2000; Napier et al, 2003.
33 Tipple, 1994.
34 Martin, 1983.
35 Renaud, 1999, p759.
36 This, however, might have much less effect in developing countries where few homeowners consider selling (Gilbert, 1999) than it would have in an industrialized country with a lively market in housing.
37 For example, Keare and Parris (1982), World Bank (1983) and numerous papers and reports emanating from the research team in the Infrastructure and Urban Department – for example, see Malpezzi and Ball, 1991.
38 For example, Laquian, 1983a; Skinner and Roddell, 1983; Rodwin and Sanyal, 1987.
39 Pugh, 2001, p409.
40 Pugh, 2001, p410.
41 Buckley, 1999.
42 Pugh, 1995.
43 Pugh, 1995.
44 World Bank, 1993.
45 Pugh, 2001.
46 The argument that housing construction is economically productive has been well made in earlier United Nations documents, especially UNCHS and the International Labour Organization (ILO) (UNCHS/ILO, 1995), and in other literature (for example, Tipple, 1995).
47 World Bank, 1993.
48 World Bank, 1993.
49 Pugh, 1997.
50 Including the first *Global Report on Human Settlements 1986* (UNCHS, 1987).
51 Pugh, 1997.
52 Pugh, 2001, p410.
53 UNCHS, 1987.
54 Pugh, 2001.
55 World Bank, 1993, 1991.
56 Pugh, 2001.
57 UNCHS, 1993, 1997, 1998; Porio, 1998
58 WCED, 1987.
59 For example, by Whittington et al, 1990.
60 DFID, 2004a.
61 Pugh, 2001.
62 Pugh, 2001.
63 UNCHS, 1990a.
64 Pugh, 2001.

65 UNCHS, 1996a.
66 UN, 1992.
67 UN, 1995b.
68 UN, 1995a.
69 UN, 1996b.
70 UN, 2001a.
71 UNCHS, 1990b, pp18–19.
72 UNCHS, 1990b.
73 Too many institutions who have given subsidies have been fatally damaged by this largesse, often imposed upon them by government.
74 UNCHS, 1990b.
75 McAuslan, 1997.
76 In Bamako, Mali; Cuenca, Ecuador; Colombo, Sri Lanka; Johannesburg, South Africa; Santo Andre, Brazil; Shenyang, China; and Tunis, Tunisia.
77 Pugh, 2001.
78 Cities Alliance, 2000.
79 Pugh, 2001.
80 These may require group guarantees where foreclosure procedures are weak.
81 World Bank, 1993.
82 World Bank, 1989.
83 World Bank, 1993, 1991.
84 Renaud, 1984.
85 Renaud, 1999.
86 Pugh, 2001.
87 Connolly, cited in UNCHS, 2001.
88 Tucker and Tomlinson, 2000.
89 Kim, 1997.
90 Especially those specializing in high-value niche markets.
91 Tucker and Tomlinson, 2000.
92 Nell et al, 2004.
93 Indeed, SDI was one of the most influential voices in organizing and hosting the Meeting of the World Urban Forum in Nairobi in 2002 and in Barcelona in 2004.
94 UN, 1948.
95 UN, 1987.
96 UN, 1993, para 31.
97 UN, 1996b, para 8.
98 UN, 1966, Article 2 (1).
99 UN-Habitat, 2002, p21.
100 UN-Habitat, 2002.
101 Kabir, 2002.
102 Republic of South Africa, 1996, Article 26.
103 Grootboom versus Oostenberg Municipality, which became Government of South Africa versus Grootboom 2000 (11) BCLR 1169 (CC).

CHAPTER 3

FINANCING URBAN DEVELOPMENT[1]

This chapter addresses the wide range of problems that face municipal authorities in financing urban development as they respond to the challenges of major shifts in their economic base, resulting from falling trade barriers and a globalizing economy. Concurrently, the devolution of administrative and financial responsibility from central governments has forced them to finance a growing proportion of their recurrent and capital expenditures at a time when, in most countries, the urban population is expanding rapidly. This chapter particularly highlights new and innovative approaches to financing urban development, as well as the contextual relevance of urban development finance to finance for shelter development. At the core of this linkage is the fact that municipal finance plays a central role in providing citywide infrastructure services, including within the slums that accommodate the majority of the urban population in developing countries.[2] Indeed, without such services, it would be very difficult and expensive to implement citywide slum upgrading programmes and, more generally, to improve access to adequate shelter for the vast majority of the urban poor.

Municipal finance plays a central role in providing citywide infrastructure services

Municipalities are only one actor in the financing of urban development; but in many ways they are the pivotal one because of their statutory powers and their ability to act on all sectors in a defined geographic space. Households and private enterprises are the developers and builders of urban communities and the owners and operators of economic activities. But unless the municipality can deliver to them the support infrastructure and services that they need, orderly development will be impaired. In developing countries, the rapid pace of urbanization and large migratory flows have increased the pressure on local government spending for urban development. In most of these countries, decentralization laws were enacted during the decades of the 1980s and 1990s amid fiscal deficits, financial crises and political unrest, eroding local revenue and disrupting access to funds for capital investment.

The chapter places emphasis on developing countries, where the challenges are the greatest and the resource constraints the most acute. They are the countries targeted by the Millennium Development Goals (MDGs) and associated 2015 targets adopted in 2001.[3] Multilateral and bilateral development organizations, as well as the individual states, are placing a priority on poverty reduction, reaffirming the world commitment to addressing the growing disparities in income and wealth among countries and within countries. The success of these efforts hinges upon democratic local governance, partnerships involving communities and stakeholders in urban development initiatives, and strengthening of the capabilities and resources of local governments as the pivotal partners in the development process.

Although differences clearly exist between developing, transitional and advanced economies, there are equally striking differences within each region. A series of cases presented in this chapter illustrates the range of issues faced by municipalities, how they have responded to them, their capacity to identify and work with strategic partners, the difficulties encountered and the results achieved. The fact that countries in different parts of the world have developed comparable approaches illustrates the emergence of several important new trends: the broadening of locally generated revenue sources; the strengthening of local financial management; partnerships to finance capital investments; and enhancement of access to long-term credit for municipalities. The cases illustrate innovative approaches to address these challenges. Some have received international recognition as 'best practices'.[4]

MUNICIPAL FINANCE AND URBAN DEVELOPMENT: THE MAIN ISSUES

In advanced economies, the combination of strong local tax bases, structured central/local fiscal relations and well-targeted transfers give local governments the means to drive their own economic, social and physical development, to partner with private-sector entities on development initiatives and to work with non-governmental organizations (NGOs) on social programmes. Their fiscal resources allow them to access a variety of financing sources, ranging from specialized municipal credit institutions and privately managed local development funds to commercial banks and international capital markets. Through strategic investments, they are able to manage growth patterns and improve the urban environment.

In transitional economies, the evolution of municipal finance for urban development reflects the path followed by each country as it integrates within the global economy. The sequencing of the reforms affecting legal and institutional frameworks and economic sectors is of paramount importance. Political, administrative and fiscal decentralization, changes in public and private roles and responsibilities, devolution of functional responsibilities, adjustments in central transfers, and privatization of land and property ownership all affect the capacity of municipalities to deliver services and manage urban development, work with local communities and enter into partnerships with the private sector. In general, municipalities have initiated jointly funded programmes with residents and developers to improve infrastructure and housing. Leading cities seek to compete in the regional and global economy. They strive to manage their finances responsibly in order to attract private investors, obtain investment-grade credit ratings and access the capital markets. Where local authorities are not empowered to borrow, as in China, they have found off-budget methods and instruments to obtain the financing needed to drive and implement urban development strategies and key projects.

In developing countries, municipal finance suffers from the fiscally destabilizing effects of asymmetrical decentralization. Where devolution is proceeding according to a planned legal, institutional and regulatory framework, local authorities benefit from more predictable finances and, in many ways, greater discretion. Successive *ad hoc* adjustments to correct fiscal imbalances tend to disrupt municipal financial management. In all cases, local authorities in developing countries lack the supportive framework enjoyed by local governments in advanced economies. They have to be creative and experiment with innovative approaches to meet their economic and social objectives, particularly in generating employment, expanding service delivery, upgrading the urban environment and improving shelter conditions in poorer communities.

In some developing countries, government-sponsored municipal development funds have provided municipalities with resources for specific categories of projects, including revenue-producing services and infrastructure. Social programmes continue to rely upon central funding and upon support from bilateral and multilateral organizations. Lack of access to long-term financing hampers their ability to fund urban development and to finance the infrastructure services that are so critical to shelter delivery. They are learning to seek partners and alliances, and the best managed municipalities have managed to launch and sustain initiatives with higher levels of government, private businesses, NGOs and community-based organizations (CBOs), as well as bilateral and multilateral organizations.

In the poorer developing countries, local authorities depend heavily upon central transfers to cover deficits in their operating expenditures and upon grants from donors to address their most pressing environmental and social problems. External funds are the main source of financing projects to upgrade and expand infrastructure and urban services. Decentralization policies have devolved functional responsibilities to them without providing them with the fiscal resources needed to discharge this mandate.[5] The general poverty of the population erodes local revenue, which relies upon a multiplicity of low-yield taxes and fees, cumbersome to manage and difficult to collect. Municipal performance is further depressed by chaotic urbanization and the proliferation of informal activities.[6] The MDGs have opened up new opportunities for poor countries to access funding through the Heavily Indebted Poor Countries (HIPC) initiatives for social and environmental programmes. While municipalities can benefit directly and indirectly from these financial resources, the lack of technical and managerial capacity hampers their ability to use efficiently the funding they receive, let alone to leverage the funds.

Around the world, globalization has aggravated uneven spatial distribution of economic activity and increased disparities in income and wealth among regions and countries, and within countries. These inequalities affect urban centres, with some benefiting from locational advantages while others, sometimes even close by, are bypassed by development. These imbalances are aggravated by the social dimension of globalization that has increased and concentrated poverty, led to massive population movements, and reduced local revenues because of the greater mobility of tax bases.[7] Within the shelter sector, the unregulated acquisition of property rights by outsiders has tended to constrict access to shelter by local populations.

The MDGs have opened up new opportunities for poor countries to access funding through the Heavily Indebted Poor Country (HIPC) initiatives for social and environmental programmes

Municipalities are hard pressed to find the resources needed to finance urban development policies fostering shelter delivery, poverty reduction and social inclusion. This challenge is further compounded by the growing concentration of wealth in the private sector brought about by globalization, the concomitant retrenchment of governmental expenditures, and the disengagement of the international community from urban issues in developing countries. Municipalities have to learn to tap private resources and access capital markets, both domestic and global, in order to fund the delivery of urban services and finance urban development programmes.

NATIONAL MUNICIPAL FINANCE SYSTEMS

Two key emerging issues are affecting municipal finance systems in both developed and developing economies. The first is the progressive decentralization of the responsibility for infrastructure investment and the delivery of services to local governments, a trend that has increased their fiscal burden. In some countries, such as Brazil and Indonesia, municipalities have taken advantage of this new autonomy to develop innovative approaches – participatory budgeting in Porto Alegre and other Brazilian municipalities, and the matching grants provided by the central government to Indonesian municipalities that show good fiscal capacities, as well as meet specified need criteria. In other parts of the world, overcoming a tradition of centralized administration is proving difficult, particularly in many African and Asian countries.

The second issue is the rapidly evolving local and regional fiscal relations. While there is a relatively smooth transition to complementary roles between regional and local authorities in the European Union (EU), the situation is far less clear in developing countries, with the exception of India where the state and provincial governments exercise a high degree of control over municipal finance.

Worldwide, there are substantial variations in both the sources of local revenues and the autonomy of local governments to determine the scope and rate of local taxes. Central transfers are still the main source of revenue for municipalities, although their contribution is diminishing in North America and the EU. With the exception of advanced economies, most local sources of revenue are still determined and collected by the central government, leaving little opportunity for local governments to assess often significant local economic activities to fund improvements in social services or invest in the infrastructure necessary to achieve sustainable urban development.

While each country is charting its own economic and social development path, shaped, to some extent, by history and tradition but determined mostly by contemporary political and economic considerations, decentralization has become a worldwide trend underlying the different approaches. Where progressive planned devolution has taken place, as in Europe, the reallocation of functions among levels of government has been guided by the concept of subsidiarity. Where political pressure has been the driving force, devolution has proceeded in a sporadic manner, resulting in serious imbalances between responsibilities and budgeting powers.

In developing countries, municipalities lack the sophisticated supportive framework from which their counterparts in the advanced economies derive technical and financial assistance. Furthermore, their fiscal autonomy is often constrained by the mismatch between devolution of control over expenditures and devolution of control over revenue, curbs on borrowing, caps on particular categories of expenditures, and limits on their discretion to reallocate funds among budget categories. Central recording of transactions relating to wealth-producing assets, including land registration and control of high-yield tax bases, has generally not been devolved, nor is it likely to be devolved in the near future since central governments are striving to strengthen their own finances.[8]

Providing adequate financing for expanding the scope of local responsibilities requires changes in taxation policies and intergovernmental fiscal relations, the development of municipal credit markets and access to long-term credit, the rationalization of expenditure patterns, and the improvement of municipal financial management. Major challenges that must be addressed include:

- large numbers of smaller, financially weak municipalities;
- asymmetrical decentralization;
- retrenchment of central transfers;
- weakness of local revenue sources;
- lack of strong domestic capital markets;
- impediments to the development of municipal credit institutions;
- inadequate capacity and rules for sound financial management at the local level;
- lack of mechanisms to finance urban investments; and
- lack of funds for maintaining existing assets.

Despite these constraints, democratic local governance has enabled local governments to address problems of poverty and exclusion, institute participatory processes, implement multi-sectoral programmes, and enter into partnership agreements with private enterprise, NGOs and CBOs to promote job creation and foster social inclusion. Most recently, concepts of 'rights to the city' and 'access to urban services' have expanded and reinforced the interaction between local governments and civil society.

The difficulty in charting an appropriate course for decentralization that does not disrupt the delivery of basic services and other functions devolved to the local level is a challenging task. The difficulties encountered often require a process of successive adjustments to correct serious imbalances that affect the economic and social life of citizens. Indonesia's experience with fiscal decentralization demonstrates that it is possible to undertake a phased reform programme of national policies that reflect national disparities and modulate the central government's role to address inequalities and national priorities (see Box 3.1).

Box 3.1 Development and equalization strategies under adverse economic conditions: Indonesia's fiscal decentralization process

Beginning in 1997, Indonesia suffered economic recession, financial crisis and political disturbances that eroded previous gains in living standards. The currency was devalued by over 80 per cent, gross domestic product (GDP) contracted by 13.8 per cent, the level of poverty doubled and political strife erupted. Prior to 2000, despite its diversity and size, the country had a highly centralized administrative and fiscal system. The central government collected 94 per cent of general government revenue and financed 60 per cent of sub-national spending. Transfers included a combination of subsidies, earmarked grants and shared taxes from central and provincial governments.

In a major drive to decentralize the country during 1999 to 2001, the share of public expenditures channelled through local governments rose from around 17 per cent to over 30 per cent. Decentralization laws in 1999 devolved wide responsibilities to local governments, including health, education, public works, communications and the management of land and other environmental resources. Further regulations enacted in 2000 mandated the provinces to undertake functions that localities were unable to perform. The devolution of responsibilities was matched by the devolution of control over expenditures; but the decentralization of revenue did not follow.

In 2001, the routine transfers of the past that were largely used to pay the salaries of local civil servants, along with general development transfers, were replaced by general purpose grants (DAUs), currently set at 25.5 per cent of net central government domestic revenues, and divided between local governments and the provinces on a 90:10 basis. The allocation formula is based on fiscal needs and capacities. The DAU, which accounted for 71 per cent of total local governments' revenues in 2001, is the most important equalization mechanism.

There are also matching grants for certain regions based on urgency of need and national priorities; but the allocation formula is still in the process of finalization. Shared revenues include taxes from land, fees on property transactions and revenues from natural resources. The regulations specify the portion distributed to provinces and districts. In 2001, shared revenues represented around 12.7 per cent of revenue in urban localities and may contribute to widening regional disparities since resource-rich jurisdictions receive the bulk of the transfers.

Source: World Bank, 2003a; Menon et al, 2003; Lewis and Chakeri , 2004.

SOURCES OF MUNICIPAL FINANCE

Municipalities obtain their finance from a wide variety of sources, but the main categories consist of financial transfers from the central government and locally generated revenue, including debt finance. Central government transfers account for the bulk of local resources in most countries, particularly for capital investments, and are usually based on a redistribution of certain centrally collected revenues: a partial redistribution of the value added tax (VAT), entitlement grants for recurrent expenditures, and grants for specific projects. These transfers bridge the gap between the revenue-raising capacity of municipalities and mandatory local expenditures.

Locally generated revenues fall into three broad categories: taxes on property and on economic activities; user fees for the delivery of services and the improvement of infrastructure; and loans borrowed to finance long-term investments, generally infrastructure. While well-managed municipalities maintain a proper balance among these sources, the rapid urbanization that is taking place in most of the world, institutional constraints and weak local management have slowed the efforts of local governments to increase their financial autonomy as part of the devolution of responsibility from the central to the local level. Increasing the yield of locally generated taxes is therefore the key challenge faced by all developing economies. The inability to do so is manifest in the fact that almost all municipalities operate at a deficit that is bridged by transfers from the central government.

Taxes on real property and, to a lesser extent, business activities are the major potential source of local revenue. A combination of factors, ranging from technical issues such as the lack of computerized databases to complex legal issues of property rights under traditional and modern tenure patterns have suppressed the yield from property taxes.[9] Although they reflect the range of economic activities found in a locality, these local revenues are often set at the national or regional level (as is the case in India), and may be collected by a central administration on behalf of the municipality. In several West African countries, a portion of the tax collected is retained by the central government. A variety of low-yield local taxes are also to be found, often the hold-overs from the colonial era.

The price structure of user fees reflects social considerations and, for the most part, does not cover the recurrent costs of delivering the service, much less the amortization of its capital cost. As a result, most developed economies have moved towards more sophisticated means to recover a varying portion of the public costs induced by private development. They range from betterment taxes, assessed on either or both existing and new development, to exactions to fund social programmes. Since the mid 1980s, the proceeds of the linkage programme that mandates payments by developers of larger commercial development has financed both the construction of affordable housing and job training for residents of lower income neighbourhoods in San Francisco and Boston, US (see Box 3.2).

Box 3.2 Linkage fees in Boston, US

In Boston, developers sign a Development Impact Project agreement with the Boston Redevelopment Authority for substantial real estate projects that require a zoning amendment. A linkage fee is levied on each additional square foot of floor space in excess of a 100,000 square feet ceiling. In 2004, linkage fees equalled US$8.62 per square foot, out of which US$7.18 subsidize affordable housing and US$1.44 job training. This rate can be adjusted every three years to follow inflation. The schedule of payments is spread out over 7 years for downtown projects and 12 years for projects in other areas, and the fees are deposited in a special fund for affordable housing and training. Alternatively, developers may choose to build affordable housing projects or create a job training programme. Between 1987 and 2004, US$79.6 million were generated for housing through linkage, adding 7604 units to the city's housing stock, 6116 of which were affordable. The programme generated US$15.2 million for job training and awarded US$12.9 million to 190 different job programmes, such as school-to-work initiatives, family literacy or workplace-based education, creating over 1000 jobs.

Source: Boston Housing Authority, 2000, 2002, 2004; Avault et al, 2000, Boston Municipal Research Bureau, 1998.

The financing of capital investments by issuing long-term bonds is a well-established practice in the developed economies and the trend is spreading to other parts of the world, except in situations of high inflation, structural adjustment or economic recession. However, access to financial markets, both domestic and international, requires efficient municipal financial management and skills. In instances where municipalities are not allowed to borrow, ingenious alternative mechanisms have frequently been used by separating revenue-producing activities from the general budget and allowing them to borrow against future revenue, as is the case with China's special purpose vehicles (see Box 3.3).

Transfers

The rising share of total public expenditures channelled through local authorities testifies to the expanding scope of their responsibilities. In Indonesia, local government expenditures jumped from 17 per cent in 2000 to 28 per cent of public expenditures in 2001 following the enactment of decentralization laws. However, wide variations in levels of decentralization and fiscal capacities among regions and within regions prevail: from under 5 per cent to over 15 per

Box 3.3 The role of special purpose vehicles in China

In China, municipalities have no borrowing power and rely upon off-budget entities to obtain the capital they need for investment, primarily in infrastructure. These special purpose vehicles (SPVs) are wholly owned companies operating on a quasi-commercial basis. SPVs raise funds by borrowing from state-owned banks and undertake investments on behalf of provincial and municipal authorities. The Shanghai Urban Development Investment Corporation (UDIC), owned by the city, has directly issued bonds to finance infrastructure projects on the financial strength of the city authority. The implicit guarantee is that the city will not allow UDIC to fail. The bonds issued by a municipality are viewed as a contingent liability of the municipal authority and are usually backed by municipal assets transferred to the SPV or by the revenue stream of a self-sustaining project.

Local authorities are prohibited from guaranteeing loans to SPVs, and the extent of their indebtedness is a major concern as China restructures its domestic financial markets and plays an increasingly bigger role in the international capital markets.

Source: Serageldin et al, 2004.

cent in Latin America; from less than 10 per cent to more than 50 per cent in Asia; and from around 10 per cent in North Africa to under 10 per cent in sub-Saharan Africa, exclusive of South Africa, where provincial and local governments account for 29 per cent and 21 per cent of public expenditures, respectively.[10] Incomplete fiscal data and uneven geographic coverage within sub-regions precludes attempts at meaningful aggregation.[11] Given the wide variations encountered in any one region, averages would be unrepresentative of most situations and have limited comparative value across regions.

In India, transfers and shared taxes bridge the gap between the revenue-raising capacity of municipalities and their expenditure needs. These transfers influence their spending patterns and help reduce geographic inequalities. State transfers are a key component of municipal revenue, contributing an average of 31.7 per cent during 2001 and 2002. They have increased by a factor of 1.7 from 1997/1998 to 2001/2002. India does not have statutory provisions defining the modalities of state transfers to municipalities. This accounts for the wide variations observed among the states and the lack of stability in state/municipality fiscal relations. State financial resources are not strained by their transfers to municipalities since this accounts for only 2.43 per cent of their budget. The allocation criteria include indicators of size, equity, need and efficiency (see Table 3.1).

In most developing economies, the taxing powers of local authorities are inadequate to meet their expenditures

In East Africa, as in most developing economies, the taxing powers of local authorities are inadequate to meet their expenditures.[12] The high-yield taxes – namely, the VAT and taxes on income, sales and business – are controlled by central governments while municipal authorities derive their revenue from property taxes and charges on services. Transfers from higher levels of government lack stability, transparency and predictability, and are subject to sudden reductions. In Botswana, municipalities receive 40 to 60 per cent of their operating budget as a formula-based block grant and the totality of their capital investment budget from the central government.[13] In Kenya, there are formula-based block transfers; in Malawi, there are general purpose block grants and specific purpose transfers; in Uganda, the constitution stipulates that localities can receive block grants, specific purpose grants and equalization grants.

Table 3.1

India: role of transfers in municipal finances 2001/2002

State	Transfers (in lakh)	Percentage of total municipal revenue	Per capita transfers (in rupees)
Maharashtra	94,177	13.8	239.6
Uttar Pradesh	77,488	74.5	232.1
Karnataka	60,859	51.9	347.7
Rajasthan	51,703	83.3	403.5
Tamil Nadu	46,770	33.7	180.7
Gujarat	31,395	17.8	175.5
Kerala	17,949	44.5	296.9
Punjab	8489	10.1	105.1
Orissa	8047	44.2	153.8
Haryana	7892	39.5	135.5
Bihar	5559	62.0	64.4
Assam	1624	29.7	65.1
Goa	941	33.6	258.6

Source: Mathur et al, 2004.

Almost all African local authorities receive shares of taxes collected by central government, but there are wide variations among countries. In Kenya, 20 per cent of the tax levies on road fees and 5 per cent of the annual income tax are apportioned to local authorities; in Uganda, the Local Government Act of 1997 stipulates that 35 per cent of total revenue is to be transferred to districts, but it is not evident that statutory transfers have actually taken place in whole or in part; and in Malawi, there is no intergovernmental tax-sharing system in operation.

In the countries of the West African Economic and Monetary Union (UEMOA), despite their lack of adequate technical, managerial and fiscal resources, local governments have become the prime providers of services and investments in basic infrastructure. Even though transfers from the central government are still dominant, the contribution of local taxes has been growing steadily. By 2003, the contribution of locally collected revenue to municipal budgets in the region ranged from a low of 45 per cent in Côte d'Ivoire to a high of 80 per cent in Niger, a marked improvement over previous years (see Table 3.2).

Taxes on property and businesses

Administration of the property tax demands a good real-estate valuation capability to perform periodic revaluations of all taxable property over a period of not more than about five years. Setting up a computerized system capable of maintaining property and valuation records greatly facilitates this task. Where these capabilities exist, it is possible to ensure that the assessed valuation of all properties is realistic relative to market conditions.

In many developing countries, property records are kept manually and valuation experts have a hard time keeping up with rapid urbanization. Tax valuations do not fully keep pace with actual values, and an increasing proportion of the urbanized area is not covered. In cities experiencing fast growth, cadastral records are obsolete and only cover a limited zone, and are unable to keep up with formal change in the use of land. Except for some regularized settlements, informal areas and squatter settlements are not covered; properties are not titled or registered and therefore are not taxed. There are exceptions to these general patterns. In Egypt, a long tradition of quasi-autonomous management of tax administration allows the taxation of real estate, whether or not it is regularized or registered. In Indonesia, an occupancy tax is levied and ensures some revenue in situations where property ownership is unclear or complex. In West Africa, a simple *adressage* system, locating and numbering properties by street address, is used as an expeditious alternative to cadastres. This method allows speedy and efficient regularization of informal settlements and registration of property, providing the basis for taxation.

The tax yield from the real estate sector is low relative to the market value of the assets and the rate of appreciation of serviced and non-serviced land. This situation is prevalent among developing countries due to a combination of factors:

Table 3.2

Structure of municipal operating revenue and expenditures in selected West African countries (percentage)

	Benin		Burkina Faso		Mali		Côte d'Ivoire	
	1996	2000	1996	2000	1996	2000	1996	2000
Operating revenues								
Municipal taxes	4	22	4	2	4	19	4	6
Transfers	50	51	53	58	60	54	65	45
State subsidies	12	3	0	0	1	14	13	14
Land revenues	2	3	9	17	0	3	1	1
Services revenues	2	10	9	9	33	7	11	14
Other	11	11	25	8	5	3	5	9
Expenditures								
Capital expenditures	20	28	30	39	30	34	20	18
Personnel	31	23	23	16	26	24	17	20
Other	49	49	47	45	44	42	63	62

Source: PDM, 1998, 1999a,b, 2000, 2001a,b

- Tenure systems are complex, with layers of primary and secondary rights derived from customary rules and successive adjustments of past colonial legal and institutional frameworks. Inheritance laws and fragmentation of property in historic centres and older neighbourhoods compound the problems of updating records, identifying taxpayers and billing and collecting taxes.
- Central governments control high-yield tax bases and the recording of wealth-producing assets, including land registries. High fees and cumbersome administrative procedures discourage regularization and the issuance of titles in informal settlements and increase the cost of updating valuations and tax rolls still managed by branch offices of central authorities. Additions, renovations and conversions are unreported and untaxed. Monitoring is sporadic due to a lack of cadastral information and updated records. Despite regulations that mandate collaboration and coordination among levels of government, central government officials are reluctant to work with municipal departments.
- Taxation systems based on real or imputed rental value, rather than capital value, understate the value of the assets, while rent and tenant protection regulations further depress property assessments based on rental valuation, thereby adding to the erosion of the municipal tax base.
- Tax rebates and exemptions granted to encourage specific segments of the housing market (such as multi-family rental units and co-operatives) or new urban development. In North and West African countries, exemptions from one or more taxes are granted for periods ranging from 3 to 15 years (see Box 3.4).
- In most countries, informal settlements on the urban fringe are not taxed until they are regularized. In a few countries, including Egypt, they are assessed by the tax administration, a central agency, independently of their status since regularization is a local function. Property owners readily pay these taxes, which are not onerous and can be used to document occupancy and possession of urban land and buildings.

Because of their buoyancy and their importance to local revenues, taxes on commercial activities also tend to heavily burden formal private enterprise (see Box 3.4). There are taxes on licences to operate the business, on the exercise of a profession or occupation, on the rental value of the premises, and on the income derived from the businesses. Market stall holders usually pay a flat rate and, except in some West African countries, hawkers and other informal activities escape local taxation.

At local government levels, taxes on income are not nearly as common as taxes on property, although in some instances provincial governments have the authority to tax income. But local governments may be allowed a surcharge on the income tax levied by provincial and national governments. Alternatively, a fixed proportion of the national income tax may be transferred to the local level.

User fees

User fees form a significant part of municipal revenues, particularly in developed economies. Although widely used, their yield in developing countries has usually been less than the operating and amortization costs of infrastructure systems as many governments have set rates below their economic level in order to alleviate hardships on the poor. Even wealthy countries have found it necessary to subsidize the cost of public transportation for environmental as well as social reasons.

Pricing of user fees is a matter of public policy, since it plays a central role in determining the financial sustainability of urban services. In many cases, charges will be levied at less than their economically efficient prices. Balancing financial and social considerations, governments at all levels have instituted measures to alleviate the hardships suffered by the poor. The most commonly used are:

Pricing of user fees is a matter of public policy, since it plays a central role in determining the financial sustainability of urban services

- allowing a minimum consumption level per capita or household free of charge, as in South Africa;
- subsidizing charges for lower income populations; and
- establishing a pricing structure that is not discriminatory for small users.

Social, economic and environmental arguments have been advanced for pricing public transportation at less than full-

Box 3.4 Côte d'Ivoire: challenges constraining the taxation of property and businesses

Côte d'Ivoire exemplifies the challenges encountered by developing countries in taxing property and businesses.

In Abidjan, the principal commercial centre, the real estate sector is overburdened. There are no less than nine direct taxes on urban property, exclusive of the taxation of rental income. Four basic taxes are levied and collected by the Ministry of Finance's Direction Générale des Impots (DGI), which transfers to the communes a portion of the receipts according to a separate formula for each tax. The tax on built property is the mainstay of the taxation system. Other real estate taxes include the tax on un-built property, a tax on underdeveloped urban property to deter speculative land holding, and a tax on property belonging to real estate development corporations and building societies. Municipal councils can levy supplemental charges not exceeding 20 per cent of the tax. Two special purpose taxes earmarked for infrastructure maintenance are also levied on all built property and no temporary or permanent exemptions are granted: the sanitation tax is collected by the state and the tax for roads and refuse removal is collected by the municipality. Communes can levy additional taxes on real estate, which are collected on their behalf by the DGI, including a tax on net income from built property; a tax on the capital value of un-built property; and a tax on the rental value of premises subject to the commercial licence fees paid to the state.

The expansion of the urbanized area during the 1970s and 1980s has not been matched by a commensurate expansion of the tax base. Three factors contribute to the erosion of the tax base:

1. temporary exemptions granted to new construction for overly long periods ranging from 5 to 20 years;
2. central control of the tax roll and rates; and
3. the proliferation of informal development on the urban fringe through the unauthorized subdivision of tribal land.

Buildings in informal settlements were not legally recognized or taxed. When a regularization policy was adopted in 1977, the process was too cumbersome and lengthy and failed to keep up with the pace of urbanization. DGI estimates the performance of real estate taxes to range between 20 per cent and 30 per cent.

Commercial taxes are the mainstay of municipal finance in West African cities. In Abidjan, they account for over 50 per cent of local revenue. There are two main taxes: the *patente* levied by the DGI on larger businesses with annual sales volume above a specified threshold, and the *Taxe Forfaitaire*, a flat-rate tax levied on small retailers and craftsmen and collected directly by the communes. Small shops and workshops pay on a monthly basis, while street vendors pay a daily fee for a ticket which allows them to trade on the sidewalks or in the designated market areas. Central authorities tend to view local commercial taxes as too numerous, difficult to manage and enforce, and low yield in comparison to other forms of taxation. Yet, their contribution to local fiscal revenue cannot be overlooked.

Source: Serageldin, 1990.

cost recovery. For water supply, social considerations and, in many cases, the reassertion of pre-colonial traditions and/or religious beliefs have thwarted attempts to raise prices to financially sustainable levels since the 1980s. Under structural adjustment programmes, price increases have led to contentious debates and civil disturbances.

Most recently, the debate over the pricing of essential services has acquired a new dimension because of the NGO-led movement to assert the legal 'right to the city'. This right includes access to urban land and urban services for all residents. The debate is ongoing in many parts of the developing world. Nevertheless, there is some consensus regarding the desirability of charging for a public service even when the charge cannot cover full financial costs. In most circumstances, user charges are not structured to take into account the recovery of capital investments, even where an operational profit materializes. Expansion of services usually takes precedence over maintenance of systems, and political pressure and rapid urbanization weigh heavily in these decisions.

Betterment taxes and development exactions

In advanced economies, an array of impact fees and betterment taxes compensate local authorities for the additional expenditures incurred in extending urban infrastructure and services to new urban development projects or to upgrade services in the urbanized area. These fees are also structured to recapture part of the unearned increment in real estate values resulting from public investment. Because they are payable over terms of up to ten years, betterment levies do not directly provide immediate funding for capital investments. Revaluation of properties affected by public works improvements makes a major contribution towards municipal revenue through property tax assessments.

Many countries with rapidly developing economies have instituted betterment fees and require developers to contribute to the costs of providing new services. They could benefit from the linkage concept as a mechanism employed in the US to redistribute the benefit of growth during periods of rapid economic development.

Borrowing

Funding for capital expenditure requires access to long-term borrowing, broadly related to the working lives of assets to be financed. Debt service can then be annually financed, either from internally generated funds for revenue-earning services or from general revenues for tax-borne services. Users of services provided by public assets are expected to pay for current use, as well as an appropriate share of the fixed asset costs, over the full working lives of the facilities, a situation that is rarely the case in developing countries or in many advanced economies, for that matter.

In situations of high inflation, economic recession, structural adjustment and other constraining factors, long-term borrowing is typically not available, although various methods have been devised to counter these constraints. The standard solution is to add the expected inflation rate to the real cost of money, adopt variable rates or index either the principal or the annuity payments to the inflation rate. Alternatively, domestic loans are linked to a stable foreign currency, as has happened in many Latin American countries.

Short-term borrowing

In the absence of long-term financing, local governments have tended to use short-term commercial debt where the option is available to them. Short-term borrowing by municipal governments is normally limited to covering capital investments. In many countries, attempts have sometimes been made to continuously roll over short-term debt used to finance capital expenditure. Debt has sometimes been used to cover recurrent budgetary deficits or for short-term cash-flow management. Accumulated debt has to be brought under control and refinanced, otherwise it can lead to financial crisis. Box 3.5 highlights some of the borrowing challenges faced by city authorities.

Credit enhancement, access to financial institutions and capital markets

Local governments need sophisticated debt management capability to draw on the range of financial options and instruments to finance their capital investment needs. These capabilities are not currently prevalent among many local administrations in the developing world. In order to strengthen local finances and enhance municipal access to medium- and longer-term credit, shared revenues are regarded as part of the local resources available to service debt and can be pledged as collateral. Thus, shared revenues serve as loan guarantees and central governments can withhold them from municipal governments and authorize lenders to intercept the transfers in order to settle arrears of debt service obligations. This arrangement enhances the credit rating of municipalities.

International capital markets and multilateral financial institutions have focused upon East Asia's credit market in light of the strength of the regional economy, anchored by Japan and China, and the Asian countries' own performance rebounding from the 1997 financial crisis. However, these countries offer sharply contrasting financial environments. The Philippines was one of the first Asian countries to devolve functions and resources to local government units. A 1991 code allowed localities to create new own sources of revenue and gave them borrowing powers. Municipalities and provinces are authorized to issue bonds to finance self-liquidating, income-generating projects, enhancing the quality of life in the city. Two government-owned banks and two municipal development funds provide local governments with credit. A steady flow of generous central transfers and the power of state-owned financial institutions to intercept these transfers to settle arrears have allowed the municipal credit market to function and a limited domestic bond market to operate.[14]

By contrast, Viet Nam is barely starting on the transition path and local authorities have little fiscal autonomy. Borrowing is restricted to capital expenditures and the state bank can extend loans to localities for up to 30 per cent of project cost.[15]

In India, the Ahmedabad Municipal Corporation became the first municipality to issue bonds on the capital market; but other municipalities have also used this method with the back-up of credit rating agencies. The nine municipalities that have accessed the capital market have thus far been able to issue bonds without requiring a guarantee from the state government or a bank, as traditionally required by lenders to municipal entities. They

Box 3.5 The challenges of borrowing

Russia

During the mid 1990s, a series of Russian laws established rather liberal borrowing rules for sub-national entities and authorized municipalities to issue bonds and lottery tickets, to extend and take out loans, and to open municipal accounts with banks and other financial and credit institutions. Municipalities borrowed from regions to cover deficits, issued municipal bonds and contracted short-term loans from banks. Municipal financial mismanagement and indebtedness led to the revocation of these laws. Following the 1998 financial crisis, the Law on Specificity in Issuance and Circulation of State and Municipal Securities and the Budget Code prohibit municipalities from contracting external debt or debt obligations exceeding ten years. The issuance of debt obligations is limited to the financing of capital expenditures. These restrictions, while justified to curb runaway municipal finances, constitute a constraint on the financing of local public infrastructure projects.

Indonesia

In Indonesia, during the aftermath of the 1997 financial crisis, widespread defaults on outstanding loans from the Indonesian National Development Fund need to be resolved and the stability of the banking system fully restored before borrowing can be meaningfully addressed. In the meantime, regional governments depend upon donor and sovereign loan funds (primarily from the World Bank and the Asian Development Bank) for regional infrastructure projects. Despite favourable loan terms, arrears reached 40 per cent in 1998. Regional and local governments were considered financially too weak to benefit from the regulatory framework authorizing sub-national entities to borrow on the financial markets. In the period leading to the 1997 financial crisis, private investors preferred to seek concessions and build–operate–transfer (BOT) contracts, fuelling a risky reliance on offshore financing. The weakness of local government finances and their reliance on transfers and shared revenue prompted the Indonesian Ministry of Finance to prohibit all new borrowing from both domestic and foreign sources. The only exceptions are borrowing through on-lending institutions for short-term working capital or profitable locally owned enterprises. Since local governments have not yet been authorized to levy new sources of revenue, their financial situation remains weak.

Sub-Saharan Africa

In sub-Saharan Africa, South Africa and Zimbabwe have led the decentralization process. Regional local governments in the two countries are empowered to borrow in order to finance capital investments. In Uganda, local authorities are allowed to borrow, but have refrained from doing so due to the lack of a municipal development bank such as South Africa's Development Bank of Southern Africa (DBSA). In most other countries, current debt burdens and legal constraints impede the development of municipal financial institutions.

Source: Chernyavsky, undated (Russia); World Bank, 2003a; Menon et al, 2003 (Indonesia); Lewis and Chakeri , 2004; Freire et al, 2004 (sub-Saharan Africa).

have raised capital on the strength of their own credit rating.[16]

Income-generating enterprises

Local governments can establish separate income-generating enterprises to enhance their overall revenue-generation capability. The advantage of using an income-generating enterprise is that its activities can be accounted for independently of general tax-borne activities. Typically, the role of revenue-earning enterprises is not to generate contributions to general public revenues, but to remove open-ended reliance upon such revenues. This approach also highlights the full costs of operation, so that these may be more appropriately covered from user charges and carefully targeted subsidies.

In China, formal government budgets account for only half of local government financial activity due to the importance of off-budget finance. Own-revenue sources consist of special fees, taxes, profit distributions from locally owned enterprises, land leases and taxes on business enterprises (VAT and income). The property tax on urban and rural land generates a meagre 2 per cent of local revenue, while the business tax contributes 34 per cent but exacts a heavy burden on businesses, representing about half their profits. As they have no borrowing power, municipalities have resorted to the ingenious mechanism of creating independent wholly owned companies, whose activities are off-budget, to finance the capital financing of development projects, particularly infrastructure. These so-called special purpose vehicles (SPVs) are allowed to borrow on the capital markets and use their revenue to amortize their debt. They have become a key instrument in implementing large-scale urban development projects (see Box 3.3).

Municipal development funds

Many countries have established municipal development funds (MDFs) that provide regional and local governments with needed capital

Many countries have established municipal development funds (MDFs) that provide regional and local governments with needed capital. The Public Works Loan Board (UK) and the Crédit Foncier (France) are among the oldest and have served as models for other countries. Typically, MDFs have been sponsored by central governments, with international development organizations initially participating in the creation of these institutions. Some poorly managed MDFs have collapsed, while others have been sustained and continue to finance development projects. Yet others have managed to leverage local capital contributions and a few have evolved into such noteworthy institutions as Colombia's Financiera de Desarrollo Territorial (FINDETER) and the Development Bank of Southern Africa.

An alternative approach has been for groups of municipalities to obtain pooled financing as members of specialized sub-national entities, such as Sweden's Kommuninvest Corporation, or by virtue of their regional location – for instance, Virginia's Resources Authority in the US. Both approaches are based on a financial intermediary whose size and managerial capacity allows it to access financial markets on better terms than its individual members. The resulting savings are passed on to the municipalities. Initially developed in Europe and the US, this model has been successfully adapted in the case of India's Tamil Nadu Urban Development Fund (TNUDF) (see Box 3.6).

Other sources

There are other sources, including social investment funds, environment funds and special funds financed by debt swaps. Social investment funds were introduced in several countries in Latin America, Asia and Africa over a decade ago to finance projects aimed at social development and poverty reduction. Environmental funds are similarly structured, but focus on environmental management, pollution control and the preservation of natural resources.

Bolivia has tried to improve the performance of its social investment fund by integrating it within the system of intergovernmental fiscal transfers aimed at promoting decentralization and redistributing fiscal revenues to the poorer areas. The country also has a programme which blends grants and loans to implement strategic actions that support decentralization, increase local resources and foster a sound fiscal management, while promoting the involvement of the private sector in municipal finance. To achieve these objectives, the programme helps to build the technical and managerial capacity of municipalities with a special emphasis on fiscal management and the administration of property cadastres and tax rolls. It is also sponsoring credit rating for the major municipalities in order to prepare them to issue bonds.[17]

Even though still an exception, targeted funding of poverty reduction and environmental projects is growing in importance, particularly in Latin America. Funding tends to be either through external donations or through debt swaps under the Heavily Indebted Poor Countries (HIPC) initiative of the Bretton Woods institutions. In a formal sense, as commonly used in financial markets, debt swaps are employed by two or more partners to exchange legal liabilities for already incurred debt. Each partner carries financial obligations; but the transaction is mutually advantageous in terms of meeting some strategic objective.

The Bolivian Strategy for Poverty Reduction, within the HIPC initiative, gives an important role to local authorities as a way of increasing the efficiency in services delivery to impoverished populations and to promote local development. It relies upon municipalities to develop and implement action plans to reduce poverty. An amount of approximately US$20 million annually is transferred to local authorities to invest within the eight national priority sectors.[18]

Governments to whom debt is owed can also agree to discount the debt and allow indebted governments to repay the balance in local currency. The debt service proceeds of these 'swap' arrangements are deposited in a fund to support new local capital investments or to promote strategic social and environmental objectives. One of the first such swaps involved Costa Rica's debt and helped to preserve the rich ecosystem of the national rainforest reservations. More recently, swaps have been used to fund poverty alleviation initiatives in accordance with the country poverty reduction strategy (PRS). In general, an agreement on social objectives requires compliance with national priorities and stipulates that projects be undertaken by NGOs.

In Egypt, a special fund for debts owed to Switzerland, Italy and Germany was set up to finance rural development, job opportunities for women and environmental improvements. Projects are to be implemented by private enterprises and civil society organizations.

Box 3.6 Tamil Nadu Urban Development Fund (TNUDF), India

The Tamil Nadu Urban Development Fund (TNUDF) has evolved from a municipal trust fund to one established and managed by the public and private sectors. The initial fund – the Municipal Urban Development Fund – was financed entirely by the public sector to reduce the massive backlog of infrastructure investment and improve the delivery of basic urban services. It was launched in 1988 with a concession loan from the International Development Association (IDA).

In 1996, with the aim of achieving managerial efficiency and attracting private capital for urban infrastructure, it was converted into an autonomous financial intermediary. Established as a trust fund with private equity participation, it was the first public–private partnership in India that provided long-term municipal financing for infrastructure without guarantees. Instead of merely channelling public funds, its purpose is to attract financing from the private sector. It also manages a separate grant fund owned by the state government to finance poverty alleviation projects.

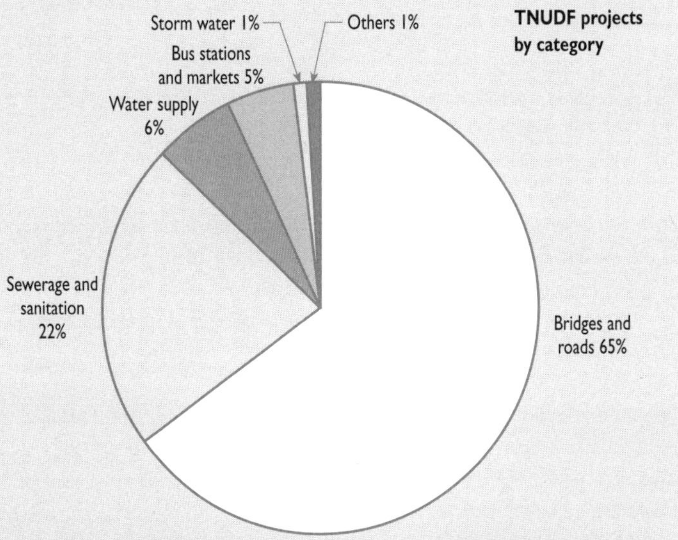

The TNUDF is managed by a private corporation: Tamil Nadu Urban Infrastructure Financial Services Ltd. Financial institutions have committed to contribute an amount equal to 44 per cent of the initial contribution of the Tamil Nadu state government. The fund's management board comprises representatives from the state government and participating financial institutions. Borrowers are required to follow conservative financial management practices and to meet performance targets, including for debt service reserves and making appropriate sinking fund contributions.

The TNUDF's debt financing depends mainly upon the surpluses of the municipal borrowers, a situation similar to revolving funds in Europe and the US. The TNUDF is making an important contribution to capital investment needs for large, lumpy and non-revenue-generating projects. For many small local governments that are unable to access the markets directly, the fund provides a pooling mechanism and indirect access to the market, together with enhanced credit. Such arrangements can be especially useful for sewerage projects that require substantial funds with repayment periods of 20 years or more.

Despite these constraints, the fund is quite creative, launching new financial products to tap the capital market for special purposes, such as the Water and Sanitation Pooled Fund. A municipal bond issued for a road development, initially funded by TNUDF, was re-financed from the bond proceeds, thus releasing funds for other capital investment.

Source: World Bank, 2004d; Singh Maini, 2004; World Bank, 2003b; Freire et al, 2004. Research on this case was also undertaken by the Center for Urban Development Studies (CUDS) team member Shannon Bassett.

MUNICIPAL SPENDING PATTERNS

Local government budgeting

The municipal budget reflects policies and strategies for the delivery of mandatory and locally approved public services. It should be capable of demonstrating the extent to which the budgeted financial results have been realized, the intended activities performed and the anticipated outcomes achieved. The lack of financial management skills at the local level often impedes the preparation of accurate and complete budgets. In many countries, local budgets are just lists of cash receipts and payments that are not usefully categorized. Often, there is no clear distinction between operating and capital expenditures. Budgets commonly respond to the mayor's priorities, requests by councillors, potential funding from higher levels of government and outside sources, and electoral promises.

Budgeting faces many challenges. First, since estimates of grant and revenue-sharing allocations are hardly ever made available to local governments in adequate time for them to prepare their own annual budgets, the practice is to assume amounts equivalent to the previous year's transfers without any assurance that the projected budget amounts will actually materialize. Fluctuations in central transfers invariably lead to *ad hoc* budget cuts or to unplanned expenditures if the funds cannot be rolled over to the following year. Whether the objective is greater efficiency in collection or greater equity in distribution, central funding will usually be accompanied by some measure of control or supervision over the local activities funded. Cumbersome controls encourage corruption and politicization of allocation decisions. Such controls can also stifle local initiative and negate some advantages of decentralization and democratic governance.

Second, in most countries in Africa, Asia and Latin America, municipalities are not able to borrow long-term funds on the capital markets and have to rely upon targeted transfers for their capital investment. But local authorities in many of these countries have limited understanding of the redistribution formulae governing central transfers. As a result, there is a tendency to consider them grants to balance the local budget irrespective of their economic or social purpose.

Third, most local capital budgets reflect immediate needs or political expediency rather than a long-term development strategy. Brazil's participatory budgeting is a notable exception and is being widely emulated. Thanks to a transparent process, it addresses immediate as well as strategic needs and provides significant infrastructure and service improvements to poorer communities. Some cities have also been able to devise coherent strategies to ensure

Box 3.7 Participatory budgeting in Brazil

The emergence and spread of participatory budgeting (PB) in Brazil is rooted in the legal mandate requiring popular participation in local decision-making. Municipalities introduced mechanisms ranging from the presentation of budget proposals for public comment to the actual involvement of residents in decision-making. Participatory budgeting was first instituted by the city of Porto Alegre in 1989 and gave the city international recognition as a leader in 'popular democracy' in local governance. The concept has now been adopted by approximately 180 Brazilian municipalities and is spreading beyond Brazil in Latin America to cities in Argentina, Uruguay, Peru, Ecuador, Colombia, Bolivia, Mexico and Chile. More recently, cities in other parts of the world are adapting the process to their own situation.

PB allows residents to have a voice in the annual allocation of capital investments. It is based on the delegation of statutory executive powers regarding the preparation of the municipal budget and has to be initiated by the mayor. There is no similar delegation of authority from the legislative branch, and the city council remains the statutory authority approving the municipal budget.

The PB concept embodies four key features:

1. It ensures representation of residents in each sub-area within the jurisdiction in the decision-making process.
2. It requires municipal officials to report on what has been accomplished with the previous year's budget and to provide estimates of revenues and expenditures for the upcoming year in order to determine the budget envelope for capital investments.
3. It is structured to ensure transparency through direct popular participation and an open voting system.
4. It ensures objectivity through the use of quantitative criteria for the prioritization of funding requests and the allocation of resources.

Participatory budgeting is primarily an instrument of empowerment and social inclusion. Participation and social impact are its most important dimensions. It covers all capital investments, which range from 5 to 15 per cent of the total budget in Brazilian municipalities. It is a flexible instrument since the rules can be amended at the end of each budget cycle, but cannot be changed during the cycle.

Popular assemblies are the cornerstone of the PB process. Attendance has grown steadily over the years in parallel with the growth of capital investments and as the importance of participation becomes evident to a wider spectrum of the population. The dynamics of attendance are complex and reflect the strategies and tactics of grassroots organizations and social movements, the mobilization efforts of groups who want to press for specific demands, and the degree of coordinated action at the community level. Outreach at the community level is needed to foster participation of lower income groups for whom the cost of attendance is high. This entails a significant commitment of resources on the part of the municipality, particularly in terms of personnel.

Source: Serageldin et al, 2003a,b.

that a stream of relatively small annual capital improvements becomes an integral component of a long-term development strategy.

Fourth, the efficient collection of taxes is a daunting problem, particularly in parts of the world that are experiencing rapid urbanization. The lack of up-to-date records, inadequately trained personnel and the prevalence of informal housing and of unstructured floating economic activities are major obstacles to an increased financial self-reliance of local governments. This has prevented the preparation of multi-year capital investment budgets that are indispensable in ensuring an adequate supply of serviced land and the delivery of improved services and, generally, in meeting the goals of sustainable urban development.

Participatory budgeting

Democratic local governance has fuelled growing demands for accountability and transparency in municipal budgeting and financial management, particularly with regard to the allocation of scarce local resources and their utilization. There is a marked trend for more rigorous financial management, clear procedures for the allocation of resources and the participation of residents in decisions affecting their communities. Of particular interest is the transparency mandated by Brazilian legislation and the spread of participatory budgeting – first instituted by Porto Alegre (see Box 3.7) – to municipalities in Brazil and other Latin American countries.

Multi-year capital budgeting

Capital investment budgets are a major undertaking for local governments. These budgets are often not well linked to development strategies and spatial plans, or such plans may not exist or may be mere wish lists of projects. There are many criteria for prioritizing capital expenditure: urgency of need; political importance; economic efficiency; availability of funding; implementation capabilities; and operation and maintenance costs of the completed assets, or life-cycle costing, to ensure that the assets and related activities will continue to operate over longer time periods. In many infrastructure projects, the relation between capital investments and operation and maintenance costs is not adequately considered and is hardly ever accounted for in choosing among options.

The rolling four-year capital investment programme of Szczecin in Poland allowed the city to improve its financial management standards to a level that enabled it to attract local and foreign investors, and to obtain a credit rating and borrow from commercial financial institutions (see Box 3.8).

Lack of funds for maintaining existing assets

In developing countries, asymmetrical decentralization has led to serious fiscal imbalances. In many such countries the funding provided barely allows for the delivery of services or coverage of settlements within the jurisdiction, thus undercutting shelter delivery. Local governments must look to other sources, domestic and external, to supplement their own.

Because they immediately impact upon day-to-day activities, operating expenditures are almost always perceived as the most urgent. Priority operating expenditures and financial constraints frequently lead to deferment of expenditures on maintaining existing assets. Unlike capital investments for which a variety of external sources of finance can be found, funding for the maintenance of existing assets is lacking. Even as it continues to perform, existing infrastructure deteriorates and becomes less efficient with the passage of time. Preventive maintenance is increasingly converted into crisis management, impairing the functional efficiency of many cities in the developing world. Particularly in the larger urban centres, authorities have to purchase expensive parts from current revenue and delay the renewal of plants, facilities and networks. When infrastructure projects carry outstanding debt, debt service often pre-empts necessary maintenance of the assets.

Managing municipal expenditures

As recurrent expenditures have increasingly dominated budgets, techniques for determining expenditures and measuring actual performance have been developed and incorporated within budgetary processes. Best practice demands that capital expenditure is budgeted and accounted for separately from recurrent operating expenditures; that operating expenditures be financed from fees, charges, regular taxes, regular shared revenues and recurrent government grants and not allowed to exceed these current revenues; and that borrowing, when permitted by law, be restricted to financing capital investments, with the possible exception of covering temporary cash-flow shortages. These principles of financial management are increasingly incorporated within legislation on national finance systems relating to state and local budgeting and provide a framework for financial management and assessment of performance, where local officials and elected representatives are held accountable for their own actions.

From 1999 to 2002, local government expenditures in Indonesia rose by a factor of 3.3 at an average rate of 55 per cent annually, in nominal terms. Capital spending increased by 60 per cent annually, slightly outpacing operating expenditure that rose by about 52 per cent. However, the structure of local government expenditure has barely changed (see Figure 3.1). Wages still constitute the most dominant component, although their share has decreased slightly from over 50 per cent to less than 45 per cent of total expenditure. Conversely, other recurrent expenditures have increased somewhat from 17 per cent to about 21 per cent of the total.

But the decision-making authority and financial autonomy that local governments obtain through decentralization policies do not necessarily lead to responsible financial management, as the experience of many cities in developing countries demonstrates. From Brazil to Morocco to India, municipalities are running budget deficits. In countries where they are empowered to borrow, many have accumulated debt and are unable to repay their loans.

In South Africa and Brazil, municipalities have constitutionally defined authority and fiscal resources. This privileged status gives them wide decision-making powers and discretion in the use of their revenues. In Brazil, dynamic mayors used their new constitutional authority to institute reforms and innovate in areas critical to sound municipal governance, including participatory planning and management, and partnerships with private enterprises, NGOs and CBOs for economic and social development initiatives in Santo Andre, Belo Horizonte and Recife, among other cities. Unfortunately, many more did not manage their affairs responsibly, forcing the federal government to intervene and rein in their runaway finances (see Box 3.9).

Box 3.8 Multi-year capital investment planning, Szczecin, Poland

During the transition towards a market economy, priority was placed on capital investments that structure and support the local economy and enhance local development, including road construction and maintenance; water supply and sewerage systems; revitalization of communal housing; and improving education and healthcare facilities. Szczecin was the first Polish city to link its city development strategy to a four-year capital investment programme (CIP). Approved by the city council in 1997, the CIP proved to be one of the most important instruments of financial management during the transition. It allowed the city to determine its financial and development capacity, and to prepare forecasts for local and foreign investors.

The first four-year CIP (1997–2000) coincided with the rapid expansion of the responsibilities of local governments as a result of devolution. In March 1998, the city council adopted a resolution detailing the principles governing the preparation of the CIP and established procedures and criteria for prioritizing and selecting projects to be funded. These included assessment of existing needs; linkages to the city development strategy; technical aspects of projects; implementation costs; financing capacity based on the city budget; and sources and conditions of potential external financing.

The programme identified each capital expenditure by year – disaggregated by project, programme and responsible department, and funding sources for each category – and proposed methods of financing. The rolling four-year CIP is submitted to the city council for annual approval. The first year's capital investment programme is integrated within the city budget.

Source: Center for Urban Development Studies, 2000; Serageldin et al, 2004.

Accountability and transparency

Accountability for performance is a cornerstone of good governance and a major tool in financial management. It places as much emphasis upon transparency as upon finance. Increasingly, mayors, councils and city managers are held accountable for financial outcomes, as well as for the qualities of the services they deliver and the projects they implement. There are increasing demands for local empowerment and for greater public participation in determining how public revenues are raised and spent. From conventional public budget hearings to participatory budgeting, people are demanding a voice in the resource allocation procedures and oversight regarding their actual application.

Demands for greater accountability and transparency by voting and taxpaying constituencies have combined with the constraints on the financial resources available to the

Figure 3.1

Structure of local expenditure in Indonesia, 1997–2002

Source: Lewis and Chakeri, 2004

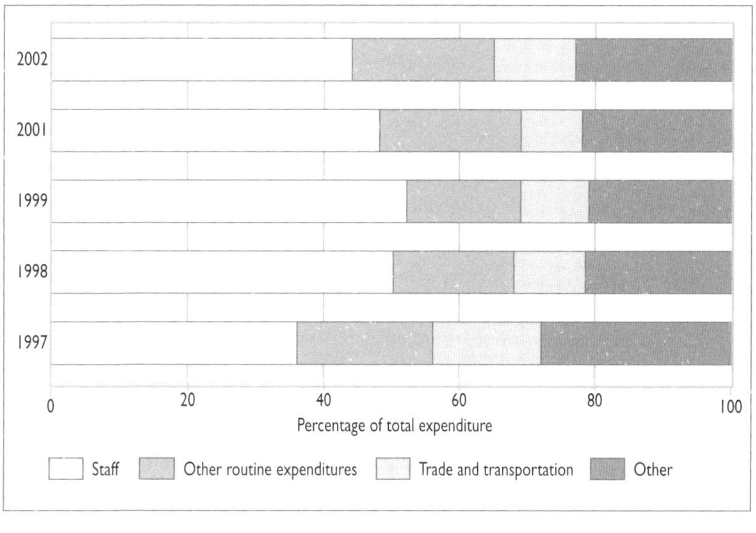

Box 3.9 Brazil's law of fiscal responsibility

In Brazil, the privileged status of state and municipal governments under the 1988 constitution strengthened the role of mayors and governors in the national administrative framework. However, these same constitutional guarantees provided an impetus for municipal mismanagement and the multiplication of municipalities through fragmentation, to reach 5559 municipalities in 2003. Dependency upon central transfers and shared revenue, and excessive politicization of local governance accounts for a focus on the short term and a general lack of coherence and continuity in municipal management. The constitutional amendment, enacted in conjunction with the fiscal stability programme adopted in October 1998, established rules for responsible fiscal management, and the passage of the Fiscal Responsibility Act in May 2000 set further rules and standards for responsible fiscal management. For the three levels of government, the law mandates multi-year budgeting with fiscal targets, contingent liabilities and cost controls, and also introduces balanced-budget principles and incentives for mobilizing own resources.

The law caps expenditures on personnel at 60 per cent and relates them to tax revenue. It mandates expenditures on education at no less than 25 per cent. It limits borrowing to the financing of capital expenditures, with the setting aside of adequate reserves to offset increases in long-term financial obligations. The law also mandates public access to fiscal and budgetary information. In 2001, the Statute of the City established general directives for urban policies and mandated regularization of informal settlements and upgrading of the living environment in areas housing lower income communities. These national priorities are, in turn, reflected in the municipal budgets.

Source: Serageldin, et al, 2003a.

public sector to exert political pressure to improve municipal financial management. Reforms of existing systems and the introduction of newer concepts and techniques have provided useful alternatives in financing and operating public services. They have also opened the public sector more widely to many innovations and efficiencies, hitherto largely confined to the private sector, prompting governments to improve their accounting and budgeting practices.

Until very recently, practices have varied in their application and enforcement among different countries. Accounting systems for activities to be funded from general revenues are often much simpler in form, but cover a large variety of activities. Unfortunately, in many countries, particularly in developing countries, local financial systems typically fall far short of the structure and rigour needed to provide instruments and indicators for policy formulation, resource allocations and strategic investment decisions. With many accounting systems currently in use in state and local governments in different countries, incompleteness is common. Therefore, unit costs and other indicators derived from these accounts will not usually account for the totality of the resources committed or consumed.

For revenue-producing activities, municipal accounting systems are often quite similar to those used in private-sector enterprises, particularly when the activities are performed by an entity legally separate from core functions, funded from budgeted general revenues. Fostered by decentralization and economic transition, the number of categories and entities financed through off-budget sources has multiplied during the past decade, particularly in Eastern Europe. Some have been established specifically for the purpose of circumventing the constraints of provincial and local governments on financial autonomy, as happened in China and is now occurring in India and elsewhere.

Box 3.10 Accounting for the financial cost of urban services

For some public services (particularly, water supply, sewerage, drainage and transport), operation and maintenance costs represent small inputs in terms of economic resource use compared to the massive quantities of land, buildings, infrastructure and equipment that are in constant use to keep the systems functioning. Yet, despite this large input of fixed assets, there has been a great reluctance, all over the world, to account for their employment. Consequently, public service decisions, especially with regard to the pricing of services, are often made on the basis of cash-flow data for operating expenses.

Currently, more recognition is being given to the need for comprehensive cost analysis and accounting for fixed assets. Depreciation costs are charged in operating statements. The net worth of fixed assets is periodically revalued to its current value and the operating statements are charged with notional interest, reflecting the opportunity cost of capital invested. Reform of existing systems and the transition to newer financial systems usually take several years to implement. To prepare and update an inventory of fully recorded and valued fixed assets, the local government or other service delivery unit requires specialized personnel whom local governments may not necessarily have in house. They must either build this capacity or procure the services by contracting out.

Worldwide, progress is being made on the institution of more transparent systems in local financial management. For example, two of the world's largest countries, Russia and Indonesia, have very different cultures and histories. Yet, in each one, during the past few years, laws have been promulgated that will require the use of full accrual accounting in state and local governments. St. Petersburg in Russia and a few other major cities began this reform during the 1990s. As housing and shelter are among Russia's most pressing social concerns, financing and budgeting for this sector need to undergo a complete overhaul. In Indonesia, capacity-building is helping local authorities to implement accrual-based budgeting; but progress is still slow.

Less ambitious trends have appeared in smaller countries. For example, in 2003 Macedonia conducted a series of national seminars sponsored by the United Nations Development Programme (UNDP) on 'Strengthening Local Self-governing Institutions in Macedonia, through Capital Development, Transparency and Financial Accountability', to build capacity as a first step in the reform of local financial systems. In the poorer countries, donor-sponsored fiscal decentralization includes the development and institutionalization of accounting reforms to ensure that the systems meet donor requirements. Capacity-building is extended to local governments to ensure proper implementation of the new systems, often starting with pilot initiatives.

Source: Serageldin et al, 2004

Accountability requires some measurement of performance, and – since the mid 1980s – local governments in Western Europe, the UK and the US have started to measure the real costs of delivering public services. Accrual-based multi-year budgeting provides more or less robust indicators of performance and is becoming a more common alternative to the traditional cash flow-based local budgets (see Box 3.10). In developing countries, most municipalities lack the capacity and resources to implement sophisticated monitoring of financial performance. Nevertheless, publicizing even crude, quantitative and qualitative indicators enhances community understanding of urban management and development challenges and promotes citizen participation in local governance.

PRIVATIZATION OF MUNICIPAL SERVICES

Key features

Starting in the 1980s, 'privatization' became an international trend embraced by countries all over the world, prompted by international and bilateral development organizations advocating the greater use of private-sector entities as the means of improving the delivery of public services. This trend was sustained by instances of policy and regulatory failure, bureaucratic impediments and public-sector inefficiencies in service delivery. Depending upon the project or the service in question, there was a gradual recognition and acceptance of the fact that private enterprise, NGOs or CBOs could undertake the task more efficiently and with greater effectiveness.

During the early years, there were massive privatizations of public utilities, in the electric power, telephone, transport, gas and other industries throughout the world, with little regard for the impact of the change of ownership upon the poor; nor was it adequately taken into account that some utilities were natural monopolies where the discipline of competition, a major justification for privatization, was substantially absent. Most of these outright privatizations concerned industries that were controlled by national or state governments. In many instances, along with its service delivery capability, the private sector has been able to supply much-needed capital investment raised by using practices that were closed to the public sector or methods that the public sector was legally barred from using, such as borrowing.

Privatization of local services entailed modifications in existing procedures and the introduction of new modalities of supply and delivery of services, including the contracting out of all or part of individual services; public–private partnerships; franchises; and forcing internal service units to compete on a commercial basis, as happened in Eastern Europe. However, the scope for privatization at the local level was limited to a relatively small number of services. These included public transport; water supply; solid waste management; a number of activities including janitorial and cleaning services; information processing and accounting; landscaping; and vehicle and plant maintenance. The success of the outcomes depends upon the particularities of each situation and the viewpoints of key stakeholders.

In both developing and advanced economies, privatization has resulted in revenue-producing services, including water supply and solid waste management being gradually taken over in the larger urban centres by specialized multinational firms serving many local government units. Although not complete monopolies, the sizes of many firms allow them to resort to predatory pricing to secure contracts in new locations and to exact costly indemnities and guarantees from local governments. Many of the activities are capital intensive and the high entry and exit costs make it difficult for potential competitors to compete against entrenched interests. Concessions granted to foreign enterprises also inhibit any substitution since the cancellation of the contract for unsatisfactory performance carries heavy political and financial risks. The contractor must usually be indemnified and the sponsoring foreign government placated, as occurred in Argentina.

Challenges of privatizing urban services

It becomes incumbent upon each locality to consider whether it should separately manage each of the services it delivers, or combine some services with one or more of its neighbouring units. Local authorities, separately or jointly, can outsource the management and delivery of one or more services to private operators, non-profit organizations or community groups. In Europe, there are strong incentives for inter-communal compacts; in some instances, as in France, national legislation mandates cooperation. In transitional and developing countries, local authorities are reluctant to engage in joint action, which typically requires some delegation of powers and sharing of revenues. In Latin America, political affiliations create divisive forces that impede the development of joint activities.

Many local authorities in developing countries have opted to establish separate operating units for some services with their own assets, staffing and management. These enterprises are managed by a 'board' or a committee where the locality is represented. In transitional countries, these semi-independent entities were viewed as an intermediate step in the process of privatization. This was particularly the case for housing maintenance and solid waste management. Similarly, the various jurisdictions can choose to jointly contract out combined service packages to a private-sector entity, which might be either publicly or privately managed or supervised. The organizational structure and the representation of partners in decisions regarding all aspects of management and finances will always be key concerns.

The experience of formal privatization in many cities is that it has not benefited lower income communities

The experience of formal privatization in many cities is that it has not benefited lower income communities, pointing to the need for the public sector to have a role in delivering essential services, especially within slum areas. The abolition of social rates and other forms of subsidization of minimum consumption levels for basic services has worked against the urban poor. Some NGOs have argued that poor urban families are unable to pay even the minimum charges required for access to basic infrastructure and

Box 3.11 Granting concessions for the operation of revenue-earning services: the experience of Abidjan, Côte d'Ivoire

Abidjan, Côte d'Ivoire, has a long history of granting concessions, having retained privately operated utilities and services. Before the disruptions and chaotic environment brought about by wars and civil strife, Abidjan's services functioned remarkably well compared to the situation prevailing in neighbouring countries. Communes within Abidjan's administrative boundaries paid the city an annual contribution for the services provided according to a formula combining population and revenue.

A French water company, la Société de Distribution d'Eau de Côte d'Ivoire (SODECI), had the concession for operating the water supply system. It was also awarded a contract for maintaining the sewerage and drainage system. These contracts contained clauses that shielded the company and shifted any risk involved in the operation of the system to the government. Even then, subsidized connections for poor households were abolished under the structural adjustment programme, and the vast majority of lower income renters now purchase their water from property owners, shopkeepers and water vendors. Despite the fact that its contract contained a clause entitling the company to compensation for any discrepancy between actual consumption and the estimates developed by the Water Directorate (the basis for negotiating concession contracts), the company contended that the maintenance of underutilized systems is inefficient, and periodically shuts off the mains supplying areas with high concentrations of low-cost rental housing and squatter settlements in a futile attempt to put the water vendors out of business.

The company's performance regarding the maintenance of the sanitation network was highly inadequate. Frequent obstructions, primarily due to defective solid waste management, were not attended to promptly despite the fact that local authorities were charged high fees for the service. However, the company's sunk investment in plant and equipment and its presence on the ground gave it a virtual monopoly, as competitors were unable to match the terms it offered.

Abidjan's solid waste management was also privatized. The different companies that were contracted covered the primary road network system and the main market areas. Their trucks were ill adapted to the high organic content of the wastes. They collected trash and garbage deposited in bins and dumpsters. The service was too infrequent for an equatorial country. Waste spilled from overflowing dumpsters was not collected.

Source: Serageldin, 1990; Center for Urban Development Studies, 2000.

services, prompting the emergence of parallel systems ranging from well-managed facilities sponsored by NGOs and charitable foundations to highly inadequate, poorly run initiatives operated on an *ad hoc* basis by local groups with or without outside support.

Côte d'Ivoire illustrates the challenges of privatizing water and sanitation services in a developing country and the difficulties of addressing the needs of lower income communities (see Box 3.11).

Joint funding of infrastructure and urban services

In China, provincial and local authorities increasingly look to public–private partnerships as an option to fund or implement infrastructure and urban development projects. Partnerships with private investors range from the granting of concessions, to joint venture agreements, to build–operate–transfer (BOT) or build–own–operate–transfer (BOOT) schemes. The public sector provides land for urban development and the construction of infrastructure and facilities (mostly new high-grade highways and toll roads). They also contribute repayable equity or loans. The private partners provide equity and shareholder loans. Concessions and BOOT agreements are more attractive to private investors – and foreign investors, in particular – because they can offer security in the form of guarantees of minimum revenue or profit, loss protection, repayment of capital, tax exemptions and other fiscal incentives, and preferential loan repayment terms. Provincial authorities can use assets and revenue-backed securities to finance their share of the investment.

Of special interest to poorer countries are solutions based on partnerships between municipalities, NGOs and CBOs. In these countries, integrating poorer communities within the city fabric and giving the poor access to basic services is hampered by the spread of chaotic urbanization, the mounting densities in the central zones, the obsolescence of existing conventional systems, and the lack of resources to maintain and upgrade existing systems.

To improve living conditions in the under-serviced communities, systems and networks using different technologies and serving different population groups and geographic areas must somehow be interlinked. Solid waste management is one of the services most affected by the need to merge traditional solutions with modern technologies. In West African cities, potable water supply could also benefit from this approach. Cotonou's (Benin) award-winning programmes demonstrate the importance of linking formal and informal service providers.

Joint funding of community-based initiatives for the delivery of basic services

Microcredit institutions have largely focused on giving microentrepreneurs the credit they need to start up and expand their businesses (see Chapter 6). Recognizing the importance of home-based income-generating activities, particularly for women, these institutions have started to offer loans for housing. They have progressively expanded their lending to help poor families access land and basic infrastructure services. Today, they have become key partners in municipal initiatives to improve the living conditions of poor households in both urban and rural areas. The experiences of Guatemala's Genesis Empresarial PROMUNI programme and the partnership between the Ahmedabad Municipal Corporation and the Self-employed Women's Association (SEWA) Mahila Trust to upgrade slums through the Parivartan programme illustrate the potential of these partnerships.

New trends in partnerships for local development

In developing countries, where decentralization is a recent or ongoing reform, municipalities are particularly reluctant to delegate authority or share revenue with their peer entities. This reluctance accounts for the difficulties encountered in getting municipalities to collaborate on joint initiatives. Formalizing collaboration through negotiated agreements and inter-municipal compacts is an even more challenging task as there are no institutional incentives that foster strategic associations other than through external aid entities. The successful initiatives mostly focus on economic development, as in the case of the ABC Region[19] in Greater São Paulo, Brazil, where seven municipalities have to cope with economic restructuring and the rebuilding of the local economy based on new growth sectors following the decline of the automotive industry.

The difficulties encountered in mobilizing and structuring alliances of stakeholders to promote local development are illustrated by the experiences from Central America. It has become clear that in poor regions bypassed by development, programmes promoting development must also foster social inclusion. Inter-municipal initiatives can significantly enhance the effectiveness of these efforts, as in the case of the Valle de Sula Metropolitan Area strategic association in Honduras. The challenge is to overcome distrust and apprehension. The participatory process required to reach consensus on objectives, operating modalities and action plans takes anywhere from two to three years, and the institutional framework must be organized before any activities can be initiated. Implementation of partnership agreements often requires the creation of a large number of assemblies, committees, boards and delegations that may become cumbersome to the point of reducing the effectiveness of the alliances. San Andres Valley, San Salvador, illustrates the benefits of forging stakeholder alliances.[20]

SUMMING UP: ASSESSING THE EFFECTIVENESS AND IMPACTS OF MUNICIPAL FINANCE SYSTEMS

Municipal finance and sustainable urban development

Municipal finance heavily influences the ability of local governments to meet the environmental and social goals of sustainable urban development and, in particular, to address issues of shelter delivery, poverty reduction and social inclusion. Sustainable urban development requires significant capital and operating expenditures, especially in situations where urban expansion depends upon the periodic extension of infrastructure systems. In particular, making services available to low-income families necessitates substantial subsidies that municipalities have been unable to generate from their own revenues. Unless the inequities generated by globalization, decentralization, central–local fiscal relations, and the dynamics of urban growth are addressed, the sustainability of urban development and shelter delivery, primarily in developing countries, will remain highly problematic.

In many parts of the world, including advanced economies, globalization has affected the financial resources of both national and local governments as taxable economic activities move to other locations. The situation is further aggravated by the increased local fiscal burden resulting from the shifting of responsibility for infrastructure investment and the delivery of services to local governments. Additional complexity is introduced by new developments that overlap municipal boundaries and impose an unexpected financial burden on the localities housing poorer populations or receiving migrants. Households in these under-serviced communities and outlying areas have to pay more per unit cost for inferior-quality services.

Municipalities are faced with a mismatch between their newly acquired responsibilities to provide services and fund capital improvements and a lack of control over their revenue sources. The resulting scaling-back of public expenditures on both capital investment and social programmes is having an adverse effect on urban development and is impeding the achievement of the Millennium Development Goals.

Municipal finance heavily influences the ability of local governments to meet the environmental and social goals of sustainable urban development

In the poorer countries, the deterioration of existing infrastructure and the inability to meet the demands created by rapid urbanization have led to chaotic urbanization, the proliferation of informal settlements and the emergence of informal providers of basic services. This has been particularly the case for water supply in Tanzania, Botswana, Kenya, Mauritania and Benin. As will be shown in Chapter 7, NGOs have contributed to the alleviation of hardships endured by the poor and provided them with some services. Their interventions have targeted specific communities selected in accordance with their own objectives and criteria.

Programmes addressing the social dimension of urban development are still largely dependent upon intergovernmental transfers or international aid. Debt swaps and discounted debt under the Heavily Indebted Poor Countries initiative are only beginning to be used to finance environmental and social programmes, mostly through local NGOs and CBOs. Bolivia is an exceptional case where funds are channelled through local authorities. The integration of these new sources into the pool of resources available to finance urban development could open up new opportunities well worth exploring.

Municipal finance and the delivery of land and services

The effectiveness of municipal authorities to improve the supply of serviced land and to deliver basic services is clearly a function of both the pace of the development they face and the country's level of economic development. Generally, the advanced and some transitional economies have both the financial and administrative resources to manage development and provide urban residents with services ranging from adequate to good. Stable or declining populations have facilitated this task. In contrast, the poorer countries have, for the most part, been unable to keep up with the demand for serviced land or provide adequate basic services to a growing percentage of their rapidly expanding urban populations. The major obstacles they face are:

Globalization has affected the financial resources of both national and local governments as taxable economic activities move to other locations

- inadequate financial resources to pay for the delivery of services to a growing population;
- limited or no access to capital resources to finance investments in infrastructure; and
- lack of institutional capacity to prepare mid- and long-term development strategies and the capital improvement programmes necessary to implement them.

Few municipalities have complete authority over taxation. In many countries, high-yield tax bases are still largely controlled by the central government and are not likely to be turned over to the local level in the near future, as stated earlier. Even though local governments are nominally responsible for managing their affairs, their real autonomy is restricted by the dominant role the national government continues to play in determining the local tax base, and in the collection and redistribution of tax revenue.

A generalized lack of resources and the difficulty in accessing capital markets impedes the preparation of long-term capital improvement programmes. Brazil's municipal reforms that imposed fiscal management standards, limited personnel expenditures and mandated the preparation of multi-year capital improvement programmes is an exceptional case. Elsewhere, the preparation of multi-year budgets is gradually being introduced as a mandatory requirement in national public finance regulations.

Financial constraints are reflected in two generalized trends: the lack of funds for maintaining existing assets and the inability of many municipalities to undertake the capital improvements needed to keep up with urban growth, let alone guide urbanization and development. While some countries, such as South Africa, have provided grants for capital investment in infrastructure, central funds are generally in short supply in most parts of the world and are often channelled to larger cities. As a result, it is not uncommon for existing infrastructure to deteriorate as a result of a lack of maintenance.

Despite adverse economic conditions, local authorities in East and West Africa have managed to increase the contribution of locally collected taxes

To circumvent legal, regulatory and fiscal constraints on their budgets, local governments in both advanced and developing countries are developing means to finance urban development and public improvements as off-budget expenditures through special purpose vehicles, as in China, and assessments and impact fees requiring private developers to pay part of the public infrastructure needed for their projects – a common practice in the US and some transitional economies.

In developing countries, medium and small municipalities lack the technical skills to prepare the coherent urban investment strategies required to access grants and loans from donors and municipal development funds. Santo Andre in Brazil and Szczecin in Poland stand out as successful examples of a forceful commitment to institute the reforms needed for financial planning and management, and a determined effort to leverage local resources, access credit finance and obtain funding from multilateral and bilateral organizations.

Strengthening the capacity of municipalities to plan and manage their economic, spatial and social development, disseminating information on successful approaches, and providing the institutional framework to support reform initiatives remain a major challenge worldwide. In adverse economic conditions or institutionally fragile environments, building the capacity of weak municipalities requires longer-term support that has to be provided by strong locally based institutions. Sponsoring local capacity-building institutions is an effective mechanism fostering the achievement of the MDGs.

Impact of decentralization upon municipal finance and service delivery

With the exception of the advanced economies where at least the larger cities have substantial experience in managing their finances, the devolution of functional responsibilities has presented local governments with a major challenge, often compounded by adverse economic and political conditions. In Eastern and Central European countries, local political autonomy, links to the West and participation in regional and international networks, and hopes of eventual accession to the EU help to cushion the burdens of devolution. Grants extended to promote social, economic and environmental objectives have provided needed funding for urban projects.

In Africa, Asia and Latin America, transfers from central governments have declined steadily, particularly for larger cities, and charting an appropriate course for decentralization without disrupting the delivery of basic services devolved to the local level has proved to be a difficult task. Only a few countries have formulated successful policies to redistribute resources that are more efficiently collected at the national level and have equalized the burden on municipalities that are economically weak or face higher per capita expenditures. Effective instruments used to foster a smooth decentralization include:

- local statutory rights guaranteed by the constitution or by national legislation;
- the mandatory transfer of shared tax revenues;
- formula-based redistribution favouring smaller and fiscally weaker municipalities;
- the sharing of fiscal revenue through formulae that take into account concentrations of poverty; and
- intergovernmental agreements and inter-municipal compacts and joint initiatives.

The experiences of Brazil, Bolivia and South Africa stand out in this respect. Other countries, such as Indonesia, have had to undertake successive adjustments to correct serious imbalances that affect the economic and social life of their citizens. Even municipalities in the poorest countries have made considerable efforts in reducing their reliance upon dwindling transfers from central governments. Despite adverse economic conditions, local authorities in East and West Africa have managed to increase the contribution of locally collected taxes. In the countries of the West African Economic and Monetary Union, these taxes now account for close to 50 per cent of municipal revenue, a significant increase over a relatively short time. In Burkina Faso, 'communes' do not receive any transfers from the national government.

A growing demand for accountability and transparency in municipal budgeting has accompanied political and fiscal decentralization. There is a marked trend for more rigorous financial management, clear procedures for the allocation of resources and the participation of residents in decisions affecting their communities. Of particular interest is the transparency mandated by the Brazilian legislation and the spread of participatory budgeting.

Impact of privatization upon municipal finance and service delivery

Privatization of public service delivery requires many years of operation for comprehensive and robust evidence to emerge regarding the extent of success or failure. But there is evidence that the outcomes have not always matched the expectations. More rigorous analysis is needed to determine in each situation whether private profits are engendered by genuine economic efficiency of operations, or by allowing the plant and equipment to continue deteriorating, or by raising prices to levels beyond the means of lower income communities, as happened in some Latin American countries. Moreover, the ability of private operators to cash out or withdraw allows them to increase profits by underfunding or deferring expenditures on replacement and preventive maintenance. When the private contractor walks away from essential services, the public sector has to pick up the operations.

Reversing or modifying a particular mode of service delivery – publicly or privately provided, or contracted out – is not simple. Many activities are capital intensive or have significant institutional implications. These entry or exit costs can be quite high and make it difficult for potential competitors to compete against entrenched interests, as happens in many concession situations in developing economies. Privatization and, in particular, the awarding of concessions have not been devoid of corruption, including lower initial bid prices to win, followed by later requests for contract amendments.

In developing economies and, in particular, in the poorer countries, there is an urgent need to address inequities in access to basic services. This is an issue that privatization will not resolve. Disparities result from a legacy of inadequate urban policies and ineffective responses, aggravated by the current dynamics of urban development. Many governments do provide subsidized access to poor families and some, like South Africa, extend these subsidies to cover minimum consumption levels. In the poorer countries, linking formal and informal service providers remains the most effective mechanism by which services to lower income communities can be provided and improved, as the experience of water supply and solid waste management in Cotonou, Benin, demonstrates.

At both the national and local levels, privatization provides an expedient way around constraints on other types of financing, especially for capital expenditures where restrictions on public-sector borrowing exist. Privatization has, to some extent, shaken local government financial management from an earlier complacency about budgetary rigour and accountability. It has forced a much greater attention upon cost recognition and control, leading to improved accounting practices and a greater concern for the recovery of costs and the collection of payments when it was previously assumed that shortfalls would automatically be covered from general public revenues.

The financial discipline and commercial outlook of competing private enterprise has forced public administrators to lower costs, achieve greater efficiency and improve the quality of outputs. Opening up public services to market participation has created more opportunities for competition in the delivery of these services. The private sector has introduced useful new products, more successful activities and labour-saving technologies to gain a greater 'return' on the huge sums of money invested in public services. While privatization has forced governments to examine entrenched practices and to consider alternatives for their modification or replacement with considerable success, it is not a panacea. There are many ways of involving the private sector in public service delivery on a rational basis short of outright privatization.

Opening up public services to market participation has created more opportunities for competition in the service delivery

Public–private partnerships require significant delegation of authority but can be very productive. Locally based partnerships involving CBOs and microenterprises have provided successful means for empowerment and social inclusion. Solid waste management and recycling have become prime mechanisms to simultaneously promote environmental and social objectives. There are numerous award-winning schemes worldwide such as Santo Andre, in Brazil, and the Scavenger communities, in the North-West Province, South Africa. Furthermore, in the poorest countries, labour-intensive activities are important in providing productive employment to impoverished populations. Partnerships between local governments, communities and microenterprises can help to achieve these objectives.

NOTES

1 This chapter is based on drafts prepared by a team of experts led by Mona Serageldin, Harvard University, US.
2 UN-Habitat, 2003a.
3 See UN Millennium Project (2005b) for detail.
4 See www.bestpractices.org.
5 UN-Habitat, 1998.
6 UN-Habitat, 2003a.
7 Alm et al, 2002; UNCHS, 2001.
8 UN-Habitat, 1998.
9 UN-Habitat, 1998.
10 Shah and Thompson, 2002.
11 See, for instance, Litvack et al, 1998.
12 See, for instance, Steffensen and Tidemand, 2004.
13 Mosha, 2004.
14 Freire et al, 2004.
15 Freire et al, 2004.
16 Mathur et al, 2004.
17 Brakarz, 2003.
18 Brakarz, 2003.
19 In 1990, the seven municipal governments of the Region established the Intermunicipal Consortium of the Greater ABC. The Greater ABC region is located in the southeastern part of the Greater São Paulo metropolitan area (Brazil) and has a population of 2.4 million inhabitants, according to the IBGE Census of 2000. Its seven municipalities are: Santo André, São Bernardo do Campo, São Caetano do Sul, Diadema, Mauá, Ribeirão Pires, Rio Grande da Serra.
20 See the Statistical Annex in Part IV for detail.

PART II

SHELTER FINANCE: ASSESSMENT OF TRENDS

CHAPTER 4

MORTGAGE FINANCE: INSTITUTIONS AND MECHANISMS[1]

Despite its recognized economic and social importance, housing finance often remains underdeveloped in emerging economies. Residential lending is typically small, poorly accessible and depository based. Lenders remain vulnerable to significant credit, liquidity and interest rate risks. As a result, housing finance is relatively expensive and often rationed. The importance of developing robust systems of housing finance is paramount as emerging economy governments struggle to cope with population growth, rapid urbanization and rising expectations from a growing middle class.[2]

HIGHLIGHTS

Cost of houses and need for mortgage finance

The cost of a complete dwelling in the North is generally 2.5 to 6 times the average annual salary.[3] Indicative costs suggest very similar figures or higher figures for the South. The Housing Indicators Programme suggested the ratio was as high as 12 for Algeria.[4] For those planning and able to purchase property, it is very difficult to finance such costs without a loan and generally such loans will need to be long term (typically over 10 years and sometimes over 20 years). When the repayment period is to stretch for such a considerable period, a legal framework is required for lenders to be confident about the security of their finance – hence, the significance of mortgage finance in which the loan is secured on property. This is the predominant context in which lending for a complete (or almost complete) dwelling takes place.

The primary emphasis in this chapter is on such mortgage finance. This is generally provided by commercial companies and/or by the state through specialist housing finance organizations. The majority of housing finance agencies only provide finance for completed units that comply with building regulations – Chapters 6 and 7 consider those institutions that are concerned with the provision of small loans. In some countries in the South, mortgage finance may be available for an 'almost complete' dwelling (together with title).[5]

Loans secured on the property only offer realistic collateral for the lender if a claim on the property can be established and the property is sold to cover any remaining monies owing on the loan in the case of default. As a result, there is a requirement for the legal capacity to register property rights, transfer titles and foreclose on loans. There are also systemic requirements for mortgage finance. Sources of funding need to be appropriate, particularly with regard to the long-term nature of the loan commitment. Such financial systems are generally also dependent upon a stable economy, notably to ensure that default rates are minimal (as borrowers maintain real incomes) and because of the multiple impacts of high levels of inflation. However, the experiences discussed in this chapter suggest that, in a number of countries, the systems have been strong enough to recover from the difficult economic situation experienced in parts of the world during the 1990s.

Mortgage finance and poverty

The size of such loans (given the cost of properties) and the requirement for a deposit or down payment to cover a significant part of the cost means that most households accessing mortgage finance are those at the top or in the middle of the income scale. As noted already, low-income households may lack the finance for the down payment and are likely to lack formal legal title deeds; therefore, they are unlikely to be able to offer acceptable collateral. The poor face further problems in their search for housing finance.[6] Other significant issues discussed in this chapter include the lack of verifiable incomes, the additional costs involved in the process of purchase, and lending policies that impose a minimum loan size.

Despite such difficulties, one emerging global trend is the effort to extend mortgage finance to lower income groups, expanding the market for housing finance and increasing formal homeownership. Such policies are partly commercial and partly state led. The commercial interest is in extending financial services to a new group of people. The last two decades have been ones of financial deregulation, with increasing numbers of financial agencies and growing competition in financial services. In many countries, governments have been behind strategies to extend mortgage finance to those who have traditionally been unable to afford such loans. Governments have multiple reasons to support homeownership, including the significance of the construction industry for economic growth and prosperity, the significance of shelter for well-being (and poverty reduction), and the political popularity of such policies. As discussed later in this chapter, they have followed numerous strategies, including providing financial support. Measures that have focused primarily on reducing the cost of lending (notably through reductions in the interest rate) and support to the system of mortgage finance (such as extending secondary markets and reducing risks) are considered in this chapter.[7] Other measures have included capital grants (direct demand subsidies), sometimes with access to mortgage finance for additional loans (see Chapter 5). While government support has been widespread, it should also be noted that there is no universal agreement on the appropriateness of encouraging homeownership.[8]

Governments have multiple reasons to support homeownership, including the significance of the construction industry for economic growth and prosperity

The focus of this chapter is threefold:

1. to consider emerging trends in the provision of mortgage finance and to summarize present terms and conditions of such finance;
2. in the context of this discussion, to look particularly at the situation with regard to lower income households who might be seeking mortgage finance and the affordability of such options for these households; and
3. to look at emerging tensions and opportunities in current mortgage finance and to assess its potential *contribution* to addressing household needs for housing finance.

Box 4.1 Reductions in general subsidies to housing

A survey of the Nordic countries, Western Europe and more highly liberalized systems shows that there are clear tendencies to restrict general subsidies and deregulate financial and housing markets. The greatest impact upon housing investment has come from the reduction in the scale of direct subsidies for housing. In most countries, targeting towards particular types of investment or households has become more significant. Two countries of particular interest are New Zealand and the Netherlands. In New Zealand, the whole range of subsidies and tax relief has been removed to be replaced with market rents and prices, together with an 'accommodation allowance' payable to low-income households of all tenures. In The Netherlands, all existing supply-side subsidies have been rolled up into a single capital grant and replaced with a system of privatized guarantees to assist both the social and owner-occupied sector to raise finance.

There are three potential impacts of these very large reductions in general assistance. In most countries there have been significant falls in output in both social and private sectors. Second, there have been significant increases in risk in the finance market. This was particularly obvious during house price falls during the early 1990s. To counter this trend, there has been some increase in credit insurance and guarantees. Finally, there has been an impact upon prices, although this is hard to assess because of other influences. In social housing, costs have increased as a result of reduced supply-side subsidies.

Source: Turner and Whitehead, 2002, pp172–173.

RECENT TRENDS

General trends related to providers

In general, governments have sought to encourage homeownership and have, in many cases, provided preferential financing to influence consumer choice. In part, this reflects the multiple benefits of housing, combined with the belief that citizens will take better care of the dwellings if they own them and the knowledge that many households wish to provide for themselves. One further factor motivating housing investment is the financial advantage arising from capital gains, as homeownership is often associated with capital appreciation.[9]

There has been a general shift towards market-based mechanisms for the provision of housing, with attempts to reduce subsidies and deregulate markets (Box 4.1).[10] This is due, in part, to the past ineffectiveness of housing strategies that have depended upon direct provision by the state. This trend is also consistent with the overall direction of macro-economic strategies during recent decades. With limited state funds (in the North and South) and few social providers beyond the state, increasing access to housing means increasing the affordability of housing provided by the market. Governments are (almost universally) seeking to stabilize or reduce state expenditures, and the scale of their support is limited. In this context, many have actively sought to encourage commercial companies to address the needs of lower income households. This fits more generally within policies to liberalize financial services and encourage competition within this service sector. It is anticipated that more providers will reduce the cost of housing finance and therefore contribute to easing affordability constraints.

As noted in the following chapters, this trend towards market provision is significant in how it has influenced strategies for social housing and has included, in at least some countries and some institutions, greater use of small loans. There was a shift towards the market for those at the lower end of the income scale in the North. Such changes are one factor encouraging more homeownership in the North. However, the example of New Zealand also warns against the dangers of generalization as, in this country, the new policy towards market provision has replaced a previous strategy that was considered to be more specifically favourable towards homeownership, while the new policy also encourages private rental markets.[11]

Traditionally, mortgage agencies have focused on a specific set of users (such as those saving regularly or making payroll contributions). The preferential circumstances favouring these groups (notably lower interest rates) mean that other financial institutions may have been reluctant to enter the market. In other cases, they were simply unable due to government policies. The shift to greater financial deregulation has meant that while mortgage finance used to be the preserve of specialist lenders (commercial mortgage companies and/or state housing banks), other providers, including more conventional financial institutions, have now been drawn into the market. In European Union (EU) countries, non-specialist financial institutions now account for more than 60 per cent of the mortgage market.[12] In some

Number	Category	Description of institution	Products	Examples
1	**Wholesale finance institutions**			
1.1	Wholesale finance institutions	Providers of wholesale finance facilities that may be used by housing institutions for internal capital needs or for retail lending activities.	Wholesale loans Institutional loans	Mutual banks Banks (e.g. Standard, Nedcor, ABSA)
1.2	Specialist housing finance institutions	Specialist DFIs established with state support in order to increase the number and capacity of housing finance organizations through providing inter alia wholesale finance. Regulated by special statutes.	Wholesale loans Institutional loans	NHFC NURCHA RHLF TUHF
2	**Retail finance institutions**			
2.1	Banks	Commercial financial institutions regulated by Banks Act and Usury Act.	Mortgage finance	Members of the banking council
2.2	Non-bank lenders	Institutions issuing medium to small loans or exempted for products of below 10,000 rand.	Securitized loans Personal equity-backed loans	NHFC (Makhulong product) South Africa home loans
2.3	Microfinance institutions	These are a subsection of non-bank lenders that grant unsecured personal loans which are exempted from the Usury Act (Usury Act Exemption Notice) and regulated by the Microfinance Regulatory Council (MFRC). These include normal microfinance institutions, niche market lenders and NGO lenders.	Unsecured small loans Savings-backed microloans	Members of the Microfinance Regulatory Council
2.4	Housing institutions	Specialist housing institutions providing end-user financing for housing products using innovative tenure arrangements. Regulated by various laws, including Instalment Sale (Alienation of Land Act, 1989).	Instalment sale products Rental tenure co-operatives	Rental housing institutions (e.g. Johannesburg Housing Company) Social housing institutions (e.g. COPE Housing Association) Instalment sale institutions (e.g. Cape Town Housing Company)
3	**Savings institutions**			
3.1	Savings-linked credit institutions	Housing savings schemes linked to the provision of credit by microfinance institutions.	Savings-linked credit	Instalment sale institutions (e.g. Cape Town Community Housing Company) Finance institutions (e.g. *uTshani* Fund)
3.2	Specialist savings institutions	Specialist institutions or schemes established to assist low-income households to accrue savings for their 'own contributions' to subsidized housing.	Savings schemes	National Savings Scheme (NURCHA)
4	**Guarantors**			
4.1	Wholesale housing finance guarantors	Institutions that underwrite or provide guarantees to the providers of wholesale loans for housing purposes.	Housing-specific wholesale finance guarantees 'Hardship cover' guarantees for rental institutions/SHIs	NHFC (specialist guarantees) NURCHA (OPIC bridging finance guarantees; Gauteng Rental Guarantee Fund guarantees for rental institutions) HLGC (hardship cover guarantees on rental income streams for rental institutions)
4.2	End-user housing finance guarantors	Institutions that provide guarantees to the providers of end-user housing finance (mortgage finance) on individual loans.	Loan default guarantees AIDS guarantees	HLGC guarantee products

Note: see pp xviii–xxii for unabbreviated forms of acronyms and abbreviations in this table

Table 4.1

The current range and diversity of providers of housing finance in South Africa

countries, providers previously came solely from the government sector. New mortgage providers may be commercial financial institutions or, in some cases, mortgage companies. Many Southern countries now have access to market-rate housing finance, which was not the case 20 years ago.[13] The section on 'Regional analysis' discusses this trend in more detail.

Table 4.1 illustrates the current range and diversity of providers of housing finance in South Africa. The table looks at all providers of housing finance both for mortgage and smaller loans. However, it does not include the kinds of programmes discussed in Chapter 5, which are significant in South Africa as there is a state-financed capital subsidy scheme to assist the poor in addressing housing need.

However, precise assessments of the extent to which there has been a de-concentration of mortgage providers away from state agencies, or those benefiting from state concessions, remains difficult. For example, while the numbers of financial institutions in India has clearly increased (including those providing housing finance), an estimated 92 per cent of India's banking sector remains under state control.[14] In addition to the state's overall involvement in the finance sector, the state may be particularly involved in the direct provision of mortgage finance. Even where this is not the case, the state may still seek to influence housing outcomes and make institutional interventions.

The aspirations of government to influence the scale and quality of the housing stock through housing finance are longstanding. Box 4.2 gives an example from Zambia of the complexity of state involvement in housing institutions and the continuing aspirations of the state for involvement. Despite these attempts, the policies have not been successful and housing need was estimated at 846,000 units in 1996.[15] More generally, the performance of state-owned housing finance institutions in the South has been widely criticized. One recent analysis of the performance of such financial institutions concludes that mortgage lending in the South has not emerged as a financially viable housing finance strategy for the poor.[16] It is suggested that 'housing banks created with the help of donor agencies over the past 30 years have gone bankrupt or moribund, evolved into full-fledged commercial banks (such as Capital Bank in Haiti), or become real estate-focused banks with very few poor clients

Box 4.2 Zambia: a brief history of state involvement in housing finance

During the period of the second and third National Development Plans in Zambia (1971–1983), the government pursued a policy of developing residential and commercial property through the parastatal firms. Among the parastatal companies that were used to increase housing stocks were the National Housing Authority (NHA), the Zambia State Insurance Corporation (ZSIC), the Zambia National Provident Fund (ZNPF) and the Zambia National Building Society (ZNBS). Apart from the National Housing Authority, these companies were supposed to build institutional houses, which their employees would rent. The NHA was allowed to build houses specifically for selling and letting out to the public. This in itself represented a shift in the general policy from encouraging homeownership to allowing renting from parastatal firms.

During the 1970s, the government removed the responsibility of housing financing from the local authorities. The government created the Zambia National Building Society in 1970 to finance property development for both residential and commercial purposes. It offers three types of property financing. First, credit is available for the outright purchase of already developed property to all prospective owners. Second, it manages a construction scheme under which it finances the construction of property on behalf of its clients. Third, it offers smaller loans for renovations, improvements and extension of already owned property. With the ZSIC, it undertakes real estate management (residential and commercial) and rents out from its own stock or on behalf of customers.

Since its inception in 1971, the NHA's core function was property development for the purposes of selling and renting to the general public, with selling being its biggest option. The NHA sought to provide minimum housing standards within the resources of the country. At the same time, it conducted research to lower the costs of low-income housing. The third National Development Plan (1979–1983) gave the NHA the responsibility of 'vetting all housing programmes' prepared by all organizations, including government. Currently, the NHA specializes in building houses for sale through outright purchase and financing of construction. A large segment of the houses built by the NHA are of low-cost type. The NHA also considers itself to be the foremost adviser to government on housing policy. The government also formed the Presidential Housing Initiative (PHI) in 1999 to spearhead the implementation of the National Housing Policy. Among other things, the PHI was expected to rejuvenate the construction of new houses. However, the programme was dissolved in 2002 under accusations of corruption.

Source: Mulenga, 2003.

(the Housing Bank of Jordan).'[17] However, it should be recognized that many were only intended for limited groups of workers.

Despite what is generally a pessimistic appraisal of the potential for direct state provision, a popular response to housing problems in the transition countries has been the establishment of national housing funds, in most cases orientated towards the provision of low-income housing.[18] Moreover, in some contexts in other nations during the last decade, government strategies to move away from direct involvement in the housing finance sector have been forced to change due to the scale of economic crisis. For example, the National Housing Bank in Thailand has sought to stabilize a difficult situation for housing finance following the financial crises during the late 1990s, and the bank has, as a consequence, become an increasingly important provider (see Box 4.3 and Table 4.2).[19] Hence, although state housing banks are perhaps less popular than previously and their role may be smaller, some governments still choose to use them as a provider of housing finance. In Mexico, the problems of the mid 1990s resulted in commercial banks reducing their exposure to mortgage lending.[20] One study of Mexico notes that banks issued 54 per cent of mortgage lending in 1994, but only 6 per cent three years later.[21] In both Thailand and Mexico, government agencies have had some success in supporting the continuation of mortgage lending.

Table 4.2

Growth of mortgage lending in Thailand: size of the primary mortgage market (million baht)

	1997	1998	1999	2000	2001	2002
Outstanding balances of mortgage loans (A)	793,521	769,379	712,401	688,544	688,884	701,700
New origination of mortgage loans (B)	204,303	103,733	64,301	108,886	111,996	120,000

Source: Kritayanavaj, 2002, pp18, 20.

Sources of finance

Access to sufficient sources of finance has long been recognized to be critical for the effective operation of housing finance markets. Mortgage finance involves the commitment of capital for long periods of time. If the only source of finance available to the mortgage lenders is deposits, then even if they can secure sufficient funds, lenders face a risk when committing long-term loans with short-term finance. In general, they minimize such risks by lending a relatively small proportion of these funds. As an alternative to short-term deposits, there are several sources of longer-term finance. One source is the state itself and the direct contributions that it might make. A second source is private funds institutionalized for housing finance, either through specialist saving schemes, such as those in Germany and Austria (and now some transition countries), and/or through the state establishing requirements for payroll deductions to capitalize housing funds. A third source is private commercial investment. Despite these multiple sources, the availability of long-term finance is limited in many countries, including the Philippines, with negative consequences:

> *In the absence of long-term finance, the large demand for housing is not translated into effective demand. As it is, the banking system has been reluctant to hold long-term mortgages as assets because of the poor match in maturities between mortgages and sources of funds. Banks thus make loans only to the high-income households to minimize risk. The low-to middle-income households, on the other hand, have been largely dependent on government social security funds; but these funds are limited and cater mainly to households in the formal sector.*[22]

The importance of deposits to the bank system is widely acknowledged.[23] Deposits account for 62 per cent of the funding of all mortgage loans within EU countries and this percentage is even higher in the transition countries.[24] As noted in 'Strengthening secondary markets', below, in a number of emerging economies secondary markets have been slow to develop because deposit funding is available to mortgage lenders. With the reduction and restructuring of state involvement, financing has potentially become a more significant issue. In theory, the withdrawal of the state, particularly from providing subsidized interest rate loans, should have encouraged additional agencies into a more commercially orientated market. Nevertheless, there are concerns, notably in Asia and Latin America, that a lack of capital will inhibit lending and reduce the effectiveness of housing finance reforms. As a result, there have been a number of efforts to strengthen secondary markets in housing finance.[25] The following discussion considers these efforts, the need for them and their success.

While the state has become less significant in some countries, it maintains a high level of involvement in others (see 'Regional analysis', below). Governments may have simply been concerned to ensure sufficient cash flow into the housing sector. In Latin America, for example, strategies to raise the amount of loan finance available include the use of special payroll taxes, taxes on fuel, surcharges on sales tax and state lottery sales.[26] A further source is the proceeds of privatization, which have been important in some countries – for example, the Housing Finance Company of Uganda in which such funds formed 50 per cent of the available capital by 2000.[27] And, as noted in the case of India, the state may provide capital finance to state-owned housing finance companies for on-lending, notably in the case of the Housing and Urban Development Corporation Ltd (HUDCO).[28] Budget allocations to 2001 were responsible for taking HUDCO's total equity to US$204.1 million.

A notable further source of finance is employer and employee contributions to payroll funds for housing.[29] Country-level analyses suggest that they are of significance in countries as diverse as Mexico, Singapore and, now, China. In Nigeria, attempts have been made to extend their significance, and there is now a mandatory contribution of 2.5 per cent for workers with monthly incomes of over 3000 Nigerian naira. Every commercial and merchant bank is mandated to invest 10 per cent of loans and advances in the fund and with further requirements on investment companies; but there is a serious problem of compliance.[30] Provident funds have also been used in some cases – with particular effectiveness in Singapore. They are being employed in Bangladesh, Namibia and South Africa as a source of loan guarantees.

Box 4.3 The role of the Government Housing Bank in Thailand

The Government Housing Bank was established in Thailand in 1953. Its major functions were intended to be the mobilization of funds for on-lending, land subdivision and the construction of houses for sale to the public. However, the bank was forced to be a developer due to a lack of alternatives. In 1972, the National Housing Authority was established to take on this role (among other activities) and this enabled the bank to focus on finance.

During the 1990s, the Government Housing Bank expanded its retail lending, and between 1990 and 1994 the number of retail branches grew from 10 to 100. Growth continued during the 1990s, and by mid 2002 the bank had 30 main branches in Bangkok, 30 main branches elsewhere and 43 sub-branches. Between 1987 and 1997, the mortgage market had expanded rapidly. In 1988, annual new home loan origination by all financial institutions in Thailand was 40 million baht; but during the mid 1990s it reached over 200,000 million baht. However, the situation became particularly difficult during the financial disasters of the late 1990s, when there was a crisis of confidence in financial institutions and several collapsed. The housing market went into a slump, in part because there was a significant oversupply as a result of speculative building. In 1994, there were 253,000 new housing units offered in the Bangkok Metropolitan Region; by 1998, this had fallen to 1000, rising to 6000 in 2001.

The total number of home mortgages outstanding in Thailand had risen to a peak of 794,000 in 1997. The consequence of a speculative market and falling prices resulted in a rapid rise in non-performing loans. In 1997, the ratio of non-performing loans reached more than 30 per cent (although by the end of 2001 it had fallen back to about 23 per cent). By June 2002, the Government Housing Bank had a non-performing loan ratio of 17.4 per cent, still considered to be too high.

As a result of the crises of the late 1990s, commercial firms tended to withdraw from the market and reduce their lending. However, the bank sought to stimulate new developments. The mortgage rate was kept low for low- and lower middle-income groups. Its share of the market in outstanding home loans increased from about 20 per cent during the early 1990s to almost 40 per cent by the first years of the new millennium. By the end of March 2002, the bank had outstanding home loans totalling about 280,000 million baht and was servicing 700,000 borrowers.

The Government Housing Bank has sought to offer low interest rates due to efficiency and a desire for growth, and in order to assist entry into homeownership. It offers lower rates on the smallest loans (less than 1 million baht and some 90 per cent of borrowers) with a cross-subsidy between high- and low-value loans. In order to increase affordability after the financial crisis, repayment periods were increased to 30 years and loan-to-value ratios rose to 90–100 per cent. This willingness to lend reflects, in part, the strategy of the government, which is to use housing development as part of its economic policy and to be willing to stimulate the economy through housing. Its strategies include a low interest rate for lower income borrowers, a further interest rate reduction for state employees and the possibility for borrowers to fix interest rates for three to five years (thereby reducing their risk).

Source: Kritayanavaj, 2002, p15.

Strengthening secondary markets

The secondary market in mortgage finance developed to cope with the risks associated with short-term deposits and longer-term loans. The US has led developments in secondary markets, which have become notably significant from the mid 1980s.[31] For the last 25 years, there have been significant changes in mortgage finance with the growth of involvement by the capital markets; this began in the US and spread to Europe and, more recently, is being explored in Latin America and Asia.[32] In the transition countries, legislation to support the development of secondary markets in housing finance has been introduced, or is being introduced, in the Czech and Slovak republics, Hungary, Poland and Latvia.[33] Such growth, in Europe and beyond, partly reflects the integration of financial markets and the attractiveness of mortgage finance for international investors. European markets now include all three major securities – structured covered bonds, agency bonds and mortgage-backed securities.[34] In addition to specific measures to enable the investment of other financial institutions in mortgage lending, there has been the related trend towards specialization. In the US, which is the global leader in this respect, mortgage finance has become increasingly complex with the growing division between aspects of the mortgage lending process: origination, servicing, funding and accepting credit risk. The shift in models is summarized in Figures 4.1 and 4.2.

The significance of the secondary market in the US is considerable, where most US mortgages are now sold – especially fixed rate mortgages, which take up 60 to 90 per cent of the market.[35] The government has supported the rise of specific institutions that have supported these financial

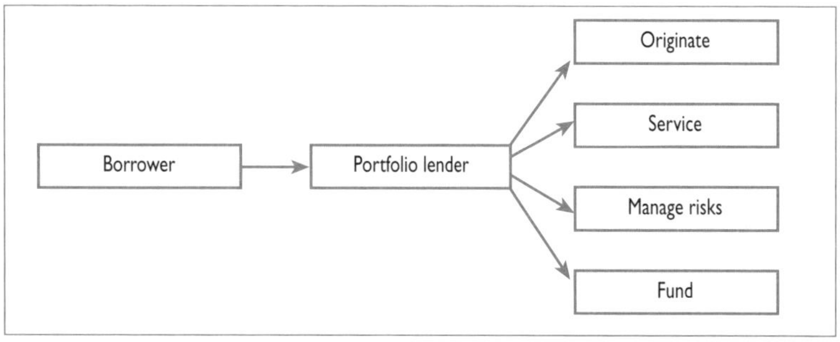

Figure 4.1

The bundled home mortgage delivery system

Source: Lea, 2000, p1.

systems (see Box 4.4) and 'Virtually all government-insured loans become mortgage-backed securities via Ginnie Mae and over 40 per cent of conventional mortgages are now sold to either Fannie Mae or Freddie Mac'.[36] The US experience shows that it is possible for the market to make money on single-family mortgages and that mortgage markets can be linked to capital markets with very little subsidy.[37] The US Office of Management and Budget argues that the liquidity added to the mortgage markets by these organizations reduces mortgage rates by as much as 0.5 per cent, reducing the interest charges on a loan of US$100,000 by about US$12,000 over the life of a 30-year loan.[38] The achievement in the US has been an elastic supply of long-run funding from the capital markets for mortgage finance. The major innovation has been the mortgage-backed security (MBS), which works as follows:

> *An MBS is a 'pass-through' security. The issuer, typically a mortgage bank, passes the payment from a pool of mortgages (both principle and interest net of fee) through to ultimate investors who typically receive* pro rata *shares of the payments. The issuer also guarantees the payment of interest and principle even if the borrower defaults (the insurer is covered by the government insurance for almost all of the foreclosure costs) and Ginnie Mae guarantees timely payment even if the issuer does not make the payment.*[39]

Despite the success in the US, there remain risks that have to be managed.[40] The government in the US appears to have played an important long-term role and has been instrumental in supporting the formalization of the secondary market.

Figure 4.2

The unbundled mortgage delivery system

Source: Lea, 2000, p2

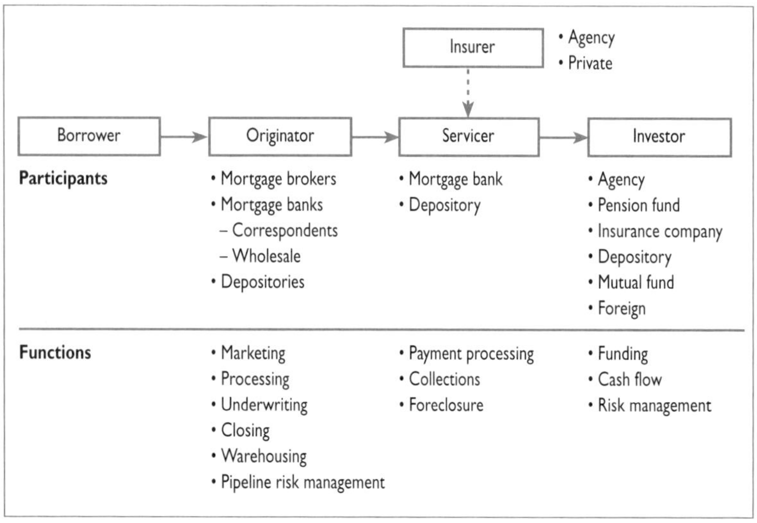

More fundamentally, it should be recognized that in the US, 80 per cent of the increase in homeownership rates occurred within a deposit-based system prior to the development of the secondary market.[41] Two further issues are relevant to considering the value of these strategies in the South.[42] First, the use of secondary markets depends upon demand from a market in long-term debt and/or deposits. Second, the efficient operation of secondary markets in the US requires the ability to use the house as an efficient loan security, which means that it is possible to foreclose and minimize losses if necessary.

Mortgage-backed securities are less significant outside of the US, although in some Northern countries there is an emerging market. In Europe, the UK was one of the first countries to have experience with the strategy and the first mortgage-backed security transaction was introduced in 1985.[43] Development was slow until 2000–2001 due, in the main, to the decline in the housing market during the late 1980s and early 1990s; and even after the rapid growth of the late 1990s, they still account for less that 5 per cent of total mortgage balances.[44] Their growth has been particularly linked to lenders in the sub-prime market and to banks' interest in preparing for diversification of funding sources.[45] However, mortgage-based securities may have limited potential in the UK for two reasons: first, the market is structured around variable rate mortgages and, hence, interest rate risks are greater; second, the retail lending institutions are not capital constrained and therefore are not looking for new sources of funds.[46]

There has been some interest in secondary market strengthening in the South, particularly in some Asian and Latin American countries. The Inter-American Development Bank (IADB) has sponsored a number of reports and argues that secondary markets are relevant to the expansion of housing finance, and particularly argues for a greater role by the private sector.[47] In respect of Asia, the International Finance Corporation held a seminar in 1998 to advance an understanding of how the capital markets could provide the required finance for an expansion of mortgage lending.[48] The World Bank also argues that mortgage securities are relevant to emerging markets to enable an increase in finance for housing investment through the capital markets.[49]

However, a number of detailed studies raise significant questions about the possible relevance of some secondary market strategies. In the case of Mexico, specific problems in relation to the development of secondary markets are macroeconomic instability; the inflation adjustment to the loan and the risks that it poses; poor credit assessment; inadequate services with high levels of default (due, in part, to few branches outside of major urban areas); and foreclosure processes that take several years.[50] Securitization in Chile began in 1994 and remained at a very low level. In 1999, there were new possibilities for expansion and the market grew to reach US$1200 million by August 2003.[51] While there are now six companies issuing securitized bonds in relation to housing, highly variable interest rates have reduced recent interest in this sector.[52] In Korea, mortgage-based securities became possible in 1997 following housing-sector reforms. Mortgage-based securitization was encouraged in 1999 with appropriate legislation and a regulatory framework. KoMoCo was then set up by the government to play a similar role to Fannie Mae/Freddie Mac in the US; by the end of 2002, it had issued about 80 per cent of all mortgage-backed securities in the Republic of Korea. Despite this encouragement, the MBS market remains small; 'commercial banks ... have dominated the mortgage market and have faced difficulties in investing funds rather than raising them'.[53]

A number of measures have been taken in Africa to strengthen secondary markets and, specifically, securitization. In Kenya, the draft national housing policy aims to create a secondary market to ensure additional capital from overseas and a reduction in the costs of borrowing.[54] Generally, mortgage bonds have not been widely used in sub-Saharan Africa, although there have been attempts in Ghana and, more recently, Kenya to raise finance in this way.[55]

A recent overview examines attempts to strengthen secondary markets in over 20 countries and looks in detail at those in Argentina, Colombia, Hong Kong, Hungary, Jordan and Republic of Korea.[56] Supported by other work,[57] a number of conclusions emerge:

- Notable successes have been achieved in Malaysia and Colombia, with multiple examples of standardized securities and an increase in funds for housing finance. Both examples are relatively simple bonds rather than more complex securitization models. Success is more likely with more simple forms of secondary market instruments. Other experiences are more limited.
- Macroeconomic stability is important. The experience in Argentina was developing well until the recent and rapid devaluation of the currency.
- Market demand from housing finance providers for wholesale funds is important and, as noted earlier, this has been lacking in the case of South Korea. The significance of this element is also reinforced by the experience in the UK, where the plentiful supply of deposits has constrained the scale of secondary market instruments.
- A demand for longer-term finance from would-be investors is also important, and this is lacking in some countries, such as Hong Kong.

State support for housing finance

A further and remaining source of finance, despite frequent criticisms on the grounds of economic efficiency and ineffectual targeting, is the state. Governments have, over many decades, intervened in housing markets with the intention of widening access to housing finance, and they continue to have a major role in housing finance through the continued use of subsidies. In general, these are designed to improve access to housing finance. This section concentrates on measures focusing primarily on assisting those in housing need through the commercialized housing finance market. Other measures, which are more reliant upon the direct state provision of housing (although they may use the commercial construction sector or specialist providers as a conduit) are discussed in Chapter 5. The division between these two strategies is a continuum, rather than a strict and unambiguous divide. Governments have explicitly sought to reach lower income households through mortgage finance, although, as argued below, they have rarely been successful.

In some cases, the scale of state support to higher and middle-income households through measures to extend homeownership (notably, interest rate subsidies) may significantly exceed more direct strategies to support housing improvements for lower income households.[58] However, whatever the specific outcomes, there is a difference between state policies to enhance housing finance markets and to extend opportunities for the purchase of dwellings, and housing policies directed at addressing the housing needs of low-income citizens.

There is a difference between policies to enhance housing finance markets and to extend opportunities for the purchase of dwellings

There are several motivations for state involvement. With regard to the welfare of households, motivations are, notably, to promote homeownership as a whole and to specifically address the needs of those with inadequate housing. The state may also have systemic interests to ensure that the financial markets for housing are stable. As noted above, in some cases state support is directly through state housing companies. However, in general, these have become increasingly commercially orientated in their use of finance. Box 4.5 summarizes the involvement of the state in the Philippines.

Although the emphasis with mortgage finance is on commercial provision, the use of subsidies is still prevalent

Box 4.4 Strategies to strengthen secondary markets in the US

The rise in the secondary market in the US during the 1970s and 1980s came about largely because of standardization of pools of mortgages brought on by three government-sponsored agencies: the Federal Home Loan Mortgage Corporation (Freddie Mac), the Federal National Mortgage Association (Fannie Mae) and for government-insured loans, the Government National Mortgage Association (Ginnie Mae). Annual sales of mortgages to these three institutions have risen from US$69 billion in 1980 to more than US$700 billion in 1998; they now own or are responsible for about half of the outstanding stock of single-family mortgages. It is these agencies that purchase mortgages and package them into securities (or fund them with debt), thereby enabling them to be traded easily with minimal risk of default.

Freddie Mac was created in 1970 to be a secondary market for thrifts. At that time it dealt with thrifts and Fannie Mae with mortgage bankers; but now both institutions deal with the same mortgage originators. It initiated the first mortgage-backed securities programme in 1970.

Fannie Mae was established during the 1930s to provide a secondary market for government-insured loans to households. During the 1970s, it switched to providing secondary conventional mortgage loans.

Ginnie Mae was created as a successor to the old Fannie Mae. Its purpose is to handle Fannie Mae policy-related tasks and provide a secondary market for government-insured loans. It also guarantees issuer payments on mortgage-backed securities, providing an extra level of insurance.

Source: Van Order, 2001, pp19–20.

Box 4.5 Government support for mortgage finance in the Philippines

In the Philippines, the government aims to address the needs of the lowest 50 per cent of income earners through the direct production of units by government, through the provision of public funds for private development and through end-user financing to entice the private sector to produce suitable housing. There are several significant state agencies that support housing finance. The Housing Guaranty Corporation provides mortgage insurance and guarantees in order to encourage private banks and financial institutions to grant housing loans on easy terms of payment. The National Home Mortgage Finance Corporation acts as a secondary market for housing mortgages. The National Housing Authority is specifically concerned with social housing. Finally, the Home Development Mutual Fund is a provident savings/pension fund for formal-sector workers. Increasingly, strategies have moved from being highly centralized to being more participatory, with the involvement of communities, local government and private-sector agencies in delivering housing. Measures continue to be taken to improve the supply of funds and the secondary mortgage market.

In housing finance, the government's role in the market remains that of a primary lender. Between 1993 and 2001, approximately 971,000 households gained homeownership through the National Shelter Programme. Fifty-one per cent of these obtained housing though private developers with loan finance provided through government programmes. About 13 per cent benefited from state-financed resettlement programmes, while a further 12 per cent secured dwellings through the community mortgage programme and other community programmes. Ownership through the presidential proclamations of public land for low-income housing accounted for a further 16 per cent. Despite such provision, however, the proportion living in informal settlements continues to rise.

Source: Ballesteros, 2002.

in some contexts. The popularity of attaching subsidies to finance continues, in part to meet the 'social goals and expectations of the middle and lower-middle classes'.[59] Their scale is often significant, even in countries in which commercial mortgage systems are advanced. In France, for example, during 1990, 23 per cent of mortgages still had a subsidy.[60] Such programmes are indicative of the support given to housing both for issues of social need and, more likely given the income groups that benefit from such measures, political popularity.

Table 4.3 summarizes common strategies to increase homeownership through the enhanced provision of finance. It draws upon experiences in the North and particularly Western Europe, although such strategies have been widely used in many other countries. One further strategy employed in some countries is the more direct involvement of the state in housing construction, with governments seeking to address housing needs by expanding the supply of suitable dwellings and/or lowering the price for owner occupiers. In the West European context, this strategy has not been significant, except in Spain, where banks were obliged to invest in housing at sub-market returns, with the cost reduction theoretically passed on to the ultimate occupant.[61] However, in some countries in the South it remains popular, although it has not often been effective at scale.

A more recent shift, discussed in Chapter 5, has been subsidies designed to augment the payment capacity of the poor (direct-demand subsidies). The strategy has been strongly associated with a number of countries, including Chile, where state-subsidized housing is a very significant component of new housing construction, with the government at least partially financing between 58 and 63 per cent of the total housing construction for each year between 1994 and 1997.[62] Of total construction, about 44 per cent was heavily financed and another 16 per cent had a less significant public contribution, being financed under the Unified Subsidy Programme and produced by the private sector on the open market.[63]

Table 4.3

Government measures to widen access to homeownership through finance

Scheme	Comments
Mortgage interest relief	Can be poorly targeted/regressive
	Can be capitalized into higher prices
Interest subsidies	Often a substitute for poor economic management
Housing savings scheme	Can be poorly targeted
	May be used as subsidized savings scheme and not used for housing
	Design can deal with these problems
Guarantees	Form of credit enhancement
	Provided by market in the UK
Subsidies for 'key' public-sector workers	Can crowd out private-sector workers and inflate prices
	May be more efficient (though possibly more costly) to vary wages by region
Intermediate tenures	Lower risk method of extending ownership

Source: Stephens, 2004.

Direct construction and loans

One of the most far-reaching systems of state intervention through direct construction has been used in the case of Singapore, where 96 per cent of the households are living in homeownership apartments (Box 4.6).[64] The strategy has been based on the provision of subsidized mortgage finance (primarily through the interest rate), combined with a dedicated supply of funds through already existing provident/pension funds.

The Singapore system appears to be a closed one in which the Housing and Development Board manages the construction (sometimes with subcontracts to the private sector) and the financing. Despite the accomplishments here, there are many other less successful attempts. Singapore was successful in part because it has one of the world's fastest growing economies, in part because the government owned so much land, so that land acquisition was not a problem (although compulsory purchase was used), and in part because there was little in-migration as the rural population was small. Nigeria is an example of how Southern governments have been committed to improving the housing situation in their countries, but have struggled to find effective policies. Between 1971 and 1995, the government actually built only 76,370 dwellings, 13 per cent of the units they intended to construct.[65] The problems can be explained thus:

> *Since the attainment of independence in 1960, and the subsequently intensified urban growth, there are some major distinct approaches to housing development and improvement in Nigeria. These include slum clearance and resettlement, public housing schemes, sites-and-services [projects], settlement upgrading and self-help housing. Apart from the last, these housing strategies are essentially public*

> *provider-orientated policies and made, at best, little impact on the housing programme... Of all the housing strategies, public direct housing was the most elaborately pursued and has cost the country billions of US dollars.*[66]

There are many further examples of failed public housing policies.[67] One similar problem was the National Housing Corporation in Kenya, whose production was also well below need, with only several thousand units a year.[68] Two parastatals in Côte d'Ivoire together constructed 41,000 units between 1960 and the 1980s before being wound up.[69] The public housing schemes generally involved completed units that were sold at a considerable discount. In one example from Nigeria, sale prices in one scheme completed during the mid 1990s were, at best, half the costs of construction and, at worst, 20 per cent of these costs.[70] Such strategies were a significant transfer of public funds to the few who received the dwellings, and they did little for the many who remained without adequate housing.

There have been further attempts by some governments at more active collaboration in the production and allocation of housing using housing finance – for example, part-equity initiatives or rent to purchase. In the North, there have been a number of targeted assistance programmes for first-time buyers, either as direct subsidy or shared equity arrangements.[71] Some Northern governments have targeted assistance on certain groups. In the UK, the problem of recruiting 'key' public-sector workers became acute in high-demand and high-cost areas, such as London.[72] This has led the government to introduce schemes to subsidize entry into homeownership for defined groups of public-sector workers. Critics of such schemes suggest (variously) that private-sector workers will be crowded out of the market, and that much greater regional pay variation in the public sector would tackle the root of the problem. However, regional pay variation is also likely to be more expensive than subsidizing housing for new recruits, as higher pay would be paid to existing workers, not just the new recruits. Intermediate tenures, such as 'right of occupancy' housing in Finland and 'shared ownership' in the UK are intended to widen access to some form of (quasi) homeownership without excessive risk to households.

Taxation-related incentives

Northern governments may provide direct subsidies (grants and interest rate concessions) and/or fiscal incentives and/or loan insurance.[73] In many West European countries, mortgage interest payments are, to some extent, tax deductible.[74] Generally, this instrument is seen as being inefficient (indeed, counterproductive as at least some of the relief will have been capitalized into higher house prices) and poorly targeted. In the Netherlands, tax deductibility is unlimited; but other countries have sought to limit the level of tax relief. For example, in Finland the tax treatment of mortgage interest relief has been restructured. Both the UK and France abolished mortgage interest relief during recent decades, a policy shift facilitated by falling nominal interest rates which reduced the burden of repayments for households. However, they continue in a number of countries, including India.[75]

There are other favourable treatments in the tax regime, with imputed rental incomes being untaxed in most European countries (except Italy) and capital gains on owners' principal house also being untaxed (although not in Japan).[76]

Box 4.6 Financing homeownership in Singapore

In Singapore, the public housing programme began prior to self-government in 1959. However, the Singapore Investment Trust (established by the British colonial government) failed to meet the housing needs of the poor. The new government was committed to improving housing, and it began during the early 1960s on a relatively small scale by providing basic rental units for the poor who were living in congested urban shop houses and as squatters. The flats, built by the Housing and Development Board, were let out at monthly rentals of between US$20–$40 and were within the paying ability of 75 per cent of the working population. In 1964, homeownership was introduced and flats were sold on 99-year leases. Once the state allowed would-be homeowners to use their savings in the Central Provident Fund to help finance their purchase, the scheme took off. The fund is a state-managed, tax-exempted compulsory social security fund for all citizens to which employees and employers contribute. The prices of the flats are subsidized so that they remain within the affordability of the majority population. The interest rate charged is 0.1 per cent above the rate paid on savings.

Among the mortgage financing policies, the significant point is that purchasers of public housing are allowed to use their provident fund savings to pay for their flats. The 20 per cent down payment may be drawn from their accumulated savings, and monthly repayments may be deducted directly as well. The board provides the mortgages. With this facility, the entire process constitutes an internal fund transfer without involving any conventional banking process. The board receives finance from the government and is charged an interest rate 0.1 per cent below the mortgage rate charged by the board for its loans. As of 31 March 2002, the total mortgage financing loans on the board's books was 63 billion Singapore dollars, of which 51 billion Singapore dollars was lending at concessionary rates. By 2001/2002, an estimated 85 per cent of the 3.3 million population in Singapore were living in Housing and Development Board dwellings (96 per cent of which are owned by their occupants and 4 per cent of which are rented).

Source: Chin Beng, 2002, pp99–114.

Interest rate subsidies

Interest rate subsidies have been a popular way of enhancing housing finance affordability. Occasionally, this policy has been criticized as acting as a substitute for prudent macro-economic management. Moreover, in the present world of flexible rates, it can look outdated; when market interest rates fell in Spain during the 1990s, they actually fell below the level at which the 'subsidized' loan rate had been set, giving rise to calls for prepayment without penalty.[77] A similar phenomenon was observed in Japan during 1996.[78] Interest rate subsidies in some countries in Europe may be associated with savings schemes for housing investments, the best known of which is the German *Bauspar* system. However, in practice, they extend well beyond this system.

Interest rate subsidies have been a popular way of enhancing housing finance affordability

Moreover, interest rate subsidies may not be effective in targeting help where it is most needed. While the data in Table 4.4 suggests that in the Philippines there is a programme which at least goes some way to meeting the housing needs of the poor, the main mechanism for reaching

Programmes	Income group		
	Low (%)	Middle (%)	High (%)
UHLP	38	33	29
EHLP	12	67	21
CMP	39	49	12
GLAD	17	56	27
LTAP	27	54	19

Notes: UHLP: Unified Home Lending Programme, open to members of the Home Development Mutual Fund (HDMF)
EHLP: Expanded Home Lending Programme, open to members of the Home Development Mutual Fund
CMP: Community Mortgage Programme (see Chapter 7)
GLAD: Group Land Acquisition Support Programme (similar to CMP)
LTAP: Land Tenurial Assistance Programme (similar to CMP for HDMF members)
Source: Llanto and Oberta, reproduced in Ballesteros, 2002, p18.

Table 4.4

The distribution of housing subsidies in the Philippines

down to low-income groups is subsidized loans to formal workers through the provident funds. A more detailed analysis highlights the distributional implications of such strategies, and the conclusions of such an analysis are summarized in Table 4.4, which depicts the distribution of housing subsidies within five housing finance programmes. The success of higher income groups in capturing even the community-based housing finance programmes – the Community Mortgage Programme (CMP), the Group Land Acquisition Support Programme (GLAD) and the Land Tenurial Assistance Programme (LTAP) – is notable. An estimated 77 per cent of the country cannot afford a loan from the formal sector even at a subsidized interest rate of 9 per cent.[79] It is such findings that have resulted in a critical perspective on the provision of interest rate subsidies in housing finance.[80] However, despite a professional acknowledgement that they are a poor tool for assisting the poor to secure housing finance and improve housing, their popularity remains significant.

The case against interest rate subsidies has been strongly made. It has been argued that direct subsidies are a preferred way of offering assistance with housing costs as they can be more precisely targeted to those in need. Interest rate subsidies inevitably favour those who can afford loans and larger subsidies go to those able to afford larger loans. Although some programmes seek to minimize this problem by offering the lowest rates only to smaller loans (for example, in the Philippines and Thailand), the essence of this critique remains. If one cannot afford a loan, one does not receive a subsidy. A related concern is that where

subsidized rates are offered only by state housing finance enterprises, they prevent the development of a commercial market. Households wait for access to a low-interest loan rather than pay a commercial price, and the commercial housing finance market does not develop because it cannot compete. Governments have tried to minimize this problem by attaching low rates to smaller loans and/or designated categories of workers.

Despite such arguments, interest rate subsidies appear to continue to be widely used.[81] Box 4.7 elaborates upon the example of Mexico where the World Bank estimates implicit subsidies (due to lower interest rates) to be 26 times the value of explicit subsidies.[82] In Sweden, the government has reduced interest rate subsidies from 36 billion Swedish kronor in 1993 to (a still sizeable) 7 billion Swedish kronor in 1999.[83] In the Philippines, four general types of subsidies are used, with interest rate subsidies being overwhelmingly the most significant and accounting for 90 per cent of the value of housing subsidies; other types are land cost subsidies (5.1 per cent), tax exemption (4.5 per cent) and cash subsidies (0.4 per cent).[84] Ironically, little of this is directed at the poor; the Community Mortgage Programme receives an estimated 3.7 per cent of the total subsidy related to interest rates. In Tunisia, subsidized loans are provided to low-income households (those earning less than three times the minimum wage), with a state-owned bank administering all subsidized loans, which account for 80 per cent of all mortgages.[85] In this case, the interest rate is between 3 and 5 per cent – about half that of non-subsidized loans.[86] In India, the mortgage rate of interest was 15 to 15.5 per cent in 1998, while the poor could get access to subsidized rates of 9 to 11 per cent.[87] In Hungary, the subsidized mortgage rate was 4 to 5 per cent in 2002, while the market rate was 18 per cent, with an estimated cost equal to 2 per cent of the government budget.[88]

Securing stability: insurance and guarantees

In addition to direct assistance to households to increase the affordability of housing finance, governments have sought to ensure the stability of the system and to reduce the risks for lending institutions when they extend services to lower income households. As the greater availability of finance has been reflected in growing levels of ownership occupation, risks have increased.

Mortgage insurance is provided in English-speaking countries in the North through a variety of mechanisms.[89] Governments may specifically provide guarantees in order to extend mortgage lending.[90] Within the 15 member states of the EU, private insurance mechanisms are well developed only in the UK, and elsewhere the state takes the lead.[91] For example, in the Dutch system a national insurance scheme, backed by government, has fulfilled a similar function since the mid 1990s: the borrower pays a supplement based on the value of their mortgage, which is paid into an insurance fund that is ultimately backed by the state.[92] Similar trends to strengthen risk management can be seen in New Zealand where the government, in September 2003, introduced a mortgage insurance scheme to encourage the private sector to extend finance to low-income households that are

Box 4.7 Mexico: interest rate subsidies

The bulk of Mexico's housing subsidies come in the form of below-market interest rates – off-budget subsidies mainly provided by Instituto del Fondo Nacional de la Vivienda para los Trabajadores (INFONAVIT) (a fund financed by a compulsory 5 per cent contribution from all private-sector workers). In 2000, interest rates subsidies from INFONAVIT amounted to an estimated US$2.2 billion (based on the net present value of the implicit interest rate subsidy for the life of the loans originated in 2000, with the implicit interest rate subsidy being the difference between the actual interest rates and an estimate of the real rate on government funds). The highest subsidies are offered on a per credit basis and increase to US$9000 per borrower. Although all formally employed households pay into these pension funds in principle, the subsidies go mainly to the moderate-income households who can afford to take mortgages necessary for a commercially produced finished house. These below-market interest rates account for about 75 per cent of all mortgages.
Source: World Bank, 2004a, p5.

'marginally out of reach of homeownership'.[93] One consequence is that on loans of up to NZ$150,000 no deposit is required and on loans between NZ$150–$280,000, only 5 per cent deposit is required.[94] While most loan insurance has been intended to protect lenders (allowing them to make loans to higher risk groups), new products are being developed to enable borrowers to insure against falls in value and loss of income.[95]

In the US and Canada, governments have developed complex systems of insurance that have supported financial flows into a system for housing based around mortgage finance. Hence, for example, the Government National Mortgage Association (Ginnie Mae) established in 1968 guarantees the payments from a number of mortgage providers so that their loans can be securitized and sold on, thereby returning cash to the housing finance system (see Box 4.4)

Mortgage insurance has been generally thought to be too risky in the transition countries, although a self-managing guarantee fund was established in Estonia in 2000.[96] Loan guarantees are being developed in Estonia, Lithuania and the Slovak Republic.[97] In the North, the South and transition countries, the role of the government (as opposed to the private sector) has been particularly important in providing support.[98] Table 4.5 summarizes the situation in a number of countries. Experience suggests that for mortgage insurance to be offered effectively, certain prerequisites are necessary; notably, there must be effective foreclosure procedures, a competitive banking sector and an efficient mortgage lending industry.[99]

In addition to planned subsidies, there are also those that occur when governments move to support commercial lending institutions in danger of collapse. For example, in Colombia:

> *... the crisis that threatened to bring down the whole financial system in 1999 was partially resolved by compensating middle-income families in default on their mortgage payments. A financial bail-out in Colombia in 1999 diverted US$2.5 billion in debt relief to 800,000 middle-class mortgage holders. When it was recalled that the Colombian government was providing housing subsidies to poor families of only US$75 million per annum, the limited resources devoted to the housing subsidy programme become obvious.*[100]

The Colombian government faced considerable problems at that time, with a housing loan system that had been devised during the early 1970s and a group of specialist savings and housing corporations that were struggling with inflation and increasing real interest rates during the 1990s.[101] Gross domestic product (GDP) growth was negative during the late 1990s and households struggled to repay rising repayments. Overdue mortgages were about 3 to 4 per cent of total mortgages in 1995; but this rose to over 18 per cent in 1999. Faced by legal as well as financial challenges, the state sought to recreate the sector. At the same time, the mortgage lending institutions had become progressively less specialist, with a group of more diversified lenders. A similar rescue process was undertaken by the Mexico government during the mid 1990s.[102]

Country	Type of mortgage insurance (MI)	Loan coverage
US: Federal Housing Authority and Veterans Administration (VA); seven private MI companies	Public and private	Public: 100% Private: 20–30%
Canada: Canada Mortgage and Housing Corporation (CMHC); private MI company	Public and private	Public: 100% Private: <100%
Australia: three MI companies	Private: 1 public until 1997	100% or less
New Zealand: three MI companies	Private	20–30%
UK: numerous general insurance companies	Private MI insurers and mortgage indemnity insurance	<100%
France	Public	100%
Italy	Private	20–40%
Spain	Private	20–40%
Netherlands	Public	Public: 100%
Sweden	Public	Varies: less than 100%
South Africa	NGO	20%
Hong Kong, Special Administrative Region of China	Public/private	30% or less
Israel	Private	20–30%
Lithuania	Public	100%
Kazakhstan (expected)	Public	30%
Latvia (expected)	Public	22%
India (expected)	Public/private/international finance corporation (IFC)	Not available
Thailand (expected)	Public	Not available

Source: Merrill and Whiteley, 2003, p12.

Table 4.5

Mortgage default insurance

REGIONAL ANALYSIS

This section assesses trends in provision of housing finance in a number of regions around the world. There do not appear to be any single sources of data about the significance of mortgage finance for homeownership across the world.

Tables 4.6 and 4.7 consider homeowners and the significance of residential debt to GDP, respectively.

Homeownership rates vary considerably, as indicated in Table 4.6. Such differences reflect many factors, one of which is the availability of finance. Interpretation is not straightforward. For example, low rates in Germany reflect, among other things, the difficulties of securing finance and the relatively high proportion of saving that is required. One recent survey provides data for the percentage of owner occupiers with mortgages in countries of the EU; in Greece, only 25 per cent of owner occupiers have mortgages, while in Belgium the figure is 56 per cent and in the Netherlands, 85 per cent.[103] In Australia and the US, the figure is 45 per cent and 62 per cent, respectively.[104]

For mortgage insurance to be offered effectively, certain prerequisites are necessary: effective foreclosure procedures, a competitive banking sector and an efficient mortgage lending industry

However, high rates in many Southern countries also reflect the high cost and related lack of opportunities for loan finance. In this case there are few alternatives to informal and, sometimes, illegal forms of incremental development. As noted before, without alternatives many build incrementally in the South using savings and, in some cases, available sources of smaller loans. While mortgage finance as a way of acquiring dwellings is relatively common in the North, it is less common elsewhere in the world.

Table 4.6

Homeownership rates (percentage)

Argentina [i]	68	1991	India	82	1990
Austria	57	2001	Ireland	77	2002
Australia	71	1998	Italy	80	2002
Belgium	68	2001	Japan	60	1998
Bolivia [i]	67	2001	Latvia	74	2002
Brazil [i]	70	1991	Luxembourg	67	2002
Canada	65	1998	Mexico	84	1999
Chile [i]	63	2002	Netherlands	53	2001
Colombia [i]	68	1985	New Zealand [ii]	68	2001
Costa Rica [i]	65	2000	Panama [i]	79	2000
Czech Republic	47	2001	Paraguay [i]	74	1992
Denmark	51	2002	Peru [i]	72	1992
Ecuador [i]	68	1990	Poland	55	2002
Finland	58	2002	Portugal	75	2003
France	56	2002	Republic of Korea [iii]	54	2002
Germany	42	2002	Spain	83	2003
Greece	83	2001	Sweden	61	2000
Guatemala [i]	65	1981	UK	70	2002
Honduras [i]	80	1988	US	68	2002
Hong Kong, SAR of China [iii]	52	1998	Uruguay [i]	63	1996
Hungary	92	2000	Venezuela [i]	78	2001

Source: unless otherwise indicated, Proxenos, 2002, p3, and European Mortgage Federation, 2004. i ECLAC, 2003. ii Stuart et al, 2004. iii Ha, 2002a.

Table 4.6 gives no indication of trends and, despite the state policies noted in the previous subsection, it should not be assumed that homeownership is rising. For example, homeownership levels in New Zealand have been falling despite financial deregulation from the mid 1980s onwards.[105] The trends in Western Europe are less clear (see Table 4.7).[106] During the last decade, demand in some Northern countries has been supported by large-scale lending and relatively low interest rates. Other factors encouraging homeownership in the North have been growing affluence and longer life expectancy.[107] Changing household structure has also had implications for the scale and nature of housing. Such increasing demand for housing has been countered by rising real housing prices (see 'The price of housing', below).

Table 4.7 shows residential debt as a percentage of GDP and offers an assessment of the significance of mortgage loans for national economies. For Northern countries, these figures are high, generally over 25 per cent, notable exceptions being Italy and Greece. For both the transition economies and Latin America, figures are considerably lower, indicative of the much lower incidence of mortgage borrowing.

The North

Homeownership is now the majority tenure across Western Europe, with only a few exceptions – notably in Germany. Nevertheless, levels of owner occupation vary considerably and are highest among some of the Southern European

Table 4.7

Residential debt as a percentage of GDP

Argentinai	4.0	2002	Ireland	45.0	2003
Austria	26.4	2003	Italy	13.3	2003
Belgium	28.5	2003	Latvia	8.3	2003
Bolivia [ii]	8.5	2004	Luxembourg	33.4	2003
Brazil [i]	2.0	2002	Mexicoi	4.0	2002
Chile [i]	12.0	2002	Panama [ii]	24.4	2004
Colombia [i]	7.0	2002	Perui	2.0	2002
Czech Republic	4.5	2003	Poland	4.7	2003
Denmark	87.5	2003	Portugal	50.6	2003
Estonia	5.0	2001	Slovenia	3.0	2001
Finland	35.6	2003	Slovakia	3.0	2001
France	24.7	2003	South Korea [iii]	13.4	2001
Germany	54.3	2003	Spain	42.1	2003
Greece	17.4	2003	Sweden	50.0	2003
Hong Kong [iv]	31.0	1998	UK	70.4	2003
Hungary	7.8	2003	US	71.0	2003
			Uruguay	7.0	2004

Notes: i Forero, 2004, p32.
ii Rojas, 2004; this is mortgage lending, not residential debt.
iii Mortgage debt to gross national product (GNP); Lee, 2003, p24.
iv Lamoreaux, 1998, p51.
Data for Austria and the Czech Republic includes non-residential mortgage loans and Portugal includes loans to individuals for housing purchase only.
Source: Yasui, 2002b, p18; European Mortgage Federation, 2004, p7.

countries (Spain and Italy), where homeownership can be described as being 'dominant' (see Table 4.8). Homeownership is relatively high in several other countries, notably the UK, at around 70 per cent. In a cluster of countries, such as France, the Netherlands, Denmark and Sweden, homeownership has been established as the 'majority' tenure without being especially high or dominant. Among members of the EU, homeownership in Germany still 'lags' behind the other countries (outside the 15 member states of the EU, but within Western Europe, similarly low levels of homeownership exist in Switzerland.)

There is little evidence of convergence in homeownership levels, either in the sense that they are moving in the same *direction*, or that they are converging towards similar *levels*.[108] As a result, since 1980, there has been strong growth in homeownership in Germany and the Netherlands, starting from relatively low bases, but also in Italy, starting from one of the highest bases. Finland exhibited a marked fall in homeownership levels, which is attributable to the coincidence of a very severe property market slump with an extremely severe economic recession partly linked to the loss of trade with the former Soviet Union. Sweden also experienced a severe housing market slump during the early 1990s, which seems to have contributed to a stagnation of homeownership levels. In the four other Organisation for Economic Co-operation and Development (OECD) countries for which data is reported in Table 4.9, levels of homeownership are relatively high and increased significantly in the US, but changed little in the other nations.

It is difficult to detect a consistent trend in mortgage lending despite a convergence in mortgage rates both within the Euro zone and outside it.[109] In general, strong growth in mortgage lending has been experienced; but there is little consistency between these countries. The Netherlands stands out as having experienced a huge rise in mortgage lending, linked to deregulation in the mortgage market during the 1990s; this took place somewhat later than in Scandinavia and the UK, while arguably it has still to occur fully in Germany, France and Italy. Having experienced big rises in mortgage lending during the 1980s, the process was thrown into reverse in Sweden, and between the years selected, it stagnated in Finland.[110] In fact, in each of these countries, a slump was followed by renewed and strong growth, so Table 4.10 is slightly misleading in this respect. Table 4.11 summarizes trends in other OECD countries, and they are also positive – although the scale of increase differs considerably.

In 2003, the European market, as a whole, continued to grow with the total value of residential mortgage debt increasing by 7.4 per cent, a little below the ten-year average of 8 per cent.[111] The total volume of mortgage loans in Europe at the end of 2003 was US$3.4 trillion.[112] This figure has grown rapidly and it now accounts for 42 per cent of the EU's GDP. This rapid expansion in lending has been encouraged by lower interest rates (both because of currency convergence and low global rates); in particular, this has helped to increase borrowing in countries such as Spain, Greece and Ireland.[113] However, it should be remembered that the rise in the volume of lending is not necessarily associated with increasing access, as one further trend has been rising house prices, with capital gains for current homeowners and increasing difficulties for those seeking to become homeowners for the first time. The final part of this chapter discusses the rise in house prices during the late 1990s and the early 21st century.

In the US, homeownership grew on average, as did income, throughout the largely prosperous 1990s and now stands at a record high. The homeownership level has, in fact, become a significant measurement of economic health.[114] However, data from the US Census Bureau and American Housing Survey's (AHS) most recent publication indicate that affordability constraints are significant. Box 4.8 shows a measure of success of government policy in reaching down to lower income households with Federal Housing Administration (FHA) support through insurance assistance. Almost 52 per cent of Fannie Mae's mortgage purchases went to low- and moderate-income (LMI) household mortgages in 2002.[115] Likewise, Freddie Mac's LMI mortgage purchases reached 51.4 per cent of its total 2002 purchases.[116] Furthermore, 2 million household units in 2002, or close to 70 per cent of the units that qualified toward Fannie Mae's LMI performance, served low-income families (those earning 80 per cent or less of area median income). Freddie Mac had similar success, purchasing 1.4 million mortgages from low-income household units, or roughly 69 per cent of its total qualifying LMI mortgage purchases.[117]

Transition countries

The transition countries face a particular problem in that commercial housing finance markets were previously non-existent. The shift in political systems resulted in considerable and continuing housing problems, with very low levels of housing construction and, in some cases, deliberate attempts to encourage building.

Table 4.8

Levels of owner occupation in Western Europe, circa 1990–2000

Country	circa 1990	circa 2000	Change
Dominant			
Spain	78	82 (1999)	+4
Italy	74 (1993)	80 (2002)	+6
High			
UK	66 (1992)	70 (2002)	+4
Finland	71 (1992)	64 (2001)	–7
Majority			
Netherlands	45	53 (1998)	+8
Sweden	55 (1991)	55 (1997)	0
Denmark	55	53 (1999)	–2
France	54	56 (2002)	+2
Low			
West Germany	37 (1987)	46 (2003)	+9
Germany	–	44 (2003)	not available

Source: Stephens, 2004.

Table 4.9

Levels of owner occupation in four Organisation for Economic Co-operation and Development (OECD) countries

Country	1990	2003	Change
Australia	72	70	–2
Canada	63	65.2	+2.2
Japan	61	62	+1
US	63.95	68.25	+4.3

Source: IMF, 2004, p73.

Country	Mortgage debt (percentage of GDP) 1990	2003	Change
Dominant			
Spain	11	42	+31
Italy	4	13	+9
High			
UK	53	64	+11
Finland	32 (1995)	32	0
Majority			
Netherlands	40	100	+60
Sweden	60 (1995)	50	-5
Denmark	59 (1995)	74	+15
France	20	25	+5
Low			
Germany	43	54	+11

Source: Stephens, 2004.

Table 4.10

Trends in mortgage lending in Western Europe, 1990–2003

There has been state support for the development of housing finance systems, with the expectation that the commercial sector will become an increasingly significant provider. Unfortunately, much of this support has been to the benefit of higher income groups who are the only ones able to afford such finance. The Slovak and Czech Republic governments pay 30 to 50 per cent of their 'budget subsidies to the *Bausparkasse* institution supporting ... middle-class savings'.[118] Tax incentives have also been used to encourage homeownership in the transition countries.[119] In the Czech Republic, Hungary, Poland and Slovakia, the German and Austrian *Bausparkassen* model was used with interest rate subsidies.[120] However, the scale of support in Hungary and the Czech Republic was estimated to cost 2 per cent or more of GDP.[121] The cost led to concerns and the subsidies were reduced. Special funds, such as the Housing Fund of Slovenia (set up in 1991), have been established to extend subsidized loans both for individual construction and for the construction of social housing by local communities and non-profit organizations.[122] For example, the Estonian Housing Foundation assists young families to secure housing. In a number of countries, such funds were established with the proceeds of privatization.[123] In Poland, direct and indirect subsidies have reached 1.3 per cent of GDP.[124] The costs of such measures are considerable and the effectiveness is difficult to evaluate at present.

While the scale of home loans is equivalent to 20 to 60 per cent of GDP in many Northern countries (see Table 4.7), volumes of housing loans are low in the transition countries. However, there are indications that housing loan markets are growing rapidly; for example, in Estonia, the scale of housing loans doubled between 1997 and 2000 and in the Czech Republic the scale of loans grew more than sixfold during the same period.[125] During 2002 and 2003, mortgage lending grew particularly strongly in Hungary, Poland and Latvia (by more than 85 per cent).[126] The growth in mortgage lending in Hungary is such that residential mortgage loans as a proportion of GDP increased from 1.3 per cent in 1998 to 6.6 per cent in 2002.[127] However, these loans have only limited reach as they are generally short term (less than ten years), with high interest rates (sometimes with repayments in hard currencies) and offered for a relatively small proportion of the value of the dwelling.[128] As such, they only address the needs of the higher income earners.

Table 4.11

Trends in mortgage lending in four OECD countries, 1990–2003

Country	Mortgage debt (percentage of GDP) 1990	2003	Change
Australia	19.90	57.30	+37.4
Canada	39.1	42.79	+3.69
Japan	30.26	36.4	+6.14
US	44.59	63.73	+19.14

Source: IMF, 2004, p73.

There have been a number of attempts to address the systemic problems related to the lack of housing finance. A number of the national housing agencies that were established in the transitional countries during the 1990s were, essentially, mechanisms to use donor finance to address urgent housing problems.[129] It was anticipated that once commercial finance moved in to fill the gap, the role of such agencies could shift to ensure sufficient secondary finance. However, while growth in housing finance is rapid in some countries, general uncertainty, falling house prices, aversion to debt and social expectations that the parents will provide accommodation remain a significant deterrent.[130]

There are two distinct housing finance systems that are developing in the transition countries – one that is similar to Southern European countries and one that shares characteristics with the German system.[131] The first system is associated with high levels of homeownership, with a housing finance system that has yet to develop. Countries in this group include Hungary, Slovenia and Lithuania. The second group includes the Czech Republic, Poland, Slovakia, Estonia and Latvia, all of whom have adopted legislation to support mortgage bonds.

The privatization process that took place resulted in the transfer of significant numbers of dwellings into private hands. However, despite the subsequent increase in homeownership, the financial systems needed for such ownership have not developed. One major reason for delay is that the necessary legal systems and structures to support mortgage finance are not in place. Title registration, for example, can take more than one year.[132] In some cases, property rights are associated with uncertainty due to property restitution initiatives; even where this only involves a small number of households, the associated uncertainty is still significant.[133] There are further problems with regard to land rights faced by the countries formed by the break-up of Yugoslavia, partly associated with the war.[134]

Owner occupation (see Table 4.7) is now close to or above 90 per cent in Hungary, Bulgaria, Estonia and Romania, while in Poland, Slovakia and Slovenia it is above 70 per cent.[135] However, to some extent this reflects the transfer of housing stock from the state to residents. For example, in Southeastern Europe, some 15 per cent of the total public housing stock was privatized to sitting tenants.[136] Generally, in the transition countries, there is a relatively large housing stock, but poor construction and, now, poor maintenance.[137] While the state has pulled out of construction, the private sector has not yet filled the gap, partly because there has been no housing finance for purchase. One indication of the problem is that, while in most EU countries between four to seven dwellings were completed for every 1000 inhabitants in 1998, in the transition countries the figure was two or less, except for Slovenia (2.5 dwellings).[138]

The South

The problems of affordability in the South are considerable. As noted above, high levels of homeownership can be misleading because while many own their homes, they are illegal and/or informal. The housing price to average income ratio in Southern countries is considerably worse than in the North. While house prices are four times average incomes in the developed world, the ratio is just under six in Latin America and the Caribbean, seven in oriental Asia, almost ten in the rest of Asia and more than ten in Africa. This subsection makes some general comments about problems that are fairly universal before looking in more detail at what is happening in specific regions within the South.

The supply of mortgages in Southern countries has been limited by a large number of factors. First, in general, there is a lack of supply of long-term funding, even in those Southern countries in which financial markets are beginning to 'emerge'.[139] This is related to many factors, including low incomes that barely cover subsistence needs for a considerable proportion of the population, a lack of formal financial institutions that can capture people's savings, and macroeconomic instability that deters households from holding savings with institutions, such as pension funds that have a particular interest in long-term finance. Low incomes and macroeconomic instability prevent institutions from developing to address problems and to facilitate the flow of long-term funds.[140] The recent financial crises have had negative impacts upon the formal housing finance systems in a number of countries and have particularly deterred commercial provision of mortgage finance. However, there are signs of a recovery in lending in both Asian and Latin American countries. It should also be recognized that (as discussed earlier) secondary markets have not developed to any large extent in a number of countries because there was no shortage of retail funds for mortgage lending.

Second, urban land and property development and urban livelihoods (labour markets) are associated with a high degree of informality that does not fit easily with the requirements of mortgage finance. The property market has not favoured mortgage systems because of uncertain property titles and difficulties in using the property as collateral, and the difficulties with which foreclosure can take place. With respect to the latter point, in some countries, there are multiple barriers to eviction that can be exemplified by political pressures on courts to restrict eviction – for example, in Zimbabwe during the early 1990s.[141] For many homeowners in the South, titles are problematic as formal registration systems may be lacking and there may be multiple claims on the land. The relevance of legal property titles to the scale of economic development and, notably, to the development of capitalism has recently been emphasized.[142] The argument is that property titles are essential if assets are to be used as productive wealth. As a consequence of this work, there has been a greater interest in titling during recent years. Box 4.9 summarizes the findings of research on a state programme that issued land titles in Peru and the relationship of such titles to the release of mortgage finance. The research took place seven years after the introduction of this policy.

The findings from Peru clearly indicate that legal title alone is unlikely to secure large-scale lending. There is growing evidence that titling programmes are only one part of what is needed to improve the definition of property rights; titling is often expensive and may be disputed.[143] A

Box 4.8 The expansion of homeownership in the US

A sample survey of loan originations made in 2002 by the US leading home mortgage lender (Wells Fargo Home Mortgage) provides further clarity on US Federal Housing Administration (FHA) clientele. From a survey size of 173,541 loans, 21 per cent (or 36,474) of originated loans were FHA insured and the remaining 79 per cent were conventional mortgages (uninsured by federal government agencies). Of FHA-insured mortgages, 35 per cent were made to moderate-income borrowers or borrowers who were purchasing a home in a neighbourhood where the median income was below 80 per cent the area median. Another 14 per cent of FHA-insured mortgages were extended to low-income households (those whose income is less than 50 per cent the area median or whose home purchase is in a neighbourhood where the median income was below 50 per cent the area median). Overall, the study implies that just less than half, or 49 per cent, of FHA-insured mortgages reach low- and moderate-income households. The conventional mortgage market only reaches 28 per cent of the population (for example, 9 per cent to low income and 19 per cent to moderate income).

Source: Carolini, 2004, p8.

Box 4.9 Land titles and mortgage finance in Peru

The policy to legalize property was established by the Peruvian government in 1996 through the Urban Property Rights Programme. A commission to legalize informal property was created and more than 1 million title deeds were distributed by 2000. The assumption was that this would enable the poor to access loans and thereby improve their standard of living. In order to maximize the potential, the commission established an information centre and offered training workshops in the use of credit for microenterprise development (although it should be noted that the government had previously legalized squatter settlements and the commission was speeding up rather than initiating a process).

There are a number of categories of insecure tenure and inadequate titles in the country. Clearly, not everyone was entitled to receive a land title. Generally, owners of unauthorized housing (those in public housing but who have not yet been given title deeds) and those living in low-income settlements which either began life as squatter settlements and which are in the process of regularization, or those which are illegal subdivisions (from agricultural land) are entitled to benefit from this policy. In the case of squatting on private land, the granting of title deeds takes longer because the commission seeks an agreement for the purchase of the land between the squatters and owners.

Taking into account all of those able to claim a land title, between 1996 and 2002, 1,269,194 title deeds were awarded, almost half of which were in metropolitan Lima. However, many of those living in squatter settlements who are in the process of improving their settlements were already reasonably confident of their tenure security. While they did not have effective possession of a title deed, improvements (both self-help and investments from service providers) had not waited on such a legal title. Perhaps as a consequence, there was very little take-up of mortgage finance. Up to 2002, 17,324 families in Peru who had obtained title deeds from the commission had gained access to mortgage loans, some 1.3 per cent of the total title deeds allocated during the process. This evidence suggests that the poor are as scared of borrowing from the banks as the banks are reluctant to lend to the poor.

Source: Calderón, 2004.

healthy housing market may exist without titling.[144] In relation to housing finance, a critical point (elaborated upon in Box 4.9) is that the granting of title may not necessarily mean that the title can be used to secure loans because, for example, formal employment may be required to obtain credit.[145] Thus, titles are valuable; but they do not necessarily 'unlock' capital.[146]

However, it is recognized that problems of titles have made foreclosure difficult and deterred lending. Overlapping customary and Western land tenure systems may further exacerbate the problem in some countries. In addition to improvements in titling, one element of housing policy reform now ongoing in some Latin American countries, including Chile, Costa Rica, Colombia, Ecuador, Guatemala and Peru, are legal changes to facilitate the recovery of collateral.[147] In Latin America, there has been a shift towards land reform and more effective land titling and land registration, which, in turn, enables more land to be used as collateral to secure loans.[148] Limited ownership rights may reduce the ability of the poor to transfer their assets.[149] However, other factors are also important. In South Africa, the ability to secure a mortgage to purchase a property in a low-income settlement may be prevented by factors other than a clear title, such as insufficient income by the purchaser, lack of formal employment and 'red-lining' (the refusal to issue mortgages in specific areas) due to generalized problems of foreclosure.[150] The informality of incomes is not highlighted in the general literature, although it did emerge as significant in research to understand the low take-up of loans in Peru and South Africa, and it also appears to be significant in Panama.[151] As discussed in 'Housing finance, affordability and lower income households', this can be a relatively significant barrier preventing mortgage lending to certain households in the North.

Low incomes and macro-economic instability prevent institutions from facilitating the flow of long-term funds

A third and further barrier is the low level of income relative to the cost of complete dwellings. There are generally two related problems: households cannot afford the deposits (which are often large as a result of the risk assessment of the financial institutions) because they have not been able to accumulate this quantity of cash, and they cannot afford to repay the loan due to their low incomes. The first problem is, in part, related to attempts by the lending institutions to reduce their risks (see Table 4.16). Lenders can reduce risk by offering to restrict the loan to a smaller proportion of the value of the dwelling. As shown in Chapter 5, a number of countries (notably, in Latin America) have introduced subsidy programmes that offer capital grants to address this problem and enable the would-be homeowner to then take up a loan.

A further indication of the problem of affordability is given by the World Bank, which reports that for Mexico 'about 40 per cent of newly formed households (300,000) earn less than three minimum wages (below US$327 per month) and cannot afford a finished house in a serviced neighbourhood'.[152] Only 12.6 per cent of the housing stock in Mexico is currently mortgaged and self-built housing accounts for roughly half of all new building in Mexico.[153] One assessment of the costs involved in borrowing money to purchase contractor-built housing in four Latin American countries noted that even a modest 40 square metre house on a 100 square metre plot is too expensive for the low-income groups under existing lending terms and conditions.[154] In Colombia, a similar percentage (40 per cent) of families earn less than two minimum salaries (US$250 each month) and are considered to be too poor to be able to afford loans for housing.[155] Other studies have also reported the lack of mortgage finance in low-income areas. In urban areas of Morocco, where just under 50 per cent of families own their own home, only 6 per cent of all formal housing loans are secured by low- and moderate-income households despite a government subsidy programme offering low-interest loans.[156] In Bangladesh, for example, the construction of a small house is affordable only for those with median incomes and above.[157] When the land costs for Dhaka are added to this cost, it increases significantly, and therefore only high-density medium rise appears affordable for this income group. Rising land prices also appear to have been a problem in some other Asian cities (for example, Manila) due to rapid economic growth and inward flows of finance for speculative property investment. In the context of Mexico, one assessment concludes:

> *... the least expensive commercially produced unit costs US$16,000 and is affordable only to families earning about five minimum salaries without subsidies. In contrast, major home improvement and/or expansion costs US$2000 to US$40,000 and is affordable to households earning 1.5 to 2.0 minimum salaries. Other relative low-cost housing solutions include construction of a core unit on a lot already owned by the households (US$6000 to US$8000) and purchase of an existing unit in a low-income settlement (US$10,000).*[158]

The kind of dwelling being referred to in Mexico is a basic unit of 40 square metres designed for further growth on a plot of, perhaps, 60 square metres and on the outskirts of the city. An indication of the scale of those who cannot afford mortgage finance is that 40 per cent of households earn less than three minimum salaries and, hence, cannot afford mortgage finance even when it is subsidized by the government.[159] In Latin America, only the upper-middle and upper-income households have access to mortgage finance. In Bolivia, Colombia, Venezuela and Suriname, low-income households make up, respectively, more than 60 per cent, 78 per cent, 80 per cent and above 70 per cent of the populations.[160] In the Philippines, one commentator concludes that the state is ineffective in targeting low-income households through a homeownership policy and an interest rate subsidy.[161] Given indicative loan thresholds, the monthly repayment of a loan of 150,000 pesos for a low-cost house is such that 77 per cent of the country cannot afford to access these loans (54.5 per cent of urban households). In Panama, 34 per cent of urban households earn less than US$300 a month and cannot afford mortgage finance (a further 43 per cent earn over US$600 and qualify without difficulty).[162] The middle group households are in an intermediate zone and may only be able to secure mortgages if they have formal employment since it is common practice in Panama for mortgage payments to be deducted from salaries.[163] As these figures indicate, even in Southern countries that have experienced rapid growth in household income, few can afford mortgage loans. Many of the attempts to provide mortgage finance to lower income groups have failed due to issues of affordability (even with subsidy support).

In addition to the cost of the property, there are significant additional costs related to the transfer of properties, securing a mortgage and associated title registration costs. Table 4.12 gives indicative costs for mortgage bond registration and the transfer duty in South Africa; legal costs and taxes amount to an average of just under 7 per cent of the purchase price of a typical middle-class home. Transaction costs in Chile are estimated to be considerably lower, at about 2.75 per cent of the cost of a typical dwelling of US$40,000, with just under half being stamp and registration fees.[164] One estimate suggests such costs equal 10 to 30 per cent of dwelling cost in sub-Saharan Africa, with stamp duty at 4 per cent in Kenya.[165] Such costs rise to 31 per cent of the estimated average transaction in Bangladesh.[166]

Informal incomes may not be acceptable to those lending mortgage finance because they cannot be verified. Mortgage companies may refuse to provide finance to those who do not work in the formal sector and/or who cannot prove their incomes. Even if some income is secured through formal labour markets, in many cases, informal employment is a further and significant source of livelihood for the household. Alternative collateral such as provident or pension funds can be used in South Africa, Bangladesh and, more recently, in Namibia; but it does not emerge as an important source of a guarantee elsewhere. A further example about the problems of informal incomes comes from a group of potters, who have legal ownership of land, in the city of Alwar, India.[167] They have saving and land collateral, but no financing institution is ready to support them. This is mainly due to the seasonal nature of their job, which does not provide a regular income throughout the year. As such, the dependence upon the indigenous money lenders remains in the range of 60 to 80 per cent.

The costs of loan services may be too expensive at US$10 a month in the US.[168] Total repayments on microfinance loans in Latin America are typically US$20–$80 a month, illustrating the difficulties that might be faced if high loan servicing costs were added:

> *... collecting on and processing a mortgage payment costs roughly US$15 for a typical savings and loan in Latin America, while the total payment on most HMF [housing microfinance] loans usually is only US$25 to US$100 per month (for families earning US$100 to US$400 per month – i.e. income range of the low-/moderate-income majority in Latin America and the Caribbean).*[169]

Table 4.12

Mortgage bond registration costs in South Africa

Registration costs of a bond of 300,000 rand					
Initial costs	**Valuation costs**	**Stamp duty**	**Administration costs per month**	**Registration**	**Transfer duty**
199.50 rand	Up to 1250 rand[i]	600 rand[ii]	5.70 rand[ii]	3500 rand[iii]	15,400 rand[iii]

Notes: i Maximum permitted by law; around 684 rand would probably be charged.
ii Defined by law.
iii Average based on quotations supplied by three banks.

Source: Hawkins, 2003, cited in Baumann, 2004

Both dimensions of affordability emerge from a more detailed analysis of the situation of the potters in Alwar. One reason why they face difficulties in accessing formal housing loans is described thus: 'Actually, the crux of the issue is that these loans are non-profitable for the banks due to small amount and high administration cost; and according to the bankers, these are high-risk loans.'[170] While a number of self-help groups in the city manage to save and access bank loans for income generation, their incomes are not adequate to access the larger loans for housing investment.[171]

For those who can afford mortgage loans and who can offer acceptable collateral, there are further barriers. In some settlements, it is difficult for low-income residents to reach the banks during opening hours due to their distance from low-income settlements. As a result, taking loans and making regular repayments is not possible. When the Self-employed Women's Association (SEWA) in India introduced its small loan programme, it sought to overcome these problems through pioneering doorstep banking.[172] This was initiated by SEWA Bank in 1978, when its first mobile van travelled to areas of high customer concentration in order to facilitate cash collection. Today, two mobile vans cover the city daily, with average daily collections of 10,000 to 15,000 rupees each. Further barriers are cultural and skill related. In many societies, including Botswana, women suffer particular difficulties in securing formal housing finance because of their lower labour market participation in formal employment and the fact that they may not be able to prove ownership of assets.[173] The formal requirements of financial institutions may be difficult for the poor, who may have limited literacy skills and not be familiar with formal processes. These general comments serve as the preface to a more detailed look at the trends in Southern regions.

Asia

The financial crisis of the late 1990s resulted in difficulties for a number of Asian countries and housing finance has been struggling to recover. There is evidence from a number of countries that the difficulties have been overcome and mortgage finance is now continuing to grow. Box 4.3 describes the increase in default rates and, hence, poor financial returns in Thailand. The total number of home mortgages outstanding in Thailand had risen to a peak of 794,000 in 1997. Mortgage finance had expanded rapidly between 1985 and 1995, growing annually at 34 per cent in the first five-year period and 33 per cent in the second.[174] As a result of the financial difficulties during the late 1990s, there was a crisis of confidence in financial institutions and several collapsed. Mortgage finance, supported by the Government Housing Bank, has picked up in recent years. In the Republic of Korea, the system has recently been

Box 4.10 Deregulation of housing finance in the Republic of Korea

Prior to the financial difficulties in the Republic of Korea in 1997, the major source of funding was the Korea Housing Bank, renamed the Housing and Commercial Bank in 1997. The state used the bank to support low-income, low-cost housing; in effect, there was a single public supplier of mortgage housing finance, with only the Korea Housing Bank being authorized to give long-term mortgages with terms exceeding ten years. Housing finance was relatively scarce and homeownership in urban areas actually fell between 1960 and 1995 from 62 to 46 per cent.

The government sought to prioritize finance for industrial development and the Housing Bank was heavily dependent upon savings. Demand for housing so exceeded supply that state housing allocations were determined by lottery, the 'winners' of which could join the bank's lending scheme after making 'subscription deposits' for two years. Little additional state resources were directed to housing, and the system was public only in so far as it was structured by the state; people provided their own finance through savings. To further assist the accumulation of resources, a very specific rental finance system developed with capital commitments thereby facilitating the accumulation of funds; in 1997, informal rental deposits were twice the amount of formal housing loans. Mortgage rates benefited from an interest rate subsidy, although the benefits were primarily realized by the middle class who could afford to accumulate sufficient funds for the required deposit and take loans.

Source: Ahn, 2002, pp255–257; Ha, 2002b, p243; Ha cited in La Grange and Nam Jung, 2004, p563.

through major changes. While the financial crisis has encouraged the trend, deregulation began significantly earlier during the late 1980s.[175] Mortgage lending rose steadily throughout the early period of the 1990s and growth was in double figures until 1996.[176] The market was further encouraged by the removal of price controls on housing in 1998.[177] Financial deregulation did not initially result in a large uptake in mortgages because 'the long-term interest rate is very high, there is no tax concession on mortgage loan repayments, and the ratio of mortgage loan to housing price is set very low'.[178] However, the housing market began to recover towards the end of the 1990s, as indicated in Table 4.13. The more active involvement of the private sector in mortgage lending after 1997 was further encouraged by the fact that there was no longer an advantage to the public sector due to lower interest rates. By 2001, the private sector accounted for 42 per cent of mortgage loans.

Strong growth is also reported elsewhere. In Hong Kong, SAR of China, growth rates have been strong during the mid to late 1990s – for example, 26 per cent growth during the first half of 1997.[179]

The economic crisis in Japan has been longer lasting than that which affected Asia during the late 1990s. The experience of Japan is particularly important because it highlights some of the risks of deregulation as increasing financing opportunities encouraged lending for housing and consumer credit.[180] Investments in homeownership were encouraged during the 1960s and the lack of public rental accommodation increased the pressure on households to become homeowners.[181] As economic problems increased for the banks' traditional industrial customers, they switched their concentration to potential homeowners. However, rapid rises in land prices caused particular problems during the 1990s – although the initial rise in prices and the associated real capital gains encouraged residential investment.[182] In 1992, prices were so high that the required average loans equalled five times the average incomes of working people.[183] Prices peaked around 1990–1991 and have fallen since then. The state has sought to offer assistance to those in particular difficulties as a result of redundancy and income falls; but take-up of options such as longer repayment periods has been minimal. Homeownership levels are now similar to the early 1960s. While homeownership was heavily concentrated among men, recent trends and, notably, lower prices and interest rates together with deregulation of lending criteria have resulted in greater access for women.

Mortgage growth has also been notable in lower income Asian countries, such as Indonesia and India. In Indonesia, housing finance grew at annual rates of over 20 per cent between 1993 and 1996.[184] In India, the 1990s were noted for the increase in the number of specialist housing finance institutions. Prior to this, developments had been slow, although the Housing Development and Finance Corporation (HDFC) had been established in 1977.[185] During the 1980s, banks were reluctant to lend for housing as they saw it as too risky. However, during the 1990s, there was a turnaround when industrial growth slowed and banks looked for alternative borrowers. Low interest rates, rising disposable incomes, stable property prices and fiscal incentives all encouraged growth in lending for house purchase.[186] One commentator summarized the situation during the late 1990s thus: 'There are now more than 370 such companies that have housing finance as their principle objective, although the majority of them play an insignificant role.'[187] Reflecting this last conclusion, only 26 of these companies worked with the National Housing Bank.[188] These institutions have been lending to middle- and higher income groups. However, the scale of finance has increased by an estimated annual rate of 30 per cent during the last five years.[189] Nevertheless, the market remains small in India at only 2 per cent of GNP, compared to 13 per cent in the Republic of Korea.[190]

This somewhat optimistic picture is not replicated everywhere. Mortgage finance has been slow to emerge in Pakistan, while traditional approaches have also dominated in Bangladesh. Box 4.11 describes the role played by the Bangladesh House Building Finance Corporation and its continuing emphasis on higher income groups.

In the Philippines, the government does appear to have been somewhat successful in extending subsidized loans to middle- and lower middle-income groups employed in the formal sector, principally through government-controlled pension and provident funds.[191] There was an

Table 4.13

Growth of mortgage lending in the Republic of Korea: size of the primary mortgage market (trillion Korean won)

	1997	1998	1999	2000	2001
Outstanding balances of mortgage loans (A)	53.0	55.5	61.3	67.6	72.9
New origination of mortgage loans (B)	13.4	12.1	17.1.	21.4	29.7
Gross domestic product (C)	453.3	444.4	482.7	522.0	545.0
A/C (percentage)	11.7	12.5	12.7	13.0	13.4
B/C (percentage)	3.0	2.7	3.5	4.1	5.4

Source: Bank of Korea, Kookmin Bank, quoted in Lee, 2003, p24.

increase in private-sector production of low-income housing during the early 1990s, which peaked in 1995 with 55.3 per cent of total residential development, involving the production of units costing less than 375,000 Philippine pesos, followed by a decline to 29 per cent in 2001.[192] This appears to have been encouraged by tax incentives and the provision of mortgage finance for low-income earners through the Unified Home Lending Programme, and discouraged following the Asian financial crisis of the late 1990s.[193] However, as always, care should be taken when generalizing. In the case of the Philippines, private-sector housing production may have increased; but with regard to housing finance, the government's role in the market remains that of a primary lender. Between 1993 and 2001, about 971,000 households gained homeownership through the National Shelter Programme. Despite such provision, however, the proportion living in informal settlements continues to rise.[194] There have been attempts to reduce the significance of the government housing finance institutions; but the reforms were abandoned in 1999, with a return to an emphasis on subsidized housing.

In China, the system of housing finance has been significantly redeveloped. The previous scheme was one in which dwellings were primarily provided through work units that housed employees in return for a nominal rent.[195] During the 1980s, an alternative system began to emerge in which the state sought to privatize and commercialize housing, shifting responsibility away from work units. Key to such a shift was a significant reduction in state housing subsidies across urban China; they fell from being equal to 18 per cent of household income in 1988 to less than 10 per cent in 1995.[196] In 1995, the government introduced two major programmes to encourage home purchase: the National Comfortable Housing Project and the Housing Provident Fund. It is difficult to assess the significance of these moves with regard to increasing access to mortgage finance and greater homeownership. One study concludes that, in 1997, 80 per cent of the population still remained in some form of state-owned housing.[197] Another assessed that, by the end of 1997, the average percentage of privatized housing in the 36 major Chinese cities was 60 per cent.[198]

The Housing Provident Fund programme in China drew on the successful experience of encouragement for homeownership in Singapore and was launched in 1991. One of the objectives was to ensure that employees made a greater contribution of the costs. The first provident fund, established in Shanghai in 1991, required a 5 per cent contribution from both employee and employer.[199] By the end of 1999, all of the 203 large- and medium-sized cities and most of the 465 small Chinese cities had started provident funds, with 69 million participants and 140.9 billion yuan having been raised.[200] However, just 10 per cent of this total had been released in mortgage loans. This is partly because of real problems in affordability, as illustrated in Box 4.12.

Box 4.11 Bangladesh House Building Finance Corporation

The Bangladesh House Building Finance Corporation (HBFC) was established in 1952 to stimulate middle-income house construction for civil servants in urban areas, and Bangladesh HBFC was recognized in 1973 after independence. While the majority of its clients are civil servants, its mandate has broadened to include all eligible private citizens and groups. It does not lend to developers or builders. During 1995/1996, the corporation's total assets were 26,218 million Bangladesh taka, of which 22,201 taka were outstanding loans and advances. Authorized capital is 1000 million taka, with 973 million taka being paid up. The main sources of funds are dedicated government bonds issues specifically floated for their programmes. The recent interest rate paid on debentures is 8 per cent, although previous issues had a lower rate. Additional transfers are provided by government on a limited scale. The HBFC is tax exempt. The government decides annually on the scale of funding and on activity. The HBFC disbursed loans of 1306.0 (provisional) million taka during 1999–2000, which was an increase of 42.3 per cent over the preceding year.

The corporation operates commercially, setting interest rates in accordance with the cost of funds and operating costs. Net profits have been increasing and since 1993/1994 have been positive (until 1999). The HBFC has financed 125,000 units since its inception, mostly for higher income households. In 1998, the bank only operated in high-income areas within Dhaka and on a limited scale in Chittagong and Rajshahi. In 1999, the corporation expanded its housing loan programme all over the country.

Recovery performance is poor and the recovery on current loans is 86 per cent, although the cumulative recovery is only 44 per cent. The HBFC recovered 2286.3 (provisional) million taka during 1999–2000, which was 16.9 per cent higher than the preceding year. Various incentive schemes are in place to encourage people to repay on time and to receive interest rate incentives. Mortgages are for 15 years, with interest rates increasing with the loan amount. This may be relaxed to 20 years in the case of small-size apartment schemes for low- and middle-income people. In Dhaka, loans above 1.5 million taka carry a simple interest rate of 15 per cent, and those below 1.5 million taka have a rate of 13 per cent. Outside Dhaka, the rate is 10 per cent. The grace period is one year. The local loan-to-value ratio is 60 per cent except for group loans, which have a loan-to-value ratio of 80 per cent.

In 1998, the institution was reluctant to move down market for fear of high levels of non-repayment. However, new apartment loans in the metropolitan cities of Dhaka and Chittagong and for 'semi-pucca' houses in the district towns, and a loan scheme for small-size flats (550–1000 square feet) for middle- and lower middle-class people have been introduced.

Source: Hoek-Smit, 1998; www.bangladesh.net/article_bangladesh/economic_trends/eco_13_house_building_finance.htm

Box 4.12 The move to homeownership in China: Guangzhou Province

Guangzhou is a city of 8 million people in southern China in an area that has experienced rapid economic growth. In 1998, Guangzhou pioneered a Housing Allowance Scheme to replace in-kind welfare housing and to move away from existing systems of housing provision. The scheme sought to reduce the responsibilities of work units and to encourage homeownership.

Despite the housing allowances, there remain considerable problems of affordability. In 1997, annual incomes for low- and middle-income groups ranged from US$1150 to US$1900. The cost of housing at that time was such that a 60 square metre unit cost US$26,000. In order to address the lack of affordability, the government designed an allowance based on rank and seniority that could be used to pay rent, to build up housing savings or to apply for a government loan that could cover up to 30 per cent of a property price. The loan would be repaid through the housing allowance. Once households have 30 per cent of the property price in their savings account, they can apply for a bank loan. Continuing problems are a lack of affordability, the lack of mortgage finance and low investment in housing.

Source: Chi-Man Hui and Seabrooke, 2000

Latin America

In Latin America, less than 30 per cent of dwellings are produced by the formal housing market.[201] As noted in Table 4.7, residential debt is, in general, a fairly low percentage of GDP, indicating that mortgage lending is not extensive. Significant difficulties of foreclosure, with long foreclosure periods taking over one year, are just one set of the problems that has reduced the attractiveness of mortgage finance in this region.[202] Some governments in Latin America established housing banks; but these concentrated on middle- and higher income housing and failed to address issues facing those with lower incomes.[203] During the last decade, the core issues facing governments in Latin America appear to be the longstanding problems of macroeconomic performance and, notably, inflation; the specific economic difficulties of the late 1990s; and the need to extend finance to those with lower incomes (Box 4.14 describes the complexities of mortgage indexing in Mexico, which has been developed to reduce the risks associated with anticipated inflation). The related strategies have been titling, direct-demand subsidies, the use of specially defined units for housing investment and the expansion of capital into the system through strengthening of the secondary market. Direct-demand subsidies have been introduced in a number of Latin American countries (including Chile, Colombia, Costa Rica, Ecuador and Mexico) to improve access and affordability (see Chapter 5).

While there are continuing problems of underdeveloped housing finance systems, in part as a result of the economic difficulties of recent decades, there are some positive trends in Chile, Costa Rica, Panama, Mexico and Peru, with uneven progress in Colombia, Bolivia and Ecuador.[204] These improvements include financial-sector reforms to facilitate the expansion of mortgage financing, judiciary reform to facilitate the recovery of collateral and an increase in housing production/finance in the private sector. They also involve attempts to have public housing agencies working more effectively with the treasuries, private banks and developers to address housing needs of beneficiaries.

Box 4.13 Extending housing finance in Mexico

In Mexico, the government has sought to increase access to mortgage finance (with subsidies) for the low- and lower middle-income group with between two to five minimum salaries. The challenge that the government has set itself is to double annual formal housing production to 750,000 dwellings. The newly created Federal Mortgage Bank (Sociedad Hipotecaria Federal, or SHF) provides secondary finance to a group of specialist housing lending agencies, SOFOLES (Sociedad Finaciera de Objeto Limitado), which were created in 1994 to serve as intermediaries in the residential mortgage market. SHF provides a guarantee in respect of loan default.

The SOFOLES originated less than 1 per cent of mortgages in 2001. By 2006, it is anticipated they will originate 19 per cent of mortgages in a market that is expected to double the number of loans that are granted. By the end of 2002, 18 SOFOLES had been set up with a total portfolio of 265,000 mortgages. Collection rates have been maintained with an average default of 2.4 per cent on total outstanding mortgage balances. The next challenge for SOFOLES is to move beyond their dependence upon funding from the SHF with the greater use of secondary market instruments.

Source: Dale-Johnson and Towle, 2002; Zaltzman, 2003.

Box 4.13 describes the creation of new housing finance institutions in Mexico and illustrates some of the challenges. In 2001, 69 per cent of mortgage loans in Mexico were given by Fondo de la Vivienda dell Instituto de Seguridad y Servicios Sociales de los Trabajadores del Estado (FOVISSTE) and Instituto del Fondo Nacional de la Vivienda para los Trabajadores (INFONAVIT), with the institutions receiving compulsory contributions of 5 per cent from public and private works for housing and pension funds. Many of their loans go to those with higher incomes; even with an interest rate subsidy, they are not affordable by the poor. It is estimated that households need to earn three times the minimum salary to be able to afford such subsidized loans.[205]

To reduce the significance and, hence, the cost of subsidized loans, and to create new possibilities for expanding lending, the government introduced a new set of housing institutions, the SOFOLES (see Box 4.13). SOFOLES, or Sociedad Finaciera de Objeto Limitado, are now estimated to be the main source of private home lending, following the withdrawal of the banks from the market after 1995; they can make loans and raise debt on the capital markets, but cannot take deposits from the public.[206] Their target market is now those who have more than five minimum salaries (about US$7500), which is already an increase on the initial target market (more than three minimum salaries) at the time of establishment in 1994.[207] SOFOLES appear to be particularly successful in reaching out to informally employed households. They have sought a means of reaching those who do not have access to payroll lending, with the achievement of lower delinquency levels than either INFONAVIT or the banks:

> *First, they have developed underwriting criteria for self-employed and informal workers: households pay a monthly sum equal to their desired mortgage payment into an account for a designated period of time, demonstrating consistent ability to pay and accumulating funds for a down payment. Second, in-person delivery of statements, acceptance of payments at on-site locations and outside of traditional business hours offer convenience and greater comfort than traditional servicing mechanisms.*[208]

In Chile, household demand for mortgage housing finance has been growing during recent years and, in 2002, loans generally started at about US$10,000 (compared to US$6000–$8000 of finance within the subsidized housing programmes, which may include a component of loan finance). It appears that the non-repayment of loans associated with subsidized housing has reduced the capacity of mortgage finance to reach further down to lower income households.[209] In 1976, there was an authorization for banks to offer mortgage-backed bonds and, since then, the banking system has been the main originators of housing loans. Although other types of mortgages have developed, these remain the most significant, with about 75 per cent of lending. An expanding market with new products and greater competition has brought down the price of housing finance, with a decline in the spread (the difference between the rate paid on the bond and that paid by the borrower) from 3 to 2 per cent between 1988 and 1997.[210]

Sub-Saharan Africa

The situation in sub-Saharan Africa divides between South Africa (and, to a lesser extent, Namibia and, until recently, Zimbabwe), where the commercial banking sector is significantly involved in mortgage lending, and the rest of the continent.[211]

In South Africa, outstanding credit extended to private households in South Africa was about 360 billion rand (US$55.8 billion[212]) in 2002 (see Table 4.14). Of this, 191 billion rand (53 per cent – US$29.6 billion) was for private mortgages. A further 7 billion rand (US$1 billion) was for mortgages extended by parastatals and non-bank institutions. South Africa's mortgage market is thus about 198 billion rand (US$30.7 billion). The South African Microfinance Regulatory Council[213] estimates that registered microlenders (including banks) currently hold 5.6 billion rand (US$868 million) in non-mortgage credit used for housing purposes.

Table 4.14 emphasizes that most housing finance is provided through bank mortgages. Despite this scale of finance, there is evidence to suggest that the lower income households remain excluded from the market. A national survey by the National Housing Finance Corporation in 2000 focused on the 1000 to 8000 rand monthly income bracket of lower to lower middle-income households.[214] The survey found that, of those seeking to buy, 41 per cent felt that financial institutions would not provide them with credit facilities due to their low income, while nearly a third (31 per cent) were unable to access credit from financial institutions due to being informally or self-employed. Only 38 per cent had applied for finance, with 13 per cent being successful. Three specific problems emerge: informality of tenure and incomes; lack of affordability; and lack of institutional reach. The informality of tenure and of incomes makes it hard for the poor to secure finance. While those who are in formal employment can use their provident funds to guarantee housing loans, many work in the informal sector. Moreover, mortgage finance is unaffordable to many. Approximately 2.28 million households live in South Africa's 'township' areas, 21 per cent of all households in South Africa. Thirty-three per cent of these households own their property (compared to a national average of 53 per cent).[215] Most lack sufficient income, estimated to be a minimum of 2500 rand, or US$390, per month, that is needed to afford a mortgage loan. The government census of 1996 estimated that 75 per cent of households have incomes below this level. There are few alternatives; those offering smaller loans charge higher interest rates. Although legislation has eased the provision of such microloans, their size is small and insufficient for housing purchase. As discussed in Chapter 6, many would be refused loans for reasons other than income.

The lack of market development in much of the rest of sub-Saharan Africa is related to similar reasons for excluding many poor South Africans from formal mortgage markets. Incomes are too low and employment is informal. Further problems include macroeconomic instability and problems around tenure insecurity. As a result of such factors, commercial housing markets remain minimal in many African cities.[216] The housing finance sector is dominated by those institutions which are state owned, receive financial support from the state, often offer subsidized loans and have poor repayment records.[217]

The original conceptualization after political independence was that the private sector would provide for higher income groups; hence, the focus of government should be on the middle- and lower income groups. Many sub-Saharan African governments established national housing agencies to directly develop houses, offer loans and establish financial systems. However, the experiences were not successful. As illustrated in the case of the National Housing Fund in Zimbabwe, there were structural and affordability problems.[218] In this specific case, the fund loaned at interest rates that were lower than the cost of funds, and had significant arrears from local authorities who managed the dwellings and who were responsible for repayment. Nevertheless, despite a technical agreement that such local authorities would be denied future loans, in practice the political decision was that investments should continue, even in the case of local authorities in arrears.[219] A further example is the Tanzania Housing Bank established in 1973, which collapsed in 1995. In this case, despite a number of specialist and general funds, relatively few loans were issued, with a total of about 36,000 units, over the 22-year period of its existence and the estimated loan recovery rate was only 22 per cent.[220]

Box 4.14 Reducing lender risk in Mexico

One of the historic problems for Mexican borrowers and lenders has been interest rate risk as a result of high inflation. During the early 1990s, escalating payments and falling incomes resulted in up to 80 per cent defaults on loans.

The Dual Index Mortgage (DIM) links the price of the house, or principal of the loan, to Unidades de Inversión (UDIs), which are the Mexican unit of investment introduced after the 1995 financial fiasco. In November 2004, the UDI was worth 3.5 pesos, or approximately US$0.30. The UDIs are indexed to the cost of living, so the amount that borrowers have to pay rises as the value of the loan rises, while the monthly payment is indexed to the minimum wage level, which also increases (although it often lags somewhat behind both the cost of living and average wage). Differences between the actual and required payments are added to the loan balance. In extreme cases it might be that the lender had a loan that could never be fully amortized. This problem has been reduced by the introduction of insurance against relative declines in the borrower's income. The insurance was originally 11 per cent of the monthly payment, but is now 5 per cent.

Source: Dale-Johnson and Towle, 2002, p23; Lea, 2000, p18.

Table 4.14

South African housing finance (by total loan book)

Type of credit	US$ billion	Percentage of housing finance market	Percentage of consumer credit market
Consumer credit	55.8	–	100
Total housing finance, of which:	30.9	100	55.4
bank mortgages	29.6	95.8	53.0
non-bank mortgages	1.01	3.3	10.0
non-mortgage loans for housing	0.87	2.8	1.6

Source: Hawkins, 2003, and Microfinance Regulatory Council (www.mfrc.co.za), both cited in Baumann, 2004.

Table 4.15

Source of funds for housing finance institutions (percentage)

	Deposits	Bonds	Foreign loans	Equity
Housing Finance Corporation of Kenya (HFCK)	79			14
Housing Development and Finance Corporation (India)	48	15	8	14
Union Homes (Nigeria)	74			7
Banque de l'Habitat du Sénégal (BHS)	63	26	5	6
Home Finance Company (Ghana)	8	80		10

Source: Okonkwo, 2002, p93.

Affordability is one of the problems faced by housing finance institutions in Africa. Even in South Africa, 75 per cent of households earn too little to be considered for mortgage loans; this is already considerably higher than the 40 per cent of households who cannot afford mortgage loans in Mexico and Panama. In Zimbabwe, nine out of ten low-income home seekers on the housing waiting list in Harare in 1996 had a monthly income of less than Zimbabwe $900, which would only qualify them to buy a plot in the Kuwadzana 5 low-income housing project that was being developed at the time.[221] Even a plot and wet core was beyond them; but this is what would be required for legal settlement. The emphasis on affordability problems continues elsewhere: 'The average cost of a decent low-income family house in Ghana (about 50 million cedi) is more than ten times the average annual salary of most key works in Ghana.'[222] Similar conclusions about affordability problems are reached for Tanzania, where a two-bedroom low-cost house required, in 2002, a monthly repayment equal to the total of a minimum monthly government salary.[223]

The consequences of such a lack of affordability have been the lack of market development. Hence, in Kenya, it is estimated that during 2004 the banks and mortgage institutions only offered 9000 loans.[224] Few loans have been given by the Housing Finance Company in Uganda; in 2000, they had 724 loans on their books.[225] The very small numbers is indicative of the scale of the problem. Such low levels of lending reflect perceptions of risk, as well as the small numbers who can afford mortgages. An illustration of the cautious nature of lending agencies is given by the Home Finance Company in Ghana, which would like to have monthly repayments in US dollars, despite the difficulties for those being paid in a local (and depreciating) currency.[226] Such lending conditionalities will inevitably result in a very small demand for mortgage loans.

While state housing finance institutions have continued in some cases, the greater emphasis on cost recovery and operating efficiency during the 1990s has given them considerable problems in securing finance. A recent review noted that while housing finance institutions exist in some African countries, in others they are lacking.[227] Generally, those that do exist have been heavily regulated and have also been seen as social instruments, rather than financial mechanisms. More recently, the state has withdrawn from this area, and some housing finance institutions have withdrawn as well. Government institutions that continued have been expected to secure higher levels of cost recovery in an effort to reorientate them to financial agencies, and alternative (commercial) institutions have been encouraged. One recent analysis of the situation across the continent highlights this process of transition.[228] Structural adjustment reduced the role of building societies and resulted in state-owned development institutions being privatized or wound up. There are a number of new initiatives emerging, notably in the Gambia and Kenya. However, apart from Ghana's Home Finance Company (and excluding South Africa), secondary mortgage finance institutions are limited.[229] Hence, a particular and continuing problem faced in Africa has been 'a lack of effective institutions and instruments to mobilize these savings and channel them into housing investment'.[230] For the most part, housing finance institutions have remained dependent upon deposits and have not been able to secure long-term finance (see Table 4.15).[231]

Despite the recognized need for additional finance, relatively little concentrated attention has been given to the private sector. In Nigeria, only 1 of 18 broad housing strategies designed to realize housing policy during the early 1990s concerned the private sector.[232] The Federal Mortgage Bank of Nigeria was established to provide additional housing finance; but between 1977 and 1990/1991, it gave only 8874 loans.[233] As noted above, attempts have been made to replicate payroll funds; however, while the National Housing Fund collected 4 billion naira from households in mandatory savings, only 300 million naira of loans was approved by the Federal Mortgage Bank, with only one third of this total actually being advanced.[234]

This regional analysis has highlighted some of the trends (opportunities and difficulties) with regard to housing finance. The following section summarizes information about lending terms and conditions and, in so doing, highlights some of the problems faced by would-be borrowers in the South.

TERMS AND CONDITIONS

Mortgage lending is associated with a standard package of terms and conditions that specify the contribution of deposits, on some occasions the period of savings, the interest rate to be charged on the loan (and if it is fixed or variable), the period of the loan (potentially with penalties for early and late repayment), and loan-to-value ratios (the maximum percentage of the loan against a verified value of the dwelling). A further important factor is the amount that the loan institution is willing to lend in relation to the borrowers' income(s).

Loan periods and loan-to-value ratios (LTVs): Accessing loans

While aspects such as interest rates are likely to be determined by macroeconomic conditions and policies, and borrower income cannot be determined by the lender, other factors make a critical difference to the affordability of the loan and the capacity of lower income households to secure mortgage finance. Longer loan periods reduce monthly repayments and higher loan-to-value ratios (LTVs) reduce the scale of the deposit that has to be saved. Table 4.16 gives indicative mortgage loan lengths and estimated LTVs for a number of countries.

Table 4.16 demonstrates that there is considerable difference even between countries in the North. Higher loan-to-value ratios may be associated with longer repayment periods if both are responding to high housing prices and the need to borrow larger proportions over longer periods to cover such costs. For example, the terms given in Table 4.16 for Thailand was introduced following the financial crises and the problem of affordability. However, risk is an important factor in addition to affordability, and it is notable that shorter repayment periods prevail in a number of transitional and Southern countries. This issue can be illustrated by Ghana, where mortgage companies want homebuyers to have a high stake in the property and generally require at least a 20 per cent deposit, although, in some cases, the required down payment is 50 per cent.[235]

Table 4.17 provides a summary of 'typical' and 'maximum' LTVs in 8 countries drawn from the 15 member states of the EU. Half of these countries' mortgage systems are able to provide LTVs of at least 100 per cent; but maximum LTVs of 90 per cent or less apply in 60 per cent of the EU-15 market.[236] Maximum LTVs may be raised by the use of secondary loans (for example, in Germany); but they may still be a considerable barrier to entry into homeownership. Rising house prices in many Northern countries have increased the pressure on the system and have resulted in increasing efforts to improve borrower affordability. In Japan, loan periods also increased during the 1990s as house prices rose.

Difficulties of foreclosure are often associated with the South, but, as Table 4.18 indicates, the process of foreclosure is often not quick even in the North. Such issues explain the significance given to verifiable incomes and other indicators of borrower reliability, as well as measures to reduce lender risk, such as red-lining. Foreclosure is, in general, a last resort that is difficult to use effectively at scale. Where lenders are under pressure to carry additional risks with longer loan periods and higher loan-to-value ratios, or with extending loan services to new groups of clients, then insurance may be increasingly significant. Table 4.18 provides data for some countries in Latin America; although, in general, periods are longer, this is not the case for every country.

Savings

Typically, mortgage finance is only available for a proportion of the purchase price of the house. As noted in Table 4.15, it is not common for mortgages to be available for the full cost of the property and LTVs are typically below 90 per cent. The remaining costs have to be met by savings or some other form of pre-existing finance. However, traditionally, saving has played a much more important part of access to mortgage finance in specialist institutions aimed at both collecting savings and issuing loans. Savings are believed to be important in preparing households for making regular payments and ensuring that the loan repayments are affordable. The increased diversification of housing loan suppliers has reduced the general significance of savings activities that are specifically linked to housing; but some form of saving remains essential if mortgage loans are offered for less than the full cost of the property.

A significant refinement of more traditional savings practices that remains important in some countries is contractual savings for housing, or *Bausparkassen*. Contractual savings schemes are dedicated savings activities undertaken by would-be borrowers who may be paid below-market interest rates on their accumulating savings. The savings period is followed by the offer of a housing loan (also at reduced interest) once the deposits have reached a certain level. The institution has been popular in Germany and

Table 4.16

Indicative mortgage lengths and loan-to-value ratios (LTVs)

Country	Usual contract length (years)	Estimated average LTV ratio (new loans) (percentage)
Australia	25	90–100
Austria	25	60
Bangladesh	up to 15	50–80
Belgium	20	80–85
Canada	25	60
Chile	8-20	up to 75
Czech Republic	less than 20	30–50
Denmark	30	maximum 80
Finland	15–20 (variable)	75–80
France	15–20 (variable)	maximum 60
Germany	20–30, with initially 5–10	70–80
Greece	15	55
Hong Kong, SAR of China	15–30 (mostly 15)	up to 70
Hungary		maximum 70
Iceland	25–40	65–70 from main lender
India	maximum 20	maximum 85
Jordan	up to 20	80–90
Lithuania	20–25	70–95
Mexico	20–30	80–90 (100 from payroll funds with contributions as implicit deposit)
Netherlands	30	87; maximum 125 for first-time buyers
Portugal	25–30	90
Slovenia	10	50
South Africa	10–20	70–100
Republic of Korea		average 41 (maximum is 50–60)
Sweden	30–40	80–90
Tanzania	15	75
Thailand	30	70–80 is typical; maximum 90–100
UK	25	70
US	30	average 76.2

Source: Scanlon and Whitehead, 2004, p18.

Except: India – Karnad, 2004; *Tanzania* – Mutagwaba, 2002; *Mexico* – Connolly, 2004b; *South Africa* – Baumann, 2004; *Chile* – Pardo, 2000 (for mortgage bonds which are 75 per cent of all mortgage loans); *Thailand* – Kritayanavaj, 2002; Aphimeteetamrong and Kritayanavaj, 1998, p229; *Republic of Korea* – Lee, 2003, p28; *Jordan* – Chiquier et al, 2004, p29; *Hong Kong* – Lamoreaux, 1998, p70; *Bangladesh* – Hoek Smit, 1998, pp29–30.

Table 4.17

Loan-to-value ratios (LTVs) in eight EU countries

Country	Typical LTV (percentage of property value)	Maximum LTV (percentage of property value)
Denmark	80	80
France	67	100
Germany	67	80
Italy	55	80
Netherlands	90	115
Portugal	83	90
Spain	70	100
UK	69	110

Source: Mercer Oliver Wyman, 2003, cited in Stephens, 2004

Table 4.18

Approximate time to take property into possession

Country	Time (months)
Netherlands i	4
Denmark i	6
Spain i	8
France i	10
Germany i	10
UK i	11
Portugal i	20
Italy i	60
Argentina ii	10–18
Chile ii	12–18
Colombia ii	45
Peru ii	31
Uruguay ii	24

Source: i Mercer Oliver Wyman, 2003, cited in Stephens, 2004; ii Rojas, 2004, p14.

Austria and has more recently spread to other countries, particularly the transition countries. Such institutions were introduced in Slovakia (1993), the Czech Republic (approximately 1994), Hungary (1997) and Croatia (2000).[237] The subsidy is often justified on the grounds that long-term savings are encouraged, that the practice of regular payment is established by the early period of saving and that interest rate changes are minimized.[238] However, one necessary precondition is low and stable inflation rates (thereby maintaining the value of the accumulating funds).

There have been concerns about the efficiency of contractual savings schemes. Once committed, the savings are tied up; as a result, such schemes suffer from their inflexibility when the broader financial and economic environment changes. The subsidies required to attract savings may be considerable, leading to the inefficient use of government funds and budgetary pressures. It is for reasons such as these that Poland is moving away from this system.[239] In Slovakia, there is some evidence that they have been used as a transitional instrument, with loan volumes rising while the subsidy burden is falling.[240] Such schemes have been poorly targeted in terms of households' incomes. However, they could potentially be limited to certain groups defined by income or age. Some schemes have been criticized for being used to subsidize savings unconnected to house purchase, although this could also be prevented by a more restrictive design.[241]

Interest rates

Interest rates reflect the cost of capital – they are the price that borrowers have to pay to the lender to make use of the funds. If the housing finance market is working effectively, interest rates should be only slightly higher than prime lending or deposit rates in the commercial banking sector.[242] However, in practice, rates may be higher and/or lower depending upon market efficiencies, perceptions of risks and state intervention. Despite the comment above that interest rates are often a 'given', set exogenously by macroeconomic trends and monetary policy, in some cases state housing institutions or those receiving subsidies charge interest rates below market rates.

State housing agencies have more flexibility in the use of funds. In Thailand, for example, the National Housing Bank undercuts commercial interest rates. It also offers differential rates (through a cross-subsidy) to those taking smaller loans in order to 'make borrowing more accessible and more affordable to a large number of home buyers'.[243] Examples of subsidized interest rates have been given in this chapter for Tunisia, India and Hungary. A further example comes from the Philippines mortgage market, where rates are variable; in 1996 the cost of commercial borrowing was 16 per cent (secure for one year), while subsidized loans charged 9 to 12 per cent.[244]

Alternatively, the way in which financial markets respond may also differ. As a result, the cost of funds may vary to reflect the relatively lower administration costs associated with larger loans. The following figures are those currently prevailing in Chile:[245]

- For loans from 800 to 1999 UF (Unidades de Fomento, a Chilean-peso denominated unit with daily adjustment to inflation) the rate is 4.8 per cent.
- For those from 1999 to 2999 UF, the rate is 4.4 per cent.
- For 3000 UF and more, the rate is 3.7 per cent.

Interest rates can be particularly problematic for affordability during periods of high inflation. High nominal interest rates tend to worsen the so-called 'front-end loading' problem, where the real burden of interest payments falls very heavily during the early years of the mortgage, which often coincides with stages in the life cycle when financial burdens are high (dependent children) and earnings have not yet been maximized. High interest rates considerably increase the cost of borrowing and make housing investments unaffordable for many families. The problem can be exemplified by Tanzania, where inflation in 2000 was between 18 and 25 per cent.[246] A loan equal to three times annual income would require total yearly payments equal to 55 to 75 per cent of annual income. A more detailed report calculates that if the interest rate 'was to drop to 10 per cent per annum, the affordability ratio, though still low, will tremendously improve'.[247]

In the North, there is discrepancy between fixed and variable rates. In general, there appears to have been a shift to flexible, variable rates, which pass more of the risks from the provider of the loan to the borrower.

Table 4.19 illustrates the situation in South Africa by providing a snapshot of terms and conditions for lenders of small loans (the first two rows) and complete loans (the following four rows). Interest rates are relatively high, reflecting two state policies not unusual in the South: first, the government wishes to encourage capital inflows to strengthen the currency and, second, it wishes to encourage saving. Table 4.19 illustrates the high cost of borrowing for those unable to secure mortgages.

Finally, lenders commonly restrict loan repayments to a maximum percentage of incomes. While a typical percentage is up to 25–30 per cent of income, higher rates have been used to increase loan acceptances as house prices rise. In Hong Kong, the rate rose to 50 per cent, in Thailand it is 30 per cent or higher for big loans and in Ghana it is about 35 per cent.[248]

Table 4.19

Terms and conditions in the South African housing finance market

Type of intermediary	Cost of funds (percentage)	Average annual charge to client (percentage)	Form of security	Average loan size (rand)	Term of loan
Microloan – NHFC incremental housing	16%	42%	Unsecured	4660 rand	21 months
Pension-backed loan	11% i	16–17%	Pension fund	20,000 rand	8 years
NHFC mortgages – homeownership	13%	17%	Property; after eight months, risk shifts to NHFC	80,000 rand	15 years
Low-end bank mortgages	11% ii	19–20%	Property	90,000 rand	20 years iii
High-end bank mortgages	11% ii	15–17%	Property	210,000 rand	20 years iii
High-end independent	13.5%	15%	Property	220,000 rand	20 years

Notes: i Opportunity costs of possible deposit rate.
ii Highest deposit rate; in reality, the average depositor earns far less.
iii Written for 20 years, but average effective term is 7 years.

Source: Baumann, 2004, p12.

HOUSING FINANCE, AFFORDABILITY AND LOWER INCOME HOUSEHOLDS

Considerable effort has been made to extend opportunities to secure housing finance during recent years. This is the product of two related factors. On the one hand, the housing finance market has become more competitive as new providers have been encouraged to enter the market. Such providers have been seeking new customers to extend their activities. Thus, the extension of mortgage services is a commercial response to market conditions. As noted earlier, this has been partly determined by growing incomes. On the other hand, the state has been looking to the market to address housing need. Faced with considerable housing problems and seeking to reduce public expenditure (see Chapter 5), governments have sought to encourage the market to address needs where possible.

The price of housing

Affordability is not just about access to and the cost of housing finance; it is also critically about the price of housing. The price of housing reflects the costs of production, but also the balance between supply and demand in the market for housing. However, much policy emphasis has been placed on extending financial services, with relatively little attention being given to increasing the quantity of housing.

The relatively high price of housing now appears to be a significant constraint on access to housing in a number of different contexts around the world. One of the most important trends in housing finance in Western Europe has been the widening 'gap' between incomes and house prices, as the latter have risen relative to the former in many countries.[249] The increase in housing prices extends beyond Europe. For example, in New Zealand, between December 2001 and December 2003, house prices rose by 27 per cent while consumer price inflation was only 4.3 per cent during the same period.[250]

This 'gap' can be characterized as the main indicator of 'underlying' affordability that housing finance systems exist to bridge. Table 4.20 shows changes in (as opposed to absolute levels of) housing affordability in a number of West European countries based on the relationship between house prices and disposable incomes per worker.[251]

Analysing Table 4.20, it is evident that 'underlying' affordability has worsened considerably in four of the seven countries included in the table since 1990, although the deterioration can often be traced as far back as 1970. The largest deteriorations in underlying affordability since 1985 have been experienced in Spain, the Netherlands and Ireland, and to a lesser extent in the UK. More modest deteriorations have occurred in France and Italy since 1985; but these have occurred within a longer-term context of relative stability. Germany stands out as having experienced consistent and marked improvements in underlying affordability since 1970.

House prices have risen particularly since 1997, notably in Australia, Ireland, Spain and the UK.[252] In 2003, the European Mortgage Federation noted particularly strong price increases in Latvia, Portugal, Spain, the UK and Ireland.[253] *The Economist* has tracked a slightly larger range of countries and data is given in Table 4.21. It notes that there is evidence of prices falling towards the end of 2004 in some countries; but growth continues in others.

Seeking to explain the rise in house prices, the International Monetary Fund (IMF) suggests that house prices are increasingly synchronized across high-income countries. There is evidence of a long-term trend in rising house prices; but prices are also linked to affordability (and, therefore, to incomes), with particularly high prices at present. One further explanatory variable is interest rates (a significant part of the cost of borrowing), and it is low interest rates that are one explanation behind the current

Table 4.20

Changes in underlying affordability since 1970 in selected West European countries

Country	1970	1980	1990	2003
Germany	129	114	95	80
France	123	125	119	125
Italy	–	135	130	131
Spain	147	127	199	289
Netherlands	137	151	111	243
Ireland	–	136	110	201
UK	97	109	137	156

Note: Change in ratio of house prices to disposable income per worker. 1985 = 100

Source: IMF, 2004.

Country	2004 i	2003 ii	1997–2004
Australia	8.2	17.6	112
Belgium	9.3	5.5	50
Canada	6.7	6.5	43
China	9.9	4.1	no data
Denmark	7.3	3.4	50
France	14.7	11.5	76
Germany	–1.7 iii	–4.5	–3
UK	13.8	11	139
Hong Kong, SAR of China	31.2	–13.6	–49
Ireland	10.8	14.8	187
Italy	9.7	10.6	69
Japan	–6.4	–4.8	–24
The Netherlands	3.3	1.9	76
New Zealand	16.4	21.2	56
South Africa	35.1	20.9	227
Spain	17.2	16.5	149
Singapore	nil	–2.3	no data
Sweden	9.8	5.5	81
Switzerland	2.2	2.4	12
United States	13	6	65

Notes: The first two columns show percentage change on a year earlier.
i Third quarter, or 2004 latest. ii Third quarter. iii Second half of 2003.
Source: The Economist, 2004.

Table 4.21

House price changes

global price boom. Overall, global developments, including those specific to housing markets (the performance of the global economy such as real stock prices, per capita output and real interest rates), explain 40 per cent of house price movements during the period of the IMF study (from 1980 to 2004).[254] The UK and the US are particularly open to such global markets as such factors explain approximately 70 per cent of house price movements in these countries, while they only explain 3 per cent of house price movements in New Zealand. There is evidence to suggest that the deepening of mortgage markets has been associated with higher global house prices (that is, efforts to expand affordability by increasing access to housing finance have resulted in increasing prices).[255]

The cost of housing – and the response of supply to increased demand

In a number of countries, housing supply appears to respond only slowly to increases in housing demand expressed through rising prices. This is clearly linked to the many stages involved in the construction process. When 'supply is inelastic, the same increase in demand … results in a much larger increase in price and a much smaller increase in quantity supplied'.[256] If supply does not increase, or only increases slowly, there is no reason to believe that a more efficient housing finance market will result in better housing (even in the short or medium term); it will simply result in rising house prices. The increase in the availability of housing finance assumes that more dwellings will be produced and/or marketed in response to increased demand and, hence, that homeownership will rise. But how responsive is supply to demand? Housing elasticity varies considerably between countries and estimates for Western Europe are given in Table 4.22.

Country	Price elasticity of supply
UK	0.5
Germany	2.1
France	1.1
Netherlands	0.3
Denmark	0.7
US	1.4

Notes: >1 = relatively strong supply response to rising prices.
0–1 = relatively weak supply response to rising prices.
Source: Swank et al, cited in Stephens, 2004

Table 4.22

International comparison of price elasticity of supply of new housing in high-income nations

A major reason accounting for the lack of responsiveness is regulation. Research has shown that local regulations that prevent housing construction are a significant cause of high house prices in US and UK cities; more evidence shows that in Malaysia and South Korea there is also an unresponsive housing supply due to regulations.[257] In Finland, one of the reasons for low housing starts is that local authorities are reluctant to sanction new housing construction because of the associated costs of infrastructure and services.[258] Similar problems emerge in Tanzania, where it is noted that in Dar es Salaam the average annual demand for plots between 1990–2001 was 20,000, while average annual supply was under 700.[259] Similar concerns emerge in the context of the Philippines:

> *… the inelastic housing supply aggravates the housing problem. Supply-side constraints arise primarily from problems in the land and financial markets. The land market has been inefficient because land administration and management is weak in various aspects: legal and regulatory framework and administration infrastructure. Land laws in the country are inconsistent… Land administration infrastructure is also poor and inadequate.*[260]

A poor and inadequate regulatory system is not the only reason for a low responsiveness of supply to demand in housing construction. In New Zealand, where prices rose rapidly between 2001 and 2004, the building sector noted that the lack of labour was a major constraint on expanding the supply for housing.[261]

Whatever the causes, the consequence is that homeownership is unaffordable to some groups. Analysing the figures in Table 4.20 and Table 4.22, one factor ensuring the continued affordability of homeownership in Germany may be the responsiveness of construction to changes in price.[262] This discussion highlights the interconnected nature of housing finance with other factors, notably land markets and regulations for housing, land development and other urban development processes.

The implications for homeownership for the young

In a context of rising prices, housing is becoming more expensive and housing finance systems have a greater job to do in bridging this gap. Young people have particular difficulties in purchasing dwellings; they have had less time to save for a down payment (deposit) and earnings are lower for those who have recently entered the labour market. They are particularly affected by rising house prices. Table 4.23 depicts changes in homeownership of young households in selected countries in Western Europe.

In the UK, the decline in homeownership among young households is very striking, with a percentage point decline of 15. Deteriorating housing affordability means that fewer young households can access homeownership, even within the context of a liberalized mortgage market that can provide 100 per cent loan-to-value ratios (LTVs).[263] Before mortgage market deregulation, LTVs were the principal constraint faced by potential first-time buyers in the UK. Although this is no longer the case, many households cannot afford to service 100 per cent mortgages, even with historically low interest rates. So the proportion of first-time buyers in the UK has fallen and their age has risen – from 27 years in the 1980s to 34 years today. A similar picture emerges in some of the other countries that have experienced large house-price rises during recent years, notably in Spain where there has been little expansion in rental alternatives to ownership, with the result that household formation has become severely inhibited. An indication of similar problems is seen in New Zealand where homeownership rates have been falling generally: 'the greatest drop in homeownership rates [between 1991–2001] was amongst 25- to 44-year-old age cohort, which experienced a 10 per cent drop'.[264] Similar consequences have been noted in Japan, even though prices have fallen from their increases during the early 1990s. Homeownership rates have been falling among the young in Japan; 'in 1978 well over a quarter of those in the aged 25–29 category were homeowners', while by 1998, the figure had fallen to one in eight.[265]

Country	circa 1990	circa 2000	Direction
Denmark	23 (1990)	20 (1999)	Down
Finland	41 (1992)	39 (1995)	Down
France	21 (1990)	17 (2002)	Down
Netherlands	43 (1993)	44 (1998)	Stable
Sweden	45 (1991)	46 (1997)	Stable
UK	74 (1994/1995)	59 (2001/2002)	Down

Source: Scanlon and Whitehead, 2004.

Table 4.23

Change in homeownership of young households (percentage)

More general problems of affordability

US data indicates that there are some 6 million households living in owner-occupied dwellings who fall below the poverty line (and with a median annual household income of US$6011).[266] This is not that much less than the 7.9 million households below the poverty line who are living in rental accommodation. While some are older households whose housing costs have been paid, just over 4 million still have a mortgage outstanding on the property. What is evident is that the numbers of owner occupiers below the poverty line with mortgages have increased significantly. From 1960 to 1985, mortgage originations for this group were below 100,000; since then the numbers with mortgages have risen fairly steadily.[267] The government has deliberately sought to reach out to low-income households; one of several programmes is the Targeted Lending Initiative, which was started in 1996 to encourage mortgage institutions to provide loans within specifically designated underserved areas, including inner-city neighbourhoods and Native American lands. Special incentives include reduced guarantee fees and increased servicing fees. Over 100,000 households have secured mortgages within this programme.

In the transition countries, there are real problems with affordability due to generally low levels of income. For example, only 10 to 20 per cent of the population in Estonia and Latvia are considered to be eligible for housing loans.[268] The transfer of properties from the public sector to private-sector households, together with the switch to a market-based economy, has resulted in considerable poverty and real problems in ensuring adequate housing with associated services. This is indicated by a recent study of Southeastern Europe, which found that for Bulgaria in 2000, the radiators of 50 per cent of those with central heating were cold.[269]

In the South, the numbers of people able to afford formal housing with the associated financing costs are limited. As discussed earlier, the clear emerging trend in a number of countries is that of the extension of mortgage finance. However, it is very difficult to assess how successful this has been. The high costs associated with large loan finance in a context in which incomes are very low suggest that the potential for down-marketing is limited.[270] However, there is little information about how successful specific initiatives have been in reaching lower income groups.

The housing finance market in India expanded during the 1990s, but did not really move down market; in particular, down-marketing was perceived by the managers of housing finance institutions as being very difficult.[271] Partly due to hesitation within primarily commercialized markets, the state changed strategy and began more systematically to explore options with non-profit lenders (such as credit unions) and the potential role of non-governmental organizations (NGOs). In India, the Asian Development Bank deliberately sought to down-market housing finance with a loan of US$300 million to create linkages between formal housing finance institutions and NGOs and community-based organizations (CBOs). One assessment has been made of several schemes designed to extend housing finance in India in order to judge their success in reaching the poorer income groups.[272] Some of the critical issues raised have also been a concern of other programmes:

Affordability is not just about access to and the cost of housing finance; it is also critically about the price of housing

- *Institutional bias*: generally, smaller loans are more useful to the poor. The focus on smaller loans aims to put in place self-discriminatory sorting systems as the higher income groups are not interested in smaller loans. However, the high administration costs mean that institutions prefer larger loans and there is an ongoing tension about trying to push down loan size. A similar problem was faced by the Community Mortgage Programme in the Philippines when the low

Box 4.15 Private development of affordable housing in India

The Parshwanath Group had developed a niche market in Ahmedabad in providing housing to lower middle-income households – generally those employed as school teachers, police constables, tailors, carpenters, bus and taxi drivers – and had developed over 20,000 units in 125 projects. During the late 1980s, they began a partnership with the government agency, the Housing and Urban Development Corporation (HUDCO). HUDCO's objective was to enable the developer to expand its operations and reach further down market. Together, the two planned to develop Parshwanath township. The group had previously targeted relatively low-income households by reducing costs through the manufacture of its own building materials and constructing minimal units, with the new residents constructing second floors and completing the finishes, such as kitchen counters, plastered walls and staircases.

HUDCO provided the Parshwanath Group with development capital for construction and agreed to offer mortgages to the residential buyers. Only the first two phases were developed. Initially, the Self-employed Women's Association (SEWA), a local NGO, had intended to be involved in targeting low-income households and in supporting repayments, but this component never fully evolved. The Parshwanath Group ran into litigation and financial troubles (when some residents refused to make repayments and challenged the quality of the buildings); the group sold the remainder of the land to developers, who now intend to target higher income groups.

The development proved acceptable to some purchasers; but others subsequently complained about the quality of the units and their size. Some residents filed a lawsuit against the developer due to the poor quality of completion, the lack of services such as street lights and the poor quality of construction. It appears that expectations had changed and that the quality was no longer considered acceptable. At the same time, the link with the public agency meant that the formal planning and regulatory procedures had to be complied with and that 'informal' practices previously used (such as the post-dating of cheques for repayment) were no longer possible.

Source: Mukhija, 2004a.

interest rate meant that the support institution was reluctant to give loans during the mid 1990s as it could make more money investing the funds.

- *Savings-related barriers*: savings-linked schemes are generally thought to require too long a time period before the release of loans.
- *Land title*: lack of clear land title is a continuing problem in India. In many cases, communities are not threatened with eviction and therefore have secure tenure; but without a legal title the land cannot be used for collateral.
- *Payroll deductions*: workers on low wages are not allowed in India to have their repayment deducted at source, and this is a further deterrent to housing finance corporations. Wage deductions are seen as one strategy to reduce risk. As noted earlier in the discussion of Panama, a problem in lower middle-income families working in the informal sector was that they could not have direct deductions and therefore were not accepted by mortgage lenders.
- *Flexible payments*: requirement for regular repayments can also be hard for the poor. This is particularly true for informal workers. It is notable that the success of the SOFOLES in reaching the informal sector in Mexico is linked to acceptance of payments at on-site locations and outside of traditional business hours.

Some of the lowest-cost housing (and, hence, smallest mortgages) have been for incomplete units, which (while being of sufficient quality to be legal dwellings) enable occupiers to finish them as and when incomes increase. The possibilities of such strategies to extend homeownership through mortgage finance in the Indian context are analysed through the experiences of a private developer in Ahmedabad (see Box 4.15).[273] This example involves a partnership between the state and the private sector in which the finance was provided by the national government agency, the Housing and Urban Development Corporation (HUDCO), for a low-cost housing development. Previously, the company had been successful in providing housing for lower middle-income households, and the objective of the development was to use a proven low-cost construction process with state mortgage finance to reach a group that had previously been excluded on the grounds of affordability. However, the experience raises questions about this strategy, with the presence of public agencies reducing the extent of informality in the development and therefore making it less attractive for the developer.[274] In particular:

> *... enabling informal-sector developers can be extremely difficult and tricky because public involvement and support can reduce their flexibility and incentives, as well as impact upon the expectations and opportunities of homebuyers.*[275]

A similar strategy for homeownership via subsidized state loans with minimal investment required for a completed unit has been tried in the Philippines, this time from a private developer that has particularly targeted the lower end of the market for social reasons. Freedom to Build is active in Manila and provides core or starter housing units of 20 square metres to those able to secure government mortgages (generally employed in low-income formal-sector work). The company argues that its model is effective. However, the profit levels are lower than those for developers aiming at the higher end of the market, and for this reason there are relatively few such providers. To date, 7000 units have been completed with a major problem being the identification of suitable land.[276] While Freedom to Build is somewhat unusual in being specifically orientated towards low-income housing, there has generally been an increase in private-sector production of low-income housing during the early 1990s.[277]

More commonly, affordability and loan repayment remain a problem in many Asian contexts. In the Philippines, the recovery rate on programmes provided by the National Housing Authority varies from 23 to 74 per cent.[278] Loan programmes that provide only plots have performed better than completed housing loan programmes, and attempts to shift towards self-help have improved loan performance. These low repayment rates have resulted in internal pressures for reform and, as a result of poor loan repayments, the pension funds that have been providing finance for the Unified Home Lending have refused to release further funds.[279] Such a situation is indicative of remaining strains in the housing finance system.

Table 4.24

Availability of mortgages to different groups in Western Europe

Country	Young household <30	Older household >50	Low equity	Self-certify income	Previously bankrupt	Credit impaired	Self-employed	Government sponsored
Denmark	A	A	C	C	B	B	A	B
France	B	B	A	C	C	B	B	A
Germany	A	B	B	C	C	C	A	B
Italy	B	B	C	C	C	B	A	B
Netherlands	B	A	B	B	C	B	B	B
Portugal	A	B	B	C	C	C	A	A
Spain	A	B	B	B	C	B	A	B
UK	A	A	A	B	B	A	A	B

Key:
Readily available A
Limited availability B
No availability C

Source: Mercer Oliver Wyman, 2003, cited in Stephens, 2004.

The continuing problem of informality

In several Northern countries such as the UK and New Zealand, it has become cheaper to borrow but harder to get through the admission requirements.[280] Despite attempts to extend affordable housing finance to those with lower incomes, many households living in the South, and at least some in the North, are not able to secure such finance. This is not just an issue of affordability, but also of the reluctance of formal-sector financial institutions to lend to those working in the informal sector. Box 4.16 summarizes this context in South Africa. While non-lending to those without formal employment is more commonly associated with the South, Table 4.24 outlines the extent to which households with specific characteristics might find it difficult to get credit in the North. Although self-employment is itself no barrier to securing mortgage finance, those who cannot verify their incomes (for example, through accounts and tax returns) fall into the category of 'self-certified' incomes and in most countries cannot be considered for mortgage finance, or only have limited access. When analysed alongside the earlier discussion of titling and access to mortgage finance, Table 4.24 highlights the fact that informal income is a major barrier. In a context in which many find employment in the informal sector, Southern countries have large numbers of citizens who have to 'self-certify' their incomes.

The authors of one study argue that 'Risk-based pricing should be desirable in mortgage markets as it allows lenders to accurately price the product for the risks and provides access to the mortgage product to a wider range of borrowers.'[281] Risk-based pricing can take several forms; but where significant differences in prices exist, lending that is termed 'sub-prime' or 'non-conforming' becomes possible. As a result, they suggest that the market can respond to this situation by allowing lenders to charge a premium (higher interest rates) for providing mortgage finance for such borrowers.

The US, since the mid 1990s, has seen the growth of sub-prime lending or lending to those borrowers who have poor credit records or who cannot verify incomes.[282] In 2000, there was US$138 million in sub-prime originations and by 2002 the figure had increased to US$213 million.[283] The expansion in homeownership rates (up to 68.4 per cent in 2003) may be partly attributable to this. Such lending now accounts for some 7 per cent of new lending in the UK, which is the only EU-15 country to have developed a substantial sub-prime market.[284] Various barriers exist in Europe that have prevented the wider adoption of risk-based pricing. These range from usury laws in Italy, to the difficulty for any one lender in making the first move, thereby risking losing market share.[285] Sub-prime products are estimated to be virtually unavailable in 70 per cent of the EU-15, and there may be significant growth in the population served by the mortgage market should risk-based pricing become more widespread.[286] This is based on the experience of the UK and the US where customers have been willing to pay additional interest to secure funds. At the same time, there have been allegations of unfair additional charges being made to borrowers in this sub-prime market.[287] There is now borrower education about the dangers of predatory prices where lenders offer low-income households favourable terms in the expectation that they will default on the loan and foreclosure will take place.

This section has considered the problems arising from down-marketing of mortgage finance. Such strategies have been one component within government strategies to address housing need. The interest of low-income households in homeownership is directly linked to a lack of alternative options. With respect to social housing, there has been a significant change in policy in many countries with the use of more market-orientated strategies. As the scale of public housing is withdrawn and as the cost of social housing rises, households consider homeownership. In one recent (2003) survey, 35 per cent of renters in the US have tried and failed to become homeowners primarily due to affordability obstacles. There are suggestions that housing inequality is increasing in at least some countries as a result of down-marketing strategies. To take the example of China, 'housing policies (privatization and subsidies combined) accounted for 37 per cent of overall inequality in the distribution of income in urban areas in 1995', while it only accounted for 30 per cent in 1988.[288] In this context, it appears that: the 'current trend in housing reform is to privatize public housing as much as possible and demolish all poor-quality welfare housing. It seems that the new emphasis on the market is incompatible with public or welfare housing.'[289]

Box 4.16 Mortgage finance: problems with down-marketing in South Africa

The preconditions for the mortgage model are that houses have exchange value and are easily traded, so banks can use them as security for a high-value, long-term mortgage, and that borrowers can make regular repayments out of a predictable income stream. These conditions, however, do not hold for South Africa's low-income majority. South African banks are undeniably correct that they cannot extend mortgage finance to the informally employed, low-income majority, most of whom do not even have bank accounts. What is only beginning to be understood is that mortgage lending at the bottom end of a 'developing country' market – which is what South Africa really is – is risky not only for banks, but also for potential low-income borrowers. Even though they can repay small loans (as some South African microfinance institutions have proved), most low-income households cannot maintain the rigid repayment schedule required by a mortgage. Moreover, South Africa's 'township' housing markets are institutionally weak, and it is very difficult to sell a house, either to move up/down the housing ladder, or in execution. To make matters worse, South African formal-sector wage employment has actually declined in absolute terms since 1994, especially in the low middle-income bracket. As a result, when they do manage to get a mortgage, many low-income black South Africans lose their houses due to factors such as income instability and retrenchment.

Source: Baumann, 2004, p6.

Assessing systemic risks

Considerable efforts have taken place in some countries to extend market reach. The 'market' may be able to extend reach by improving its efficiency; but, ultimately, there is likely to be a trade-off between extending 'reach' and risk arising from the increased likelihood of a borrower with a large loan defaulting.[290] The risks with regard to individual borrowers can be reduced through insurance. However, there is also a need to recognize that such risks may be systemic rather than random (for example, they occur because of a general economic recession or rise in interest rates), and therefore can endanger the financial system itself. This, in part, explains the willingness of the state to provide assistance to households who find themselves in financial difficulties at the time of a financial crisis. The market itself may provide ways of mitigating against risk to protect itself, or allow individual borrowers to shift risk to third parties.

In the absence of falling prices assisting in affordability, the mortgage finance industry has to balance its response to consumer demand together with requests by governments to expand lending against pressure from shareholders, members and regulators, and start to lend prudently. The new lending undertaken by mortgage providers in the North has introduced new risks into the lending process.[291] Even in high-income countries, the housing market may be volatile partly due to the scale of financial deregulation. A recent IMF survey suggests that strong regulation of the banking sector is necessary to minimize these risks and that a deregulated banking system can encourage speculative investment in property.[292] The IMF highlights the specific problems faced by Thailand and (to a lesser extent) Malaysia.

In the US and UK, there have been problems with housing market 'booms and busts'.[293] Policy changes in the UK have shifted risks from institutions to borrowers. Several factors, notably increasing interest rates and very high loan-to-value ratios, resulted in a crisis during the late 1980s, with a significant increase in foreclosures. The 1980 foreclosure rate (as a percentage of outstanding mortgages) was 0.06 per cent, while the rate of 6 to 12 months' arrears was 0.25 per cent and the rate of 12-month-plus arrears was 0.08 per cent.[294] By 1989, these figures had risen to 0.17, 0.73 and 0.15, and by 1991 they were 0.77, 1.87 and 0.93 per cent, respectively. A related problem to 'boom-and-bust' house prices combined with high loan-to-value ratios is negative equity – that is when the value of the remaining loan exceeds the price of the house (for example, following a fall in prices). The fall in the Japanese market during the early 1990s offers an illustration of the potential scale of this problem: 'The total amount of negative equity for the whole of the Tokyo area was estimated [1995] to be about UK£7 billion.'[295] The consequences are considerable. One immediate problem is less housing mobility, as households simply cannot afford to repay their mortgage and take another because of the additional capital that they have to raise. A second problem is that foreclosure becomes less effective for the lending company since the value of the property will not fully cover the debt. Other problems relate to a lack of confidence in the housing finance system and housing markets in general. The dependence of the Japanese banking system upon real estate collateral resulted in considerable financial instability when land prices fell.[296] The message is that in addition to assessing the effectiveness of extending mortgage finance for their poverty reduction goals, governments also need to consider the implications and risks for housing market stability.

NOTES

1 This chapter is based on a draft prepared by Diana Mitlin, University of Manchester, UK.
2 Chiquier et al, 2004, p1.
3 Yasui, 2002a, p15.
4 Nuri Erbas and Nothaft, 2002, p15.
5 It is only such dwellings that are likely to meet the need for potential repossession and resale. Even if incremental dwellings have a legal land title, they may contravene building and/or zoning regulations.
6 Lohse, 2002, p42.
7 Governments have sought to control inflation for many reasons; but success in this area is likely to have particularly beneficial effects on mortgage lending.
8 For example, some argue that homeownership limits labour mobility and/or the need is for household savings (with appropriate interest rate policies) to be directed to the benefit of enterprise investment rather than personal assets.
9 Stephens, 2003, p1015. Stephens also notes that this pattern is associated with the housing finance history of Western Europe in recent decades. During the last decade, consistently lower inflation (likely to continue given current macroeconomic policies) means that the real value of the mortgage does not rapidly erode. Hence, consumer preferences may change.
10 Renaud, 1999.
11 Stuart at al, 2004.
12 Yasui, 2002a, p14.
13 Buckley and Kalarickal, 2004, p2.
14 Cities Alliance, 2002, p2.
15 Government of the Republic of Zambia, cited in Mulenga, 2003, p52.
16 Daphnis, 2004a, p2.
17 Daphnis, 2004a, p2.
18 Hegedüs, 2004, p8.
19 See Kritayanavaj, 2002, p15. Nevertheless, the bank's non-performing loans are at 17.4 per cent (Kritayanavaj, 2002, p25), and this suggests that the

weakness referred to by Daphnis (2004a) has not been fully addressed.
20 Lea, 2000, p17.
21 Joint Center for Housing Studies, 2004, p8.
22 Ballesteros, 2002, p3
23 Dübel, 2004, p28.
24 Yasui, 2002a, p12.
25 The primary market is retail lending to households. The secondary market is wholesale lending to retail providers.
26 Rubinstein, 2002, p15.
27 Okwir, 2002, p94.
28 Suresh, 2002, p119.
29 These are funds that receive mandatory payments, generally from employers and employees, and from which the employees can draw on for housing finance under particular circumstances.
30 Gadzama, 2002, p74.
31 Van Order, 2001, p16.
32 Dübel, 2004, p28.
33 Yasui, 2002a.
34 Dübel, 2004, p28.
35 Van Order, 2001, p21.
36 Van Order, 2001, pp20–21.
37 Van Order, 2001, p29.
38 Carolini, 2004.
39 Van Order, 2001, p20.
40 Van Order, 2001, p17.
41 Van Order, 2001, p29.
42 Van Order, 2001, p19.
43 Karley and Whitehead, 2002, p31.
44 ODPM, 2003, p1.
45 Karley and Whitehead, 2002, p32.
46 Karley and Whitehead, 2002, p36.
47 Lea, 2000, unnumbered Foreword.
48 Watanabe, 1998.
49 Chiquier et al, 2004, p2.
50 Lea, 2000, pp20–21.
51 D'Cruz, 2004a, p19.
52 D'Cruz, 2004a.
53 Lee, 2003, p26.
54 Gitau, 2004, p2.
55 Gitau, 2004, p9.
56 Chiquier et al, 2004.
57 Dübel, 2004, p29; Lea, 2000, pp3–5.
58 Connolly, 2004b.
59 Hoek-Smit and Diamond, 2003, p7.
60 Dymski and Isenburg, 1998.
61 Stephens, 2004, p11.
62 Pardo, 2000, p3.
63 Pardo, 2000, p3
64 Chin Beng 2002, p100.
65 Ogu and Ogbuozobe, 2001, p476.
66 Ogu and Ogbuozobe, 2001, p477.
67 Hardoy and Satterthwaite, 1989, pp107–111.
68 Stren, cited in Gitau, 2004, p4.
69 Mabogunje, cited in Gitau, 2004, p4.
70 Ogu and Ogbuozobe, 2001, p478.
71 Williams, 2004.
72 Stephens, 2004.
73 Stephens, 2003, p1020.
74 Stephens 2004, p11.
75 Suresh, 2002, p120.
76 Stephens, 2003, p1020.
77 Stephens, 2004.
78 Watanabe, 1998, p135.
79 Ballesteros, 2002, p18.
80 See, for example, Okpala, 1994, and Renaud, 1999.
81 As illustrated by Rubinstein (2002, p16) for Brazil, Mexico and Panama.
82 Quoted in Connolly, 2004b, p2.
83 Turner and Whitehead, 2002, p176.
84 Ballesteros, 2002, p18.
85 Nuri Erbas and Nothaft, 2002, p22.
86 Nuri Erbas and Nothaft 2002, p22.
87 Kumar Garg, 1998, p106; Smets, 2002, p138.
88 Lea, 2004b, p24.
89 Stephens, 2003, p1014.
90 Stephens, 2004, p12.
91 Scanlon and Whitehead, 2004
92 Stephens, 2004, p9.
93 Stuart et al, 2004, p9.
94 Stuart et al, 2004, p9.
95 Scanlon and Whitehead, 2004, p20.
96 Kahrlik, cited in Hegedüs, 2004, p7.
97 Yasui, 2002b, p27.
98 Merrill and Whiteley, 2003, pp11–12.
99 Merrill and Whiteley, 2003, p18.
100 Gilbert, 2004, p35.
101 Forero, 2004, pp34–38.
102 Connolly, 2004b.
103 Scanlon and Whitehead, 2004, p18.
104 Scanlon and Whitehead, 2004, p18.
105 Stuart et al, 2004, p3.
106 Stephens, 2004.
107 Williams, 2004, p20.
108 Stephens, 2004, p3.
109 Stephens (2004, p4) notes that nominal interest rates fell throughout the advanced economies, a phenomenon linked to the worldwide fall in inflation; however, although the nominal interest rate is the same throughout the Euro zone, different levels of inflation between member countries mean that real interest rates continue to vary.
110 Stephens, 2004, p4.
111 Earley, 2004b, p4.
112 Earley, 2004b; Lambert, 2004.
113 Earley, 2004b.
114 Pitcoff, cited in Carolini, 2004, p2.
115 HUD, 2003, cited in Carolini, 2004.
116 Carolini, 2004.
117 HUD, cited in Carolini, 2004, p11.
118 Hegedüs, 2004, p6.
119 Hegedüs, 2004, p6; Yasui, 2002b, p25.
120 Lea, 2004b, pp22–24.
121 Lea, 2004b, pp22–24.
122 Yasui, 2002b pp29–30.
123 Yasui, 2002b, p30.
124 Hegedüs, 2002, p56.
125 Yasui, 2002b, p19.
126 Earley, 2004b.
127 Chiquier et al, 2004, p28.
128 Yasui, 2002b, p19.
129 Hegedüs, 2002, p10.
130 Hegedüs, 2002, p49.
131 Stephens, 2003, p1021.
132 Yasui, 2002a, p11. These delays are partly due to the extensive transfer of properties from state to household in many countries (Hegedüs and Teller, 2003).
133 Hegedüs and Teller, 2003.
134 Hegedüs, 2002, pp18, 23.
135 Yasui, 2002b, p22.
136 Hegedüs and Teller, 2003.
137 Yasui, 2002a, p8.
138 Yasui, 2002b, p23.
139 Bugie, 2004, pp32–33.
140 An example of the scale of the problems is given by Zambia where, between 1985 and 2000, the average mortgage interest rate oscillated between 20 and 90 per cent per annum (Groves, 2004).
141 Kamete, 2000, p255.
142 De Soto, 2002.
143 Buckley and Kalarickal, 2004, pp21–22; Lincoln Institute of Land Policy, 2002.
144 Gilbert, 2002b, p16.
145 Buckley and Kalarickal, 2004, p22.
146 Buckley and Kalarickal, 2004, p23.
147 Rojas, 2004.
148 Vance, 2004, p127.
149 Daphnis, 2004b, p107.
150 Nell et al, cited in Baumann, 2004.
151 Calderón, 2004.
152 World Bank, 2004a, p2.
153 Joint Center for Housing Studies, 2004, pp12–14.
154 Ferguson, 1999, p186.
155 IADB, 2003.
156 Davies and Mahony, 2001, p25.
157 Hoek-Smit, 1998, p18.
158 World Bank, 2004a, p3.
159 World Bank, 2004a, pp2–3.
160 Ferguson, 1999, pp186–187.
161 Ballesteros, 2002, p18.
162 Jacobs and Savedoff, 1999, p5.
163 Jacobs and Savedoff, 1999, p6.
164 Pardo, 2000, pp23–24.
165 Gitau, 2004, p13.
166 Hoek-Smit, 1998, p18.
167 Lall and Lall, 2003, pp15–16.
168 Ferguson, 2004a, p22.
169 Ferguson, 2003.
170 Lall and Lall, 2003, p16.
171 Lall and Lall, 2003, pp20–21.
172 Biswas, 2003.
173 Datta, 1999, pp192–193.
174 Aphimeteetamrong and Kritayanavaj, 1998, p227.
175 Ahn, 2002.
176 Lee and Lee, 1998, p162.
177 Ha, 2002b, p245.
178 Kim and Ahn, 2002, p224.
179 Lamoreaux, 1998, p69.
180 Itoh, 2002, p157.
181 Oizumi, 2002, p170.
182 Oizumi, 2002, p181.
183 Itoh, 2002, p166.
184 Seki and Watanabe, 1998, pp118–119.
185 Karnad, 2004.
186 Karnad, 2004, pp8–9.
187 Kumar Garg, 1998, p98.
188 Kumar Garg, 1998, p99.
189 Karnad, 2004, p8.
190 Karnad, 2004, p8.
191 Gallarado, 1998, p204.
192 Ballesteros, 2002, p28.
193 Ballesteros, 2002, p28.
194 Ballesteros, 2004, pp15–16.
195 Zhao and Bourassa, 2003, p722.
196 Zhao and Bourassa, 2003, p738.
197 Ballesteros, 2002.
198 Zhao and Bourassa, 2003, p724.
199 Zhao and Bourassa, 2003, p733.
200 Zhao and Bourassa, 2003, p733.
201 Rojas, 2004.
202 Rojas, 2004.
203 Rubinstein, 2002, p15; Rojas, 2004.
204 Rojas, 2004.
205 World Bank, 2004a. Minimum salaries are set in many Latin American countries. However, they have not kept pace with inflation and, hence, the assessment of what is required to afford a mortgage even on a very basic unit.
206 World Bank, 2004a, p4.
207 Joint Center for Housing Studies, 2004, p35.
208 Joint Center for Housing Studies, 2004, p35.
209 World Bank, 2004a.
210 World Bank, 2004a.
211 Coovadia, 2004, pp10–11.
212 At the exchange rate of US$1 = 6.45 rand, as of Thursday, 7 October 2004.
213 See www.mfrc.co.za/detail.php?s=91 downloaded on 7 October 2004.
214 Moss, 2001, pp33–34.
215 Nell el al, cited in Baumann, 2004.
216 Groves, 2004.

217 Coovadia, 2004, pp10–11.
218 Kamete, 2000, p252.
219 Kamete, 2000, p254.
220 Government of Tanzania and UN-Habitat, 2003, pp44–47.
221 Kamete, 2000, pp249–251.
222 Kofi Karley, 2002, p27.
223 Government of Tanzania and UN-Habitat, 2003, p32.
224 *Sunday Nation*, 2004, cited in Gitau, 2004, p2.
225 Okwir, 2002, p95.
226 Kofi Karley, 2002, p28.
227 Shelter Afrique, 2002, pp50–51.
228 Baëta Ansah, 2002, pp55–59.
229 Okonkwo, 2002, p87.
230 Baëta Ansah, 2002, p57.
231 Although, as observed earlier, Van Order (2001) argues that, in the US, 80 per cent of the increase in homeownership rates occurred within a deposit-based system and prior to the development of the secondary market.
232 Ogu and Ogbuozobe, 2001, p479.
233 Ogu and Ogbuozobe, 2001, p480.
234 Nubi, cited in Gitau, 2004, p4.
235 Kofi Karley, 2002, p28.
236 Mercer Oliver Wyman, cited in Stephens, 2004, pp7–8.
237 Hegedüs, 2004, p7.
238 Yasui, 2002a, p13.
239 Yasui, 2002a, p13; Yasui, 2002b, p29.
240 Zehnder, 2004.
241 Stephens, 2004, p12.
242 Arimah, 2000, p2562.
243 Kritayanavaj, 2002, p21.
244 Gallarado, 1998, p212; Ballesteros, 2002.
245 Fernandez, 2004.
246 UN-Habitat, 2002, p8.
247 Government of Tanzania and UN-Habitat, 2003, p72.
248 See, respectively, Lamoreaux, 1998, p51; Aphimeteetamrong and Kritayanavaj, 1998, p229; Kofi Karley, 2002, p27.
249 Stephens, 2004, p5.
250 Stuart et al, 2004, p3.
251 This is not a perfect guide to 'underlying' affordability because the growth of dual-income households in some countries increases the number of incomes that can be called upon to finance house purchase or pay interest charges on mortgages.
252 IMF, 2004, p72.
253 Earley, 2004b, p11.
254 IMF, 2004, p84.
255 IMF, 2004, p86.
256 Buckley and Kalarickal, 2004, p12.
257 Stephens, 2002.
258 Buckley and Kalarickal, 2004, p12.
259 Government of Tanzania and UN-Habitat, 2003, p26.
260 Ballesteros, 2002, p2.
261 Stuart et al, 2004, p5.
262 Stephens, 2004.
263 Stephens, 2004, p5.
264 Stuart et al, 2004, p6.
265 Forrest et al, 2003, p286.
266 Carolini, 2004, p4.
267 Carolini, 2004, p4.
268 Yasui, 2002b, p31.
269 Hegedüs and Teller, 2003.
270 Down-marking is a term used to refer to the practice of reaching lower income groups.
271 Smets, 2002, p175.
272 Smets, 2002, p175.
273 Mukhija, 2004a.
274 Mukhija, 2004a, p2235.
275 Mukhija, 2004a, p2241.
276 Freedom to Build, 2004, p77.
277 Ballesteros, 2002, p28.
278 Ballesteros, 2002, p21.
279 Ballesteros 2002, p23.
280 Dymski and Isenburg, 1998; Stuart et al, 2004.
281 Mercer Oliver Wyman, 2003, quoted in Stephens, 2004.
282 Lea, 2004a, p13.
283 Carolini, 2004.
284 Stephens, 2004, p10.
285 Mercer Oliver Wyman, cited in Stephens, 2004.
286 Mercer Oliver Wyman, cited in Stephens, 2004.
287 Lea, 2004a, p13.
288 Khan, cited in Zhao and Bourassa, 2003, pp738–739.
289 Zhao and Bourassa, 2003, p742.
290 Stephens, 2004, p1.
291 Williams, 2004, pp20–21.
292 Collyns and Senhadji, 2002, p73.
293 Stephens, 2003, p1014.
294 Dymski and Isenburg, 1998; Stephens, 2003, p1014.
295 Forrest et al, 2003, pp285–286.
296 Forrest et al, 2003, p282.

CHAPTER 5

FINANCING FOR SOCIAL AND RENTAL HOUSING[1]

As already indicated in the discussion of subsidies within Chapter 4, there is a widespread acceptance of the need for subsidies. This does not simply reflect political ideology, nor is it only a popularist response by politicians in need of votes. The willingness of governments to consider housing subsidies reflects the significance of shelter and a home to citizens, the recognized importance of this to society, and the importance of residential construction for the economy. More specifically, a number of reasons can be identified to explain the prevalence for state subsidies for shelter (which explicitly includes services and the dwelling):[2]

- *Improving public health and, more specifically, ensuring that living conditions do not cause outbreaks of diseases.* This relates particularly, but not exclusively, to the provision of water and sanitation services.
- *Improving fairness, justice and social stability.* This set of objectives reflects the poverty orientation of some housing programmes. It is understood that children need places in which to study and to be safe, and equally that social exclusion and poverty may be characterized by living in an inadequately resourced neighbourhood. It may simply be that incomes are too low to afford the basic standard of living that society wishes to provide to its members or that households under-provide from their income – hence the need for subsidies.
- *Providing some aspects of housing considered to be a 'public good' that is not adequately coped with by the private market.* For example, the high level of informality in Latin America suggests that 'It is a public responsibility to devise and implement the legal systems and policies required to bring housing into compliance with land and building regulations.'[3] Only such tenure security will encourage private investment in housing.
- *Overcoming market inefficiencies that may result in monopoly profits and undersupply by developers, poor housing quality, or an insufficient volume of construction, particularly low-income housing.* Financial subsidies are only one possible response to such problems; others would include facilitating the supply of land and reforming the regulatory framework.
- *Reducing housing costs.* This can be achieved, for example, by developing a system for mortgage insurance in primary or secondary markets, or encouraging competition in the building materials sector.
- *Stimulating economic growth.* The construction industry is a very important sector.

The breadth of the appeal of subsidies is illustrated later in this chapter by the government of the Republic of Korea, which, even as it considers how to deregulate the housing finance market, is looking at alternative ways to assist those in housing need. Moreover, as indicated by housing-support strategies in the North, increasing prosperity does not necessarily result in the state doing less in housing markets.

While a narrow definition of housing finance may focus only on the provision of credit, the scale and significance of housing finance subsidies – primarily through rental housing, subsidized loan finance and direct demand (capital) subsidies – makes this component difficult to ignore. An understanding of how the financing of social housing can fit within a broader system of housing financing is needed.[4] This chapter looks specifically at some strategies that have recently been used to provide financial subsidies. Financial subsidies seek to provide incentives 'to enable and persuade a certain class of producers or consumers to do something they would not otherwise do by lowering the opportunity cost or otherwise increasing the potential benefit of doing so'.[5] Some argue that such financial subsidies are best avoided and should 'be a policy of last resort'.[6] These concerns focus on the potential distortion of markets and are often accomplished by recommendations on institutional and regulatory reforms, such as those elaborated upon in Box 5.1. As already noted in Chapter 4, such subsidies, especially those offered on interest rates, may have a huge hidden cost.

Increasing prosperity does not necessarily result in the state doing less in housing markets

Although subsidies tend to be criticized by economists seeking to encourage a greater realization of the potential effectiveness of markets, they remain popular with governments. One critical assessment of the potential of subsidies in Latin America is forced to also recognize, in a

Box 5.1 Regulations, policies or subsidies?

Subsidy should be used as a policy of last resort or, more precisely, should only be used in conjunction with other policy steps. The hierarchy of complementary government actions needed to improve the housing conditions for the majority of housing in an economy are as follows:

- Develop or reform institutions and policies to facilitate the role of private and non-profit lenders and developers in expanding the moderate-/low-income housing supply, and provide education and training to consumers and producers to improve the operation of the housing finance industry;
- Improve the regulatory system in the different supply markets (land, finance and infrastructure) to allow more households to acquire authorized and healthful housing;
- Provide subsidies to address well-defined objectives.

Simply put, if government does not do what is necessary to encourage housing construction and finance industries to function efficiently, housing supply cannot respond to price signals, and higher incomes or subsidies will not translate into better housing.

Source: Hoek-Smit and Grigsby, cited in Hoek-Smit and Diamond, 2003, p5.

footnote, that 'it appears that countries at the level of economic development in Latin America allocate from 1 to 5 per cent of government budgets for housing subsidies'.[7] The interest in subsidies has resulted in multiple approaches to their delivery of subsidies, which notably include direct interest-rates reductions, allowing mortgage interest to be deducted from income taxes; support for housing savings; support for insurance in the primary market; and support for insurance in secondary markets and direct grants.[8]

Nevertheless, concerns remain, notably that such subsidies rarely reach the poor. This concern has been widely recognized and is validated in Chapter 4. As discussed in Chapters 6 and 7, recent housing policy in some countries of the South has been associated with a growing interest in small loans to enhance the process of incremental or progressive housing. Furthermore, as discussed in Chapter 6 (which deals with smaller loans), many of the poor, particularly those living in the South, face highly distorted markets for housing, especially in the markets for credit and land. Further problems arise because of the constraining impact of the regulatory systems. In such a context, governments have made use of finance as a way to address need. This chapter looks specifically at financial subsidies that have particularly sought to reach the poor and provide them with access to a complete dwelling. Governments in the North and the South have primarily used two financing strategies to assist families to obtain housing: assistance for ownership and/or the assistance to afford adequate rental accommodation. Despite this focus on the poor, the limitations of these approaches should be recognized. The Chilean programme, for example, gives a majority of subsidy funds to subsidy streams that include loan components and are for higher income households.[9]

Prior to discussing specific experiences in the provision of subsidized housing finance to low-income families for complete dwellings, several predominant trends should be recognized. As is the case with Chapter 4, there are always exceptions to such trends. Nevertheless, three specific trends are well established in a number of countries:[10]

1. There is now less direct provision managed by the state or agencies associated with the state. Governments have shifted away from the direct construction and management of public housing. They have also used several strategies to reduce their stocks with, in some cases, large-scale transfers to occupiers.
2. There is increasing assistance for homeownership through direct-demand (capital) subsidies. The scale and costs of interest rate subsidies have already been noted. In an effort to reduce costs and increase the effectiveness of expenditure, several countries have introduced capital subsidies for those with low incomes to assist them in purchasing complete (or almost complete) dwellings. The use of targeted financial benefits for housing presupposes the institutional capacity to identify households in need. This may not exist in all Southern countries.
3. Consistent with the two trends above is the greater use of housing allowances (rather than direct provision) to assist low-income families renting accommodation in private or not-for-profit sectors.

All these options involve considerable subsidy finance and therefore their use is limited to a number of countries. No consideration is given in this chapter to loan finance, as interest rate subsidies have been considered in Chapter 4 with regard to larger loans and are considered in Chapters 6 and 7 in the light of smaller loans. However, it should be noted that some of the direct-demand subsidies have loan components. Despite their focus on lower income households, funding for direct subsidies is often smaller in scale than interest rate subsidies when the full costs of the latter over the life of the loan are considered. The different strategies for supporting the housing costs of the poor depend considerably upon state capacity to pay; for this reason, this chapter is divided by world region.

CONDITIONS AND TRENDS

State rental housing in the North

Although the state in the North is generally playing a less direct role in economic intervention, this is not necessarily the case in housing. Despite the shift to income-related support, the social rented sector (defined as housing let at below-market prices and allocated administratively on the basis of housing need, rather than on the ability to pay) remains a significant tenure in several of the 15 European Union (EU-15) member states, including the UK, France, Denmark, Finland, Sweden and the Netherlands. However, there have been significant changes in policy and the nature of housing support has shifted in Western Europe:

> *The existing support system with large, general interest subsidies for new construction and*

rehabilitation has been phased out. Targeted, income-related, subsidies have become relatively more important, as have subsidies to depressed housing areas.[11]

Such changes partly reflect the success of housing systems in addressing housing need.[12] However, what is also evident is that, despite a commonality of trends with regard to more limited funding, considerable diversity continues within Europe and there is no single approach to addressing housing need.[13]

In the US, the direct provision of social housing has not been a popular strategy, with just 1.7 per cent of the population living in public housing.[14] Just over half of the funding to support low-income housing from the Housing and Urban Development Department goes to the Section 8 Housing Choice Voucher Programme, which initially focused on rental housing, but which has now been extended to enable support for ownership occupiers. This scheme is means tested by income and family size. Within this programme, there is evidence of similar trends to those in Europe, with a shift away from designated housing units and towards greater market choice, with the individual selection of accommodation. Public housing also remains an option (see Box 5.2), albeit somewhat limited. There are 1.8 million occupied units across the country owned by public housing authorities. There is also limited assistance, such as tax credits for private-sector developers building rental housing for low- and moderate-income housing. However, public housing is not perceived as the most suitable option for low-income families; rather, it is a route that will lead, in the longer term, 'toward self-sufficiency and homeownership'.[15]

There has been a general marked decline in the levels of new housing units in this sector. Subsequent problems include those faced by women in Canada as reductions in state funding in 1993 resulted in the loss of 325,000 subsidized rental units.[16] The decline in new housing units reflects the fulfilment of the mission to remove 'crude' housing shortages (when the number of households exceeded the number of dwellings), although regional shortages have often re-emerged.[17] As noted earlier, the government still plays an important role in housing people who are unable to access housing through market mechanisms, although the emphasis placed on the *safety net* function (assistance to the very poor) and wider *affordability* (assistance to those who are not so poor) objectives varies greatly. In the UK, the emphasis is very much on the safety net function, which has contributed to the concentration of very poor households in the sector. Elsewhere, the tenure is much more mixed, although sometimes the most marginalized households have difficulty in accessing social housing. The incomes of social renters averaged at least 70 per cent of the average in France, Germany, the Netherlands and Sweden, but were less than 50 per cent of the average in the UK.[18]

As the numbers of designated social housing and/or public properties fall, there are concerns that the scale of social disadvantage associated with such accommodation will rise. It is feared that the shifts in housing policy in Europe and, notably, a more limited housing stock will result in a high concentration of social disadvantage, thereby exacerbating social exclusion, reducing mobility and creating greater marginalization for tenants.[19] One further concern is that the growth of means-tested housing allowances (also encouraged by use of private finance) has resulted in higher rents.[20] However, these are considered to offer better incentives in terms of labour mobility and to enable more effective targeting.

Box 5.2 Public housing in New York

The New York City Housing Authority (NYCHA) is the largest public housing authority in the country, with roughly 181,000 apartments in 2698 residential buildings throughout the city (as of September 2004). The public housing residential population represents roughly 5 per cent of the city's total, and on average pays US$311 in monthly rent. This same population's average annual income is US$18,334, and almost 18 per cent of households are on public assistance.

NYCHA has more than 10,000 apartments that are for the elderly alone, and about 33 per cent of NYCHA households are headed by persons over 62 years of age. Working families account for 40 per cent of NYCHA residents; but with an extremely low vacancy rate of only 0.43 per cent of apartments available for all public housing households, it is not very surprising that over 136,000 families are on NYCHA's waiting list.

Source: Information from NYCHA Fact Sheet (revised 2 December 2004) quoted in Carolini, 2004, accessible online at www.nyc.gov/html/nycha/pdf/factsheet.pdf.

One of the most significant developments in social rented housing has been the increased use made of private finance for social rented housing in much of Western Europe.[21] Despite this use, there has been limited private-equity investment, although there is some evidence of greater interest in the UK.[22] Box 5.3 discusses changes in the financing of social housing in the EU countries. An analysis of margins suggested that despite a degree of sophistication, UK housing associations pay more for finance than their counterparts in the Netherlands, Denmark and Sweden (see Table 5.1). This could be attributable to the absence of a state guarantee system in the UK.

One of the most significant developments in social rented housing has been the increased use made of private finance

One of the key trends during recent years has been the emergence of surpluses in the social rented sector as a whole in many countries.[23] Declining debt burdens arising from lower levels of construction and the repayment of older debt have coincided with rising rents to create these surpluses. Several countries have attempted to establish 'revolving-door' systems of finance whereby surpluses are reinvested in the sector. This may happen informally (as in the Netherlands where redistribution between landlords occurs through the informal mechanism of merger) and more formally (through the Housing Fund in Finland and the building funds in Denmark). However, it seems that revolving-door finance alone does not stimulate increased construction, either because funds are inadequate or incentives are absent. Without subsidy mechanisms, governments appear to lack the leverage with which to stimulate the social rented sector.

At the same time, the shift from state provision to state financing of a range of providers means that government has reduced its risk. However, the market for social housing is heavily influenced by political choice. Whatever the housing system for lower income households, governments appear to be highly involved; even if they are

Box 5.3 Funding social housing in the European Union (EU)

At the highest level of generality, European Union (EU) social providers (particularly not-for-profit providers) typically raise private-sector loans collateralized on the housing stock (although the UK still uses extensive capital grants). The financial basis of the funding is supervised by local authorities or dedicated public agencies and by the financial supervisors who follow lenders' practices. Unlike the constraints facing mortgage markets, there is some evidence of a European-wide market for social housing finance.

The classic model of social housing finance in Western Europe involved significant public commitments to underpin, insure, subsidize or provide public loans (or some combination of the above). This meant that providers could repay loans at below-market terms or have to fund investment on only a proportion of the capital value (rather than the private-sector provider who needs to raise market finance on the entire capital value). The growth in the use of market instruments, buttressed by housing allowances and some subsidy in the form of capital grants, has many important consequences:

- the opening up of the source of social housing funds to the global capital market and to a diverse range of social instruments;
- 'professionalizing' the voluntary housing sector (arguably to the detriment of tenant participation);
- expecting most providers in EU countries to use their own funds (reserves), which can be as large as 33 per cent of funding;
- the fact that, despite the growth in private funding, public funding remains important in the UK, Germany, Belgium, the Netherlands, France and the Nordic countries; and
- the diversity of the sources of private funding, with an increase in risk.

Source: Gibb, 2002, p331.

not significant operationally, they are significant with regard to finance. In such a context, it is important for the private sector to:

> *... understand both the current situation in relation to government safety nets for the sector and the extent to which what is on offer is truly open to the usual risks of changing costs and demand ... it is political risk rather than market risk which determines the value of the investment.*[24]

Table 5.1

The cost of private finance to social landlords

Country	Spread (basis points)	Benchmark rate	Cost of guarantee to landlord	Estimated value of guarantee (basis points)
Denmark	20–30	Government bond	0	20
Finland	30–40	IBOR (inter-bank offered rate)	0	–
Netherlands	20–40	Government bond	Initial membership fee/commission	100
Sweden				
• strong	20–25	Government bond	0	20
• weak	100	Government bond	0	20
• securitization	40	Government bond	0	20
UK				
• VR (variable rate) LIBOR (London inter-bank offered rate)	53.4	IBOR	not available	not available
• FR (fixed rate) <7 years	164	5-year government bond	not available	not available
• FR 7–16 years	180	10-year government bond	not available	not available
• FR >20 years	170	20-year government bond	not available	not available
• Bond issues 1998–2001	126.4	Government bond	not available	not available

Source: Stephens et al, 2002, cited in Stephens, 2004.

State rental housing in transition countries

Prior to transition, in most Eastern European countries housing was provided by state institutions (workplace, local government and/or housing co-operatives). Essentially, the system was one in which state-provided social rental systems dominated, with low rents and administrative allocation systems.[25] However, there was also considerable diversity with, for example, Albania having 35 per cent of its housing stock in public hands compared to Bulgaria, with only 7 per cent public housing.[26]

The transition phase included the transfer of some of these dwellings to their occupants under privatization programmes. In some countries, more than 90 per cent of the stock was sold, while in others the percentage was as low as 6 per cent.[27] In most cases, the share of the public sector in the housing stock has fallen to 5–10 per cent, with some exceptions such as Poland and the Czech Republic.[28] In some countries, this transition began during the 1970s and 1980s when pressure for improved housing increased and experiments were made in market provision.[29] However, housing markets were very limited. Even where people owned their dwellings, it appears to have been difficult to trade them. While such transfers of public housing to occupants are particularly associated with the transition countries, the policy is not exclusive to them. Similar transfers are currently taking place in China; and in the UK, the homeownership rate rose from 54 to 65 per cent between May 1979 and November 1990 as a result of the Conservative government's 'right to buy' policy.[30] Similar opportunities have now been introduced in Sweden.[31]

By the end of the 1990s, there was some interest in reinvestment in rental housing – for example in Poland, Slovakia, the Czech Republic and Hungary.[32] A significant scale is planned – between 10 and 30 per cent of new construction in Poland, Romania and Hungary.[33] However, a considerable problem remains, which is that the institutional strategies for addressing the housing needs of the poorest have 'collapsed', with no alternative being developed. Although there has been much debate, little has come forward to develop solutions at scale. Support for the private sector seems to be politically more acceptable; but it appears to be both expensive and rarely orientated towards the social rental sector.[34] Housing allowance systems have been considered, but appear to be too expensive given the scale of need.[35] Moreover, a recent assessment of the effectiveness of this approach in Russia is pessimistic and suggests that it is failing to fulfil the safety net function that was intended.[36] An alternative used in Hungary sought to provide subsidized capital to entities (such as local government) to set up agencies that provide social housing which would be let under controlled rents to eligible households.[37] In the countries of Eastern Europe:

> *Although there was no absolute shortage in housing, there was a significant need for more housing that was affordable for low-income groups. The low-income social groups will not be able to afford to finance homeownership, thus support to these groups by public housing*

will be needed. As a result of the extreme privatization policy, no substantial public sector remains.[38]

Despite such needs, it appears that social housing is becoming a residual category.[39]

Rental housing in the South

Large-scale public housing has not been that significant in the South despite exceptions such as Hong Kong. While many countries have experimented on a minor scale, in general the scale of provision reflects the limited funds available to invest in public housing initiatives and the high standards that are required. As noted in Chapter 4 vis-à-vis housing for sale, units have been expensive and scarce. Usually, they have not been allocated to the poor, nor would they necessarily have been affordable even if they had been allocated. In some cases, these properties have now been privatized following the increased emphasis on market provision.[40] As with the transition countries in Europe, China has relatively recently begun a policy to transfer to homeownership dwellings that had previously been rented primarily from state-owned enterprises, but also from other state housing providers. Box 5.4 describes this process in the city of Jinan.

Despite this general trend against direct provision in the South as well as the North, there is some continuing support for rental housing. In Hong Kong, the Housing Authority actually increased its stock by 18,000 units between 1991 and 2001; this is also in spite of the simultaneous sale of public rental housing during this period.[41] The authority continued building and increased the entitlement threshold in real terms, thereby adding to its potential clients. However, a considerable subsidy is required; tenants pay about 9 per cent of their income in rent compared to 29 per cent in the private sector.[42] In the Republic of Korea, since 1989 there has been a growing interest in a permanent rental dwelling programme for those on low incomes.[43] Progress has been slow and, by the end of 1999, public rental units only accounted for 2 per cent of the total housing stock; however, the policy reflects government recognition that homeownership is not a viable solution for all of those on low incomes.[44] In South Africa, there has also been a policy (albeit as a secondary strategy subsidiary to the main emphasis on homeownership that is discussed in the next section) to support the development of a social housing sector and, more specifically, to encourage the development of housing associations to manage low-income estates and rental accommodation. The government estimates that there are 60 institutions offering 25,000 rental units.[45] The institutional housing subsidy programme is used to assist with the financing of developments. In this case, a further benefit has been the use of finance to rehabilitate inner-city buildings. There is a recognition within the government that rents should not be more than 25 to 30 per cent of income, and this may make future financing complex. Even more recently, the municipal government in São Paulo, Brazil, introduced further measures in Jaunary 2004 to provide benefits to low-income households renting accommodation in the city.

Box 5.4 The right to buy in China

In Jinan, a city of 1.5 million in eastern China, the percentage of work-managed housing was still at 63 per cent in 1998, with 18 per cent living in state-managed housing and 19 per cent in private housing. Nominal rents in public housing rose during the 1990s from an average of 0.11 yuan to about 6.75 yuan per square metre. The Comfortable Housing Programme was aimed at assisting those in particular need, and by 1999, 10,800 (just under half of the 24,500 low-income households with special housing problems) had bought – at cost price – or were renting comfortable housing.

Attempts to sell public housing began in 1994, but did not really take off until conditions were made more favourable; by the end of 1995, only 5 per cent of all units had been sold. The subsidy on sale was further increased until it became almost a free allocation in many cases, and by the end of 1999, 80 per cent of public housing units had been privatized.

Source: Zhao and Bourassa, 2003.

The majority of renters in developing country cities are in the informal housing sector. In some parts of West Africa and Asia, the incidence of renting is very high. It is estimated that 80 per cent of households in Abidjan, Côte d'Ivoire, were tenants in the 1980s and that 88 per cent were tenants in Port Harcourt, Nigeria, in 1984. Comparable percentages in 1981 for Calcutta and Madras, India, were 76 and 68 respectively.[46] In spite of this reality, most low-income shelter policies, programmes and projects have tended to promote homeownership and have paid little attention to rental housing, either in terms of understanding and addressing the needs of tenants or encouraging the development of this type of housing. However, there is now increasing recognition of the significant role of rental housing in meeting the shelter needs of the many urban poor households who cannot afford homeownership (see Box 9.3).

Social housing and homeownership

In practice, the high costs of constructing rental public housing and the ongoing costs of maintenance, often in a context in which rents remain very low, has resulted in large-scale rental programmes being considered impossible in many Southern countries. Housing budgets in Southern countries can 'seldom carry universal housing subsidy programmes and very few new programmes are created that are structured as an entitlement'.[47] Despite these problems, there are some governments that have sought to introduce subsidy programmes of a significant scale. There is often widespread popular support for measures to address housing needs. Box 5.5 describes the pressure that social movements in Brazil have been exerting over a number of years in order to increase state commitment to this area. Given the financial constraints, governments have a limited range of choices. In some cases, they have chosen to use limited funds to support small loan programmes that enhance the process of incremental housing development. These strategies are considered in Chapter 6 on shelter microfinance and Chapter 7 on community funds.

Housing budgets in Southern countries can seldom carry universal housing subsidy programmes

In other cases, governments have chosen to subsidize a minimum complete dwelling. The remainder of this chapter considers financing strategies that have incorporated capital grants (direct-demand subsidies), in some cases together with mortgage loans.

Box 5.5 The National Fund for Popular Housing, Brazil

During the early 1990s in Brazil, the popular housing movements acting in the National Forum of Urban Reform presented to the Brazilian Congress a popular initiative subscribed to by 1 million voters,[48] hoping to create the National Fund of Popular Housing and the National Council of Popular Housing. This project has been a long time in gestation (over 12 years); but was finally passed in the Brazilian Chamber of Deputies in June 2004 and is now awaiting approval of the senate.

The objective is to make access to housing easier for low-income populations in both urban and rural areas through the use of subsidies. Land policies will need to facilitate this programme. The target population are those living in insecure conditions, in slums, collective-renting accommodation, tenement houses and risk areas, or individuals with an income equal to or lower than ten minimum wages. It is proposed that the main resources for the fund will be the national budget, together with the investment resources of the government's Severance Indemnity Fund for Employees (FGTS). These resources will be invested in social programmes such as the production of serviced land; slum improvement; the upgrading of tenement houses and co-operative rental housing; the construction and reform of community and/or institutional facilities connected with housing projects; land regulation; and the purchase of building materials.

It is proposed that a National Council of Popular Housing be established to draft guidelines and design programmes to allocate the fund's resources, to carry out the economic management of these resources and to determine objective criteria for resource distribution. The membership of the council will be drawn from the federal government, the trade unions and legally constituted popular housing organizations. The system, as a whole, must include the Brazilian Urban Ministry and other federal, state and municipal organizations of public administration.

The federal government already manages various social housing programmes of benefit to low-income rural and urban populations, which provide land for housing and smallholdings. These programmes include:

- the efficient production of economical housing and infrastructure improvement (Better Living and Pro-Housing; Residential Leasing);
- regularization of informal settlements; and
- slum upgrading (Habitar Brazil).

These are all subsidized programmes controlled by Programme for Social Housing (PSH), a federal entity. In addition to financing self-help and co-operative construction, they endeavour to give some priority to women who are heads of household, to families with the lowest incomes, and to rural and poor urban populations. There is also a low-cost credit aid programme (Solidarity Credit) directed at family groups organized into formal co-operatives or housing associations where the members' incomes ranges from zero to three times the present minimum wage, with 542 million Brazilian real for 2004.

Source: Nelson Saule, pers comm, 2004

Occasionally, effective capital subsidies have been given through supposed low-interest loans. The poor performance of state-owned housing finance companies has already been discussed in Chapter 4; but what was not elaborated upon are the reasons for such a poor performance. The limited resources that exist for housing finance mean that allocations may be made as political favours rather than universal entitlements. Governments have been reluctant to be seen to agree to foreclosure, as noted in the example from Zimbabwe in Chapter 4.[49] In other cases, state loans may simply be written off (perhaps as part of an election campaign). In such contexts, one reason for low repayment rates on government loans is that borrowers do not expect to be held to their repayment commitments. The dynamics around such lending are illustrated in Box 5.6.[50] In this case, the scheme sought to assist the poor, identified by the Indian classification system of 'economically weaker sections' (EWS), with additional and explicit criteria specifying inclusion of scheduled castes, scheduled tribes and backward classes. In order to participate in the schemes, beneficiaries had to own land; furthermore, to enable the inclusion of the poorest, land was allocated free to some squatting on public land with plots of less than 85 square metres. A basic permanent structure was provided using funds provided by the Housing and Urban Development Corporation (HUDCO) at a subsidized interest rate of 9 per cent, with the loans to be repaid by beneficiaries and guaranteed by the state government. In one project, in 1994, used for purposes of illustration, the cost of each unit was 13,000 rupees, of which 11,700 rupees comprised a loan. The reason for a recovery rate of less than 15 per cent is explained in Box 5.6.

Box 5.6 The politicization of housing finance in India

By building as many housing units for 'economically weaker sections' (EWS) of the Indian social hierarchy, the Indian government has attempted to demonstrate that it is doing a lot to benefit the poor. However, almost all of the actors involved try to manipulate the creation of policy, the selection of beneficiaries and/or the implementation of housing schemes for personal gain. Almost none of the government officials are really bothered whether or not the target group is helped.

The recovery rate of EWS housing loans is also poor, which implies that the schemes can only be implemented at the expense of the taxpayer. Party-political leaders allocate and sell pattas (land titles) and half-completed houses to people who do not necessarily belong to the target group. For this purpose, beneficiaries have to pay slum leaders.

The leaders in cooperation with political leaders create a vote bank by getting the housing scheme sanctioned. Later on, these politicians try to maintain their vote bank by telling the beneficiaries that they do not need to repay the housing loans provided by the government. The leaders have to bribe bureaucrats and other political leaders to get housing units allocated to people of their choice. Bureaucrats who do not cooperate face being transferred to unpopular districts. Despite payments, which have to be made to (political) leaders and government officials, EWS housing schemes tend to be gift schemes.

Source: Smets, 2002, p150.

Box 5.7 The Chilean approach to housing subsidies

Since the mid 1980s, housing policy in Chile has been orientated towards subsidizing demand for housing. There are now a number of different housing programmes; but the financial principle is the same in each, with finance being based on three components: beneficiaries' savings, government subsidy and loans. The proportion of these three components varies according to the cost of the house and according to each housing programme. The lower the price of the housing, the higher the proportion provided by the subsidy – although the actual subsidy per housing unit could be almost the same amount. One of the most important aspects of Chilean housing policy is its continuity. It has been based on this approach for almost 20 years, and during the last 15 years the average number of subsidies provided has been nearly 100,000 per year.

In most programmes, people apply through the regional office of the Chilean Ministry of Housing or through the local government. Each programme has its own regulations that are primarily related to who can apply, what they will need to submit in order to be eligible for financial support and what they obtain. The process of selection of the applicants is a very important part of the housing process. One of the reasons for the success of the Chilean model is that almost everyone believes that the process is transparent. This process is computerized and, in general terms, people know what the criteria are according to which they will be selected (for example, level of poverty as indicated by a socio-economic survey of each family and the amount of initial saving). The result of this selection is published in a local and/or a national newspaper so that people can be informed.

There are basically two types of programmes:

1 *Modalidad SERVIU (SERVIU way)*: the regional government will contract the construction of a housing scheme to a private contractor (usually through a process of tendering) and then sell the units to the applicants who have subsidy certificates.
2 *Modalidad privada (private way)*: each applicant manages the construction of the housing themselves or purchases an existing unit in the market. Each person receives the subsidy certificate for a specified amount of money (typically the equivalent of around US$4500). For those who are building new units, they will need to hire a building enterprise (it is difficult for those who would like to do self-build to get this funded).

All programmes require the families (even the poorest) to have a certain amount of savings. This is to make people feel that they have made an effort and that they are not wholly dependent upon the state. At the same time, most programmes included a credit system or support for a loan system (private mortgage). This has meant that it is very important to make the terms and conditions of the loan clear. If the government considers that a certain housing programme is orientated towards the poorest families, it may decide that it is better that the programme does not include a loan component.

The Solidarity Fund for Low-income Housing is a programme that has no loan component as it seeks to reach the poorest households. It is based only on family savings and a subsidy that varies regionally. The housing programme generally restricts the proportion of the subsidy that can go on land to below 30 per cent – largely because a certain level of quality for the house is considered necessary (in terms of size, building materials, etc.). Most applicants are families; but people living on their own can apply if they are older than 60 years or if they are disabled (and registered with the National Disabled Register) or are Indigenous people (registered with the National Register of Indigenous Peoples). Single-person households cannot be more than 30 per cent of the families in the whole group. Groups need to be organized in at least ten families. The organization of the group is managed by an external institution that could be the municipality, a non-governmental organization (NGO), the regional housing office, a housing co-operative or a housing foundation, among others; this institution must be registered with the Ministry of Housing. This institution will prepare the housing project as it is requested. Each project needs the approval of the municipality (in terms of urban planning regulations) and the feasibility of urban infrastructure/services (such as water, sewerage and electricity). If the group is buying the land, it will need to show the ownership as a group or the fact that the site is owned by the institution in charge.

Source: Fernandez, 2004.

Such programmes demonstrate some of the difficulties of low-interest loans for the poorest households. As already noted, loans may simply be unaffordable, but may be targeted at the poorest groups (as those most in need of housing). The contradiction encourages the type of practices described earlier, whereby such subsidies are diverted to higher income groups and/or loans suffer from high levels of default. In other strategies, there has been a greater emphasis on grant finance, and one alternative has been the direct-demand subsidies that are associated particularly with the Chilean housing subsidy system, but which are now also being used in a number of other countries. As noted in Box 5.7, one aspect of this programme that is considered essential is its clarity of

Table 5.2

Three nation comparison: Chile, Colombia and South Africa

	Chile	Colombia	South Africa
Housing subsidies as percentage of central government expenditure	5.8	0.6	1.3
Housing subsidy as percentage of GDP	1.25	0.1–0.46	0.38
Number of subsidies per year	91,130	45,000 [i]	196,030
Subsidies to population ratio (percentage)	2.2	0.4–0.65	2.4
Subsidies to the housing deficit ratio (percentage) [ii]	10–12	2–3	7.5
Subsidy value at purchasing power parity PPP (US$)	10,111	11,776	6904
Subsidy value to GDP per capita ratio (percentage)	86	175	83

Notes:
i Official estimates range between 37,977–58,755.
ii Figures for 1996, 1993 and 1998, respectively.

Source: Gilbert, 2004, pp21, 25.

Box 5.8 Costa Rica: savings, subsidies and loans

Costa Rica has a population of 3.3 million, with 786,600 housing units of which about 100,000 are informal and an estimated housing deficit of 164,000. A direct-demand subsidy programme was introduced in 1987 which, modelled on the Chilean system, offered access to a subsidy and a mortgage loan in return for a down payment (savings). The lowest-income households up to one minimum salary do not have to make a down payment. The process works largely through 'authorized entities' that support households to acquire a house.

In contrast to Chile and most other countries that have adopted direct-demand subsidies, the programme of Costa Rica has succeeded in reaching low-income groups. The main reason is that a group of sophisticated non-governmental organizations (NGOs), experienced in housing development, have become the main developers under the programme. At first, many for-profit developers where involved; but they have now withdrawn from the programme. Some NGOs have become authorized entities, forming communities, extending credit and building the units. These NGO-authorized entities even issue bonds to raise money on public markets for housing finance. Between 1988 and 1998, the programme delivered just over 93,000 dwellings reaching 13 per cent of households in the country.

Source: Ferguson, 2002, p169.

conditions and transparency of selection. Previous programmes had been characterized by public-sector provision, inadequate scale and, subsequently, by political favouritism and corruption in their allocation.[51] In general, such programmes are small, although in both Chile and South Africa there have been extensive programmes of grant finance to access homeownership. This has been linked to loans in the case of Chile and, more recently, South Africa. Capital grant subsidies have also been offered in a number of other countries, although at a smaller scale. By 1999, five other Latin American countries had introduced owner-orientated direct-demand subsidies: Costa Rica (1986), Colombia, El Salvador, Paraguay and Uruguay (all in 1991).[52]

As noted in Box 5.7, the Chilean subsidy programme requires a period of savings, which is then rewarded by access to a subsidy to be used to purchase housing. Families compete for subsidy vouchers, with the funds being allocated on the basis of four criteria: savings, poverty level of the family, family size and geographic location.[53] Savings is the variable that they can most easily affect, and savings levels have grown considerably to 1.38 million savings accounts by the end of 1997. Savings contributions are becoming recognized as being more important in South Africa. The South African capital subsidy scheme has recently been amended to require a mandatory upfront savings contribution of 2479 rand for all subsidies, unless the beneficiary chooses the People's Housing Process (self-build) route, in which case they must contribute 'sweat equity', although there are not yet fixed guidelines for what this means in practice.

Despite the initial political commitment, a recent comparative study argues that the Chilean, Colombian or South African governments have not put large-scale funding into this process.[54] As shown in Table 5.2, the percentage of state expenditure for these three countries does not exceed 1.25 per cent, while 2 per cent has been considered typical in the South. The Chilean state was committed to provide a complete house, rather than support incremental development, and for that reason gave fewer and larger subsidies.[55] Colombia concurred with the emphasis on complete housing (except for a period between 1994 and 1998 when upgrading was also included). In South Africa, the emphasis has been on scale, although it is also considered necessary that a complete house be offered; minimum size requirements were introduced during the late 1990s reflecting concerns about the small size of the units.

Arguably, the strong focus on capital subsidies responded to the needs of the construction industry. The construction companies in Chile appear to have favoured higher standards and have been opposed to self-help housing.[56] In South Africa, while the focus on housing reflected political priorities, the strategy for addressing housing need emerged from the business representatives and consultants who dominated the National Housing Forum between 1992 and 1994.[57] The forum saw low-income housing finance in terms of a new capital subsidy deployed by private developers in large-scale construction projects. The Costa Rican programme profile in Box 5.8 is particularly interesting because it appears to have avoided these problems, being less concerned with construction volume and more orientated towards addressing the needs of the poor.

The interest in these programmes is highlighted in Box 5.9, which summarizes an analysis by the World Bank of the merits of the approach. As noted earlier, similar programmes have been introduced in a number of countries, including Ecuador and Colombia. In Colombia, a recent Inter-American Development Bank (IADB) loan is to provide additional financing, with an anticipated 10,000 subsidies for housing improvement and 61,000 subsidies for complete housing aimed at the poorest 40 per cent of households with monthly incomes of less than two minimum salaries. A specific component aims to support shelter microfinance.[58] In Ecuador, the Housing Incentive System (SIV) offers households access to a subsidy if they can provide savings. There is state assistance to purchase a new house and also for housing improvements. In the case of housing improvements that are seen as being appropriate for the lower income groups, the take-up of a loan is optional. Between 1998 (the beginning of the programme) and October 2002, approximately 25,000 families were given support for housing improvement and a further 25,000 higher income families received support for housing purchase.[59]

The influence can also be seen in current discussions in Mexico where the theoretical arguments have increasingly favoured direct subsidies, although, as described in Chapter 4, interest rate subsidies have, in practice, been given much emphasis. The government now intends to put in place a single unified system of housing subsidies linked to savings and loans with (for those with low incomes) *Tu Casa* and, for those with slightly higher incomes, a more market-orientated linked subsidy and loan (such as the special programme for housing loans and subsidies, PROSAVI).[60] In 2003, just over 13,000 loans were provided through this second programme. Plans for *Tu Casa* highlight the tension between small subsidies and loans for incremental improvements and more substantial loans for home improvements and purchase. Within this programme, there is a strong emphasis on the 'formal' housing solution, with 92 per cent of these funds being earmarked for the purchase of a completed minimal house (about 60 per cent of the loans).[61] The average subsidy in 2004 was US$4540 for finished minimum houses and US$184 for home improvements. At present, high unit subsidies of *Tu Casa* and PROSAVI (which the World Bank estimate to be US$6000 and US$5000, respectively) limited the reach of the programmes to about 33,000 in 2002.[62]

For the most part, such large subsidy programmes have been driven by state agencies and state funds. In some cases, such as in Chile and Ecuador, NGOs may play a role in the programme – for example, to assist groups and individuals to prepare themselves. In Chapter 6, Box 6.6 describes the use of a fund in Ecuador to help applicants acquire their 'savings' so that they can secure their subsidy entitlement. Another approach is illustrated by the People's Dialogue on Land and Shelter in South Africa who pioneered use of the People's Housing Process subsidy stream through the utilization of bridge funding and demonstrated the effectiveness of self-build options. A similar strategy is that used by the Society for the Promotion of Area Resource Centres (SPARC) and the National Slum Dwellers Federation (NSDF), who have raised bridge funds to advance developments in a number of Indian cities with the understanding that once development is fully or partially complete they will be able to draw down the subsidy funds. The funds are sufficient for land, infrastructure and a small but complete dwelling of about 200 square feet. In 2001, the government of India came up with a scheme of subsidy for housing the urban poor in India – the *Valmiki Ambedkar Yojna* (VAMBAY). VAMBAY allocations were initially used by politicians to benefit their supporters and do not involve the participation of the poor in any way. SPARC supported local communities to demonstrate how the subsidy can be used most effectively to address their needs. In several cities they have demonstrated that the communities can do it at much lower costs – for example, 50,000 rupees rather than 70,000 rupees. In the last two years, they have extended this work (see Chapter 6).

Similar loan and subsidy schemes to support low-income housing have been developed in other contexts. While the programmes discussed above have been state programmes, municipal governments have also been interested in innovation. One recently established scheme in Mexico City offers loans and subsidies to those with single incomes below 4.7 minimum wages and joint incomes less than 7 minimum wages.[63] Loans are for land acquisition, improvements and new housing. The maximum loan is US$10,500, with an attached subsidy of US$2000. An additional subsidy is payable if repayments are made on time. The deposit is 5 per cent and the annual interest is 6 per cent above the annual wage increment. Repayments are tied to a maximum of 20 per cent of the income. More than 5000 families were assisted in 1999 and 2000.

Box 5.9 An assessment of direct-demand subsidies by the World Bank

Direct-demand subsidies have proved the most efficient type of homeownership subvention for moderate- and middle-income households in Latin America. Essentially, direct-demand subsidies are portable vouchers that bridge the gap between the amount that households can afford (by joining an affordable mortgage, a down payment and the subsidy) and a housing solution. This form of subvention most effectively stimulates competition among supply agents (developers and financial institutions) and furthers development of the financial sector. Securitization of accompanying market-rate home credit becomes feasible, although it is generally unviable when subvention takes the form of below-market interest rates. Once subsidy programmes reach a significant size and continuity, they develop important economies of scale necessary for the systemic improvement of housing conditions. However, developers, financial institutions and other formal-sector institutions often find serving low-income groups uneconomic if they have other options, even with families obtaining direct-demand subsidies.

As a result, there is a need to supplement these programmes with other policy changes. Supply bottlenecks, such as a lack of lending institutions and land development standards, need to be addressed.

Source: World Bank, 2004a, p8.

CHALLENGES

Despite the widespread recognition that has been given to the subsidy approaches discussed above, their limitations should also be recognized.

Reaching the poor and the poor quality of developments

Despite intentions, the evidence from Chile and Colombia is that such programmes have struggled to reach the lowest-income households.[64] As noted in Box 5.7, the government of Chile created new (non-loan) options in 2000 because they recognized that the programmes were not reaching the poorest.[65] Subsidies of a similar value (with greater financial requirements on the household) have also been offered in programmes aimed at encouraging middle-class households to remain in inner-city areas. One study of the Chilean programme reported that 8.7 and 5.7 per cent of households in the highest-income quintiles were receiving a subsidy.[66] In part, this was because savings were required.

Other problems include the small size of the housing units and the poor quality of housing construction. The remote location of the land has resulted in isolation and costly access to jobs and services for lower income families. Box 5.10 summarizes some recent concerns about the programme in Chile. One analysis of trends in Europe suggests that where subsidies are tied to the purchase of new housing (presumably in the hope of stimulating construction), significant problems can arise, including the housing being built in unpopular locations to take advantage of lower land costs.[67] This is similar to the emerging conclusions about the situation in South Africa:

> *The result of this system is that local authorities and private developers have consistently produced low-quality houses in cheap dormitory suburbs far from higher-cost land in the urban core. This raises long-term public and private non-housing costs (transportation,*

Box 5.10 The Chilean housing subsidy and the quality of dwellings

A considerable accomplishment of the Chilean government has been achieving a high rate of housing construction, which has controlled the housing deficit through using public resources to leverage private contributions. However, while significant numbers of dwellings have been constructed, concerns have also been raised. In particular, the policy offers few location options for the urban poor. The construction focuses on new housing developments that have primarily been built in the urban periphery where land costs are lowest. This has promoted a rapid process of urban expansion. Today, social housing is only available in a few very distant areas of the capital city of Metropolitan Santiago.

However, the peripheral setting of these units, together with the size of the complexes (estates), has resulted in serious problems for the residents' well-being, with implications for the quality of life in Santiago. The externalities of building on the periphery have not been fully taken into account and no allowance has been made for the costs of new transportation networks and other urban infrastructure and services. Nor has any consideration been given to the additional transport costs faced by families who often have limited employment possibilities. A further problem is the consequences arising from a high concentration of vulnerable families in remote areas. The result is greater urban and social segregation, an increase in the disparity in access to urban services, a worsening of local living conditions, increased environmental damage, urban security problems, and the deterioration of urban and historic centres.

Source: Jiron and Fadda, 2003.

schooling, etc.) and creates numerous negative externalities, including household- and community-level economic decline, increased crime and so on. This is entirely in keeping with the logic of private-sector housing delivery under a fixed output price (the subsidy), but also reflects a broader failure to see housing delivery in terms of integrated human settlement development rather than the physical production of 'top structures'.[68]

Cost for households

One problem in South Africa is that some households are beginning to abandon their subsidy houses, partly because of their poor quality and location, but also because households are now liable for rates and other service charges. It is not clear that capital subsidies are the way to go for the poorest households. A more effective strategy might be to ensure access to serviced plots in well-located areas where the poor choose to live and then to provide small loans to finance incremental housing.

How much of a problem is affordability in Latin America? There are some indications in Chile that affordability is not a serious problem as service bills are being paid, although the repayment of housing loans received in association with capital subsidies is poor.[69] However, it should also be recognized that only 17 per cent of subsidies go to the poorest income group.[70] The financing model in Colombia anticipated that households earning less than two minimum salaries with an average monthly income of US$117 will be able to save US$710 and repay US$35 a month.[71] This seems somewhat unlikely and suggests that affordability may be an issue. In Ecuador, there is also evidence that suggests the lowest-income families find it hard to participate, particularly in the larger towns. The cheapest dwellings are now priced at around US$2400 in smaller towns and US$4500 in the larger cities.

There are those who believe that such programmes are unaffordable to the poor in Latin America, given that there are 18 million indigent poor in the continent and that these families cannot provide themselves with enough to eat, let alone save for housing.[72] However, solutions can be developed. In Chile, Hogar de Cristo has provided more than 330,000 shelters. One of the key activists behind the Latin American and Asian Low-income Housing Service (SELAVIP), an NGO which has supported many housing initiatives for the poor argues that:

> *What is required … is that the poorest of the poor have access to locate themselves on urban property. A bit of their own land permits the families to advance by their own means in the building of a house.*[73]

Costs for the state

The potential scale of such strategies for financing housing appears to be limited by the high and explicit costs: 'few governments can afford to grant ample per-unit subsidies for complete units' and, generally, these strategies lead to small and insignificant programmes.[74] In some countries, such as Venezuela, this is funded by specific taxes on salaries; however, the Ley de Politica Habitacional results in only one in a hundred of the contributors being assisted each year.[75]

In Chile, Colombia and South Africa, the intention was that the commercial banks would be involved in providing credit (small loans) to supplement the subsidies. 'Unfortunately, all three countries have faced major problems in convincing the banks to lend to the poor.'[76] Clearly, in a financial context in which the ambition is to keep the subsidy to a minimum, the option of supplementary loan finance is attractive. However, it appears that commercial institutions used to mortgage finance find the low-income market difficult due to a lack of conventional collateral and lack of affordability.[77] In addition, initial attempts to draw in private finance may have failed in Chile because loan recovery on state loans was poor.[78] One additional factor is that, despite the political situation during the 1980s, it was considered unacceptable to evict people:

> *… government efforts to recover due payments or collect by exercising its rights through the court system have been minimal. For example, despite arrears in the order of 65–75 per cent, there have been few efforts to repossess properties.*[79]

For such reasons, in 1992, the State Bank of Chile (as the private sector had avoided offering loans) had 62 per cent of borrowers in this programme who were more than four payments late.[80] However, the state has now passed over the loans to the banks, together with a guarantee of repayment, as the banks know that past repayment rates have been low. A similar strategy to persuade the banks to offer loans for housing to low-income households occurred in South Africa, where it was believed that South Africa's mainline banks would extend the middle-class mortgage model 'downwards'. This was, in part, based on the supposition that finance market behaviour had largely reflected racial discrimination. In this case, there was also opposition to incremental housing on political grounds and a reluctance to accept 'second-best' strategies for the poor (black) majority in housing need.[81]

Poor location due to market choice and financial shortage

There are concerns with regard to social housing (including both Northern rental and Southern direct-demand subsidy options) about the concentration of the poor in specific spatial areas. It is recognized that remote location can add to problems of social exclusion, while a high concentration of very poor households can increase some of the problems of poverty. In programmes that place emphasis on market mechanisms, the poor may have relatively little choice about the kind of housing solution that is offered. The locations appear to be a result of greater reliance on the market, which chooses the location according to a range of factors but which has no particular incentive (in most cases) to maximize locational advantage to the poor. The emphasis placed by government on the adequate standard of the dwelling (as in Chile and South Africa), combined with the wish for contractors to maximize profits, tend to orientate the solution towards lower land costs and greater construction investment.

There are repeated concerns about the lack of finance in these systems except, perhaps, vis-à-vis the North. Even in the North, there are expressed concerns about the quality of provision, which is related to the scale of finance. In the South, there is some evidence of a lack of provision even among those countries that do have programmes, as well as concerns about the quality of the social housing that is provided. Many are not reached by the systems of capital subsidies discussed earlier. Even in the countries in which they are operating, it can be hard to secure subsidies, with numbers considerably below need. In every case, there are many who remain in need. In the South, many low- and low middle-income households build incrementally because this is all that is affordable (see Chapter 6). Much of this building (as is shown in Chapters 6 and 7) is financed by saving and virtually none by the formal financial sector.

With regard to social housing, there are concerns about the concentration of the poor in specific areas

NOTES

1 This chapter was prepared by a team of experts led by Diana Mitlin, University of Manchester, UK.
2 Mayo, 1999; Hoek-Smit and Diamond, 2003, pp3–5.
3 Mayo, 1999, p9.
4 Renaud, 1999, p756.
5 Hoek-Smit and Diamond, 2003, p5.
6 Hoek-Smit and Diamond, 2003, p5.
7 Mayo, 1999, p40.
8 Hoek-Smit and Diamond, 2003, pp11–12.
9 Fernandez, 2004.
10 Renaud (1999, p758) argues that the superiority of demand-side subsidies had been shown in the US experience during the 1970s. He argues that there is a strong case for saying income transfers were needed more than expenditure on improved housing.
11 Turner and Whitehead, 2002, p171.
12 Whitehead, 2003; Stephens, 2004.
13 Whitehead, 2003.
14 Taylor-Hayford, 2002, p149.
15 HUD, cited in Carolini, 2004, p16.
16 Farha and Goba, 2003, p22.
17 Stephens, 2004.
18 Stephens, 2002.
19 Priemus and Dieleman, 2002, p198.
20 Gibb, 2002, p332.
21 Stephens, 2004.
22 Whitehead, 2003.
23 Stephens, 2004.
24 Whitehead, 2003, p6.
25 Stephens, 2003, p1021.
26 Hegedüs and Teller, 2003.
27 Hegedüs et al, cited in Stephens 2003, p1021.
28 Hegedüs, 2004, p1.
29 Stephens, 2003, p1021.
30 Proxenos, 2002, p5.
31 Turner and Whitehead 2004, p175.
32 Hegedüs, 2004, p4; Yasui 2002b, p25.
33 Hegedüs, 2004, p4.
34 Hegedüs, 2004, p3.
35 Hegedüs, 2004, p3.
36 Lykova et al, 2004, p633.
37 Hegedüs, 2004, p5.
38 Hegedüs, 2002, p24.
39 Stephens, 2002, p180.
40 See Mulenga, 2003, for an illustrative discussion of this process in Zambia.
41 Ho, 2004, p486.
42 Lamoureaux, 1998, p71.
43 Ha, 2002b, p202.
44 Ha, 2002b, p200.
45 Department of Housing, 2003.
46 UN-Habitat, 2003c.
47 Hoek-Smit and Diamond, 2003, p6.
48 According to the Brazilian constitution, citizens have the right to present bills through the instrument of popular initiative. In the case of national bills, 1 per cent of the national electorate must subscribe to the initiative through signing a petition.
49 Kamete, 2000.
50 Smets, 2002, p150.
51 Gilbert, 2004, p15; Gilbert, 2002b, p310.
52 Mayo, 1999, p36.
53 Pardo, 2000, p5.
54 Gilbert, 2004, p20.
55 Gilbert, 2004, p23.
56 Gilbert, 2004, p28.
57 Baumann, 2004, p6; Huchzermeyer, 2003, p604.
58 IADB, 2003, p2.
59 Frank, 2004, p173.
60 World Bank 2004a, p6.
61 Connolly, 2004b, p4.
62 World Bank, 2004a, p9.
63 Solis and Ortiz, 2002, pp157–158.
64 Gilbert, 2004, p27.
65 Fernandez, 2004.
66 Cummings and Di Pasquale, 1997, p13.
67 Bosvieux and Vorms, cited in Scanlon and Whitehead, 2004.
68 Baumann, 2004, p17.
69 Pardo, 2000, p6.
70 Fernandez, 2004.
71 IADB, 2003, p3.
72 Van der Rest, 2003, p8.
73 Van der Rest, 2003, p7.
74 Ferguson, 1999, p190.
75 Ferguson, 1999.
76 Gilbert, 2004, p32.
77 Tomlinson, cited in Gilbert, 2004, p33.
78 Gilbert, 2002a, p315.
79 Pardo, 2000, p6.
80 Cummings and Di Pasquale, 1997, p8.
81 Baumann, 2004, p6.

CHAPTER 6

SMALL LOANS: SHELTER MICROFINANCE[1]

SMALL LOAN CHALLENGES

Shelter has become a commodity for increasing numbers of low-income households, especially those living in urban areas of developing countries. Those who build incrementally (or progressively) are a very significant group in many countries in the South. However, loan finance for shelter-related investments in incremental dwellings made by low-income households whose income comes from the informal economy is rarely available through the formal commercial financial sector. In the vast majority of cases, these households are ineligible for commercial mortgage finance. Households seeking to invest in their shelter (land, infrastructure and housing) have been forced to use their own limited income, seek additional resources from family and friends, and borrow on informal credit markets or, in some cases, from groups such as credit unions. Sources of longer-term finance are extremely limited and interest rates may be high. Box 6.1 illustrates sources of finance used by low-income households in Hyderabad, India.

Shelter microfinance and community finance mechanisms have grown considerably during recent decades

There have been several institutional efforts to assist these households in obtaining secure access to some kind of loan finance. In particular, shelter microfinance and community finance mechanisms have grown considerably during recent decades. Based predominantly in Asia and Latin America, there have been multiple explorations and innovations over the last 20 years.[2] Initial activities were developed by non-governmental organizations (NGOs) working in housing and urban development, and by microfinance organizations interested in supporting housing investment. Agencies responsible for these activities now span the voluntary and public sectors. There are now a small number of larger programmes that involve multi-sectoral initiatives, with some also having a role for the private sector. As the effectiveness of small loans has become more evident, some innovative state programmes have sought to secure similar development benefits by replicating such programmes, albeit within different structures and systems. A small number of private-sector initiatives have been launched, generally building on microfinance approaches and seeking to expand into what is perceived to be a potentially profitable market. Urban dwellers in a wide range of different countries may now be offered such opportunities related to savings and loans for shelter investments.

What is characteristic of these initiatives is that they involve small-scale lending for shelter improvements. In many cases, they also encourage savings (although this may be constrained by the rules and regulations of the financial system). The growing interest in such programmes is reflected in the launch by the Cities Alliance of the Shelter Finance for the Poor Initiative in 2001, which focuses on emerging practices of providing housing finance to poor clients on commercially viable terms.

These initiatives are of particular significance in the urban sphere where land, housing, infrastructure and basic services are all marketed commodities. However, in some cases, lenders have extended into rural areas, notably in Bangladesh, where traditional materials are not sufficient for a secure dwelling. Community funds for utilities such as electricity and water management may also be associated with rural areas.

The programmes share a common perspective in that they work with the realities of urban development in the South (and, in some cases, in transitional economies), rather than the Northern model of urban development in which a house is constructed and then sold (often through a financing package) to a family or individual. Their underlying model of housing investment is one of incremental shelter development. Housing is secured over time as improvements are made when funding is available. The dwelling is gradually consolidated, made more secure and services and infrastructure are obtained. As is the case with micro-enterprise development, there is not a big market for such lending in the North.[3] This is partly due to much higher levels of affordability, but also arises because building regulations prevent the extensive use of incremental shelter strategies. In the North, conventional modern housing is complete in one single stage even if later investments expand, renovate and/or modify the dwelling.

Low- and many middle-income urban households in the South use incremental strategies. Underlying incremental housing development is the issue of affordability; as already noted in Chapter 4, many struggle to afford mortgage finance and lack the capital to purchase a completed house outright. In 1991, one study in nine Asian countries concluded that between 40 and 95 per cent of all households had no possibility of living in a dwelling produced by the formal sector.[4] Estimates of cement producers conclude that 70 per cent of housing investment in Mexico is occurring incrementally.[5] In Tanzania, it is estimated that 98 per cent of the housing stock in urban areas is constructed on an incremental basis.[6] This is unchanged from the figures quoted for 1978.[7] In the Philippines, a similar estimate is that 93 per cent of owner-occupied houses have been built through an incremental building process.[8] Such figures emphasize the significance of incremental development.

This chapter considers a distinct approach to delivering small loans to low-income households (almost universally in the South): microfinance. Another significant approach – community funds – is discussed in Chapter 7.[9] Microfinance loans are almost universally to individuals, generally to those with some security of tenure, for investment in housing (construction, improvement and extension). Chapter 7 examines the community fund approach in which lending is typically to communities for land purchase, infrastructure and service investment, and (in some cases) for housing construction. In both cases (although most likely in the first), shelter lending may be accompanied by opportunities to borrow for micro-enterprise development. Prior to considering these lending strategies, the strategy of incremental development of shelter and the strategies used by the poor to secure finance are introduced.

Incremental development

For individuals or households with limited incomes, the only possibility of homeownership (even in an illegal settlement) is through shelter investment made in several stages. Land purchase, service installation and upgrading, as well as housing construction, consolidation and expansion, are all made at separate times. For higher income households, the land purchase may be first, with subsequent investments made as incomes increase and assets accumulate over a period of years. In the lower income families, the first investments may be in shelter on a piece of land with uncertain security. Subsequent investments are made as security increases. Infrastructure may be installed (perhaps with state assistance). A shack may be transformed into a more robust dwelling, with rooms being added, and flooring and roofing improved with the use of permanent materials.

Such incremental shelters, often initially built of temporary materials, frequently require repairs because of damage – for example, from natural forces. In Hyderabad, about one quarter of a sample of 224 households had recently repaired their house.[10] No less than 64 per cent had repaired the roof (essential against monsoon rains). Box 6.15 on the Grameen Bank's loan package highlights the high cost of repeat repairs for houses built of traditional materials; with loan finance, scarce funds can be allocated more effectively.

Box 6.1 describes the strategies that are used in Hyderabad, India. The lack of contact with formal financial institutions that is illustrated within this example is evident in many parts of the world.

Despite its significance, incremental development may be discouraged by more formal housing finance agencies. The Kenyan Banking and Building Societies Act explicitly forbids financial institutions from lending for plots of land with no or partially constructed housing on it.[11] Households allocated land by the state Self-help Housing Agency in Botswana were expected to replace traditional building materials within two years – a very short period of time for those with low incomes to accumulate sufficient funds.[12] One study of housing strategies for the poor in Zimbabwe also highlights the resistance of some politicians and residents to incremental housing.[13] The lending conditions of the Housing Finance Company of Uganda require land title, together with a number of further conditions: the development must be located in an urban area, have full services, be constructed of permanent materials and have local authority approval for construction.[14]

Low- and many middle-income urban households in the South use incremental strategies

In general, this resistance to incremental housing by formal finance companies is because of the risks associated with the building processes (particularly potential illegality) and because of uncertainty about house value and, hence, problems of mortgage valuation. However, one general policy concern about incremental strategies is that investment is wasteful because small improvements are made that might have to be repeated when a further extension is added.[15] However, the financial implications are also clear. Low-income households cannot afford to pay the high interest charges on a complete loan, but are more likely to be able to cover the relatively small interest charges from repeat borrowings of much smaller amounts of finance.

Access to financial services

What research and practice during the early 1990s emphasized was that the quality of self-help investment could be enhanced by financial institutions that enabled the accumulation of savings and/or offered small loans. However, little finance is available for the poor in the South. Several examples from different countries all point to the high dependency of the poor upon non-mortgage sources of housing finance.

In India, according to the National Statistical Survey's (NSS's) 44th round survey, more than 80 per cent of housing finance comes from private savings, sale of assets and non-formal sources of credit.[16] In a number of households studied in Hyderabad, 45 per cent of those living in 13 low-income settlements were in debt for housing (but less than 2 per cent borrowed from formal financial institutions).[17] This is higher than that reported in low-income settlements in Amritsar, where it was estimated that 10 per cent of the credit taken out by low-income households was for housing.[18] A further example comes from South Africa, a country widely noted for having an extended financial sector. As noted in the discussion of mortgage finance, within one group of low to lower-middle earners in South Africa, only 38 per cent had applied for finance, with 13 per cent being successful.[19] For those unable to secure mortgages, in the non-mortgage

Box 6.1 Housing finance for low-income households in Hyderabad, India

What are the strategies of low-income households for obtaining housing finance? This question was studied in detail by Peer Smets in Hyderabad, India. This Indian city was chosen because it is in a state that had moved away from a managed economy towards liberalization. The information was collected between 1993 and 1996 in 13 low-income neighbourhoods, each with between 76 and 530 households. There were no housing schemes by external agencies in the chosen settlements. The focus was on low-income groups, notably the economically weaker sections (which at that time had a monthly income of below 1250 rupees) and the low-income groups (with a monthly income of between 1250 and 2650 rupees).

In 2002, the city population was about 5 million, with considerable numbers of the poor squatting or living in illegal subdivisions. Despite the interest during this period by the national government in exploring the role of innovative savings and lending instruments, both with regard to housing and, more generally, the housing finance systems, practices and outcomes in Hyderabad could only be understood with reference to local land and housing markets. Important factors included how competing elite interest in land development have been reconciled, the presence of ongoing ethnic tensions between Muslims and Hindus, local political interests, and the changes that resulted from Hyderabad being made the capital of the newly formed state of Andhra Pradesh in 1956. By the 1970s, the land market in Hyderabad was uncertain, with an inadequate registration process and many disputes. In 1970, 60 per cent of residents lived in rental accommodation, and by 1981 this percentage had fallen to 55 per cent. In 1981 the population living in illegal settlements was 19.6 per cent; but ten years later it had increased to 29 per cent.

Considering the urban poor in the 13 study settlements, 53 per cent of the households are above the poverty line and 47 per cent below. Some 38 per cent are tenants and 62 per cent are homeowners with no significant differences in income. The physical quality of the shelter can be divided into *kaccha* (traditional materials, corrugated iron, cloth and wood) semi-*kaccha* (partly or completely constructed with concrete or cement-plastered walls, with asbestos or iron sheets or tiles on the roof) and *pucca* (concrete or brick masonry with a concrete roof). Over 80 per cent of tenants and homeowners are living in semi-*kaccha* houses, with only 4 per cent of the sample living in *pucca* houses.

A sample of 242 households has been surveyed in greater detail. These are either homeowners or tenants who have bought elsewhere in the city. Sixty-five per cent of those with land in the low-income settlements (illegal land) have bought their rights. About half made a single payment for the land and the other half paid in instalments. In terms of construction materials, just under 50 per cent have made some use of second-hand materials. Forty-five per cent are in debt because of an investment in housing, of which the majority live close to the poverty line. The biggest single source of funding for the first step of incremental building is savings and the second most significant source is friends/relatives/neighbourhoods. This is closely followed by the third source of finance: chit funds. Chit funds involve a given number of participants who each commit to paying an equal monthly amount. There are a number of different systems for selecting the order according to which members receive the funds. For second investments in incremental housing, savings and money lenders/pawnbrokers are the most important, and for further steps, savings is the source of finance in 75 per cent of cases. Considered across all financing stages, employers are a fourth source of funds. Finance or credit co-operatives and banks are used very rarely, if at all.

Source: Smets, 2002.

housing finance sector 89 per cent of loans by value are personal loans secured by ceding a pension and payroll deduction (only available to formally employed persons). The remaining 11 per cent of housing loans by value are unsecured personal loans. Approximately 60 per cent of South African households fall into income and employment categories that would make them potentially eligible for *only* this kind of loan under current South African conditions.[20] And in a further African example, the overwhelming source of housing finance in Tanzania during the 1980s were people's own savings, and this was true for the formal and informal sectors.[21]

The importance given to savings is repeated elsewhere. A study of 198 households in low-income settlements in Pereira, Colombia, found that savings was the most common method of financing land purchase and construction, with only 10 per cent of households using loan finance.[22] In Botswana, savings were once more found to be a critical source of funding for housing investment, with few other alternatives being used.[23]

This information points fairly clearly to a lack of housing finance. Would more finance increase investment in low-income areas and assist in a more speedy development of incremental housing? The evidence is somewhat mixed. In one area in Colombia, about one third of these households could secure public-sector loans as they had plots in a sites-and-services project.[24] Despite this possibility, these groups did not have a higher incidence of borrowing, and even within these projects those who secured loans did not appear to be faster at consolidating their housing than other households. Another scheme in Mauritania provides land security to the urban poor, together with further assistance for development.[25] The assistance programme includes housing finance, technical assistance for enterprise development and literacy and skills-enhancement classes for residents. The housing finance package is divided into three components: room, latrine and perimeter wall. Participants make a deposit of 25 per cent of the cost, the municipality gives a subsidy of 25 per cent and the remainder is repaid over two years at 0 per cent interest. Due to poor uptake, subsidies were increased for the second phase (which started in 2002). During the first 18 months, the programme was successful in increasing housing development. Those who did not obtain shelter finance but who secured land from the programme invested an average of US$178 in their housing, while those who secured the loan and subsidy invested an average of US$349. Clearly, affordability remains an important issue. At the same time, the speed with which some microfinance initiatives for shelter have grown suggests that, in at least some households, there is a considerable demand for loan capital.

What is also notable is that limited access to mortgage finance means that there are few alternatives to incremental development for households wishing to secure housing. The problem is exemplified by the low-income settlements in South Africa where, even if someone wants to sell a house in a low-income settlement (even with legal tenure), it is difficult to secure mortgage finance. There are no financial products in South Africa appropriate for those who wish to purchase housing that has been developed incrementally from a sites-and-services programme, or that has been recently constructed and financed under the capital subsidy programme or formal houses built for Africans between 1948 and 1960.[26] Current lenders to low-income households offer secured and unsecured microloans and pension-backed loans of between 5000 and 15,000 rand (US$775–$2325). This is not enough to purchase existing houses in any of the housing sub-markets mentioned above: the mean selling price for houses in each is between 13,000 and 52,000 rand (US$2000–$8000). The specific problems resulting in mortgage refusal include lack of adequate land title, insufficient income by the purchaser, lack of formal employment and red-lining (the refusal to issue mortgages in specific areas) due to generalized problems of foreclosure.

This is the situation in which low-income householders find themselves. Unable to afford fully developed houses with established legal title, they develop housing incrementally. In the absence of commercial or state finance for complete houses, they invest when and as they are able. To fill this gap, a number of different initiatives have developed. This chapter looks particularly at the provision of small loans for shelter to individual households provided primarily, but not exclusively, by the group of microfinance agencies that emerged during the 1980s and 1990s to supply enterprise finance. It concentrates on the financial sector that works primarily with individuals, while Chapter 7 considers the separate but related tradition of community finance. This chapter focuses largely on microfinance institutions because that is where considerable innovation has taken place, and where there are indicative signs that further value might be added. However, the discussion also considers other small-scale lending through civil society groups, such as credit unions, as well as commercial loans from small commercial lending firms and building material suppliers.[27] Chapter 7 then turns to community funds, a further financial strategy developed within socially orientated development agencies working particularly on urban poverty and/or addressing housing need.

Table 6.1 highlights the differences between these two strategies and those of mortgage and microfinance for enterprise development. In essence, community funds seek to address the needs of poorer groups and, thus, use collective loans both to build the capacity of the poor to act together and because the priorities of secure land tenure and infrastructure cannot be afforded individually. Shelter microfinance responds to the needs of the poor with reasonably secure tenure to upgrade their dwellings using strategies that have developed for lending to small and medium-sized enterprises.

Table 6.1

Lending strategies for housing development

	Mortgage finance	Microenterprise finance	Shelter microfinance	Community funds
Objective	Provide long-term housing finance	Provide investment finance for enterprise development and enable income growth	Provide housing improvement and improve well-being	Enable the poor to secure shelter assets, particularly land and infrastructure
Borrowers	Upper- and middle-income households	Micro- and small entrepreneurs	Those with land who need to improve the dwelling	Those without secure tenure, basic services and adequate housing
Use of loan funds	Acquisition of property	Development of business	Housing improvement	Land, infrastructure and occasionally housing improvement
Role of savings	Deposit required; savings process not important	May be required	Savings may be required; deposit may be required	Savings generally essential; deposit may be required
Additional support	Irrelevant	Generally not	Possible	Nearly always considered necessary because of complexities of land development
Attitude to the very poor	Avoid	Generally avoid; some specialist programmes	Depends upon orientation; but requirement for land likely to exclude the poorest	Generally seeks to help the very poor if they are residentially stable
Purpose of the collective (community organization)	None	May be used as guarantor	May be used as guarantor; sometimes additional community support is a part of the process	Lending is collective and the role of the group is seen as essential to address the exclusion of the poor
Amount	Generally over US$10,000	Generally under US$500	Generally between US$100–$5000	Generally under US$1000
Interest rate	Inflation plus a margin of 8–15%	Inflation plus a margin of 15–45%	Inflation plus a margin to cover costs of 10–20%	Inflation plus administration
Term	15–30 years	Less than 1 year	1–8 years	3–20 years (generally shorter)
Collateral	Mortgage	Personal guarantees, goods, co-signers	Personal guarantees, goods, co-signers, mortgage	Can be title deeds but emphasis placed on collective loan management
Financial sustainability	Generally considered essential, but may be state subsidies	Desired – support for product development	Desired – support for product development; occasionally integrated with subsidies for land development	Seek state support to offer subsidies for land development and services in order to include lower income families
Linking role	None	To other financial institutions	To other financial institutions; may involve the municipality in slum upgrading programme	To state and municipality

Source: adapted from ACHR, 2002, p6, and Ferguson, 2004b, p5.

Microfinance: what is it?

As emphasized above, many in the South develop housing incrementally and the need for small loans is considerable. An estimated 70 per cent of housing investment in developing countries occurs through such progressive building.[28] Microfinance for shelter addresses a gap that larger-scale mortgage lenders are unwilling to provide for and, arguably, for which they lack the skills and capacities.

Table 6.2

Consultative Group to Assist the Poor (CGAP): typical terms and conditions for shelter microfinance

Size	Varies, but generally two to four times larger than average working capital loans
Term	Usually 2 to 24 months for home improvements and two to five years for land purchase or construction
Interest	Same as standard working capital loans or slightly lower
Delivery method	Almost always provided to individuals rather than to groups
Collateral	Mostly unsecured; co-signers often used; real guarantees may be used; formal ownership of dwelling or land may be required; savings sometimes used as guarantee (may be compulsory)
Target clientele	Low-income salaried workers; microentrepreneurs primarily in urban areas; poor people
Other services	Sometimes accompanied by land acquisition, land registration and construction (including self-help building techniques)

Source: CGAP, 2004.

The main issues discussed in this section are the growth of shelter microfinance, including the sources of funding, the terms and conditions of lending and the challenges that this sector faces.

Microfinance for shelter offers small loans suitable for significant housing improvements. Terms and conditions are summarized in Table 6.2. Loan sizes are between US$1000 and US$5000, although they may be smaller in some countries where construction costs are lower and/or building standards do not prevent low-cost housing options. Loan terms are generally between one and eight years, although in most cases they are at the shorter end of this range. Hence, although these loans are often given by existing microfinance lenders and are seen as falling within this category of financial services, they are often considerably larger than enterprise loans (especially those taken by new borrowers when entering this market).[29]

Shelter microfinance responds to the needs of the poor with reasonably secure tenure to upgrade their dwellings

Security conditions vary considerably depending upon local circumstances. In some cases, they are similar to those required for enterprise development (that is, group guarantees and co-signers). In other cases, they involve holding the para-legal documents to the property and other non-mortgage collateral. Some shelter microfinance lenders follow a process similar to that of a conventional mortgage for larger loans. The Consultative Group to Assist the Poor (CGAP) is a consortium of 28 public and private development agencies seeking to expand access to financial services (microfinance) for the poor in the South. In 2004, they recognized the significance of shelter microfinance with a briefing for members.

Loans are generally taken to build additional rooms (often turning space constructed using wood and traditional materials into concrete built structures), improve roofs and floors, and add kitchens and toilets. Investing in improved facilities is very popular and the Self-employed Women's Association (SEWA) in India estimates that 'almost 35 per cent of housing loans from SEWA Bank are utilized for installing infrastructure, such as a private water connection or toilet'.[30] The emphasis is very much on improvements for homeowners. The terms and conditions of microfinance lending in the context of incremental development favour those who already have some degree of tenure security and housing structure. For this reason, these loans are often referred to as housing loans, or housing microfinance. In some cases, they are also for land – for example, the Grameen Bank will lend for land purchase if the borrower does not have legal tenure. However, lending for land purchase is much less likely because of the high costs and other problems with individualized solutions to tenure and infrastructure needs, and because some degree of land security may be a prerequisite for such a loan.

Microfinance for shelter addresses a gap that larger-scale mortgage lenders are unwilling to provide for

There is a vibrant rental market in many low-income settlements in most Southern cities. Such rental activities are, in general, informal; in addition to the fact that the income is not taxed or declared, the rental agreements are managed outside of the formal legal system. Tenants may be particularly vulnerable and may face difficult terms and conditions, with few alternative affordable options. They generally enjoy restricted access to services.[31] In some cases, microfinance loans are used by the landlords to construct additional rooms for rent. However, there is not much information about such purposes and it does not appear to be happening at scale. In one housing loan scheme in low-income settlements in Mauritania, two-thirds of households used the home for some kind of enterprise activity, including renting space. The percentage renting space to others among the group who took housing loans is twice the percentage of those who did not take loans – but it still remains low at 6 per cent of households.[32] In a few cases, small loan programmes have been orientated towards the landlord sector to improve the living conditions of tenants. However, there are relatively few intentional initiatives of this kind. One difficult issue is that, although the project may be intended to improve living conditions for tenants, in practice, the improvements may be associated with rent increases and the displacement of one (poorer) group of tenants by another (higher income group). Box 6.2 describes a small revolving fund in Kitale, Kenya, which offers loans for improved sanitation to plot owners, many of whom are also renting rooms. The objective is to improve environmental health, although the risk of potential rent increases and the displacement of tenants is recognized.

THE GROWTH OF MICROFINANCE FOR SHELTER

The growth of microfinance agencies since their inception during the 1980s has been considerable and there are now many such organizations. To exemplify the situation in one country, in India the number of such grassroots-level organizations engaged in mobilizing savings and providing microloan services to the poor is estimated to be in the range of 400 to 500 organizations.[33] However, some 60 million families in India (approximately 36 per cent of the country's population) are in need of financial services, while the cumulative outreach by microfinance agencies is no more than 1.5 million households (2.5 per cent).[34]

The developments in shelter microfinance follow the development of a growing microfinance sector. During the 1980s, several agencies demonstrated success in offering small loans for enterprise development. The underlying and emerging argument was that small entrepreneurs were constrained by a lack of credit. The availability of credit, it was argued, would enable businesses to expand and development opportunities to emerge from within the small-scale, invariably informal, business sector.

Early and continuing evaluations demonstrated that, whatever the loans were taken for, a proportion as large as 25 per cent could be diverted for shelter investments. For example, *Centro de Fermento a Iniciativas Economicas* (FIE), a Bolivian microfinance agency, estimates that 20 per cent of its enterprise loans are allocated to housing investments.[35] An assessment made by the Association for Social Advancement (ASA) in Bangladesh suggests that 15 per cent of borrowers for income generation use these loans for improving housing.[36] Findings such as these have encouraged the exploration of microfinance lending specifically for shelter. Box 6.3 describes how one microfinance agency sought to develop a specific product to address the housing needs of borrowers.

Although much emphasis of the early microfinance lending was on enterprise development, shelter has been a possible reason for lending since the mid 1980s, much the same time as enterprise lending was expanding. For example, the Grameen Bank started lending for housing in 1984;[37] while in 1985, for example, the US Agency for International Development (USAID) offered finance for the Co-operative Housing Foundation to implement credit programmes in a number of Central American countries.[38] The foundation developed its work with local organizations such as CACIEL (a credit union in Honduras) to expand shelter lending. Between 1985 and 1990, US$11 million was invested in activities with 28 organizations to offer 4653 home improvement loans and a further 2828 construction loans.[39] Within the same programme, experimentation also occurred (on a much smaller scale) with community loans for infrastructure improvements (such as water systems).

There are a considerable number of NGOs that have been working with housing issues, generally for lower income groups, and that have been drawn into loan financing in order to scale up their activities and/or to provide assistance to residents who have been successful in acquiring land. In such cases, NGO loan programmes are part of a more substantive programme to improve housing conditions that may involve the provision of technical assistance; community development training; grants for improving infrastructure and services; building materials production; and support in negotiations with local authorities.[40] Most of these initiatives emerged from Southern NGOs seeking to address the needs of the poor more effectively. Agencies working with housing, urban poverty and urban development issues were aware that self-builders faced major problems in securing the finance they needed for incremental development, and the NGO professionals were also aware of the long-term cost of short-term temporary improvements.

Shelter NGOs looked to the examples of microfinance agencies seeking to bring financial markets to those who traditionally had been excluded from opportunities for savings and credit. Others concentrated on the individualized lending systems of enterprise microfinance, but orientated the loans towards housing improvements. One example of this heritage is Proa in Bolivia, an NGO that started work in 1988 with a concentration on urban development and which evolved a programme of housing loans (see Box 6.4).[41]

Even within the housing NGO sector, there are two distinct groups of such NGOs working in housing finance in Mexico.[42] The first group is professional urban development NGOs who have primarily been drawn into finance programmes in order to influence state policies and the demands of low-income communities. Such programmes are illustrated in Box 6.6.[43] The second group are humanitarian agencies who have worked to improve housing conditions in low-income areas. Recognizing that families are able and willing to invest in their own dwellings, they have directly developed small loan programmes at scale. Their work is illustrated in Box 6.5 (it is estimated that households below five minimum salaries cannot afford a fully completed dwelling paid for with unsubsidized mortgage finance).[44]

Box 6.2 Sanitation revolving fund in Kitale, Kenya

The sanitation revolving fund has been initiated by the Intermediate Technology Development Group in two settlements in Kitale (Tuwani and Shimo la Tewa). The first phase has included 23 loans, all to plot owners, some of whom rent rooms within their plots. Many plot owners wished to take loans and the successful applicants were selected on the basis of their willingness to accept the loan in the form of materials, as well as according to their capacity to contribute towards the cost. The loans are to be repaid over two to three years. The amounts loaned are between 27,000 and 60,000 Kenyan shillings, and the interest rate charged is 12 per cent (if the repayment period is two to three years), or 11 per cent for a one-year repayment. A one-month grace period on repayments is offered. To assist in securing repayments, an affidavit has to be signed by each recipient. A further incentive for repayment may be that people have bigger dreams (better housing) and seek further opportunities to borrow. A remaining question is whether they see the additional facilities as an opportunity to raise rents.

The Catholic Diocese of Kitale has agreed to manage the sanitation revolving fund on behalf of Intermediate Technology Development Group. The diocese already has some expertise in microfinance. A board of trustees oversees the loans and includes three members from the diocese, along with community members.

Source: L. Stevens, pers comm, 2004.

Box 6.3 Launching a housing microfinance product: Mibanco, Peru

With 70,000 active borrowers, Mibanco in Peru is one of the largest microfinance institutions (MFIs) in Latin America. The organization started as a non-governmental organization (NGO), but became a commercial bank in 1998. The conversion into a deposit-taking institution gave Mibanco the funding necessary to expand from microenterprise lending into other areas. During mid 2000, Mibanco added a housing product, Micasa, in the form of a loan for improvement, expansion, subdivision, or rebuilding or replacement of existing housing.

After 12 months of operation, Micasa had 3000 clients, with portfolio at risk greater than 30 days of 0.6 per cent and a return on loan portfolio of 7 to 9 per cent. Loan size ranged from US$250–$4000, and averaged US$916. Interest rates were 50 to 70 per cent per annum. These rates are less than those Mibanco charges on microenterprise loans. Loan periods were as much as up to 36 months; but most households preferred loans of 6 to 12 months, and the average loan period was 11 months. Mibanco uses its analysis of repayment potential and household assets to guarantee most loans. Mortgage liens are sometimes taken, but only on larger loans (those above US$4000) if the client already has clear legal title. In total, mortgage liens secure only 7 per cent of Mibanco's home loans. The housing loan product has strong profitability and demand, and Mibanco expects such loans to represent half of its portfolio within three years.

Source: Ferguson, 2003.

Box 6.4 Proa: learning how to offer shelter loans

When the non-governmental organization (NGO) Proa in Bolivia moved into housing finance in 1991, its original strategy was small loans for home improvements using solidarity groups to guarantee repayments. For this and subsequent strategies, it secured funding from Mutual La Paz, a mutual savings association. This first strategy failed and Proa was forced to cover some of the losses with Mutual La Paz; however, there was an enthusiasm to carry on.

The second strategy was to use some form of individual guarantee using landownership. The costs (and time) of registering a mortgage with the Office of Property Rights were considered too high; but even without this measure some claim over the property could be secured. In addition, procedures to follow up repayments were strengthened. This system worked relatively well and a refined, but broadly similar, strategy was introduced in 1993.

Most loans are for housing improvements including access to water and sanitation services. However, some are for the regularization of properties and new construction by small contractors. One measure of success has been that foreclosure and late payment rates are now below those for Mutual La Paz's overall mortgage lending and are low for Bolivia. Repayments that are more than 90 days late account for 1.09 per cent of the portfolio compared to 4.1 per cent for Mutual La Paz's middle- to higher income mortgage lending.

Source: Ferguson, 1999, p193.

However, it is also important to recognize that not all housing and urban development NGOs have chosen to develop financial services for housing. In Mumbai, for example, at the end of the 1990s there were 18 NGOs addressing issues broadly related to housing and community finance, but only four specifically providing housing loans.[45] Urban development NGOs in Mexico have tended to develop housing finance initiatives as exemplar projects, not necessarily intending to take them to scale, but seeking to use the experiences to influence the ways in which housing policy is being developed.[46] This strategy extends well beyond Mexico, and many other NGOs who are advocating for more successful housing policies and strategies have introduced demonstration projects to show the effectiveness of small loan provision.[47] Another significant and influential group are the community organizations and their representatives, and NGO-initiated programmes have sought to switch community demands away from clientalist favours and towards effective development interventions that can go to scale. The Step-by-Step programme in Ecuador and Peru is a recent example of such a programme (see Box 6.6).

As illustrated by the Step-by-Step programme, in the case of some NGO programmes the desire to influence policy is combined with a wish to respond to the needs of those seeking to improve their housing and to improve access to loan finance. Despite widespread discussions about the value of microfinance, need remains acute, and in many cases there are few providers. In Ecuador there is a subsidy programme; but as illustrated in Box 6.6, the requirement for a savings contribution means that it cannot be accessed by many low-income households.

A further illustration of the continuing responsiveness of the NGO sector is given by the launch of South Africa's Kuyasa Fund (see Box 6.12). In South Africa, there is considerable state subsidy for housing provision and a commercial banking sector that has been under significant pressure to expand lending to the poor. Hence, the context appears to be one in which there are opportunities for low-income communities to secure both housing improvements and financial services. Despite this apparently favourable context, there is a further need for small housing loans. A Cape Town-based NGO, the Development Action Group, launched the Kuyasa Fund in 2001 after beginning trial housing loans in 1999. It did so because the communities with whom it was working needed finance to upgrade their dwellings, and there were few alternative accessible and affordable sources of finance.

Box 6.5 Humanitarian housing interventions in Mexico

One of the most significant of the humanitarian housing agencies operating in Mexico is *Habitat para la Humanidad México A.C.*, the Mexican branch of Habitat for Humanity. This agency began operating in Mexico in 1987 and currently works in the federal district and 13 other states, with 20 active affiliate groups. The organization provides credit to previously formed mutual aid groups of selected families, who supply the labour for their own and other group members' house construction on their own land. Until now, it has financed 14,388 houses in 600 communities in both rural and urban areas.

Another non-governmental organization (NGO) which provides home improvements finance for workers in the bonded industries (*maquiladores*) in Ciudad Juárez, on the Mexico–US border, is *Fundación Habitat y Vivienda A.C.* (FUNHAVI). This was set up in 1996 as a branch of Co-operative Housing Foundation International with the help of a Ford Foundation donation as seed capital. It is also sponsored by the Inter American Foundation, from which it received two loans for a total of US$500,000 last year and donations from local businesses. Its target population comprises homeowners earning between two and eight times the minimum wage, although the average income of beneficiaries was four minimum wages in 2001; 38 per cent were women. The same source quotes that loans ranged from US$500 to $2500 (average loans of US$1623), interest rates were 2.5 to 3 per cent a month, and a 2 per cent commission is charged by the organisation, as well as a US$20 mandatory technical assistance fee. The technical assistance provider or 'architect' decides what sort of loan is needed. Loan terms vary from 6 to 36 months, with repayments being paid monthly at the local supermarket chain, with which FUNHAVI has a special arrangement. Another special arrangement with construction material distributors enables FUNHAVI to purchase them at wholesale prices, although recipients of the loans have to buy them from FUNHAVI at retail prices; this covers 11 per cent of FUNHAVI's running costs.

Source: Connolly, 2004b.

Links to formal financial agencies

During the 1980s, some programmes had the explicit intention of preparing their clients for entry into formal housing finance either in the short or the longer term.[48] There was an underlying expectation that the poor could borrow from the formal financial systems once appropriate modifications had been identified and implemented. For example, in the case of the Central American programmes supported by the Swedish International Development Agency (SIDA), links have been sought. However, in practice, it has proved difficult to convince such formal financial institutions that they should participate in direct lending; this is due, in part, to the small loan size and associated high administration costs.[49] Generally, this expectation has changed and there is now greater recognition that it might be preferable to build significant institutions that specialize in small loans. Such institutions might link to the more formal commercial financial institutions to secure capital; but the formal financial institutions would not be expected to interact directly with the poor.

Box 6.6 Step-by-Step programme in Peru and Ecuador

The Step-by-Step programme is located in Peru and Ecuador and is being implemented by Centro de Investigaciones (CIUDAD) and Centro de Escudios y Promoción del Desarrollo (DESCO), with contributions from the European Union (EU), Centre for Ecology and Development (KATE), Instituto de Estudios Políticos para América Latina y Africa (IEPALA), Alternativas Sostenibles de Desarrollo, España (ASDE) and La Asociación para la Cooperación con el Sur/Las Segovias (ACSUD-Las Segovias). Activities include the establishment of a revolving loan fund with the related construction of safe and affordable housing through incremental development and the promotion of savings among participants. The revolving loan fund for shelter production seeks to establish a credit system that is adaptable to, and appropriate for, the needs of self-building families. Technical assistance in the building of affordable, healthy and safe houses is also being provided. Training programmes for the people involved in the construction of low-income housing are offered, together with the dissemination of good practices on progressive shelter financing schemes through a training and dissemination centre. In addition to the direct benefits, a further intention is to improve housing policies for low-income families through the targeted dissemination of the programme's achievements.

The total budget for the programme is 1.8 million Euros. In Peru, the project is taking place in Villa el Salvador (part of metropolitan Lima), with its 1 million residents. In Ecuador, the project is located in Quito, Riobamba, Alausí and Cotacachi. In total, 0.54 million Euros are allocated to the revolving fund and it is anticipated that just over 2000 loans will be provided.

In Ecuador there is a national housing subsidy system that offers families a grant of US$1800. However, families have to be able to save 10 per cent of the value of the house to qualify, and experience suggests that it is difficult to save the required amount. Generally, they are not eligible for loans and they do not trust formal credit institutions. As a result, one use of the revolving fund is for the down payment to secure the subsidy. Additional uses are part payment for new houses in existing housing programmes, housing improvement, down payments or deposits for commercial loans and providing community facilities.

Local financial strategies involving the fund can be exemplified through the women's association *Luchando por la Vida.* The 36 families have an average income of US$185 per month, with 94 per cent of households falling below the official poverty line (US$360 per month). The housing programme involves the construction of 6 buildings and 36 apartments (of 60 square metres at a unit cost of US$5100). The total costs are paid thus: 33 per cent by the government housing subsidy and 67 per cent by the families (using a combination of savings, commercial loan and a Step-by-Step deposit to access the housing subsidy).

From 2001 to 2004, Step-by-Step in Ecuador has granted more than 930 loans and 550 families have secured new houses of good quality. In addition, 62 per cent of the users of the loans are women, and 72 per cent of families who have secured houses through the programme have incomes below the poverty line. Step-by-Step's loans (for a total amount of US$750,000) have already mobilized more than US$2.5 million from government subsidy (25 per cent) and private bank loans (75 per cent).

Source: M. Vasconez, pers comm, 2004.

There remains the tradition of guarantee funds, although their use is somewhat limited to a few specific examples, and scaling up such examples into regular practice appears difficult.[50] A number of NGOs have specifically sought to use guarantee fund strategies to release financial capital from the formal (mainly commercial) financial sector. Such guarantee systems have a dual rationale. On the one hand, they are intended to build links between the formal and informal financial systems, encouraging further lending (with no or lower guarantee ratios) once a positive experience has occurred. Second, they are a way of leveraging finance if the guarantee is accepted to be less than 100 per cent. Examples of guarantee funds include the Latin American and Asian Low-income Housing Service (SELAVIP), the Society for the Promotion of Area Resource Centres (SPARC), Homeless International and a number of other Southern NGOs. Such guarantees can be illustrated by SPARC (an Indian NGO), the state-financed Housing and Urban Development Corporation (HUDCO) and a housing co-operative in Dharavi (a large low-income area in Mumbai).[51] In this case, the funding was only released after SPARC guaranteed the repayments (with the financial support of a Northern NGO) and 25 per cent was withheld from the first loan instalment as a contribution to interest payments. More recently, SPARC has had more successful experiences based on the increasing interest of the private sector to find a way of investing in the development of low-income urban areas.[52] One experienced commentator concludes that despite difficulties around the release of additional finance for the local development activities of NGOs and community organizations 'it is too early to give up on banks yet'.[53]

In this context, the more recent interest by commercial financial agencies, such as the Colombian Banco Davivienda, in developing a small loan facility is notable.[54] However, what is not yet clear is the extent to which the state will have to support such initiatives. What is evident from the following discussion is that the commercial banking sector in some countries is seeking more involvement in what is considered to be a potentially profitable sector.

Microfinance agencies appear to be diversifying rapidly into housing micro-credit in at least some regions

The microfinance institution (MFI) experience: enterprise to housing loans

In addition to NGO initiatives, there has been considerable interest in housing lending shown by the microfinance sector. It is difficult to assess the significance of the growth of microfinance agencies into small shelter lending, but it appears to be significant. For example, three significant microfinance agencies were profiled in a 1996 study when, at that time, none of them were working in housing.[55] Four years later, two of the three were working in this area.

Box 6.7 Assessing the demand for housing finance

Demand for housing and small-scale lending for housing investment is likely to increase, as is illustrated by the following examples:

- *Peru*: 82 per cent of the 8 million people living in greater Lima are classified as poor. At least half of poor households and 60 per cent of the poorest households express a strong desire to expand or improve their home within the next 12 months. Only 10 to 15 per cent are borrowing from formal or informal sources. The potential market in metropolitan Lima for housing finance loans is estimated at 610,000 home improvements annually.
- *Indonesia*: during 2000, the country's urban population of 85 million already represented 40 per cent of the total. By 2010 it will represent 50 per cent, with 120 million people. Annual projections for housing needs for the next ten years are approximately 735,000 new units and an additional 420,000 in need of improvement. An estimated 70 to 80 per cent of all housing in Indonesia is constructed informally and incrementally, with minimal access to formal financial markets.
- *Morocco*: two surveys found that 88 per cent of households have or are planning a productive activity in the home, and more than 83 per cent of households are willing to take a loan to finance home improvement. Ninety-two per cent of urban and 94 per cent of rural households constructed their own homes without access to formal finance.
- *Mexico*: one market study of microfinance in three Mexican cities (Tijuana, Matamoros and Juarez) bordering the US found that 14 per cent of all households both qualified for and wanted housing microcredit at terms of 35 per cent amortized over three years. The effective demand for shelter microfinance (US$122 million) amounted to five times that for microenterprise loans (US$20 million) in these cities.

Source: Malhotra, 2003, pp218–219.

Microfinance agencies appear to be diversifying rapidly into housing microcredit in at least some regions.

Over the last three years, most leading microfinance agencies in Latin America and the Hispanic Caribbean have established a housing product. Cases in point include Banco Sol in Bolivia, Banco Solidario in Ecuador, Mibanco in Peru, Banco Ademi in the Dominican Republic, Calpia in Honduras, and Genesis Empresarial in Guatemala.[56]

One study funded by the International Finance Corporation (IFC) identifies 141 institutions providing shelter-finance loan products to the poor.[57] Another, focusing on Latin America, identifies 57 microfinance agencies as offering housing loans, just under 30 per cent of the total number of such institutions.[58] Of these agencies, about 18 per cent of their total loan portfolio is related to housing loans, amounting to about US$160 million.[59] Among the 27 financial institutions in the Accion Network, seven have housing portfolios totalling almost 10,000 active clients and US$20 million in outstanding balances.

A further potential role for shelter microfinance is within more comprehensive slum upgrading programmes

The speed with which housing loans have been integrated within such agencies appears to have been facilitated by the similarity of lending practice. For example, in the case of one Peruvian agency, Mibanco, adding a home improvement loan product was easier than originally anticipated.[60] Traditional microfinance agencies treat housing loans broadly as they treat microenterprise lending, with small repeat loans that are not (in many cases) conditional upon collateral.

Reasons for expansion of MFIs into housing

One reason for the diversification of microfinance agencies into housing is commercial advantage. Such diversification may increase the financial stability of their loan portfolio, enable them to take advantage of opportunities for growth, and avoid losing clients to other microfinance agencies that provide housing loans.[61] A further notable advantage is that the longer repayment period associated with housing loans helps to draw the borrowers into a longer-term relationship with the lending agency and increases the likelihood that further loans will be taken (for example, for enterprise development). Thus, lending for land and housing has commercial benefits for a microfinance industry seeking to extend its niche and strengthen performance. The need for diversification may be particularly important in countries such as El Salvador and Bolivia, in which microfinance agencies are facing considerable competition for clients.[62]

It appears likely that there is significant scope for expansion, at least in most of Latin America and Asia. Given the scale of housing need, microfinance for shelter remains significantly underdeveloped in many countries in which market conditions appear favourable, such as Mexico and Brazil.[63] In Central America, the SIDA has been financing a number of market assessment studies to identify what people want, both in terms of demand for housing loans and other financial services beyond credit.[64] Generally, demand has been diverse and has included infrastructure loans, as well as demand for microinsurance and housing. The market may also be significant in Africa; but it is likely that the income group will be different. In Africa, where many of the middle class may not be able to access formal loans due to land title problems, microfinance may not reach down the income groups so far and scale may be smaller but still valuable. Box 6.7 summarizes a recent analysis of the potential for growth in a number of countries. These assessments are only indicative of potential. However, they illustrate some of the reasoning that lies behind new initiatives in shelter microfinance.

Neighbourhood improvement (slum upgrading)

A further potential role for shelter microfinance is within more comprehensive slum upgrading programmes. There appears to be a growing interest in using microfinance agencies to provide specialist financial services within more comprehensive neighbourhood improvement and poverty reduction programmes. Within this strategy, the development agency, central government and/or municipality finances a process to upgrade the low-income area with components to regularize tenure and provide and/or upgrade infrastructure and services. The upgrading programme then contracts with an organization to offer small-scale housing loans for those who wish to upgrade their homes. At the broadest level, such programmes are similar to best practice elsewhere, involving local government and public–private partnerships to address housing and community development activities.[65]

Box 6.8 The local development programme (PRODEL) in Nicaragua

In order to address the need to improve the physical environment and the socio-economic conditions of the poor in Nicaragua, Programa de Desarollo Local (PRODEL), a local development programme, established the following kinds of support:

- infrastructure and community works, including the introduction, expansion, repair and improvement of infrastructure and services through small-scale projects costing up to US$50,000;
- housing improvement through small loans (of between US$200–$1400) targeted at low-income families who can afford to enlarge and improve houses and to repay their loans;
- financial assistance to microenterprises with small short-term loans (of between US$300–$1500) for fixed and working capital; these loans are directed, in particular, at microenterprises owned and operated by women; and
- technical assistance and institutional development to strengthen the capacities of local governments and encourage institutionalized financial entities to become involved in non-conventional lending programmes for housing improvements and microenterprise loans.

Between April 1994 and December 1998, 260 infrastructure and community projects were carried out in 155 different neighbourhoods, benefiting more than 38,000 families. Total investment has been US$4.4 million (an average of US$16,972 per project). Contributions from municipal governments and the beneficiary communities (in kind, cash, materials, tools, labour, administration and supervision) totalled 43.1 per cent, with the remaining 56.9 per cent coming from the programme. Thirty-five per cent of the projects were for improving roads, gutters and sidewalks; 10 per cent for improving and expanding potable water and sewage systems; 14 per cent for rainwater and storm water drainage; 18 per cent for electrification (public lighting and/or household connections); and 23 per cent addressed community infrastructure (including construction, improvement, expansion and repair of primary schools, daycare centres, health centres, parks and playgrounds). The communities contributed approximately 132,000 days of work to these 260 projects, both volunteer and paid, using their own resources.

In five years, more than 4168 loans were given for housing improvements (total disbursed funds reached US$2.7 million). By 2003, the total had grown to over 11,000 loans and annual disbursements during this year exceeded US$2.5 million. These benefited approximately the same number of families. Families contributed their own resources, construction materials, labour, transportation and project administration to an amount equivalent to at least 15 per cent of the total value of the labour, transport and building materials. Seventy per cent of the families have monthly incomes of US$200 or less, including many with monthly incomes below US$100.

More than 12,451 loans to microentrepreneurs were allocated to communities in which PRODEL is active, with almost US$5.5 million being disbursed, benefiting approximately 2400 existing families. Seventy new microenterprises have been created, giving jobs to some 210 people.

Source: Stein, 2004, pp117–118; PRODEL, 2004.

A number of different variants of this model have developed. Box 6.8 describes the Local Development Programme (Programa de Desarollo Local, or PRODEL) in Nicaragua that was set up to enhance development in smaller towns and cities with a number of components, including infrastructure improvements, housing loans and loans for microenterprises. The activities received the support of SIDA, who signed an agreement with the Nicaraguan government in 1993 for the implementation of a programme to address basic needs and support development in a number of urban centres. In this case, the programme worked with Banco Crédito Popular, a state commercial bank, and selected two existing NGOs, Asociacíon de Consultores para el Desarrollo de la Pequeña, Mediana y Microempresa (ACODEP) and Nilapán-FDL, both of whom were already active in lending for micro-enterprises and who wished to expand their activities.[66] Although the physical areas for the different components of the programme do not necessarily overlap exactly, the cumulative effects are illustrated by the change in the number of those receiving housing loans who have land titles. In 1994, only 15 per cent of those receiving housing loans had title deeds; in 2002, the figure had increased to 73 per cent as the titling programme expanded.[67] Although communities do not pay directly for the improvements in basic services and infrastructure, they contribute self-help estimated at 13 per cent of the costs.

A more focused (and smaller-scale approach) is illustrated in Ahmedabad, India, where the Slum Networking Project (undertaken within the municipality) wished to include a credit component to help households afford to contribute to infrastructure improvements. In establishing this programme, they drew upon the local expertise of SEWA, a local agency lending to the poor. More recently, the Parivartan Programme has been established to upgrade slums in and around Ahmedabad through the joint participation of government entities, NGOs, the private sector and low-income residents themselves. The programme was initiated by the Slum Networking Cell within the Ahmedabad city government. Parivartan means 'transformation' in Gujarati and Hindi. The programme seeks to offer improved infrastructure and better communication between the local residents and the authorities. It provides a water supply to every house, an underground sewerage connection, toilets in the home and an efficient storm water drainage system. Further benefits are street lighting, paved roads and pathways and basic landscaping, together with solid waste management. Costs are divided between the residents (2000 rupees, or US$42) and the municipality (8000 rupees, or US$170). SEWA helps the lower income residents with loans.[68]

Box 6.9 Community-led Infrastructure Financing Facility (CLIFF) and bottom-up neighbourhood development

The Community-led Infrastructure Financing Facility (CLIFF) is an urban poor fund capitalized by donors that has been designed to act as a catalyst in slum upgrading through providing strategic support for community-initiated housing and infrastructure projects that have the potential for scaling up. The overall goal is to reduce urban poverty by increasing the access of poor urban communities to commercial and public-sector finance for medium- to large-scale infrastructure and housing initiatives. The first initiative is in India with the Society for the Promotion of Area Resource Centres (SPARC), the National Slum Dwellers Federation (NSDF) and *Mahila Milan*.

Scaling up citywide requires an engagement with the formal development process and the establishment of working relationships with formal-sector institutions. This is usually problematic, largely because public-sector financing is severely constrained and has a proven record of being reluctant to lend to the poor. A further problem is that the formal sector has continued to be unable to adapt their systems to accommodate non-formal investment processes. In December 2002, Cities Alliance approved a proposal to establish CLIFF with a seed capital of US$10 million from the UK Department for International Development (DFID) and an additional US$2 million from the Swedish government. Homeless International (a UK NGO) is the implementing agent and works with *Samudaya Nirman Sahayak*. The main function of CLIFF is to:

- provide bridging loans, guarantees and technical assistance;
- initiate medium-scale urban rehabilitation in cities in the South;
- work in partnership with community-based organizations (CBOs)/and non-governmental organizations (NGOs) who have or can be assisted to develop a track record in delivering urban rehabilitation;
- seek to attract commercial, local and public-sector finance for further schemes, thus accelerating or scaling up the response to the challenge of urban renewal; and
- establish local CLIFF agencies that can operate as lasting local institutions.

The example of SEWA gives some indication of the potential for housing finance agencies to work in alliance with groups seeking sources of funds and organizational potential for upgrading. One further programme is the Comprehensive Kampung Improvement Programme (KIP) introduced in Surabaya, Indonesia, during the late 1990s and following on from earlier improvement strategies for these low-income areas. In these earlier strategies, the experience was that housing investment took place as the local environment was upgraded. In the Comprehensive KIP, revolving funds within communities have been capitalized to provide a source of finance for income generation and housing investment.[69] In Comprehensive KIP 2003, some 30 per cent of the initial investment revolving fund (US$33,000) per area was used to capitalize a revolving fund specifically allocated to housing. Between 2001 and 2003, an estimated 860 households had borrowed for housing improvements.[70] The delivery of housing loans was integrated with the provision of enterprise lending, as well as physical improvements to the area. Similar strategies have been used in a number of other programmes, including the Programme for Integrated Urban Renewal in El Salvador to assist in the rehabilitation of *mesones* in San Salvador after the earthquake. These are old houses now subdivided with tenants in each room. The programme provided for the improvement of infrastructure (with substantial finance) and then offered loans for housing improvement and micro-enterprise development.[71]

Although most slum upgrading initiatives have been led by the state, an alternative approach is that developed from an Indian alliance of SPARC (an NGO), the National Slum Dwellers Federation (NSDF) and *Mahila Milan* (a network of women's collectives). Their strategy is to develop the capacity of local communities to manage a comprehensive upgrading and redevelopment process that is financed primarily by the state (through subsidies), with additional monies through loans taken by communities and repaid by individual members. Through a not-for-profit company, *Samudhaya Nirman Sahayak*, communities draw down the funds they need to pre-finance land, infrastructure and housing development. The scale of activities has resulted in additional donor finance being drawn into the process through the Community-led Infrastructure Financing Facility (CLIFF), which is described in Box 6.9.

Land development

A further model offering a more comprehensive development strategy than shelter microfinance is the strategy of combining small loans for housing improvement with land development.[72] One illustration is the case of El Salvador where low-cost subdivision regulations established during the early 1990s have helped to stimulate a low-income land development industry of 200 firms.[73] After

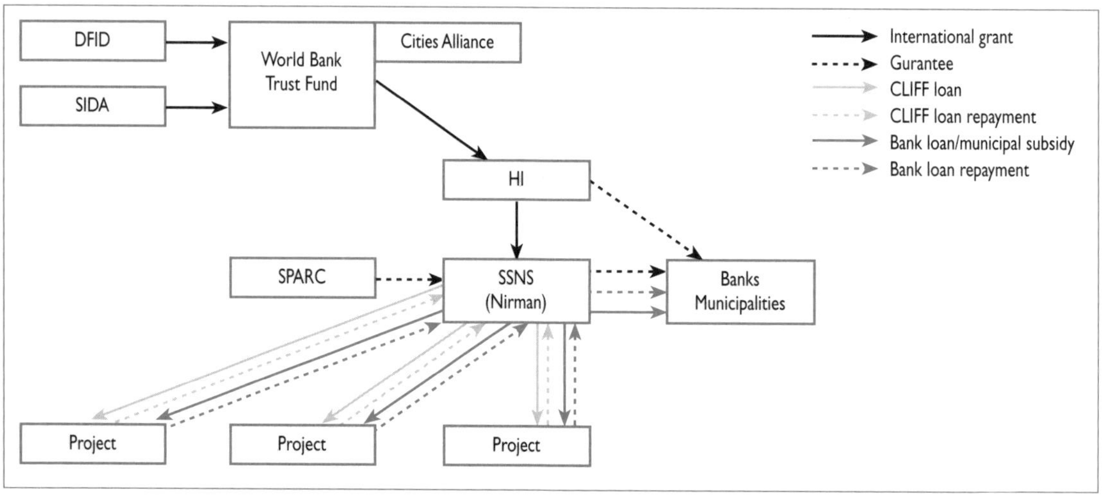

Figure 6.1

The Community-led Infrastructure Financing Facility (CLIFF) process

Note: DFID = Department for International Development (UK)
SPARC = Society for the Promotion of Area Resource Centres
HI = Homeless International
SSNS = Samudaya Nirman Sahayak

Source: D'Cruz, 2004b.

developing the area and selling the household a serviced plot, many of these developers offer a small loan (often around US$1,000) to build an initial core unit. It appears that this strategy has resulted in affordable secure tenure over the last decade, and – with greater supply – has lowered real estate prices in real terms. However, there are concerns about housing quality, and households who face difficulties at the end of the period may fail to secure a legal title.[74] A similar system is used by the Salvadoran Integral Assistance Foundation (FUSAI), a microfinance agency that has also started to be operational in land development in order to address the needs of clients. FUSAI acquires the title to the land and undertakes the cost of infrastructure development. Once serviced, the land is subdivided and allocated to families who have been accepted by FUSAI according to income and capacity to pay criteria. Families receive the land title once they pay back the loan. The amount to be financed by the loan equals the price of the house, including road and infrastructure development, minus the subsidy received from the state, minus the value of the self-help contribution by the family.[75] Similar initiatives are ongoing in Bolivia where Banco Sol has an agreement with a major developer and construction company in Santa Cruz.[76]

The discussion here highlights the growing diversity of approaches that are grouped together within shelter microfinance. This final discussion on neighbourhood development (slum upgrading), together with the servicing of greenfield sites, has suggested a number of distinct neighbourhood and housing strategies that include a role for small-scale housing loans:

- *Improvements of existing housing units*: this is the dominant approach at present within shelter microfinance. Small-scale loans are provided to households with reasonably secure land tenure to enable the extension and/or improvement of accommodation.
- *Linked land purchase and housing loan developments*: private development companies prepare serviced land (and, perhaps, basic housing units) for sale with additional loans for housing development.
- *Linked land development and/or upgrading paid for with a capital subsidy and housing loan developments*: this has been discussed in Chapter 5 in the context of complete housing (paid for by saving, subsidy and loan); but the subsidy funds might be used to prepare a serviced plot with additional loans being taken as the household can afford to improve the dwelling.
- *Linked settlement upgrading and housing loan*: a further option may be for the government (either development agency and/or municipality) to upgrade the area, with households then taking additional loans to improve the dwelling.

In the case of the final three options, there are two distinct strategies that are considered in this chapter and Chapter 7. Shelter microfinance considers those strategies that are based on individual lending to the household by the microfinance agency. Without community capacity (and in the absence of state upgrading programmes), it is not possible for shelter microfinance to do more than loans for housing improvement.[77] Chapter 7 looks at an alternative approach, community funds, which places more emphasis on collective capacity and which lends to groups of low-income households within a defined area and/or group. In some cases, the approaches within community funds have led into much larger-scale upgrading or land development strategies with the involvement of a much greater number of agencies. Notable examples are the *Baan Mankong* programme in Thailand (which has emerged from the work of the Community Organization Development Institute, or CODI) and the upgrading of 100 settlements in Phnom Penh, Cambodia, which was catalysed by lending from the Urban Poor Development Fund.

OTHER PROVIDERS AND SOURCES OF FINANCE

The preceding discussion concentrated on the growth in provision of small-scale loans for housing by NGOs and microfinance agencies. However, there are numerous sources of finance for small loans, although there are few large programmes that offer opportunities to finance incremental housing development at scale. One reason for the lack of scale is a lack of capital. The discussion of the development of this sector has concentrated on microfinance agencies and NGOs, both of whom receive external development assistance. Many of the providers considered below have had no external source of finance. The lack of loan capital is relevant to all providers and is discussed further in Chapter 8 as one of the challenges facing the sector.

There are numerous sources of finance for small loans, although there are few large programmes that offer opportunities to finance incremental housing development at scale

Small loans tend to be offered by less formal financial markets and they may have a number of characteristics that differ from formal financial markets.[78] Access to finance may depend upon social networks based on religion or ethnicity. In some cases, households secure finance from neither formal nor informal financial markets, but borrow or otherwise obtain from friends and family. In this case, there may be further obligations in addition to repayments, with the loan being simply one component within a dense set of reciprocal exchanges. The following discussion focuses primarily on small loans being offered by institutions and organizations, rather than those being offered through entirely personal networks. Table 6.3 draws on one recent analysis that identified several key types of providers.[79]

The potential significance of commercial micro-lenders can be illustrated in the case of South Africa. Like most countries in the South, South Africa has always had informal money lenders who ignore official interest rate restrictions. During the mid 1990s, however, revisions to the Usury Act created the possibility of formal commercial microlending at unregulated interest rates. These commercial microlenders, shown in Table 6.4, now comprise 64 per cent of registered institutions with the Microfinance Regulatory Council. Table 6.4 also illustrates the importance of larger banks. These commercial micro-lenders serve a market that is predominantly formally employed, with access to a bank account. The council estimates that about 11 per

Table 6.3

Sources of small housing loans

Institutional type	Area of focus
Microfinance agencies (large)	Those already working with more than 100,000 clients. Housing loan programmes may have emerged from disasters and may be a 'reward' for successful enterprise lending.
Microfinance agencies (medium)	Medium scale with 10,000 to 100,000 clients. May use similar principles for housing as for enterprise lending. May be short of suitable longer-term capital for such lending.
Northern NGOs	Some lend directly and some provide wholesale funds. They may provide limited technical assistance.
Co-operatives, mutuals and municipals	Locally owned and locally started housing programmes. May be part of networks for the sharing of experiences.
State housing programmes	May have limited capacity to offer small loans. Major source of second-tier funding, but limited outreach.
Commercial agencies	Some downscaling to housing generally faster than microcredit. Security and collateral is a major issue. Could mobilize large amounts of capital.
Local NGOs	Mainly involved in housing from a community perspective. Most are small with less than 1000 clients.

Source: adapted from Escobar and Merrill, 2004, pp38–39.

cent of disbursements from such institutions are used for housing.

In South Africa and other countries, there are also examples of commercial banks seeking to reach the lower-income market with smaller loans for housing. One example is the Banco de Desarrollo in Chile, which has a small lending programme for housing with 15,000 current loans and an average size of US$1200 per loan.[80] As noted earlier, Banco Davivienda in Colombia is now considering developing a small loan facility for housing.[81] However, such initiatives appear to be limited since many banks do not see it as profitable to develop lending into the small-loan housing finance sector.

In addition to the commercial microlender industry, there are some alternative forms of housing finance that have emerged, including lines of credit from building materials suppliers and hire purchase of individual items such as sanitary ware. In some cases, there are longstanding practices within these or associated industries (such as furniture). In Chile, companies such as Easy, Homecenter and Home Depot provide people with building materials and have credit systems to which it is very easy to have access, providing that proof of income can be offered. Home building materials supply chains (such as Elektra in Mexico) may also enter this business on a more significant scale. Elektra (a large electrical appliance chain) has now formed a bank that provides credit for building material packages suitable for starter homes. A further Mexican programme, Patrimonio Hoy, is run by Cemex and encourages women to save together for the purchase of building materials. At the end of five weeks, the programme will advance raw materials worth ten weeks of savings. After three years of operation, *Patrimonio Hoy* had 36,000 customers and over US$10 million in extended credit; the customer base is reported to be growing at the rate of 1500 to 1600 individuals per month.[82]

Table 6.4

Registered micro-lenders, 2003

Type	Branches	Percentage of total
Banks	2387	32.7
Publicly listed, non-bank	15	0.2
Private commercial microlenders	4687	64.2
Trusts	116	1.6
Section 21 (non-profit) companies	54	0.7
Co-operatives	42	0.6
Total	7301	100.0

Source: www.mfrc.co.za/detail.php?s=95.

Although remittances are not a provider of small-scale investments in housing finance, they are emerging as a significant source of finance for housing investment. Their current scale is estimated to be US$200 billion a year, placing remittances as the second largest inflow to the South after foreign direct investment.[83] The largest receivers of remittance income are India, Mexico, the Philippines, Morocco and Egypt. Their growing scale has resulted in a number of institutional innovations to capture these financial flows and to more efficiently enable housing investment.

For example, Mexico's remittance income equalled 1.5 times the tourist income in 2002.[84] Although precise data is hard to come by, it appears that a significant proportion of such remittances are invested in housing.[85] An indication of the scale of such funds is the interest shown by financial agencies and building material companies in facilitating such investment. Box 6.10 describes the commercial systems that have been established to assist in housing investment in Mexico for workers based in the US.

The other set of institutions that may be concerned to provide small-scale loans are traditional home lenders. Traditional home lenders face substantial barriers in engaging in microfinance due to the relatively high costs associated with lending, which have been noted earlier.[86] Such institutions may require a mortgage lien as security for their home loans, while most shelter microfinance agencies work with other sorts of collateral. The culture and underwriting standards of traditional home-lending institutions suit lending to the middle class and those with higher incomes, while these institutions have difficulty with the practices required for lending to low-income households, such as reconstructing informal income and securing alternative forms of collateral.

State programmes offering small loans are potentially important, although they have not featured much in the development of the sector. In general, there has not been large-scale state finance for small-scale lending to support incremental housing development, although there are some exceptions to this situation, including the programmes discussed in Chapter 7 in which small loans are offered through collective mechanisms. Further exceptions are where small housing improvement loans have been associated with larger-scale upgrading (slum improvement programmes). In other cases, governments have sought to provide capital for NGOs interested in providing small loans for housing development. In India, the government has sought to provide capital through HUDCO from the early 1990s. A number of NGOs have taken up these funds, while some have struggled to manage the restrictions within the programme.[87] The Colombian government has recently taken a loan from the Inter-American Development Bank (IADB) that includes financing for 10,000 microloans for housing improvement. There may be a significant number of other programmes. Households buying serviced land from the city of Windhoek in Namibia can ask to repay over eight years at an interest rate of 15 per cent.[88]

There are signs that there is a growing interest in financing these approaches and more groups interested in participating in activities. In Peru, the state housing authority is channelling housing funds to microfinance agencies, municipal savings and loan co-operatives, as well as some microfinance banks, in an effort to provide appropriate finance.[89] There also appears to be increasing interest at the municipal level in Latin America. The municipal funds in Peru offer little direct lending for housing, although the scale of their activities suggests that they have a major impact upon the financial choices of many of the residents. There are now 14 such funds throughout the country, with total deposits of US$200 million and an annual growth in deposits of US$40 million.[90] Belem in Brazil provides a further example of the potential role of the municipality. Collaboration between the municipality, civil society, the Banco de Povo and the community itself has resulted in a flexible loan programme offering loans of up to US$500 for a variety of activities, and housing loans have also been made available through a new programme.[91] One quarter of borrowers have improved their sanitation provision, reflecting urgent and pressing needs in the low-income neighbourhoods.

There have been some deliberate attempts to draw formal financial institutions closer to the microfinance sector. The discussion of social housing in Chapter 5 highlights the programme *Tu Casa* in Mexico, and there is a very similar component within an IADB loan to Colombia.[92] In both cases, small home improvement grants are a minor part of loan and subsidy programmes that are primarily concerned with funding complete houses.

Box 6.10 Mexico and remittances

Cemex is a Mexican company and the world's third largest cement producer. Since 2002, Mexican residents in the US can buy cement and other building materials directly in eight Cemex branches in the US (a subsidiary called Construmex) and have the materials delivered directly to a chosen address in Mexico. Since it began this service (early 2002 to October 2004), US$3 million have been taken in construction sales. The company estimates that the building materials needed for a 100 square metre completed two-bedroom house cost US$6700.

The new mortgage banks, the Sociedad Finaciera de Objeto Limitado (SOFOLES), have also sought to capitalize on similar funds and two have opened branches in the US, with a third operating in the US via an intermediary. However, the sales of mortgages have been slow, in part, because Mexican migrants come from communities with self-build traditions. Presidents Bush and Fox launched a bilateral organization, Partners in Prosperity, in 2001. In November 2004, the programme stated:

> *BANSEFI [Banco del Ahorro Nacional y Servicios Financieros], together with housing finance public institutions INFONAVIT [Instituto del Fondo Nacional de la Vivienda para los Trabajadores] and FONHAPO [Fondo Nacional de Habitaciones], have continued working under the Programa de Recepción de Aportaciones de Mexicanos en el Extranjero to allow Mexican migrants living in the US to transfer money to their families in order to obtain housing benefits and pay mortgage debts. Sociedad Hipotecaria Federal (SHF) is funding the Raíces programme where mortgage intermediaries (SOFOLES) grant loans to Mexicans living in the US to acquire a house in Mexico.*

Source: Connolly, 2004a, b.

Cooperatives and other voluntary sector agencies

There is a range of voluntary sector agencies, such as co-operatives, and credit unions, that seek to extend credit to their membership and that may offer small loans for housing. These may also include less formal rotating savings and credit associations (ROSCAs). In general, the loans offered by such providers are not intended for housing improvements; but in some cases they are used for this purpose. A significant problem for such small-scale lenders is that the size of the loans is generally not sufficient for housing improvements. The issues are illustrated by an analysis of the Women Credit Union in Sri Lanka.[93] The housing needs of the members led to external finance being raised to enable the union to offer housing loans. However, such credit was limited and, thus, few loans could be allocated. The Kenya Union of Savings and Credit Co-operatives established a housing fund in 1998 through an agreement with the National Co-operative Housing Union (NACHU). However, funds also appear limited, and by 2003 the fund had extended 33 loans valued at 40 million Kenyan shillings.[94]

Although informal financial mechanisms are used for incremental improvements in Hyderabad, such finance often cannot be accessed by the poorest.[95] Many of the ROSCAs require regular payments that are difficult for the poor to meet. The more flexible systems that do not require monthly payments have higher participation from the poor.[96]

Housing and/or savings and loan co-operatives and mutuals are a further source of loans in Latin America.[97] Also notable are the housing and mutual aid co-operatives of Chile (Federacíon Unificadora de Cooperativas de Vivienda por Ayuda Mutua, FUCVAM), which provide loans and assist with construction. Although it might be anticipated that housing co-operatives would provide appropriate sources of finance, in practice many seem to concentrate on the provision of complete houses. This might be explained by their need to build 'officially' and conform to building regulations and/or by their own need for collateral. Box 6.11 discusses a scheme in Kenya to provide both housing and income support to low-income groups in Nakuru and highlights some typical problems of affordability that have been experienced elsewhere. Housing People in Zimbabwe faced very similar difficulties and found that many of those turning to housing co-operatives had higher incomes. Although such organizations often make considerable efforts to reach down to low-income groups – for example, Housing People helped one group of domestic workers – this tends to be exceptional. NACHU in Kenya has made some efforts to offer loans for land purchase and (household-level) infrastructure development to its member co-operatives. However, it is hard to assess the scale and affordability of this programme, and other loans are orientated towards those who have landownership.[98] The Nala Makazi Housing Co-op in Dodoma, Tanzania, has also managed to raise capital for housing construction and is currently developing housing for those living in informal settlements.[99] However, the scale is again very small. Similar problems appear to be prevalent in Latin America where credit unions will extend loans for housing improvement and purchase to lower income

Although remittances are not a provider of small-scale investments in housing finance, they are emerging as a significant source of finance for housing investment

Box 6.11 From self-help group to housing co-operative in Kenya

Between January and February 2003, members of the Nakuru Housing and Environment Co-operative (NAHECO) in Kenya have accessed seven housing loans from the National Housing Co-operative Union (NACHU) amounting to 360,000 Kenyan shillings and microcredit loans amounting to 140,500 Kenyan shillings. The membership of the co-operative has increased from the initial number of 15 groups from the three low-income settlements to 30 groups drawn from seven low-income settlements. The increased membership to NAHECO has resulted in increased savings. NAHECO has taken up a role of coordinating local self-help activities and people show confidence and trust in the operations of the group.

However, the poorest within the area are unable to benefit from this programme. The participatory needs assessment results showed that 92.6 per cent of people living in the three project settlements were tenants living in dilapidated housing; 70.9 per cent of them were very poor, with no land on which to construct own housing. One of the criteria for accessing credit for housing through NAHECO is possession of land or the ability to save enough to buy some. This is a major weakness in identifying the target group and formulating the guidelines for accessing credit through NAHECO. This implies that the poorest of the people in the target area may be excluded from benefiting from the project.

Source: Ng'ayu, 2003.

households; but they require that households have savings deposits equal to about 25 per cent of the loan, which the poorer households are unlikely to find affordable.[100] One exception to lending for incremental housing is the co-operative Jesus Nazareno in Bolivia, which provides small loans with a solidarity group guarantee for the purchase of land.[101] However, titles are held by the co-operative until repayment is completed, and this suggests that the loans are to those able to afford secure tenure and title.

Despite such difficulties, the significance of many small providers is emphasized by a recent assessment of the microfinance sector in Peru.[102] Major institutions offering small loans include self-managed communal funds and co-operatives, NGO programmes, local microfinance agencies, municipal funds, rural funds and the protection funds of some workers' unions. An estimated US$25 million may be loaned each year to housing, of which about 67 per cent comes from the savings and loan co-operatives.

Box 6.12 Acquiring loan finance in South Africa

The Kuyasa Fund is a non-profit microfinance institution based in Cape Town, South Africa. Since 2001, it has reached more than 2643 clients with US$1.8 million of housing loans. Portfolio at risk is 15 per cent and write-offs are 5 per cent of cumulative disbursements. Women constitute the vast majority of Kuyasa borrowers at 72 per cent, and account for 70 per cent of the value of loans taken.

The Kuyasa Fund has been unable to obtain any loan equity locally, and the wholesale equity and start-up grants have all come from offshore donor sources. Although the parastatal National Urban Reconstruction and Housing Agency (NURCHA) has assisted with loan guarantees, none of South Africa's housing-related parastatals have been willing to lend or grant Kuyasa any funds on the grounds of 'high risk'. Kuyasa, however, has already demonstrated conclusively that its lending performance is better than that of mortgage lenders operating in the same market. Recently, the National Housing Finance Corporation has courted Kuyasa management with the offer of a loan, but on terms that made it unviable for Kuyasa. Once again, the parastatal cited risk as its main concern. Kuyasa's difficulty in attracting local equity, even in the face of solid performance, reflects the continuing dominance of the mortgage mindset and risk aversion in South Africa's parastatal housing finance sector.

Source: Baumann, 2004; Van Rooyan, 2004.

Sources of capital finance

How do microfinance agencies secure capital for their lending? Some providers draw on their own capital, notably the private sector and, for the most part, the small-scale voluntary organizations, such as credit unions. However, most agencies who wish to expand their lending have to find significant sources of capital.

Although consumers in South Africa have been successful in accessing and using small loans and targeted savings for incremental housing improvement, the policy and regulatory environment has not been developed with this approach in mind, and there is no source of wholesale finance or technical support for such institutions.[103] The NGOs who have developed this model cannot drive the development of a pro-poor housing finance sector alone. Groups such as the Kuyasa Fund now face a major constraint in the lack of capital to expand lending (see Box 6.12).

Such NGOs and other microfinance agencies have four sources of funds: deposits, development assistance, governments and the private sector. The problem remains even in countries with a well-developed microfinance sector, such as Bangladesh. Despite the creation of an apex financing institution, the Palli Karma-Sahayak Foundation (PKSF), agencies such as the Grameen Bank remain short of capital to finance microloans for housing.[104]

Although many agencies encourage deposits and, as noted in Box 6.14, in SEWA's case these savings provide 80 per cent of capital, availability of medium-term capital is recognized to be a constraint. This is a problem even in the context of the Central American agencies funded by SIDA that generally receive medium- to long-term support (an average of nine years per programme).[105]

Microfinance organizations, for the most part, seek to be viable commercial enterprises. The small number of agencies studied by Cities Alliance are broadly successful in this aspiration.[106] Micasa (the housing programme of Mibanco in Bolivia) broke even on a cash-flow basis, including the initial investment in adjusting the management information system, within nine months; if performance continues at current levels, it is expected to generate a return on loan portfolio of between 7 and 9 per cent, compared with its overall return on loan portfolio of 3.4 per cent. FUNHAVI, the Mexican agency, was operationally self-sufficient after six years of business and moving towards full financial sustainability.

However, both these agencies appear to have had sufficient capital to expand their activities to a profitable level. Proa (also in Bolivia) has a model that would work without a subsidy only if volumes increased.[107] The programme has money from a mutual savings association at 9 to 10 per cent and on-lends at 13.5 to 15 per cent. Given current volumes, a higher fee (margin) is required; but this is not allowed by the mutual association providing the funds. The expansion of the programme from US$175,000 to US$500,000 of new loans per month would allow costs to be covered. The success of this strategy is critically dependent upon securing adequate capital to expand lending.

This aspiration to be financially viable without access to financial support has a number of implications for the nature and development of microfinance. Many microfinance organizations face a balance between reaching down to the poorer households with smaller loans and minimizing administration and management costs by offering larger loans. In general, the emphasis has been greater on cost-effective lending. There is a widespread belief (supported by many experiences) that access to credit is rather more important than the price of credit and, hence, that microenterprise lending can charge interest rates that are relatively high in comparison to the formal financial markets (although low compared to informal money lenders). However, housing loans are often considerably larger and therefore the interest rate charges are more significant. In some cases, lenders have developed specific housing products with lower interest rates; these are generally commercially viable even if they are not fully market based.[108]

Some bilateral donors have funded shelter microfinance activities for a considerable period (almost 20 years) including Swedish Assistance (Box 6.13) and USAID. However, the multilateral donors – such as the IADB and the World Bank – have only begun to learn about and develop programmes in this area over the last few years. In their absence, Northern NGOs have played a very significant role in supporting such initiatives. These NGOs have included Misereor (Germany) and CordAid (the Netherlands), as well as specialist housing and urban development groups such as SELAVIP (Belgium) and Homeless International (the UK).

Shelter microfinance and subsidies

There is a difference of opinion between microfinance agencies about the need for housing subsidies. On the one hand, there is a belief that subsidies are necessary because of the traditional association between subsidies and low-income housing and because of the larger size of housing loans.[109] On the other hand, it is widely accepted that microfinance needs to perform without subsidy finance in order to be able to expand as market conditions permit. Sector commentators suggest that subsidies should not be offered through interest rates or permitted defaults, and that subsidies, if offered, should be managed separately outside of the loan operation.[110] For example, subsidies might be provided through capital grants for housing investment or through the provision of water and sanitation services. Chapter 5 discussed the use of small loans to top up housing subsidy finance.

Despite such recommendations, this is not necessarily common practice. In situations in which there is no state support, there appears to be an effective cross-subsidy from enterprise to shelter lending, as the interest rates are lower in the latter. In some countries, particularly in Asia, subsidies are available through reduced interest rates and microfinance agencies have become a conduit to deliver state support to the poor. In some cases, the subsidy is provided in the form of an interest rate reduction. Grameen Bank and SEWA have both accessed low-interest sources of funds and pass on this subsidy.

Box 6.13 Swedish International Development Agency (SIDA) assistance to low-income housing in Central America

Since 1988, the Swedish International Development Agency (SIDA) has financed housing and local development programmes in Central America with total resources of US$50 million. By the end of 2003, the programmes had helped approximately 80,000 low-income families, or about 400,000 people, in the main urban areas of the region to improve their habitat conditions. The resources from SIDA have been channelled through different institutions and programmes – namely, the Foundation for Housing Promotion (FUPROVI) in Costa Rica, the Local Development Programme (PRODEL) in Nicaragua, the Salvadoran Integral Assistance Foundation (FUSAI) in El Salvador, the Urban and Rural Social Housing Development Foundation (FUNDEVI) in Honduras and the Local Development Trust Fund (FDLG) in Guatemala.

SIDA's policy throughout the region has been that housing subsidies are primarily the responsibility of national governments, who act as counterparts to the international agency. That is why most of the funds allocated by SIDA have been channelled to finance three main components of these programmes: loans (including microloans for housing improvements and new housing), technical assistance (both to executing agencies and the target population) and institutional development, especially of those institutions that manage the Swedish funds.

Source: Stein with Castillo, 2005.

TERMS AND CONDITIONS

There is a considerable diversity in the nature of shelter microfinance as provided by the many different organizations who are active in this sector. One commentator illustrates such differences thus:

> *In Mexico, CHF International and FUNHAVI [Fundación Habitat y Vivienda A. C.] have developed a home improvement loan that features an average loan amount of US$1800, a repayment period of 18 months for first-time borrowers and a 54 per cent effective annual interest rate. The Grameen Bank's housing loans typically are repaid over ten years. They are offered at an interest rate that is 10 per cent below rates assessed for microenterprise loans, and first-time clients are not eligible for such loans.*[111]

The average size of the Grameen Bank housing loan is 13,386 Bangladesh taka (US$224).[112] This contrast demonstrates the significance of local context in developing appropriate housing finance solutions. The difference between these approaches reflects the type of housing solution that is acceptable and affordable to the borrowers, and the solution that is likely to be approved by the authorities if they have a significant presence. The contrast also reflects the target group for lending activities and the operating constraints and choices of the agency. For example, as is sometimes the case for microenterprise lending, some microfinance agencies prefer to give fewer larger loans, thereby reducing their administration costs and increasing their financial returns for a given amount of loan capital.

Savings

The link between housing investment and savings extends well beyond the microfinance sector. In the North, traditionally families have saved for several years simply to access conventional mortgage finance. Savings is a particularly significant component of the contract-savings schemes in Western Europe, notably the German Bausparkasen and UK building societies.[113] Similarly, many microfinance programmes for housing, particularly in Asia and Africa, have savings requirements.

Savings has a place in microfinance for many reasons. Savings is a strategy to assist with repayments in which borrowers have to demonstrate a capacity to make regular payments and accumulate sufficient funds for the required down payment or deposit. Microfinance agencies may try to get would-be borrowers to save at a rate equal to loan repayments, in part to reduce the risk to lender and borrower. The required savings period typically lasts between 6 to 12 months before a loan is granted.[114] One notable example is Bank Rayat Indonesia (BRI), which has mobilized more than US$2.7 billion in voluntary savings through 16.1 million savings accounts; however, saving on this scale is very unusual. A further reason to encourage savings is to assist the agencies themselves in acquiring funds.[115] In SEWA's case, the bulk of the bank's loan portfolio arises from client deposits, although additional finance for housing loans is provided by the government though HUDCO.[116] The importance of saving can be illustrated for the case of SEWA:

> *In order to be eligible for any loan from SEWA Bank, for example, the would-be borrower must have a regular savings record at SEWA Bank for at least one year. What is important for SEWA is that the savings history is stable and consistent. SEWA Bank's experience is that facilitation of a strong savings habit correlates significantly with high loan repayment rates – hence, a client's savings record serves as the main form of collateral for loans.*[117]

The significance of savings to the clients of microfinance agencies has long been recognized. The experience of the Kuyasa Fund in South Africa is that clients use their savings to augment the subsidy that they receive from the state. A very notable estimated 65 per cent of Kuyasa clients only save and do not take loans.[118]

Collateral and security

Collateral is an asset pledged to a lender until the borrower pays back the debt. Its major role is in reducing lender risk and it is widely recognized that a key challenge for shelter microfinance is that of loan security.[119] Many microfinance agencies seek to minimize the need for collateral by using existing client history (enterprise lending). A further strategy used for lending for income generation is small repeat loans as a way of building up repayment skills and capacities and providing an incentive for repayment. However, the larger size of shelter microfinance makes this strategy more difficult to follow.

Another strategy used by microenterprise lenders is that of group guarantees. However, this strategy has been found to be problematic for housing loans, again because of the bigger loans and longer loan period.[120] This may explain the problems faced by the Group Credit Company in South Africa (which tried and failed to replicate Grameen Bank strategies in offering small loans). Difficulties are related to the longer period of the loans and, hence, the lack of need for the group unless repeat income-generation lending is also taking place. The use of group guarantees should not be confused with group loans, which include a collective responsibility to manage and repay the loan (see Chapter 7).

In the absence of such strategies, a wide range of collaterals are used, including mortgages, personal guarantees, group guarantees, fixed assets and/or pension/provident fund guarantees.[121] Pension fund collateral is used particularly in South Africa and Bangladesh, and more recently in Namibia, but is not significant elsewhere. In a recent study of microfinance agencies' practices, the following are identified as collateral:[122]

- land title and buildings;
- chattel mortgage/lien on assets;
- obligatory savings;
- assignment of future income (wages);
- personal guarantees (co-signers);
- joint liability and group guarantees (character-based lending); and
- other financial assets (for example, life insurance policies and pension funds).

One difficult area is the extent to which legal title is a requirement of lending. One commentator argues that 'Client ownership of the home or land is preferred: it is against the policy of some lenders to provide credit for housing on squatted land.'[123] Moreover, in some countries such as the Dominican Republic, lenders may not be legally allowed to extend housing loans without a formal property title.[124] However, despite an emphasis on land ownership, the use of title deeds as collateral for microfinance loans is limited, and one study of 80 such organizations found that only one quarter use it.[125] For example, the experience of Mibanco in Peru is also to avoid the use of land titles. The agency relies on the same informal collateral of household assets and co-signers used for microenterprise loans (despite the mass land-titling programme that has taken place in Peru, discussed in Chapter 4). Mibanco found that land titles are expensive to use as guarantees, and that poor clients do not want to use title as collateral for a loan of less than US$1000.[126] Banco Sol uses such collateral but considers that there are major risks because of the poor standard of deeds and title documentation.[127]

Alternative strategies are varied. In some cases, such as the Grameen Bank, home loans are only given to those who have experience in enterprise lending and a good repayment record. Alternatively, social collateral such as guarantees from other residents involved in the programme may be used. A further option is holding the para-legal documents to the property, or other non-mortgage collateral such as jewellery. Some lenders take a mortgage lien when the costs and legal structure permit for larger loans, such as for the construction of a core unit. In the case of PRODEL in Nicaragua, experience suggests that for loans under US$700, there are other types of collateral as effective as a mortgage.[128] PRODEL gives loans to families who do not have full land ownership, but that are able to demonstrate security of tenure – for example, co-signers who could put up their properties for mortgage, valuable objects and municipal certificates that show security of tenure, although not necessarily land title. Only half of the more than 5000 loans provided up to the year 2000 were mortgaged, and delinquency rates were still very low.

Although not collateral, a further common requirement is to specify the maximum percentage of income that can be used for housing loan repayment. A maximum percentage of 25 to 30 per cent of income in housing repayment is widely used by agencies. However, the effectiveness of this constraint can be questioned as precise incomes are not that easy to establish. Lenders may have different conditions for salaried workers and entrepreneurs.[129]

Interest rates

In many cases, interest rates for shelter loans are lower than those for enterprise development, even when offered by the same agency.[130] In most cases, the rates are fixed as the loans are for relatively short periods and it is very difficult for low-income households to cope with the uncertainty of variable rates. In a study of four Bangladeshi microfinance agencies offering loans for housing, the interest rate was lower in every case.[131] Although the Grameen Bank's explanation rests on the social significance of housing, it is also notable that higher interest rates would be unaffordable for the target group, given loan size and repayment periods.[132]

Setting the level of interest rates is clearly a difficult issue. Interest rates must be acceptable to borrowers and one report on SIDA's experience suggests that interest rates cannot diverge greatly from (even if they are not identical to) mortgage rates.[133] Most agencies seek to at least cover the cost of inflation and administration, with an allowance for defaults and bad loans. Box 6.14 summarizes SEWA's experience in setting interest rates for housing loans. An alternative approach used by Habitat for Humanity in Africa and the Middle East is to use a variable inflation index on the loan, which is pegged to the price of a bag of cement.[134] This allows repayments to maintain their real value.

Loan periods

There is a very significant difference in the loan periods of different shelter microfinance programmes. One recent survey of 15 agencies offering small loans for shelter finds that the loan periods differ by between 20 months and 15 years.[135] It might be anticipated that longer loan periods would be used for larger loans, potentially secured on the property, as the incentive for small repeat lending could not be used. In practice, this does not appear to be the case and some of the small loans have long repayment periods, with some larger loans featuring shorter repayment periods. However, the longer loan periods may be misleading. For example, one case is People's Dialogue in South Africa, where in most cases the loans are bridge financing for the state housing subsidy and are paid off rapidly once the subsidy entitlement has been accepted and finance released.

Box 6.14 Self-employed Women's Association (SEWA) interest rates for housing, India

When the Self-employed Women's Association (SEWA) first started lending for housing in India, it did not differentiate between housing and enterprise loans (in practice, the housing loans were bigger and were often the third or fourth loan that was taken). However, due to the size of housing loans (and the fact that they did not necessarily generate an instant higher income flow), they have been differentiated as a separate loan product since 1999, since which time they attract a lower interest rate of 14.5 per cent. Income generation loans – which typically account for 50 per cent of SEWA Bank's total loan portfolio and are usually of a lower loan amount and generate faster returns, charge interest at 17 per cent, thus partially cross-subsidizing the housing loan portfolio. SEWA's average cost of capital is 8 per cent and this primarily reflects the interest that it pays on members' savings. To secure housing loans, clients must have a regular savings record of at least one year. SEWA's experience is that a strong savings record correlates to good repayments and the regularity of payments is more important than the amount.

Source: Biswas, 2003.

Technical assistance

A further area related to the provision of subsidies is that of technical assistance. Many of those lending for shelter microfinance seek to provide assistance in construction activities. For example:

- FUSAI is an NGO in El Salvador that is working in housing-related activities. In 2002, it decided to separate its housing financing activities from construction support in order to maximize the efficiency of both operations.[136]
- Proa, a Bolivian NGO lending for housing improvements, has technical staff who prepare plans and budgets. They receive a commission on each loan (US$40) and secure additional payments from the households if required.[137]
- SEWA found that its members were increasingly asking for other services related to housing (in addition to loans). The Gujarat Mahila Housing SEWA Trust (MHT) was established to provide SEWA members with technical services related to housing, including advice on improving and extending existing houses, building new houses and infrastructural services. The MHT plays a key role as an intermediary with government departments in accessing schemes, including those related to infrastructural facilities and environmental improvement.

Box 6.15 Grameen Bank loan package, Bangladesh

In Bangladesh, the families who are members of the Grameen Bank typically live in small shelters of jute stick, straw, grass thatch, bamboo and dried mud. Each year a family has to spend about US$30 to repair the house after the monsoons. For an equal amount of money, a family can repay a housing loan for a strong, well-constructed house with a floor area of 20 square metres. The bank views housing loans as investment rather than consumption since a secure and well-constructed house aids the health and well-being of the family and helps them to break the vicious circle of poverty. The house can be used for storage for their small businesses, and time and money are saved in not having to continually repair the jute-stick shelters.

The Grameen Bank has developed two standard house designs. The smaller one costs US$300 and a larger version costs US$625. In many cases, the family adds their own savings to the loan and spends up to US$800–$1000 on their home and its furnishings. The houses vary in appearance throughout the country, but have the same basic structural components. There are four reinforced concrete pillars on brick foundations at the corners of the house and six intermediary bamboo or concrete posts, with bamboo tie beams, wooden rafters and purlins supporting corrugated-iron roofing sheets. This provides stability in the flood and strong monsoon wind and protection from the heavy rain during the monsoon season. In cases of severe flooding, the house can be dismantled and the components stored and reassembled later. A sanitary latrine must be provided with each house. Families can build the houses themselves with the help of friends and neighbours. Local skilled carpenters carry out the roof construction.

Source: www.bshf.org and www.grameen-info.org.

- FUNHAVI (Mexico) goes one step further and requires borrowers to buy construction materials from it (as well as providing technical advice). However, this is also a financial measure, as it buys at wholesale and sells at retail prices.[138]

Opinions differ about the viability of such services for microfinance agencies. One argument is that the more developed microfinance agencies do not offer such services.[139] A related view is that 'Construction assistances in the context of housing microfinance does not appear to be a predictor of financial performance.'[140] Some, such as Associación para el Desarollo de Microempresas (ADEMI) (Dominican Republic), argue that it is up to clients to manage their own affairs. Groups such as the Co-operative Housing Foundation argue that it is a necessary service and the content helps to reduce default rates. Another position is that of the Kuyasa Fund in South Africa, which does not want to provide these services itself, but recognizes the need to work alongside those who can provide technical assistance around construction issues.

In some cases, such as the Grameen Bank in Bangladesh, the loan is for a defined package of building materials, which minimizes the need for technical assistance (or greatly eases its provision) (see Box 6.15).

Orientation towards women

There is an emerging preference to lend to women in many of these institutions, based on the reliability of repayment.[141] Women borrowers are 'current good practice' and there is a particularly strong predisposition towards lending to women in Asia.[142] The Grameen Bank, for example, argues that the title to the house constructed with loan finance is vested with the borrower, and in 95 per cent of cases this is the woman. By having title to the house, the woman obtains financial security and an improved status within the family and society. In the case of FUNHAVI in Mexico, 38 per cent of the clients are women.[143] According to the Kuyasa Fund, South Africa, women are 72 per cent of the borrowers.[144] In the case of PRODEL in Nicaragua, more than 60 per cent of the housing improvement loan recipients and 70 per cent of the microentrepreneurs are women.[145] Such figures are indicative of the more general position: women are often predominant among borrowers, but few funds exclusively serve women.

In the case of shelter, the role of home carer is often defined by gender and given to women. Hence, women may have a greater interest in investing in housing even if they are less likely to be the formal 'owner' of the dwelling.

Income generation

Although the primary focus of the initiatives discussed above is on savings and lending for shelter improvement, some of these programmes recognize the evident links between shelter and livelihoods. Some agencies, such as SEWA, have long recognized the close connection between home-based enterprise lending and housing improvement loans.[146] Improving the infrastructure in the areas in which SEWA is working resulted in an average 35 per cent increase in small enterprise earnings.[147] Through experiences such as these, there is a growing awareness of the links between enterprise and shelter investment.

There are three notable ways in which these programmes are linked to enterprise lending. The first is through lending for income generation. In many cases, shelter microfinance is offered along with income-generation loans. In some cases, it is a condition of the lending organization that income-generation loans are taken first, in other cases, one or other might be taken. The justification for the first strategy is that successful income generation is needed to be able to afford housing investment and related loan repayments. The argument in favour of the second strategy is that many 'enterprise' loans are diverted to housing investments and repayments proceed successfully.

Second, housing investments are more directly linked to income generation in a number of ways. Housing construction activities may be to improve a business or production area, such as a small shop or a workroom. In some cases, they may not even be related to a productive or vending enterprise directly, but may be providing a room to rent. Finally, the more ambitious schemes have explored the possibility of creating commercial centres to improve local livelihoods and to strengthen the local economy. Generally, these strategies belong to initiatives with more ambitious development objectives (see Chapter 7).

FORESEEN CHALLENGES

Although shelter microfinance might not be effective in every context, there is now widespread experience and understanding of the process and considerable appreciation of the approach in many countries. There are two notable challenges facing the shelter microfinance sector. The first is the nature of the beneficiary group and the difficulties faced by very poor households due to problems of affordability and lack of secure tenure. The second is sources of funding. Although other issues may be of specific concern to particular programmes, these two subjects are those that appear to be the most significant.

Affordability

Microfinance for shelter may contribute to a more holistic approach to development than that generally associated with microfinance. In so doing, it may be addressing some of the concerns raised about its ability to assist some of the poorer families.[148] By reducing expenditure on basic needs (such as rent, repairs to housing and water costs), lending for land, infrastructure and housing may increase remaining income and reduce vulnerability. As demonstrated in the case of the Grameen Bank (see Box 6.15), housing investment reduced repair costs and essential expenditures.

These programmes appear, in general, to reach the income groups served by microfinance agencies lending for enterprise development and families with similar incomes in the formal sector. The bias of microfinance agencies towards the somewhat higher income groups has been recognized for some time. This bias reflects the need of the agencies to secure high levels of repayments and give out larger loans (with the administration costs therefore being a smaller proportion of the loan). It also reflects the self-selection of their clients, with the more vulnerable avoiding the problems of debt, or beginning and dropping out of the programmes. Many shelter microfinance programmes appear to be targeted at the higher income urban poor, sometimes those with formal employment (at least one member of the family) and often those with diversified household livelihood strategies. As is the case with SEWA, successful income-generation borrowing may be required prior to housing loan applications. In many cases, land tenure is required.

The target group of those agencies reviewed by Cities Alliance is profiled thus:

> *...these financial institutions describe their clients as the economically active poor in the informal sector. They are largely serving their existing poor clients with this new loan product, and most provide housing loans as a reward for good past performance on microenterprise loans.*[149]

In the cases of the agencies considered, Mibanco's clients have an income that is around or below the poverty line for Peru (where 50 per cent of the population have incomes below the poverty line). FUNHAVI in Mexico serves clients who earn between two and eight times the local monthly minimal wage of US$125. SEWA Bank's clients are all poor self-employed women – predominately street vendors, labourers or home-based workers. In 1998, an estimated 76 per cent of SEWA borrowers had annual household incomes below US$415 and half of these had annual incomes below US$276. Clearly, the group that is being reached is poor and in need of housing investment. However, these are large income categories and they may say little about how far below the poverty line such programmes are able to extend.

In some cases, shelter microfinance is linked to state subsidy programmes (notably in Latin America), and this may extend their reach downwards towards lower income groups. The Step-by-Step programme in Ecuador, for example, helps households to raise the deposit they need in order to secure the direct demand subsidy and therefore afford improved housing. However, as noted in Chapter 5, such programmes may include further loans and, hence, the poorest may not be able to afford the costs of inclusion.

The use of other mechanisms and, notably, the requirement for secure tenure, may further define the client group as being the poor, but not so poor. The greatest difficulty faced by the poor is that, in general, these programmes offer small loans for housing improvement and therefore cannot address the large numbers who do not have tenure security (if not a full title). A further illustration of such restrictions is given for one housing loan programme in India in which only those households who were occupying the house on an ownership basis were selected and tenants on rent were excluded; this was based on the consideration that such households would not be in a position to join the shelter upgrading programme.[150]

It might be argued that any household able to afford a loan is not going to be the very poorest; therefore, the shelter microfinance programmes will inherently struggle to reach down to those with lower incomes. The group that is being reached by these programmes is clearly benefiting from the assistance. Moreover, without access to loans, housing investment is very inefficient. For those who do secure loans, the benefits can be considerable. In addition to the income benefits discussed above, Box 6.16 describes some of the health consequences. Shelter microfinance appears to be effective in improving the housing conditions of a group eager to invest in its own dwellings. It has a significant role in a system of housing finance, while, at the same time, there is a need to be realistic about the limitations of the strategy in reaching the poorest.

Securing capital

As noted above, securing sufficient loan capital is difficult. Lack of capital emerges as being a very significant constraint on expansion. Banco ADEMI (in the Dominican Republic) cited lack of capital as the principal challenge that the organization faces in providing housing credit, for which there has been substantial demand.[151] These difficulties reflect a general constraint on the microfinance sector and usually do not appear to be specifically related to housing lending; however, as illustrated in the example of Bangladesh, there may be even more limited sources in the case of housing. As noted earlier, in the case of some

Box 6.16 Improving shelter, improving health

The few impact evaluations conducted of shelter finance point to positive results for the poor. An evaluation of Plan International's Credit for Habitat programmes in Bolivia and Guatemala showed that clients invested their US$200–$800 loans in roofing, walls, floors, tiling, water, sewage and electrical connections, as well as additional rooms. Seventy-eight per cent of clients said that home improvements improved family health. Clients with Grameen-financed homes in Bangladesh – equipped with Grameen's construction standards of cement pillars and sanitary latrines – had 50 per cent fewer incidences of illnesses than those without Grameen houses. Their houses suffered far less structural damage during the devastating floods of 1987 and since, compared with non-Grameen homes. An impact assessment of the Self-employed Women's Association (SEWA) Bank's slum upgrading programme in India, which included progressive housing loans, reported increases in literacy (school children enrolment), productivity (increase in number of working hours), income and health (lower incidences of illness and, thus, lower health expenditures), and increased marriage opportunities, higher status and respect in the community for women borrowers. In sum, housing finance loans serve poor households and help them to improve their livelihoods.

Source: Malhotra, 2003.

agencies, viability is related to the scale of activities, and capital for expansion will result in profitable lending and potentially an easing of capital constraints.

Very little is known about the aggregate balance of sources of funding for shelter microfinance. A recent study of the total capital of the larger microfinance agencies in Bangladesh highlights some interesting trends.[152] It is notable that finance from the commercial banking sector increased from 3 to 11 per cent of total capital between 1996 and 2002. Donor finance has dropped fairly dramatically through a similar period (from 58 to 17 per cent), although this partly reflects the growing significance of the Palli Karma Sahayak Foundation, a public–private apex body that channels funds to microfinance agencies, which has increased its significance by providing 12 per cent of capital in 1996 and 24 per cent of capital in 2002. However, the analysis suggests that the strategy used by these agencies may not be easy to replicate in other countries and it is not so evident that shelter microfinance can succeed in ensuring a growing and secure capital base. A further specific suggestion is that Palli Karma Sahayak Foundation should extend its activities and provide finance for housing.[153]

It is not so evident that shelter microfinance can succeed in ensuring a growing and secure capital base

Shelter microfinance agencies may face a particularly difficult balance in setting interest rates that weigh borrowers' demands against their own financial needs. Interest rates must be acceptable to borrowers.[154] In some countries, subsidized interest rates for mortgage loans may increase pressure for reduced interest rates. Such factors, as well as longer-loan terms and required concessions for affordability, may explain the use of favourable interest rates in the case of small loans for housing.

As is evident from this discussion, microfinance agencies face an issue of scale. To be profitable, they have to increase the quantity of lending. There is evidence that this is driving their expansion into shelter microfinance; but for the smaller agencies, lack of capital to expand operations appears to be a significant constraint. One view is that the shorter lending terms of shelter microfinance may better fit the short-term funding sources (with the bulk of financial liabilities often one year or less) available to financial institutions in the South; therefore, more conventional housing lenders should be active in this area. Such a match of demand and supply may help to account for the strong interest being shown in this area. The greater interest demonstrated by the private sector may assist in reducing the capital constraint; however, it is equally evident that this is unlikely to happen in all countries. The Banco Davivienda in Colombia is currently working with the government to examine the possibility of offering loans of less than US$2800 to be repaid in up to five years for homes valued at less than US$15,000.[155]

Nevertheless, it is equally apparent that longer-term loan repayment periods are also common in shelter microfinance agencies, despite the small size of the loans. Raising funds for shelter microfinance may be more complicated than for enterprise lending because of these longer loan periods. In the case of microenterprise lending, donor support has placed emphasis on building the institutional capacity of lending agencies and assisting in the accumulation of their capital base. There has been a resistance to providing concessional funds for on-lending. Despite this, it has been argued that one problem is that such agencies have had access to funds at a modestly concessional rate, which have been built into the cost basis of their operation. As a result:

> *... one recent ambitious effort to raise funding for major MFIs [microfinance institutions] on international capital markets ran squarely into this problem – lack of demand for the funds. Very few MFIs wanted funds on the resulting market terms.*[156]

Shelter microfinance products continue to be developed, and there are reasons to believe that more agencies are entering this area and that those that are here already are expanding their activities. Can shelter microfinance continue to scale up? Lack of financial capital does appear to be a significant constraint. However, there are more agencies interested in this area in some countries, notably the private sector, municipal government and central government. In some cases, they are working with existing microfinance agencies; in others, they are developing their own products. In part, the growth of shelter microfinance has been driven by the commercial interests of existing microfinance agencies and the need to consolidate and extend their own market base. In the Latin American context, this has happened in a number of countries in which direct-demand subsidies already exist or are being introduced. Microfinance can help to secure subsidies and add value to the construction process. In other cases, microfinance agencies have responded to their own analysis of need and have been able to secure funds from the state to extend their services. As a result, shelter microfinance as a sector is witnessing the expansion of existing agencies, new NGO and microfinance agency initiatives and new interest from groups that were not previously involved in offering small loans.

NOTES

1 This chapter is based on a draft prepared by Diana Mitlin, University of Manchester, UK, with assistance from a number of urban researchers listed in the Acknowledgements.
2 See, for example, those discussed in ESCAP, 1991; *Environment and Urbanization*, 1993; Arrossi et al, 1994; Mitlin, 1997; Jones and Datta, 1999; Center for Urban Development Studies, 2000; *Environment and Urbanization*, 2001; ACHR, 2002; Daphnis and Ferguson, 2004; Malhotra, 2003.
3 There has been some experimentation and the case for housing microfinance is explored in Daphnis and Ferguson, 2004.
4 ESCAP, 1991.
5 Ferguson, 2004b, p4.
6 Mutagwaba, cited in Government of Tanzania and UN-Habitat, 2003, p31.
7 See Okpala, 1994, p1572.
8 Ballesteros, 2002, p3.
9 The Center for Urban Development Studies (2000) divides the groups into two based on the nature and purpose of the originating agency (microfinance or shelter advocacy). The alternative division used here, which divides by the terms and conditions of the loan and, in particular, by whether loans are collective or individual, has the advantage of distinguishing those agencies able to lend for land and infrastructure (which must necessarily be collective) and those for whom shelter finance is primarily restricted to housing improvement.
10 Smets, 2002, p77.
11 Malhotra, 2003, p225.
12 Datta, 1999, p204.
13 Kamete, 2000, p254.
14 Okwir, 2002, p95.
15 Okonkwo, 2002, p97.
16 Biswas, 2003.
17 Smets, 2002, pp65, 87.
18 Smets, 2002, p65.
19 Moss, 2001, p33-4.
20 Baumann, 2003, p88.
21 Government of Tanzania and UN-Habitat, 2003, pp53–54.
22 Gough, 1999.
23 Datta, 1999, p203.
24 Gough, 1999.
25 Wahba, 2001.
26 Nell et al, cited in Baumann, 2004.
27 Civil society is a term used to refer to the not-for-profit and voluntary sector. It is also referred to as the third sector in some texts. The distinctive features of such agencies are that they are not part of the state, nor are they commercial companies. Although not all such organizations are registered (for example, as charities and/or voluntary associations), many of those offering loans and/or savings facilities are likely to have some kind of registration. The exception is the large number of less formal savings groups including those that fall under the title of ROSCAs (rotating savings and credit associations). They are not discussed here as few offer sums substantial enough for shelter investment.
28 Ferguson, 2003.
29 CGAP, 2004.
30 Biswas, 2003, p51.
31 Smets, 2002, p75; Mohamed, 1997.
32 Wahba, 2001, Appendix 1.
33 SANMFI, cited in Biswas, 2003.
34 Biswas, 2003.
35 Ferguson, 1999, p191.
36 Hoek-Smit, 1998, p41.
37 Arrossi et al, 1994, p58.
38 Co-operative Housing Foundation, 1993, p38.
39 Co-operative Housing Foundation, 1993, p41.
40 Jones and Mitlin, 1999, p27.
41 Ferguson, 1999, p93.
42 Connolly, 2004b, p9.
43 A further Mexican example is FOSOVI, an NGO active in Mexico City. Between 1998 (when it was set up) and 2000, FOSOVI granted 1266 housing loans to families (SELAVIP, 2003, p43). The maximum loan per family is US$1000 and the loan period is 36 months. Capital has been secured through a partnership with local government, local savings and loan societies, NGOs and popular movements (residents' associations). About one quarter has been for the construction of a core house and half for the extension of an existing house; the remaining loans were for the improvement of facilities such as toilets or the improvement of housing quality. Families organize themselves into groups to receive the loans and this group helps in the material purchasing and construction process.
44 World Bank, 2004a, p3.
45 Smets, 2002, p181.
46 Connolly, 2004b.
47 Center for Urban Development Studies, 2000.
48 Arrossi et al, 1994, p54.
49 Stein with Castillo, 2005.
50 McLeod and Mitlin, 1993.
51 Smets, 2002, pp195–197.
52 Sheela Patel (director of SPARC), pers comm, 2004.
53 McLeod, 2002, p204.
54 Forero, 2004, p41.
55 Mutua et al, 1996.
56 Ferguson, 2003, pp26–27.
57 Malhotra, 2004, p222.
58 Escobar, undated, p21.
59 Escobar, undated, p24.
60 Malhotra, 2003, p222.
61 Mutua et al, 1996, p182; Escobar and Merrill, 2004, p36; Ferguson, 2004a, pp24–25.
62 Ferguson, 2003.
63 Ferguson, 2003.
64 Vance, pers comm, 2004.
65 See Renaud, 1999, p760, for a discussion of such processes in the US.
66 Stein, 2004, p116.
67 PRODEL, 2002.
68 Cities Alliance, 2002.
69 Silas, 2004.
70 Septanti, 2004, p8.
71 Murcia de López and Castillo, 1997, p173.
72 Ferguson, 2003.
73 Ferguson and Haider, cited in Ferguson, 2003.
74 Escobar, undated, p36.
75 Stein with Castillo, 2005.
76 Escobar, undated.
77 Stein with Castillo, 2005.
78 Smets, 2002, p9.
79 Escobar and Merrill, 2004, pp37–38.
80 Escobar and Merrill, 2004, p41.
81 Forero, 2004, p41.
82 Prahalad, cited in Connolly, 2004b.
83 Ratha, 2003.
84 Ratha, 2003.
85 Connolly, 2004b, p3.
86 Ferguson, 2003.
87 Cities Alliance, 2002, p3; Smets, 2002.
88 Gold et al, 2002.
89 Escobar and Merrill, 2004, p40.
90 Cabannes, 2002.
91 Cabannes, 2004.
92 IADB, 2003.
93 Albee and Gamage, 1996.
94 Gitau, 2004.
95 Smets, 2002, p129.
96 Smets, 2002, p130.
97 Escobar and Merrill, 2004, p39.
98 Gitau, 2004.
99 Gitau, 2004.
100 IADB, 2003, p4.
101 Vance, 2004, p142.
102 Escalante, 2004, p59.
103 Baumann, 2004.
104 Hoek-Smit, 1998, p39.
105 Stein with Castillo, 2005.
106 Malhotra, 2003.
107 Ferguson, 1999, p196.
108 Escobar and Merrill, 2004, p58.
109 See, for example, Christen, 2004, pxiii.
110 CGAP, 2004.
111 Daphnis, 2004a, p3.
112 Grameen Bank, 2004.
113 Ferguson, 2004b, p4.
114 Vance, 2004, p141.
115 Escobar and Merrill, 2004, pp45, 48.
116 Biswas, 2003.
117 Biswas, 2003.
118 Van Rooyan, 2004.
119 Christen, 2004, pxiii.
120 Jones and Datta, 1999, p21; Escobar and Merrill, 2004, p58.
121 Escobar and Merrill, 2004, p61.
122 Vance, 2004, p139.
123 Escobar and Merrill, 2004, p62.
124 Daphnis, 2004b, pp108, 110.
125 Vance, 2004, p135
126 Malhotra, 2003.
127 Escobar, undated, p26.
128 Stein with Castillo, 2005.
129 Escobar, undated.
130 Escobar and Merrill (2004, p57) note that six of the eight agencies they profile offer lower interest rates, and one of the other two agencies may also offer lower rates.
131 Hoek-Smit, 1998.
132 Hoek-Smit, 1998, p38.
133 Stein with Castillo, 2005.
134 Escobar, undated, p19.
135 Escobar and Merrill, 2004, p56.
136 CGAP, 2004.
137 Ferguson, 1999, p196.
138 Malhotra, 2003, p221.
139 Escobar and Merrill, 2004, p62.
140 Daphnis, 2004b, p105.
141 Arrossi et al, 1994, p63.
142 Escobar and Merrill, 2004, p51. This emphasis on women is also true for microenterprise lending, although in some cases it has resulted in the woman in a family taking the loan but not being in control of the investment.
143 Malhotra, 2003.
144 Van Rooyan, 2004.
145 Stein, 2004, pp117–118.
146 Biswas, 2003.
147 Center for Urban Development Studies, 2000.
148 See concerns expressed by Hulme, 2001.
149 Malhotra, 2003, pp219–220.
150 Lall and Lall, 2003, p15.
151 Davies and Mahony, 2001, p15; Pedro Jimenez, executive vice-president, Banco ADEMI, Housing Microfinance Questionnaire, 7 March 2001.
152 Zaman, 2004, pp9–12.
153 Hoek-Smit, 1998.
154 Stein with Castillo, 2005.
155 Forero, 2004, p41.
156 Ferguson, 2003, p27.

CHAPTER 7

COMMUNITY FUNDS[1]

Community funds are of growing significance in assisting the poor to address their shelter needs. As the role of the state has diminished, increased emphasis has been placed on alternative strategies to support secure tenure, access to basic services and improved dwellings. The increase in microfinance has resulted in a growing diversity of approaches to providing the small loans required to help self-build communities address their multiple needs. Community funds offer small loans to households but route these loans through community organizations. The emphasis on collective loans is for many reasons; but one is that the loans support investments in land and infrastructure, which are necessarily made by a group working together. This chapter describes community funds, identifying their key characteristics, and discusses trends within this sector. It looks specifically at a number of key challenges, notably the affordability of their strategies and sources of funds.

It should be said immediately that it is difficult to assess their changing significance for several reasons. First, although the strategy is not new, there have been few overviews to date. Without an established baseline, it is not possible to consider what has changed. Second, the distinctions with microfinance are often not that clearly drawn, with a graduation rather than a clear dividing line. As shown in Chapter 6, both community funds and microfinance seek to assist an incremental development process through the use of small loans. Community funds work with group loans, thereby enabling them to address the needs of those without land and/or infrastructure. As a result, they place greater emphasis on the priorities of the lower income families. They may also offer loans for housing; in general, these are also managed at the community level, although the investment takes place at the household level. Some community funds lend for income generation and use more conventional microfinance approaches for their income-generation loans, further confusing the distinction.

Community funds offer small loans to households but route these loans through community organizations

WHAT ARE COMMUNITY FUNDS?

The growth of shelter microfinance initiatives has been paralleled by a further development – that of socially orientated savings and loans for shelter improvement. Community funds are financial mechanisms that encourage savings through establishing and strengthening local savings groups, providing collective finance for shelter improvement (which may include any one or more of the following activities: land purchase, land preparation, infrastructure installation and service provision, as well as housing construction, extension and improvement). Community funds offer loans to groups due to their interest in supporting land and service acquisition. Their most distinguishing characteristic is the way in which funding is perceived – rather than the mechanisms of the financing process. Community funds use savings and loans to trigger a development process – not simply to increase the access of the poor to financial markets. They seek to strengthen the social bonds between community members (building social capital) so that existing finance within the community can be used more effectively and external finance can be integrated within community development strategies. Significantly, they believe that small loans for individualized investment in private dwellings cannot address the multiple needs of the poor, and that finance and financial skills are required for tenure and investments in infrastructure and services. Community funds are targeted at group borrowing and therefore may include those with lower incomes.

One approach common to some of the programmes grouped together in this chapter is an emphasis on savings for shelter improvement and the use of collective strategies both to reduce the risks for the individuals involved and to build relations between low-income citizens and development agencies and/or the state. Collective saving and lending seeks to offer a number of administrative and, sometimes, political advantages. The programmes go beyond the simple role of the credit agency to integrate financial and social approaches in the search for long-term development that works for the poor. Box 7.1 describes how such approaches have catalysed pro-poor social change in Phnom Penh, Cambodia. In this case, the management of the fund built relationships between civil society and the municipality which resulted in a common recognition that upgrading was a better development strategy than relocation. In other cases, community funds have a more limited conceptualization and offer loans only for one (or sometimes two) specific activities.

As with many such development trends, there is no single source for the innovations around community funds and the approach has emerged from a combination of factors. And as with shelter microfinance, one of these has been the recognition by housing professionals of the inefficiencies in housing investment that arise from a lack of access to loan capital. Other factors of notable importance have been the following:

- Non-governmental organizations (NGOs) are seeking to use donor monies more effectively; there is also a recognition of people's willingness to invest in their own neighbourhood (land and infrastructure) and dwellings, suggesting an interest in repayment of external finance.
- State agencies are attempting to find more effective ways of addressing housing need and building based on their experience of what has not worked in the past. The growth of community-managed infrastructure, such as in water, indicates that development agencies (including national governments) are looking for new mechanisms to extend access to essential services.
- There is a growing expertise in poverty reduction and a greater awareness of the role of assets in securing improved livelihoods. This has been coupled with a longstanding recognition that basic infrastructure is important in improving health with multiple benefits.
- More recently, there has been an awareness of the scale of differentiation within low-income groups. As the importance of reaching the poorest has grown within development, so has a willingness to look at new methods that might be effective in securing inclusion.

Box 7.1 The Urban Poor Development Fund in Cambodia

Since the first democratic election in 1993, and increasingly after the economic crisis and greater political stability after 1997, development and investment in Phnom Penh have escalated significantly. As a consequence, commercial and public development agendas have collided with the needs of the poor within the city. As elsewhere, the poor have been left worse off as a result; they have been struggling to secure a place in the city in the face of aggressive commercialization of land markets.

In 1998, the Urban Poor Development Fund was formed. The fund is a collaboration between the Squatter and Urban Poor Federation (SUPF), the municipality and local non-governmental organizations (NGOs). The fund was initially intended for shelter loans for a community relocated in an inner-city development, but has diversified into other areas in response to community needs. Between 1998 and 2003, more than 18 relocations of low-income communities took place, with great variance in the viability of the new sites. The development of the fund has had to respond to such needs. Relocation was the only option offered to communities facing eviction.

Frustrated with the lack of alternatives, several organizations considered a new City Development Strategy. Building on the relationships within the fund, this emerged as a joint programme of the Municipality of Phnom Penh (MPP), the United Nations Human Settlements Programme (UN-Habitat) and the Asian Coalition for Housing Rights (ACHR), the SUPF and the Urban Resource Centre, a local NGO. The organizations initiating the strategy believed that developing a shared vision of the city's development between various stakeholders was essential. Preparatory studies for the strategy led to a consensus that *in situ* upgrading needed to be an option.

The fund used its fifth anniversary event (24–26 May 2003) to promote the strategy of on-site community improvement. The approaching national election provided added incentive for the government to launch the pro-poor upgrading initiative. Prime Minister Hun Sen gave the opening speech, in which he announced his policy for the upgrading of 100 settlements in one year in Phnom Penh with 500 settlements in five years.

Source: ACHR, 2004.

Many microfinance enterprise initiatives are premised on the understanding that increasing incomes is an effective strategy to reduce poverty. Shelter lending is, in part, consistent with that strategy, but also seeks to enable households to reduce expenditure, using their monies more effectively to achieve their goals. Community funds that offer comprehensive borrowing 'windows' are designed around the premise that increasing incomes is simply one component of a poverty reduction strategy. A number of dimensions of urban poverty have been identified and Box 7.2 outlines specific poverty reduction strategies to address such features, which are embedded within the community fund approach.[2]

While Table 6.1 differentiates between microfinance and community fund approaches, the relationship between microfinance and community funds can best be represented as a continuum. At one extreme are agencies who seek to operate according to the criteria of financial markets; at the other are those who offer highly subsidized loan programmes, with a premium being placed on the inclusion of those most in need. In between lies a range of agencies who seek to blend a commitment to improved financial services with the recognition that poverty has multiple causes that cannot all be addressed through finance. As noted in Chapter 6, many shelter microfinance agencies use lower interest rates for shelter lending. Some have linked up with more comprehensive development programmes that offer support for neighbourhood development and (slum) upgrading. Equally, community funds seek to use more stringent (market-orientated) financial conditions with regard to their lending for enterprise development, while placing greater development emphasis on lending for tenure security, infrastructure improvements and housing.

In practice, there is considerable overlap of interest between community funds and microfinance. Microfinance institutions are anxious to consider new ways of reducing

Box 7.2 Addressing urban poverty with community funds

Aspect of poverty	Poverty reduction strategy
Income	Enterprise development
Assets	Housing and land investment
Poor-quality housing	Housing and infrastructure investment
Inadequate public infrastructure	Negotiations with authorities; improved infrastructure from community investment; community-managed investments
Inadequate basic services	Negotiations with authorities; direct investment by the community; community-managed investments
Limited or no safety net	Emergency funds and savings
Inadequate protection of poor groups	Stronger community organizations; political negotiations
Voiceless/powerless	Stronger community organizations; federations and networks; political negotiations

Box 7.3 Catholic Social Services in Pakistan

Catholic Social Services began their housing loan programme in Karachi, Pakistan, in 1981 when a group they were working with in Benaras Colony was resettled on the edge of the city following eviction. The community of 200 households had had their houses demolished. They were offered land far from where they were living; without any other resources, the community remained homeless. The non-governmental organization (NGO) provided interest-free loans of 4000 rupees (US$160) to each household with a repayment period of three years. The loan size later increased to 6000 rupees.

As the programme expanded, it worked with more communities. Individuals in need who came to the NGO were encouraged to form co-operatives that were able to manage the finances. In general, the NGO worked through these co-operatives, which took collective responsibility for loan management, including repayments. Maximum loans were just sufficient to build a single room. By 1993, the programme had expanded to 830 families, with some 347 loans having been successfully repaid.

Source: Ghouri and Nihal, 1993, pp18–25.

poverty – many of them remain mission-led development agencies – while community funds face similar issues of loan and debt management and are anxious to learn about new tools and mechanisms so that they are better able to address such management challenges. The continuum includes programmes that place more emphasis on collective aspects (including strengthening local organizations and improving relationships with political/state agencies) and others that highlight market-orientated financial investments. Some microfinance agencies recognize that money is just one aspect of what is needed. Banco Sol in Bolivia and others in Ecuador and elsewhere have separated their credit activities from technical assistance services as they have grown; one group has concentrated on credit and another on technical assistance (particularly marketing).[3] Some conventional microfinance agencies are very serious about seeking to add value to their financial strategies; they are careful to assess the needs of their clients and adapt their programmes accordingly.

TRENDS

Securing land and services requires a collective effort and savings provides a good organizing basis for such efforts

As noted above, community funds are embedded in a social development approach to addressing need. The small scale of traditional housing programmes for the poor has led to a search for more effective ways of improving housing and addressing the shelter needs of the poorest at scale. The challenge has been to use the relatively small amount of funds effectively and to ensure that those benefiting from the programme have a strong sense of ownership, driving and developing the programme to meet their needs: savings and loans programmes offer these advantages. While slightly higher income groups can be assisted with programmes that offer only housing improvements, lower income groups require more holistic development interventions. Securing land and services requires a collective effort and savings provides a good organizing basis for such efforts. Many of these programmes were piloted by NGOs who were working with groups in acute need of housing, perhaps under threat of eviction. Box 7.3 offers an example of the kinds of activities that lie behind the development of some community funds. While such programmes developed in tandem with the evolution of microfinance, they already had a significantly different approach, with an emphasis on the collective and a comprehensive position on addressing development needs that expanded beyond purely financial services.

As communities, sometimes supported by NGOs, became successful at securing land, they needed to access funds for upgrading and improvement. Some of the money they could raise themselves, and they could provide their own labour; but this was not enough to finance the houses without any loan capital. At this point, securing finance becomes a major issue. NGOs have been using revolving funds as one option to assist families with finance. One example is the work of the Carvajal Foundation in Colombia, which set up a number of programmes to assist with housing improvements. Its approaches included setting up material banks in low-income settlements to assist small businesses involved in the production of building materials to secure their market, thus helping to ensure that house builders can get access to what they need without high transportation costs.[4] Other traditions are characterized by the *Fundación Vivienda y Comunidad* in Argentina, which raised approximately US$600,000 from one Northern NGO in 1987 for a fund that offered money under three distinct funding 'windows': full subsidy; part loan and part subsidy; and full loan. Activities included income generation, improvements in services such as education, and neighbourhood improvements such as water supplies.[5]

The success of such initiatives built up confidence among NGOs, and more ambitious plans were developed. NGOs (and other civil society groups) began to consider ways in which families could be assisted to save and to develop mechanisms to draw in state subsidy funds. The scale and effectiveness of NGO innovation began to be reflected in government programmes. NGOs argued that such programmes deserved state support because they offered a real sense of capacity and confidence to low-income communities. Problems of selection and dependency (which were associated with more traditional welfare assistance) were avoided as participants were 'self-selected', perhaps through savings activities. Further benefits were low administration costs as management roles were taken on by the community, and the fact that loan repayments enabled the available subsidies to be 'stretched' much further than was previously possible when the full costs of housing were subsidized. The vision was one of pro-poor, inclusive poverty-orientated development. Such a tradition is in keeping with the principles of social justice that are at the root of many of the NGOs who instigated microfinance programmes. NGO experiences, together with those of the Uruguayan housing co-operatives during the late 1960s, led to the design and development of a programme in Mexico, Fondo Nacional de Habitaciones (FONHAPO), which is one of the earliest examples of state support for flexible collective loans channeled through multiple agencies for shelter improvements (see Box 7.4).

The willingness of some governments to explore these processes has increased ambition among those interested in working with these funds. Funding support

Box 7.4 Fondo Nacional de Habitaciones (FONHAPO), Mexico

FONHAPO is a state institution which still has a role in Mexican government housing policy; but its most significant international influence stems from its work in the early and mid 1980s. FONHAPO sought a strategy that would enable it to reach the 60 to 70 per cent of the population whose incomes were below 2.5 times the minimum wage. During this period it provided loans to intermediate organizations, either public, private (such as financial institutions and development trusts) or social (co-operatives and other legally constituted social organizations). Five types of housing project were financed: sites and services; incremental housing; home improvements; finished dwellings; and production and distribution of building materials. FONHAPO, in contrast to the other housing institutions, progressively favoured financing partial housing solutions over finished dwellings.

FONHAPO offered a flexible range of credit packages, including small loans, on a large scale. The value of the loans was expressed in terms of multiples of the local daily minimum wage, the maximum value being 2000 minimum wages (about US$6000 in 1988). The amount of money loaned depended upon the income of the head of household. Those earning less than the minimum wage could be loaned up to 1200 daily minimum wages (about US$3700 in 1988), those earning between 1 and 1.5 minimum wages could be loaned up to 1600 daily minimum wages (US$4900) and those earning between 1.5 and 2.5 minimum wages could receive up to the maximum loan of 2000 minimum wages. The credit limits for sites and services, incremental housing, home improvements and finished housing were 600, 2000, 1150 and 2000, respectively (US$1847, US$6157, US$3540 and US$6147 in 1988).

A deposit of between 10 and 15 per cent had to be paid by the final beneficiaries. An initial subsidy of between 15 and 25 per cent was offered on the value of all loans. Additionally, a further 15 per cent would be offered for prompt repayment. This implied a direct subsidy of 30 per cent of the loan value for the larger loans for incremental or finished housing, and up to 40 per cent of the loan value for smaller loan packages. On the basis of a maximum payment of 25 per cent of the beneficiary's monthly income, the amount and number of repayments were calculated in terms of percentages of minimum wages at the time of contracting the loan. These payments would escalate according to the increase in minimum wage. In this way the real value of loans repayment was maintained approximately in line with inflation. In all, it was estimated that the total subsidy to the beneficiaries would average at 50 per cent – that is, the repayments from two loans would finance one more of similar amount.

Between 1982 and 1988, just over 10 per cent of new dwellings, including core houses, financed by the public sector can be attributed to FONHAPO, using just 4 per cent of the available funds. This was accomplished by giving high priority to smaller loan packages for core housing and site and services, and to public and private housing organizations. Between 1982 and 1994, FONHAPO finished 203,657 core housing units, 115,870 sites-and-services projects, 179,661 home improvement loans and 1730 finished houses.

Source: Connolly, 2004a.

has spread from being primarily Northern NGO, notably those with the larger budgets in Holland and Germany, to include national governments. In some cases, notably the UK and Holland, the programmes overlapped with self-help housing traditions that had emerged during the 19th century and with long-established state support for owner occupation. There were sufficient synergies to enable the expansion of funding for these programmes. In a limited number of cases, funds were also sought from the commercial banking sector within countries. The Society for the Promotion of Area Resource Centres (SPARC) accessed first the Housing and Urban Development Corporation (HUDCO), a state housing bank, and then Citibank funds; however, in both cases guarantees were needed from European NGOs (see Chapter 6). These initiatives benefit from a further trend, which was the increasing realization by NGOs focusing on infrastructure improvements that, in an era of cost recovery, soft loan funds offered the best possibility to secure development assistance to expand access to services. NGOs such as WaterAid began to undertake increasing numbers of programmes to improve access to water services that combined community management with soft loans to repay water infrastructure investments.[6]

The growing interest of state agencies in community funds has been due, in part, to the movement of staff between the two sectors and, in part, to the recognized mutual benefits from close collaboration. In countries such as Chile, Mexico, the Philippines and South Africa, professionals with experience in housing NGOs have moved to posts in government poverty-reduction programmes. They have begun to draw on multiple experiences to design housing loan programmes to address the needs of the poor. It should be emphasized that this discussion is not about government programmes to provide conventional mortgage finance to lower middle-income households, but about non-conventional lending programmes. A further example is the Community Mortgage Programme (CMP) in the Philippines (see Box 7.5).

Part of the motivation for state involvement in such programmes has been an awareness of the need for poverty reduction in urban areas, coupled with the knowledge that neighbourhood and housing improvement is essential. Previous solutions were recognized to have failed and from the 1980s onwards there was a growing interest in working with the self-help capacities of the poor. The earlier generation of NGO programmes was restricted to a specific group that the programme works with and/or a predetermined spatial area. State programmes have to grow beyond such restrictions in order to achieve scale and inclusion (within the specific rules of the programme). Box 7.6 explains the evolution of the community fund process in Thailand as it emerged from more traditional approaches to addressing housing need.

Box 7.5 Community Mortgage Programme (CMP), the Philippines

The Community Mortgage Programme (CMP) is a housing finance programme in the Philippines that allows poor families and households living on public and private lands without security of tenure to have access to affordable housing. Between 1989 and 2003, it assisted 140,650 poor families in securing housing and tenure in 1126 communities, with a total loan volume of 4.404 billion Philippine pesos and an average loan size of 31,000 Philippine pesos.

The CMP was established in the post-Marcos era of the Philippines in an attempt to address the housing needs of the poor. Lending is for residents at risk of eviction who have organized themselves into a community association. Each group has an 'originator,' generally a non-governmental organization (NGO) or local government that is responsible for assisting with the development of the land. The average loan size in 2001 was US$665 per household. The repayment period is 25 years and the (state-subsidized) interest rate is 6 per cent. While originally conceived of as a housing loan programme for groups of the urban poor, the high price of land (especially in Manila) means that many groups borrow only for land purchase. In these circumstances, residents and community associations use multiple strategies to secure infrastructure and improve their homes.

Source: Porio et al, 2004; *CMP Bulletin*, 2004.

There has been increasing interest in community funds during the last decade. The growth is supported by a general acknowledgement that small-scale lending has been somewhat successful and that urban poverty is growing. The trend towards small loans for shelter improvements has received a considerable boost by the popularity of microfinance. For NGOs and governments seeking to put in place comprehensive and integrated programmes to address urban poverty, experimentation with loan packages that incorporate savings and building collective community capacity have been popular. There are two noteworthy current trends related to the development of such funds: first, the growing interest by local government in these approaches, in part related to the use of such funds to extend essential infrastructure; and, second, the expansion of Shack or Slum Dwellers International (SDI), a community/NGO network whose strategies incorporate savings and lending activities for shelter improvements.

Decentralization to local government in both Asia and Latin America is opening new possibilities, both in terms of funding and of meeting responsibilities towards their citizens. In Latin America, democratization and decentralization appear to be associated with increasing support for shelter improvements, including community funds and microfinance. In Forteleza, Brazil, the local government was willing to contribute to innovations using the *mutirão* tradition of collective building.[7] The longstanding participatory budgeting process in Belo Horizonte, Brazil, has extended outwards from infrastructure and services to address housing need; the municipality built 1600 units up to 2002, just under half as a result of consultations within the participatory budgeting process.[8] As the quality of consultation has improved, so municipal housing strategies have begun to reflect the priorities of the poor, moving away from medium-rise construction to land titling in squatter and informal areas. In Maracaibo, Venezuela, the plight of the poor has continued despite oil wealth. Recognizing the need to address poverty, a new municipal programme has offered loan finance; additional funds were then offered by a local NGO, *Nuevo Amanecer*. A first round of 50 loans demonstrated the ease of the process. The municipality, NGOs and grassroots organizations are committed to expanding this fund and making it available to other neighbourhoods. Financial support has recently been obtained from the *Fondo Intergubernamental para la Descentralización* through the local municipality, and the programme has been expanded to reach 267 households.[9]

In Asia there is a similar interest at some local levels. In Kathmandu, the Urban Community Support Fund (UCSF) is a pool of resources which the urban poor can draw upon to assist them with the development of their communities. The UCSF was launched on 30 May 2004 at the city hall, with a financial contribution from the mayor.[10] In the Philippines, local authorities have been drawn into the funding process over a longer period through the CMP, which has allowed them to be 'originators' (that is, to support local communities through the process and provide technical assistance with a small fee payment attached). In some cases, they have made their own resources available – for example, in the city of Muntinlupa in Metro Manila, over US$1 million has been provided to assist families within the programme.[11]

A further area of interest is the use of community funds for utility investment, for which the local authority may be formally responsible. Infrastructure investments and land purchase that involve loan finance have generally required some level of external development support because the technical issues may be more complicated and because a collective investment is generally required.

Box 7.6 The evolution of shelter improvement strategies in Thailand

The concept of upgrading slums in Thailand began during the late 1970s. At first there were attempts to secure cost recovery for the improvements; but there was little support within low-income communities. As a result, a subsidy model was used and 128,000 households benefited from improvements financed by the National Housing Authority. However, land tenure was not offered and the community had little say in what was done.

During the early 1990s, the conventional strategies of medium-rise rental flats and relocation were used by the state to address the needs of those being evicted from inner-city land as rapid economic growth took place. In keeping with other trends, there was a willingness to decentralize these funds for upgrading to municipalities. However, at the same time, the Urban Community Development Office (from 1992) began to build up the capacity of local communities through savings and loan funds, which offered finance for income generation and shelter improvements. Several hundred savings schemes rapidly emerged and these communities began to negotiate with their local municipal offices. The office included the Urban Community Environment Activities Project, which offered small grant funds to savings groups to undertake further neighbourhood improvements. This project required communities to work with municipalities and other city-based professionals (such as university and NGO staff), and the results demonstrated just how effectively communities could use grants.

As the national funds for upgrading were decentralized, some municipalities began to work with the communities who were already improving their own situation. When the government made a commitment to address the needs of 300,000 households in 2000 urban-poor communities in 200 cities within five years (the *Baan Mankong* programme), the strategy of offering infrastructure grants together with subsidized housing loans to organized local communities was accepted.

Source: CODI, 2004.

However, there has also been experimentation (and increasing interest) in lending for infrastructure. Box 7.7 describes a fund for microhydro investments in remote Peruvian villages, while Box 7.10 describes a fund for water investments in Faisalabad, Pakistan. In both cases, new relationships with local authorities needed to be secured. Even where the local authority does not directly offer financial support, it may be interested in working with the fund (once they realize the potential) to improve local services. In the case of microhydro investments, a further linked component has been lending to individuals for enterprise development once the electricity supply has been secured. A similar example is Genesis Empresarial in Guatemala, which also lends for electrification (in rural areas) and potable water projects (sometimes with public assistance).[12] In this case, the groups are very small, between 4 to 12 members. *Fundación Pro Vivienda Social* in Argentina primarily provides housing loans, but will extend these to provide infrastructure loans to small groups where there is clear evidence of solidarity and strong cooperation.[13] WaterAid is a UK NGO that assists in the provision of water. In its work in Bangladesh, WaterAid finances seven local NGOs working in Dhaka and Chittagong to provide services using a full-cost recovery strategy.[14] Local communities are provided with a range of facilities, including water points and sanitation blocks. Management committees collect fees that repay construction and installation costs, and which cover maintenance. The capital costs are repaid to the NGOs who use these monies to finance further investment.

Contrasting approaches to community funds can be seen in Namibia, where there is both a government fund (the Build Together programme) and civil society fund (the *Twahangana* Fund) managed by a local NGO, the Namibia Housing Action Group, on behalf of the Shack Dwellers Federation of Namibia. Box 7.8 describes the Build Together programme and the work that it does to support housing development. The Build Together fund is relatively close to shelter microfinance in that it supports individual housing investments, albeit through a local committee. The *Twahangana* Fund is financed by international development assistance (Northern NGOs) and the Namibian government. It provides loans to savings groups in order to develop services and income-generation activities. To date, the government has contributed Namibian $2 million (US$300,000) in loan finance to the fund and almost Namibian $2.5 million (US$ 385,000) has been donated by international development assistance. In addition, the government has routed Namibian $4.35 million (US$670,000) of Build Together loans through *Twahangana* to help to reach lower income households who are typically involved in Build Together. The civil society fund gives smaller loans (for land purchase, infrastructure development and enterprise investment) and is acknowledged by the government to provide essential support to assist low-income groups in benefiting from the state programme.

The Shack Dwellers Federation of Namibia is a member of Shack/Slum Dwellers International (SDI). Within the NGO sector, there are numerous individual initiatives in this area; but there is one multi-country initiative of particular significance. SDI is a network of grassroots organizations and support NGOs who share a focus on savings and credit as one component of a programme to transform relations within low-income communities, and between local communities and local authorities. Within SDI, collectively organized and locally managed savings funds comprise a strategy to reconstitute grassroots organizations into democratic and accountable organizations. Through savings, communities learn financial skills and how to manage systems of financial accountability. Lending for housing, land and infrastructure responds to the local priorities of members.

Through savings, communities learn financial skills and how to manage systems of financial accountability

Shack/Slum Dwellers International has emerged from an NGO–community-based organization (CBO) partnership between SPARC, the National Slum Dwellers Federation and *Mahila Milan* in India, and their peer exchanges with similar groups that emerged in South Africa. Over the last 15 years this has evolved into an international movement with affiliates in more than 12 countries. SDI groups have spawned a host of local community-owned and NGO-administered funds. In Cambodia, the Philippines, South Africa, Nepal, Sri Lanka, Zimbabwe and Kenya, federation groups have established their own funds, which they lend to savings schemes. State contributions have been obtained in South Africa, Namibia and, more recently, Nepal. Otherwise

Box 7.7 A community fund for electricity services in Peru

A community fund to assist in the extension of electricity through small hydro installations was started in 1994 in Peru under an agreement between Intermediate Technology Development Group (ITDG) and the Inter-American Development Bank (IADB). The finance model has developed over time and has demonstrated that loan finance to small villages and private farmers can leverage local capital and government funds for locally owned and sustainable rural electrification. The financial model combines subsidized loans and technical assistance through shared efforts between technical cooperation agencies and government institutions (local, regional and central governments). Its purpose is to meet the small-scale electricity requirements in isolated rural areas of Peru that cannot be served with the conventional grid system. To date 26 loans, totaling US$850,000, have been made for the same number of installations, which has leveraged US$3.5 millions – a total installed capacity of 1.6 megawatts benefiting 5000 families

The loans range from US$10,000 to US$50,000, with a 10 per cent interest rate, reimbursement terms of one to five years and variable periods of grace depending upon the financial situation of the client(s). Guarantees vary slightly depending upon clients' circumstances and whether they belong to the public or private sector. Borrowers include local governments, small entrepreneurs (mostly farmers and/or livestock breeders), farming co-operatives and peasant communities. The installations have been ranging from 4 kilowatts to 130 kilowatts; the larger ones in villages, the smaller for privates businesses. Villages (the public sector) must show a positive cash flow, including short- and medium-term investment plans, whereas private entrepreneurs must submit actual and collateral guarantees.

The project's total capital now stands at US$700,000, of which US$400,000 represents the initial capital (under the 1994 agreement) and US$300,000 the increase approved by the IADB in 2000. During the first part of the project, the focus had been the implementation of hydro schemes, while since 2001 there has been a very important component of promoting small-scale business and employment-generating initiatives, utilizing the power generated.

Loan recovery is a significant and complex task that requires careful monitoring of clients, frequent consultations with the bank and notices of payment deadlines. In the event of any delay or non-payment, the loan agreements contain regulations that permit legal recovery actions. So far, no enforcement actions have been required. A small consulting firm, AFIDER, is used for this work and to conduct financial appraisals of each project.

Source: Sánchez-Campos, 2004.

Box 7.8 Build Together, Namibia

The Build Together programme in Namibia was established in 1991 (operational from 1992) in order to offer financial support to people who use self-help efforts to construct their own housing. The programme lends money to low- and very low-income groups and families in urban and rural areas who are thought to be too risky by the commercial financial institutions. The programme offers loans for land purchase, housing and a range of infrastructure and services. Loans vary between US$460 and US$4900, with a graduating interest rate and repayment period of 20 years. The interest rate is 5 per cent for loans of between US$460–$3700 and rises to 9 per cent for the maximum loan of US$4900. The implementation of the programme has now been decentralized to local authorities. Local Build Together committees with multi-stakeholder membership, including representatives of those receiving loans, are established to oversee the implementation of the programme. The role of these groups is to identify communities and families in need of housing or housing improvement in their area. Groups should also consult with individuals on how the community wants to solve their problems, prepare an implementation programme and submit it for funding. The committee checks the credibility of loan applicants and monitors their building. It also plays a key role in monitoring the repayments of the borrowers.

There has been a very high degree of participation of women in the programme, with over 45 per cent of the beneficiaries being women-headed households. The programme seeks to encourage more women to take part, thus enabling them to learn building skills and to be involved in the process. They will also be encouraged to form savings and credit societies to meet their regular credit needs, as well as to improve their houses. Families who wish to benefit from the programme are encouraged to set up a local organization for their settlement. The rules stipulate that only those living within the settlement can be office bearers, although external advisers can be appointed. This group negotiates with the Build Together committee to secure loan finance to develop the area.

Since 1992, 11,187 families have been supported to improve their shelter. Local authorities have been assisted to build 323 houses for those in special need and 2830 dwellings have been created from the redevelopment of previous 'single quarters' areas. A further 13,656 families have benefited from the upgrading of informal settlements.

Source: Helao, 2004.

these urban poor funds are financed by international development assistance and by local fundraising. In some cases, such as in Zimbabwe, the savings scheme members also contribute to these national funds. The Indian Federation has developed a further model that integrates loan and subsidy finance within the construction process. More recently, it has been pioneering the Community-led Infrastructure Financing Facility (CLIFF) programme (see Chapter 6).

Lending for housing, land and infrastructure responds to the local priorities of members

SDI affiliates attempt to secure state contributions in order to enable the poor to afford adequate improvements in shelter. Box 7.9 describes how the People's Dialogue on Land and Shelter and the South African Homeless People's Federation used the subsidy funding that they secured in South Africa. Through their own community fund (*uTshani* Fund), local savings schemes facilitated access to state subsidies by providing bridging finance, thereby enabling community groups to develop for themselves and at their own pace. The analysis of their experience suggests that this approach is effective, generating secure assets for some of the poorest households. However, during recent years problems have been caused by considerable and continuing delays in securing the subsidy funds.[15]

This example (and others) demonstrates the potential of such strategies; but it also highlights the issue of funding. Securing an adequate capital base is difficult for non-state (and, sometimes, state) initiatives, as has already been discussed in the case of shelter microfinance (see Chapter 6). The situation is more complex for community funds because of the interest in providing subsidy and increasing affordability.

FUNDING SOURCES

The importance of mixed funding sources is evident from a number of examples and, notably, the study of a number of community fund programmes.[16] In some cases, funds have been established by government and located within a state agency with access to subsidies. In other cases, the fund has been set up by civil society organizations and financed through a combination of state funds, NGO monies, community contributions and, generally, international development assistance agencies. In both cases, the communities may make direct contributions to the fund through deposits to secure loans.

An important and common characteristic of community funds is that some subsidy is provided – either through state funds or international development assistance. This is a further significant difference with regard to conventional microfinance and its individualized housing loans.[17] While conventional microfinance programmes may offer a subsidy, in general there is an understanding that this should be avoided. Within community funds, greater priority is placed on achieving poverty reduction goals and neighbourhood improvement. Subsidies may be needed for institutional survival if interest rates are below the level required to maintain the real value of the fund. Equally or alternatively, subsidies may be required to reach everyone in a community or to reach very low-income communities. These funds are viewed as an alternative strategy for achieving equitable development, rather than an attempt to bring financial markets down to a traditionally excluded group. In this context, rather than the perception being that money is lost through a subsidy, it is considered that funds which simply grant finance are used effectively because ownership is strong and some of the investment made is returned through repayments.[18]

There are several routes through which subsidies are delivered. The primary sources are direct subsidies, interest rate subsidies, additional support (for example, community development and technical assistance) and unintended subsidies when delayed payment and/or default occur. Some of the different approaches can be exemplified thus:

- In Faisalabad, the *Anjuman Samaji Behbood* (ASB) has not been charging interest on loans from their fund to improve water supplies (see Box 7.10). Technical assistance was initially provided by another NGO, the Orangi Pilot Project, to ASB free of charge. ASB has also been assisting the community in which it works free of charge.
- In the Urban Community Development Office (now the Community Organization Development Institute) in Thailand, the associated housing loan activities

charge an interest rate of 3 per cent, which is cross-subsidized by a higher interest charged on commercial lending. The aggregate interest charges aim to cover inflation and administration, not to provide an equivalent market return on capital. Technical support is provided free of charge. Shortly after the office merged with another organization and became the Community Organization Development Institute, the government introduced the *Baan Mankong* programme, which offers grants for infrastructure with the community, with additional monies for re-blocking and relocating.

- In Peru, the ITDG fund to extend electricity supplies through microhydro is designed to facilitate the process of leveraging additional resources from local authorities, with success in some cases. The interest rate charged to borrowing communities is 10 per cent a year, well below microfinance rates.

Direct subsidies. As noted above, grant-based subsidies may be offered to supplement loans and extend the scope of the programme. In Fortaleza, Brazil, the *Cearah Periferia* developed two programmes during the mid 1990s. In Casa Mehlor, Brazil, with local authority participation, the funding delivered to households was one -third saving, one third subsidy and one third loan.[19] A further programme, PAAC (Programa de Auto Ajuda e sistenciana Casa), was undertaken without local authority financial support and the subsidy fell by 50 per cent to one sixth of the available finance, with an additional loan element making up the difference. In Thailand, the *Baan Mankong* programme of the Community Organization Development Institute, a parastatal development agency, offers infrastructure subsidies to organized communities for each family of US$625 for *in situ* upgrading, US$1125 for re-blocking and US$1625 for relocation.[20] Additional loan funds are available for housing improvements. In Guatemala, Genesis Empresarial assists the groups who receive loans for water and electrical supplies to apply for public grants.[21]

Box 7.9 Adding value: The *uTshani* Fund, South Africa

The *uTshani* Fund of the South African Homeless People's Federation was set up in 1994 to provide an opportunity for federation members to experiment with a self-build approach to housing. It was hoped that success in this regard would lead to greater government willingness to release housing subsidies directly to organized poor communities rather than through commercial developers. From 1995 to 1999, the *uTshani* Fund received substantial grant funding, including 10 million rand (US$1.5 million) from the South Africa Department of Housing and many millions more from European donors who supported the federation's strategy. It on-lent this money to federation members who used it to start building houses while waiting for subsidy approval. During this period the *uTshani* Fund facilitated the construction of almost 15,000 houses, all of them larger and of better quality than comparable developer-built products.

The *uTshani* Fund provides several positive examples of a way forward for South African low-income housing finance. First, accessing finance directly and controlling its use allowed federation members to produce much better houses than the Reconstruction and Development Programme (RDP) driven model that has dominated the post-1994 housing drive. Second, *uTshani* showed that ordinary households could manage external housing finance successfully and at low cost if supported by an appropriate institutional framework with clear rules. Third, *uTshani* was able to act as a financial management tool for community-based residential land acquisition and development, allowing the federation to produce some of South Africa's best examples of community-driven housing.

Taking a somewhat conservative view of the benefits secured, making modest assumptions about the value that has been generated and only considering those benefits that can be quantified financially, the development investment in the People's Dialogue on Land and Shelter and the South African Homeless People's Federation has created a net present value of 540 million rand (in 2000 prices) or US$47 million. In just eight years, the *uTshani* process has created assets worth seven times the value of the original investment. With average monthly incomes for federation members of 700 rand, these assets have directly contributed to adding to the well-being of some of South Africa's poorest urban citizens. The overwhelming bulk of the value added is attributable to the housing that has been developed. In contrast to much privately developed state housing in South Africa, a federation house is worth considerably more than the resources put into it. Values of three to eight times the cost of the building materials and skilled labour have been suggested and sometimes offered by potential non-federation purchasers, although few federation members have been interested in selling. The value of federation houses stands in sharp contrast to the experience of many RDP housing developments, where beneficiaries have resold their new houses at far less than the amount spent on them by the state.

Source: Baumann and Mitlin, 2003.

Bridging finance for state funding. In a small number of cases, community funds have been used to bridge finance state direct subsidies, enabling them to be used by communities in ways that more closely follow a locally driven development process (see Chapter 5). In these cases, the direct (capital) subsidy is not attached to the community fund as such; but the fund is a means of obtaining the subsidy. In South Africa, the South African Homeless People's Federation and the People's Dialogue pioneered a new route for the state subsidy that funds land, infrastructure and a dwelling unit (as described in Box 7.9). The loan fund of the federation, the *uTshani* (or grassroots) Fund, helped to spread the use of the People's Housing Process subsidies – a particular form designed for self-help housing but not widely used, accounting for only 2 per cent of the total number of subsidy releases.[22] In India, SPARC, the NGO that works with the National Slum Dwellers Federation, provides local groups with development finance (bridging loans) to enable them to build and, hence, secure access to state subsidies that can only be drawn down once developments are complete. In both cases, communities add to loan releases with their own savings. In the Philippines, delays with the Community Mortgage Programme (CMP) resulted in the NGOs raising international development assistance to enable them to establish a fund to bridge finance CMP funds. In other cases, such as in Chile, NGOs such as Cobijo have also been working with low-income residents to assist them in accessing the state housing subsidy programme.[23]

One advantage for the communities involved in community management options within such programmes (or in the context of any self-help initiative) is lower costs or – for a fixed subsidy amount – improved housing. For example, the housing developed by the National Slum Dwellers Federation in India is designed to maximize the use of the available subsidies. In Sholapur, Maharashtra, the National Slum Dwellers Federration (NSDF) has developed a design and building strategy that secures terraced houses

Box 7.10 Funding water improvements in Pakistan

Faisalabad is one of Pakistan's largest cities. Two-thirds of Faisalabad's population live in areas with little or no official provision for services, and most new housing and land developments take place without official approval. Less than half the city's population have piped water and less than one third are connected to the sewer system. The *Anjuman Samaji Behbood* (ASB) is a non-governmental organization (NGO) active in the city. The area in which they are working is Dhuddiwala – one among many informal settlements in Faisalabad – with a population of 8080 in 1999.

In 1994, ASB developed a successful microcredit programme for local businesses. The NGO agreed to help the community secure water improvements. Staff used and adapted the model developed by the Kararchi-based NGO, Orangi Pilot Project. The model requires that those inhabitants of each lane within a settlement that want improvements have to organize and work out how to pay for the immediate cost of the water supply and sewer infrastructure and the connection charges. The Water Supply Committee felt that before such a process could happen, it needed funds to lay the main pipeline to the water mains. Then, individual lanes' inhabitants could lay their own distribution lines and households would connect to them and pay their share, so the project costs would be recovered. A loan for a revolving fund was received from WaterAid to cover the cost of laying 1100 running feet of main pipeline. The community invested 1,028,367 rupees to complete this work (around US$18,700) which was only one third of the cost of water authority initial estimates for this project (3.2 million rupees). A self-financing piped water supply and underground sewer system were developed between 1995 and 1999, with 253 houses benefiting from in-house connections to water and 1300 houses with sewers. By 1999, 73,500 rupees had been recovered from the WaterAid loan (300 rupees per household). Within the first three years, slightly more than 30 per cent of households had been connected to the system. The Water Supply Committee was responsible for collecting payments for water connections, keeping accounts, purchasing construction materials and supervising the construction of the main line and the distribution lines in the lanes.

Many other communities are now asking ASB for technical assistance in laying sewage lines, and a second phase of the programme is under way, developing a new collector sewer to serve 1000 households.

Source: Alimuddin et al, 2004.

for 62,000 rupees. There is a subsidy of 40,000 rupees, and households use savings or borrow to cover the additional 22,000 rupees. While the NSDF has built 350 houses, ten times this number have been built by local trade unions and financed by the state. Until the NSDF started building houses, the cost of such a basic unit was 100,000 rupees – with a subsidy of 40,000 rupees, this left a large amount for the families to find. After seeing what the NSDF could do, the costs in the other projects fell to 75,000 rupees.[24]

Interest rate subsidies. As noted in Chapters 4, 5 and 6 of this report, there is widespread use of lower interest rates in the case of shelter loans because of the longer periods of repayment and in order to improve affordability, recognizing that while shelter improvements may assist income generation, this is not necessarily the case. State-financed community funds are associated with subsidized interest rates. This discussion is elaborated upon in 'Terms and conditions'.

Delayed repayment. In the more successful programmes, it is evident that community groups generally take repayment responsibilities very seriously. Even if the subsidy is greater than for other programmes, higher collection rates may assist in making up this shortfall. For example, in the Philippines, the CMP has the highest collection efficiency rate (CER) of 75 per cent compared to the other government housing loan programmes, such as the Unified Home Lending Programme (UHLP), which has a lower collection rate of 54 per cent.[25] By 2004, the CMP collection rate had risen to 78.67 per cent.[26] The CMP is assessed as being among the most cost effective of state housing programmes, with an overall average loan amount of 27,946 Philippine pesos (about US$665) per family, which accounts roughly for 15 per cent of the average loan amount of other housing programmes.

Subsidies may be offered through measures to allow delayed repayments. Several experiences suggest that there are significant delayed repayments that reflect the economic situation at the household, local, city and national level, and that communities are unlikely to be able to manage to secure repayments from all their members at any given point in time.[27] In part, this reflects the ability of communities to manage collective repayments for the benefit of all members:

- SPARC (India):
  Our system never says that repayment is 100 per cent! We discovered that about 65–70 per cent of communities were able to repay on time in any single month. The others have a problem and need longer to repay. Now we assume that, at any given time, there will be 30–40 per cent of people who don't have money in their pocket for that period. It's not designed in this fantasy that it is 98 per cent. We are not saying that people don't repay that money; but we always find that about 30 per cent of people need to extend beyond the initial point. (ACHR, CODI and IIED, 2004)
- Build Together (Namibia):
  Our general experience is that women are very good at completing the programme; but men are not so good. The loan recovery rate is about 75 per cent. The groups that work with the Shack Dwellers Federation of Namibia, they are better able to manage these problems. (ACHR, CODI and IIED, 2004)
- Maracibo (Venezuela) has a savings process that has developed into a loan programme. Approximately 30 per cent fall into a grey zone, and there are many reasons for this. One reason comprises the economic difficulties that have been experienced by some Latin American economies. People have to manage this economic crisis and it is difficult for them all to manage it easily. Generally, after some time, when people begin to cope with their difficulties, repayments start again.

In Thailand, several groups were forced into difficulty at the time of the financial crisis during the late 1990s. The Urban Community Development Office offered rescheduling loans at zero interest rate to enable communities to sort out their problems.[28] This was successful in offering a period in which people could re-establish their livelihoods and continue paying.

While the need for a subsidy might imply a lack of scale, some of the programmes described here have been successful in reaching large numbers of those in shelter need. Rather than attempt to be viable within financial markets, such programmes have sought expansion through state poverty reduction programmes. In some cases, the programme use loan finance to access subsidies; in other cases, the state subsidy is integrated within the programme. The belief is that community funds should be able to demonstrate their advantages and mobilize the political support needed for their continuation. Sources of funding are both national governments (in some instances) and development assistance. While many of the original supporters of this work were Northern NGOs (notably, Cordaid, Homeless International, Misereor and SELAVIP), international development assistance agencies have become increasingly interested in supporting such initiatives. Funding for the initiatives described here has been provided by the UK Department for International Development (DFID), the European Union (EU), the Inter-American Development Bank (IADB) and the Swedish International Development Agency (SIDA).

A further source of finance is that of commercial financial institutions. A number of groups who manage community funds have sought to draw in commercial banks. At a minimal level, loan funds are released through banks, thereby encouraging the poor to see such institutions as something that they might use. In CLIFF, a donor-financed programme working with SPARC, the National Slum Dwellers Federation and *Mahila Milan* in India, there is an expectation that urban poor groups will become strong enough to be able to borrow from the banks. There is also the assumption that the banks will recognize their financial responsibilities and develop ways of reaching the poor. However, there is an increasing recognition that the answer may not be to extend formal banking services to low-income communities since this may be expensive and it may be better for the community to organize it for themselves. In response to the economic crisis and the recognized need to restructure the financial system, there is an ongoing review in Thailand. Communities explained to the review group that they had access to financial services which they provided for themselves. The committee had been thinking of taking the banking system to the grassroots level; but after the meeting they changed their minds and were looking at how the banks should work with the grassroots financial systems. There was no longer talk of formal and informal systems – there was a recognition that all groups are part of a whole and the best solution may not be to integrate the informal with the formal.

TERMS AND CONDITIONS

The emphasis on local funds has resulted in a complexity of arrangements within community funds themselves. In the simplest form, the fund passes a loan to a community for a specifically defined shelter-related activity. The community then collects repayments and passes them back to the fund. In some cases, communities also manage local revolving funds (capitalized by their own savings), which are used to give small loans to members for multiple purposes and which are then augmented by the larger-scale community fund. As a result, a wide variety of terms and conditions may be found.

Strengthening collective capacity: savings

Savings plays a central role in community funds. However, the programmes may differ in the speed and the intensity of savings. This difference reflects both the orientation of the programme itself and the possibilities within different countries. For example, in a large number of countries (including those with experience of informal savings and loan mechanisms), communities have been sceptical about the value of savings for shelter investment, and loan finance has been provided rapidly once the savings commitment was fulfilled. This is particularly true of countries that have experienced rapid inflation and/or where the state has confiscated or temporarily frozen savings.

These programmes are primarily orientated towards urban-poor neighbourhoods which often have insecure tenure and inadequate services, with families who are using self-build strategies to provide themselves with housing. They are intended to benefit those without secure land tenure, adequate basic services and/or suitable housing. As already noted, in many cases, emphasis is put on collective benefits and on reaching the poorest. In some cases, where funds are restricted, benefits may be limited to particular improvements. For example, some funds, such as the *Twahangana* Fund in Namibia, may prioritize land tenure and basic services with the understanding that a full package is likely to be too expensive for many residents.[29]

As noted above, while finance is integral to these approaches, the role of finance is set within a comprehensive development approach. Finance becomes the means to build strong communities, as well as the resource needed to improve material conditions. The emphasis is on using savings (occasionally lending activities are the primary mechanism) to build the collective capacity of the community to address their development needs. There are several reasons for this. First and foremost, there is the understanding that development that is affordable for the urban (and, sometimes, the rural) poor will need to include local authorities to secure state subsidies (where possible) and/or to negotiate reductions from unaffordable regulations. Such changes are only possible when the poor engage the state as a group; changes in rules, regulations and/or financial procedures are unlikely to happen for (poor) individuals. The savings process equips communities with new skills and an associated new consciousness, enabling them to strategically engage with the state to obtain the redistribution of resources and regulatory reforms that assist in their access to secure tenure, basic services and housing.[30] In the case of the example illustrated for Faisalabad (see Box 7.10), the community had to negotiate with the water authorities and with local politicians who sought to develop an alternative process.

Communities are encouraged to work together to save money?

Second, with an emphasis on solutions that work for the poorest, land purchase and infrastructure development

Box 7.11 Alternatives to relocation in Thailand

The experience of Thai urban poor groups has been that communities cannot afford the costs of land purchase if they also need to construct housing, even with the subsidized interest rate that the Community Organization Development Institute (CODI) provides. During the mid 1990s prior to the financial crisis in Thailand, groups did buy land. The first communities threatened with eviction were eager to purchase land and resettle. In these first housing schemes funded by the Urban Community Development Office (UCDO) in Thailand (1992–1996), some 54 per cent had previously been renting land and the remainder had been squatters.

The high prices meant they could only afford plots outside the city centre. Even before the financial crisis, some families struggled to secure their livelihood in these areas. Unable to find alternative sources of income, they continued with their existing work and managed either high transport costs or renting minimal accommodation closer to their previous inner-city locations. Other savings groups learned about these experiences through the community networks that had been established. They realized that relocation was a difficult strategy and that families would have been better remaining in their existing locations. Now networks actively discourage households from relocating. As the financial crisis came to an end, the community networks developed alternatives. Rather than lend money for relocation, they would work with communities threatened with eviction to strengthen their capacity to negotiate with their landowners. The costs are lower and the location is better with regard to income-earning opportunities.

Source: Boonyabancha, 2004.

become important, perhaps more important than housing improvement. Land purchase and infrastructure development can only be undertaken with groups – they are unaffordable for the poor (even for the not so poor) as individualized developments. The activities of securing land (either by purchase, lease or rent) and installing infrastructure need strong groups with financial management capacity. Land purchase may be to secure existing land or to purchase new land if a community is threatened with eviction. In some cases, the communities can afford to purchase land on the market (or with their own negotiating capacity securing a discount from the owners). In other cases, savings provides the means to bring communities together and successfully negotiate a subsidy or change in policy from the state. Box 7.11 explains how communities in Thailand found that although peripheral land was affordable for communities, in the longer term it was too expensive. A more effective strategy was to join together into city networks and then use collective strength to negotiate for communities to remain in their existing locations. In these first housing schemes funded by the Urban Community Development Office (UCDO) in Thailand (1992–1996), some 54 per cent had previously been renting land and the remainder had been squatters.[31] A higher proportion (72 per cent) had owned the structure on the land.

Infrastructure is similar to land in that it is likely to benefit from a greater collective capacity. In this case, there are also issues related to installation and ongoing management. While some improvements to infrastructure can be made by individual borrowing (for example, water storage tanks to take account of irregularly supplied water), many infrastructure improvements require group efforts. For instance, in a typical project, families in a low-income settlement in Dakar, Senegal, borrowed to install a water supply system and drainage channels; the investment paid for itself within a year due to savings in medical bills.[32]

Third, there is the recognition that collective action can save money. Communities are encouraged to work together to save money – perhaps through group purchase of building materials (with associated discounts) and/or through joint work programmes. Even where lending is for housing improvements, collective involvement may offer additional benefits. In some cases, community funds enable groups to construct units for each of their members. In many cases, construction is organized collectively, with all participating in the construction process.

A fourth reason for the emphasis on savings is that managing collective finance builds within communities an understanding of how to manage money. Many development programmes that seek to be people centred want to give communities financial responsibility. However, building this capacity once a large-scale externally funded project has begun is very difficult. Local community leaders often fail and that failure knocks their confidence, while associated allegations of corruption and mismanagement further divide communities. Locally managed savings and loan programmes ensure that communities embed financial management within their own organizations and associated social relationships. Groups learn by trial and error to set up robust systems, to call for assistance when needed and to manage problems along the way. By starting with their own funds, they increase their ownership of this learning process. Finally, these approaches often encourage the community to use their savings to set up local funds, capitalized by savings, which can lend to members for emergencies and/or enterprise development and thereby offer immediate material benefits. This further develops the skills and experiences of financial management as fund managers learn from successes and mistakes. Typical emergencies are health expenditures when a family member falls sick or transport costs to get to work or to take up a livelihood opportunity.[33]

Despite the merits in saving with lending activities, in some countries this is not possible due to financial regulations. This is a problem both for conventional microfinance as well as community funds. A recent report from ACHR, CODI and IIED suggests that:

> *... in Nicaragua, government regulations prevent loan agencies, except for a few authorized by the superintendency, from taking savings. Today, there are some 300 non-profit organizations lending to the poor; but none are allowed to collect savings.*[34]

Interest rates

Interest rates are generally subsidized, especially for land purchase and infrastructure, but often also for housing investment. Three major reasons emerge for this policy: practical, political and social. On the practical side, many of these early programmes evolved with an interest rate subsidy because the relatively large size of the loan made affordability difficult if market rates were used. Even land

and infrastructure are often sizeable investments. Additional costs were incurred in some cases because of the involvement of local authorities and other state agencies who had standards and regulations that needed to be complied with. Politically, the policies may have been influenced by communities who were familiar with state support for housing through a reduced interest rate. This appears to be particularly strong in Asia where, for example, the Bangladeshi, Indian, Thai and Philippine governments all have programmes with interest rate subsidies for low- (and low-medium) income households. Inevitably, this influenced the expectations of the communities participating in the funds. For example, when the Urban Community Development Office (UCDO) (now the Community Organization Development Institute, or CODI) in Thailand first met to discuss interest rates, the community members of the board negotiated for 3 per cent. This was considerably below inflation at the time. Box 7.12 describes the decision-making process. Interest rates for water investment in Bangladesh and Pakistan are both set to zero (see Box 7.10 for Pakistan).[35]

From a social development perspective, inclusion of the poorest and affordability are critical. As noted above, interest rate subsidies are common and, in some cases, they have been preferred to capital subsidies despite the discussions against this strategy in some of the literature and the position of some international agencies. The preference for interest rate subsidies is because there is no direct grant involved. The concern is that if something is offered for free, there will be a struggle within the community to secure such a free resource. The advantage of interest rate subsidies is seen as being that the subsidy depends upon action that the community takes by participating in the programme. A further advantage is that communities are believed to be more motivated to repay when they can see that most of their contribution reduces their loan balance. In this context, community funds rarely seek to charge rates that are equivalent to market rates for commercial lending. The interest on shelter-related loans may be set in order to cover inflation costs and administration charges (thereby maintaining the real value of the fund) or may be below this amount.

The state funds demonstrate a willingness to offer subsidized interest rates. In Namibia, the Build Together programme recently reduced its interest rate to 5 per cent.[36] Clearly, it is much easier for state programmes to offer interest rate subsidies than it is for NGO initiatives to set interest rates to cover inflation and administration. While the need to raise continued funding might have been thought to deter NGOs from using subsidized interest rates, this does not always appear to be the case. As noted in the discussion of SIDA's programme in Chapter 6, interest rate subsidies appear to be important, in part, because they are considered alongside mortgage rates in many countries, and the practices in the formal housing finance institutions influence those in the small loan market. In India, the state housing agency, the Housing and Urban Development Corporation (HUDCO), has made some subsidized loans through NGOs and other civil society organizations for housing development, aware of the benefits of such an approach.[37]

Community funds may carry on even in very difficult economic contexts if there appear to be strategic advantages. In Zimbabwe, the loan fund of the Zimbabwean Homeless People's Federation (the Gungano Fund) is continuing to offer loans despite the present economic difficulties and the high current rates of inflation (600–800 per cent). Continued lending is taking place because the difficult political climate has enabled a number of councils to negotiate development standards and, hence, to lower the costs of improvements with higher densities, partial infrastructure and delayed housing construction. By 2002, nine local authorities had committed themselves to releasing land that they own to the urban poor, and seven had released plots with tenure to more than 2000 households.[38]

Locally managed savings and loan programmes ensure that communities embed financial management within their own organizations and associated social relationships

Collateral and security

There are two distinctive characteristics of the collateral strategies used by community funds. First, there is reliance upon community systems and community collateral rather than claims over the individual borrowers. Second, in cases of land purchase, legal title deeds may be used.

However, the difficulties of loan security are considerable because of the different attitude towards non-repayment. How can programmes distinguish between those who genuinely need more time to pay and the free riders who are exploiting a poverty-reduction orientation for their personal gain? The microfinance agencies described in Chapter 6 solve this problem through a combination of incentives (access to additional loans) and threats (for example, foreclosure). Community funds may use these strategies; but they also rely on local knowledge to address the problems of information for those issuing the loans. Local loans managers help to institute checks and balances within the system to ensure that abuse is minimized. In the Community Mortgage Programme in the Philippines, 61 per cent of accounts are over six months overdue, although (in terms of collection efficiency) the programme performs relatively well, with a rate that exceeds that of most housing loan programmes in the Philippines.[39] Box 7.13 suggests some measures to reduce these problems, including greater emphasis on the individualization of plots. This last measure may weaken incentives to strengthen group practice in community funds.

NGOs may find themselves taking on the role of guarantor to give the communities space to develop systems and to gain confidence, and because links with more conventional financial institutions require it. For example, in India SPARC found that a role emerged around maintaining books and providing information about the performance of local revolving funds. Community leaders were worried that they would be pressurized into giving loans, or that they would have other problems. Therefore, as the NGO, SPARC set up a fund financed by grants, and this fund operated like a guarantee for the savings. Communities established revolving funds using their savings.

Box 7.12 Determining housing interest at the Urban Community Development Office (UCDO), Thailand

When the Urban Community Development Fund (UCDF) was established, the UCDO board calculated that it could be self-sustainable with an annual average interest rate of 7 per cent. These monies would cover all administration expenses, including the community development process (an estimated 4 per cent), with a small allowance for inflation (which was relatively low). The setting of the terms and conditions of the loan processes was immediately a political rather than a technical issue. The idea of a 'shared' interest rate with a proportion remaining with the community organization developed during the initial study phase from the experience with earlier loan funds. These groups (and, later, the networks) were allowed to add a margin to cover their own costs and to provide funds for development costs or their community welfare fund. The decision on this margin or on an additional rate depends upon agreement made within the community and ranges between 2 and 10 per cent.

Achieving the aggregate figure of 7 per cent return across all loans was an objective used to design the interest rate structure for the various loans, considering the amount of capital, repayment period and use made of the loans. The more conservative board members were anxious that UCDO loans did not undercut existing financial markets. When they understood that the reason why they did not undercut existing financial institutions was because the community itself added to the interest rate of the office, there was a discussion about why the office itself should not benefit from high interest rates. Eventually the board agreed that the interest charges would be shared with the savings schemes.

In reality, the actual average interest gained across all lending was only 5 per cent. This shortfall was caused by the high percentage of housing loans requested during the initial years. The interest rate on housing loans is only 3 per cent. However, only one third of the total fund was being loaned to communities and the rest remained on deposit. The interest earned on deposit was generally sufficient to compensate for the shortfall. Therefore, annual average interest gained from all the monies in the fund has averaged 7 per cent. Total expenses for all development activities and management costs have averaged 3 per cent a year.

Source: Boonyabancha, 2004.

If thefts occurred, then the community saving was supported through additional resources provided by SPARC. In effect, SPARC acted as guarantor and this gave communities the courage to carry on. As activities increased, the NGO came under pressure from the communities to secure more capital, thereby enabling them to expand their local funds with external capital, and with that came a system of peer accountability. If one community failed to repay the capital that they had borrowed, another investigated the non-repayment and supported the community to resolve any problems. SPARC became a wholesale banker; each transaction was identified and the information sent back to communities. Like a bank, every transaction is identified and that information is provided each month to the national federation.

As is the case with shelter microfinance, community funds seek to ensure that households do not overburden themselves with debt, and most do not let households borrow such that repayments are more than 25 per cent of their income. However, there are problems with estimating incomes and, in practice, this restriction may not be effective.

Box 7.13 Group credit for housing loans: strengthening the Community Mortgage Programme (CMP) in the Philippines

Within the Community Mortgage Programme (CMP) in the Philippines, repayment performance is unsustainable and highly variable. The strength of the community is affected by its size, with smaller communities having a better repayment performance, and by whether or not the project is on site or off site. Off-site projects have a lower repayment rate as there are problems with cooperation (members come from different areas) and livelihoods may not be well established in the new area. To improve the repayment rate, there is a need to establish and strengthen collective action and joint liability in CMP community organizations as an anchor of programme sustainability. This requires the CMP to take into consideration key principles that have evolved from the experience of group lending. Groups have to agree on internal rules; they have to monitor loan performance and uncooperative behaviour; and they must rely upon members' deposits rather than external sources to increase the borrower's incentive to repay.

There is also a need to resolve land issues in group lending for housing. Site selection and planning are necessary conditions for a CMP scheme to work. Government has to act on ownership conflicts and titling problems and include the individualization of plots as an important part of the incentive system.

Source: Ballesteros and Vertido, 2004.

Loan periods

Loan periods seek to recognize the fact that considerable care is needed in any loan programme for low-income groups since the capacity of such groups to repay is obviously limited. They also have a limited capacity to cope with sudden stresses (such as higher interest rates) or shocks (such as maintaining repayments when their income falls). 'Good practice' among loan programmes for low-income groups should actually support them in avoiding loans or in taking the smallest loans they need with rapid repayment periods (to minimize interest charges), rather than maximizing the size and number of loans (which would be the conventional measure of 'success' for most loan programmes). Such loan programmes should also ensure that they have measures to help those who find it difficult to repay. And, obviously, loan programmes work best for low-income groups where the cost of what is to be funded by a loan is kept down.

Loan periods appear to be longer than those used for shelter microfinance with, for example, terms of 25 years in the Philippines and 10 years in Thailand. In part, this is because of the large size of the loan relative to family incomes. It is also acknowledged that land purchase, for example, may be only a part of the investments that the family needs to make. NGO loan periods are lower and are generally less than five years. While some appear longer, such as those of the *uTshani* Fund in South Africa, the design reflects the fact that funds are primarily released as bridge finance for the state subsidy.

Technical assistance

Community funds generally place some emphasis on technical assistance, in part because access to land and infrastructure may be more difficult than simple house construction. However, advice is not limited to the difficulties of land purchase and subdivision and/or infrastructure installation. Support is often given to forging links with the local authority both with regard to the professional staff responsible for municipal rules and regulations, as well as the politicians. It appears that once it is accepted that a subsidy is part of the process, some of the subsidy is allocated to technical and professional advice.

In general, technical advice concerning land and infrastructure development is provided by professional staff attached to the government department and/or local NGOs. In many cases, such as in Namibia, Zimbabwe and the Philippines, support may be given by local authority staff even if they do not make a financial contribution. These relationships are important to the development of future opportunities, and the strategies have been successful, most recently in Cambodia.[40] One agency using community funds, Shack/Slum Dwellers International, has developed an alternative strategy, using the need for technical assistance to further build the confidence of communities through skill-sharing exchanges. Communities teach one another to survey land, install water pipes and construct houses. This has the double advantage of being low cost and strengthening relationships between communities. Such exchanges generally take place within the city and help to develop stronger city-based networks that can offer further assistance.[41]

Types of loans	Annual interest (percentage)	Maximum term
Revolving fund loan	10	3
Income generation	8	5
Community enterprise	4	7
Housing improvement	8–10	5–15
Housing project	3–8	15
Network revolving fund loan	4	5
Revival loan	1	5
(Miyazawa) Loan to reduce community crises and debt	1	5
Guarantee loan	Fixed rate +2	Flexible

Source: Boonyabancha, 2004.

Table 7.1

Summary of Urban Community Development Fund loans (from 2000)

Income generation

Community funds differ significantly in their attitude towards income-generation lending. Some funds have a specific focus on a particular activity and have no interest in lending beyond that activity. More conventional microfinance lending may take place alongside the work supported by the community funds with a different set of staff, procedures and, often, clients. In other cases, the funds have developed a number of windows offering an integrated lending package for their members, almost universally with more conventional microfinance strategies being used for the enterprise component. Interest rates are generally higher, loan periods are shorter and the size of loans is smaller. One of the most complex is the Community Organization Development Institute in Thailand.[42] The Urban Community Development Fund managed by the institute has developed a number of lending windows (see Table 7.1). Revolving fund loans top up small community-managed savings funds and may also be used for small microenterprise loans. All of these loans are managed by the local savings schemes; in most cases, they will add a margin of up to 5 per cent from this rate charged by CODI to provide funds for essential community administrative expenditures and to provide a pool for selected projects. The scale of these funds depends upon the additional charge chosen by the savings scheme.

The more ambitious schemes have explored the possibility of creating commercial centres to assist with income generation. This reflects the priority within some local communities to create employment opportunities and increased incomes. While the better-off households may be able to benefit from individual income-generation loans, more inclusive strategies require more comprehensive attempts to strengthen the local economy. The schemes recognize that many small enterprises have marketing difficulties. By creating commercial centres, such initiatives seek to offer generalized opportunities that draw larger numbers of consumers to one place. The evident intention is to increase expenditure within the locality, thereby helping to ensure that more income circulates locally and seeking a virtuous economic cycle. For example, *Cearah Periferia* constructed small neighbourhood shopping centres in Fortaleza, Brazil, that provided a mix of productive units with space for selling. Similar strategies were tried in South Africa by the People's Dialogue and the South African Homeless People's Federation. The objective in both cases was to enable entrepreneurs to more easily sell their goods and to encourage residents to buy locally, thereby increasing demand for local products and seeking a community multiplier effective. In Fortaleza, this was taken one step further with the development of a community credit/debit card, which was managed within one neighbourhood and which added to the circulation of finance within the local economy as families used it to buy purchases from local retailers. An alternative strategy to enhance income-generation potential has been to increase the demand for specific goods. In Thailand, the Community Organization Development Institute (CODI) has enabled groups of tradespeople in individual income-generation activities to come together to make larger investments. For example, waste collectors in Khon Khan developed a wholesale company to buy their goods at a fair price and to prevent them from being cheated by existing wholesalers.

CHALLENGES

Community funds face very similar challenges to those faced by agencies supporting shelter microfinance initiatives. How can they secure the funding they need for long-term viability and how can they be effective in reaching out to those in need of shelter investment?

Long-term strategies for continued viability

A particularly different challenge faces community funds as they develop – what should their strategy be with respect to the state? Fundamentally, this is about strategies that maximize possibilities for scaling up funds while retaining a process that can be controlled by local communities. Links to the state are almost certainly essential if funding on the required scale is to be available. However, there is a concern that funds will be bureaucratized. There are broadly three models in the programmes reviewed here:

1. state agency;
2. independent agency with state contributions to a central fund;
3. independent agency with state contributions to local activities supported by the fund.

The experiences in Thailand and the Philippines have been discussed above. UCDO started life under the National Housing Authority and CODI (UCDO's successor) is now a public agency with its own funds. There are advantages to being within government, such as preferential access to state finances and legitimacy when convening other groups – for example, local government. However, the agency can also be vulnerable to political pressures, and the process may need to be managed carefully. In the Philippines, there has been considerable support for community fund approaches, with a high level of institutionalization of people's organizations and NGOs within state housing strategies:

> *In recent years, NGOs, in particular, have also provided housing communities with financing and services for site and home development. The NGOs, through funds from private and international donors, offer bridge-financing facilities to housing communities… Community-based programmes have raised a need, which apparently cannot be adequately supported by government housing programmes, by the formal financial markets or by the business sector.*[43]

However, there are also difficulties in raising the required funds. One source of difficulties, evident in the Philippines, comes from a lack of acceptance of incremental housing strategies:

Community fund programmes are designed for relatively stable communities that are in need of finance to secure land tenure and to upgrade their neighbourhood

> *… the CMP has also failed to obtain the support of government officials, including heads of housing agencies, because of the perception that it legitimizes the existence of squatters and degraded neighbourhoods in urban areas… At the heart of this issue are the different perspectives informing what constitutes a valid housing solution.*[44]

As a consequence, the CMP has, at times, been starved of funds. For example, between January 1993 and September 1998, only 19.5 per cent of the total expenditure on housing was allocated to poverty-orientated housing projects (socialized housing) and only 1.33 per cent to the CMP.[45] It has now been proposed that a social housing finance corporation should be established in the Philippines to enable the CMP and other initiatives to be managed within a supportive state framework. The advantage of being independent and somewhat removed from government is that a positive political context can offer benefits; but if and when state strategies shift to other approaches, the fund can consolidate without being threatened. One of the reasons for the reduction of support for FONHAPO's innovative programme in Mexico was that the general trend shifted in favour of market-based solutions and the agency was unable to protect its approach.[46]

Nevertheless, a critical strategy of community funds is to secure state support both for central lending activities and to subsidize local development initiatives so that they can be inclusive and affordable. It is very difficult for a process that does not secure national funds to achieve scale even if it is successful in attracting donor support. In South Africa, the South African Homeless People's Federation, based around a network of savings schemes, became very strong. At one point, the intention was to set up a state fund. However, government distanced itself from the federation, claiming that it was difficult for it to support a single initiative.

The challenge of inclusion

Community fund programmes are designed for relatively stable communities who are in need of finance to secure land tenure and upgrade their neighbourhood. In some cases, communities choose to resettle. In other cases, they remain where they are and invest in their existing location. Such investments do not necessarily imply land purchase. Many communities have taken small loans to make improvements that are designed to improve the quality of their immediate lives and the visual appearance of the settlement and, hence, the likelihood of longer-term residency even if legal tenure cannot be secured. With regard to the challenge of inclusion, community funds may struggle to include all residents living within the settlement. They may also find it difficult to assist those who do not live permanently in the city.

Throughout Asia, Latin America and Africa, conventional development processes have failed to deal with many groups of poor people. In some cases, these are the poorest; but this is not always the case. There are particular groups who are vulnerable, such as illegal migrants. For example, Nicaraguans living in Costa Rica, Peruvians in Ecuador or West Africans in South Africa are often treated as non-citizens. Such groups often fall outside of any development scheme and are excluded from the benefits that others can secure. Community funds struggle to reach these groups and others who live in very distinct geographical areas or who do not have a permanent location. A major reason is that savings schemes build up links between neighbours in geographical areas. It is difficult for those who are working but not living in the city to join in, or for those who are very mobile. In Latin America, the Urban Management Programme tried to set up savings schemes with a group of street sellers in Quito; but it failed, in part, due to the attitude of local government.[47]

In respect of activities within the settlements, policies for inclusion in savings and loans schemes may be difficult to operate effectively. To take a very different example from Asia, the Grameen Bank in Bangladesh has very strict criteria and tries to ensure that only the very poor take part. It is nervous that the richer groups within the community will be too strong and will determine the rules and regulations. In other countries, such as Thailand, such a highly targeted policy would not work easily.[48] Within urban-poor communities, there is a lot of sharing between residents. CODI seeks to look at the community more holistically and inclusively, with rich and poor alike. However, CODI staff recognize that there is the danger that the process will be difficult for the poor. The difficulty with more inclusive groups is that the rules they adopt are hard for the poor to comply with. The practice of daily saving in India helps to ensure that even the poorest can participate. The livelihoods of the poor are generally managed daily (or in three- to five-day cycles), not monthly. Groups who save monthly exclude the poor. At the same time, richer households may not be interested in a process that requires them to save daily.

A group who may face exclusion is tenants. It may be difficult to ensure that tenants are granted equal rights as tenure is secured and development takes place. One area that has managed to overcome its differences and work together to develop their area equitably is Huruma in Nairobi, Kenya.[49] In this case it was facilitated by the requirement that agreement between all residents had to be reached before development could occur.

A further aspect of inclusion is that of gender. There is a widespread understanding that the centrality of women is important. In part, this is because women are concerned about their neighbours, about who is sick and who needs what; it is also related to the level of poverty and vulnerability experienced by women. Women's community role means that if women are central to managing the savings process, then it is likely that there will be fewer problems with exclusion within the community. However, this requires that the process is orientated towards women taking up a leadership role. While this seems prevalent in the case of savings and loans, in some contexts the shift to construction encourages higher levels of involvement by men. In the experiences of the Gungano Fund, Zimbabwe, and the *uTshani* Fund, South Africa, women are members of the savings schemes and are among those who take the loans; but a significant percentage of titles are registered in the name of the man. Nevertheless the high level of activity from women often continues. In the Community Mortgage Programme, for example, 70 to 90 per cent of community board members and officers are women and the assessment from research is that women are considered to be the more reliable managers.[50] Some of the groups have a demonstrated capacity to move from housing on to other needs, such as daycare centres.

The microfinance agencies have noted the difficulties that they have in reaching some of the poorest groups, and such problems have been recognized in the case of community funds. For example, while even the poorest in the settlements supported by WaterAid in Bangladesh are better off as a result of the investments in water facilities, some individuals cannot afford to pay for adequate supplies of clean water.[51] With a requirement for full-cost recovery, local communities have to cover the costs that are required. Inclusion issues may be particularly strong in the case of more formal processes, such as those associated with government funds. The situation within the CMP is assessed thus:

> *If we take the income level of beneficiaries at the time of CMP application, the programme has reached those coming from the bottom three income deciles (3178 Philippine pesos and below) ... with the majority coming from the second- and third-income deciles (2600 Philippine pesos to 3178 pesos)...*[52] *Only a small percentage (7 per cent) of the beneficiaries came from the bottom segment or the first-income decile (2600 Philippine pesos and below)... [Moreover], substitution of beneficiaries*[53] *and/or selling of rights have occurred (ranging from a low 5 per cent to a high 35 per cent) because of inability to pay the amortization due to loss of income because of sickness, death or unemployment. In some cases, the beneficiary has moved to another place because of marital separation, death and job transfer... That the CMP beneficiaries do not come from the poorest of the poor is further supported by their occupational profile and income sources. Almost half (45 per cent) derived their income from low-wage work (e.g. employee, nurse/teacher, factory worker and services) or from the informal sector (vending/selling, transport service workers). Most families have several income earners who pool together their earnings in order to pay the amortization, as well as meet their basic survival needs.*[54]

NOTES

1 This chapter is based on a draft prepared by Diana Mitlin, University of Manchester, UK.
2 Mitlin and Satterthwaite, 2004b, p15.
3 ACHR, CODI and IIED, 2004.
4 Arrossi et al, 1994, pp130–134.
5 Arrossi et al, 1994.
6 Hanchett et al, 2003.
7 Cavalcanti et al, 2004.
8 Cabannes, 2004, p30.
9 Gonzáles de Kauffman and Rincón, 2004.
10 Lumanti, pers comm (2004).
11 Porio et al, 2004, p63.
12 Escobar, undated, pp40–41.
13 Escobar, undated, p43.
14 Hanchett et al, 2003, p44.
15 Baumann and Bolnick, 2001.
16 Mitlin and Satterthwaite, 2004b, p13.
17 Mitlin, 2003.
18 Mitlin, 2003.
19 Cavalcanti et al, 2004, pp172–173.
20 CODI, 2004.
21 Escobar, undated, p41.
22 Baumann and Bolnick, 2001.
23 Saborido, pers comm (2004).
24 SPARC, pers comm (2004).
25 Porio et al, 2004.
26 *CMP Bulletin*, 2004, in SELAVIP, 2004, p93.
27 ACHR, CODI and IIED, 2005.
28 Boonyabancha, pers comm (2004).

29 Mitlin and Muller, 2004.
30 Mitlin and Patel, 2005.
31 Boonyabancha, 2004.
32 See Gaye and Diallo, 1997.
33 Patel and D'Cruz, 1993.
34 ACHR, 2004, pp3–4. Some financial regulations prevent organizations from lending and collecting savings. While this may be well intentioned, there are evident problems in lending without saving opportunities. In addition to the benefits described here, without savings people are less likely to build up assets to enable them to repay loans in times of difficulty, or to develop the habit of regularly making payments. Hence, they may be more vulnerable.
35 Hanchett et al, 2003, p47.
36 Ministry of Regional, Local Government and Housing, 2003.
37 Escobar and Merrill, 2004, p66.
38 *HiFi News*, 2002; SELAVIP, 2004, pp129–134.
39 Ballesteros, 2002, pp21–23.
40 ACHR, 2004.
41 Patel and Mitlin, 2002.
42 Boonyabancha, 2004.
43 Ballesteros, 2002, p12.
44 Porio et al, 2004, p60.
45 *CMP Bulletin*, January 1998, cited in Porio et al, 2004.
46 Connolly, 2004a, b.
47 Cabannes, pers comm (2004).
48 ACHR, CODI and IIED, 2004.
49 Weru, 2004.
50 Porio et al, 2004, p75.
51 Hanchett et al, 2003, pp48–49.
52 This study opted to use the lowest three mean income decile criteria (bottom 30 per cent), rather than the poverty threshold definition of poverty (4945 Philippine pesos in 1994 and 6231 pesos in 1997). However, comparing the two indicators of poverty shows how much deficit the poor suffer in terms of their income and basic needs for survival (for example, almost 100 per cent deficit of the third decile's average monthly income of 3544 Philippine pesos versus the poverty threshold of 6321 Philippine pesos).
53 Substitution of beneficiaries occurs when an original member of the organization cannot/refuses to fulfil his duties to the association and decides to forfeit his access rights to the CMP project. Reasons include death, migration, inability to pay or loss of faith in the project.
54 Porio et al, 2004, pp72–73.

PART III

TOWARDS SUSTAINABLE SHELTER FINANCE SYSTEMS

CHAPTER 8

ASSESSING SHELTER FINANCE SYSTEMS[1]

The analysis in the previous chapters of this Global Report highlights a number of specific issues that have policy implications with regard to the value of housing finance in addressing the world's housing needs. This chapter brings together a discussion of these issues across the different approaches to housing finance that have been addressed. Several themes are considered:

- affordability and the difficulties of reaching the poor;
- access to capital and the lack of loan finance;
- the move to markets and what the market cannot manage, including the issues of maintaining financial viability; and
- connections and diversity within globalization, as well as risk management within the market.

Housing finance is critical to the process of development: 'cities are built the way they are financed'.[2] While urban form reflects other factors, such as land regulations, building codes, cultural values and demographic change, finance is a powerful influence on the kind of cities and settlements in which people can expect to live. Hence, the development of urban areas reflects who has money, how much they have and on what conditions.

The challenge is to ensure that finance contributes to the equitable and sustainable development of cities. Clearly, as indicated in earlier chapters of this report, finance for the dwelling is only a part of the picture. Finance for other components of urban development is also important. At the level of the settlement, municipal finance is important, as demonstrated in Chapter 3. Households need to consider finance for land and for services in addition to the dwelling itself. While the typical model of urban development in the North is where the household purchases a complete unit (dwelling, serviced site, land tenure), this is not the reality for much of the South (see Chapter 6). In this context, housing finance has to be appropriate to the multiple needs of incremental development (land, services, infrastructure and dwelling). This raises a further and very significant complexity since investments in land and infrastructure are rarely affordable on an individual basis – as discussed in Chapter 7 and considered further in this chapter.

It no longer seems true to say, as in a 1993 study, that most developing countries do not have a sustainable and viable institutional housing finance system.[3] In most parts of Asia and Latin America, this does exist in some shape and form and it has been growing significantly during the last 10 to 15 years. In some cases, the state remains a very significant influence on the market for housing finance (through regulation, direct lending activities or, as in the case of Chile, other subsidy finance strategies). In others, governments' significance appears to be decreasing as the number of alternative providers increases and more market-orientated policies begin to gain more influence (see Chapters 4 and 5). This 'formal' housing finance system, orientated towards the provision of mortgage finance, is limited in scale, with low-income households being excluded. Arguably, it is not as cheap or as flexible as is required. In sub-Saharan Africa, it still appears to be lacking on a significant scale. But it does, for the most part, exist in many Latin American and Asian countries. In general, it appears to be growing, and it has demonstrated a capacity to survive the financial stresses of the 1990s. While macro-economic stability is widely acknowledged to be important for the health of the housing finance sector, housing finance systems have demonstrated some resilience as they have recovered successfully from financial crises during the 1990s (see Chapter 4).

Cities are built the way they are financed

The challenge is to ensure that finance contributes to the equitable and sustainable development of cities

Unable to afford mortgage finance or complete dwellings, many low-income residents finance homeownership through incremental development, making small investments over a considerable time period. 'Formal' institutions providing small loans for shelter improvements have become more significant during the last 15 years. During the early 1980s, the distinction between non-institutional and institutional almost entirely replicated the small loans/big loans division, with the majority of institutional sources supplying big loans for complete (or almost complete) dwellings and non-institutional sources supplying small loans used for incremental shelter development. This is no longer the case. As discussed in Chapter 6, there has been a significant growth in non-governmental organizations (NGOs), microfinance agencies and government programmes offering small loans to assist in financing incremental shelter strategies. Many in low-income countries in the South still develop their housing incrementally; for the poorer households, this remains the only viable strategy, even in relatively wealthy Southern countries. As a result, the provision of appropriate funding is a development priority. However, small loans from microfinance agencies, in general, go to those with land tenure for housing improvement and extension, limiting once more their contribution to addressing the needs of many in the South. Community funds with an emphasis on collective loans have recently emerged to address the needs of the urban poor. However, much of their work remains experimental and it rests somewhat uneasily between financial approaches and poverty reduction programming.

The greater emphasis on the market has brought benefits, but also problems

The integration of neighbourhood upgrading and slum improvement programmes with small loan programmes offers significant support to the poor. Within such programmes, in general, subsidy funding (sometimes together with small loan finance) is orientated towards land tenure, infrastructure and services, while small loans assist families in finding the funds for housing improvements. Although not always the case, there are clear further benefits if small loan funds are also provided for enterprise development. Two emerging models exist for such upgrading. In one model, the local authority, or some other professional development agency, takes the lead, with small loans being provided through subcontracting arrangements with microfinance agencies. In the other model, exemplified by the work of the Community Organization Development Institute (CODI) in Thailand and the Community-led Infrastructure Financing Facility (CLIFF) in India, the community build up their financial management expertise through the use of community funds and they take the lead in managing the process, with appropriate support from government agencies and professional NGO staff.

If the needs of higher income groups are not met, they will occupy the shelter opportunities created for the poor

Despite its lack of immediate relevance for the poor, great emphasis has been placed, by governments and development agencies, on mortgage finance. This is represented in the weight of the discussion in this report, which, in turn, reflects research, documents, institutional investments and financial capital related to mortgage finance. However, it is not directly relevant to those most in need in the world – at its crudest, their incomes are simply too low. This is not to say that this work is insignificant to the poor. There is evidence that housing finance has to be treated as a system. If the needs of higher income groups are not met, they will occupy the shelter opportunities created for the poor.

With a growing global dependence upon the market for the delivery of finance, how have housing finance systems responded? There are a growing number of providers in numerous countries. Consumers who can access mortgage finance have been able to benefit from competition, with some indications of improving loan-to-value ratios[4] and smaller loan margins.[5] While loan periods have also lengthened in some countries, this seems to be more concerned with the crisis of affordability than with competition *per se*. The benefits seem, in part, to have been taken up in rising dwelling prices, and increases in the scale of mortgage lending are less impressive once price increases are taken into account. Yet there does appear to be more money for housing finance in most regions of the world, with sub-Saharan Africa being a notable exception. While there have been initiatives in this region (for example, in Ghana and Nigeria), they remain small scale and relatively insignificant.

The greater emphasis on the market has brought benefits, but also problems. A number of specific issues arising from too great a dependence upon the market that have been highlighted in previous chapters of this report. None of these themes are new; but they have, perhaps, been overlooked in the eagerness of policy-makers to move from ineffective strategies to increase access to housing finance towards something that appears to work. These are areas where the market cannot be expected to respond effectively; by its very nature, it produces outcomes that reflect individual decision-maker's choices rather than grander plans. The areas are systemic risks within the financial system; ensuring that institutional frameworks are in place for multi-family dwelling and neighbourhood development and maintenance; and urban planning and land-use management. They are all areas which require a role for government (and governance) in developing appropriate structures for planning, regulation and institutional development.

Finally, recent development discussions have placed much emphasis on globalization. While globalization means many things to many people, the two specific areas relevant to this debate are the relationship between global financial flows and housing finance, and the ways in which 'global' ideas about housing finance are permeating solutions and strategies to address housing needs. The final theme considers these issues.

AFFORDABILITY AND THE DIFFICULTIES OF REACHING THE POOR

The discussion in Chapter 4 highlights the difficulties that the poor have in affording mortgage finance to purchase a complete dwelling through a single purchase that is funded primarily (but rarely exclusively) by a loan. Significant numbers of people in the North remain in rental accommodation and cannot afford the costs of homeownership, even in a context in which subsidies have been provided. The indications are that rising house prices have made affordability more difficult in the North, although the ratio of current prices to incomes is high when compared to long-term trends, and greater affordability may be anticipated in the short term. There have been very considerable attempts supported by government to extend homeownership to lower income groups – for example, through the more extensive use of mortgage insurance. There are some indications of success (higher homeownership rates) and some areas of concern as households may find it difficult to manage the associated risks. Northern governments seek to supplement commercial housing finance for homeowners with a range of measures in order to assist the poor in securing adequate accommodation, primarily through rental markets.

In the South, the percentage of those who cannot afford mortgage loans is significantly higher in many countries, reflecting high levels of poverty. The estimates in Chapter 4 suggest that these numbers may be over 70 per cent in sub-Saharan Africa and the lower income countries of Asia, and at or above 40 per cent in the higher income countries of Asia and Latin America. The problems are not simply related to lack of income (looking at restrictions on mortgage lending in the North); they are also related to the nature of the economy and its high dependence upon informal as well as low-paid employment.

The costs of being poor are considerable. There is no doubt that the poor wish to save and accumulate assets. The World Bank estimates that 60 per cent of households in Mexico save for housing.[6] That figure appears low. A very detailed analysis of the overwhelming importance of savings in housing investment in Hyderabad has been done,[7] while it has also been noted that 65 per cent of those who join a shelter microfinance facility in Cape Town, the Kuyasa Fund, do so only to use its savings facilities.[8] The scale of informal saving appears to be very significant. The success of microfinance in providing essential financial services to the poor has been noted. There is a willingness to save among the poor, and as the discussion of community funds explains, programmes have been able to build on such experiences to increase take-up of financial services (see Chapter 7).

While the poorest may not be able to afford to invest much in housing, the costs of squatting, of purchasing water and of repairing temporary dwellings are very significant. Given the opportunity, the poor readily take up opportunities to save and acquire small loans through microfinance agencies and/or community funds. Programme reports discuss many issues; but none have ever referred to a lack of demand for their services. Opportunities to acquire small loans for land acquisition, infrastructure and housing do appear to have grown significantly during the last two decades, particularly during the last ten years. However, provision still appears very small, given potential demand (and in the context of estimated housing deficits).

Small loan agencies have been established and have contributed to addressing shelter needs. They have been extensively discussed in Chapters 6 and 7. Incremental development is all that is affordable to the poor and is a viable strategy that has helped to develop housing for millions. Incremental development requires finance and is, for the most part, primarily financed through savings at present. Loan finance can reduce the time taken for such development and the overall scale of the investment. The interest in this sector is reflected by a growth in sources of provision (as well as the scale), with municipal and national governments, commercial financial institutions and other private-sector groups such as building material suppliers all becoming involved.

The growth of microfinance agencies for enterprise development pre-dates the specific rise of shelter microfinance. These agencies have been encouraged to move into the shelter sector due, in part, to the scale of enterprise loans that were 'misdirected' at housing investment. In other cases, they have extended their loan services to respond to explicit needs and requests, and because of their own commercial needs to expand their markets. While not all microfinance programmes for housing have been successful, there is a body of experience that demonstrates the possibilities. The major problem faced by these agencies appears to be a lack of capital for expansion.

The particular focus of shelter microfinance agencies on individualized lending for housing improvements limits their value to many of the poorest urban dwellers. It is indicative that the Grameen Bank in Bangladesh, which lends to low-income rural dwellers (mainly women) for housing, except where land tenure is uncertain (in which case they lend for land purchase prior to lending for housing investment), does not consider this model to be transferable to urban areas where land costs are so much higher. This does not mean that shelter microfinance is unimportant. It provides essential assistance in enabling urban improvements to take place in many areas in which tenure is secure and in some urban informal settlements in the South. It may also be of significance in illegal subdivisions, where the tenure is not in dispute but where additional investment is required for infrastructure and services, as well as upgrading of dwellings. But in seeking to address the Millennium Development Goals (MDGs), the limitations of microfinance strategies as well as their potential have been recognized. Shelter microfinance assists in the consolidation of urban poor areas; it helps households to build up their assets, investing their savings in dwellings that provide both a place of shelter and a source of enterprise development for many working in the informal sector. In other cases, it adds directly to income when families rent rooms. However, its value is predominantly for those who already have tenure (although this may not be formal legal tenure).

In the South, the percentage of those who cannot afford mortgage loans is very high, reflecting high levels of poverty

The tradition of community funds has grown up to respond to the needs of urban poor groups to invest in land purchase and to develop infrastructure on such land. Community funds offer collective loans to organized communities to enhance their development capacities. While many loans are for secure tenure and infrastructure, the financial systems are also used for more individualized lending both for housing and income generation. The strategy seeks to strengthen local institutions to address investment needs that individual households, and individualized solutions, cannot tackle.

However, once more, there are indications that the poorest find it difficult to participate. Such problems are evident in assessments of the Community Mortgage Programme (CMP), a group-lending scheme in the Philippines that has provided almost 150,000 households with secure tenure, but which finds it difficult to include the poorest households. The solution used by some agencies such as the Society for the Promotion of Area Resource Centres (SPARC), an Indian NGO, is to seek to develop models that work for the poorest within a residential group, and then allow higher income groups to join in if they wish. However, it has to be recognized that the use of loans carries inherent risks for those who are too poor to manage repayment risk. The vulnerability of the poorest may be too great to successfully manage these risks (despite the capacity of an organized community to provide support), and greater emphasis may need to be placed on savings and grant combinations. While there have been some attempts to develop microinsurance schemes with microfinance initiatives, relatively little attention has been given to such strategies in the context of shelter microfinance. Another limitation is that bulk investments are still required by the local authority to enable communities to develop infrastructure. In Namibia, the collaboration between the government (through the Build Together programme) with the Shack Dwellers Federation of Namibia (and its community-based *Twahangana* Fund) have allowed improved housing, tenure and infrastructure to be extended to several thousand households. However, land purchase is becoming increasingly difficult due to the need for bulk infrastructure investments in urban areas such as Windhoek and Walvis Bay.[9]

Bulk investments are still required by the local authority to enable communities to develop infrastructure

Both shelter microfinance and community funds have been integrated with neighbourhood improvement (slum upgrading) programmes for a more comprehensive approach to address the needs of the urban poor. In such a model, subsidy (sometimes augmented by household loan repayments, such as in Ahmedabad, India) contributes to the improvement of the area, with secure tenure and improvements to essential services such as water, sanitation, drainage and pathways. Small loan funding will then assist households that can afford to take loans to improve their dwellings. In some cases, very similar subsidy/loan strategies are also associated with greenfield site development. Additional loan finance may be provided to help households invest in enterprise development. Both 'top-down' and 'bottom-up' models have developed in which development is led by state agencies (local and/or national government) and community groups, respectively. In addition to the work of CODI (in Thailand) and SPARC/National Slum Dwellers' Federation (NSDF) (in India) in supporting bottom-up approaches, the experiences supported by the Swedish International Development Agency (SIDA) in Central America (through alliances of local government and civil society organizations) are also notable. Such programmes provide subsidies for integrated upgrading, enhanced by small loans, and ensure the significant participation of both the community and the local authority. While finance is a very significant direct aspect to the success of these programmes, it is more critical in supporting changes in relationships between the citizens (through community organizations) and the urban development agencies (including state and, in some cases, the private sector).

Collectively managed savings and loan finance, together with upgrading strategies, help to strengthen local governance

The role of finance: relationship-building

The significance of social networks and relationships in helping those in need of housing is remarked upon in one pro-market analysis of social housing.[10] The analysis highlights the networks that individuals need to avoid homelessness in the US. However, there is a wider relevance to the argument when analysed in the context of destitution in the South. In this case, those in housing need are rarely in need of specific social support (such as dealing with mental illness and drug addiction); rather, they face much wider system failings in the lack of affordable legal opportunities to acquire adequate shelter. The notable point about the strategy used by community funds and by neighbourhood upgrading programmes, such as those supported by SIDA in Central America, is the greater use of finance to build improved social relationships. The pattern of urban development in the South, with the extensive settlements of informal housing, patron–client relationships within such settlements, and (sometimes) weak and unaccountable government structures, is such that the relationships necessary for urban development are missing. The experiences here suggest that collectively managed savings and loan finance, together with upgrading strategies, help to strengthen local governance, as well as provide the means for investments in individual and collective physical improvements.

Within the community fund programmes described in Chapter 7, savings strengthen relations between community members, enabling them to be more effective (skilled and cohesive) groups, while the joint development of land and infrastructure for the poor are the basis for new relationships between urban-poor communities and local authorities. As SPARC has found with the CLIFF programme, private commercial financial institutions are interested in finding ways to link to the urban poor, but need local institutional strengthening to be able to do this successfully.

THE ROLE OF MORTGAGE FINANCE: ACCESS TO CAPITAL AND THE LACK OF LOAN FINANCE

As noted earlier, mortgage finance is unaffordable for many of those living in the South and a significant minority in the North. Despite this, great emphasis has been placed by both governments and development agencies on mortgage finance and state subsidies for mortgage finance still appear to be at a considerable scale in more than a few countries. The fairly extensive use of interest-based subsidies for mortgage finance is likely to be reducing competition significantly in some countries and, hence, may be delaying the development of more extensive private provision of mortgage finance. Such interest rate subsidies appear to reach only the higher income levels among the poor, if they reach the poor at all. Even when they are affordable, other factors (notably, informality in property and labour markets) prevent access by those with low incomes. There is reason to believe that the reduction in interest rates is likely to be accompanied by the more extensive development of the market. However, some households may not be able to afford the subsequent rates and, thus, may not be able to access housing finance. While there appears to be good reason to press for the reduction of interest rate subsidies on mortgage loans since it does little to assist the poor to secure access to housing finance, it should also be recognized that such a reduction has been suggested many times before and governments still persist in favouring this strategy.

In some countries (and particularly in Latin America) there has been a shift to direct-demand subsidies. They are associated with large-scale programmes, notably in Chile and South Africa, which address housing need through the provision of finance. In other countries, programmes are significantly smaller. However, as noted in Chapter 5, issues of quality remain. Programmes in Colombia and Mexico appear to be placing considerable emphasis on larger unit subsidies for complete houses (as is also the case in the Chilean and South African programmes), while, arguably, more extensive programmes to support smaller loans for incremental development would spread the available finance more widely, be appropriate to lower income households and be less attractive an option for higher income groups to capture. The strong association with dwelling construction within these programmes appears to be influenced by the involvement of construction companies in their execution. It is clearly not a priority of the poor.

Governments do need to be concerned about the development of appropriate systems for housing finance, and the existence of strong mortgage lenders is important to both higher income groups as well as low-income groups. Different housing markets are not necessarily distinct, and if possibilities are not created for higher income groups to secure the housing improvements that they seek through the market, they are likely to take up those that are being offered to the poor.

While subsidies are often justified by the expectation that they will assist the poor to secure housing improvements, in practice, higher income groups have been successful in gaining access to such subsidies. This suggests that programmes to address the housing needs of the poor need to be more carefully designed.

Returning to the role of mortgage finance and support for such finance, in both Latin America and Asia, there have been initiatives at the government and multilateral agency level to support the development of secondary markets to increase wholesale finance to mortgage lenders. Generally, these efforts appear to be overdone. As discussed in Chapter 4, in many cases these have not been successful because market conditions have not been right. While it is possible that it is a shortage of capital that is preventing the expansion of mortgage finance, many other reasons have been identified in this report. What appears to be of most significance is the scale of informality in property and labour markets. Hence, there is a group excluded from mortgage finance, not for reasons related to the scale of their incomes (or lack of land title), but due to the informal nature of their employment.

It appears that much emphasis has been placed on formalizing land titles; but, as seen in Peru, this has not necessarily increased the take-up of either mortgages or enterprise loans. A detailed examination of sources of income in the context of Europe demonstrates that this problem has not been solved, and those who cannot verify their incomes (due to small-scale or informal entrepreneurship) are also unable to get loans in most countries and have limited access in others. The problem is less evident because this group is proportionally much smaller in the North due to the nature of the labour market. This suggests that access to loans may be limited in ways that cannot be addressed by reforms to property titles, increasing the ease of foreclosure or the scale of finance and competition in the sector. Land titling should not be relied upon as a single solution to the lack of loan finance reaching groups who can apparently afford to take mortgage loans. The example of the new housing banks in Mexico, Sociedad Finaciera de Objeto Limitado (SOFOLES), and their apparent ability to reach such groups is important (see Chapter 4). However, the information that they have moved up income groups since their creation should also be acknowledged. This implies that they may be successfully working with higher income levels in the informal sector – but still not reaching the poor.

Despite these problems, mortgage lending does appear to have expanded in a number of countries. This may be associated with economic growth and with growing affluence. Competition has increased and the market for mortgage finance is moving beyond a small number of lenders in several countries. As shown above in the case of India, even in these circumstances, down-marketing mortgage finance can be difficult. However, there appears to be a significant group that is being reached by the market due to more extensive housing finance in some Northern countries and the wealthier countries of Asia and Latin America. More competition in the finance sector and greater efficiency in the delivery of loans, together with increases in real incomes, have increased the numbers and percentages of people who can afford mortgage finance.

There are risks for individual households in taking on these loans, and some of these risks have been evident when housing prices have fallen, notably in the UK and Japan. If mortgage finance continues to be extended to low-income households, there is a strong case for more attention being given to the potential negative consequences for low-income households. While mortgage insurance has been extended, it appears that much emphasis has been placed on protecting the lender rather than the borrower.

While mortgage insurance has been extended, it appears that much emphasis has been placed on protecting the lender rather than the borrower

At the national level, mortgage finance has survived difficult circumstances in Asia and Latin America during the last decade. As seen by the examples of Colombia, Mexico and Thailand, there is evidence of systemic strain and of recovery. Governments have been involved in managing the outcomes of the financial crises that took place during the 1990s and mortgage lending is continuing (albeit with a high level of state involvement in some contexts).

THE BIGGER PICTURE AND WHAT THE MARKET CANNOT MANAGE

Despite a general emphasis on the expansion of market-orientated mortgage finance and housing support, more generally, the analysis does point to a number of areas in which markets alone appear to be struggling. Three have emerged as being particularly important: systemic financial risk, institutional failings related to necessarily collective rather than individual investments in shelter, and issues related to urban planning and land-use management.

Financial risks

As suggested in the discussion of house prices above, there is evidence that the expansion of housing finance has helped to fuel house price increases. This suggests that sufficient consideration has not been given to measures to address the restrictions that have prevented an increase in the supply of housing.

Expansion of housing finance has helped to fuel house price increases

In addition to inefficiencies in the construction markets, as noted in Chapter 4, a recent survey suggests that strong regulation of the banking sector is necessary to ensure that financial deregulation does not permit speculative investment in property.[11] Experiences have been mixed, with some evidence of weak regulation in Thailand and (to a lesser extent) Malaysia, but few problems in Singapore and Hong Kong, Special Administrative Region of China. In the US, housing finance has become closely linked to the capital markets, with government involvement (in some form) in both primary and secondary markets.[12] Total mortgage debt in the US is now US$6.2 trillion. If house prices fell rapidly in a number of countries, resulting in the risks of negative equity and a sharp reduction in housing investment, then the effects might be felt on a larger scale within the global economy.

The need for local organization

The housing finance market is strongly orientated towards providing loans to individual households. In two of the situations discussed in this Global Report, there is a need for collective investment – to maintain multi-family dwellings in transition countries and to invest in land and infrastructure for those without tenure in the South. In both cases, it appears that the market is unable to make an adequate response due, in part, to reasons of affordability, but also because local institutions that can manage the finance are missing.

If housing prices fall rapidly, there are risks of negative equity and a sharp reduction in housing investment

There is a significant problem in the transition countries with the very poor quality of much of the multi-family dwelling housing stock (that is, apartment blocks). During the transition process, there was a significant transfer of dwellings into homeownership; but a lack of household incomes and institutional weaknesses have meant that little maintenance has taken place. Indications of the scale of the problem are given in a 2003 study, which reports that in Romania only 17 per cent of the housing stock was assessed in 1992 as being likely to provide reliable shelter in 2020.[13] The cost of renovations is estimated to be 30 per cent of gross domestic product (GDP) in Latvia and 8 per cent of GDP in Poland.[14] The problems of maintenance are exacerbated by poor construction technology, lack of maintenance prior to transition and a lack of affordability during recent years. But a core problem is simply that there is no appropriate institutional structure.[15] Even when households can afford to maintain their dwellings, they often do not have an appropriate institution that enables them to do this.

These buildings were previously managed by state-owned companies. With the transfer of ownership to the individual households, such companies no longer had a demand for their services. By the middle of the 1990s (after some delay), new laws were introduced to support the development of homeownership organizations. Further problems are that the administrative procedures may be complex and the laws often provide inadequate guidelines regarding voting procedures, cost-sharing mechanisms and enforcement possibilities. For example, in Romania, the Housing Act of 1996 meant that the multi-dwelling properties had to establish a Homeowners' Association, a legal entity, to ensure property management. However, in 2003, it was reported that only an estimated 20 per cent had done so.[16] In addition, there remain problems of affordability for many households.

Similar problems can be found in multi-family dwellings in the South. In Mumbai, for example, some of the families resettled in medium-rise buildings after the clearance of shacks alongside the railway have been struggling to pay the running costs (electricity bills).[17] While the suggestion proposed by government agencies is often the establishment of formal management committees, care needs to be given that these do not discriminate against the poor.[18]

Moreover, as discussed above and considered in detail in Chapters 6 and 7, mortgage finance is for higher income formal workers and small loans are orientated towards those with secure tenure. Many in the South rent accommodation or squat in precarious situations with little security of tenure. In numerous cases, improvements are unaffordable because individual purchase (even of an insecure site) is beyond the cost of such households. Collective land purchase may be affordable (particularly if households are renting in the informal housing markets). However, such collective land purchase requires financial capital. It may also require relationship-building with the local authority in order to ensure that building regulations are flexibly enforced and, hence, that the development remains affordable. This is the process that community fund mechanisms have often sought to support. However, there remain many areas in which such strategies are not being used and, in this case, there are few alternatives offered to the poor.

To address the housing needs of the poor, housing finance systems need to provide loans for such collective purposes, and appropriate local structures need to be in place if this is to occur.

The issue of urban development

Finally, the market seems to struggle with ensuring the quality of the urban environment (in a physical and social sense). In the discussion above, the problems associated with urban development patterns and form seem to be greatest in relation to the extended reliance on the market in social housing programmes, and two specific issues have arisen. First, the greater emphasis on targeting and reduced social provision in the North appears to have resulted in a greater concentration of low-income households in specific areas. This applies both in the case of the transition countries and for richer countries of Western Europe. In the case of the transition countries, it is also linked with the lack of investment possibilities in multi-family dwellings. Hence, the privatization of state housing has resulted in the increasing spatial segregation of rich and poor. The richer groups have tended to move to detached houses and more up-market housing estates, while the poorest have been drawn together in areas that lack maintenance. In the context of Western Europe, 'lower levels of owner occupation seem to facilitate less polarized housing systems because the rental sectors can be less residualized'.[19]

The second issue is the nature of the developments that are being supported by the direct demand subsidies, for example in South Africa and Chile. In both cases, the private sector is constructing housing paid for by government-financed capital subsidies. In Chile, the amount that can be spent on (serviced) land is explicitly limited to 30 per cent. In South Africa, there is no such limit; but a minimum size of house has been introduced, encouraging investment in the dwelling itself. A consequence in both countries is that low-income housing has been located on low-cost sites often a considerable distance from jobs, services and other facilities, with little consideration of the social cost that results from such physical exclusion. This suggests that the market is unable to respond to the needs of the poor without greater interventions from the state – either the funding agency and/or the local authority. This suggests that a key task for government is to ensure adequate supplies of well-located and well-serviced land – which could fit well with the small loan-based strategies discussed earlier in this chapter.

In the North, there are also environmental (as well as social) issues about the patterns of development emerging from the housing market. At the end of World War II, roughly 70 per cent of the US population lived in central cities; but in the decades since, that figure has dropped to below 40 per cent.[20] This has been partly fuelled by the accessibility of the home mortgage. However, environmental problems are emerging. In addition to the problems of air pollution and high energy use from the dependence upon cars, the quick construction of mass settlements in greenfield sites outside urban centres often relied upon the use of septic systems rather than sewers. Yet, the failure of septic tanks in many parts of the country has been responsible for outbreaks of infectious diseases, as well as the pollution of groundwater, streams and lakes.[21]

CONNECTIONS AND DIVERSITY WITHIN GLOBALIZATION

The broad context within which this discussion is situated is one in which financial markets are deregulating and the state is withdrawing from direct involvement in the economy. It should be recognized that there are distinct limitations to this model. Governments continue to invest in housing support in order to meet poverty reduction goals and for social reasons. There are also continuing programmes, in a number of countries, to support homeownership among higher income groups. In addition, governments have intervened to stabilize difficult financial situations and have, in some cases, offered support to housing finance institutions. However, despite this, in general there is a broad trend in favour of greater reliance upon financial markets and less direct state involvement.

No global financial flows in housing

Despite this financial deregulation, there is relatively little evidence that financial globalization is taking place in the housing sector.[22] Markets for housing finance have internationalized rather than globalized.[23] Hence, at present, while money can flow across borders and assets are sold offshore as well as domestically, there is not a globalized market in which there is a continuous flow of funds into assets whose risks and returns are independent of national regulatory and banking structures and where prices are identical across national borders (for areas with similar risks).

The market is unable to respond to the needs of the poor without interventions from the state

Internationalization, it has been argued, has occurred in place of globalization because, although the state has withdrawn to some extent, it remains involved and housing finance markets are still particular, depending upon their specific historical and structural contexts. As a result, rather than there being a single market, many national markets exist. Moreover, it has been noted that in European markets 'attempts at cross-border lending have been small scale, frequently loss-making and often brief'.[24] It is the scale of local diversity and the lack of understanding of the local context that deter such investments. For example, mortgage lending involves a security on a property which is very fixed and valuation systems vary between countries, as does the ease of foreclosure. 'The evidence from advanced economies suggests that not only do housing finance systems play an important role in determining the nature of housing systems, they are also fairly resistant to convergence.'[25] These conclusions are reinforced by other studies which conclude that there is little international investment in the UK market for mortgage-backed security[26] and that international funding of social housing in Europe is an exception.[27]

Markets for housing finance have internationalized, economies are becoming more interdependent and this is affecting housing finance markets

Despite these conclusions about specific investment flows that are directly concerned with housing, there is evidence that economies are becoming more interdependent and this is affecting housing finance markets. A recent study emphasizes that there is evidence of the synchronization of housing price increases in Northern markets.[28] The growing significance of international capital flows has affected housing markets through exchange and interest rates.[29] There are also commonalities in housing markets due to the increased use of market mechanisms in addressing housing need.

However, with regard to state activities, the global trend is very difficult to establish. National and regional experiences are different. It has been argued that, in the context of Western Europe, 'it is not possible to detect a general, unidirectional and irreversible retreat by government from financial assistance for homeowners'.[30]

The creation of the Euro zone in the European Union (EU) has reduced the variation in national-level monetary policies. Increased incomes and, thus, affordability have made a real difference for some households (and therefore opened up new market-based opportunities), notably in Asia but also elsewhere. The experience of New Zealand highlights the potential of governments to change policies. While in 1991, the government moved away from homeownership and towards 'a tenure-neutral form of income supplementation called the accommodation supplement, available at the same rate to all eligible households', a few years later it moved back to create a mortgage insurance system that encouraged the extension of mortgage finance possibilities for lower income households.[31] Although the scale of instability in financial markets during the late 1990s encouraged some governments to be proactive in ensuring that finance for housing was available (illustrated earlier in the case of Colombia, Mexico and Thailand), such instability was not experienced by all countries.

Instability in financial markets encouraged some governments to be proactive in ensuring availability of finance for housing

In summary, with respect to financial flows, studies of Asia and Europe find that housing finance markets remain distinct despite the presence of international investment. There is evidence of the convergence of housing markets, notably around current price increases; but local factors remain important, particularly in some countries. With regard to housing policy, there has been a widely accepted trend of relying more upon market mechanisms; but many governments still intervene for multiple reasons.

CONCLUDING REMARKS

It is evident that many of the poor cannot afford access to mortgage loan finance to improve their shelter because of the conditions attached to loans and the scale of poverty. This presents a significant challenge to the world as it seeks to achieve the Millennium Development Goals. This is not to say that mortgage finance is unimportant. Shelter finance is critical to improving the situation of urban and rural citizens across the world. Mortgage finance systems have to address the needs of those who can afford financial markets and have to do so efficiently. But the groups that are targeted by the MDGs are not those who can afford mortgage finance.

Additional measures are needed for those who cannot afford mortgage finance and/or who live and work in informal markets and who cannot obtain mortgages. Small loans will help these households to address their desire and need for shelter improvements. However, the experience of shelter finance suggests that it is limited in what it can contribute directly to the MDGs. Most small loans through shelter microfinance agencies go to households with land tenure. Moreover, such loans are rarely used for infrastructure, partly because such loans are not on offer and because, without support, few communities have a suitable social organization through which to borrow for infrastructure improvements. Hence, these loans improve dwellings but do not address other development priorities. The experiences with community funds are particularly interesting because their target group is people with low incomes and few assets. However, development may be slow and limited if finance depends upon loans to assist the incremental building process. As noted above, with respect to the needs of the poor in the South, the greatest potential appears to lie in integrating neighbourhood development strategies with small loan packages (including income generation, housing improvement and community fund methodologies for additional needs). Loans and grant packages that enable the poor to identify and collectively develop land may also be useful, in addition to support for the upgrading of existing areas.[32] It should be noted that neighbourhood development packages tend to concentrate on those who already have some claim to land within the designated areas (even if it is not a legal title), and tenants may be neglected even if they are also interested in securing tenure.

Housing finance markets have developed significantly during the last two decades. The extension of the market for housing finance has offered assistance to more affluent citizens, particularly urban dwellers. However, the problems for the poor remain and difficulties related to the scale of income, the degree of informality and the affordability of housing mean that mortgage housing finance markets offer little to the poor. If the MDGs are to be achieved, much greater consideration has to be given to how this group can access effective financial systems and strategies that build assets and do not increase vulnerability.

NOTES

1 This chapter is based on a draft prepared by Diana Mitlin, University of Manchester, UK.
2 Renaud, 1999, p761.
3 Okpala, 1994.
4 As the loan-to-value ratio moves closer to 100, the down payment required to secure the property falls.
5 Pardo, 2000.
6 World Bank, 2004a, p13.
7 Smets, 2002.
8 Van Rooyan, 2004.
9 Muller, pers comm (2004).
10 Renaud, 1999, p759.
11 Collyns and Senhadji, 2002, p73.
12 Carolini, 2004, pp5–6.
13 Hegedüs and Teller, 2003.
14 Yasui, 2002b, p23.
15 Hegedüs and Teller, 2003.
16 Hegedüs and Teller, 2003.
17 Railways Slum Dwellers Federation, pers comm (2004).
18 There is evidence that the poorest members are less likely to participate in formal organizations. See, Cleaver, 2004; Thorp et al, forthcoming; D'Cruz and Mitlin, 2005.
19 Stephens, 2003, p1020, and Priemus and Dieleman, 2002, p198, substantiate these concerns.
20 Frey and Fielding, cited in Carolini, 2004.
21 Rome, 2001, p89.
22 Stephens, 2003; Dymski and Isenberg, 1998, 2002.
23 Dymski and Isenburg, 1998.
24 Stephens, 2003, p1018.
25 Stephens, 2003, p1021.
26 Kofi Karley and Whitehead, 2002, p35.
27 Gibb, 2002.
28 IMF, 2004.
29 D'Arista, 1998.
30 Stephens, 2003, p1020.
31 Stuart et al, 2004, p8.
32 In Phnom Penh, many communities were evicted in 2003 and they were only offered land some distance from the city centre with very limited transport facilities. The stronger communities negotiated with the city for a contribution and, using additional savings and a loan, purchased land much closer to the city (Urban Poor Development Fund, pers comm., 2004).

CHAPTER 9

POLICY DIRECTIONS TOWARDS SUSTAINABLE URBAN SHELTER FINANCE SYSTEMS[1]

The scale of the need for urban services and housing in the coming decades is both huge and unprecedented. Starting from a position characterized by backlogs, developing countries will add about 2 billion new urban residents during the next 20 years, all of whom will need services and shelter in some form. They will be concentrated in 48 countries, mostly in South, Southeast and East Asia, with 660 million in China and India. In most countries, in the absence of some major global change, there will be continuing and deepening urbanization of poverty. As stated in Chapter 1, the current backlog of people living in slums is approximately 925 million. They will probably be joined by a further 1900 million (more than twice as many again), resulting in 2.8 billion slum dwellers by 2030.

The bureaucratic institutions currently in place in most countries are too unwieldy for rapid and efficient urban development. The costs of bypassing regulations and providing services that city authorities fail to provide (including water, electricity, waste disposal and security) or only provide intermittently (for example, with frequent power failures) are not insignificant and reduce the competitive position of many cities in the global economy.

Urban development and housing policies often appear to be unconcerned with whether any goods are actually supplied and often appear to be really targeted at stopping anything regarded as undesirable by policy-makers. For example, if an occupant of a plot decides to build a second dwelling on it to rent out, they may well discover that it is illegal to have two dwellings on a plot. Housing supply is less important than maintaining plot ratios. Similarly, water-connection pricing policy based on actual cost rather than average cost can severely discourage providers from extending the mains system. In another vein, taxation systems that tax rental income more highly than 'earned' income, or rent control that reduces the profitability of providing rooms to low-income households, can severely affect housing supply, especially for those in need. There is a fundamental need to put the supply of housing and other urban goods at the centre of urban development policy and its financing.

Although there has been a great deal of recent focus on establishing well-functioning financial markets into which householders can dip in order to finance their dwellings, most households in most developing countries have no access to housing finance, nor are they likely to feel that they have access to any. There are many societies in which low-income people are too risk averse to borrow money.

In the supply process followed by millions of householders, if low-income people want to own a house they must build one, employing a local contractor to do the work incrementally. They must save up enough money to be able to pay the contractor for each stage of the work, in cash, as expenses are encountered. The contractor is unlikely to give credit, even in the form of wages paid to workers ahead of a payment by the owner. Indeed, most small contractors cannot raise credit for their operations and therefore must pass on all costs to the client immediately or in advance. It is not unusual for the client to have to pay the workers' wages at the end of each day or each week. In addition, the client may have to purchase and arrange delivery of the materials to site, the contractor going along to advise, but not to meet any costs. As the savings run out, so the work stops, often mid process, in a hiatus that will last until more money is saved. In this way, as a result of lack of capital, many homes which could be completed within a few months take many years to reach a stage where they can be occupied. This ties up peripheral land around countless cities under haphazard and wasteful quasi-residential land uses, with few people in residence and under-use of any service lines fitted ahead of development. In consequence, authorities are loath to fit services ahead of the development process and pioneer residents may have to wait many years before service lines are installed.

The scale of the need for urban services and housing in the coming decades is unprecedented

In an ideal world, there is a compact between householders and the public realm represented by city authorities and the providers of services. Householders expect that their dwelling will exist within an efficient public environment that supplies them with convenience and location. They will receive the benefits of road access; water supply; sanitation; waste disposal; energy and telecommunications; commercial, educational and social services; and the other benefits of city life. In exchange, they will pay for what they receive at a level that is both affordable and recompenses the providers for the public services they provide. This will not only happen at the beginning of the development of their dwelling, but will also persist through their lives and those of their children in perpetuity.

In order to fulfil this compact, the following are required:

- efficient and well-funded city authorities and service providers;
- appropriate and affordable technologies;
- appropriately distributed service lines and locations;
- appropriate charges for services, agreed to by both users and providers;
- the ability and willingness of the city authorities and service providers to levy and collect the charges; and
- the ability and willingness of householders to pay for services received.

This is the ideal; but the preceding chapters have shown that this is not usually the reality, especially for low-income households.

This chapter will, on the basis of the experiences reviewed in this Global Report, discuss the ways in which shelter finance systems could be strengthened in terms of both performance and sustainability. Its main purpose will be to point the way forward, highlighting best policies and practices. Currently, the great majority of households in many countries are unlikely ever to afford a formal-sector dwelling, but are usually left financially unassisted in their struggle for shelter in the informal sector. Furthermore, the scale of need for shelter is and will remain at levels unparalleled in the past, requiring finance in much greater quantities than ever before. The implications of failure to provide finance for shelter for all are stark. This must form the context of the following discussion of the way forward.

Unless urban areas produce sufficient income, the resources to develop infrastructure and build shelter will not be available

TOWARDS INCLUSIVE URBAN INFRASTRUCTURE AND SERVICES

The essential basis of the municipal side of the compact is a system of financing public goods so that they can be provided across the city in appropriate quality and quantity, and at affordable cost, and so that the city can be managed effectively. Unless urban areas can produce more income at the same rate that they absorb more people, the resources to develop infrastructure and build shelter will not be available.

Pro-poor municipal financing requires that effective levels of finance reach the municipality to enable services to be provided to all neighbourhoods and households regardless of their influence or income. Thus, funding for municipalities should be adequate to the task, paid on time and reliable over the medium term, and should allow the municipality some flexibility over its level and source.

The means by which municipalities receive their finance and the balance between their funding and obligations are considered below.

Financing for municipalities and service providers

It is vital that powers, duties and revenues are congruent. If the municipal authority is responsible for social housing, it should have the power to take policy decisions on how it will act and receive the required revenue or be able to raise the finance. Furthermore, it is important that the balance should express where power is best exercised and revenue can be most effectively disbursed. This is in line with the current trend to decentralize power to municipalities.

Public-sector inadequacy to the task

Most developing countries labour under large public budget deficits, with public resources scarcely able to meet salaries of civil servants and operating costs of schools and hospitals. Infrastructure maintenance is regularly deferred and new infrastructure cannot remotely keep pace with development. Reliance upon official development assistance (ODA) for new infrastructure leaves it prey to competition from other countries for the scarce resources on offer. When events such as the 2003 Bam Earthquake and the 2004 tsunami in the Indian Ocean occur, ODA is inevitably diverted to relief efforts because public opinion in donor countries drives the political agenda.

Without a revolution in how it is raised and managed, public-sector finance is unlikely to be an appropriate resource for service and housing provision for the majority, or even any significant fraction of the population. The macro-economics of how currently poor countries become richer tend to be determined by trade terms and the flow of international finance, which are largely outside the remit of this Global Report. The following sections discuss how improvements can be made in how governments, municipalities and service providers raise and manage their resources; but only major restructuring can remove the underlying causes of urban servicing and housing shortfalls – the effect on poorer countries of the inequalities in global resource distribution.

Balancing local, provincial and national financing

There are many ways to balance different levels of government, with services provision and responsibilities for such issues as housing, education, policing and many others residing in municipalities or provinces with more or less equal effectiveness. Incongruities, such as municipalities having most of the duties but provinces receiving most of the revenue, fundamentally affect the ability of households living in poverty to improve their circumstances.

The needs of local government bodies to raise revenues are expressed in many different ways, and it is not the purpose of this report to recommend a single way forward. However, the balance of argument seems to favour municipalities being able to raise at least part of their revenue from local taxation, at levels which reflect local conditions. As a consequence, municipalities and governments need to build the institutional capacity to levy and collect these taxes, and to spend them responsibly. Indeed, legislation may be necessary to guide the responsible use of municipal revenues.

Importance of a municipal capital financing fund

It is vital that there is some source of loans for capital projects to which municipalities can apply to allow them to develop major projects that cannot be financed out of annual budgets. There are many models. Funds may be made available through loans from central government or an agency thereof, a mortgage bank, a finance company, a provincial-level institution, or a group of municipalities working cooperatively. Such an institution can be used for raising and passing on grants and loans from commercial banks and/or multilateral and bilateral funders. If there is central control, care can be taken that the projects funded fit into a national strategy; but smaller municipalities may miss out in favour of larger, more internationally competitive, cities. However, local discretion is required so that municipalities can compete and work on managing local differences to their advantage.

Debt swaps

Just as protecting endangered environments can be funded through debt swaps, so such exercises can be used to fund housing and urban services, as shown in the case of Bolivia described in Chapter 3. As in many other financing arrangements, having a poverty reduction strategy paper (PRSP) in place that influences urban policy enables debt swapping in that it gives the parties confidence that the money will be spent within a strategy for poverty reduction rather than *ad hoc*.

Betterment levies

The rising value of urban land is a significant potential source of finance for cities. It is argued that landowners who benefit from the increased value of their land as a result of its conversion from agricultural to urban uses, or as a result of the provision of infrastructure, should contribute to the costs of new infrastructure from their 'windfall' gains. This revenue could finance interventions to increase access to land for the poorest groups. Extracting public value out of the development process has been practised in many countries, some with great success. The US linkage process, in which city authorities leverage funds from the profits derived by developers of real estate to fund social projects, might be effective in cities in the South.

Improving tax collection

As a means of increasing revenue for a municipality, it is important to actually collect the taxes and revenues to which it is entitled from those who are liable to pay. Many municipalities have abysmal records in collecting taxes and service charges. To enable this to improve, there is a need for:[2]

- up-to-date information on who should pay (this should be in a form that is easy to access; many municipalities will need assistance to change from outdated paper methods to computerized record-keeping – this is especially important for property taxes, but is also applicable to market traders' and hawkers' licences);
- transparent charging structures adhered to during collection and recording;
- efficient collection methods with regard to reaching all who should pay (ranging from cash daily to monthly or annual bank standing orders);
- career progression prospects and other reward systems for tax and charge collectors so that they have incentives to collect efficiently;
- effective penalties for those who do not pay, especially those who exploit positions of power to escape payment; and
- appropriate means to keep tax levels in line with inflation and changes in costs.

Strengthening property tax systems

Transparency and efficiency of tax collection are particularly important

The above characteristics of currency of records, transparency and efficiency of collection are particularly relevant with respect to property taxes where systems are often poorly provided with records, where tax levels appear arbitrary and have not kept pace with property values, and where taxes are inefficiently collected. The level of accuracy required in land records for collection of property taxes is lower than that for avoidance or resolution of land disputes. Thus, such systems as half cadastres and the use of regular low-resolution aerial photography can provide a level of accuracy well able to support property taxation systems at relatively low cost compared with an expensive, high resolution land survey. Where available, geographical information systems (GIS) and satellite imaging can provide an ideal basis for property tax records. Tax levels and payment records could be seeded into one layer of a GIS dataset, with access limited to tax collection staff as appropriate.[3]

It is also important that the tradition of allowing informal settlement occupants to free-ride on the property tax base should be abandoned. The dilemma that this presents of taxing people for occupying land that is not recognized as theirs to occupy, and from which services are withheld for that reason, should be addressed instead of continuing to ignore it. In Egypt, the link between taxing and regularizing has been broken, and residents of peripheral settlements pay up in exchange for receipts that provide them with documentary evidence of occupation. Other locally appropriate solutions are required elsewhere.

Managing borrowing and debts

There is a need for municipalities to raise capital and there are several methods in use around the world. However, many have become severely embarrassed by debt-servicing burdens. Debt management is a field in which there is an urgent need for capacity-building within local authorities in rapidly developing countries.

Adjusting charges for local services

It is important that municipalities are paid economic charges for their services. Thus, functions such as land registry, building regulation and planning control should be subject to a charge that covers the cost. This is essential if the institutions are to survive and attract high-quality staff on progressive career paths.

Similarly, user fees for municipal services (markets, abattoirs, car parks, transport interchanges, bus services, assembly halls, etc.) should cover life-cycle costs and, where appropriate, generate revenue. Where concessions are to be granted, this should be done through demand-side interventions, such as tokens for low-income users supplied centrally rather than by compelling the service to give supply-side concessions to some users. The exchange of recyclable waste for transport tokens in Curitiba, Brazil, is a good example of a method of granting concessions while maintaining the profitability of a transport system.

Improving maintenance to reduce expenditure

It is important that municipalities are paid economic charges for their services

In many cities, there is a culture of replacing regular maintenance with irregular capital projects. Rather than annual road repair cycles, keeping them up to standard, roads are allowed to disintegrate over a few years and are then rebuilt using capital funds, often sourced through ODA.[4] It is better practice to cost infrastructure over its whole life (life-cycle costing) and put aside money for periodic maintenance over a long life. The savings are considerable compared with rebuilding at the end of a short life. In this way, low capital cost solutions that involve expensive maintenance or have short life can be avoided in favour of those with a lower life-cycle cost, even though their initial capital costs are higher.

There are also gains to be made from servicing costs through maintenance. When New Delhi loses 40 per cent of its water through leakages and unauthorized connections,[5] there are obvious savings to be made through following up leaks and stopping them. New technologies, including in-pipe monitors, which reduce the inevitability of major leaks escaping attention are now available. More efficient use of the current water flow will also delay the need for, and limit the size of, new reservoirs and other major capital investments.

Private finance

Private-sector finance is probably the most important engine for urban development

Private-sector finance is probably the most important engine for urban development, providing large shopping malls and corner shops, high-rise apartments and informal housing. However, it cannot keep pace with demand, especially where there is insufficient profit to make it worthwhile for outside investors to participate (that is, most housing developments). Foreign direct investment (FDI) is vital in most countries; but in all regions, it averages less than 6 per cent of gross domestic product (GDP).

One of the most important segments of the private sector in financing shelter is the domestic (household) economy, in which households save money and invest incrementally in their housing and the services around it. Not only will this improvement affect the dwelling and its water, sanitation and energy services, it will also affect the supply of shops, social facilities such as crèches, schools, clinics and employment opportunities. It is likely that this will continue to be a vital part of shelter supply and should be encouraged as a matter of priority. The ability of the small-scale private sector to run local supplies of water, waste collection and other services in partnership with the public authorities is well documented and should be explored by municipalities not already using such partnerships.

Improving the efficiency of resource use

Multi-year programmes and budgets

Just as life-cycle costing is important to maintain the momentum of maintenance,[6] planning budgets ahead of the next financial year also allows for programmatic investment. As stated in Chapter 3, multi-year capital investment planning has proved very successful in Szczecin, Poland, as the city carried out a programme of transformation during the 1990s. The confidence established through the medium-term planning allowed the city to leverage non-municipal resources for its capital investment programme, which could be adopted in many other cities to improve efficiency.

Participatory budgeting

Where municipalities in Brazil have implemented popular participation in budgeting, four key features have been introduced in the budgeting process:[7]

1. representation of residents through popular assemblies;
2. accountability by officials;
3. transparency, with open voting; and
4. objectivity in prioritization – for example, through a quality-of-life index.

Participatory budgeting has changed the dynamics of citizen–municipality relationships from confrontation and corrupt political bargaining to trust and constructive engagement. Its success depends, however, upon there being sufficient funding to give people participating in the process some hope that they will see improvement in their own lives, as well as those of others.

Government as creditor of local authorities and service providers

It has become almost established practice for governments and their agencies to delay payments to municipal councils. This is also the case for service providers who may wait years for government ministries to pay for electricity, water, waste disposal and other services. The service providers may have little ability to use their usual tactics to ensure payments. For example, when a prison is disconnected from the water supply, inmates may die of dysentery. The minister of prisons is unlikely to tolerate disconnection of supply and the water authority will continue supply even without the bill being settled. Multiplied by the many other ministries – and good reasons for not cutting off supply – arrears build up to unsustainable proportions. Similarly, if government fails to pay the agreed proportion of municipalities' revenues on time, or the property taxes on its premises in a city, it impoverishes local government. When changes in levels of cost chargeable for service delivery are ordered by government, it is quite likely that funding for the service will not increase. Even where governments recognize the importance of local government through devolution, these practices are all too common.

Such exploitation of its position by central government should be stopped in the interest of effective local government and service provision. Similarly, municipalities should pay service providers on time and at the levels agreed.

Eliminating corruption

Wherever it occurs, corruption saps the ability of central and municipal governments to meet the needs of their constituents through diverting money away from the development and maintenance of services.[8] The eradication of corruption would allow greater benefit to be passed on to people living in poverty, instead of benefits simply passing into the hands of small elite groups. Not only could international finance perform more effectively, but people trying to obtain small loans would receive better value, and all cases in between could be more effective per unit of finance involved.

International advocacy – such as through the United Nations Convention against Corruption, the work of Transparency International in, among others, publishing the annual *Global Corruption Report*, UN-Habitat's Global Campaign on Urban Governance and the World Bank Institute's theme on governance and anti-corruption – are all steps in the right direction. However, only when real progress is made on making corruption simply unacceptable in business and government, and involving people in eradicating it wherever it is found, will the vicious cycle be broken.

Reducing the cost of urban services

It is likely that government funding can have the greatest effect if it is directed towards infrastructure and services for low-income neighbourhoods and welfare services for the poorest. In the provision of land, basic infrastructure and social services to the poor and poorest, subsidy is likely to be required unless the cost of services is low indeed. Public taps, public toilets and neighbourhood waste collection points have all been utilized to reduce cost per household. However, there are often seemingly insuperable problems arising from maintenance and payment when such services are shared among many people. A mid point at which services are shared among a limited group of people who all know each other, especially those who live in a multi-occupied house of the type common in cities in Nigeria and Ghana, may provide a means of sharing without the usual problems of public services.

Enhancing households' willingness and ability to pay

Income and employment

Unless urban areas can produce more income at the same rate that they absorb more people, per capita incomes will fall and urban poverty will deepen. Thus, employment and income are central to the financing of urban development. It is, therefore, vital that employment and economic opportunities are available for as many people as possible in the cities. Improved income allows people to better afford services and to achieve more choice in their housing. Housing and service provision present important potential for employment.[9] The potential of shelter provision to generate employment for low-income workers should be utilized to generate income to improve people's ability to pay for housing. The income multipliers (the number of times income circulates in the local economy before being saved, paid in tax or spent on imported items) are very high for construction and even higher for low-technology, labour-intensive construction.[10] In addition, backward linkages (in which economic activity is generated in other sectors) and forward linkages (in which the building is used in generating economic activity either in equipping and maintaining it or by using it for work) are also high in construction.[11] Thus, the very activity that the housing finance allows is capable of generating further wealth and economic development very effectively, largely concentrated in low-income households.

Improved income allows people to better afford services and to achieve more choice in their housing

In parallel, the provision of efficient infrastructure and appropriate shelter is critical in ensuring the economic productivity of the work force in urban areas and countries as a whole. Although it is very difficult to demonstrate empirically, it is intuitively evident that where people are well housed, they can be more productive. In addition, workshops, offices and other workplaces need good service connections. Where workplaces are in or adjacent to the home, services to residential neighbourhoods are additionally important for employment and productivity. Thus, investment in urban infrastructure and shelter are essential components of national economic success.

Reducing transaction costs

Local governments should reduce the costs of economic activity by streamlining land allocation, development control and other regulatory activities while retaining appropriate ability to act in the public good. Municipalities should carry out audits of their regulatory procedures and reduce their complexity for the user. One-stop shops allowing planning and building control to be streamlined are capable of radically reducing the transaction costs of development and encourage more people to take the formal development route. Despite high initial set-up costs, record-keeping on GIS and other electronic systems can reduce bureaucratic complexity in addition to their primary task in land registry, urban planning and infrastructure planning.

STRENGTHENING THE SUSTAINABILITY AND PERFORMANCE OF SHELTER FINANCE SYSTEMS

There is both a need and a demand for different types of finance for different sectors of the housing supply process. Mortgage finance, for relatively large sums over a long period of repayment, is essential for those well off enough to buy a complete formal dwelling. However, small loans, taken out over short terms of between one and eight years, loaned at market rates, are growing in importance in the housing sector, as shown in Chapters 6 and 7.

Reducing housing costs

The problem in many developing and even in some developed countries is not that housing is too expensive but that incomes are too low. It should be noted that in many countries housing is very inexpensive in international terms and it is difficult to significantly reduce the cost any further. The real problem is that incomes are too low. As seen in Chapter 2, more than 60 per cent of the population of South Asia and sub-Saharan Africa survive on less than US$2 per day. Thus, the locus of attention should not only be on the minimum quality and cost of housing, but also on the level of payment received by workers. This demand-side focus is in line with current trends in subsidies and concentrates attention on the systemic problem of poverty, which is responsible for generating poor housing conditions.

The problem is not that housing is too expensive but that incomes are too low

In many countries in the South, the cost of urban housing is increased significantly by the high standards to which it must comply. The standards in force often specify the use of building materials and components that use imported materials and/or inputs. This not only increases the cost substantially, but also necessitates expenditure of scarce foreign exchange. It is often the case that these standards are either a colonial legacy or have been adopted from a foreign context, and are therefore of little practical relevance to the prevailing socio-economic situation. The introduction of lower standards that are more appropriate to the local context could potentially make housing more affordable to a far greater proportion of the urban population. Lower standards would still, however, have to safeguard the health and safety of the occupants and protect the public interest.[12]

Enabling household decision-making through more effective policy

The context of shelter provision can be summed up thus: households will make housing arrangements that they can afford for the amount of their income that they are willing to spend on housing. This may vary through many household circumstances, including:

- spending the occasional dollar on bribing a policeman to allow them to sleep in a sheltered place on the pavement;
- renting an un-serviced room in an informal settlement;
- spending about half the household's income on the rent of a flat so that they can have a secure base in the city;
- building a shack in a land invasion on the edge of the city;
- after years of saving, engaging a builder to construct a cement-block dwelling in an informal settlement; and
- using a mortgage to buy a formal dwelling in a fully serviced area.

Although there may seem to be an upward income gradient from the first to the last of the above circumstances, this may not be the case as the old idea of households devoting a fixed amount of their income to housing is no longer plausible.

Housing decisions depend upon the proportion of income that a household is willing to spend and how they are willing to spend it. Thus, destitute households may choose to pay for a room in a shack or may prefer to sleep rough and use the rent money another way, including sending it back to their home village. Similarly, households who could easily afford a formal-sector dwelling may choose to stay in an informal settlement and use their money to put a child through college overseas. A similar household may choose to own a large informal dwelling rather than a small formal one, or to stay in the squatter settlement among friends and business clients rather than move to better housing on the periphery, or any of a multitude of circumstances. All households need a policy environment in which these choices can be taken and sustained.

Addressing the need for rental accommodation

Most policies behind ODA and national policies are based on the provision of independently serviced, single-household dwellings, owned by their occupants. However, this is by no means the main form of occupation by households living in poverty. Instead, large numbers of households live in buildings occupied by many households. These may be, at the upper end of the market, spacious fully serviced apartments or, at the lower end, houses with many households sharing services and having a single room each.[13] Except for their development by entrepreneurs for sale or renting, there is little finance available for co-operative construction and ownership. For example, tenants wishing to redevelop their tenements (*chawls*) in Mumbai had to become involved in 'black' money to finance the project because of restrictive rules over selling prices.[14] There is much to be gained from encouraging multi-occupied housing development where it fits in with local norms. If someone is willing to build accommodation for many people, financing conditions should take account of rental income or the combining of many incomes to assess the scale of a loan for construction.

Small-scale landlords in informal settlements are a major source of affordable housing for a growing majority of households living in poverty in the urban South; but there are few initiatives to assist them.[15] In many cities, over half the population live in such settlements, and the proportion of those occupying rental accommodation is increasing by the day. Evidence from past experience shows that *in situ* upgrading to improve access to water supply, sanitation and other basic urban services often results in higher rent levels. When this happens, there is little to prevent displacement of poorer tenants by higher income households. The former, consequently, have to move to another settlement where living conditions are less satisfactory but within their means. It is imperative, therefore, to understand how best to assist the informal rental sector, and at the same time to preserve affordability in order to preclude gentrification (see Box 9.3).

Contractor financing

In the spirit of the Habitat Agenda, and if the housing backlog is to be cleared at all, it is vital that all actors in the housing process are involved in the role in which they are most efficient. The most important suppliers of the dwellings themselves, and their ancillary services, are the millions of small-scale building contractors, the single artisans or small groups of skilled people and the labourers who service their needs. However much demand there is for housing, it can only be supplied as quickly as the construction industry can build it. The small-scale contractors take on most of the work but are ill equipped to operate efficiently because they are underfinanced. It is far too common for a client to have to pay the workers and buy the raw materials because the contractor cannot even borrow enough money for a week's work ahead of payment. For the same reason, technological improvements are slow in coming – even the smallest power tools are unusual on small-scale construction sites.

The resources provided in the past to self-help builders involved in sweat equity consolidation should now be provided to those individuals who do not stop when they have built a single house for their own use, but who will go on to construct several each year for the rest of their career as contractors.[16] Finance to provide healthy liquidity among small-scale contractors and single artisans is an essential prerequisite to effective housing supply to scale. Unless finance and other assistance are available, the contractors, whose efforts build vast swathes of our cities, are unlikely to be able to adopt efficient methods of employment, material purchasing and customer payment schedules. Neither are they likely to adopt tools and technologies appropriate to their making best use of local materials and labour conditions. Suitable finance is urgently needed to allow them to buy tools and materials, and to pay their workers for periods before being paid for a job, and to retain them between jobs. They are likely to be able to pay market rates for loans, so there is no need for tax revenue to be expended in helping them to make better profits (see Box 9.1).[17]

Development of 'developers'

In countries where the housing supply system is efficient and speculative of what the market demands, developers are often an important part of the process. In this sense, developers are not builders. Instead, they are investors who locate and buy land, engage and brief designers, gain permissions and infrastructure provision, engage and supervise contractors, and sell the completed properties. They drive the process of housing development, especially when it uses private-sector funds.

The process of development can be taught, typically at management schools, but is also one that some people can do instinctively. However, they need finance for their risky, but often highly lucrative, business. Some mechanism for recognizing their contribution with financial assistance, especially for bridging loans, may be very beneficial for the housing supply process and could institute the efficient speculative building of housing that is common in industrialized economies.

Box 9.1 Pitfalls of providing financial support to private developers in India

The following is a cautionary tale from Ahmedabad in India where the state housing finance company funded a large private developer to build low-income housing. Although the developer was well known for its cost-cutting low-income housing, its involvement with officialdom and the expectations that built up in the customers caused severe problems and drove the developer out of low-income development. No longer able to cut corners with regard to land acquisition and finishes, and under pressure to use the secure tenure land for higher income groups, the developer cut down on the cheaper dwellings to make more profit from better-off clients. This example of a large contractor being assisted in carrying out a very large contract provides some caution for helping small contractors, mainly with regard to the changes wrought by enabling secure tenure and providing government agency imprimatur. Most of the problems found in the Ahmedabad case would be avoided by arms-length loans from commercial banks to small-scale contractors. Self-interest-orientated and opportunistic behaviour from each of the actors in the housing process, rather than naively hoping that everyone will act for the common good, should be expected.

Source: Mukhija, 2004a.

Reducing financing constraints and risks

Where the housing supply system is efficient, developers are an important part of the process

Financing informal development

Following a long history of increasing acceptance of the validity of informal development and that which does not conform to prevailing high standards, it is easier to finance the informal housing development efforts of people living in poverty now than it was 20 years ago. There is still a need, however, for a pro-poor enabling policy environment in which households living in poverty can obtain secure land tenure and build housing within their affordability range. Recent research into regulatory frameworks for urban upgrading and new housing development has recommended the removal of constraints that prevent the poor from borrowing from financial institutions or accessing credit through other formal channels. In particular, administrative procedures that delay investments and/or increase risks should be reviewed as they add to the cost and deter the poor from conforming.[18]

Savings and debt

The countries in which most of the urban growth will take place in the next 25 years have very low domestic savings, measured as both per capita and as a percentage of GDP (13 and 14 per cent, respectively, in South Asia and sub-Saharan Africa). As savings are the foundation for investment, this does not auger well for urban development. These countries are heavy with debt, especially external debt to public and private institutions in developed countries. Many of the countries, especially in sub-Saharan Africa, are unable to offer the environment required by private investment and must rely upon ODA and loans from international development agencies.

There is a need for a pro-poor enabling policy environment

It is important that developing countries maintain as much of the investment and savings arising from local economic activity within their borders or benefit from net inflows from investments overseas. In many countries, assets are stripped out as profits are stored in foreign exchange in Swiss or other Northern banks, or used to buy property and education in the North in a way that does not lead to benefits back home. Such capital flight contributes to investments in shelter and infrastructure in Europe or America, but not in cities at home. It is difficult to overstress the importance of reliable banks and low inflation in discouraging capital flight.

Improving the accessibility of mortgage finance

Mortgage finance, in the sense of long-term fixed or variable interest rate loans sufficient to buy a whole dwelling when combined with a deposit, is helpful to the middle- and upper-income groups in most societies. It is in governments' interests to extend mortgage markets down the income scale since homeownership is beneficial economically, socially and politically. Measures adopted have included:

- reducing the cost of lending, especially through lowering interest rates;
- supporting the system of mortgage financing, especially through extending secondary markets and reducing risks; and
- direct capital grants to reduce the size of the household's mortgage in comparison with the dwelling cost.

Some governments are still heavily involved in mortgage finance; but experiences vary from great success to embarrassing failure. In the transitional countries, national housing funds offering loans to lower income groups have become very popular.[19] In addition, some Southeast Asian countries have major government housing finance programmes. The Thai Government Housing Bank lends to about 40 per cent of homeowners. It offers some lessons in:

- making loans to lower income groups at lower rates subsidized by higher rates charged to higher income groups; and
- offering fixed rates to borrowers for three to five years to reduce their risk.

The Thai government uses housing development as part of its economic strategy and is willing to stimulate its economy through shelter development.[20] The Philippine government also has the role of primary lender for housing and has helped nearly 1 million households into homeownership between 1993 and 2003. Even so, the number of households not served and living in informal housing grows, and this must be noted while attempting to use mortgages to reach low-income groups.[21]

There are examples, particularly in Latin America, where mortgage companies have arrangements to reduce risks in lending to the informally employed, particularly through establishing a savings record before the loan is granted and the lender is willing to receive repayments out of normal banking hours.[22]

Secondary mortgage markets have been successful in providing funding outside the 'borrowing short, lending long' cycle of deposit funding. In the US, Europe and transitional countries, secondary mortgage markets are in place or are being set up. They are also being instituted in many countries in Latin America and Asia, sometimes with multilateral donor support. The limited experiences with secondary mortgage markets in developing countries allow some conclusions to be drawn:

- Keep it simple – success is more likely with simple bonds and simple forms of secondary mortgage instruments.
- Macroeconomic stability is essential.
- There must be demand from housing finance providers for secondary mortgage market funds.
- Investors must want longer-term financial arrangements.
- Standardized mortgages simplify pooling for selling on to the secondary lender.[23]

Within the fraction of the population for whom they are helpful, mortgages inevitably lead to issues about land tenure and the need for long-term security, even freehold, owing to the lenders' need to be able to foreclose and liquidate the asset in the case of default. The importance of legal property titles for developing sound economies cannot be overemphasized.[24] In itself, the need for secure tenure disqualifies hundreds of millions of low-income households from mortgage finance. Providing secure tenure for the poor is seen to be a key to opening the door to leveraging household expenditure on the dwelling. A recent study shows that willingness to invest in housing is likely to be over 30 per cent for owners with secure tenure, but no more than 15 per cent for those with poor tenure or renters. Less than full title may be sufficient, however, and even beneficial in that it may reduce raiding by higher income groups. Many microfinance institutions do not use title deeds as collateral; therefore, secure land title is not a prerequisite.[25]

Nevertheless, not all experience has supported the idea that legalizing land holdings leads to a greater availability of some of the benefits of capitalism, including bank finance. Many countries have no loans for people wishing to buy existing low-income housing. For example, resale of formal housing in South Africa's former 'black townships' is hampered by a lack of suitable loans.[26] It must be remembered, however, that many cultures and urban circumstances preclude the development of a market in second-hand housing; once bought or built, low-income housing is rarely sold.[27]

In Peru, many squatters without title deeds were improving their settlements in the confidence that they were secure; but only 1.3 per cent of the 1.25 million households who had obtained legal title were applying for mortgage loans.[28] The link between investment and legal security seems much more tenuous and localized than is often argued. Indeed, other characteristics may be more important, such as lack of formal employment, transaction costs, and, vitally, low income in comparison with the cost of a dwelling.

Even where they can gain access to it, long-term lending implicit in mortgaging may be very unsuitable for low-income households as they are unlikely to be able to keep up an unrelenting stream of payments over many years owing to irregular incomes or external circumstances, such as economic recession leading to unemployment and/or increases in interest rates. Mortgages tend to have substantial transaction costs that can put them outside the affordability of most households. There is a need to reduce such costs.

Well-run mortgage facilities are undoubtedly important to the health of the housing supply system in the North and may be a major contributor to housing improvement in transitional countries. They are also important in providing upper- and middle-income groups with housing finance, without which they would claim the shelter provision directed at those lower down the income scale. However, the introduction or continuation of mortgage schemes in developing countries must not be thought of as a way of financing more than a minority of households' need for shelter.

Since mortgage finance is unlikely to assist the majority of the people, it must not be allowed to divert attention from financing that is helpful to lower income groups, or to drain resources away from low-income households towards those in the middle- or upper-income groups. In the past, it has commonly done this in several ways. Perhaps the most influential has been when governments have supported mortgages in order to stimulate the formal building industry and improve homeownership rates, especially among their own power base. However, such supported mortgages have, typically, underperformed on numbers, especially those directed towards even the higher echelons of the lower income majority, and have transferred large sums from the majority to the better-off minority. Even in developed and transitional countries, mortgages redistribute resources from the poor to the not so poor where there is government assistance in the form of tax relief on interest payments (as there still is in France) or any other concessions for mortgage holders. Where such transfers occur, they are usually much greater than any direct subsidies offered to support low-income housing and are insupportable on equity grounds.

In transitional and developing countries, it is not unusual for governments to subsidize interest rates on mortgages, or to fix rates arbitrarily so that the mortgage lender cannot maintain liquidity. A further significant concession is the tolerance of large amounts of arrears from borrowers. Although they only deal with relatively well-off households and eschew moving down the market because of fears of default, many mortgage companies have relatively poor loan recovery rates. In sum, in the South, mortgages should avoid blanket concessionary interest rates, tax relief and tolerance of arrears as these all favour the better off at the expense of the poor. Their political sponsors should also be clear that they in no way assist the poor majority.

Terms of housing loans

Loan periods and loan-to-value ratios (LTVs) are vital components of mortgage loans that are determined by the lender rather than the global macroeconomic environment. Decisions about them can be the difference between success and failure of the mortgage company and can determine who can afford to borrow, at least at the margins. Low LTVs (and, therefore, high initial deposits) reduce risk but increase the need for upfront capital. However, the UK Department for International Development (DFID) experience in Indore shows that a low LTV may simply drive borrowers into the clutches of dealers in unsecured, high-interest loans to cover the gap between price and formal loan, greatly increasing risk of default and impoverishment of the borrowers through high monthly payments.[29]

The level of repayments can be varied to help households meet their obligations. Variable-interest loans allow low payments at the beginning, increasing as income improves to repay the loan on time. Loan repayments can be linked to cost of living, with payments indexed to minimum wage levels. All 'save now, pay later' programmes such as these, however, are vulnerable to economic fluctuations that adversely affect household incomes.

Well-run mortgage facilities are undoubtedly important to the health of the housing supply system

The price of housing

In some contexts, recent rises in housing prices compared with incomes and other prices have occurred. Particularly sharp rises have transpired in Australia, Ireland, Spain and the UK.[30] The picture in the developing world is, however, less easy to determine and may not present the same rise in property prices against others. There was an understanding that it was becoming more difficult to own a dwelling during the 1980s and 1990s; land was no longer available free for the invading. This was accompanied by an assumption that housing was more expensive than before, which was not dented by the early housing indicators results that showed very high house cost-to-income ratios in many countries.[31] However, detailed studies in Ghana gave no support to this idea that households need to be better off now in order to be owners than they had to be in the past. They demonstrated that recent owners were no better off than more established owners and that, although prices had risen sharply, they were not out of step with other price rises and those of incomes from all sources.[32]

Recognizing the need for incremental loans

The majority of housing in developing countries is developed incrementally in stages, separated by many months or years. In new building, this is usually implemented a room or a few rooms at a time; but it may, less commonly, occur in construction stages (for example, all the foundations, followed by all the walls, etc.). In the ongoing process of consolidating and improving an existing dwelling, or replacing worn-out materials, there is investment in newer, stronger and more durable materials – perhaps dismantling a wood-and-tin structure and replacing it with bricks and tiles. It is imperative that national and international institutions recognize that low-income people build incrementally and provide microfinance suitable for that process. This may also call for reform of building regulations that often do not allow incremental building in formally recognized dwellings. Currently, they rarely tend to legalize a more incremental approach even if it is planned to produce a fully compliant structure in the end. Thus, it is time to remove the assumption that a single process will complete a dwelling and to accept the reality of incremental building over many years so that lending can be tailor-made for incremental construction.

There are many incremental activities that add to the housing stock, and extension activity is one of the most important. A study of extension activity in former government estates in four countries found that finance had been the most important problem facing extenders; but most had coped despite having to pay cash.[33] Household income characteristics had relatively little influence on the decision to extend, but they did constrain what was actually built. Larger and better-quality extensions could be built and the process could be much more efficient if suitable loans could be raised to allow one or two rooms to be added efficiently and without delay. Short-term, small-scale loans, on one-year to eight-years loan terms and in amounts of US$500–$5000 are more useful for incremental development than the long-term, large value loans favoured by the mortgage markets.

Experience shows that there is great demand for microfinance

Improvements and efficiency gains possible through incremental building with small loans, rather than with savings, include:

- greater likelihood of building well (though on a small scale), building immediately and avoiding high annual maintenance costs arising from poor construction;
- avoiding the wasteful process of improvising a dwelling in temporary materials and then discarding them as they are replaced with permanent materials; and
- reducing the age at which a householder can afford to be an owner as stages do not have to wait for money to be saved but can be paid for in arrears.[34]

Problems regarding the valuation of incrementally constructed dwellings may be avoided if building cost, rather than resale value, is taken as the measure for valuation.

Lending based on the idea of housing as a productive good

There is a well-documented link between finance for income generation and improvements in housing. Many homeowners operate one or more home-based enterprises from the structure on which they raise housing finance. In their household portfolio, such enterprises are important as a contributor of about half the household income, on average, or all the household income for a large minority of operators.[35] Without the home-based enterprise, the household would not be able to afford the house. Many such households should have their home-based enterprise income-factored into the loan affordability criteria.

The same goes for rental income. One of the most important sources of low-cost rental property, which is becoming more important as the years pass, is the extra room built on to a home and rented out to a stranger for rent, or to a co-villager or relative for no rent but for some other benefit (if only to satisfy family obligations).[36] Such petty landlord behaviour is very common and often involves an owner who has a lower per capita household income than the tenants.[37] In societies where rents approximate to a good return on capital investment, such activity can increase a household's ability to pay for housing, and plans to rent out rooms should be factored into their affordability calculations when considering a housing loan. The buy-to-let loans available in the UK may be a model for this.

Many of the large microlenders are quite sanguine about their enterprise loans being used for improving housing. It is obvious that improvements in housing can benefit home-based income generation, including room rentals. Thus, lenders should take account of the likelihood of income improvements in the application procedure through a process which factors in future income generated by the housing goods to be provided under the loan.

Enhancing pro-poor formal housing finance systems

It is important that financiers recognize that the poor are more concerned about access to credit than its cost. Experience shows that there is great demand for microfinance even if interest rates are high. Interest rate ceilings distort the lending environment, as do forgiveness of arrears and default, as well as subsidies. Since housing is a productive asset for many low-income households (30 to 60 per cent of housing finance clients have a home-based enterprise), borrowers are able to service their loans.[38]

A hospitable macroeconomic, financial and regulatory framework is necessary for the development of sound and sustainable housing finance institutions. In Bolivia, freedom from unfair competition from a state-run bank and temporary waiving of regulations helped financial providers to become established.

Subsidies

In the past, subsidies were the accepted way to help the poor. The theory was that if goods could be cheaper, people living in poverty could afford them. Thus, reducing the price would make housing more accessible to the poor. However, this did not work out as planned. As the subsidy increased real cost to the government, only a few could be provided in comparison with the need or demand. The scarce subsidized dwellings were then rationed – vertically, by being only available to some income groups, and horizontally, by being in insufficient quantities to serve all who qualified. This was further distorted as the subsidized housing tended to be captured by households who were not living in poverty, but who had influence or were regarded as 'deserving' through some criteria other than income. These criteria may be income neutral, for example, having lived in the city for a time, or involve some indirect income redistribution, for example, by numbers of dependants (redistribution towards the poor) or by having secured a loan (redistribution away from the poor). Indeed, subsidies rarely reach the poor.[39]

Subsidies come in many guises, including:

- direct interest rate reductions;
- allowing mortgage interest payments to be deducted from income tax;
- supporting housing-related savings;
- supporting insurance of mortgages;
- supporting the secondary mortgage markets; and
- direct grants for shelter.[40]

The last can be through housing allowances paid with salaries, a mark-down of the house purchase price, or the provision of a bundle of shelter benefits at cut price or free.

Subsidized loans are still offered by many governments, including Brazil, Hungary, Mexico, Panama, the Philippines, India, Tunisia, Thailand and many more. However, to qualify, a household must be able to afford the loan. This may disqualify a majority of the population from benefiting from the subsidy and increases inequity. Subsidies offered by governments tend to prevent the development of a commercial market, not only in loans but also, in extreme cases, in house building. Indeed, free government housing offered to citizens in the oil-rich Gulf States can even reduce the quality of the current housing stock through allowing the older stock to fall into disrepair in order to qualify for new housing.[41]

Interest rates are often subsidized to increase affordability – indeed, some ODA finance has been used to fund interest rate subsidies. However, this has been seen to be both unsustainable at a large scale or in the long run and to redistribute income towards the upper-income groups. However, market rates may be so high (perhaps above 20 per cent per annum) that they make it impossible for all but a very few households to afford repayments, leading to political pressure to reduce rates through subsidies.

Subsidy is a function of the failure to afford the market price of shelter solutions. If appropriate housing finance is in place, the proportion of households requiring subsidy should be minimized to only those too poor to afford the real cost of the shelter available. The need for subsidy can, thus, be reduced by adopting effective financing systems.

The work of some non-governmental organizations (NGOs) in providing funding for the individual's contribution to attract a subsidy is very helpful to many households. In Ecuador, a revolving fund provides the down payment necessary to obtain a national housing subsidy grant. NGOs in South Africa, such as the Kuyasa Trust, lend money for improvements to be made to housing provided by the subsidy programme. Although the amounts per household are often quite small, such loans are frequently pivotal in providing improved housing to low-income households. The Community-led Infrastructure Financing Facility (CLIFF) in India provides grants so that professional help can be acquired to help communities 'package' projects in a way that will attract loans from banks and draw down applicable subsidies from state authorities. Then, CLIFF bridging loans are granted to slum development projects so that initiatives can start while negotiations go on with formal finance institutions and public officials. Housing finance institutions should be vigilant for such opportunities to enable target groups to benefit from their entitlements.

Box 9.2 Hogar de Cristo, Chile

> *Hogar de Cristo is a non-governmental, non-profit, Church institution, whose mission is to provide appropriate and loving shelter to the poorest among the poor and, particularly, to the helpless aged, to the homeless, to the terminally ill and irrecoverable who lack any form of support, and to children and youths who are abandoned, excluded and lacking in opportunities. It also seeks to generate an awareness of the real extent of the problems of the poor in order to encourage drives to relieve them, and to denounce what can be solved.*[i]

Founded in Chile over 50 years ago, and featuring many programmes to help the poor, Viviendas Hogar de Cristo (VHC) has grown into a major provider of wooden sectional housing to the poor. Its Ecuadorian branch produces 100 dwellings daily from bamboo, which it grows in its own plantations. Seventy-seven per cent of its beneficiaries have incomes of less than US$20 per month. About half are widows or female single parents.[ii]

The overall costs of the house are US$450; but there is a government subsidy of US$144 (US$4 per month for three years). The client has to pay US$186 through payments of US$4–$5 per month. If they pay at the VHC office, the client can simultaneously receive medical attention and lunch for themselves and their youngest children, subsidized by the government. They can pay with their social welfare of US$11 per month or with other income. Some are supported by VHC's charitable funds.

Currently, VHC has 16,000 clients, of whom 80 per cent pay every month; some even pay several months in advance. Only 1 to 2 per cent of clients are regarded as permanent defaulters.

Notes: i Hogar de Cristo, undated.
ii Costa, 2002.
Source: INBAR, undated.

Social housing

Social housing is, almost by definition, subsidized housing. As stated earlier, the reasons that governments subsidize shelter include improving fairness and social stability, especially in ways that do not occur through market mechanisms. The subsidy element is a financial credit to the occupier and, thus, often constitutes an important element in a nation's housing finance system. Many countries have followed the example given by several European countries during the early 20th century in their large state rental sectors. Former colonies inherited systems of social housing from their respective colonial powers.

The subsidy element is a financial credit and, thus, often constitutes an important element in a nation's housing finance system

In Europe, recent shifts from government as provider to government as funder has reduced the level of its risk,

Box 9.3 Low-income rental housing: encouraging self-help landlords

Few developing countries have in the past put in place incentives to encourage private landlords to develop or improve the quality of rental housing. A recent review proposes the following ways of encouraging self-help landlords to create more and better rental accommodation for low-income households:

- **Providing subsidies to poor owners, or poor private landlords, who create living space for others.** If landlords are as poor as their tenants, equity objections to this approach do not present a problem. Subsidies could also be in the form of tax relief, the difficulty being, of course, that very few small landlords pay formal taxes.
- **Building rental incentives into upgrading programmes.** Planners and managers of slum upgrading programmes should take the needs of tenants into consideration and encourage homeowners to increase the supply of rental housing by, for example, offering credit or subsidies. Good examples of this approach are the Plan Terrazas Programme in Colombia, implemented in the 1970s in the cities of Medellin, Cali and Bogotá, as well as the more recent Mawani Squatter Resettlement Programme in Voi, Kenya.
- **Providing microcredit for self-help landlords.** The idea of extending credit to informal sector landlords is now widely recommended, particularly since the emergence and rapid growth of shelter microfinance during the last decade. Governments should also encourage banks to move into the low-income housing sector and to lend to landlords wishing to enlarge or improve their rental properties.
- **Modifying planning regulations.** House extensions are often discouraged by planning regulations on maximum use of plots. In addition, the projected impact of densification on the supply of urban services is often used as a reason for prohibiting owners from adding rental rooms to their existing houses. Incorporating rental housing into upgrading programmes or encouraging its development in upgraded settlements may therefore require some modifications to existing building regulations.
- **Reassuring self-help landlords.** Existing and potential landlords often feel threatened by government policies that either give tenants the right to claim a house that has been rented to them illegally or that do not sufficiently protect them when tenants fail to pay rent. The adoption of rental regulations that protect the rights of both landlords and tenants, subject to the housing meeting specified minimum standards, will go a long way in encouraging landlords to invest more in rental housing. Governments and local authorities could also facilitate use of standard written lease agreements and establish mediation and reconciliation tribunals to address tenant-landlord disputes.
- **Application of more carefully designed rent control measures.** Many governments have in the past used rent control measures to achieve housing affordability. Unfortunately, such measures have often turned out to be inequitable and inefficient, as they tend to distort market values. They have also tended to discourage good maintenance, as they often rendered rental housing unprofitable, and have sometimes been applied in a haphazard way. Where it is necessary to apply rent control measures, care should be taken to avoid these negative results.

Source: UN-Habitat, 2003c

but has not removed the necessity for government to be involved in housing for lower income groups.

Although social housing is becoming residual in Europe and transitional countries, the need to provide more housing that is affordable to low-income households is still present. Those who cannot afford homeownership or market rents in the private market need shelter through public rental housing. In the South, however, few countries have been successful in large-scale public rental housing. It is unlikely that any country which does not already have a considerable stock could successfully develop public rental housing as a major component of housing supply during the 21st century.

Building for occupant ownership, either in whole or combined with a housing association or some other not-for-profit partner, is practised in some countries – for example, Brazil, South Africa, Chile, Colombia, Costa Rica and India – with reasonable success, but still carries the problem of how to target subsidies and how to reach the low-income group that is the target population. The effective target group is those who have been described as 'moderate and middle income households'.[42] Reaching the lower income groups is especially difficult when considerable contributions are required from the recipients or the move into the formal sector involves paying taxes and service charges, where none were required in their previous, informal, neighbourhood. Costa Rica seems to have reached the target population most effectively through collaboration with an active NGO sector.[43] NGOs, especially faith-based organizations, appear to be better at targeting the poor than governments. Hogar de Cristo (Hearth of Christ) has been particularly effective with simple timber dwellings; but other successful programmes are often featured by the Latin American and Asian Low-income Housing Service (SELAVIP) in its newsletter.

Incentives for investment in low-income rental housing

As pointed out in Chapter 5 and earlier in this chapter, most low-income shelter policies and programmes in developing countries focus on promoting homeownership, in spite of the preponderance of rental housing among urban poor households. While little attention has been paid to rental housing in the past, there is now increasing recognition of its importance to the many urban poor households who cannot afford homeownership. Box 9.3 summarises some of the ways that have been proposed to support self-help landlords, who are the suppliers of most low-income rental accommodation in developing country cities.

Small loans and housing microfinance

As stated earlier, the links between housing finance and income generation are many and should be taken into account in policy-making.[44] Numerous agencies offering housing microfinance may require housing borrowers to have a successful credit record on enterprise loans before raising a housing loan. This also has the advantage that enterprise loans are likely to increase income and, therefore, the ability to repay the larger housing loans. Indeed, some microfinance institutions (MFIs) came into the housing loans business because it was acknowledged that house improvements to enable more effective home-based enterprises were a valid use for their loans.

Small housing loans, disbursed through housing microfinance institutions (HMFIs), are some of the most promising developments in housing finance during the last decade. They are suitable for extending existing dwellings, building on already serviced land, adding rooms (often for renting out), adding services such as toilets, and housing improvements within *in situ* neighbourhood upgrading. Only in a few cases – for example, from the Grameen Bank in Bangladesh – are they intended for land purchase because secure land is often a prerequisite for collateral. They tend to reach much further down the income scale than mortgage financing, but not to the households close to or below poverty lines.

Small loans are seen as a way of lifting many low-income households out of the necessity to build their housing with cash or savings. As pointed out earlier, the incremental building process, carried out in a cash-only context, tends to begin with poor-quality materials that need replacing repeatedly and demolishing when the next stage of construction is carried out. This is a wasteful use of resources and expensive in relation to the total investment. Small loans, even when the market rate is quite high, provide the capital to make incremental building more efficient through more durable materials earlier in the process. Repeatedly borrowing small amounts is good for a household's credit rating and imbues confidence in lenders and their guarantors. Fully secure tenure has not been found to be essential for improving housing through microfinance, as highlighted above.

In the context of large numbers of new low-income households in cities over the next two decades, it is important to increase the number of lenders in the housing microfinance sector rather than to concentrate only on mortgage finance which, inevitably, serves the middle- and upper-income groups. Many HMFIs have come in from enterprise-focused microfinance as it is a simple 'next step' and the commercial advantages are evident. Currently, housing microfinance tends to be a small portion of the current business of enterprise MFIs; but they are growing quickly. Their loans tend to be small and short term, reflecting their enterprise loans and a reluctance to saddle the poor with much debt.

However, there is room for other financial institutions, governments, NGOs and community groups to be involved. The number of HMFIs is very large – there are between 400 and 500 in India alone – but their reach is currently quite small. A recent study in India reports that HMFIs reach no more than 2.5 million of the 60 million households in need of microfinance.[45]

There is a serious issue of funding for on-lending by HMFIs. Many have received concessionary funds and their lending reflects the low price of the capital. If they are to expand their operations, they will need to cope with borrowing at international market rates and to reflect this in their loans.

HMFIs may charge very high interest rates. For example, the very successful Mibanco MFI in Peru launched Micasa for housing microfinance, which lends at between 50 and 70 per cent per annum.[46] Some MFIs that offer housing microfinance charge lower interest rates for the housing loans than for their enterprise loans. Where concessionary finance can be accessed, however, interest rates can be lower than the market would dictate. Where MFIs (even large ones such as the Grameen Bank in Bangladesh and the Self-employed Women's Association, or SEWA, in India) receive preferential loans from governments, they can keep interest rates and costs as low as possible to reach as far down the income scale as possible. This could be a very effective use of government subsidies and is a good reason to divert them from mortgages and other finance, which is more difficult to target to the low-income group.

There are cogent arguments about why HMFIs should operate without subsidies, especially so that they can expand as the market allows. Where subsidies are made available, they should be through capital grants or service provision, rather than through interest rate discounts or the tolerance of arrears.

Housing microfinance is an important potential resource for increasing the rate, scale and quality of housing supply. Small loans should be incorporated within policy in a number of contexts, as follows:

- loans to improve and extend existing units, to supply services within the dwelling, and to add rooms for more generous domestic space or for renting out or for active home-based enterprises;
- loans linked to land development, whether it be led by private enterprise, NGOs or government;
- loans linked to developments for which a capital subsidy is payable; and
- loans linked to neighbourhood upgrading and available to improve the dwellings affected.

Housing microfinance is an important potential resource for increasing the rate, scale and quality of housing supply

In comparison to enterprise microfinance, however, these are long-term and large loans, and they generate a need for group security or some security of tenure backed by documentation. Some microlenders only offer housing loans to those who have had enterprise loans and have successfully established a credit rating through their payment history. Others gain a lien on pension funds, future income or movable assets; or require savings, sometimes at a monthly level of payment equivalent to the loan repayments, for a year or so in advance; or accept group or co-signers' guarantees. These mechanisms address different sectors of the low-income population, small entrepreneurs and formal-sector workers, demonstrating that a palette of acceptable collateral methods could cover just about everyone.

In the context of group lending, mandatory savings periods before loans are issued not only build up an understanding of finance, but also strengthen community ties among savers through regular group meetings. Then the group becomes the collateral as the members will support each other in times of difficulty and take the complication of following up defaulters away from the lender.

There is a need for an international exchange of experience about how different forms of collateral perform with regard to default levels and feasibility of recovering value in case of irredeemable default.

The issue of default among low-income borrowers

While it may seem self-evident that lower income borrowers are more likely to default on their loans than those with higher incomes, the evidence does not support this. In contrast, many housing microfinance agencies achieve very low levels of default, indeed. The repayment rates can be further improved by flexibility in where and when payments are made. Travelling banking vans visiting low-income neighbourhoods, banks which are open outside office hours, repayments through local supermarkets: all these and others can assist lenders to minimize defaults and encourage borrowers to keep up with their payments.

The Kuyasa Fund in South Africa has an innovative way of dealing with defaults. It uses the same means as the furniture hire-purchase companies so familiar to its clientele: it sends in bailiffs to take possession of household goods, such as televisions and furniture in distraint until housing repayments are up to date again. It does not, however, repossess the home since the result of this could be catastrophic.

Habitat for Humanity International, which gives interest-free loans through grants from Christian institutions in the North, relies upon group pressure to ensure that individuals keep up with their repayments. It also does not repossess dwellings from defaulters.

Guarantees

Notwithstanding the above, guarantees are important in broadening the appeal of housing microfinance to lenders as they will look for ways of reducing their risks, even though the lowest income groups tend to be assiduous at repayment. The catalytic value of guarantees is evident in the Dharavi housing co-operative process, in India, in which a formal housing finance company (the Housing and Urban Development Corporation, or HUDCO) would only lend when an NGO (the Society for the Promotion of Area Resource Centres, or SPARC) guaranteed the community's repayments. This is being continued in a wider context through CLIFF, which has a guarantee fund to reduce banks' perceived risks in lending to groups of low-income people. The National Urban Reconstruction and Housing Agency (NURCHA) in South Africa guarantees a portion of loans at a cost of 2 per cent of the portion covered. In the absence of government action, some NGOs have sufficient institutional capacity to act as guarantors for community groups.

In many circumstances, the establishment of formal guarantee organizations is an important prerequisite to lending. Governments have much to gain from setting up guarantee funds to allow HMFIs to lend to low-income households at reduced risk. ODA should be directed towards them so that the full value of guarantees as catalysts for shelter development can be captured for low-income groups.

Widening the scope of housing microfinance

There has been comparatively little government involvement so far; but some recent developments in Colombia and Peru demonstrate that there is a great potential for central and local government to channel housing funds through small loans. Voluntary-sector organizations often find their efforts hampered by the lack of funding on which they can draw. Funding from below, such as from savings associations and rotating savings and credit associations (ROSCAs), is mostly inadequate to the task (Indonesia's Bank Rayat Indonesia, or BRI, and India's SEWA are major exceptions). Funding from financial agencies is often lacking because of the default risk perceived by the potential funder even though actual defaults can be shown to be low. Medium-term funding is required and tends to be in short supply. Some HMFIs resist government involvement, while others welcome it. There is scope for governments to consult HMFIs and to respond in an appropriate manner as to whether their financial backing would be welcome or not.

Credit for building materials

Throughout the days of sites-and-services projects and other aided self-help, efforts were made to reduce the financial burden of low-income homeowners by allowing materials to be drawn from dedicated warehouses, or to be supplied on credit through local commercial suppliers. Recent experience in Mexico and elsewhere has shown how there may be great potential for this to expand alongside housing microfinance and the downscaling of mortgages to lower income households, using the longstanding credit culture operated by furniture and household goods retailers.

Remittances

Remittances from overseas residents of local nationality are an important part of housing finance in numerous countries. Many people can remit enough to build a house in a few years overseas in quite lowly employment, which would be impossible if they stayed at home in higher level employment. Indeed, in countries such as Ghana, remittances have been a substantial contributor to housing supply for at least 20 years.[47] In many African cities, it is often only the 'been-to', '*wa-Benzi*' and 'burger' (former expatriate) populations who can afford palatial housing, alongside their peers who have become rich through opportunism. This is good news for a country's gross fixed capital formation; but there is a danger that tastes, standards and ability to pay from a different context take over the local markets and drive other residents into poorer housing than they would otherwise have. In Ghana, formal-sector housing developments in Accra are likely to be sold to residents of London and Hamburg and are way above the prices that Accra residents can afford.

The role of charity in low-income housing

Some of the initiatives that have been successful in reaching households living in poverty have had considerable funding from charity. Many charities give large amounts of money towards housing improvement and shelter for the poorest. Habitat for Humanity International augments such monetary support with volunteering, recruiting groups of short-term volunteers, mainly from the North, who offer free and enthusiastic labour for a week or two in exchange for a feeling of doing something of worth and seeing an unfamiliar country at first hand. There has recently been a flurry of charitable support for shelter and urban development following the tsunami in Asia in December 2004.

There is a place in funding shelter for the poor for that which arises from altruistic humanitarian support. However, there is a need to target such support towards those who need it most and to avoid reinforcing dependency. Most charities would probably admit that, however hard they try, they do not always manage this as well as they would wish.

Strengthening community-based funding mechanisms

Community-based financing of housing and services has been used for both settlement upgrading and for building on greenfield sites. In a context where small loans are evidently successful and where there is an increase in poverty, it has many advantages for low-income and otherwise disempowered households. It provides the benefits of scale – strength in lobbying, the ability to affect neighbourhoods comprehensively, rather than just single dwellings, and the ability to raise capital funding – and it builds the cohesion of the community because its members act together. It takes strength from the willingness of people to work together as communities through traditions such as *gotong royong* in Indonesia.

The experience of the affiliates of the Shack or Slum Dwellers' Federation (SDI) has demonstrated that there is great potential for community-based organizations to manage development finance to the benefit of large numbers of relatively poor households. Community-based funding is focused on the comprehensive development process, not just on raising finance. Through cooperation in this way, low-income households can raise finance and influence policy, even changing by-laws, in a way unthinkable if they acted individually.

Through the growth in community-focused NGOs, particularly the SDI network, development funds are now regularly directed towards community initiatives. Grassroots organizations demonstrate a high degree of ownership of improvements achieved through channelling assistance directly to their members and neighbourhoods. They have achieved high levels of added value and low levels of drop-out and default. They have been effective in directing existing funding sources and maximizing the direction of subsidies to their members.

If community-based funding is to be successful, the following must occur:

- NGOs should act as intermediaries with funders and assist in providing links with local authorities, government departments, local funding institutions and other stakeholders. In some cases – for example, the Build Together programme in Namibia – this role is taken by a government or quasi-government institution. The appropriateness of this will vary among countries and hinges on the balances between such characteristics as funding, control, influence and independence.
- A guarantor should safeguard funding so that financial institutions feel confident enough to lend.
- Decision-making should be decentralized and funds disbursed to community-based organizations (CBOs).
- Community organizations should be able to act as legal entities. This, in turn, requires a history of working together, which is often achieved through savings groups.
- Finance sources should exist to augment savings and local resources.
- There must be help for prospective borrowers to take the smallest loans over the shortest period possible, or not to borrow at all. This is contrary to conventional banking practice where the assumption is to maximize the loan.
- Stable interest rates should continue through the life of the loan as low-income households can be severely affected by upward fluctuations in payments. This increases the appropriateness of short-term loans since they are less vulnerable to interest rate fluctuations over time.
- Care must be taken not to lend so that a household has total debt repayments of more than 25 per cent of income.
- Technical advice on infrastructure installation and house improvement should be provided. When offered free, this becomes a subsidy. SDI avoids this subsidy element by encouraging group exchanges where a successful community group in the network shares experience with newly established groups.
- Policy on defaults is vital as some community funds experience serious default levels – for example, the Community Mortgage Programme (CMP) in the Philippines has 61 per cent of its accounts more than six months overdue.[48] In serious cases of group money being embezzled, peer review has been used in India where the NGO involved will send one community in to investigate another. This may be impossible in many cultures.

Community-based funding is focused on the comprehensive development process

Working in groups allows communities to negotiate cheaper building materials, to buy land in large plots for subdivision, and to install infrastructure without the piecemeal, wasteful approach inherent in individual connections. The long period of community loans may prove to be a problem, however, especially with the issues of fixed interest rates and ensuring continuity of committed leadership over periods of up to 25 years.

The evident success of community funds has attracted some governments to take part in their financing. The

Philippines Social Housing Finance Corporation is a good example. Community funding tends to benefit from a number of funding sources, including members' savings, ODA, government grants and subsidies, bank loans, short-term credit from suppliers and contractors, and leveraging of property values through development rights transfers. Often, subsidies can only be accessed by a group.

The expectation behind the CLIFF programme is that community groups of low-income households will be able to establish enough strength and creditworthiness that they will be able to negotiate loans directly with banks.

Nevertheless, there are issues about how far non-members of such community groups are excluded by the activities of groups who so successfully lay claim to limited resources. Are the groups simply capturing rationed benefits at the expense of the majority in the same way that the middle- and upper-income groups have done for decades? Even if benefits are potentially open to all comers, in reality, most benefits are rationed because of limited budgets. In this context, those who successfully receive benefits reduce the chances of others. Similarly, where groups negotiate particularly favourable terms – for example, in low interest rates – they may exacerbate the intrinsic rationing. In economies of shortage, there will be winners and losers. How it is determined whether particular groups win or lose should be as transparent as possible, and measures should be taken to remove obstacles and give everyone as near an equal chance of benefiting.

Care must be taken not to transfer problems that would happen at government or municipal level down to a community level where they may be more difficult to control. For example, community group leaders are probably as likely to act factionally or to defraud funds as are national politicians and officials, but social pressures may inhibit criticism or censure. Community groups formed around confronting or negotiating with state bodies may find resolving sensitive internal conflicts beyond their ability.

Savings are now seen as not only one of the most important prerequisites for obtaining finance, but also one of the most effective ways of building social cohesion in neighbourhoods. They are central to housing microfinance and community funds. The savings process can be used to:

- Establish lender confidence in the group of borrowers, thus reducing risk in the transaction. The ability of prospective borrowers to save consistently over several months is a valuable measure of reliability for the lender.
- Equip communities with the cohesion, skills and consciousness to engage with the state over the distribution of resources and regulations in order to gain better tenure, services and housing.
- Form the groups to which land is allocated, subsidies granted, funds loaned and infrastructure provided.
- Build an understanding of the management of money.
- Set up internal funds for lending to those in greatest need or going through crises.

Where regulations limit the establishment of savings groups, careful attention should be directed to whether they can be withdrawn so that the benefits arising from community savings groups can be garnered.

Interest rates are often subsidized for community funds; but this is likely to reduce their sustainability and ability to expand to cover most people living in poverty. The balance of advantage arising from such subsidies should be kept under review, especially with regard to whether the recipients are drawn from the poorest households.

NOTES

1 This chapter is based on a draft prepared by Graham Tipple, University of Newcastle upon Tyne, UK.
2 UN-Habitat, 2004.
3 UN-Habitat, 2003a.
4 Satterthwaite, 2000.
5 Sharma, 2005.
6 Ashworth, 1993.
7 See Chapter 3 for detail.
8 UN-Habitat, 2003a.
9 UNCHS/ILO, 1995.
10 UNCHS/ILO, 1995.
11 Klaassen et al, 1987.
12 Payne and Majale, 2004.
13 Or, even further down the market, shared dormitories with 'hot beds' slept in by several people in a 24-hour period. Tipple and Willis, 1991; Schlyter, 2003.
14 Mukhija, 2004b.
15 UN-Habitat, 2003b.
16 Tipple, 1994.
17 This is similar to the experience in Malaysian developments, where higher income dwellings can only be built in developments including a certain percentage of low-income dwellings. The contractors build the more expensive ones and then neglect to build the cheaper ones.
18 Payne and Majale, 2004.
19 Hegedüs, 2004.
20 Kritayanavaj, 2002.
21 Ballesteros, 2002.
22 Joint Center for Housing Studies, 2004.
23 Lea, 2000; Chiquier et al, 2004.
24 De Soto, 2002.
25 Malhotra, 2003.
26 Nell et al, cited in Baumann, 2004.
27 Tipple and Korboe, 1998; Gilbert, 1999.
28 Calderón, 2004.
29 See Chapters 6 and 7 for detail.
30 IMF, 2004.
31 UNCHS (Habitat), 1993b.
32 Even though formal-sector salaries appeared to be lower. Tipple et al, 1999.
33 Tipple, 2000.
34 The mean age of becoming an owner in urban Ghana, where no incremental housing finance is available, is in the late 40s. See Tipple et al, 1999.
35 Tipple, 2005.
36 UN-Habitat, 2003b.
37 UN-Habitat, 2003b; Tipple, 1991; Tipple et al, 1999.
38 Tipple (2005) suggests that 25 to 40 per cent of households may be a reasonable comparable figure in low-income neighbourhoods as a whole. Since many loans are connected with home-based working (for example, SEWA) and others tend to be offered to clients who have had micro-enterprise loans before (such as the Banco Sol and the Grameen Bank), these could influence the high frequency of home-based enterprises among borrowers.
39 Hoek-Smit and Diamond, 2003.
40 Hoek-Smit and Diamond, 2003.
41 Al-Mansoori, 1997.
42 World Bank, 2004c, p8.
43 Ferguson, 2001.
44 UNCHS/ILO, 1995.
45 Biswas, 2003.
46 Ferguson, 2002.
47 Diko and Tipple, 1992.
48 Ballasteros, 2002.

TOWARDS SUSTAINABLE URBAN SHELTER[1]

Among the issues addressed in this *Global Report on Human Settlements 2005* is the financing of shelter for the urban poor. This focus is but the latest manifestation of a broader concern that has been at the centre of the preoccupation of social activists, reformers and public authorities since the dawn of the Industrial Revolution, when the issue arose of providing humane living conditions to workers and poor families crowded in the rapidly growing cities of Europe. The same issue has become one of a global nature after the concept of 'human settlements' found its place in the international development agenda as one of the main challenges facing countries experiencing similar processes of rapid urbanization, but without the resources to provide adequate living conditions to their low-income urban populations.[2]

Until recently, the classical response to the shelter problems of the urban poor was social housing, both in developed and developing countries. However, the massive demand for affordable housing in developing countries, coupled with the limited resources of the public sector, would have made this solution inapplicable, even in the presence of a well-organized and transparent public housing delivery sector. Notable exceptions were states such as Singapore, which implemented huge and very successful public housing programmes, as well as successful policies in other larger countries such as Tunisia and isolated exemplary projects in many others. By and large, however, social housing was abandoned. Unfortunately, none of the alternative solutions developed during the 1970s and 1980s proved capable of addressing the problem. Sites-and-services programmes, for example, simply lowered shelter standards without reaching the scale required. In the absence of adequate solutions, and with city authorities being incapable of guiding development or preventing uncontrolled growth, shelter delivery for the poor was largely left to 'spontaneous', informal mechanisms.

The notion of 'financing shelter for the poor' corresponds, in a way, to the abandonment of the traditional concept of public responsibility embedded in the 'social role of the state'. With the commodification of the economy, where housing is but another good to be produced, sold and bought, the solution to the shelter dilemma is based on the notion that 'the poor' will always exist, and that their access to a fundamental human need, adequate shelter, will always require special measures and special solutions. At the same time, this premise implies that there will always be a category of citizens who will never, on their own, have access to decent shelter – hence the need for special approaches and solutions aimed at 'helping the poor'.

> The classical response to the shelter problems of the urban poor was social housing, but the massive demand for housing, coupled with the limited resources of the public sector, would have made this solution inapplicable

This Epilogue starts from the premise that 'special approaches' and *ad hoc* solutions, however ingenious, will never work at the scale required. Three points are made. First, the percentage of the urban poor in the cities of the developing world is far too high to be considered a residual issue. Second, the demand for affordable shelter is increasing at an extremely fast pace, notably in the rapidly growing cities of the developing world.

Third, the standards and costs that city life requires are high and complex. Shelter is only one, albeit the central, requirement of all citizens. Given the rapid spatial growth of cities in the developing countries, transport, for example, becomes a crucial necessity for survival. The living, working and spatial circumstances of city life require standards and services for all that are far superior in quality and sophistication to those usually associated with minimal shelter – a roof over one's head.

The definition of 'adequate shelter' in the Habitat Agenda alludes to the multiple and complex characteristics of minimum standards in an urban setting:

> *Adequate shelter means more than a roof over one's head. It also means adequate privacy; adequate space; physical accessibility; adequate security; security of tenure; structural stability and durability; adequate lighting, heating and ventilation; adequate basic infrastructure, such as water supply, sanitation and waste management facilities; suitable environmental quality and health-related factors; and adequate and accessible location with regard to work and basic facilities: all of which should be available at affordable cost.*[3]

This definition highlights the idea that all citizens should be able to afford adequate shelter, as described. Affordability goes beyond the ability to secure some form of tenure – that is, a title of ownership or rental of a legal dwelling unit. It also means the capacity to hold on to this asset through a regular source of income, to pay taxes and utility user fees, as well as to absorb recurrent costs of maintenance.

Given these considerations, the issue is not simply financing shelter for the poor. The issue is making adequate shelter affordable to the poor. This approach may be called 'sustainable shelter': shelter that is environmentally, socially and economically sustainable because it satisfies the Habitat Agenda requirements of adequacy. Its acquisition, retention and maintenance are affordable by those who enjoy it. It does not overburden the community with unaffordable costs. Finally, it is located in areas that do not constitute a threat to people or to the environment.

There is no single magic formula to achieve this. Individual self-help can only produce solutions that are admirably suited to the harsh circumstances of urban migration, but are also the most fragile of all. Community-based funding has proven a valuable and indispensable asset, particularly for improving services and, in some cases, infrastructure in informal settlements; but it is not likely to reach the scale required, at least in the short term. It must also be noted that the admirable solidarity mechanisms found in poor urban communities stem from the common will to stave off a common threat, often rooted in a state of illegality and a risk of eviction. They also depend upon the cultural and ethnic composition of the informal settlement. Strongly desirable and supported outcomes such as regularization, infrastructure upgrading and the improvement of economic circumstances can also bring the attenuation of community solidarity and mutual self-help mechanisms. Therefore, they cannot be assumed to work in all cases and for indefinite periods of time.

One of the major inadequacies is the inability of the market to provide adequate, secure housing at affordable prices for poor people

At the opposite end of the spectrum, one of the major inadequacies is the inability of the market to provide adequate, secure housing at affordable prices for poor people.[4] There is no need for sophisticated analysis to prove this argument. If this were not the case, 43 per cent of the urban population of developing countries would not be living in slums – an indicator that is estimated to be as high as 78 per cent in the least developed countries. It is interesting to note, in this regard, that the private sector does not ignore the poor – it simply provides housing only when circumstances make it profitable. In many slums, shacks are built by private investors on public land illegally appropriated by them to extract rent from the poor. Many argue that this kind of housing market, thanks to the rapid turnover of the 'investment', can be even more profitable than formal housing. Often it is the connivance between private interests and unscrupulous public authorities, rather than humanitarian concerns, which permit the consolidation of informal urban settlements and the perpetuation of their fragile tenurial balance between silent acquiescence and sudden forced eviction.

Other informal shelter delivery systems found everywhere, but particularly in Latin America, are illegal subdivisions. This is also a thriving market, where private landowners cut out tracts of land in small lots to be sold to low-income families. The occupants own their land, but still in a situation of illegality, often with insufficient infrastructure. There, two examples of 'unsustainability' are found: an individual one, due to the illegality of the settlement; and a public one, as municipalities are eventually forced to bring necessary infrastructure to settlements that were never meant to be developed for residential purposes.

Ironically, neither example presents a problem of 'financing' or 'affordability'. Rental fees in slums accurately reflect the maximum affordability level of slum dwellers: if this were not the case, this particular market would not exist. The prices of plots in illegal subdivisions are tailored to the affordability levels of the buyers, while investments in layout and basic infrastructure are kept to a minimum to maximize profits.

So far, the unsuitability of two kinds of existing mechanisms – informal and 'legal'– for providing sustainable shelter has been highlighted. The first one is unsuitable because it is 'affordable', but not adequate. The second – conventional housing built by the private sector – is adequate but not affordable. What solutions can then be found for sustainable shelter for the poor – including the two basic components of adequacy and affordability?

Slum upgrading is the solution offered to make 'affordable shelter' adequate. This solution has been championed by all international agencies and is strongly supported by the United Nations Millennium Project Task Force on Improving the Lives of Slum Dwellers. It is seen as a necessary and humane remedy to consolidated situations where the urban poor have created communities. The main argument is that the costs of regularization and upgrading to be borne by society can be largely offset by the benefits that can accrue to the residents and to the city as a whole. There are many elements of sustainability involved in this process. One of them is that regularization and the granting of secure tenure creates a sense of security and a solid justification for self-help investment in the improvement of housing and its immediate environment. Therefore, investment in regularization and physical upgrading releases important resources on the part of the residents. Moreover, it creates hope and self-esteem, which are the basis for expanding small business activities and, in turn, for generating higher income. With increases in income, residents can begin to afford basic utilities (water, electricity and solid waste management). With time, therefore, at least part of public investments in basic infrastructure can be repaid and the delivery of services and utilities can become more sustainable. Upgrading also achieves two important objectives: it allows more successful residents to be able to access the conventional housing market, and it eliminates demand for other sites suitable for low-cost housing, which can therefore be reserved for new residents and low-income in-migrants. Therefore, the two solutions advocated by the task force – upgrading and the development of assisted self-help housing on greenfield sites – are mutually reinforcing. Existing slum dwellers are given the option of not encroaching on new land, and new city dwellers have an alternative to squeezing in already overcrowded informal settlements.

Ultimately, the affordability question hinges on costs and real demand. Therefore, a good starting point is to act on all the elements that make adequate housing unaffordable to the poor, keeping in mind that the whole enterprise is an oxymoron of sorts: making adequate shelter an increasingly expensive commodity, affordable to people who, at best, have only enough to survive on a daily basis. Making adequate shelter affordable to the poor has two requirements: reducing housing production and delivery costs and increasing income levels. These are examined in succession.

FIRST ELEMENT: ABATING HOUSING COSTS

Housing is becoming an increasingly expensive commodity in all countries. As in other socio-economic areas, information and data are more readily available for industrialized countries. Between 1997 and 2004, according to a very recent survey, average housing prices grew by 131 per cent in Spain, 147 per cent in the UK, 179 per cent in Ireland, 113 per cent in Australia, 90 per cent in France and 65 per cent in the US. The only developing country listed in the survey is South Africa, which registered the highest growth in the sampled countries: 195 per cent.[5]

Of course, these sharp increases in housing prices can, in many cases, be due mainly to speculative bubbles. But there is little that policies can do to prevent or control these phenomena. On the other hand, while average housing prices are lower in the developing countries, they are also influenced by steeply rising costs of land, building materials and other cost components.

Affordability, therefore, rests to a large extent on policies capable of bringing down housing production costs. Housing production cost components are known: capital, land, infrastructure, building materials, standards, design, location and modes of production. To be affordable, all of these elements will require a substantive element of subsidy; but in some cases they will only need intelligent policy changes. Some examples are offered below.

Capital

Activities that create wealth for the richer segments of the city population must be tapped in order to subsidize sustainable shelter. The obvious one is an important source of wealth in rapidly growing cities: the rapid increase in land values. Efficient collection of property taxes, as well as taxation of land and property transactions, is the basic capital resource that cities can tap in order to cross-subsidize social investment, including sustainable shelter. Subsidies of various types, in turn, can encourage the private sector to produce less expensive housing while still retaining a profit, the co-operative sector to expand its activities, and the community sector to play a larger role in what it does best – building cheap housing.

The report of the Millennium Project Task Force on Improving the Lives of Slum Dwellers argues that development aid will be necessary in order to finance part of the costs of slum upgrading and new low-cost housing. The difficult part is to justify it. This can be done if donors are made to perceive that aid funds for sustainable shelter are an investment, and not an expenditure. The fundamental argument here is that improving the lives of the urban poor and turning them into citizens by regularizing and improving their shelter conditions is the best investment in 'making cities work', which is a precondition for sustainable national development and, ultimately, the gradual elimination of aid as a necessary, and often major, component of many national budgets of developing countries.

One factor that still stands in the way of greater flows of development aid is the perception that the governance performance of most developing countries is too low to allow for external funds to be employed fairly and effectively. The Millennium Project argues that if the Millennium Declaration Goals, including improving the lives of slum dwellers, are to be met, there is no luxury of waiting for perfect governance to be in place. The important thing is for countries who want to receive development aid to give substantive signals that they are reorienting their budget allocations to the social sector. This can be done in many ways. One of them is the reduction of military budgets. Another, particularly important for the sustainable shelter agenda, is to increase budget allocations to the social housing sector. This does not mean massive public housing projects – although, as mentioned before, not all large-scale public housing projects have been a disaster – but, more generally, to develop nationwide enabling policies for cities, shelter and related infrastructure, as argued in *The Global Strategy for Shelter to the Year 2000*.[6]

Affordability rests to a large extent on policies capable of bringing down housing production costs

The argument for donor assistance to housing for the urban poor is implicitly confirmed by the fact that 'rich' countries have the same problems themselves. For example, one of the main conclusions of a recent report to the US Congress by the Millennium Housing Commission, released in May 2002, states that:

> *... there is simply not enough affordable housing. The inadequacy of supply increases dramatically as one moves down the ladder of family earnings. The challenge is most acute for rental housing in high-cost areas, and the most egregious problem is for the very poor.*

The same report highlights some of the built-in biases of domestic subsidies to owner-occupied housing. In the US, about 90 per cent of the total benefits of the mortgage interest deduction system accrue to homeowners with more than US$40,000 annual income. This observation is an important reminder of the need for subsidies to be concentrated on the neediest. This principle was stated clearly in The Global Strategy for Shelter to the Year 2000, which recognized that economic growth and the creation of well-functioning housing markets are not always sufficient to ensure that shelter conditions are adequate for specially disadvantaged households, and that such subsidies should be 'targeted' (designed to focus on, and reach, the people in need whom they are devised to help).

Land

Cities in developing countries still hold large tracts of unused land, both publicly and privately held. Although some efforts to avoid land hoarding for speculation purposes have proven unsuccessful, as in the case of the Land Ceiling Act of India, other countries have enacted legislation to encourage the utilization of idle urban land. This is the case in Brazil, whose 'Statute of the City'[7] recognizes the social value of property and provides disincentives for landowners who deliberately hold land, hoping to accrue unearned gain on its value arising from the investments of other public and private actors in urban development.

The task of planners is to identify suitable locations in the city for sustainable shelter development for the urban poor

Cities must engage, as a first priority, in identifying public land to be developed for sustainable shelter and related income-generating activities. Unused land is unused capital; but keeping land idle when half of the city's population is housed in appalling conditions and new potential slum dwellers are on their way is irresponsible. Paradoxically, the idea stems from the concept of 'sustainable slum': a greenfield site, preferably already owned by a public body or institution, developed from scratch, but retaining the same incremental characteristics that make informal settlements an affordable settlement solution for the urban poor. Accordingly, sites would be identified and reserved for sustainable shelter development, furnished with essential basic infrastructure and services, and used as a 'building platform' for minimal, low-cost housing solutions to be developed according to the principles of assisted self-help housing. The sustainability factor, in this case, would be guaranteed by the fact that the choice of the site would be governed by sound environmental criteria, excluding, for example, ecologically fragile locations and reserved sites, such as water catchment areas; by social criteria, as they would cater to the economic circumstances of the urban poor; and by economic criteria, as their development would follow principles of the most economic use of land and infrastructural investment. In fact, public sites can remain in public hands as long as their users are granted a long-term title for their occupation. Private land could also be used this way through a number of incentives: property tax exemptions, 'leasehold swaps', building rights vouchers, and rental fees subsidized by municipalities, government, donors, foundations and other stakeholders. Intelligent innovations for the use of public land can also have unexpected results. The United Nations Human Settlements Programme (UN-Habitat), in cooperation with the government of Finland, is testing an innovative approach in Kenya whereby part of that country's bilateral debt would be forgiven in exchange for the earmarking of a tract of public land of equivalent value for low-income housing.

Now is the time to establish realistic and reasonable minimal standards for sustainable shelter

Infrastructure and land-use planning

With sound planning, trunk infrastructure developed for upper- and middle-income housing and commercial development can be extended at marginal additional costs to nearby areas reserved for sustainable shelter for lower income groups. There could be nothing more intelligent and environmentally, socially and economically sound than locating sustainable low-cost shelter in the proximity of industrial and commercial areas. One must only think of the hours saved in commuting and the advantages for easing traffic congestion and pollution.

Upgrading does not leave the planner much choice as the task is dictated by existing functions in an existing location. But an equally challenging task is to plan ahead of development, instead of regularizing *post-facto* situations. The task of planners is to identify suitable locations in the city for sustainable shelter development for the urban poor.

As argued in *Investing in Development: A Practical Plan to Achieve the Millennium Development Goals*, the Millennium Project's overview report,[8] community-based slum upgrading and earmarking idle public land for low-cost housing is one of the 'quick wins' that need to be embedded within the longer-term investment policy framework of Millennium Development Goal (MDG)-based poverty reduction strategies.

Building materials

Assisted self-help housing is the most affordable and intelligent way of providing sustainable shelter. It is cheap because it is based on minimum standards and incorporates a substantive amount of sweat equity. It is useful because individuals and communities engaged in it acquire precious skills. It is practical because it responds to people's actual need and levels of affordability. It is flexible because dwelling units are often designed to be able to expand over time. But all construction, and particularly incremental upgrading, requires a suitable supply of building materials, components and fittings. These markets already exist and thrive in virtually every city of the developing world because they respond to a huge solvent demand. They have to be supported by the public and large-scale private sector because they abate housing costs and provide precious jobs and incomes.

Standards

For decades, UN-Habitat and other international agencies have recommended reforming building codes and standards in order to allow for housing construction that is affordable for the poor.[9] Now is the time for developing-country central and local governments to engage in sweeping reforms to establish realistic and reasonable minimal standards for sustainable shelter. This reform alone would cut housing production costs considerably and, equally importantly, legalize a huge chunk of the existing and future housing stock.

Regulations both for upgraded and new shelter should allow, and indeed encourage, the development of small-scale manufacturing and service activities in the home (such as tailoring and small repairs) and in workshops especially designed for the purpose, and all kinds of other activities that do not endanger public health (for example, kiosks, small restaurants and cinemas). Of particular value are all non-housing activities that can enhance the dynamism of any given settlement and encourage social interaction: they often constitute the best 'acupuncture' against boredom and crime.[10]

Design

Design is a cost factor that has also been neglected for too long. Often, large-scale, high-rise housing projects result in very high costs per unit because they entail high overheads and are a typical target for corrupt contracting practices. The scale, brutality and anonymity of the high-rise housing found in most developing countries also often accounts for social traumas in people and communities engaged in a difficult transition from rural to urban settings and accustomed to a more minute and 'horizontal' scale of human interaction. At the other end of the spectrum, non-assisted self-help housing can be cheaper in the long run, but can result in flimsy and hazardous construction. The happy medium are design practices that combine the skills and briefs of clients/users with the abilities of dedicated trained professionals (architects, engineers, planners, surveyors) and reconcile the need for an efficient use of land with human-scale design. Sustainable design can also help to identify the best and cheapest building materials and components and reconcile the needs for stability and durability with the imperative of efficient and low-cost construction solutions. Architects, planners and public-sector professionals from all over the world must be mobilized in this effort.[11]

Location

Although, as a rule, land and housing costs tend to decrease with distance from the city, it is important for sustainable low-cost shelter to be located as close as possible to the widest range and concentration of income-earning opportunities, which is found in or near the cities' central areas. This is why it is important for slum dwellers located in central and peri-central parts of the city to be able to hold on to their most important asset – consolidated settlement in a favourable location. This is the imperative of *in situ* slum upgrading, and this is why the retention of established settlers in centrally located informal settlements through regularization and upgrading is the best investment that public authorities can make in guaranteeing the economic survival of their poorest citizens. It is also possible to take advantage of lower land costs in parts of the city more distant from prime locations for greenfield development of low-cost housing, but only on the condition that such development includes good income-earning opportunities and affordable and efficient transport services.

Modes of production and delivery

Clearly, the final cost to the user also depends upon the mode of production and delivery of a housing unit. The cheapest form of housing, for example, is shelter built or assembled by individuals on a piece of land occupied without any formal title. This is the mode of housing production commonly found in the conventional slum. But its drawbacks are also well known – insecurity, lack of services and poor construction. This mode of construction is the cheapest available, but also the most expensive in terms of health and security. The most expensive mode of production, on the other hand, is standard and legal housing produced on a market basis. This kind of housing incorporates all the costs found in all contexts, developed and developing, including land, capital, various fees and construction, as well as the profit component. And by its nature, it is this mode of construction that is the least eligible for government subsidies.[12]

However, there are other modes of housing construction that, by their own nature, involve lower costs to the purchaser/user. One of them is self-help housing, which replaces built-in labour, time and resources employed in conventional housing with the labour, time and materials provided by its future occupants. 'Assisted self-help housing', which incorporates a large component of donor and domestic government technical and financial inputs is, in fact, the mode of production recommended by the United Nations Millennium Project's Task Force on Improving the Lives of Slum Dwellers as the best and cheapest alternative to new slum formation in the developing countries.[13]

Another successful approach is cooperative housing. This approach does not necessarily reach the poorest of the poor, but it does produce housing that is more affordable, by virtue of the elimination of the profit component and the advantage of government subsidies granted by law by virtue of its social nature. Its traditional form of organization is based on affiliation to the same trade or profession: often, however, the aggregation of cooperators can reach beyond affiliation and be based on kinship. This later element is a strong factor in creating a sense of community around the 'build together' concept. This important social asset is not found in conventional housing, which is bought, sold or rented on an individual basis.

Another mode of production, or delivery, is social housing. Traditionally, social housing involves the construction, with public funds, of low-cost housing units, usually as comprehensive projects, for rental to deserving low-income families. A recent report stresses the importance of rental housing as a far too neglected means of satisfying the shelter needs of lower income groups.[14] Social housing is built on the premise that public funds should be employed for the provision of housing to the neediest on a subsidized rental basis. This approach, however, has come under severe criticism during recent years on several grounds. One of them is efficiency. But it must be remembered that social housing – or public housing, or council housing, as it is known in different countries who pioneered it on a vast scale – historically drew its justification from different grounds. One of them is the sense of collective responsibility that nations felt towards the shelter needs of the less fortunate members of society. Other reasons were social stability, political support, public health and hygiene. And another was purely of a macroeconomic nature – the advantages of using large public funds to revive the economy, support the domestic construction and building materials sector, and create employment. Some of these factors still exist today, and it is, indeed, remarkable that social housing programmes have been virtually abandoned where people need them most – the developing countries.

Rental housing is important in terms of affordability

because it is particularly suited

to the economic circumstances of the urban poor

Rental housing is important in terms of affordability because it is particularly suited to the economic circumstances of the urban poor: lack of capital and lack of access to it. It is not surprising that in most slums, particularly in sub-Saharan Africa, the poorest of the poor are not owner occupiers, but renters. The solution here is to abate the costs of rental housing by devising a system of subsidies capable of stimulating the production of rental housing for the poor by accessing all possible and practicable avenues – built-for-rental housing; housing purchased or built as an income-producing asset; housing built by companies for their workers; and social housing.

The urban poor could not be reached without abating housing production costs and reducing the price of sustainable shelter

So far, a variety of approaches that can help to abate housing production costs and reduce the price of sustainable shelter to the target client – the urban poor – has been discussed. However, sustainability also has to do with the increase of purchasing power. The higher the disposable incomes of the urban poor become, the wider will their access be to housing markets. The next section addresses this second element of adequate shelter affordability strategies: increasing the purchasing power of the urban poor.

SECOND ELEMENT: INCREASING PURCHASING POWER

Is this goal too ambitious? The 2003 issue of the *Global Report on Human Settlements* offered some prudent scepticism:

Making shelter affordable to the poor depends upon increasing the poor's income

> *It has to be remembered that slums have always been part of market societies. In the long run, the goal of cities without slums is only going to be achieved in a predominantly market economy once a good majority of the urban work force has middle-class incomes. How to achieve this major aim of development is rooted in controversy and is somewhat beyond the scope of this report.*[15]

A recent observation portrays one of the many slum families in New Delhi.[16] A shack, about 2 metres long and 2 metres wide, is home to a family composed of husband, wife and four children. It is just one of 7700 such shacks in a street behind the residential area where the mother of this family works as a domestic help. Her husband is a plumber and her children study at a nearby government school.

The striking aspect of this situation is that the wife holds a steady job, and her husband has a skill that is considered to be highly rewarding in industrialized countries. Yet, they are forced to live in a shack with considerably less than 1 square metre of space per household member. By the same standard, a small 100 square metre apartment in a rich country could hold roughly 150 people – all of whom, however, would enjoy the considerable advantage of protection from the elements, a well-functioning communal toilet, the luxury of running water and electricity, and protection against forced evictions (at least as long as public health officials did not report the intolerable overcrowding condition of that particular dwelling unit).

The circumstances described above are very similar to those experienced by the vast majority of the more than 900 million slum dwellers all over the world, whose adult members often hold jobs or rely upon some kind of regular revenue-generating activity. In the developed world, a household with two sources of income, wife and husband, however humble the occupation or the source of income may be, normally can gain access to decent shelter on the market, however modest. In the developing world, this is virtually impossible – hence the virtual necessity of finding affordable inadequate shelter in a slum. People who live in slums are known as 'slum dwellers'. In reality, they are 'working poor': people who work for a living, but whose income cannot guarantee them access to the basic needs that everybody in developed countries take for granted – adequate shelter, proper nourishment, health, education and decent and non-threatening living environments.

The Delhi example shows that there is something terribly wrong about the inability of the working poor in developing countries to gain access to adequate housing. Part of the problem is the rising costs of conventional housing addressed in the previous section; but an equally important issue is the extremely low income in both the formal and informal sectors. This is why making shelter affordable to the poor also depends upon increasing the poor's income.[17]

The issue, of course, is not simply that of higher wages. A regular income is also a standard prerequisite for accessing mortgage or shelter microfinance markets. Continuity in income earning is also important once one enters a mortgage agreement in order to avoid the risk of losing all of one's investment through the painful process of repossession. But a decent income is the minimum basis for accessing decent shelter, particularly in the situations of virtually all developing countries where workers' benefits and pensions are virtually non-existent and where the prices of basic necessities rise as rapidly as those of housing.

It is often argued that low wages in developing countries, particularly in sub-Saharan Africa, are justified by a variety of factors, including the low skills of the work force, low productivity, the volatility of the economy, capital restrictions and various forms of risks for the capital invested. However, some of these negative factors may not play such a large role today as they did previously. Rising levels of literacy, even in most of the poorest countries, coupled with the rapid removal of capital and profit-repatriation restrictions, have introduced much more favourable conditions for domestic and foreign direct investment (FDI) in the industrial and services sector. The fact that migrants with little or no formal education tend to find all sorts of jobs in developed countries shows that their skills are dramatically underutilized in their countries of origin. China, which boasts an extremely skilled and active pool of labour, still registers very low wages in comparison with the massive and rapid growth of its economy. From the point of view of sheer equity, it is hard to explain to a construction worker in a developing country that he may never afford to live in any of the houses he builds or drive on any of the roads he paves, while his counterparts in richer countries can.

On the other hand, economists and policy-makers tend to disregard important factors that dramatically lower productivity in developing countries, all linked to the residential circumstances of the working poor. Among them are lack of hygiene, leading to health vulnerability and consequent loss of working days and, more dramatically, high mortality rates; living environments that are the least conducive to decent recuperation after a day's hard work; constant exposure to the risks of violence, assault, theft and forced eviction, leading to mental stress, physical injury and long-term traumas; long commuting times spent, at best, in crowded, dangerous and unreliable means of public or para-public transport and, at worst, walking at pre-dawn, dusk and after sunset on often unpaved paths. Is it unrealistic to assume that improving the residential circumstances of the working poor would ultimately lead to higher productivity, higher profits, higher wages and, more generally, to a virtuous cycle that could ultimately make the living and shelter conditions of workers more comparable across the North–South divide?

The argument above is in favour of investments in improving the living conditions of the urban poor through sustainable shelter as a precondition for sustainable economic and social development.

A second argument is questioning the level of working wages and benefits in developing countries. An informed guess is that there is no reason why wages in the sectors where the urban poor are usually employed – domestic work, retail shops, warehouses, security services, factories, construction, repairs and maintenance, public institutions, schools, hospitals, and so on – should be so abysmally low all across the board. It may well be that this relates more to a non-signed understanding among all kinds of formal and informal employers than to a real reflection of the costs and benefits of decently paid work. More likely, wages are generally set on the basis of the classic parameter of the 'reproduction of the work force' – the bundle of expenditures required to survive, rather than to live a dignified life. On the other hand, it is reasonable to assume that well-to-do families could very well afford to pay more for domestic help. Most factories could probably well absorb reasonable increases in workers' salaries and benefits; and even public employers could raise low-end salaries to a decent level and provide in-house training in exchange for more efficient, reliable and regular delivery of the required services.[18] All of this would certainly result in more productive and efficient outcomes with benefits for all: the earning power of the employed and a better quality of products and services.

Transnational corporations, for example, are making growing recourse to job outsourcing in order to take advantage of the huge salary differential between salaries at home and those in developing or transition economies. This is an inescapable trait of globalization. However, such corporations are also under strong pressure to show that their activities are not over-exploitative. In this particular area, is it unrealistic to assume that some of the most important and visible of them, while retaining this comparative advantage, could give the good example of paying their workers salaries that allow them to lead a decent life for themselves and their children? The suggestion here is that salaries should not follow a 'race to the bottom', but the inverse route. It is quite likely that all of this would result, in addition to the achievement of adequate shelter conditions, in a less violent and threatening world for all.

Many specialists also point at ways of easing the burden and increasing the earning capacity of the huge numbers of people who draw their livelihood from the so-called 'informal sector'. The following recommendations have been made by such specialists:[19]

- providing the physical infrastructure for business development and job creation, including home-based enterprises;
- adopting pro-poor and labour-based methods when creating and maintaining infrastructure and providing basic services;
- easing the regulatory and fiscal burden for starting and growing enterprises;
- facilitating financial and business support for local enterprises;
- adopting community contracting on a much larger scale; and
- facilitating the regularization and operations of informal-sector activities.

Investments in improving the living conditions of the urban poor through sustainable shelter is a precondition for sustainable economic and social development

SYNERGIZING THE TWO: LOWER HOUSING PRICES AND HIGHER INCOMES

One important aspect is the synergies between lower housing prices and higher incomes. This section considers the mutually supporting benefits of acting on both sides of the spectrum.

Capital

Increasing both wages and income opportunities for the working poor augments the saving potential of the same earning group. As documented in the Millennium Project Task Force report, the urban poor show a marked propensity and ability to pool part of their incomes into community funds and other forms of saving arrangements. This triggers virtuous circles: the more capital is saved, the more is available for improving shelter conditions, productivity, skills formation and income-earning activities. With upgrading and adequate shelter solutions, more disposable income can become available to contribute to basic infrastructure and services, thus making public capital investment in this area more sustainable.

Infrastructure and land-use planning

Investments in infrastructure and land-use planning can provide important income-earning opportunities for the working poor. One of them is 'community contracts', whereby contracts for physical improvements are offered to the communities themselves, thus internalizing at least part of public investments in upgrading and rehabilitation.

Building materials and standards

The revision of standards in favour of locally produced building materials, in addition to enabling 'home-grown' construction practices, can give a strong impetus to the local building-materials industry, which typically employs low-income workers and a large part of the so-called informal sector. Similarly, the revision of planning regulations in favour of home-based and community-based economic activities can stimulate local economies and enhance the income opportunities of the working poor. Women, in particular, have proven particularly active and able in the production of simple and low-cost building materials, such as bricks and tiles. More generally, stepped-up public and private investment in infrastructure development and maintenance and citywide services, essential to improving urban productivity (roads, transport, utilities, health and educational structures), typically create income for the working poor and create and improve badly needed skills.

Stepped-up public and private investment in infrastructure development and maintenance and citywide services, essential to improving urban productivity

Design

The development of appropriate design solutions for urban living, from fixtures and furniture, to new building material production techniques, shelter design and residential and other development schemes – including environmentally sound solutions for waste management and energy sources and use – can open up wide avenues for employment and skills training. The Cinva Ram machine, for example, developed decades ago in a Colombian appropriate technology centre for the production of compressed earth blocks, proved to be one of the most effective and universally used means for the local production of affordable building materials. Similar, and much improved, solutions in design are being developed in many parts of the world. Their wider dissemination would provide a great impetus to efficiency in sustainable solutions encompassing both cost reduction and employment creation.

Modes of production

The more participatory assisted upgrading and new housing development programmes and projects are, the greater the chance they have to improve the access of the working poor to the foundations of a modern urban economy: from credit to design, planning, management, trade and so on. Participation in the design of collaborative schemes, such as upgrading, assisted self-help and cooperative housing, can bring into clearer focus the strongly perceived need on the part of the working poor to integrate housing functions with income-earning facilities, such as shops, workshops, food processing, arts and crafts, repair shops, carpentry and skills incubators, and light manufacturing.

FORMULATING AND IMPLEMENTING URBAN SHELTER POLICIES: SHELTERING THE POOR FROM 'MARKET POACHING'

The identification of sustainable ways of guaranteeing adequate and affordable shelter for the urban poor requires close attention to a third aspect, in addition to reducing costs and improving incomes. This third aspect has to do with the fact that all shelter sub-markets are permeable, and that different levels of demand (from very low income, to low income, up to middle income) can come into conflict and/or competition with one another. In these cases, it is always the poorest who lose. This undesirable outcome can be defined as 'market poaching': an outcome whereby more affluent social groups, taking advantage of their more favourable positions in the land and housing markets, can end up, voluntarily or not, absorbing resources (financial, spatial and otherwise) that are of vital importance in satisfying the shelter needs of the more vulnerable members of society.

'High-end poaching' in attractive urban locations

Competition among income groups and different land uses can occur in many different ways. Classic examples are drawn from forced evictions of poor populations living in un-regularized informal settlements. In some cases, such evictions are determined by attempts to satisfy the perceived needs of the city as a whole (such as improvements in the road infrastructure and public services). In others, they are motivated by the desire to put the land to a more profitable use (for example, commercial or attractive private housing development). In this latter case, a utilization of high social value (affordable shelter for the poor) mutates into another type of use that satisfies a smaller and selected cluster of higher income city dwellers, often with large profits for very few (the landowner and the developer). City authorities, at least in theory, also stand to gain from higher property values and real estate tax revenue.

Similar cases of 'locational poaching' occur in the all-too-frequent instances of 'market evictions'. In these cases, the dislocation of the urban poor does not occur because of forced evictions; but the results are similar. Whether or not in possession of a legal title, the poor who occupy a piece of land in a central location can be easily persuaded to clear out and transfer their property to higher income location seekers. The new occupants usually find it much easier to obtain a title, and as they are imitated by others, a low-income settlement is quietly transformed into a middle- or high-income neighbourhood. In all cases, these transformations are motivated by the value of a location which, with the expansion of the city, has become highly attractive.

Ironically, this kind of competition is, on the one hand, highly penalizing for the poor because choice central locations are the ones that offer them the best opportunities for income generation and are hardly affected by the availability or not of conventional housing mortgage financing. This is because choice locations attract high-end market uses for which capital financing is generally available.

The obvious antidote to this undesirable outcome is to adopt policies that accord top priority to the regularization and upgrading of consolidated informal settlements, save for the cases where their existence constitutes a permanent threat to the residents or can cause the irreversible loss of ecological resources.

'Residential poaching' in the urban periphery

Location is not the only factor that can determine 'residential poaching'. One very important grey area is represented by the more peripheral parts of the city, where potential competition between low- and middle-income housing is more acute. A classic case is that of subdivisions, legal or informal. The system works through the actual purchase of building plots and the construction of residential units, whether by the purchasers themselves or by the subdivider/developer. In this case, the discriminating factor can be the availability of finance to purchase the plot, which is obviously beyond the means of the poorest of the poor. Although this kind of acquisition is typically conducted through informal channels such as family or kinship connections, the unplanned way in which it often occurs places the poorest residents in a position of weakness with regard to access to new residential opportunities in the city.

This kind of competition reveals the unsustainability of 'spontaneous' informal settlements as a means of satisfying the shelter needs of the poorest citizens. The antidote is anticipatory land-use planning policies capable of increasing the total amount of land available for residential purposes and encouraging mixed development schemes, particularly of public land, that can provide a good social mix and ensure an appropriate combination of affordable shelter, employment opportunities, basic infrastructure and accessible community services. Cross-subsidies can be devised to ensure a sufficient amount of land for assisted self-help housing development for the lowest income groups.

'Mortgage finance poaching'

Direct and indirect means of providing financial access to shelter can result, deliberately or not, in higher income groups taking advantage of government subsidies and incentives created to address the needs of the most vulnerable groups of society. The case has already been mentioned of the utilization of tax expenditures in countries such as the US, which result in higher deductions for higher mortgages and, therefore, the upper end of the housing market.

In most developing countries, tax deductions on mortgages tend to be less widely used; where they exist, the fairness of their application is more vulnerable to less accountable practices. That leaves a greater burden on classic mortgage financing. However, ratios of outstanding mortgage loans to gross domestic product (GDP) range from around 35 per cent to 70 per cent in developed countries, and from 1 per cent to 17 per cent in developing countries.[20]

The lack of mortgage financing for shelter purposes in the developing countries is compounded by difficulties in accessing proper information and reliable professional services. In addition, cases abound of favourable loans being obtained through cronyism and manipulation of the banking sector. Patronage and connections are additional elements that broaden the access-to-financing gulf between the well-to-do and the poor, in addition to the well-known barriers represented by creditworthiness and the existence of collateral. The result is that in developing countries, limited mortgage financing resources tend to be monopolized even more severely by those who normally have much better economic access to adequate shelter.

Limited mortgage financing resources tend to be monopolized even more severely by those who normally have much better economic access to adequate shelter

However, the trend with regard to the use of mortgage financing in the developing countries is on the rise, and it can be hoped that in many of them the availability of financing for the shelter sector will increase. This can, in the long run, bring about beneficial results as 'mortgage finance poaching' may become less severe.

One mechanism for financing the shelter needs of formally employed workers – the ones most likely to compete for adequate and affordable shelter with the poor – is the creation of a housing development fund, based on contributions from the government, the employers and the workers themselves. It is through mechanisms of this nature that so many countries, in all continents, made dramatic breakthroughs in improving the housing conditions of their populations. Provided that they are managed in an efficient and transparent manner, such funds can create win–win situations for everybody – the construction sector; the banking sector; the employment situation; the efficiency of cities; the improvement of infrastructure and services; and the improvement in the quality of life of an important sector of the working population.

Political commitment and policy reform as the key to sustainable shelter

While shelter mortgage financing may improve in the future, the destinies of the urban poor cannot be left to the expansion of the markets. No serious and responsible approach to this problem can ignore the necessity for a much stronger financial and policy involvement on the part of central and local government.

The Millennium Project, in developing a practical plan for the achievement of the Millennium Development Goals, pointed out that developing countries, and particularly the poorest among them, can achieve the MDGs only if they manage to devote much greater resources to sustainable policies for the reduction of poverty and the improvement of the living conditions of people. The report of the Millennium Project Task Force on Improving the Lives of Slum Dwellers identifies official development assistance as an indispensable component of this effort, and suggests that all countries should develop, as a matter of urgency, MDG-based poverty reduction strategies indicating the domestic and international resources required to achieve the goals.

Cities are the key to sustainable development. It is through the development of commerce, services and industry in the framework of a diversified economy that significant gains in economic growth can be made. This, in turn, can generate the resources and the opportunities that the poor need in order to improve their own lives and to optimize their contribution to national development. The urban poor have an indispensable role to play because they are the ones who work in cities and who make cities work. Nowhere is this positive concatenation more evident than in those developing countries that have made the greatest strides in modernization and GDP formation.

Recent trends indicate that more donor countries may be willing to increase the level of their official development assistance as a means of reaching the MDG goals and targets. However, the best catalyst to bring this about and to attract flows of aid will be the proven commitment to invest in sustainable development. Key to this goal are the urban poor, and central to improving the lives of the urban poor is sustainable shelter.

Therefore, governments should consider, as a priority matter, adopting the innovative policy changes required to improve the shelter conditions of the urban poor and to achieve sustainable shelter development. Among them are:

Cities are the key to sustainable development: in the framework of a diversified economy significant gains in economic growth can be made

- reallocating a reasonable level of domestic resources to the shelter sector, particularly to programmes specifically geared to slum regularization and upgrading and the provision of low-cost housing;
- mobilizing public resources for urban and shelter development through a transparent and rigorous use of existing public revenue-generation mechanisms, including property taxes;
- actively seeking donor support for funding pro-poor programmes linked to increased public-sector and administrative efficiency, taking advantage of the MDG-based poverty reduction strategy approach;
- identifying blockages and introducing incentives for the expansion of housing mortgage financing;
- creating or strengthening funding mechanisms for the provision of adequate shelter to the urban poor through, for example, national housing funds and direct subsidies; and
- involving the working poor and their organizations in every step of policy review, reform and implementation, from the national to the local level.

Local engagement in the pursuit of the Millennium Development Goals (MDGs): the Millennium Towns and Cities Campaign

The above recommendations apply to central governments and local governments alike, within their distinctive spheres of responsibility. Legislative reform remains a prerogative of central governments, but steady advances in decentralization of powers and responsibilities has greatly increased the range of action of local governments. Ultimately, progress under the sustainable shelter agenda rests on positive synergies among all spheres of government.

One such synergy is represented by the role that local governments can play in achieving the Millennium Development target of improving the lives of slum dwellers – and, at the same time, creating viable alternatives to new slum formation. The report of the Task Force on Improving the Lives of Slum Dwellers argues that the MDG-related poverty reduction strategies should be based on local concerns (both those expressed by the poor themselves and by the local governments that have the direct responsibility of addressing them) and should generate local poverty reduction strategies. In a way, this suggestion is drawn from the Agenda 21 experience and the success registered by local Agendas 21. The level of global attention that the MDGs are currently receiving provides a great opportunity for local governments to engage in the process and to attract the support and the resources, both domestic and international, that they need in order to discharge their responsibilities in a more sustainable and equitable way. Cities are now offered the opportunity to engage in the MDG implementation process by following the example of pioneering municipal administrations in the North and in the South (Los Angeles and Curitiba, among them) which have voluntarily endorsed the Millennium Development Goals and activated mechanisms for monitoring their performance in this respect. International agencies are shaping initiatives around this goal.[21] In this regard, cities are becoming key agents in formulating and implementing local MDG-based poverty reduction and sustainable development strategies.[22] The new world organization United Cities and Local Governments has taken an important step in this direction by endorsing the MDGs and committing to the organization of an action-orientated global Millennium Towns and Cities Campaign. The potential of this approach is high, particularly in terms of the approach advocated in this Epilogue: an integrated, citywide strategy to the central issue of securing sustainable shelter development opportunities for the urban poor.

CONCLUDING REMARKS

Financing shelter is only a component of the broader goal of securing solutions that can make shelter truly sustainable and fill the gap between the two extreme outcomes that are being witnessed today: affordable shelter that is inadequate and adequate shelter that is unaffordable. One starting point is to look at the inhabitants of informal settlements not simply as 'slum dwellers', but as 'working poor'. Important opportunities exist for addressing the affordability gap by acting on both ends of the sustainable shelter equation – reducing housing production costs and increasing the incomes of the working poor. Given the urgency and growing significance of the 'urbanization of poverty' challenge, it is difficult to think of other areas of development that deserve more attention and investment on the part of the local, national and international institutions committed to reaching the Millennium Development Goals, including the target of improving the lives of at least 100 million slum dwellers by 2020 and, more generally, of finding practical and sustainable solutions to the global fight against poverty. Cities can lead the way, and the urban poor, who are the targets of the Millennium Development Goals, can become the protagonists, leading actors and living examples of a brighter future for all of humanity.

NOTES

1 This Epilogue is based on a paper prepared by Pietro Garau, University of Rome, Italy.
2 The identification of urbanization and the urbanization of poverty as one of the fundamental challenges facing development is not restricted to human settlements scholars and policy-makers. See, for example, Sir Hans Singer in Meyer and Stiglitz, 2000, p518: 'Soon, the majority of the population and the majority of the poor will live in towns, often in megacities. This will give added urgency to the problem of local government, civic participation, the urban informal sector, and urban infrastructure and environment.'
3 UNCHS, 1996a.
4 UN-Habitat, 2003a.
5 *The Economist*, 2004; IMF, 2004.
6 UNCHS, 1990a.
7 UN Millennium Project, 2005a.
8 UN Millennium Project, 2005b.
9 As remarked at one of the meetings of the United Nations Millennium Project's Task Force on Improving the Lives of Slum Dwellers, Italian hill towns could be classified as inadequate by a stern public health official or planner applying conventional 'modern' standards.
10 UN-Habitat, 2004.
11 Following up on a recommendation by the Task Force on Improving the Lives of Slum Dwellers during the World Congress of the International Union of Architects in Istanbul in June 2005, teams of architectural students in partnership with residents of a low-income community sought architectural solutions to improve the living environment.
12 Although in several countries all housing construction, including built-for-profit housing, is eligible for subsidies. For example, tax expenditures benefiting all owner occupants in the US and the housing voucher system adopted in Chile.
13 UN Millennium Project, 2005a.
14 UN-Habitat, 2003b.
15 UN-Habitat, 2003a.
16 Sood, 2003, p14.
17 Much has been said and written about the obstacles that the poor face in accessing conventional housing loans. However, this is only a small part of the picture and there is evidence that the issue is far wider than 'shelter finance'. The dramatically high level of repossessions of mortgaged housing in many industrialized countries reveals that accessing credit and obtaining a loan is only the first step in the long process towards shelter security. Moreover, insufficient incomes also prevent access to decent rental housing, which continues to be an important way of securing adequate shelter in all countries. See UN-Habitat, 2003a, for detail.
18 UN Millennium Project, 2005b.
19 UN Millennium Project, 2005a.
20 Mintz, 2003.
21 United Cities and Local Governments (UCLG) has coordinated the local government contribution to the United Nations five-year review of the implementation of the Millennium Development Goals, stressing the importance of the local implementation of the MDGs.
22 Advanced cities should be honoured with the title of Millennium City.

PART IV

STATISTICAL ANNEX

General disclaimer

The designations employed and presentation of the data do not imply the expression of any opinion whatsoever on the part of the Secretariat of the United Nations concerning the legal status of any country, city or area or of its authorities, or concerning the delimitation of its frontiers or boundaries.

TECHNICAL NOTES

The Statistical Annex comprises 16 tables covering three broad categories: (i) demographic indicators and households data; (ii) housing and housing infrastructure indicators; and (iii) economic and social indicators. These tables are divided into three sections presenting data at the regional, country and city levels. Tables A.1 to A.3 present regional-level data grouped by selected criteria of geographic, economic and development aggregation. Tables B.1 to B.9 contain country-level data and Tables C.1 to C.4 are devoted to city-level data. Data have been compiled from various international sources, from national statistical offices and from the United Nations.

EXPLANATION OF SYMBOLS

The following symbols have been used in presenting data throughout the Statistical Annex:

Category not applicable ..
Data not available ...
Magnitude zero –
Provisional data is given in *italics* and bracketed numbers have a negative value.

COUNTRY GROUPINGS AND STATISTICAL AGGREGATES

World major groupings

More developed regions: All countries and areas of Europe and Northern America, as well as Australia, Japan and New Zealand.

Less developed regions: All countries and areas of Africa, Latin America, Asia (excluding Japan) and Oceania (excluding Australia and New Zealand).

Least developed countries (LDCs): The United Nations currently designates 49 countries as LDCs: Afghanistan, Angola, Bangladesh, Benin, Bhutan, Burkina Faso, Burundi, Cambodia, Cape Verde, Central African Republic, Chad, Comoros, Democratic Republic of the Congo, Djibouti, Equatorial Guinea, Eritrea, Ethiopia, Gambia, Guinea, Guinea-Bissau, Haiti, Kiribati, Lao People's Democratic Republic, Lesotho, Liberia, Madagascar, Malawi, Maldives, Mali, Mauritania, Mozambique, Myanmar, Nepal, Niger, Rwanda, Samoa, Sao Tome and Principe, Senegal, Sierra Leone, Solomon Islands, Somalia, Sudan, Togo, Tuvalu, Uganda, United Republic of Tanzania, Vanuatu, Yemen, Zambia.

Landlocked developing countries (LLDCs): Afghanistan, Armenia, Azerbaijan, Bhutan, Bolivia, Botswana, Burkina Faso, Burundi, Central African Republic, Chad, Ethiopia, Kazakhstan, Kyrgyzstan, Lao People's Democratic Republic, Lesotho, Malawi, Mali, Mongolia, Nepal, Niger, Paraguay, Rwanda, Swaziland, Tajikistan, TFYR of Macedonia, Turkmenistan, Uganda, Uzbekistan, Zambia, Zimbabwe.

Small island developing states (SIDS): Antigua and Barbuda, Aruba, Bahamas, Bahrain, Barbados, Belize, Cape Verde, Comoros, Cook Islands, Cuba, Cyprus, Dominica, Dominican Republic, Fiji, Grenada, Guinea-Bissau, Guyana, Haiti, Jamaica, Kiribati, Maldives, Malta, Marshall Islands, Mauritius, Micronesia (Federated States of), Nauru, Netherlands Antilles, Niue, Palau, Papua New Guinea, Saint Kitts and Nevis, Saint Lucia, Samoa, Sao Tome and Principe, Seychelles, Singapore, Solomon Islands, Saint Vincent and the Grenadines, Suriname, Tokelau, Tonga, Trinidad and Tobago, Tuvalu, United States Virgin Islands, Vanuatu.

United Nations Regional Groups[1]

African States: Algeria, Angola, Benin, Botswana, Burkina Faso, Burundi, Cameroon, Cape Verde, Central African Republic, Chad, Comoros, Congo, Côte d'Ivoire, Democratic Republic of the Congo, Djibouti, Egypt, Equatorial Guinea, Eritrea, Ethiopia, Gabon, Gambia, Ghana, Guinea, Guinea-Bissau, Kenya, Lesotho, Liberia, Libyan Arab Jamahiriya, Madagascar, Malawi, Mali, Mauritania, Mauritius, Morocco, Mozambique, Namibia, Niger, Nigeria, Rwanda, Sao Tome and Principe, Senegal, Seychelles, Sierra Leone, Somalia, South Africa, Sudan, Swaziland, Togo, Tunisia, Uganda, United Republic of Tanzania, Zambia, Zimbabwe.

Asian States: Afghanistan, Bahrain, Bangladesh, Bhutan, Brunei Darussalam, Cambodia, China, Cyprus, Democratic People's Republic of Korea, Fiji, India, Indonesia, Iran, Iraq, Japan, Jordan, Kazakhstan, Kuwait, Kyrgyzstan, Lao People's Democratic Republic, Lebanon, Malaysia, Maldives, Marshall Islands, Micronesia (Federated States of), Mongolia, Myanmar, Nauru, Nepal, Oman, Pakistan, Palau, Papua New Guinea, Philippines, Qatar, Republic of Korea, Samoa, Saudi Arabia, Singapore, Solomon Islands, Sri Lanka, Syrian Arab Republic, Tajikistan, Thailand, Tonga, Turkmenistan, Tuvalu, United Arab Emirates, Uzbekistan, Vanuatu, Viet Nam, Yemen.

Eastern European States: Albania, Armenia, Azerbaijan, Belarus, Bosnia and Herzegovina, Bulgaria, Croatia, Czech

Republic, Georgia, Hungary, Latvia, Lithuania, Poland, Republic of Moldova, Romania, Russian Federation, Serbia and Montenegro, Slovakia, Slovenia, TFYR Macedonia, Ukraine.

Latin American and Caribbean States: Antigua and Barbuda, Argentina, Bahamas, Barbados, Belize, Bolivia, Brazil, Chile, Colombia, Costa Rica, Cuba, Dominica, Dominican Republic, Ecuador, El Salvador, Grenada, Guatemala, Guyana, Haiti, Honduras, Jamaica, Mexico, Nicaragua, Panama, Paraguay, Peru, Saint Kitts and Nevis, Saint Lucia, Saint Vincent and the Grenadines, Suriname, Trinidad and Tobago, Uruguay, Venezuela.

Western Europe and Other States: Andorra, Australia, Austria, Belgium, Canada, Denmark, Finland, France, Germany, Greece, Iceland, Ireland, Israel, Italy, Liechtenstein, Luxembourg, Malta, Monaco, Netherlands, New Zealand, Norway, Portugal, San Marino, Spain, Sweden, Switzerland, Turkey, United Kingdom.

Countries in the Human Development aggregates[2]

High human development (*HDI 0.800 and above*):[3] Antigua and Barbuda, Argentina, Australia, Austria, Bahamas, Bahrain, Barbados, Belgium, Brunei Darussalam, Canada, Chile, Hong Kong SAR of China, Costa Rica, Croatia, Cuba, Cyprus, Czech Republic, Denmark, Estonia, Finland, France, Germany, Greece, Hungary, Iceland, Ireland, Israel, Italy, Japan, Kuwait, Latvia, Lithuania, Luxembourg, Malta, Mexico, Netherlands, New Zealand, Norway, Poland, Portugal, Qatar, Republic of Korea, Saint Kitts and Nevis, Seychelles, Singapore, Slovakia, Slovenia, Spain, Sweden, Switzerland, Trinidad and Tobago, United Arab Emirates, United Kingdom, United States, Uruguay.

Medium human development (*HDI 0.500–0.799*):[4] Albania, Algeria, Armenia, Azerbaijan, Bangladesh, Belarus, Belize, Bhutan, Bolivia, Bosnia and Herzegovina, Botswana, Brazil, Bulgaria, Cambodia, Cameroon, Cape Verde, China, Colombia, Comoros, Dominica, Dominican Republic, Ecuador, Egypt, El Salvador, Equatorial Guinea, Fiji, Gabon, Georgia, Ghana, Grenada, Guatemala, Guyana, Honduras, India, Indonesia, Iran (Islamic Republic of), Jamaica, Jordan, Kazakhstan, Kyrgyzstan, Lao People's Democratic Republic, Lebanon, Libyan Arab Jamahiriya, Malaysia, Maldives, Mauritius, Mongolia, Morocco, Myanmar, Namibia, Nepal, Nicaragua, Occupied Palestinian Territory, Oman, Panama, Papua New Guinea, Paraguay, Peru, Philippines, Republic of Moldova, Romania, Russian Federation, Saint Lucia, Saint Vincent and the Grenadines, Samoa, Sao Tome and Principe, Saudi Arabia, Solomon Islands, South Africa, Sri Lanka, Sudan, Suriname, Swaziland, Syrian Arab Republic, Tajikistan, TFYR Macedonia, Thailand, Tonga, Tunisia, Turkey, Turkmenistan, Ukraine, Uzbekistan, Vanuatu, Venezuela, Viet Nam.

Low human development (*HDI 0.500 and below*):[5] Angola, Benin, Burkina Faso, Burundi, Central African Republic, Chad, Congo, Côte d'Ivoire, Democratic Republic of the Congo, Djibouti, Eritrea, Ethiopia, Gambia, Guinea, Guinea-Bissau, Haiti, Kenya, Lesotho, Madagascar, Malawi, Mali, Mauritania, Mozambique, Niger, Nigeria, Pakistan, Rwanda, Senegal, Sierra Leone, Timor-Leste, Togo, Uganda, United Republic of Tanzania, Yemen, Zambia, Zimbabwe.

Countries in the income aggregates[6]

High income (*GNP per capita US$9386 or more*): Andorra, Aruba, Australia, Austria, Bahamas, Bahrain, Belgium, Bermuda, Brunei Darussalam, Canada, Cayman Islands, Channel Islands, Cyprus, Denmark, Faeroe Islands, Finland, France, French Polynesia, Germany, Greece, Greenland, Guam, Hong Kong SAR of China, Iceland, Ireland, Isle of Man, Israel, Italy, Japan, Kuwait, Liechtenstein, Luxembourg, Macao SAR of China, Malta, Monaco, Netherlands, Netherlands Antilles, New Caledonia, New Zealand, Norway, Portugal, Puerto Rico, Qatar, Republic of Korea, San Marino, Singapore, Slovenia, Spain, Sweden, Switzerland, United Arab Emirates, United Kingdom, United States, United States Virgin Islands.

Upper-middle income (*GNP per capita US$3036–9385*): American Samoa, Antigua and Barbuda, Argentina, Barbados, Belize, Botswana, Chile, Costa Rica, Croatia, Czech Republic, Dominica, Estonia, Gabon, Grenada, Hungary, Latvia, Lebanon, Libyan Arab Jamahiriya, Lithuania, Malaysia, Mauritius, Mexico, Northern Mariana Islands, Oman, Palau, Panama, Poland, Saint Vincent and the Grenadines, Saudi Arabia, Seychelles, Slovakia, Saint Kitts and Nevis, Saint Lucia, Trinidad and Tobago, Uruguay, Venezuela.

Lower-middle income (*GNP per capita US$766–3035*): Albania, Algeria, Armenia, Azerbaijan, Belarus, Bolivia, Bosnia and Herzegovina, Brazil, Bulgaria, Cape Verde, China, Colombia, Cuba, Djibouti, Dominican Republic, Ecuador, Egypt, El Salvador, Fiji, Georgia, Guatemala, Guyana, Honduras, Indonesia, Iran (Islamic Republic of), Iraq, Jamaica, Jordan, Kazakhstan, Kiribati, Maldives, Marshall Islands, Micronesia (Federated States of), Morocco, Namibia, Occupied Palestinian Territory, Paraguay, Peru, Philippines, Romania, Russian Federation, Samoa, Serbia and Montenegro, South Africa, Sri Lanka, Suriname, Swaziland, Syrian Arab Republic, TFYR Macedonia, Thailand, Tonga, Tunisia, Turkey, Turkmenistan, Ukraine, Vanuatu.

Low income (*GNP per capita US$765 or less*): Afghanistan, Angola, Bangladesh, Benin, Bhutan, Burkina Faso, Burundi, Cambodia, Cameroon, Central African Republic, Chad, Comoros, Congo, Côte d'Ivoire, Democratic People's Republic of Korea, Democratic Republic of the Congo, Equatorial Guinea, Eritrea, Ethiopia, Gambia, Ghana, Guinea, Guinea-Bissau, Haiti, India, Kenya, Kyrgyzstan, Lao People's Democratic Republic, Lesotho, Liberia, Madagascar, Malawi, Mali, Mauritania, Mongolia, Mozambique, Myanmar, Nepal, Nicaragua, Niger, Nigeria, Pakistan, Papua New Guinea, Republic of Moldova, Rwanda, Sao Tome and Principe, Senegal, Sierra Leone, Solomon Islands, Somalia, Sudan, Tajikistan, Timor-Leste, Togo, Uganda, United Republic of Tanzania, Uzbekistan, Viet Nam, Yemen, Zambia, Zimbabwe.

Sub-regional aggregates

Africa

Eastern Africa: Burundi, Comoros, Djibouti, Eritrea, Ethiopia, Kenya, Madagascar, Malawi, Mauritius, Mozambique Réunion, Rwanda, Seychelles, Somalia, Uganda, United Republic of Tanzania, Zambia, Zimbabwe.

Middle Africa: Angola, Cameroon, Central African Republic, Chad, Congo, Democratic Republic of the Congo, Equatorial Guinea, Gabon, Sao Tome and Principe.

Northern Africa: Algeria, Egypt, Libyan Arab Jamahiriya, Morocco, Sudan, Tunisia, Western Sahara.

Southern Africa: Botswana, Lesotho, Namibia, South Africa, Swaziland.

Western Africa: Benin, Burkina Faso, Cape Verde, Côte d'Ivoire, Gambia, Ghana, Guinea, Guinea-Bissau, Liberia, Mali, Mauritania, Niger, Nigeria, Saint Helena, Senegal, Sierra Leone, Togo.

Asia

Eastern Asia: China, Hong Kong SAR of China, Macao SAR of China, Democratic People's Republic of Korea, Japan, Mongolia, Republic of Korea.

South-central Asia: Afghanistan, Bangladesh, Bhutan, India, Iran (Islamic Republic of), Kazakhstan, Kyrgyzstan, Maldives, Nepal, Pakistan, Sri Lanka, Tajikistan, Turkmenistan, Uzbekistan.

Southeastern Asia: Brunei Darussalam, Cambodia, Indonesia, Lao People's Democratic Republic, Malaysia, Myanmar, Philippines, Singapore, Thailand, Timor-Leste, Viet Nam.

Western Asia: Armenia, Azerbaijan, Bahrain, Cyprus, Georgia, Iraq, Israel, Jordan, Kuwait, Lebanon, Occupied Palestinian Territory, Oman, Qatar, Saudi Arabia, Syrian Arab Republic, Turkey, United Arab Emirates, Yemen

Europe

Eastern Europe: Belarus, Bulgaria, Czech Republic, Hungary, Poland, Republic of Moldova, Romania, Russian Federation, Slovakia, Ukraine.

Northern Europe: Channel Islands, Denmark, Estonia, Faeroe Islands, Finland, Iceland, Ireland, Isle of Man, Latvia, Lithuania, Norway, Sweden, United Kingdom.

Southern Europe: Albania, Andorra, Bosnia and Herzegovina, Croatia, Gibraltar, Greece, Holy See, Italy, Malta, Portugal, San Marino, Serbia and Montenegro, Slovenia, Spain, TFYR Macedonia.

Western Europe: Austria, Belgium, France, Germany, Liechtenstein, Luxembourg, Monaco, The Netherlands, Switzerland.

Latin America and the Caribbean

Caribbean: Anguilla, Antigua and Barbuda, Aruba, Bahamas, Barbados, British Virgin Islands, Cayman Islands, Cuba, Dominica, Dominican Republic, Grenada, Guadeloupe, Haiti, Jamaica, Martinique, Montserrat, Netherlands Antilles, Puerto Rico, Saint Kitts and Nevis, Saint Lucia, Saint Vincent and the Grenadines, Trinidad and Tobago, Turks and Caicos Islands, United States Virgin Islands.

Central America: Belize, Costa Rica, El Salvador, Guatemala, Honduras, Mexico, Nicaragua, Panama.

South America: Argentina, Bolivia, Brazil, Chile, Colombia, Ecuador, Falkland Islands (Malvinas), French Guiana, Guyana, Paraguay, Peru, Suriname, Uruguay, Venezuela.

Northern America

Bermuda, Canada, Greenland, Saint-Pierre and Miquelon, United States.

Oceania

Australia/New Zealand: Australia, New Zealand.

Melanesia: Fiji, New Caledonia, Papua New Guinea, Solomon Islands, Vanuatu.

Micronesia: Guam, Kiribati, Marshall Islands, Micronesia (Federated States of), Nauru, Northern Mariana Islands, Palau.

Polynesia: American Samoa, Cook Islands, French Polynesia, Niue, Pitcairn, Samoa, Tokelau, Tonga, Tuvalu, Wallis and Futuna Islands.

NOMENCLATURE AND ORDER OF PRESENTATION

Tables A.1 to A.3 contain regional, income and development aggregates data. Tables B.1 to B.9 and C.1 to C.4 contain national- and city-level data, respectively. In these tables, the countries or areas are listed in English alphabetical order within the macroregions of Africa, Asia, Europe, Latin America, Northern America and Oceania. Countries or area names are presented in the form commonly used within the United Nations Secretariat for statistical purposes. Due to space limitations, the short name is used – for example, the United Kingdom of Great Britain and Northern Ireland is referred to as 'United Kingdom', the United States of America as 'United States'.

DEFINITION OF STATISTICAL TERMS

Access to improved drinking water supply: 'Improved' water supply technologies are household connection, public standpipe, borehole, protected dug well, protected spring, rainwater collection. Availability of at least 20 litres per person per day from a source within 1 kilometre of the user's dwelling. 'Not improved' are unprotected well, unprotected spring, vendor-provided water, bottled water (based on concerns about the quantity of supplied water, not concerns over the quality of water), tanker truck-provided water.

Access to improved sanitation: 'Improved' sanitation technologies are connection to a public sewer, connection to septic system, pour-flush latrine, simple pit latrine, ventilated improved pit latrine. The excreta disposal system is considered adequate if it is private or shared (but not public) and if it hygienically separates human excreta from human contact. 'Not improved' are service or bucket latrines (where excreta are manually removed), public latrines, latrines with an open pit.

Access to water: Percentage of households with access to water. Access is defined as having water located within 200 metres of the dwelling. It refers to housing units where the piped water is available within the unit and to those where it is not available to occupants within their housing unit, but is accessible within the range of 200 metres. This assumes that access to piped water within that distance allows occupants to provide water for household needs without being subjected to extreme effort.

Aid dependency ratios: Calculated using values in US dollars converted at official exchange rates. *Aid per capita* includes both official development assistance (ODA) and official aid (OA).

Commercial energy production: Commercial forms of primary energy – petroleum (crude oil, natural gas liquids and oil from non-conventional sources); natural gas; solid fuels (coal, lignite and other derived fuels); and primary electricity – all converted into oil equivalents.

Commercial energy use: Apparent consumption, which is equal to indigenous production plus imports and stock changes, minus exports and fuels supplied to ships and aircraft engaged in international transport.

Development assistance: Consists of disbursements of loans made on concessional terms (net of repayments of principal) and grants by official agencies of the members of the Development Assistance Committee (DAC), by multilateral institutions, and by non-DAC countries to promote economic development and welfare in countries and territories in part 1 of the DAC list of aid recipients. It includes loans with a grant element of at least 25 per cent (calculated at a rate of discount of 10 per cent).

Domestic gross savings: Calculated as gross domestic product (GDP) less total consumption.

Domestic credit to private sector: Refers to financial resources provided to the private sector – such as through loans, purchases of non-equity securities, and trade credits and other accounts receivable – that establish a claim for repayment. For some countries these claims include credit to public enterprises.

Electric rail lines: The length of line with electric traction. This line can include overhead catenary at various direct current or alternating current voltage and third-rail direct current systems.

Energy use per capita: Refers to apparent consumption, which is equal to indigenous production plus imports and stock changes, minus exports and fuels supplied to ships and aircraft engaged in international transport.

Foreign direct investment (FDI): Net inflows of investment to acquire a lasting management interest (10 per cent or more of voting stock) in an enterprise operating in an economy other than that of the investor. It is the sum of equity capital, reinvestment of earnings, other long-term capital and short-term capital as shown in the balance of payments.

Foreign direct investment (FDI) in–out flows: Data are on a net basis (capital transactions' credits less debits between direct investors and their foreign affiliates). Net decreases in assets (outward FDI) or net increases in liabilities (inward FDI) are recorded as credits (recorded with a positive sign in the balance of payments), while net increases in assets or net decreases in liabilities are recorded as debits (recorded with a negative sign in the balance of payments). FDI flows with a negative sign indicate that at least one of the three components of FDI (equity capital, reinvested earnings or intra-company loans) is negative and is not offset by positive amounts of the other components. These are instances of reverse investment or disinvestments.

The United Nations Conference on Trade and Development (UNCTAD) regularly collects published and unpublished national official FDI flows data directly from central banks, statistical offices or national authorities on an aggregated and disaggregated basis for its FDI/transnational corporations (TNC) database. These data constitute the main source of reported data on FDI flows.

Female-headed households: Percentage of households with a female head.

Fuel prices: Pump prices of the most widely sold grade of petrol and diesel fuel. Prices have been converted from the local currency to US dollars.

Gini index: Measures the extent to which the distribution of income (or, in some cases, consumption expenditure) among individuals or households within an economy deviates from a perfectly equal distribution. A Lorenz curve plots the cumulative percentages of total income received against the cumulative number of recipients, starting with the poorest individual or household. The Gini index measures the area between the Lorenz curve and a hypothetical line of absolute equality, expressed as a percentage of the maximum area under the line. Thus, a Gini index of 0 represents perfect equality, while an index of 100 implies absolute inequality.

Gross capital formation: Consists of outlays on additions to the fixed assets of the economy, plus net changes in the level of inventories. Fixed assets include land improvements (for example, fences, ditches, drains), plant, machinery and equipment purchases, and the construction of roads, railways and the like, including schools, offices, hospitals, private residential dwellings, and commercial and industrial buildings. Inventories are stocks of goods held by firms to meet temporary or unexpected fluctuations in production or sales, and 'work in progress'.

Gross domestic product (GDP): At purchaser prices, this is the sum of the gross value added by all resident producers in the economy, plus any product taxes, minus any subsidies not included in the value of the products. It is calculated without making deductions for depreciation of fabricated assets or for depletion and degradation of natural resources. *GDP per capita*: GDP divided by the mid-year population. Growth is calculated from constant price GDP data in local currency.

Gross national savings: Calculated as the difference between gross national income and public and private consumption, plus net current transfers.

Gross school enrolment ratio: Number of students, by sex, enrolled in a level of education, whether or not they belong in the relevant age group for that level, as a percentage of the population in the relevant group for that level.

Hospital beds: Include in-patient beds available in public, private, general, and specialized hospitals and rehabilitation centres. In most cases, beds for both acute and chronic care are included.

Household: Estimations and projections prepared by the United Nations Human Settlements Programme (UN-Habitat). Household statistics were collected through the Human Settlements Statistical Questionnaires. The concept of household is based on the arrangements made by persons, individually or in groups, for providing themselves with food or other essentials for living. A household may be either:

1. A one-person household – that is to say, a person who makes provision for his or her own food or other essentials for living without combining with any other person to form a part of a multi-person household; or
2. A multi-person household – that is to say, a group of two or more persons living together who make common provision for food or other essentials for living. The persons in the group may pool their incomes and may, to a greater or lesser extent, have a common budget; they may be related or unrelated persons or constitute a combination of persons both related and unrelated. This concept of household is known as the 'housekeeping' concept. It does not assume that the number of households and housing units is equal. Although the concept of housing unit implies that it is a space occupied by one household, it may also be occupied by more than one household or by a part of a household (for example, two nuclear households that share one housing unit for economic reasons or one household in a polygamous society routinely occupying two or more housing units).

Household final consumption expenditure: The market value of all goods and services, including durable products (such as cars, washing machines and home computers), purchased by households. It excludes purchases of dwellings but includes imputed rent for owner-occupied dwellings. It also includes payments and fees to governments to obtain permits and licences. Here, household consumption expenditure includes the expenditures of non-profit institutions serving households, even when reported separately by the country. In practice, household consumption expenditure may include any statistical discrepancy in the use of resources relative to the supply of resources.

Household projection methods: Determined by availability and reliability of data. The five types of projection approaches followed by the lists of countries, for which the respective approach has been applied, are:

1. *Total headship rate-based projection*: Albania, Algeria, Austria, Bangladesh, Belarus, Benin, Bolivia, Botswana, Brazil, Brunei Darussalam, Bulgaria, Burkina Faso, Cambodia, Cape Verde, China Macau SAR, Colombia, Cyprus, Denmark, Dominican Republic, Ecuador, Estonia, Fiji, Finland, France, French Polynesia, Gambia, Georgia, Germany, Greece, Guatemala, Haiti, Honduras, Hungary, Ireland, Italy, India, Indonesia, Iraq, Jamaica, Japan, Kazakhstan, Kenya, Kuwait, Latvia, Lesotho, Libyan Arab Jamahiriya, Lithuania, Luxembourg, Malaysia, Maldives, Malta, Madagascar, Malawi, Mali, Mauritius, Mexico, Netherlands, New Caledonia, Nicaragua, Niger, Pakistan, Paraguay, Peru, Poland, Portugal, Republic of Korea, Rwanda, Singapore, Solomon Islands, South Africa, Spain, Sudan, Switzerland, Thailand, Tunisia, Turkey, United Republic of Tanzania, United States, Venezuela, Viet Nam, Yemen, Zambia and Zimbabwe.
2. *Headship size rate-based projection*: Argentina, Armenia, Australia, Azerbaijan, Bahamas, Bahrain, Barbados, Belgium, Belize, Burundi, Canada, Central

African Republic, Chile, Congo, Costa Rica, Egypt, El Salvador, Guadeloupe, Guam, Guyana, Iran (Islamic Republic of), Israel, Jordan, Kyrgyzstan, Liberia, Martinique, Morocco, Nepal, Netherlands Antilles, New Zealand, Norway, Panama, Philippines, Puerto Rico, Republic of Moldova, Réunion, Romania, Russian Federation, Serbia and Montenegro, Samoa, Sweden, Syrian Arab Republic, Tajikistan, Trinidad and Tobago, Turkmenistan, Ukraine, United Kingdom, Uruguay, Uzbekistan and Vanuatu.

3 *Estimation on country level not possible*: Afghanistan, Angola, Bosnia and Herzegovina, Democratic People's Republic of Korea, Lebanon, Occupied Palestinian Territory, Sierra Leone, Timor-Leste and Western Sahara.

4 *Estimation on the basis of one data point*: Cameroon, Comoros, Côte d'Ivoire, Croatia, Czech Republic, Democratic Republic of the Congo, Eritrea, Ethiopia, Gabon, Ghana, Guinea, Guinea-Bissau, Iceland, Mauritania, Mongolia, Mozambique, Myanmar, Namibia, Nigeria, Oman, Papua New Guinea, Qatar, Senegal, Slovakia, Slovenia, Suriname, TFYR Macedonia, Togo, Uganda and United Arab Emirates.

5 *Estimation with no data point*: Bhutan, Chad, Djibouti, Equatorial Guinea, Lao People's Democratic Republic, Saudi Arabia, Somalia and Swaziland.

The following countries or areas are not included in the total number of households calculated for regions and other aggregates: American Samoa, Andorra, Anguilla, Antigua and Barbuda, Aruba, Bermuda, British Virgin Islands, Cayman Islands, Channel Islands, Cook Islands, Dominica, Faeroe Islands, Falklands, French Guiana, Gibraltar, Greenland, Grenada, Holy See, Isle of Man, Liechtenstein, Marshall Islands, Micronesia (Federal States of), Monaco, Montserrat, Nauru, Northern Mariana Islands, Palau, Pitcairn, Saint Helena, Saint Kitts and Nevis, Saint Lucia, Saint-Pierre and Miquelon, Saint Vincent, San Marino, Sao Tome and Principe, Seychelles, Tokelau, Tonga, Turks and Caicos Islands, Tuvalu, United States Virgin Islands, and Wallis and Futuna Islands.

For the following countries the estimates are extremely rough and cannot be interpreted on their own; they have only been calculated for completeness reasons on the aggregate (regional and global) level: Afghanistan, Angola, Bosnia and Herzegovina, Democratic People's Republic of Korea, Lebanon, Occupied Palestinian Territory, Sierra Leone, Timor-Leste and Western Sahara.

Investment in infrastructure projects with private participation: Covers infrastructure projects in telecommunications, energy (electricity and natural gas transmission and distribution), transport and water and sanitation that have reached financial closure and directly or indirectly serve the public. Incinerators, movable assets, stand-alone solid waste projects and small projects such as windmills are excluded. The types of projects included are operation and management contracts with major capital expenditure, greenfield projects (in which a private entity or a public–private joint venture builds and operates a new facility) and divestiture.

Level of urbanization: Percentage of the population residing in places classified as urban. Urban and rural settlements are defined in the national context and vary among countries (the definitions of urban are generally national definitions incorporated within the latest census).

Life expectancy at birth: Number of years a newborn infant would live if prevailing patterns of mortality at the time of birth were to stay the same throughout the child's life.

Literacy rate: Percentage of persons aged 15 and above who can, with understanding, both read and write a short, simple statement about their everyday life. In practice, literacy is difficult to measure. To estimate literacy using such a definition requires census or survey measurements under controlled conditions. Many countries estimate the number of literate people from self-reported data. Some use educational attainment data as a proxy, but apply different lengths of school attendance or level completion. As definition and methodologies of data collection differ across country – and even over time within countries – data need to be used with caution.

Local government revenue and expenditures: Total annual *local government revenue* from all sources in US dollars, both capital and recurrent, divided by population (three-year average) and capital expenditure in US dollars per person, by all local governments in the metropolitan area, averaged over the last three years. *Per capita expenditures*: Include both fixed capital and plant as per the capital account.

Motor vehicles: Include cars, buses and freight vehicles but not two-wheelers. Population figures refer to the mid-year population in the year for which data are available. Roads refer to motorways, highways, main or national roads, and secondary or regional roads. A motorway is a road specially designed and built for motor traffic that separates the traffic flowing in opposite directions.

Ownership: *Owner:* A household who owns the living quarters that it occupies, whether used wholly or partly for own occupation by the owner. This may include living quarters being purchased in instalments or mortgaged, according to national legal systems and practice. Other arrangements, such as living quarters in co-operatives and housing associations, may also be included depending upon national practices. *Tenant in publicly owned housing unit*: A household residing in a housing unit that it does not own, but is owned by a public institution (disregarding whether or not the institution is sponsored by central or local government). These institutions may be co-operatives, housing associations or government agencies. *Tenant in privately owned housing unit*: A household residing in a housing unit that it does not own, but is owned by the private sector. This includes households renting a housing unit from individuals – for example, a landlord – or units owned by a private corporation.

Persons in housing units: Number of persons resident in housing units. *Persons per room*: Figures are derived by dividing the number of occupants by the number of rooms in a given housing unit. The number of rooms is obtained by multiplying the number of units by the number of rooms in the unit. The calculations were done by the United Nations Secretariat.

Poor households: Percentage of women- and men-headed households situated below the locally defined poverty line. The poverty line is usually an 'absolute' poverty line, taken as the income necessary to afford a minimum nutritionally adequate diet, plus essential non-food requirements, for a household of a given size.

Population, total: Mid-year population estimates for the world, region, countries or areas. The Population Division of the United Nations Department of Economic and Social Affairs updates, every two years, population estimates and projections by incorporating new data, new estimates and new analysis of data on population, fertility, mortality and international migration. Data from new population censuses and/or demographic surveys are used to verify and update old estimates of population or demographic indicators, or to make new ones and to check the validity of the assumptions made in the projections. Total population refers to the estimates and projections (medium variant) of the total population for each country region and major area. *Annual growth rate*, calculated by UN-Habitat, refers to the average annual percentage change of population during the indicated period for each country, major regions and global totals. The formula used throughout the Annex is as follows:

$$r = [(1/t) \times \ln(A2/A1)] \times 100,$$

where 'A1' is a value at any given year; 'A2' is a value at any given year later than the year of 'Al'; 't' is the year interval between 'Al' and 'A2'; and 'ln' is the natural logarithm function.

Population, urban and rural: Mid-year estimates and projections (medium variant) of the population residing in human settlements classified as urban or rural.

Poverty definitions: *National poverty rate*: Percentage of the population living below the national poverty line. National estimates are based on population-weighted sub-group estimates from household surveys. Survey year is the year in which the underlying data were collected. *Population below US$1 a day* and *Population below US$2 a day*: Percentages of the population living on less than US$1.08 a day and US$2.15 a day at 1993 international prices (equivalent to US$1 and US$2 in 1985 prices, adjusted for purchasing power parity). Poverty rates are comparable across countries, but as a result of revisions in purchasing power parity (PPP) exchange rates, they cannot be compared with poverty rates reported in previous editions for individual countries.

Purchasing power parity (PPP) gross national income: Gross national income (GNI) converted to international dollars using purchasing power parity rates. An international dollar has the same purchasing power over GNI as a US dollar has in the United States.

Refugees, asylum-seekers and IDPs: Data are provided by governments based on their own definitions and methods of collection. Total asylum-seekers, refugees and others of concern to the United Nations High Commissioner for Refugees (UNHCR) include the following. *Refugees*: Persons recognized as refugees under the international conventions, in accordance with the UNHCR Statute; persons allowed to stay on humanitarian grounds and those granted temporary protection. *Asylum-seekers*: Persons whose application for refugee status is pending in the asylum procedure or who are otherwise registered as asylum-seekers. The total number of asylum-seekers is underestimated due to a lack of data from a number of countries. *Returned refugees*: Refugees who have returned to their country of origin during the year. *Internally displaced persons (IDPs)*: Persons who are displaced within their country and to whom UNHCR extends protection or assistance, generally pursuant to a special request by a competent organ of the United Nations. *Returned IDPs*: IDPs of concern to UNHCR who have returned to their place of origin during the year.

Roads: Motorways, highways, main or national roads, and secondary or regional roads. A motorway is a road specially designed and built for motor vehicles that separates the traffic flowing in opposite directions. *Total road network*: Includes motorways, highways and main or national roads, secondary or regional roads, and all other roads in a country. *Paved roads*: Roads surfaced with crushed stone (macadam) and hydrocarbon binder or bitumized agents, with concrete or with cobblestones, as a percentage of all of the country's roads measured in length.

Squatter household: A household who built a structure that it occupies on land on which it does not have a title. Squatter settlements are usually built on the fringes of large cities without a predetermined plan and without any legal validation. Most of the structures of these settlements usually fall into the category of 'marginal housing unit', although they may also consist of more solid structures.

Total health expenditure: Sum of public and private health expenditure. It covers the provision of health services (preventive and curative), family planning activities, nutrition activities and emergency aid designated for health, but does not include provision of water and sanitation.

Transport used for work trips: Percentage of work trips undertaken by private car (A); train, tram or ferry (B); bus or minibus (C); other (motorcycle, bicycle and other non-motorized modes) (D). When several modes of transport are used for a given trip, the principal mode is selected.

Travel time: Average time in minutes for a one-way work trip. This is an average over all modes of transport.

Type of living quarters: Living quarters are structurally separate and independent places of abode. They may (i) have been constructed, built, converted or arranged for human habitation, provided that they are not used wholly for other purposes and that, in the case of improvised housing units and collective living quarters, they are occupied at the time of the enumeration; or (ii) although not intended for habitation, actually be in use for such a purpose. Living quarters are either housing units or collective living quarters. *Housing unit*: A separate and independent place of abode intended for habitation by a single household, or one not intended for habitation but occupied as living quarters by a household at the time of the enumeration. It may be an occupied or vacant dwelling, an occupied mobile or improvised housing unit or any other place occupied as living quarters by a household at the time of the census. This category includes housing of various levels of permanency and acceptability.

Value added: The net output of an industry after adding up all outputs and subtracting intermediate inputs. The industrial origin of value added is determined by the International Standard Industrial Classification (ISIC) revision 3. Agriculture includes forestry and fishing. Industry comprises mining, manufacturing (also reported as a separate sub-group), construction, electricity, water and gas. Manufacturing refers to industries. Services sector is derived as a residual (from GDP, less agriculture and industry) and may not properly reflect the sum of service output, including banking and financial services.

Under-five mortality: Percentage of female children and male children who die before reaching their fifth birthday. Child mortality = (number of deaths for children below five years of age during the year)/(average number of live births during the last five years).

Urban agglomeration: The contours of contiguous territory without regard to administrative boundaries. It comprises the city or town proper and also the suburban fringe lying outside of, but adjacent to, the city boundaries. Table B.1 contains revised estimates and projections for all urban agglomerations comprising 750,000 or more inhabitants. *Annual growth rate*: Average annual percentage change of population during the indicated period for each country's major regions and global totals.

Wastewater treated: Percentage of all wastewater undergoing some form of treatment.

Water consumption: Average consumption of water in litres per day per person for all domestic uses (excludes industrial use) in settlements.

Water supply system: 'Housing units with piped water inside the housing unit' refers to the existence of water pipes within the walls that constitute a housing unit. Water can be piped from the community source – that is, one that is subject to inspection and control by public authorities. Water can also be piped into the unit from a private source, such as a pressure tank, a pump or some other installation. The category 'piped water outside unit, but within 200 metres' refers to units where the piped water is not available to occupants within the unit they reside in, but is accessible within the range of 200 metres, assuming that access to piped water within that distance allows occupants to provide water for household needs without being subjected to extreme effort. 'Other' refers to units that do not have access to piped water at all, whose occupants depend upon springs or wells, or to units where piped water is located beyond 200 metres.

Women-headed household: Households headed by women. In identifying the members of a household, a common approach is to identify, first, the household head or reference person and then the remaining members of the household according to their relationship to the head or reference person. The head of household is defined as that person in the household who is acknowledged as such by other members. However, it is recognized that national practices in identifying household headship vary significantly on the basis of customs and cultural traditions.

SOURCES OF DATA

The Statistical Data Tables have been compiled from the following UN-Habitat databases: Human Settlements Statistics Database, Global Urban Observatory (GUO) Database, CitiBase and Habitat's Household Projections Project.

Various statistical publications from the United Nations and other international organizations have been used as well. Notable among them are International Energy Agency (IEA), *Energy Balances of OECD Countries*, Paris, various years. International Labour Organization (2003) *Economically Active Population Estimates and Projections: 1950–2010*, 4th edition, Geneva. International Road Federation (IRF) (2001) *World Road Statistics 2001*, Geneva. Organisation for Economic Co-operation and Development (OECD) *International Development Statistics*, CD-ROM, various years, Paris. United Nations (2001) *Compendium of Human Settlements Statistics 2001* (United Nations publication sales No E01.XVII5), UN, New York. UNDP (2004) *Human Development Report*. UNDP/Oxford University Press, New York. United Nations Population Division (2004) *World Urbanization Prospects: The 2003 Revision*, UN, New York. UNESCO (2002) *Estimated Illiteracy Rate and Illiterate Population Aged 15 Years and Older, by Country, 1970–2015: July 2002 Assessment*, Institute for Statistics (UIS), Montreal. United Nations High Commissioner for Refugees (UNHCR) (2002) *Statistical Yearbook 2001*, Geneva. United Nations Human Settlements Programme (UN-Habitat) (2002) *Global Urban Indicators*

Database 2, UN-Habitat, Nairobi. United Nations Statistics Division (2002) *Energy Statistics Yearbook 2002*, New York. United Nations Statistics Division (UNSD) *National Accounts Statistics: Main Aggregates and Detailed Tables*, parts 1 and 2, various years, New York. World Bank (2002) *World Development Indicators, 2002*, World Bank, Washington DC. World Bank (2004) *World Development Indicators 2004*. World Bank, Washington DC. World Health Organization (WHO), United Nations Children's Fund (UNICEF) and Water Supply and Sanitation Collaborative Council (2000) *Global Water Supply and Sanitation Assessment, 2000 Report*, Geneva and New York. WHO/UNICEF Joint Monitoring Programme for Water Supply and Sanitation (2004) *Meeting the MDG Drinking Water and Sanitation Target: A Mid-term Assessment of Progress*. WHO/UNICEF, Geneva. World Resources Institute (WRI) (2000) *World Resources 2000–2001*, Washington, DC.

NOTES

1 All members of the United Nations General Assembly arranged in Regional Groups. According to the *United Nations Handbook 2003* (2003), this grouping is unofficial and has been developed to take account of the purposes of General Assembly Resolution 1991 (XVIII) (1963), 33/138 (1978) and 2847 (XXVI) (1971). The US is not a member of any regional group, but attends meetings of the Western European and Other States Group (WEOG) as an observer and is considered to be a member of that group for electoral purposes. Turkey participates fully in both the Asian and WEOG groups, but for electoral purposes is considered a member of WEOG only. Israel became a full member of WEOG on a temporary basis on 28 May 2000. As of 31 May 2002, Estonia and Kiribati were not members of any regional group. In addition to member states, there is also a non-member state, the Holy See, that has observer status in the United Nations. By General Assembly Resolution 52/250 (1998), the General Assembly conferred upon Palestine, in its capacity as observer, additional rights and privileges of participation. These included, *inter alia*, the right to participation in the general debate of the General Assembly, but did not include the right to vote or to put forward candidates.

2 As classified by the United Nations Development Programme (UNDP); see *Human Development Reports* for detail.

3 55 countries or areas.

4 86 countries or areas.

5 36 countries or areas.

6 As classified by the World Bank; see *World Development Reports* for detail.

DATA TABLES

TABLE A.1

Demographic Indicators

	Level of urbanization (%)		Urban population						Rural population		Total population	
			Estimates and projections (000)				Rate of change (%)		Estimates and projections (000)		(000)	
	2000	2030	2000	2010	2020	2030	2000–2010	2020–2030	2000	2030	2000	2030
World Total	47.1	60.8	2,856,927	3,505,347	4,215,397	4,944,679	2.0	1.6	3,213,654	3,185,470	6,070,581	8,130,149
WORLD MAJOR AGGREGATES												
More developed regions	73.9	81.7	882,465	928,632	974,228	1,014,773	0.5	0.4	311,407	227,505	1,193,872	1,242,278
Less developed regions	40.5	57.1	1,974,462	2,576,716	3,241,169	3,929,906	2.7	1.9	2,902,247	2,957,965	4,876,709	6,887,870
Least developed regions	25.2	43.3	167,957	257,330	381,129	544,304	4.3	3.6	499,800	712,511	667,757	1,256,815
Landlocked developing countries	25.9	38.1	84,462	114,292	161,568	228,657	3.0	3.5	240,396	367,169	326,225	599,807
Small island developing states	54.8	63.4	28,037	32,839	37,889	43,137	1.6	1.3	23,094	24,891	51,132	68,026
UNITED NATIONS REGIONAL GROUPS												
African States	37.1	53.5	295,348	417,186	568,199	748,158	3.5	2.8	500,323	649,846	795,671	1,398,004
Asian States	37.1	54.5	1,366,980	1,770,494	2,214,364	2,664,282	2.6	1.8	2,312,757	2,222,364	3,679,737	4,886,647
Eastern European States	68.3	74.3	207,850	200,624	196,183	191,976	(0.4)	(0.2)	96,688	66,281	304,538	258,257
Latin American and Caribbean States	75.5	84.6	392,982	471,708	542,392	601,726	1.8	1.0	127,247	109,332	520,229	711,058
Western European and Other States	72.7	79.6	529,058	533,808	540,068	545,369	0.1	0.1	198,928	140,070	727,986	685,440
HUMAN DEVELOPMENT AGGREGATES												
High human development	76.6	84.2	901,011	983,241	1,058,287	1,122,972	0.9	0.6	275,302	210,793	1,176,312	1,333,768
Medium human development	41.1	57.8	1,688,509	2,133,279	2,604,927	3,064,454	2.3	1.6	2,416,847	2,235,381	4,105,359	5,299,833
Low human development	31.3	49.3	216,584	324,409	470,027	652,554	4.0	3.3	474,819	672,117	691,402	1,324,667
INCOME AGGREGATES												
High income	77.3	84.7	722,636	782,919	837,366	885,084	0.8	0.6	212,075	160,056	934,711	1,045,142
Middle income	50.8	69.0	1,494,433	1,847,789	2,188,966	2,473,662	2.1	1.2	1,447,655	1,110,360	2,942,091	3,584,020
Upper-middle income	74.9	84.1	243,436	285,489	325,256	360,017	1.6	1.0	81,525	68,125	324,959	428,139
Lower-middle income	47.8	67.0	1,250,997	1,562,300	1,863,710	2,113,645	2.2	1.3	1,366,130	1,042,235	2,617,132	3,155,881
Low income	29.1	45.3	637,926	872,391	1,186,558	1,583,217	3.1	2.9	1,553,718	1,914,890	2,191,643	3,498,102
GEOGRAPHIC AGGREGATES												
Africa	37.1	53.5	295,348	417,186	568,199	748,158	3.5	2.8	500,323	649,846	795,671	1,398,004
Eastern Africa	24.4	41.0	61,501	93,562	135,788	189,215	4.2	3.3	191,014	272,320	252,515	461,535
Middle Africa	35.2	54.4	32,738	49,640	73,212	104,041	4.2	3.5	60,222	87,257	92,960	191,298
Northern Africa	48.4	63.4	84,045	109,269	138,277	169,347	2.6	2.0	89,570	97,902	173,615	267,249
Southern Africa	52.4	67.0	26,421	29,451	31,169	32,634	1.1	0.5	24,026	16,092	50,448	48,725
Western Africa	40.1	58.9	90,642	135,264	189,752	252,920	4.0	2.9	135,491	176,277	226,133	429,197
Asia	37.1	54.5	1,366,980	1,770,494	2,214,364	2,664,282	2.6	1.8	2,312,757	2,222,364	3,679,737	4,886,647
Eastern Asia	40.4	62.6	598,413	766,054	921,854	1,039,087	2.5	1.2	882,697	620,302	1,481,110	1,659,389
South-central Asia	29.5	43.7	438,694	565,020	739,066	959,121	2.5	2.6	1,047,355	1,233,232	1,486,049	2,192,353
Southeastern Asia	39.6	60.7	206,228	282,547	359,842	432,014	3.1	1.8	314,128	279,222	520,355	711,236
Western Asia	64.3	72.3	123,646	156,874	193,602	234,060	2.4	1.9	68,577	89,608	192,222	323,669
Europe	72.7	79.6	529,058	533,808	540,068	545,369	0.1	0.1	198,928	140,070	727,986	685,440
Eastern Europe	68.3	74.3	207,850	200,624	196,183	191,976	(0.4)	(0.2)	96,688	66,281	304,538	258,257
Northern Europe	83.0	87.7	78,150	80,922	84,254	87,586	0.3	0.4	15,974	12,256	94,123	99,842
Southern Europe	65.4	74.1	95,325	98,084	100,321	102,465	0.3	0.2	50,497	35,797	145,822	138,261
Western Europe	80.5	86.4	147,734	154,178	159,309	163,342	0.4	0.3	35,769	25,737	183,502	189,079
Latin America	75.5	84.6	392,982	471,708	542,392	601,726	1.8	1.0	127,247	109,332	520,229	711,058
Caribbean	63.3	73.3	23,838	27,111	30,344	33,216	1.3	0.9	13,836	12,102	37,673	45,318
Central America	68.4	77.5	92,483	112,379	132,055	150,192	1.9	1.3	42,729	43,607	135,213	193,799
South America	79.7	88.6	276,661	332,218	379,992	418,317	1.8	1.0	70,682	53,624	347,343	471,941
Northern America	79.1	86.9	249,995	286,479	321,968	354,081	1.4	1.0	65,920	53,451	315,915	407,532
Oceania	72.7	74.9	22,564	25,673	28,405	31,063	1.3	0.9	8,479	10,405	31,043	41,468
Australia/New Zealand	89.9	94.9	20,617	23,194	25,214	26,842	1.2	0.6	2,320	1,448	22,937	28,290
Melanesia	19.3	27.2	1,348	1,736	2,289	3,153	2.5	3.2	5,648	8,439	6,996	11,592
Micronesia (Federated States of)	67.3	81.2	336	429	522	608	2.4	1.5	163	141	499	748
Polynesia	43.1	55.0	263	314	381	461	1.8	1.9	348	377	611	838

Note: Rates of change for the periods indicated in this table and tables that follow show the average annual rates of change. Lists of countries in aggregates are presented in the Technical Notes, pp177–179.

Source: Data in regional aggregates are calculated on a basis of country/area level data from Tables B.1 and B.2.

TABLE A.2

Shelter Indicators

	Access to urban services						Number of households						
	Improved water (%)		Improved sanitation (%)		House connections (%)		Estimates and projections (000)			Five-year increment (000)			
	1990	2002	1990	2002	1990	2002	2005	2015	2025	2005–2010	2010–2015	2015–2020	2020–2025
World Total	92.1	92.4	81.1	81.2	73.3	71.6	1,743,640	2,116,248	2,461,422	191,930	180,678	175,481	169,694
WORLD MAJOR AGGREGATES													
More developed regions	99.8	99.6	99.4	98.0	97.9	96.4	497,505	547,104	582,358	27,161	22,438	18,896	16,357
Less developed regions	89.0	89.9	73.8	75.4	63.5	62.9	1,246,135	1,569,144	1,879,065	164,769	158,240	156,584	153,337
Least developed regions	74.9	79.2	49.0	57.8	32.9	34.7	134,798	179,679	239,473	21,416	23,465	27,327	32,468
Landlocked developing countries	83.2	86.2	54.8	61.6	43.3	53.2	72,437	93,677	121,838	10,016	11,224	13,064	15,098
Small island developing states	93.7	94.2	85.8	86.1	80.2	76.0	11,187	12,882	14,375	839	856	777	716
UNITED NATIONS REGIONAL GROUPS													
African States	78.7	83.4	55.3	57.8	42.5	43.3	188,308	248,991	321,124	30,867	29,816	33,993	38,140
Asian States	91.3	90.8	82.1	81.0	69.4	70.3	937,383	1,164,423	1,368,331	116,316	110,725	105,331	98,576
Eastern European States	97.5	97.7	97.6	93.3	90.9	88.9	139,769	147,013	147,129	5,384	1,860	471	(355)
Latin American and Caribbean States	94.4	96.3	82.6	86.4	82.9	83.8	142,689	175,549	206,351	16,644	16,215	15,749	15,054
Western European and Other States	98.5	98.5	99.4	99.7	98.8	99.6	209,865	231,808	248,799	11,384	10,560	9,050	7,941
HUMAN DEVELOPMENT AGGREGATES													
High human development	99.0	99.2	98.2	98.4	96.6	96.1	461,648	518,920	566,193	29,490	27,782	24,769	22,504
Medium human development	93.4	92.6	80.4	81.1	70.6	72.1	1,134,804	1,396,006	1,623,226	136,728	124,473	118,068	109,153
Low human development	74.3	81.9	47.5	53.9	33.7	34.8	147,188	201,322	272,003	25,712	28,423	32,644	38,037
INCOME AGGREGATES													
High income	99.8	99.8	99.6	99.6	98.9	98.8	386,518	433,249	472,107	23,984	22,747	20,349	18,509
Middle income	95.2	95.5	98.9	88.4	83.4	84.5	891,644	1,083,250	1,247,057	101,780	89,827	85,217	78,590
Upper-middle income	95.7	95.9	92.7	89.9	86.3	86.0	93,028	109,385	124,323	8,259	8,098	7,649	7,290
Low-middle income	93.9	94.2	83.6	85.5	77.3	78.8	798,616	973,865	1,122,734	93,520	81,729	77,569	71,300
Low income	79.7	81.7	50.7	58.3	37.3	40.5	465,479	599,749	742,258	66,167	68,104	69,914	72,595
GEOGRAPHIC AGGREGATES													
Africa	78.7	83.4	55.3	57.8	42.5	43.3	188,604	249,358	321,562	30,902	29,853	34,029	38,174
Eastern Africa	85.2	84.5	51.1	53.8	42.9	42.3	56,357	72,812	96,066	7,637	8,819	10,661	12,593
Middle Africa	67.9	74.9	46.0	43.2	30.0	30.8	22,129	31,268	44,370	4,144	4,994	5,987	7,115
Northern Africa	91.0	91.4	89.6	90.6	78.4	84.8	34,070	43,207	52,890	4,885	4,252	5,198	4,485
Southern Africa	94.0	94.2	68.8	69.6	62.0	63.6	18,711	21,932	22,194	2,759	462	144	118
Western Africa	95.6	81.6	46.2	57.0	27.8	32.8	57,337	80,139	106,041	11,477	11,326	12,039	13,863
Asia	91.3	90.8	82.1	81.0	69.4	70.3	962,492	1,194,550	1,402,896	118,823	113,236	107,657	100,690
Eastern Asia	96.8	95.2	82.0	75.5	80.8	83.0	480,753	593,113	690,509	59,045	53,315	50,415	46,981
South-central Asia	94.0	88.9	76.9	74.4	62.9	63.9	303,843	381,645	451,755	38,779	39,023	36,374	33,736
Southeastern Asia	90.6	85.5	71.9	78.7	49.0	42.7	135,880	166,502	193,391	15,585	15,037	14,197	12,693
Western Asia	94.1	94.4	95.5	93.9	85.2	85.7	42,015	53,291	67,242	5,414	5,862	6,671	7,280
Europe	99.7	99.5	99.3	97.5	97.7	96.0	302,806	323,017	331,902	12,323	7,888	5,298	3,588
Eastern Europe	99.3	98.6	98.6	73.9	93.0	88.0	125,626	132,180	132,129	4,965	1,589	368	(418)
Northern Europe	100.0	100.0	100.0	97.7	98.9	98.7	42,179	47,064	51,179	2,486	2,399	2,125	1,990
Southern Europe	99.7	99.7	99.0	99.0	96.7	98.4	53,614	56,055	57,033	1,401	1,040	625	353
Western Europe	100.0	100.0	100.0	100.0	100.0	100.0	81,387	87,717	91,561	3,471	2,860	2,181	1,663
Latin America	94.4	96.3	82.6	86.4	82.9	83.8	144,416	177,484	208,475	16,746	16,321	15,848	15,143
Caribbean	96.4	97.4	87.8	90.4	81.8	79.3	11,230	13,189	14,767	1,035	924	838	739
Central America	93.3	97.3	73.2	82.0	86.0	88.0	34,455	43,243	51,722	4,349	4,439	4,365	4,114
South America	92.2	94.2	81.0	84.5	81.5	86.9	98,731	121,052	141,985	11,361	10,959	10,644	10,290
Northern America	100.0	100.0	100.0	100.0	100.0	100.0	133,819	158,218	180,848	12,076	12,323	11,597	11,033
Oceania	93.3	91.9	83.9	88.6	79.3	75.5	11,504	13,621	15,739	1,060	1,056	1,053	1,065
Australia/New Zealand	100.0	100.0	100.0	100.0	100.0	100.0	9,600	11,254	12,790	837	817	782	755
Melanesia	90.5	89.0	88.0	85.5	72.3	70.0	1,647	2,056	2,584	198	212	243	284
Micronesia (Federated States of)	88.8	88.2	71.7	83.7	...	...	116	141	166	11	13	13	13
Polynesia	99.7	97.0	99.0	99.0	...	81.7	142	170	199	14	15	15	14

Note: Lists of countries in aggregates are presented in the Technical Notes, pp177–179.

Source: Data in regional aggregates are calculated on a basis of country/area level data from Tables B.3 and B.5.

TABLE A.3

Social Indicators

	Poverty		Vital data		Health services					Communications				
	(below US$/day) $1 (%)	$2 (%)	Life expectancy (years)	Under five mortality /1000	Expend-iture US$/cap	Physicians /1000		Hospital beds /1000		Adult literacy (%)	Radios /1000	TV sets /1000	PCs /1000	Mobile phones /1000
			2002	2002	2001	1980	1995–2002	1980	1995–2002	2002	2001	2001	2002	2002
World Total														
WORLD MAJOR AGGREGATES														
More developed regions	...	...	73.3	10.6	1,203	2.1	3.0	9.8	7.5	98	893	563	282	571
Less developed regions	20.5	48.8	63.2	75.0	173	0.7	1.1	2.9	2.6	78	305	188	66	137
Least developed regions	46.1	80.9	47.8	162.4	18	0.0	0.1	1.0	0.6	56	193	48	5	18
Landlocked developing countries	28.9	62.0		112.0	42	1.0	1.1	5.9	4.3	73	230	114	13	46
Small island developing states	...	...	70.5	37.4	916	1.0	1.7	5.0	4.1	79	598	356	286	311
UNITED NATIONS REGIONAL GROUPS														
African States	36.6	65.1	47.7	152.4	37	0.2	0.3	1.7	0.0	63	245	80	16	50
Asian States	15.9	48.5	67.3	55.9	222	0.9	1.3	4.2	4.1	81	278	211	93	161
Eastern European States	3.3	13.2	71.7	21.5	184	2.5	3.0	9.0	7.0	99	475	408	98	319
Latin American and Caribbean States	13.6	33.2	70.4	35.7	212	0.6	1.6	1.7	2.2	86	421	251	60	178
Western European and Other States	...	...	77.9	7.3	1,965	2.0	3.1	9.3	7.2	...	1,119	643	377	763
HUMAN DEVELOPMENT AGGREGATES														
High human development	...	...	76.6	8.5	1,272	1.9	2.7	8.0	6.4	96	905	538	295	618
Medium human development	14.7	39.2	66.0	53.5	93	1.2	1.5	4.9	3.5	84	308	223	35	125
Low human development	43.1	74.8	46.1	171.5	15	0.1	0.1	1.3	0.6	58	297	67	7	32
INCOME AGGREGATES														
High income	...	...	78.2	5.7	1,836	1.9	2.7	8.5	7.0	95	1,050	595	396	740
Medium income	8.6	26.6	69.6	31.8	173	1.5	1.9	5.4	4.0	90	403	299	61	217
Upper-middle income	7.0	17.8	71.7	20.7	299	1.4	2.2	5.8	4.5	94	535	365	104	339
Low-middle income	9.5	31.8	68.4	38.3	100	1.5	1.8	5.2	3.7	88	327	261	36	146
Low income	38.3	71.6	51.8	139.2	20	0.4	0.5	3.1	2.1	64	214	73	9	21
GEOGRAPHIC AGGREGATES														
Africa	40.3	75.7	57.9	162.0	54	0.2	0.3	2.1	0.7	78	303	104	25	66
Eastern Africa	37.5	74.5	43.2	158.7	22	0.1	0.2	1.7	0.9	70	265	49	17	33
Middle Africa	43.5	76.0	45.1	172.8	18	0.1	0.1	1.6	0.7	57	264	51	13	31
Northern Africa	2.9	21.3	70.3	39.3	78	0.7	0.9	1.7	2.2	64	286	207	18	60
Southern Africa	30.7	54.7	41.0	93.5	117	0.1	0.3	2.4	...	82	168	112	52	146
Western Africa	49.4	77.4	47.0	186.9	14	0.1	0.1	1.4	0.5	45	264	52	8	28
Asia	13.2	43.2	69.4	49.5	319	1.2	1.6	4.9	5.2	83	339	252	127	249
Eastern Asia	10.9	34.2	74.3	24.8	651	1.1	1.9	6.6	8.4	95	537	374	283	502
South-central Asia	20.5	57.8	65.3	75.8	54	1.5	1.6	4.6	4.7	77	193	151	17	18
Southeastern Asia	11.3	52.2	65.9	54.7	148	0.3	0.7	2.3	1.9	75	232	157	96	193
Western Asia	5.2	22.8	71.1	41.1	354	1.8	2.0	4.6	3.0	83	344	305	64	260
Europe	...	...	74.9	10.7	1,214	2.2	3.2	10.0	8.2	99	801	547	260	576
Eastern Europe	3.6	15.9	70.5	16.2	169	2.5	3.2	9.4	8.2	99	615	465	91	333
Northern Europe	...	3.6	75.6	7.9	1,499	2.3	3.0	12.7	7.6	99	1,518	762	376	728
Southern Europe	...	...	75.4	12.3	686	1.8	2.8	6.3	4.7	97	374	365	145	571
Western Europe	...	...	78.8	5.7	2,381	2.1	3.4	11.1	10.3	99	843	612	427	747
Latin America	13.6	33.2	70.4	35.7	212	0.6	1.6	1.7	2.2	86	421	251	60	178
Caribbean	6.3	26.7	65.0	60.3	166	...	2.0	...	3.0	75	495	263	55	226
Central America	16.3	36.0	71.0	33.7	186	0.4	1.1	1.8	1.5	84	384	189	57	130
South America	14.2	33.6	71.5	29.7	253	0.8	1.7	1.8	2.3	92	487	297	63	196
Northern America	...	...	77.2	7.9	4,615	2.0	2.6	6.1	3.6	...	2,010	913	642	477
Oceania	...	...	...	...	...	...	...	...	...	...	...	...	...	...
Australia/New Zealand	...	...	78.7	6.0	1,518	...	2.4	11.6	7.3	...	1,661	673	515	634
Melanesia	...	...	...	...	...	...	...	...	...	...	...	...	...	...
Micronesia (Federated States of)	...	...	...	...	...	...	...	...	...	...	...	...	...	...
Polynesia	...	...	...	...	...	...	...	...	...	...	...	...	...	...

Note: Lists of countries in aggregates are presented in the Technical Notes, pp177–179.

Source: Data in regional aggregates are calculated on a basis of country/area level data from Table B.9

TABLE B.1

Urbanization, Urban Population and Urban Slum Dwellers

	Level of urbanization (%)		Urban population: Estimates and projections (000)				Urban population: Rate of change (%)		Urban slum dwellers: Estimated number (000)		Urban slum dwellers: Rate of change (%)	Urban slum dwellers: Percentage of urban	
	2000	2030	2000	2010	2020	2030	2000–2010	2020–2030	1990	2001	1990–2001	1990	2001
WORLD	**47.1**	**60.8**	**2,856,927**	**3,505,347**	**4,215,397**	**4,944,679**	**2.0**	**1.6**	**721,608**	**923,986**	**2.2**	**...**	**31.6**
AFRICA	**37.1**	**53.5**	**295,348**	**417,186**	**568,199**	**748,156**	**3.5**	**2.8**	**122,692**	**187,532**	**3.9**	**...**	**61.3**
Algeria	57.1	72.6	17,285	22,281	27,468	32,032	2.5	1.5	1,508	2,101	3.0	11.8	11.8
Angola	33.4	55.9	4,135	6,919	10,723	15,971	5.1	4.0	2,193	3,918	5.3	83.1	83.1
Benin	42.3	63.5	2,630	4,022	5,756	7,675	4.2	2.9	1,288	2,318	5.3	80.3	83.6
Botswana	50.2	65.7	866	972	1,002	1,025	1.2	0.2	311	466	3.7	59.2	60.7
Burkina Faso	16.7	33.0	1,991	3,318	5,592	9,220	5.1	5.0	987	1,528	4.0	80.9	76.5
Burundi	9.0	22.6	561	1,078	1,881	3,088	6.5	5.0	294	394	2.7	83.3	65.3
Cameroon	49.0	69.2	7,403	10,059	12,540	15,050	3.1	1.8	2,906	5,064	5.0	62.1	67.0
Cape Verde	53.3	72.7	232	325	422	513	3.4	2.0	106	193	5.4	70.3	69.6
Central African Republic	41.2	60.5	1,531	1,995	2,633	3,315	2.6	2.3	1,038	1,455	3.1	94.0	92.4
Chad	23.8	42.2	1,870	2,971	4,811	7,470	4.6	4.4	1,218	1,947	4.3	99.3	99.1
Comoros	33.2	54.1	234	366	538	747	4.5	3.3	91	151	4.6	61.7	61.2
Congo	52.2	67.4	1,800	2,572	3,692	5,096	3.6	3.2	1,050	1,852	5.2	84.5	90.1
Côte d'Ivoire	43.6	60.4	6,902	8,940	11,355	14,054	2.6	2.1	2,532	4,884	6.0	50.5	67.9
Democratic Republic of the Congo	30.3	51.0	14,713	23,408	36,659	54,536	4.6	4.0	5,366	7,985	3.6	51.9	49.5
Djibouti	82.2	90.1	548	667	807	967	2.0	1.8	...	...	...	...	...
Egypt	42.1	54.1	28,559	35,664	45,916	58,986	2.2	2.5	14,087	11,762	(1.6)	57.5	39.9
Equatorial Guinea	45.1	67.6	206	321	452	601	4.4	2.8	112	201	5.3	89.1	86.5
Eritrea	18.7	37.4	696	1,229	1,969	2,967	5.7	4.1	342	510	3.6	69.9	69.9
Ethiopia	14.9	28.7	9,771	14,841	23,353	36,466	4.2	4.5	5,984	10,159	4.8	99.0	99.4
Gabon	81.4	91.5	1,024	1,322	1,603	1,870	2.6	1.5	357	688	5.9	56.1	66.2
Gambia	26.2	35.7	344	448	597	835	2.6	3.4	155	280	5.4	67.0	67.0
Ghana	43.9	58.3	8,607	11,750	15,271	19,034	3.1	2.2	4,083	4,993	1.8	80.4	69.6
Guinea	32.6	55.3	2,647	4,033	5,990	8,246	4.2	3.2	1,145	1,672	3.4	79.6	72.3
Guinea-Bissau	31.5	54.9	431	724	1,145	1,731	5.2	4.1	210	371	5.2	93.4	93.4
Kenya	35.9	62.7	10,965	16,429	21,533	25,807	4.0	1.8	3,985	7,605	5.9	70.4	70.7
Lesotho	17.6	29.8	314	340	389	464	0.8	1.8	168	337	6.3	49.8	57.0
Liberia	44.9	63.4	1,321	2,104	3,071	4,331	4.7	3.4	632	788	2.0	70.2	55.7
Libyan Arab Jamahiriya	85.2	91.2	4,463	5,580	6,623	7,410	2.2	1.1	1,242	1,674	2.7	35.2	35.2
Madagascar	26.0	40.7	4,152	6,027	9,079	13,624	3.7	4.1	2,562	4,603	5.3	90.9	92.9
Malawi	15.1	32.0	1,716	2,691	4,188	6,342	4.5	4.1	1,033	1,590	3.9	94.6	91.1
Mali	30.2	52.0	3,594	6,037	9,880	15,390	5.2	4.4	1,968	3,361	4.9	94.1	93.2
Mauritania	57.7	81.1	1,527	2,452	3,447	4,445	4.7	2.5	827	1,531	5.6	94.3	94.3
Mauritius[1]	42.7	55.8	506	586	686	804	1.5	1.6	...	...	...	...	...
Morocco	55.5	72.5	16,144	21,076	26,129	30,824	2.7	1.7	4,457	5,579	2.0	37.4	32.7
Mozambique	32.1	60.0	5,735	9,135	12,683	15,976	4.7	2.3	2,722	5,841	6.9	94.5	94.1
Namibia	30.9	50.9	584	773	988	1,231	2.8	2.2	155	213	2.9	42.3	37.9
Niger	20.6	41.1	2,211	4,047	7,229	12,453	6.0	5.4	1,191	2,277	5.9	96.0	96.2
Nigeria	44.1	65.0	50,603	75,748	104,339	134,398	4.0	2.5	24,096	41,595	5.0	80.0	79.2
Réunion	89.9	96.0	650	771	859	920	1.7	0.7	...	...	...	...	...
Rwanda	13.6	58.5	1,050	2,983	5,606	7,866	10.4	3.4	296	437	3.5	82.2	87.9
Saint Helena[2]	34.7	50.5	2	2	2	3	0.0	4.1	-	-	...	...	2.0
Sao Tome and Principe	37.6	48.7	56	74	99	134	2.8	3.0	-	1	...	...	2.0
Senegal	47.4	67.1	4,456	6,472	8,801	11,350	3.7	2.5	2,276	3,555	4.1	77.6	76.4
Seychelles	49.7	61.7	39	44	51	58	1.2	1.3	...	...	...	...	...
Sierra Leone	36.7	58.7	1,619	2,570	3,579	4,813	4.6	3.0	1,107	1,642	3.6	90.9	95.8
Somalia	33.3	53.9	2,905	5,057	8,314	13,144	5.5	4.6	1,670	2,482	3.6	96.3	97.1
South Africa	55.5	70.1	24,416	27,094	28,476	29,540	1.0	0.4	8,207	8,376	0.2	46.2	33.2
Sudan	36.1	60.2	11,355	17,321	23,563	30,408	4.2	2.6	5,708	10,107	5.2	86.4	85.7
Swaziland	23.2	36.6	242	272	314	373	1.2	1.7	...	...	...	...	...
Togo	33.4	54.6	1,523	2,272	3,276	4,431	4.0	3.0	796	1,273	4.3	80.9	80.6
Tunisia	62.8	74.4	5,975	7,001	8,156	9,193	1.6	1.2	425	234	(5.4)	9.0	3.7
Uganda	12.0	20.4	2,825	4,336	7,329	13,035	4.3	5.8	1,806	3,241	5.3	93.8	93.0
United Republic of Tanzania	32.3	58.2	11,236	17,787	25,225	33,144	4.6	2.7	5,601	11,031	6.2	99.1	92.1
Western Sahara	92.9	96.3	265	345	423	495	2.6	1.6	-	5	...	-	2.0
Zambia	35.1	50.2	3,660	4,526	5,902	7,638	2.1	2.6	2,284	3,136	2.9	72.0	74.0
Zimbabwe	33.6	51.8	4,253	5,008	5,785	6,620	1.6	1.3	116	157	2.8	4.0	3.4
ASIA	**37.1**	**54.5**	**1,366,980**	**1,770,494**	**2,214,364**	**2,664,282**	**2.6**	**1.8**	**...**	**...**	**...**	**...**	**...**
Afghanistan	21.9	41.9	4,683	8,484	13,674	20,920	5.9	4.3	2,458	4,945	6.4	98.5	98.5
Armenia	65.0	69.2	2,024	1,908	1,908	1,928	(0.6)	0.1	47	51	0.7	2.0	2.0
Azerbaijan	50.5	59.5	4,123	4,504	5,280	6,235	0.9	1.7	278	301	0.7	7.2	7.2
Bahrain	89.6	92.9	607	753	891	1,018	2.2	1.3	...	...	...	...	...
Bangladesh	23.2	39.3	31,996	45,298	63,224	86,500	3.5	3.1	18,988	30,403	4.3	87.3	84.7
Bhutan	7.7	20.1	159	292	500	810	6.1	4.8	61	70	1.2	70.0	44.1
Brunei Darussalam	73.9	87.0	247	334	415	489	3.0	1.6	...	...	...	...	...
Cambodia	16.9	36.9	2,223	3,792	5,981	8,697	5.3	3.7	870	1,696	6.1	71.7	72.2
China[3]	35.8	60.5	456,247	616,228	765,597	877,623	3.0	1.4	137,929	178,256	2.3	43.6	37.8
China, Hong Kong SAR[4]	100.0	100.0	6,807	7,537	8,188	8,781	1.0	0.7	113	139	1.9	2.0	2.0
China, Macao SAR[5]	98.9	99.2	445	486	526	558	0.9	0.6	7	9	2.3	2.0	2.0
Cyprus	68.8	76.5	539	591	643	687	0.9	0.7	-	-	-	-	-
Democratic People's Republic of Korea	60.2	72.8	13,414	14,794	16,507	18,186	1.0	1.0	117	95	(1.9)	1.0	0.7
Georgia	52.7	58.1	2,772	2,476	2,428	2,473	(1.1)	0.2	558	252	(7.2)	18.4	8.5
India	27.7	41.4	281,255	355,205	455,823	586,052	2.3	2.5	131,174	158,418	1.7	60.8	55.5
Indonesia	42.0	67.7	88,863	126,739	160,775	187,846	3.6	1.6	17,964	20,877	1.4	32.2	23.1
Iran (Islamic Republic of)	64.4	79.7	42,799	53,784	66,011	75,253	2.3	1.3	17,094	20,406	1.6	51.9	44.2
Iraq	67.9	71.3	15,759	20,134	25,714	32,344	2.4	2.3	6,825	9,026	2.5	56.7	56.7

TABLE B.1

continued

	Level of urbanization (%)		Urban population						Urban slum dwellers				
			Estimates and projections (000)				Rate of change (%)		Estimated number (000)		Rate of change (%)	Percentage of urban	
	2000	2030	2000	2010	2020	2030	2000–2010	2020–2030	1990	2001	1990–2001	1990	2001
Israel	91.5	93.6	5,527	6,687	7,600	8,392	1.9	1.0	81	113	3.0	2.0	2.0
Japan	65.2	73.1	82,794	85,150	86,977	88,482	0.3	0.2	6,117	6,430	0.5	6.4	6.4
Jordan	78.7	84.6	3,963	5,117	6,216	7,311	2.6	1.6	388	623	4.3	16.5	15.7
Kazakhstan	55.8	65.7	8,733	8,580	9,297	10,018	(0.2)	0.7	2,835	2,664	(0.6)	29.7	29.7
Kuwait	96.0	97.5	2,157	2,942	3,542	4,091	3.1	1.4	60	56	(0.6)	3.0	3.0
Kyrgyzstan	34.4	44.6	1,692	1,914	2,349	2,993	1.2	2.4	858	885	0.3	51.8	51.8
Lao People's Democratic Republic	19.3	38.2	1,018	1,603	2,451	3,549	4.5	3.7	422	705	4.7	66.1	66.1
Lebanon	86.6	92.0	3,013	3,566	3,991	4,317	1.7	0.8	1,142	1,602	3.1	50.0	50.0
Malaysia	61.8	77.6	14,212	18,768	23,218	27,324	2.8	1.6	177	262	3.6	2.0	2.0
Maldives	27.5	45.9	80	126	194	282	4.5	3.7	-	-	-	-	-
Mongolia	56.6	66.9	1,415	1,658	1,988	2,336	1.6	1.6	886	940	0.5	68.5	64.9
Myanmar	28.0	49.1	13,290	18,147	23,921	30,086	3.1	2.3	3,105	3,596	1.3	31.1	26.4
Nepal	13.7	29.4	3,220	5,253	8,082	11,976	4.9	3.9	1,574	2,656	4.8	96.9	92.4
Occupied Palestinian Territory	70.0	80.5	2,233	3,324	4,686	6,246	4.0	2.9	...	...	...	...	...
Oman	76.0	86.3	1,982	2,796	3,658	4,509	3.4	2.1	671	1,214	5.4	60.5	60.5
Pakistan	33.1	49.8	47,220	67,140	96,952	135,347	3.5	3.3	26,416	35,627	2.7	78.7	73.6
Philippines	58.5	76.1	44,327	59,294	73,763	86,615	2.9	1.6	16,346	20,183	1.9	54.9	44.1
Qatar	91.5	94.8	532	623	708	778	1.6	0.9	8	11	2.9	2.0	2.0
Republic of Korea	79.6	86.2	37,291	40,200	42,070	43,120	0.8	0.2	11,728	14,385	1.9	37.0	37.0
Saudi Arabia	86.2	92.9	19,083	26,282	33,265	40,124	3.2	1.9	2,385	3,609	3.8	19.8	19.8
Singapore	100.0	100.0	4,016	4,574	4,812	4,934	1.3	0.3	-	-	-	-	-
Sri Lanka	21.1	29.9	3,927	4,309	5,118	6,481	0.9	2.4	899	597	(3.7)	24.8	13.6
Syrian Arab Republic	50.1	59.8	8,289	10,640	13,627	17,188	2.5	2.3	629	892	3.2	10.4	10.4
Tajikistan	25.8	32.6	1,568	1,602	2,032	2,787	0.2	3.2	942	951	0.1	56.0	56.0
Thailand	31.1	47.0	18,974	22,994	28,569	35,420	1.9	2.1	1,998	...	...	19.5	...
Timor-Leste	7.5	15.2	52	82	127	189	4.6	4.0	1	7	16.4	2.0	12.0
Turkey	64.7	77.7	44,206	54,308	63,395	71,415	2.1	1.2	14,633	19,080	2.4	42.6	42.6
Turkmenistan	44.8	59.6	2,080	2,571	3,308	4,071	2.1	2.1	...	...	...	...	...
United Arab Emirates	84.6	89.6	2,386	2,904	3,332	3,633	2.0	0.9	...	...	...	...	...
Uzbekistan	37.3	44.6	9,282	10,462	12,502	15,632	1.2	2.2	4,170	4,689	1.1	50.7	50.7
Viet Nam	24.3	43.2	19,006	26,221	35,809	46,863	3.2	2.7	8,100	9,197	1.2	60.5	47.4
Yemen	24.7	42.2	4,452	7,321	12,718	21,370	5.0	5.2	1,787	3,110	5.0	67.5	65.1
EUROPE	**72.7**	**79.6**	**529,058**	**533,808**	**540,068**	**545,369**	**0.1**	**0.1**	**...**	**...**	**...**	**...**	**...**
Albania	42.0	60.7	1,306	1,603	1,929	2,233	2.0	1.5	...	...	...	...	...
Andorra	92.4	92.1	61	77	96	116	2.3	1.9	...	...	...	...	...
Austria	65.8	72.3	5,331	5,363	5,497	5,723	0.1	0.4	...	...	...	...	...
Belarus	69.8	80.2	7,003	7,057	7,082	6,959	0.1	(0.2)	...	...	...	...	...
Belgium	97.1	97.9	9,955	10,158	10,257	10,295	0.2	-	...	...	...	...	...
Bosnia and Herzegovina	43.0	61.0	1,708	2,051	2,315	2,495	1.8	0.7	...	...	...	...	...
Bulgaria	68.8	79.0	5,569	5,390	5,208	5,004	(0.3)	(0.4)	...	...	...	...	...
Channel Islands	30.5	30.5	44	44	43	43	-	-	...	...	...	...	...
Croatia	57.7	72.1	2,566	2,704	2,815	2,877	0.5	0.2	...	...	...	...	...
Czech Republic	74.1	77.4	7,607	7,634	7,597	7,439	-	(0.2)	...	...	...	...	...
Denmark	85.1	89.0	4,529	4,672	4,774	4,866	0.3	0.2	...	...	...	...	...
Estonia	69.4	76.6	949	861	794	722	(1.0)	(1.0)	...	...	...	...	...
Faeroe Islands	37.8	52.6	17	20	24	28	1.6	1.5	...	...	...	...	...
Finland	61.1	67.9	3,164	3,218	3,362	3,565	0.2	0.6	...	...	...	...	...
France	75.7	83.0	44,897	48,135	51,062	53,581	0.7	0.5	...	...	...	...	...
Germany	87.5	91.9	72,036	73,729	74,621	74,907	0.2	0.0	...	...	...	...	...
Gibraltar	100.0	100.0	27	27	27	26	0.0	(0.4)	...	...	...	...	...
Greece	60.1	72.4	6,552	6,937	7,339	7,646	0.6	0.4	...	...	...	...	...
Holy See[6]	100.0	100.0	1	1	1	1	-	-	-	-	-	-	-
Hungary	64.0	75.9	6,406	6,496	6,551	6,559	0.1	0.0	...	...	...	...	...
Iceland	92.4	95.1	261	283	301	314	0.8	0.4	...	...	...	...	...
Ireland	59.1	70.1	2,259	2,612	2,985	3,339	1.5	1.1	...	...	...	...	...
Isle of Man	51.8	51.8	38	40	41	41	0.5	0.0	...	...	...	...	...
Italy	67.2	74.3	38,677	38,570	38,315	38,278	0.0	0.0	...	...	...	...	...
Latvia	66.8	72.0	1,586	1,420	1,330	1,260	(1.1)	(0.5)	...	...	...	...	...
Liechtenstein	21.4	32.0	7	8	10	12	1.3	1.8	...	...	...	...	...
Lithuania	67.0	72.4	2,344	2,212	2,151	2,126	(0.6)	(0.1)	...	...	...	...	...
Luxembourg	91.0	95.3	396	461	521	581	1.5	1.1	...	...	...	...	...
Malta	90.9	95.0	354	376	392	396	0.6	0.1	...	...	...	...	...
Monaco	100.0	100.0	33	36	39	41	0.9	0.5	...	...	...	...	...
Netherlands	64.3	77.2	10,230	11,470	12,467	13,305	1.1	0.7	...	...	...	...	...
Norway	75.8	90.1	3,392	3,901	4,223	4,428	1.4	0.5	...	...	...	...	...
Poland	61.7	69.9	23,846	24,103	24,840	25,649	0.1	0.3	...	...	...	...	...
Portugal	53.0	68.7	5,312	5,875	6,315	6,674	1.0	0.6	...	...	...	...	...
Republic of Moldova	45.8	59.5	1,961	2,019	2,216	2,387	0.3	0.7	...	...	...	...	...
Romania	54.6	59.0	12,274	12,206	12,178	11,997	(0.1)	(0.1)	...	...	...	...	...
Russian Federation	73.3	78.3	106,758	101,218	97,201	93,736	(0.5)	(0.4)	...	...	...	...	...
San Marino	88.9	91.1	24	26	28	30	0.8	0.7	...	...	...	...	...
Serbia and Montenegro	51.6	63.7	5,444	5,634	6,003	6,432	0.3	0.7	...	...	...	...	...
Slovakia	56.8	64.9	3,062	3,228	3,377	3,470	0.5	0.3	...	...	...	...	...
Slovenia	50.8	59.8	1,011	1,007	1,033	1,085	0.0	0.5	...	...	...	...	...
Spain	76.3	81.7	31,078	31,910	32,315	32,657	0.3	0.1	...	...	...	...	...
Sweden	83.3	86.7	7,377	7,488	7,668	7,831	0.1	0.2	...	...	...	...	...
Switzerland	67.6	73.6	4,849	4,816	4,835	4,896	(0.1)	0.1	...	...	...	...	...
TFYR Macedonia[7]	59.4	68.9	1,202	1,284	1,398	1,520	0.7	0.8	...	...	...	...	...
Ukraine	67.1	73.9	33,363	31,274	29,935	28,777	(0.6)	(0.4)	...	...	...	...	...
United Kingdom	88.9	92.0	52,189	54,151	56,559	59,024	0.4	0.4	...	...	...	...	...

LATIN AMERICA	**75.5**	**84.6**	**392,982**	**471,708**	**542,392**	**601,726**	**1.8**	**1.0**	**...**			
Anguilla	100.0	100.0	11	13	15	17	1.7	1.3	3	5	3.7	40.6	40.6
Antigua and Barbuda	36.8	54.0	26	31	36	42	1.8	1.5	2	2	0.8	6.9	6.9
Argentina	89.5	93.7	33,181	37,895	42,054	45,568	1.3	0.8	8,597	10,964	2.2	30.5	33.1
Aruba	46.7	50.3	44	49	60	77	1.1	2.5	...	...	...	...	...
Bahamas	88.5	93.3	268	306	335	356	1.3	0.6	...	...	...	...	...
Barbados	50.0	68.1	134	155	175	192	1.5	0.9	...	...	...	...	...
Belize	48.0	60.4	115	145	183	225	2.3	2.1	48	69	3.2	54.2	62.0
Bolivia	61.9	75.3	5,149	6,664	8,311	9,994	2.6	1.8	2,555	3,284	2.3	70.0	61.3
Brazil	81.1	91.3	139,403	167,039	188,143	202,686	1.8	0.7	49,806	51,676	0.3	45.0	36.6
British Virgin Islands	61.1	78.3	12	16	20	24	2.9	1.8	...	...	...	...	...
Cayman Islands	100.0	100.0	37	49	61	72	2.8	1.7	...	...	...	...	...
Chile	85.9	92.3	13,084	15,243	17,193	18,750	1.5	0.9	432	1,143	8.8	4.0	8.6
Colombia	74.9	85.2	31,553	38,929	45,774	51,860	2.1	1.2	6,239	7,057	1.1	26.0	21.8
Costa Rica	59.0	73.8	2,318	3,024	3,698	4,333	2.7	1.6	195	313	4.3	11.9	12.8
Cuba	75.2	82.2	8,424	8,818	9,165	9,322	0.5	0.2	...	...	...	...	...
Dominica	71.0	81.1	55	59	63	65	0.7	0.3	8	7	(1.2)	16.6	14.0
Dominican Republic	58.2	72.0	4,862	5,974	7,104	8,133	2.1	1.4	2,327	2,111	(0.9)	56.4	37.6
Ecuador	60.3	74.1	7,489	9,306	11,149	12,846	2.2	1.4	1,588	2,095	2.5	28.1	25.6
El Salvador	58.4	71.3	3,626	4,441	5,325	6,277	2.0	1.6	1,126	1,386	1.9	44.7	35.2
Falkland Islands (Malvinas)	78.8	94.2	2	3	3	3	4.1	0.0	...	...	...	...	...
French Guiana	75.1	81.7	123	159	198	239	2.6	1.9	11	16	3.5	12.9	12.9
Grenada	38.5	59.6	31	36	40	43	1.5	0.7	2	2	1.4	6.9	6.9
Guadeloupe	99.6	99.9	426	460	478	488	0.8	0.2	27	30	1.0	6.9	6.9
Guatemala	45.1	60.6	5,155	7,208	9,742	12,724	3.4	2.7	2,192	2,884	2.5	65.8	61.8
Guyana	36.3	54.9	275	316	356	381	1.4	0.7	12	14	1.3	4.9	4.9
Haiti	35.6	56.0	2,851	3,841	4,997	6,215	3.0	2.2	1,728	2,574	3.6	84.9	85.7
Honduras	44.4	60.0	2,864	3,913	5,108	6,434	3.1	2.3	488	638	2.4	24.0	18.1
Jamaica	52.1	61.3	1,343	1,500	1,753	2,072	1.1	1.7	356	525	3.5	29.2	35.7
Martinique	94.9	98.0	366	392	409	418	0.7	0.2	...	...	...	...	...
Mexico	74.7	82.9	73,899	87,701	100,375	110,770	1.7	1.0	13,923	14,692	0.5	23.1	19.6
Montserrat	12.9	25.4	1	1	1	1	-	-	...	...	...	...	...
Netherlands Antilles	69.2	78.5	149	166	184	198	1.1	0.7	...	...	...	...	...
Nicaragua	56.1	70.6	2,848	3,849	5,031	6,305	3.0	2.3	1,638	2,382	3.4	80.7	80.9
Panama	56.2	69.2	1,659	2,098	2,594	3,123	2.3	1.9	397	505	2.2	30.8	30.8
Paraguay	55.3	71.8	3,027	4,239	5,642	7,104	3.4	2.3	756	797	0.5	36.8	25.0
Peru	72.8	82.6	18,885	22,897	26,971	30,690	1.9	1.3	8,979	12,993	3.4	60.4	68.1
Puerto Rico	94.6	99.4	3,611	3,934	4,043	4,021	0.9	(0.1)	...	...	...	...	...
Saint Kitts and Nevis	32.8	40.0	14	13	13	15	(0.7)	1.4	1	1	(0.7)	5.0	5.0
Saint Lucia	29.3	47.9	43	53	67	81	2.1	1.9	6	7	1.4	11.9	11.9
Saint Vincent and the Grenadines	54.8	76.1	65	81	92	100	2.2	0.8	2	3	3.6	5.0	5.0
Suriname	74.1	85.5	315	365	398	418	1.5	0.5	18	22	1.6	6.9	6.9
Trinidad and Tobago	74.1	84.1	955	1,039	1,094	1,115	0.8	0.2	292	310	0.5	34.7	32.0
Turks and Caicos Islands	45.2	63.1	8	13	18	23	4.9	2.5	...	...	...	...	...
United States Virgin Islands	92.6	96.7	101	112	121	126	1.0	0.4	...	...	...	...	...
Uruguay	91.9	95.5	3,071	3,354	3,587	3,778	0.9	0.5	191	4	...	6.9	6.9
Venezuela	86.9	91.9	21,103	25,808	30,211	33,999	2.0	1.2	6,664	8,738	2.5	40.7	40.7
NORTHERN AMERICA	**79.1**	**86.9**	**249,995**	**286,479**	**321,968**	**354,081**	**1.4**	**1.0**	**...**	**...**	**...**	**...**	**...**
Bermuda	100.0	100.0	80	85	89	91	0.6	0.2	...	...	...	...	...
Canada	79.4	87.2	24,429	27,324	29,958	32,251	1.1	0.7	...	...	...	...	...
Greenland	81.6	88.3	46	48	50	51	0.4	0.2	...	...	...	...	...
Saint-Pierre and Miquelon	88.9	91.5	6	6	6	6	0.0	0.0	...	...	...	...	...
United States	79.1	86.8	225,434	259,016	291,865	321,682	1.4	1.0	...	...	...	...	...
OCEANIA	**72.7**	**74.9**	**22,564**	**25,673**	**28,405**	**31,063**	**1.3**	**0.9**	**...**	**...**	**...**	**...**	**...**
American Samoa	88.8	95.2	51	67	83	98	2.7	1.7	...	...	...	...	...
Australia [8]	90.7	96.0	17,375	19,686	21,466	22,874	1.2	0.6	...	...	...	...	...
Cook Islands	65.2	88.6	12	15	16	16	2.2	0.0	...	...	...	...	...
Fiji	49.4	68.8	402	505	594	675	2.3	1.3	204	280	2.9	67.8	67.8
French Polynesia	52.7	61.0	123	141	167	200	1.4	1.8	...	...	...	...	...
Guam	93.2	96.1	145	170	195	215	1.6	1.0	...	...	...	...	...
Kiribati	43.0	72.2	36	54	71	84	4.1	1.7	14	18	2.2	55.7	55.7
Marshall Islands	65.8	75.3	34	39	44	50	1.4	1.3	...	...	...	...	...
Micronesia (Federated State of)	28.3	46.2	30	37	47	60	2.1	2.4	...	...	...	...	...
Nauru	100.0	100.0	12	15	18	21	2.2	1.5	...	...	...	...	...
New Caledonia	60.7	71.5	131	162	198	237	2.1	1.8	...	...	...	...	...
New Zealand	85.7	89.0	3,242	3,507	3,748	3,968	0.8	0.6	28	33	1.3	1.0	1.0
Niue	33.7	53.5	1	1	1	1	0.0	0.0	...	...	...	...	...
Northern Mariana Islands	93.3	97.0	65	97	127	153	4.0	1.9	...	...	...	...	...
Palau	69.5	73.4	13	16	19	24	2.1	2.3	...	...	...	...	...
Papua New Guinea	13.2	20.4	704	896	1,233	1,847	2.4	4.0	107	165	3.9	19.0	19.0
Pitcairn	-	-	-	-	-	-	...	...	...	...	...	...	...
Samoa	22.1	32.7	38	45	57	76	1.7	2.9	3	3	0.3	9.8	9.8
Solomon Islands	15.7	30.0	69	108	167	255	4.5	4.2	4	7	6.5	7.9	7.9
Tokelau	-	-	-	-	-	-	...	...	...	...	...	...	...
Tonga	32.7	48.3	33	40	49	60	1.9	2.0	...	...	...	...	...
Tuvalu	52.2	72.8	5	7	8	10	3.4	2.2	...	...	...	...	...
Vanuatu	21.7	39.0	43	65	96	138	4.1	3.6	10	17	4.3	37.0	37.0
Wallis and Futuna Islands	-	-	-	-	-	-	...	...	...	...	...	...	...

Notes:

1 Including Agalega, Rodrigues and Saint Brandon.

2 Including Ascension and Tristan da Cunha.

3 For statistical purposes, the data for China do not include Hong Kong and Macao Special Administrative Regions (SAR) of China.

4 As of 1 July 1997, Hong Kong became a Special Administrative Region (SAR) of China.

5 As of 20 December 1999, Macao became a Special Administrative Region (SAR) of China.

6 Refers to the Vatican City State.

7 The former Yugoslav Republic of Macedonia.

8 Including Christmas Island, Cocos (Keeling) Islands and Norfolk Island.

Source: UN Population Division, 2004; UN-Habitat, 2003a,b.

TABLE B.2

Total and Rural Population Size and Rate of Change

	Total population						Rural population				
	Estimates and projections (000)					Rate of change (%)	Estimates and projections (000)				Rate of change (%)
	2000	2005	2010	2020	2030	2000–2030	2000	2010	2020	2030	2000–2030
WORLD	**6,070,581**	**6,453,628**	**6,830,283**	**7,540,237**	**8,130,149**	**0.97**	**3,213,654**	**3,324,936**	**3,324,840**	**3,185,470**	**(0.03)**
AFRICA	**795,671**	**887,964**	**984,225**	**1,187,584**	**1,398,004**	**1.88**	**500,323**	**567,040**	**619,385**	**649,846**	**0.87**
Algeria	30,245	32,877	35,549	40,479	44,120	1.26	12,960	13,268	13,012	12,087	(0.23)
Angola	12,386	14,533	16,842	22,036	28,588	2.79	8,251	9,923	11,314	12,617	1.42
Benin	6,222	7,103	8,068	10,122	12,091	2.21	3,592	4,046	4,366	4,416	0.69
Botswana	1,725	1,801	1,767	1,665	1,562	(0.33)	860	796	663	536	(1.58)
Burkina Faso	11,905	13,798	16,018	21,403	27,910	2.84	9,914	12,700	15,811	18,690	2.11
Burundi	6,267	7,319	8,631	11,072	13,652	2.60	5,705	7,552	9,191	10,563	2.05
Cameroon	15,117	16,564	17,775	19,874	21,760	1.21	7,713	7,716	7,334	6,710	(0.46)
Cape Verde	436	482	529	623	705	1.60	203	204	201	193	(0.17)
Central African Republic	3,715	3,962	4,265	4,900	5,475	1.29	2,184	2,270	2,267	2,160	(0.04)
Chad	7,861	9,117	10,543	13,890	17,722	2.71	5,991	7,572	9,079	10,252	1.79
Comoros	705	812	927	1,154	1,382	2.24	471	561	616	635	1.00
Congo	3,447	3,921	4,532	5,960	7,558	2.62	1,647	1,960	2,268	2,462	1.34
Côte d'Ivoire	15,827	17,165	18,526	21,026	23,258	1.28	8,925	9,586	9,671	9,204	0.10
Democratic Republic of the Congo	48,571	56,079	64,714	84,418	106,988	2.63	33,858	41,306	47,758	52,452	1.46
Djibouti	666	721	773	912	1,073	1.59	118	106	105	106	(0.36)
Egypt	67,784	74,878	82,590	96,852	109,111	1.59	39,224	46,926	50,935	50,126	0.82
Equatorial Guinea	456	521	590	736	888	2.22	250	269	284	287	0.46
Eritrea	3,712	4,456	5,256	6,584	7,942	2.54	3,016	4,027	4,615	4,975	1.67
Ethiopia	65,590	74,189	83,530	104,797	127,220	2.21	55,819	68,689	81,444	90,754	1.62
Gabon	1,258	1,375	1,509	1,781	2,044	1.62	234	187	179	174	(0.99)
Gambia	1,312	1,499	1,680	2,015	2,338	1.93	968	1,232	1,417	1,504	1.47
Ghana	19,593	21,833	24,117	28,521	32,648	1.70	10,987	12,366	13,249	13,614	0.71
Guinea	8,117	8,788	9,990	12,478	14,921	2.03	5,470	5,957	6,488	6,675	0.66
Guinea-Bissau	1,367	1,584	1,827	2,421	3,154	2.79	936	1,104	1,276	1,422	1.39
Kenya	30,549	32,849	34,964	38,507	41,141	0.99	19,584	18,535	16,974	15,334	(0.82)
Lesotho	1,785	1,797	1,757	1,663	1,555	(0.46)	1,471	1,417	1,274	1,092	(0.99)
Liberia	2,943	3,603	4,130	5,367	6,830	2.81	1,622	2,025	2,296	2,499	1.44
Libyan Arab Jamahiriya	5,237	5,768	6,332	7,378	8,123	1.46	774	752	755	714	(0.27)
Madagascar	15,970	18,409	21,093	27,077	33,464	2.47	11,818	15,066	17,998	19,840	1.73
Malawi	11,370	12,572	13,796	16,668	19,834	1.85	9,655	11,105	12,479	13,492	1.12
Mali	11,904	13,829	16,208	22,140	29,572	3.03	8,310	10,171	12,261	14,182	1.78
Mauritania	2,645	3,069	3,520	4,473	5,482	2.43	1,117	1,068	1,026	1,038	(0.24)
Mauritius[1]	1,186	1,244	1,294	1,382	1,441	0.65	680	708	695	637	(0.22)
Morocco	29,108	31,564	34,066	38,726	42,505	1.26	12,964	12,990	12,597	11,680	(0.35)
Mozambique	17,861	19,495	21,009	24,004	26,620	1.33	12,126	11,874	11,321	10,643	(0.43)
Namibia	1,894	2,032	2,120	2,276	2,418	0.81	1,309	1,347	1,287	1,186	(0.33)
Niger	10,742	12,873	15,388	21,731	30,337	3.46	8,531	11,341	14,502	17,884	2.47
Nigeria	114,746	130,236	145,922	177,158	206,696	1.96	64,143	70,174	72,819	72,298	0.40
Réunion	723	777	821	900	958	0.94	73	50	41	38	(2.18)
Rwanda	7,724	8,607	9,559	11,557	13,453	1.85	6,674	6,575	5,951	5,587	(0.59)
Saint Helena[2]	5	5	5	5	5	-	3	3	3	3	-
Sao Tome and Principe	149	169	190	232	275	2.04	93	116	134	141	1.39
Senegal	9,393	10,587	11,869	14,422	16,926	1.96	4,937	5,397	5,621	5,577	0.41
Seychelles	79	82	86	91	95	0.61	40	42	40	36	(0.35)
Sierra Leone	4,415	5,340	5,859	6,979	8,206	2.07	2,796	3,289	3,400	3,393	0.65
Somalia	8,720	10,742	12,948	17,928	24,407	3.43	5,815	7,890	9,613	11,263	2.20
South Africa	44,000	45,323	44,939	43,683	42,170	(0.14)	19,584	17,845	15,207	12,630	(1.46)
Sudan	31,437	35,040	38,323	44,493	50,525	1.58	20,082	21,002	20,930	20,118	0.01
Swaziland	1,044	1,087	1,084	1,062	1,020	(0.08)	802	812	747	647	(0.72)
Togo	4,562	5,129	5,730	6,962	8,117	1.92	3,039	3,458	3,686	3,686	0.64
Tunisia	9,519	10,042	10,581	11,621	12,351	0.87	3,544	3,580	3,465	3,158	(0.38)
Uganda	23,487	27,623	32,996	46,634	63,953	3.34	20,662	28,661	39,305	50,918	3.01
United Republic of Tanzania	34,837	38,365	41,931	49,784	56,903	1.64	23,601	24,144	24,560	23,759	0.02
Western Sahara	285	324	363	441	514	1.97	20	18	19	19	(0.17)
Zambia	10,419	11,043	11,768	13,558	15,224	1.26	6,760	7,242	7,656	7,586	0.38
Zimbabwe	12,650	12,963	13,024	12,963	12,773	0.03	8,397	8,017	7,178	6,154	(1.04)
ASIA	**3,679,737**	**3,917,508**	**4,148,948**	**4,570,131**	**4,886,647**	**0.95**	**2,312,757**	**2,378,454**	**2,355,767**	**2,222,364**	**(0.13)**
Afghanistan	21,391	25,971	31,232	40,067	49,987	2.83	16,708	22,748	26,393	29,067	1.85
Armenia	3,112	3,043	2,991	2,926	2,786	(0.37)	1,088	1,083	1,018	859	(0.79)
Azerbaijan	8,157	8,527	8,983	9,876	10,486	0.84	4,034	4,479	4,597	4,251	0.17
Bahrain	677	754	828	969	1,095	1.60	70	76	78	77	0.32
Bangladesh	137,952	152,593	167,170	195,215	220,321	1.56	105,955	121,872	131,991	133,821	0.78
Bhutan	2,063	2,392	2,712	3,374	4,030	2.23	1,904	2,421	2,874	3,220	1.75
Brunei Darussalam	334	374	415	490	563	1.74	87	81	76	73	(0.58)
Cambodia	13,147	14,825	16,612	20,197	23,555	1.94	10,924	12,820	14,216	14,858	1.03
China[3]	1,275,215	1,322,273	1,364,875	1,429,473	1,450,521	0.43	818,969	748,648	663,876	572,898	(1.19)
China, Hong Kong SAR[4]	6,807	7,182	7,537	8,188	8,781	0.85	-	-	-	-	-
China, Macao SAR[5]	450	472	491	531	563	0.75	5	5	5	5	-
Cyprus	783	813	838	879	898	0.46	244	248	237	211	(0.48)
Democratic People's Republic of Korea	22,268	22,876	23,270	24,203	24,974	0.38	8,854	8,476	7,696	6,788	(0.89)
Georgia	5,262	5,026	4,843	4,585	4,258	(0.71)	2,490	2,367	2,157	1,784	(1.11)
India	1,016,938	1,096,917	1,173,806	1,312,212	1,416,576	1.10	735,684	818,601	856,389	830,525	0.40
Indonesia	211,559	225,313	238,374	261,053	277,567	0.91	122,696	111,635	100,278	89,721	(1.04)
Iran (Islamic Republic of)	66,443	70,675	75,537	86,746	94,441	1.17	23,644	21,753	20,735	19,189	(0.70)
Iraq	23,224	26,555	30,290	37,992	45,338	2.23	7,465	10,156	12,278	12,994	1.85
Israel	6,042	6,685	7,266	8,196	8,970	1.32	515	580	596	578	0.38

Japan	127,034	127,914	127,998	125,617	121,017	(0.16)	44,240	42,847	38,640	32,536	(1.02)
Jordan	5,035	5,750	6,385	7,560	8,643	1.80	1,073	1,267	1,344	1,332	0.72
Kazakhstan	15,640	15,364	15,130	15,422	15,258	(0.08)	6,906	6,549	6,125	5,240	(0.92)
Kuwait	2,247	2,671	3,043	3,647	4,198	2.08	90	100	105	107	0.58
Kyrgyzstan	4,921	5,278	5,621	6,235	6,711	1.03	3,229	3,707	3,886	3,718	0.47
Lao People's Democratic Republic	5,279	5,918	6,592	7,967	9,282	1.88	4,261	4,989	5,516	5,733	0.99
Lebanon	3,478	3,761	4,000	4,395	4,692	1.00	465	435	403	375	(0.72)
Malaysia	23,001	25,325	27,513	31,580	35,191	1.42	8,790	8,745	8,362	7,867	(0.37)
Maldives	291	338	391	503	614	2.49	211	265	310	332	1.51
Mongolia	2,500	2,667	2,860	3,223	3,491	1.11	1,085	1,202	1,235	1,154	0.21
Myanmar	47,544	50,696	53,388	57,880	61,308	0.85	34,255	35,241	33,959	31,222	(0.31)
Nepal	23,518	26,289	29,148	34,901	40,740	1.83	20,298	23,895	26,820	28,764	1.16
Occupied Palestinian Territory	3,191	3,815	4,506	6,064	7,758	2.96	958	1,183	1,378	1,512	1.52
Oman	2,609	3,020	3,459	4,349	5,223	2.31	627	663	692	714	0.43
Pakistan	142,654	161,151	181,753	227,395	271,600	2.15	95,434	114,613	130,443	136,254	1.19
Philippines	75,711	82,809	89,674	102,716	113,795	1.36	31,384	30,380	28,953	27,180	(0.48)
Qatar	581	628	670	752	821	1.15	49	47	45	43	(0.44)
Republic of Korea	46,835	48,182	49,081	50,026	50,042	0.22	9,545	8,881	7,955	6,921	(1.07)
Saudi Arabia	22,147	25,626	29,176	36,253	43,193	2.23	3,064	2,894	2,988	3,069	0.01
Singapore	4,016	4,372	4,574	4,812	4,934	0.69	-	-	-	-	-
Sri Lanka	18,595	19,366	20,046	21,121	21,670	0.51	14,668	15,738	16,003	15,190	0.12
Syrian Arab Republic	16,560	18,650	20,835	25,077	28,750	1.84	8,271	10,196	11,450	11,561	1.12
Tajikistan	6,089	6,356	6,743	7,756	8,548	1.13	4,521	5,141	5,724	5,761	0.81
Thailand	60,925	64,081	66,946	71,913	75,424	0.71	41,951	43,952	43,344	40,004	(0.16)
Timor-Leste	702	857	976	1,138	1,243	1.90	650	894	1,011	1,054	1.61
Turkey	68,281	73,302	77,967	85,707	91,920	0.99	24,075	23,659	22,311	20,505	(0.54)
Turkmenistan	4,643	5,015	5,412	6,211	6,825	1.28	2,564	2,841	2,903	2,754	0.24
United Arab Emirates	2,820	3,106	3,363	3,786	4,056	1.21	434	459	454	423	(0.09)
Uzbekistan	24,913	26,868	28,837	32,335	35,031	1.14	15,630	18,375	19,834	19,399	0.72
Viet Nam	78,137	83,585	89,128	100,079	108,374	1.09	59,131	62,906	64,270	61,511	0.13
Yemen	18,017	21,480	25,662	36,537	50,584	3.44	13,565	18,342	23,819	29,214	2.56
EUROPE	**727,986**	**724,722**	**719,714**	**705,410**	**685,440**	**(0.20)**	**198,928**	**185,906**	**165,342**	**140,070**	**(1.17)**
Albania	3,113	3,220	3,335	3,548	3,680	0.56	1,807	1,732	1,619	1,448	(0.74)
Andorra	66	75	85	105	126	2.16	5	8	9	10	2.31
Austria	8,102	8,120	8,094	8,023	7,911	(0.08)	2,771	2,731	2,526	2,188	(0.79)
Belarus	10,034	9,809	9,612	9,208	8,678	(0.48)	3,030	2,555	2,126	1,719	(1.89)
Belgium	10,251	10,359	10,429	10,500	10,512	0.08	296	270	243	216	(1.05)
Bosnia and Herzegovina	3,977	4,209	4,269	4,253	4,089	0.09	2,268	2,218	1,937	1,594	(1.18)
Bulgaria	8,099	7,763	7,462	6,882	6,335	(0.82)	2,529	2,072	1,675	1,331	(2.14)
Channel Islands	144	145	145	143	140	(0.09)	100	101	99	97	(0.10)
Croatia	4,446	4,405	4,349	4,187	3,990	(0.36)	1,880	1,645	1,372	1,113	(1.75)
Czech Republic	10,269	10,216	10,161	9,957	9,608	(0.22)	2,662	2,528	2,360	2,169	(0.68)
Denmark	5,322	5,386	5,425	5,459	5,469	0.09	793	753	685	603	(0.91)
Estonia	1,367	1,294	1,226	1,089	943	(1.24)	419	365	295	221	(2.13)
Faeroe Islands	46	47	49	51	53	0.47	28	29	28	25	(0.38)
Finland	5,177	5,224	5,258	5,295	5,253	0.05	2,013	2,041	1,933	1,688	(0.59)
France	59,296	60,711	61,889	63,597	64,577	0.28	14,399	13,754	12,535	10,997	(0.90)
Germany	82,282	82,560	82,575	82,294	81,511	(0.03)	10,247	8,845	7,673	6,603	(1.46)
Gibraltar	27	27	27	27	26	(0.13)	-	-	-	-	-
Greece	10,903	10,978	10,992	10,840	10,567	(0.10)	4,351	4,055	3,501	2,921	(1.33)
Holy See[6]	1	1	1	1	1	-	-	-	-	-	-
Hungary	10,012	9,784	9,553	9,091	8,636	(0.49)	3,606	3,057	2,541	2,078	(1.84)
Iceland	282	294	303	318	330	0.52	21	19	18	16	(0.91)
Ireland	3,819	4,040	4,221	4,549	4,762	0.74	1,560	1,609	1,565	1,422	(0.31)
Isle of Man	74	75	77	79	80	0.26	35	37	38	39	0.36
Italy	57,536	57,253	56,560	54,264	51,546	(0.37)	18,859	17,989	15,949	13,268	(1.17)
Latvia	2,373	2,265	2,162	1,962	1,750	(1.02)	787	742	633	490	(1.58)
Liechtenstein	33	34	35	37	39	0.56	26	27	28	26	-
Lithuania	3,501	3,401	3,311	3,131	2,935	(0.59)	1,157	1,099	980	809	(1.19)
Luxembourg	435	465	494	550	609	1.12	39	33	30	29	(0.99)
Malta	389	397	405	416	418	0.24	35	28	24	21	(1.70)
Monaco	33	35	36	39	41	0.72	-	-	-	-	-
Netherlands	15,898	16,300	16,583	16,970	17,224	0.27	5,668	5,114	4,503	3,919	(1.23)
Norway	4,473	4,570	4,649	4,790	4,913	0.31	1,081	748	567	485	(2.67)
Poland	38,671	38,516	38,367	37,840	36,680	(0.18)	14,826	14,264	13,000	11,031	(0.99)
Portugal	10,016	10,080	10,082	9,941	9,721	(0.10)	4,704	4,207	3,626	3,047	(1.45)
Republic of Moldova	4,283	4,259	4,230	4,163	4,011	(0.22)	2,322	2,211	1,947	1,624	(1.19)
Romania	22,480	22,228	21,972	21,255	20,328	(0.34)	10,206	9,766	9,077	8,331	(0.68)
Russian Federation	145,612	141,553	137,501	129,018	119,713	(0.65)	38,854	36,282	31,817	25,976	(1.34)
San Marino	27	28	29	31	33	0.67	3	3	3	3	-
Serbia and Montenegro	10,555	10,513	10,498	10,357	10,094	(0.15)	5,111	4,864	4,354	3,663	(1.11)
Slovakia	5,391	5,411	5,434	5,428	5,344	(0.03)	2,329	2,206	2,051	1,874	(0.72)
Slovenia	1,990	1,979	1,959	1,897	1,814	(0.31)	979	952	864	729	(0.98)
Spain	40,752	41,184	41,284	40,815	39,951	(0.07)	9,674	9,374	8,500	7,294	(0.94)
Sweden	8,856	8,895	8,940	9,028	9,033	0.07	1,479	1,452	1,360	1,202	(0.69)
Switzerland	7,173	7,157	7,095	6,914	6,655	(0.25)	2,323	2,279	2,078	1,759	(0.93)
TFYR Macedonia[7]	2,024	2,076	2,122	2,185	2,205	0.29	822	837	787	685	(0.61)
Ukraine	49,688	47,782	46,038	42,605	38,925	(0.81)	16,325	14,764	12,670	10,148	(1.58)
United Kingdom	58,689	59,598	60,392	62,274	64,183	0.30	6,500	6,241	5,715	5,158	(0.77)
LATIN AMERICA	**520,229**	**558,281**	**594,436**	**659,248**	**711,058**	**1.04**	**127,247**	**122,728**	**116,856**	**109,332**	**(0.51)**
Anguilla	11	12	13	15	17	1.45	-	-	-	-	0.00
Antigua and Barbuda	72	74	75	77	78	0.27	45	45	41	36	(0.74)
Argentina	37,074	39,311	41,443	45,317	48,611	0.90	3,893	3,548	3,262	3,043	(0.82)
Aruba	93	103	113	133	152	1.64	50	64	73	76	1.40
Bahamas	303	321	336	363	382	0.77	35	30	28	26	(0.99)
Barbados	267	272	276	282	282	0.18	134	122	107	90	(1.33)
Belize	240	266	291	337	373	1.47	125	146	154	148	0.56
Bolivia	8,317	9,138	9,987	11,673	13,275	1.56	3,168	3,323	3,362	3,281	0.12
Brazil	171,796	182,798	192,879	209,793	222,078	0.86	32,394	25,840	21,651	19,392	(1.71)
British Virgin Islands	20	22	24	27	30	1.35	8	7	7	7	(0.45)

TABLE B.2

continued

	Total population						Rural population				
	Estimates and projections (000)					Rate of change (%)	Estimates and projections (000)				Rate of change (%)
	2000	2005	2010	2020	2030	2000–2030	2000	2010	2020	2030	2000–2030
Cayman Islands	37	43	49	61	72	2.22	-	-	-	-	0.00
Chile	15,224	16,185	17,114	18,879	20,311	0.96	2,140	1,871	1,685	1,561	(1.05)
Colombia	42,120	45,600	48,959	55,277	60,843	1.23	10,567	10,030	9,503	8,982	(0.54)
Costa Rica	3,929	4,327	4,702	5,338	5,872	1.34	1,611	1,678	1,640	1,539	(0.15)
Cuba	11,202	11,353	11,458	11,539	11,338	0.04	2,778	2,640	2,374	2,016	(1.07)
Dominica	78	79	80	80	80	0.08	23	20	18	15	(1.42)
Dominican Republic	8,353	8,998	9,595	10,570	11,290	1.00	3,491	3,621	3,466	3,157	(0.34)
Ecuador	12,420	13,379	14,274	15,968	17,335	1.11	4,931	4,968	4,819	4,489	(0.31)
El Salvador	6,209	6,709	7,154	8,005	8,802	1.16	2,583	2,713	2,680	2,525	(0.08)
Falkland Islands (Malvinas)	3	3	3	3	3	-	1	-	-	-	-
French Guiana	164	187	208	252	293	1.93	41	49	53	54	0.92
Grenada	81	80	79	75	72	(0.39)	50	43	35	29	(1.82)
Guadeloupe	428	446	460	478	489	0.44	2	1	-	-	-
Guatemala	11,423	12,978	14,584	17,835	21,002	2.03	6,268	7,376	8,093	8,278	0.93
Guyana	759	768	769	746	695	(0.29)	483	453	390	313	(1.45)
Haiti	8,005	8,549	9,132	10,206	11,094	1.09	5,155	5,291	5,209	4,880	(0.18)
Honduras	6,457	7,257	8,028	9,457	10,715	1.69	3,593	4,115	4,349	4,281	0.58
Jamaica	2,580	2,701	2,834	3,128	3,380	0.90	1,237	1,334	1,375	1,308	0.19
Martinique	386	397	404	419	427	0.34	19	12	10	9	(2.49)
Mexico	98,933	106,385	113,320	125,176	133,591	1.00	25,034	25,618	24,801	22,821	(0.31)
Montserrat	4	4	4	4	4	-	3	3	3	3	-
Netherlands Antilles	215	224	233	246	253	0.54	66	67	62	54	(0.67)
Nicaragua	5,073	5,727	6,378	7,679	8,929	1.88	2,225	2,529	2,648	2,624	0.55
Panama	2,950	3,235	3,520	4,047	4,514	1.42	1,291	1,422	1,453	1,391	0.25
Paraguay	5,470	6,160	6,893	8,419	9,890	1.97	2,443	2,654	2,777	2,786	0.44
Peru	25,952	27,968	29,988	33,870	37,170	1.20	7,067	7,091	6,899	6,481	(0.29)
Puerto Rico	3,816	3,915	3,990	4,073	4,046	0.20	204	56	29	26	(6.87)
Saint Kitts and Nevis	42	42	41	39	37	(0.42)	28	28	26	22	(0.80)
Saint Lucia	146	152	157	165	168	0.47	103	104	98	88	(0.52)
Saint Vincent and the Grenadines	118	121	124	129	131	0.35	53	43	37	31	(1.79)
Suriname	425	442	458	480	489	0.47	110	93	82	71	(1.46)
Trinidad and Tobago	1,289	1,311	1,331	1,346	1,327	0.10	334	292	252	212	(1.52)
Turks and Caicos Islands	19	22	26	32	37	2.22	10	13	14	14	1.12
United States Virgin Islands	109	113	118	126	130	0.59	8	6	5	4	(2.31)
Uruguay	3,342	3,463	3,577	3,783	3,958	0.56	270	223	196	180	(1.35)
Venezuela	24,277	26,640	28,955	33,300	36,991	1.40	3,174	3,146	3,089	2,993	(0.20)
NORTHERN AMERICA	**315,915**	**332,156**	**348,139**	**379,589**	**407,532**	**0.85**	**65,920**	**61,660**	**57,621**	**53,451**	**(0.70)**
Bermuda	80	83	85	89	91	0.43	-	-	-	-	-
Canada	30,769	31,972	33,069	35,166	36,980	0.61	6,340	5,745	5,208	4,729	(0.98)
Greenland	56	57	58	58	57	0.06	10	9	8	7	(1.19)
Saint-Pierre and Miquelon	6	6	6	6	6	-	1	1	1	1	-
United States	285,003	300,038	314,921	344,270	370,396	0.87	59,568	55,905	52,405	48,715	(0.67)
OCEANIA	**31,043**	**32,998**	**34,821**	**38,275**	**41,468**	**0.97**	**8,479**	**9,148**	**9,869**	**10,405**	**0.68**
American Samoa	58	65	72	88	103	1.91	6	5	5	5	-
Australia[8]	19,153	20,092	20,945	22,501	23,833	0.73	1,778	1,259	1,036	960	(2.05)
Cook Islands	18	18	19	18	18	-	6	4	3	2	(3.66)
Fiji	814	854	890	940	982	0.63	411	385	346	307	(0.97)
French Polynesia	233	252	270	303	328	1.14	110	129	135	128	0.51
Guam	155	168	180	204	224	1.23	11	10	9	9	(0.67)
Kiribati	84	90	96	107	116	1.08	48	42	36	32	(1.35)
Marshall Islands	51	54	57	62	67	0.91	17	18	18	16	(0.20)
Micronesia (Federated State of)	107	111	115	121	130	0.65	77	78	74	70	(0.32)
Nauru	12	14	15	18	21	1.87	-	-	-	-	-
New Caledonia	215	237	258	297	332	1.45	85	95	99	95	0.37
New Zealand	3,784	3,932	4,059	4,280	4,457	0.55	542	551	532	488	(0.35)
Niue	2	2	2	2	1	(2.31)	1	1	1	1	-
Northern Mariana Islands	70	86	102	132	158	2.71	5	4	4	5	-
Palau	19	21	24	28	32	1.74	6	8	9	9	1.35
Papua New Guinea	5,334	5,959	6,565	7,797	9,075	1.77	4,630	5,670	6,564	7,228	1.48
Pitcairn	-	-	-	-	-	-	-	-	-	-	0.00
Samoa	173	182	192	214	234	1.01	135	147	157	157	0.50
Solomon Islands	437	504	574	713	850	2.22	368	466	546	595	1.60
Tokelau	2	2	2	1	1	(2.31)	2	2	1	1	(2.31)
Tonga	101	106	110	118	123	0.66	68	71	69	64	(0.20)
Tuvalu	10	11	11	13	13	0.87	5	4	4	4	(0.74)
Vanuatu	197	222	249	301	353	1.94	154	184	206	215	1.11
Wallis and Futuna Islands	14	15	15	16	16	0.45	14	15	16	16	0.45

Notes:

1 Including Agalega, Rodrigues and Saint Brandon.

2 Including Ascension and Tristan da Cunha.

3 For statistical purposes, the data for China do not include Hong Kong and Macao Special Administrative Regions (SAR) of China.

4 As of 1 July 1997, Hong Kong became a Special Administrative Region (SAR) of China.

5 As of 20 December 1999, Macao became a Special Administrative Region (SAR) of China.

6 Refers to the Vatican City State.

7 The former Yugoslav Republic of Macedonia.

8 Including Christmas Island, Cocos (Keeling) Islands and Norfolk Island.

Source: United Nations Population Division, 2004.

TABLE B.3

Households: Total Number and Rate of Change

	Estimates and projections (000)					Annual rate of change (%)			Five-year increment (000)			
	2005	2010	2015	2020	2025	2000–2010	2010–2020	2020–2030	2005–2010	2010–2015	2015–2020	2020–2025
WORLD	**1,743,640**	**1,935,570**	**2,116,248**	**2,291,729**	**2,461,422**	**2.10**	**1.70**	**1.36**	**191,930**	**180,678**	**175,481**	**169,694**
AFRICA	**188,604**	**219,505**	**249,358**	**283,387**	**321,562**	**2.98**	**2.67**	**2.51**	**30,902**	**29,853**	**34,029**	**38,174**
Algeria	5,372	5,974	6,184	7,322	7,901	2.25	2.03	1.31	602	209	1,138	580
Angola	2,894	3,420	4,009	4,757	5,693	3.50	3.30	3.62	526	589	748	936
Benin	1,286	1,526	1,778	2,054	2,371	3.49	2.97	2.88	239	252	276	317
Botswana	430	426	417	415	417	0.87	(0.26)	0.14	(5)	(9)	(2)	2
Burkina Faso	1,797	1,994	2,236	2,520	2,848	2.02	2.34	2.45	197	242	284	328
Burundi	1,642	2,120	2,566	3,057	3,632	3.92	3.66	3.53	478	445	491	576
Cameroon	3,944	4,504	5,083	5,718	6,453	2.91	2.39	2.48	560	578	635	735
Cape Verde	108	125	145	167	189	2.95	2.89	2.32	17	20	22	23
Central African Republic	861	969	1,085	1,216	1,369	2.27	2.27	2.41	108	116	131	153
Chad	1,300	1,479	1,693	1,941	2,230	2.58	2.71	2.80	180	214	247	289
Comoros	120	143	167	194	226	3.62	3.06	3.01	22	24	27	32
Congo	991	1,222	1,516	1,882	2,320	3.95	4.32	4.12	231	295	365	438
Côte d'Ivoire	3,398	3,856	4,287	4,793	5,429	2.32	2.18	2.51	459	431	507	636
Democratic Republic of the Congo	11,627	14,088	17,201	20,957	25,404	3.28	3.97	3.84	2,461	3,113	3,756	4,447
Djibouti	145	164	185	211	240	1.60	2.51	2.70	18	22	25	30
Egypt	15,544	18,296	20,938	23,477	25,847	3.21	2.49	1.76	2,752	2,641	2,539	2,370
Equatorial Guinea	125	150	180	215	254	3.67	3.58	3.33	25	30	34	40
Eritrea	924	1,146	1,364	1,618	1,919	4.93	3.45	3.42	221	218	255	301
Ethiopia	14,913	17,247	20,102	23,564	27,658	2.91	3.12	3.20	2,334	2,855	3,462	4,094
Gabon	355	403	457	521	590	2.38	2.56	2.50	48	54	64	70
Gambia	201	236	273	313	356	3.58	2.81	2.52	35	37	40	43
Ghana	4,723	5,492	6,310	7,176	8,156	3.08	2.67	2.57	770	818	866	981
Guinea	1,184	1,458	1,841	2,076	2,353	2.89	3.61	3.83	274	383	235	277
Guinea-Bissau	184	234	295	351	393	2.43	2.62	2.47	50	61	56	42
Kenya	8,780	10,228	11,535	12,953	14,488	3.30	2.36	2.16	1,448	1,307	1,418	1,534
Lesotho	352	346	339	336	336	0.14	(0.29)	0.09	(6)	(7)	(3)	0
Liberia	574	664	744	874	1,086	8.41	2.76	4.18	89	80	130	212
Libyan Arab Jamahiriya	814	884	935	990	1,058	1.82	1.13	1.48	71	51	55	67
Madagascar	3,769	4,370	5,221	6,101	7,026	2.85	3.34	2.77	601	851	880	925
Malawi	1,718	1,619	1,549	1,659	1,886	(1.13)	0.24	2.60	(98)	(71)	110	227
Mali	2,276	2,698	3,233	3,889	4,699	3.32	3.66	3.78	422	535	656	810
Mauritania	424	482	547	618	697	2.66	2.48	2.38	58	65	71	79
Mauritius	306	322	341	354	365	1.19	0.94	0.57	16	19	13	11
Morocco	6,229	6,976	7,684	8,468	9,180	2.32	1.94	1.48	747	708	784	713
Mozambique	3,092	3,156	3,174	3,298	3,478	0.75	0.44	1.14	64	17	124	180
Namibia	398	419	426	440	461	1.72	0.51	1.00	21	7	15	20
Niger	1,504	1,742	2,045	2,390	2,800	2.86	3.16	3.20	238	303	345	409
Nigeria	36,458	44,615	52,169	60,104	69,100	4.37	2.98	2.78	8,156	7,554	7,935	8,997
Réunion	230	256	283	307	329	2.26	1.80	1.29	26	27	24	22
Rwanda	2,269	2,624	3,014	3,482	4,048	5.82	2.83	3.07	354	391	468	566
Senegal	1,058	1,225	1,414	1,620	1,849	2.86	2.79	2.66	166	190	205	229
Somalia	1,369	1,701	2,057	2,548	3,193	4.38	4.05	4.54	332	357	491	644
South Africa	17,270	19,988	20,444	20,567	20,651	4.05	0.29	0.04	2,718	457	122	85
Sudan	3,822	4,325	4,795	5,323	5,932	2.02	2.08	2.19	503	470	527	609
Swaziland	261	292	306	318	328	2.82	0.85	0.66	30	15	11	11
Togo	1,097	1,276	1,491	1,727	1,997	3.03	3.02	2.93	180	214	236	270
Tunisia	2,224	2,425	2,587	2,730	2,864	1.88	1.19	0.88	201	163	143	134
Uganda	4,830	5,811	7,157	8,942	11,232	3.01	4.31	4.51	981	1,346	1,785	2,290
United Republic of Tanzania	6,659	7,149	7,747	8,368	9,013	1.40	1.57	1.50	490	598	621	645
Zambia	2,019	2,115	2,297	2,519	2,779	1.11	1.75	2.02	95	182	223	260
Zimbabwe	3,554	3,808	4,036	4,279	4,532	1.78	1.17	1.09	254	229	243	253
ASIA	**962,492**	**1,081,314**	**1,194,550**	**1,302,207**	**1,402,896**	**2.35**	**1.88**	**1.43**	**118,823**	**113,236**	**107,657**	**100,690**
Armenia	576	563	547	523	502	(0.66)	(0.74)	(0.77)	(13)	(16)	(24)	(21)
Azerbaijan	1,744	1,893	2,034	2,111	2,182	1.39	1.09	0.67	149	141	77	71
Bahrain	124	138	152	161	166	2.26	1.55	0.61	14	14	9	5
Bangladesh	30,611	35,130	38,869	43,190	47,628	3.09	2.07	1.79	4,519	3,739	4,321	4,438
Bhutan	423	493	574	661	752	3.16	2.92	2.57	70	81	87	91
Brunei Darussalam	61	68	75	79	82	2.16	1.42	0.63	7	6	4	3
Cambodia	3,145	3,792	4,449	5,157	5,894	3.77	3.08	2.62	647	657	708	737
China	405,474	460,902	511,168	558,867	603,485	2.46	1.93	1.47	55,428	50,266	47,699	44,617
China, Hong Kong SAR	2,253	2,513	2,739	2,944	3,154	2.56	1.58	1.35	260	226	205	210
China, Macao SAR	180	208	234	257	277	3.49	2.13	1.43	28	26	23	20
Cyprus	211	221	228	230	231	1.05	0.40	0.03	10	7	2	1
Democratic People's Republic of Korea	5,612	6,061	6,483	6,909	7,320	1.59	1.31	1.07	448	423	426	411
Georgia	1,310	1,273	1,245	1,212	1,177	(1.11)	(0.49)	(0.62)	(37)	(28)	(33)	(35)
India	209,389	234,345	259,658	281,906	300,831	2.28	1.85	1.14	24,956	25,313	22,248	18,925
Indonesia	57,869	63,740	69,139	74,132	78,261	2.05	1.51	0.98	5,871	5,399	4,993	4,129
Iran (Islamic Republic of)	18,149	20,777	23,598	25,635	27,633	3.34	2.10	1.48	2,629	2,820	2,038	1,997
Iraq	3,006	3,351	3,737	4,340	5,049	2.03	2.59	2.96	345	386	602	710
Israel	1,858	2,081	2,291	2,464	2,625	2.54	1.69	1.13	223	209	173	160
Japan	51,281	53,206	54,616	55,836	56,818	0.90	0.48	0.28	1,924	1,410	1,220	982
Jordan	578	665	758	862	977	3.02	2.58	2.45	88	92	104	115
Kazakhstan	5,734	5,928	6,252	6,526	6,775	0.74	0.96	0.72	194	323	274	249
Kuwait	384	462	510	548	584	4.42	1.71	1.19	78	48	38	36
Kyrgyzstan	1,032	1,103	1,178	1,236	1,276	1.18	1.14	0.58	71	75	57	41
Lao People's Democratic Republic	1,093	1,271	1,468	1,672	1,901	2.86	2.75	2.59	177	197	205	228
Lebanon	734	798	861	931	1,001	1.92	1.53	1.43	64	62	70	70
Malaysia	5,706	6,532	7,517	8,422	9,216	2.85	2.54	1.61	826	985	905	795

TABLE B.3

continued

	Estimates and projections (000)					Annual rate of change (%)			Five-year increment (000)			
	2005	2010	2015	2020	2025	2000–2010	2010–2020	2020–2030	2005–2010	2010–2015	2015–2020	2020–2025
Maldives	50	60	71	83	98	3.82	3.20	3.18	10	11	12	15
Mongolia	560	635	688	727	760	2.39	1.36	0.84	75	53	40	33
Myanmar	11,681	12,713	13,492	14,283	15,053	2.09	1.16	0.99	1,032	779	791	771
Nepal	4,880	5,686	6,548	7,509	8,621	3.05	2.78	2.69	806	863	960	1,112
Oman	425	487	541	603	677	2.78	2.15	2.38	62	55	62	74
Pakistan	16,550	19,457	22,948	26,857	31,221	3.13	3.22	2.91	2,907	3,491	3,909	4,364
Philippines	18,009	20,750	23,834	27,213	30,406	2.85	2.71	2.00	2,742	3,084	3,379	3,193
Qatar	109	114	118	121	125	1.11	0.58	0.50	6	3	3	4
Republic of Korea	15,393	16,275	17,185	17,988	18,695	1.38	1.00	0.69	882	910	803	707
Saudi Arabia	3,431	3,860	4,342	4,926	5,590	2.62	2.44	2.56	429	482	584	664
Singapore	867	890	905	899	881	0.82	0.11	(0.59)	22	16	(6)	(18)
Sri Lanka	4,130	4,338	4,487	4,626	4,745	1.27	0.64	0.47	207	150	139	120
Syrian Arab Republic	3,109	3,659	4,133	4,652	5,218	3.34	2.40	2.16	549	475	519	566
Tajikistan	1,145	1,231	1,322	1,442	1,548	1.25	1.58	1.27	86	91	120	107
Thailand	17,366	18,940	20,170	21,312	22,409	1.87	1.18	0.95	1,574	1,230	1,141	1,097
Turkey	18,641	20,694	22,829	24,948	26,916	2.46	1.87	1.41	2,053	2,134	2,119	1,969
Turkmenistan	661	707	753	838	913	1.16	1.70	1.54	45	46	85	75
United Arab Emirates	1,058	1,153	1,206	1,244	1,270	1.86	0.76	0.30	95	54	38	25
Uzbekistan	4,717	5,231	5,686	6,073	6,376	1.90	1.49	0.89	515	455	387	303
Viet Nam	19,850	22,494	25,145	27,192	28,925	2.62	1.90	1.17	2,643	2,651	2,047	1,733
Yemen	3,972	5,117	6,684	8,802	11,433	4.90	5.42	5.13	1,145	1,567	2,118	2,631
EUROPE	**302,806**	**315,128**	**323,017**	**328,315**	**331,902**	**0.87**	**0.42**	**0.15**	**12,323**	**7,888**	**5,298**	**3,588**
Albania	650	684	715	742	759	0.47	0.82	0.38	34	32	27	17
Austria	3,407	3,534	3,648	3,727	3,787	0.77	0.53	0.28	127	113	80	60
Belarus	3,144	3,198	3,186	3,129	3,081	0.40	(0.22)	(0.28)	54	(13)	(56)	(48)
Belgium	4,500	4,702	4,882	5,024	5,144	0.90	0.66	0.45	202	180	142	121
Bosnia and Herzegovina	1,176	1,225	1,258	1,280	1,292	1.31	0.44	0.12	49	33	22	13
Bulgaria	3,233	3,240	3,199	3,139	3,089	0.02	(0.32)	(0.36)	7	(41)	(60)	(50)
Croatia	1,658	1,682	1,679	1,668	1,653	0.41	(0.09)	(0.15)	24	(4)	(11)	(15)
Czech Republic	4,525	4,662	4,767	4,797	4,821	0.61	0.28	0.07	137	104	30	25
Denmark	2,554	2,639	2,742	2,828	2,899	0.61	0.69	0.40	84	103	86	71
Estonia	580	596	580	566	543	0.45	(0.52)	(0.77)	16	(16)	(14)	(23)
Finland	2,358	2,461	2,552	2,614	2,662	0.90	0.61	0.33	102	91	63	48
France	25,678	26,995	28,127	29,073	29,928	1.07	0.74	0.56	1,317	1,132	946	856
Germany	36,938	38,151	38,991	39,525	39,786	0.60	0.35	0.10	1,213	840	534	262
Greece	4,266	4,456	4,596	4,695	4,770	1.09	0.52	0.27	190	140	100	74
Hungary	3,992	4,016	4,037	4,018	3,990	0.12	0.01	(0.17)	24	21	(19)	(28)
Iceland	121	131	141	150	160	1.62	1.39	1.17	9	10	10	10
Ireland	1,405	1,523	1,623	1,726	1,832	1.94	1.25	1.18	118	100	102	107
Italy	23,340	23,877	24,289	24,501	24,554	0.53	0.26	(0.03)	537	412	213	53
Latvia	878	886	869	835	807	0.10	(0.59)	(0.64)	8	(17)	(33)	(29)
Lithuania	1,288	1,334	1,355	1,356	1,351	0.69	0.16	(0.06)	46	21	0	(5)
Luxembourg	186	206	226	246	267	2.08	1.80	1.57	20	20	20	21
Malta	141	149	157	163	169	1.25	0.86	0.66	9	7	6	6
Netherlands	7,316	7,777	8,234	8,615	8,916	1.25	1.02	0.60	461	457	381	301
Norway	2,095	2,217	2,350	2,475	2,593	1.07	1.10	0.85	122	134	124	118
Poland	13,525	13,809	13,896	13,806	13,717	0.59	(0.00)	(0.14)	284	87	(90)	(89)
Portugal	3,882	4,002	4,116	4,201	4,268	0.78	0.49	0.28	119	115	84	67
Republic of Moldova	1,275	1,324	1,343	1,340	1,335	0.80	0.12	(0.02)	48	19	(2)	(5)
Romania	8,292	8,633	8,731	8,721	8,714	0.75	0.10	(0.01)	342	98	(10)	(7)
Russian Federation	69,526	73,116	74,237	74,818	74,640	1.15	0.23	(0.31)	3,589	1,121	581	(178)
Serbia and Montenegro	3,529	3,639	3,715	3,768	3,813	0.73	0.35	0.26	110	76	54	45
Slovakia	2,143	2,239	2,311	2,342	2,379	0.96	0.45	0.26	96	72	31	37
Slovenia	753	774	782	784	783	0.66	0.12	(0.06)	21	8	2	(1)
Spain	13,585	13,856	14,046	14,144	14,209	0.60	0.21	0.08	272	189	98	65
Sweden	4,432	4,687	4,937	5,117	5,246	0.96	0.88	0.45	255	250	180	129
Switzerland	3,334	3,462	3,577	3,653	3,694	0.76	0.54	0.13	128	115	76	40
TFYR Macedonia	580	609	634	658	679	1.07	0.77	0.60	29	25	23	22
Ukraine	15,972	16,354	16,475	16,437	16,361	0.46	0.05	(0.11)	382	121	(38)	(76)
United Kingdom	26,356	28,073	29,792	31,395	32,956	1.23	1.12	0.99	1,718	1,719	1,603	1,560
LATIN AMERICA	**144,416**	**161,162**	**177,484**	**193,332**	**208,475**	**2.31**	**1.82**	**1.42**	**16,746**	**16,321**	**15,848**	**15,143**
Argentina	11,635	12,727	13,848	15,002	16,134	1.86	1.64	1.38	1,092	1,121	1,154	1,132
Bahamas	72	74	76	78	79	0.59	0.57	0.05	2	3	2	1
Barbados	89	93	98	100	103	1.04	0.70	0.40	4	4	3	2
Belize	56	64	75	86	95	2.86	2.91	1.82	8	11	11	9
Bolivia	1,794	2,003	2,233	2,486	2,744	2.16	2.16	1.88	208	230	253	258
Brazil	51,679	57,224	62,103	66,596	70,828	2.25	1.52	1.18	5,546	4,879	4,493	4,231
Chile	4,680	5,309	5,950	6,609	7,258	2.49	2.19	1.77	628	642	659	649
Colombia	10,004	11,347	12,817	14,282	15,721	2.62	2.30	1.82	1,343	1,470	1,465	1,439
Costa Rica	1,201	1,408	1,602	1,795	1,993	3.40	2.43	2.00	207	194	193	198
Cuba	4,357	4,714	5,017	5,268	5,455	1.51	1.11	0.62	357	303	251	187
Dominica	20	22	23	23	24	1.23	0.79	0.66	1	1	1	1
Dominican Republic	2,338	2,646	2,942	3,217	3,472	2.53	1.95	1.44	308	296	275	255
Ecuador	3,541	4,042	4,574	5,109	5,632	2.81	2.34	1.79	501	532	535	523
El Salvador	1,920	2,184	2,473	2,788	3,122	2.75	2.44	2.14	264	289	315	334
Guadeloupe	141	150	158	165	172	1.32	1.00	0.74	9	9	7	7
Guatemala	2,056	2,342	2,661	3,022	3,399	2.65	2.55	2.22	286	320	360	378
Guyana	165	166	165	161	154	0.34	(0.32)	(0.90)	1	(1)	(4)	(7)
Haiti	1,735	1,967	2,157	2,354	2,557	2.44	1.80	1.70	232	190	198	203
Honduras	1,405	1,657	1,935	2,219	2,504	3.39	2.92	2.27	252	277	284	284

Jamaica	522	539	558	573	581	0.63	0.62	0.21	17	19	15	8
Martinique	131	139	147	154	160	1.20	1.01	0.68	8	8	7	6
Mexico	25,973	28,997	31,998	34,823	37,345	2.32	1.83	1.25	3,024	3,001	2,825	2,522
Netherlands Antilles	74	81	88	95	100	1.82	1.60	1.13	7	7	7	6
Nicaragua	996	1,174	1,389	1,633	1,893	3.44	3.29	2.80	178	214	244	260
Panama	848	978	1,111	1,243	1,371	2.91	2.40	1.84	130	133	132	128
Paraguay	1,401	1,678	1,985	2,315	2,675	3.70	3.22	2.79	277	307	330	360
Peru	6,424	7,187	7,944	8,678	9,363	2.29	1.89	1.39	763	758	734	685
Puerto Rico	1,230	1,288	1,349	1,406	1,455	1.03	0.88	0.58	58	62	57	49
Suriname	115	120	127	132	136	1.23	0.97	0.52	4	7	5	4
Trinidad and Tobago	317	331	335	334	333	1.17	0.09	(0.03)	14	4	(1)	(2)
Uruguay	1,085	1,150	1,216	1,287	1,355	1.15	1.12	0.99	65	66	71	69
Venezuela	6,160	7,083	8,023	8,964	9,903	2.88	2.36	1.85	923	940	941	939
NORTHERN AMERICA	**133,819**	**145,895**	**158,218**	**169,815**	**180,848**	**1.76**	**1.52**	**1.22**	**12,076**	**12,323**	**11,597**	**11,033**
Canada	13,801	15,058	16,321	17,440	18,520	1.83	1.47	1.18	1,258	1,263	1,119	1,080
United States	119,959	130,775	141,831	152,306	162,257	1.74	1.52	1.22	10,815	11,057	10,475	9,951
OCEANIA	**11,504**	**12,565**	**13,621**	**14,674**	**15,739**	**1.84**	**1.56**	**1.39**	**1,060**	**1,056**	**1,053**	**1,065**
Australia	8,090	8,810	9,517	10,189	10,841	1.78	1.45	1.21	720	706	673	652
Fiji	169	181	191	199	207	1.53	0.92	0.72	12	10	8	9
French Polynesia	59	66	72	78	83	2.10	1.73	1.10	7	6	6	5
Guam	37	40	44	47	49	1.33	1.72	0.75	3	4	3	2
New Caledonia	63	70	78	87	94	2.32	2.07	1.45	7	8	8	7
New Zealand	1,509	1,627	1,737	1,846	1,949	1.51	1.27	1.02	118	110	109	102
Papua New Guinea	1,290	1,449	1,623	1,828	2,073	2.39	2.32	2.43	160	174	206	245
Samoa	36	39	43	48	53	1.38	2.03	1.88	3	4	5	5
Solomon Islands	84	99	114	131	149	3.22	2.81	2.54	14	15	17	18
Vanuatu	40	45	50	55	60	2.44	1.98	1.74	5	5	5	5

Source: UN-Habitat, 2005.

TABLE B.4

Household's Consumption Indicators

	Household final consumption expenditure								Female-headed households		Share of consumption		
			Annual rate of change				Proportion of GDP					Lowest 10%	Highest 10%
	Total US$ millions		Total (%)		Per capita (%)		(%)		(%)		(%)		
	1990	2002	1980–1990	1990–2002	1980–1990	1990–2002	1990	2002					
AFRICA													
Algeria	35,265	24,745	1.5	0.9	(1.4)	(0.9)	57	44		...	1995	2.8	26.8
Angola	3,674	...	*(3.6)*	...	...	...	36	61		...		...	...
Benin	1,602	2,183	1.9	3.4	(1.2)	0.7	87	81	2001	20		...	...
Botswana	1,260	1,537	6.3	4.1	2.7	1.5	33	28		...	1993	0.7	56.6
Burkina Faso	2,284	2,556	2.6	3.9	0.1	1.4	82	82	1998-99	6	1998	1.8	46.3
Burundi	1,070	655	3.4	(1.7)	0.5	(3.7)	95	92		...	1998	1.7	32.8
Cameroon	7,423	6,394	3.5	3.5	0.6	0.9	67	71	1998	22	2001	2.3	35.4
Central African Republic	1,274	815	1.5	...	...	...	86	78	1994-95	21	1993	0.7	47.7
Chad	1,538	1,719	*2.9*	*2.0*	*0.2*	*(1.1)*	88	86	1996-97	21		...	...
Congo	1,746	955	2.3	1.7	(0.9)	(1.5)	62	32		...		...	...
Côte d'Ivoire	7,766	7,048	1.5	3.1	(2.1)	0.2	72	60	1998-99	14	1998	2.2	35.9
Democratic Republic of the Congo	7,398	5,269	3.4	*(2.9)*	0.4	*(5.4)*	79	92		...		...	...
Egypt	30,933	71,236	4.6	4.3	2.0	2.3	73	79	2000	11	1999	3.7	29.5
Eritrea	496	592	...	*(0.3)*	...	*(2.9)*	*104*	92	1995	30	...	...	...
Ethiopia	6,382	4,756	*0.7*	5.6	*(2.4)*	3.2	74	78	2000	23	2000	3.9	25.5
Gabon	2,961	3,040	1.5	2.1	(1.6)	(0.6)	50	52	2000	25		...	...
Gambia	240	296	(2.4)	5.3	(5.9)	1.8	76	83		...	1998	1.5	38.0
Ghana	5,016	5,093	2.8	1.3	(0.6)	(1.1)	85	83		...	1999	2.1	30.0
Guinea	2,068	2,625	...	3.6	...	1.1	73	82	1999	12	1994	2.6	32.0
Guinea-Bissau	212	213	0.8	1.5	(1.9)	(1.4)	87	105		...	1993	2.1	39.3
Kenya	5,320	8,819	4.7	2.2	1.2	(0.3)	67	71	1998	31	1997	2.3	36.1
Lesotho	746	585	1.3	(0.4)	(0.8)	(1.5)	121	82		...	1995	0.5	48.3
Liberia	...	...	...	...	...	...	...	...		...		...	...
Libyan Arab Jamahiriya	13,999	10,970	...	...	...	...	48	58		...		...	...
Madagascar	2,663	3,703	(0.7)	2.3	(3.4)	(0.6)	86	84	1997	21	2001	1.9	36.6
Malawi	1,345	1,665	1.5	4.9	(1.7)	2.9	72	88	2000	26	1997	1.9	42.2
Mali	1,943	2,230	0.6	3.2	(1.9)	0.7	80	77	2001	11	1994	1.8	40.4
Mauritania	705	762	1.4	3.9	(0.9)	1.1	69	79	2000-01	29	2000	2.5	29.5
Mauritius	1,519	2,983	6.2	4.8	5.3	3.6	64	66		...		...	...
Morocco	16,833	23,952	4.3	2.7	2.0	0.9	65	62	1992	16	1998-99	2.6	30.9
Mozambique	2,481	2,124	(1.6)	1.5	(3.1)	(0.7)	101	59	1997	26	1996-97	2.5	31.7
Namibia	1,204	1,377	1.3	5.1	(1.9)	2.2	51	48	1992	30	1993	0.5	64.5
Niger	2,079	1,814	0.0	*1.8*	(3.1)	*(1.7)*	84	84	1998	13	1995	0.8	35.4
Nigeria	15,816	24,135	(2.6)	*0.2*	(5.5)	(2.7)	56	55	1999	16	1996-97	1.6	40.8
Rwanda	2,162	1,503	1.2	2.2	(1.8)	0.8	84	87	2000	36	1983-85	4.2	24.2
Senegal	4,353	3,820	2.1	2.9	(0.8)	0.2	76	76	1997	18	1995	2.6	33.5
Sierra Leone	546	728	(2.7)	(5.2)	(4.7)	(7.3)	83	93		...	1989	0.5	43.6
Somalia	...	...	*1.3*	...	...	...	112	...		...		...	...
South Africa	64,251	64,741	2.4	2.7	(0.2)	0.5	57	62	1998	41	1995	0.7	46.9
Sudan	...	8,339	0.0	...	...	...	...	79		...		...	...
Swaziland	547	883	5.3	3.5	2.1	0.4	62	74		...	1994	1.0	50.2
Togo	1,158	1,184	4.7	3.6	1.3	0.8	71	86	1998	24		...	...
Tunisia	7,152	13,152	2.9	4.5	0.3	2.9	58	63		...	2000	2.3	31.5

TABLE B.4

continued

	Household final consumption expenditure								Female-headed households		Share of consumption		
			Annual rate of change				Proportion of GDP					Lowest 10%	Highest 10%
	Total US$ millions		Total (%)		Per capita (%)		(%)		(%)		(%)		
	1990	2002	1980–1990	1990–2002	1980–1990	1990–2002	1990	2002					
Uganda	4,002	4,528	2.6	6.0	(0.6)	3.0	92	78	2000-01	27	1999	2.3	34.9
United Republic of Tanzania	3,526	7,365	...	3.5	...	0.7	81	77	1999	23	1993	2.8	30.1
Zambia	2,078	3,110	1.8	(2.3)	(1.3)	(4.5)	64	84	2001-02	22	1998	1.1	41.0
Zimbabwe	5,543	6,020	3.7	0.4	(0.0)	(1.5)	63	72	1999	33	1995	1.8	40.3
ASIA													
Afghanistan	...	...	...	...	...	...	...	108		...		...	...
Armenia	1,097	2,121	...	1.1	...	2.5	46	87	2000	28	1998	2.6	29.7
Azerbaijan	3,186	3,587	...	11.3	...	10.3	51	60		...	2001	3.1	29.5
Bangladesh	24,988	36,548	3.0	2.8	0.4	1.0	86	77	1999-2000	8	2000	3.9	26.7
Cambodia	1,016	3,287	...	4.7	...	2.2	91	80	2000	25	1997	2.9	33.8
China	174,249	586,381	8.8	8.7	7.2	7.6	50	43		...	2001	1.8	33.1
China, Hong Kong SAR	42,723	93,401	6.6	3.5	5.2	1.8	57	58		...	1996	2.0	34.9
Dem. People's Rep. of Korea	...	...	...	...	...	...	...	...		...		...	...
Georgia	5,231	2,799	...	4.6	...	5.0	65	81		...	2001	2.3	27.9
India	215,762	328,706	4.2	4.9	2.0	3.1	66	65	1998-99	10	1999-2000	3.9	27.4
Indonesia	65,010	122,193	5.3	5.8	3.4	4.3	59	71	1997	12	2002	3.6	28.5
Iran (Islamic Republic of)	74,476	54,403	2.8	3.3	(0.6)	1.7	62	50		...	1998	2.0	33.7
Iraq	...	...	...	...	...	...	...	...		...		...	...
Israel	32,112	61,552	...	4.2	...	1.7	56	59		...	1997	2.4	28.2
Japan	1,618,040	2,282,911	3.6	1.5	3.0	1.2	53	56		...	1993	4.8	21.7
Jordan	2,978	7,622	1.9	5.2	(1.9)	1.4	74	75	1997	9	1997	3.3	29.8
Kazakhstan	12,856	14,392	...	(5.5)	...	(4.6)	52	60	1999	33	2001	3.4	24.2
Kuwait	10,459	19,720	(1.4)	...	...	...	57	56		...		...	...
Kyrgyzstan	1,896	1,083	...	(4.7)	...	(5.6)	71	67	1997	26	2001	3.9	23.3
Lao People's Democratic Republic	...	...	...	...	...	...	...	...		...	1997	3.2	30.6
Lebanon	3,961	16,921	...	2.4	...	0.7	140	95		...		...	...
Malaysia	22,806	41,971	3.3	4.9	0.4	2.4	52	44		...	1997	1.7	38.4
Mongolia	...	744	...	...	...	...	58	64		...	1998	2.1	37.0
Myanmar	...	...	0.6	3.9	...	...	89	88		...		...	...
Nepal	3,060	4,336	...	...	...	...	84	78	2001	16	1995-96	3.2	29.8
Oman	2,810	8,752	...	...	...	...	27	43		...		...	...
Pakistan	29,512	43,936	4.3	4.4	1.6	1.8	74	74	1991	7	1998-99	3.7	28.3
Philippines	31,566	53,307	2.6	3.7	0.2	1.4	72	69	1998	14	2000	2.2	36.3
Republic of Korea	132,113	286,818	7.9	4.9	6.7	4.0	53	62		...	1998	2.9	22.5
Saudi Arabia	54,508	69,666	...	...	...	...	47	37		...		...	...
Singapore	17,019	37,360	5.8	5.5	3.9	2.6	47	42		...	1998	1.9	32.8
Sri Lanka	6,143	12,736	4.0	4.7	2.9	3.4	76	77		...	1995	3.5	28.0
Syrian Arab Republic	8,458	12,289	3.6	2.0	0.2	(0.8)	69	59		...		...	...
Tajikistan	1,940	932	...	0.9	...	(0.3)	74	82		...	1998	3.2	25.2
Thailand	48,270	71,743	5.9	3.3	4.1	2.5	57	58		...	2000	2.5	33.8
Turkey	103,324	130,631	...	3.1	...	1.2	69	71	1998	10	2000	2.3	30.7
Turkmenistan	1,616	2,918	...	...	...	...	49	49	2000	26	1998	2.6	31.7
United Arab Emirates	12,726	...	4.6	...	...	...	39	...		...		...	...
Uzbekistan	8,204	4,569	...	...	...	...	61	58	1996	22	2000	3.6	22.0
Viet Nam	5,485	22,780	...	5.0	...	3.6	84	66	1997	24	1998	3.6	29.9
Yemen	3,561	6,882	...	3.6	...	0.3	74	70	1997	9	1998	3.0	25.9
EUROPE													
Albania	1,271	4,496	...	4.2	...	4.8	61	93		...	2002	9.1	22.4
Austria	89,789	117,605	2.4	2.3	2.2	2.0	55	58		...	1997	3.1	23.5
Belarus	8,223	8,781	...	0.9	...	1.2	47	61		...	2000	3.5	24.1
Belgium	109,154	135,445	2.0	1.9	1.9	1.6	55	55		...	1996	2.9	22.6
Bosnia and Herzegovina	...	...	...	...	...	...	...	113		...	2001	3.9	21.4
Bulgaria	12,401	10,742	3.1	(1.0)	3.2	(0.3)	60	69		...	2001	2.4	23.7
Croatia	13,527	13,483	...	3.0	...	3.5	74	60		...	2001	3.4	24.5
Czech Republic	17,195	36,165	...	2.7	...	2.8	49	53		...	1996	4.3	22.4
Denmark	65,430	82,827	1.4	1.8	1.4	1.4	49	48		...	1997	2.6	21.3
Estonia	2,539	3,727	...	1.2	...	2.5	62	58		...	2000	1.9	28.5
Finland	68,341	66,204	3.9	2.1	3.4	1.8	50	51		...	2000	4.0	22.6
France	672,960	784,209	2.2	1.6	1.7	1.2	55	55		...	1995	2.8	25.1
Germany	950,047	1,168,773	2.3	1.6	2.2	1.3	57	59		...	2000	3.2	22.1
Greece	60,164	89,446	2.0	2.4	1.5	2.0	72	67		...	1998	2.9	28.5
Hungary	20,290	42,860	1.3	0.9	1.7	1.1	61	67		...	1999	2.6	22.8
Ireland	27,957	47,973	2.2	5.7	1.9	4.8	58	47		...	1996	2.8	27.6
Italy	634,194	713,186	2.9	1.7	2.8	1.5	58	60		...	2000	2.3	26.8
Latvia	3,365	5,274	2.3	(1.6)	1.8	(0.4)	53	63		...	1998	2.9	25.9
Lithuania	5,826	8,577	...	4.9	...	5.6	57	62		...	2000	3.2	24.9
Netherlands	145,871	209,068	1.7	2.8	1.1	2.2	50	50		...	1994	2.8	25.1
Norway	57,047	73,067	2.2	3.5	1.9	2.9	49	67		...	2000	3.9	23.4
Poland	28,281	123,535	...	4.8	...	4.7	48	65		...	1999	2.9	27.4
Portugal	44,679	67,078	2.6	2.8	2.4	2.5	63	61		...	1997	2.0	29.8
Republic of Moldova	1,780	1,403	...	8.6	...	8.9	77	86		...	2001	2.8	28.4
Romania	25,232	34,785	...	1.9	...	2.2	66	76		...	2000	3.3	23.6
Russian Federation	252,561	177,362	...	0.3	...	0.5	49	51		...	2000	1.8	36.0
Serbia and Montenegro	...	13,915	...	...	...	...	...	89		...		...	...

Slovakia	8,350	13,133	3.8	1.8	3.5	1.6	54	55		...	1996	3.1	20.9
Slovenia	6,917	11,697	...	*3.5*	...	*3.5*	55	55		...	1998-99	3.6	21.4
Spain	306,953	378,319	2.6	2.5	2.3	2.0	60	58			1990	2.8	25.2
Sweden	116,475	116,993	2.2	1.6	1.9	1.3	47	49		...	2000	3.6	22.2
Switzerland	130,900	*149,886*	1.6	*1.1*	1.1	*0.5*	57	76		...	1992	2.6	25.2
TFYR Macedonia	3,021	2,924	...	2.1	...	1.4	72	77		...	1998	3.3	22.1
Ukraine	46,497	23,251	...	(4.7)	...	(4.1)	57	56		...	1999	3.7	23.2
United Kingdom	619,782	1,034,301	4.0	3.3	3.8	3.1	63	66	...		1999	2.1	28.5
LATIN AMERICA													
Argentina	109,038	62,158	...	0.5	...	*(0.7)*	77	61		...	2001	1.0	38.9
Bolivia	3,741	5,835	1.2	3.4	(0.9)	0.9	77	75	1998	19	1999	1.3	32.0
Brazil	273,952	263,710	1.2	4.7	(0.7)	3.2	59	58	1996	20	1998	0.5	46.7
Chile	18,759	39,211	2.0	6.2	0.3	4.7	62	61		...	2000	1.2	47.0
Colombia	26,357	53,046	2.6	1.8	0.5	(0.1)	66	66	2000	27	1999	0.8	46.5
Costa Rica	3,502	11,521	3.6	4.4	0.6	2.2	61	68		...	2000	1.4	34.8
Cuba	...	...	...	...	...	...	...	70		...		...	...
Dominican Republic	5,633	16,408	3.9	5.6	1.7	3.8	80	76	1999	32	1998	2.1	37.9
Ecuador	6,988	16,837	1.1	2.2	(1.5)	0.3	67	69		...	1998	0.9	41.6
El Salvador	4,273	12,847	0.8	4.8	(0.2)	2.8	89	90		...	200	0.9	40.6
Guatemala	6,398	19,794	1.1	4.1	(1.4)	1.4	84	85	1998-99	19	2000	0.9	48.3
Guyana	...	...	...	...	...	...	...	...		...	1999	1.3	33.8
Haiti	2,332	*3,334*	0.9	...	...	...	81	103	2000	42		...	...
Honduras	2,026	4,858	2.7	3.1	(0.5)	0.3	66	74		...	1999	0.9	42.2
Jamaica	2,980	5,859	...	...	...	...	65	67		...	2000	2.7	30.3
Mexico	182,791	445,791	1.1	2.8	(1.0)	1.1	70	70		...	2000	1.0	43.1
Nicaragua	592	3,123	(3.6)	6.1	(6.2)	3.2	59	78	1997-98	30	2001	1.2	45.0
Panama	3,022	5,673	2.1	4.1	(0.0)	2.4	60	63		...	2000	0.7	43.3
Paraguay	4,063	4,649	2.4	3.2	(0.5)	0.8	77	84	1990	16	1999	0.6	43.6
Peru	19,376	40,717	0.7	3.6	(1.5)	1.7	74	72	2000	19	2000	0.7	37.2
Puerto Rico	19,827	...	3.5	...	...	...	65	...		...		...	...
Saint Lucia	...	...	...	...	...	...	...	...		...	1995	2.0	32.5
Trinidad and Tobago	2,975	6,424	(1.3)	2.0	(2.5)	1.5	59	69		...	1992	2.1	29.9
Uruguay	6,525	8,836	0.7	3.2	0.1	2.5	70	73		...	2000	1.8	33.5
Venezuela	30,170	60,977	1.3	0.4	(1.2)	(1.7)	62	65		...	1998	0.6	36.3
NORTHERN AMERICA													
Canada	322,564	*391,155*	3.2	2.7	2.0	*1.7*	56	56		...	1998	2.5	25.0
United States	3,831,500	7,303,700	3.8	3.5	2.9	2.3	67	70		...	2000	1.9	29.9
OCEANIA													
Australia	182,448	247,950	2.9	3.7	1.4	2.5	59	60		...	1994	2.0	25.4
New Zealand	26,632	34,955	2.1	3.1	1.2	2.0	61	60		...	1997	2.2	27.8
Papua New Guinea	1,902	...	0.4	5.2	(2.1)	2.6	59	...		...	1996	1.7	40.5

Notes:

Data, unless otherwise indicated, are for the most recent year available. Household final consumption expenditure includes statistical discrepancy. Data for Tanzania cover mainland only.

Source: World Bank, 2004e.

TABLE B.5

Environmental Infrastructure

	In-house connection						Improved drinking water coverage						Improved sanitation coverage					
	Total (%)		Urban (%)		Rural (%)		Total (%)		Urban (%)		Rural (%)		Total (%)		Urban (%)		Rural (%)	
	1990	2002	1990	2002	1990	2002	1990	2002	1990	2002	1990	2002	1990	2002	1990	2002	1990	2002
AFRICA																		
Algeria	62	76	83	87	39	60	95	87	99	92	92	80	88	92	99	99	76	82
Angola	1	5	1	13	0	1	32	50	11	70	40	40	30	30	65	56	19	16
Benin	6	12	17	26	1	1	60	68	71	79	54	60	11	32	31	58	1	12
Botswana	25	46	40	62	13	28	93	95	100	100	88	90	38	41	61	57	21	25
Burkina Faso	4	4	25	23	1	0	39	51	63	82	35	44	13	12	47	45	8	5
Burundi	3	4	31	41	1	1	69	79	96	90	67	78	44	36	42	47	44	35
Cameroon	11	15	25	28	2	2	50	63	77	84	32	41	21	48	43	63	7	33
Cape Verde	...	24	...	41	4	4	...	80	...	86	...	73	...	42	...	61	...	19
Central African Republic	1	4	2	9	0	0	48	75	70	93	35	61	23	27	32	47	18	12
Chad	1	5	6	19	0	0	20	34	45	40	13	32	6	8	27	30	1	0
Comoros	18	25	32	47	12	14	89	94	99	90	85	96	23	23	41	38	16	15
Congo	...	33	...	58	5	5	...	46	...	72	...	17	...	9	...	14	2	2
Côte d'Ivoire	24	33	52	65	5	9	69	84	74	98	66	74	31	40	52	61	16	23
Democratic Republic of the Congo	25	10	89	32	0	1	43	46	92	83	24	29	18	29	56	43	3	23
Djibouti	32	35	40	40	11	11	78	80	82	82	67	67	48	50	55	55	27	27
Egypt	61	80	89	98	40	67	94	98	97	100	92	97	54	68	70	84	42	56
Equatorial Guinea	4	8	12	17	0	0	...	44	...	45	...	42	...	53	...	60	...	46
Eritrea	6	8	40	42	0	0	40	57	60	72	36	54	8	9	46	34	0	3
Ethiopia	1	4	4	23	0	0	25	22	80	81	16	11	4	6	14	19	2	4
Gabon	...	45	...	52	...	8	...	87	95	95	...	47	...	36	...	37	...	30
Gambia	...	12	...	39	3	3	...	82	95	95	...	77	...	53	...	72	...	46
Ghana	14	24	35	50	2	3	54	79	85	93	36	68	43	58	54	74	37	46
Guinea	10	8	37	23	2	1	42	51	70	78	32	38	17	13	27	25	13	6
Guinea-Bissau	...	5	...	15	0	0	...	59	...	79	...	49	...	34	...	57	...	23
Kenya	22	29	58	56	11	12	45	62	91	89	30	46	42	48	49	56	40	43
Lesotho	7	7	31	31	2	2	...	76	...	88	...	74	37	37	61	61	32	32
Liberia	11	1	21	1	3	0	56	62	85	72	34	52	38	26	59	49	24	7

TABLE B.5

continued

	In-house connection						Improved drinking water coverage						Improved sanitation coverage					
	Total (%)		Urban (%)		Rural (%)		Total (%)		Urban (%)		Rural (%)		Total (%)		Urban (%)		Rural (%)	
	1990	2002	1990	2002	1990	2002	1990	2002	1990	2002	1990	2002	1990	2002	1990	2002	1990	2002
Libyan Arab Jamahiriya	54	54	54	54	55	55	71	72	72	72	68	68	97	97	97	97	96	96
Madagascar	8	5	30	14	1	1	40	45	82	75	27	34	12	33	25	49	8	27
Malawi	6	9	33	45	2	2	41	67	90	96	34	62	36	46	52	66	34	42
Mali	2	10	8	27	0	1	34	48	50	76	29	35	36	45	50	59	32	38
Mauritania	9	22	18	29	3	11	41	56	19	63	57	45	28	42	31	64	26	9
Mauritius	...	78	98	74	...	82	100	100	100	100	100	100	99	99	100	100	99	99
Morocco	41	57	75	92	9	12	75	80	94	99	58	56	57	61	87	83	28	31
Mozambique	...	11	...	28	2	2	...	42	...	76	...	24	...	27	...	51	14	14
Namibia	31	39	83	76	12	21	58	80	99	98	43	72	24	30	68	66	8	14
Niger	3	8	19	35	0	0	40	46	62	80	35	36	7	12	35	43	2	4
Nigeria	13	11	31	20	3	3	49	60	78	72	33	49	39	38	50	48	33	30
Rwanda	1	6	24	34	0	1	58	73	88	92	57	69	37	41	49	56	36	38
Sao Tome and Principe	...	25	...	34	...	19	...	79	...	89	...	73	...	24	...	32	...	20
Senegal	22	40	50	71	4	11	66	72	90	90	50	54	35	52	52	70	23	34
Seychelles	...	87	100	100	...	75	...	87	100	100	...	75	...	...	...	...	100	100
Sierra Leone	...	12	...	30	1	1	...	57	...	75	...	46	...	39	...	53	...	30
Somalia	1	1	3	3	0	0	...	29	...	32	...	27	...	25	...	47	...	14
South Africa	58	60	94	82	23	31	83	87	99	98	67	73	63	67	85	86	42	44
Sudan	34	26	75	46	19	13	64	69	85	78	57	64	33	34	53	50	26	24
Swaziland	...	26	...	67	...	13	...	52	...	87	...	42	...	52	...	78	...	44
Togo	4	4	14	12	0	0	49	51	81	80	37	36	37	34	71	71	24	15
Tunisia	64	70	91	93	28	30	77	82	93	94	57	60	75	80	95	90	47	62
Uganda	3	1	24	8	0	0	44	56	79	87	40	52	43	41	54	53	41	39
United Republic of Tanzania	10	16	30	44	4	2	38	73	79	92	27	62	47	46	51	54	45	41
Zambia	22	18	51	47	2	2	50	55	86	90	27	36	41	45	64	68	26	32
Zimbabwe	33	35	95	91	8	5	77	83	99	100	69	74	49	57	69	69	40	51
ASIA																		
Afghanistan	...	2	...	8	0	0	...	13	...	19	...	11	...	8	...	16	5	5
Armenia	...	85	97	97	...	64	...	92	99	99	...	80	...	84	96	96	...	61
Azerbaijan	41	47	63	76	16	19	66	77	80	95	49	59	...	55	...	73	...	36
Bahrain	...	...	100	100	...	...	...	...	100	100	...	...	...	...	100	100	...	...
Bangladesh	6	6	28	26	0	0	71	75	83	82	68	72	23	48	71	75	11	39
Bhutan	...	...	...	81	...	...	...	62	...	86	...	60	...	70	...	65	...	70
Cambodia	...	6	...	31	1	1	...	34	...	58	...	29	...	16	...	53	...	8
China	49	59	80	91	37	40	70	77	100	92	59	68	23	44	64	69	7	29
Cyprus	100	100	100	100	100	100	100	100	100	100	100	100	100	100	100	100	100	100
Democratic People's Republic of Korea	...	77	...	81	...	71	100	100	100	100	100	100	...	59	...	58	...	60
Georgia	...	58	...	83	...	30	...	76	...	90	...	61	...	83	96	96	...	69
India	17	24	51	51	5	13	68	86	88	96	61	82	12	30	43	58	1	18
Indonesia	10	17	26	31	3	5	71	78	92	89	62	69	46	52	66	71	38	38
Iran (Islamic Republic of)	84	87	96	96	69	69	91	93	98	98	83	83	83	84	86	86	78	78
Iraq	76	74	94	94	33	33	83	81	97	97	50	50	81	80	95	95	48	48
Israel	100	100	100	100	98	98	100	100	100	100	100	100	...	...	100	100	...	...
Japan	95	96	98	98	91	91	100	100	100	100	100	100	100	100	100	100	100	100
Jordan	95	87	99	89	87	81	98	91	100	91	91	91	...	93	97	94	...	85
Kazakhstan	62	61	88	88	27	27	86	86	96	96	72	72	72	72	87	87	52	52
Kyrgyzstan	...	48	...	87	...	28	...	76	98	98	...	66	...	60	...	75	...	51
Lao People's Democratic Republic	...	8	...	25	4	4	...	43	...	66	...	38	...	24	...	61	...	14
Lebanon	...	98	100	100	...	85	100	100	100	100	100	100	...	98	100	100	...	87
Malaysia	...	...	...	...	...	64	...	95	96	96	...	94	96	...	94	...	98	98
Maldives	20	22	78	76	0	0	99	84	100	99	99	78	...	58	100	100	...	42
Mongolia	28	28	49	49	1	1	62	62	87	87	30	30	...	59	...	75	...	37
Myanmar	3	8	11	23	1	2	48	80	73	95	40	74	21	73	39	96	15	63
Nepal	6	14	42	48	3	8	69	84	94	93	67	82	12	27	62	68	7	20
Occupied Palestinian Territory	...	83	...	91	...	63	...	94	97	97	...	86	...	76	...	78	...	70
Oman	21	25	30	30	7	7	77	79	81	81	72	72	83	89	97	97	61	61
Pakistan	28	23	61	50	13	9	83	90	95	95	78	87	38	54	81	92	19	35
Philippines	21	44	37	60	6	22	87	85	93	90	82	77	54	73	63	81	46	61
Qatar	...	...	100	100	...	...	100	100	100	100	100	100	100	100	100	100	100	100
Republic of Korea	...	84	96	96	...	39	...	92	97	97	...	71	...	...	...	...	...	...
Saudi Arabia	89	...	97	97	60	...	90	...	97	97	63	...	...	...	100	100	...	...
Singapore	...	...	100	100	...	...	...	...	100	100	...	...	...	...	100	100	...	...
Sri Lanka	11	10	37	35	4	4	68	78	91	99	62	72	70	91	89	98	64	89
Syrian Arab Republic	...	...	...	...	...	...	79	79	94	94	64	64	76	77	97	97	56	56
Tajikistan	...	40	...	82	...	26	...	58	...	93	...	47	...	53	...	71	...	47
Thailand	28	34	69	80	11	12	81	85	87	95	78	80	80	99	95	97	74	100
Timor Leste	...	9	...	26	...	8	...	52	...	73	...	51	...	33	...	65	...	30
Turkey	50	52	64	64	30	30	81	93	92	96	65	87	84	83	96	94	67	62
Turkmenistan	...	52	...	81	...	29	...	71	...	93	...	54	...	62	...	77	...	50
United Arab Emirates	...	...	...	...	...	...	...	...	...	...	...	...	100	100	100	100	100	100
Uzbekistan	54	53	85	85	33	33	89	89	97	97	84	84	58	57	73	73	48	48
Viet Nam	11	14	51	51	1	1	72	73	93	93	67	67	22	41	46	84	16	26
Yemen	31	33	64	64	22	22	69	69	74	74	68	68	21	30	59	76	11	14

EUROPE																		
Albania	...	68	96	96	...	46	97	97	99	99	95	95	...	89	99	99	...	81
Andorra	...	...	100	100	...	...	100	100	100	100	100	100	100	100	100	100	100	100
Austria	100	100	100	100	100	100	100	100	100	100	100	100	100	100	100	100	100	100
Belarus	...	61	...	78	...	22	100	100	100	100	100	100	...	...	...	...	...	...
Belgium	100	...	100	100	90	...	...	...	100	100	...	...	...	...	...	...	...	...
Bosnia and Herzegovina	...	82	98	98	...	69	98	98	100	100	96	96	...	93	99	99	...	88
Bulgaria	98	...	100	100	94	...	100	100	100	100	100	100	100	100	100	100	100	100
Denmark	100	100	100	100	100	100	100	100	100	100	100	100	...	...	...	...	...	...
Estonia	...	87	96	96	...	67	...	...	...	...	...	...	...	...	...	93	...	...
Finland	92	97	96	100	85	93	100	100	100	100	100	100	100	100	100	100	100	100
France	99	99	100	100	95	95	...	...	100	100	...	...	...	...	...	...	...	...
Germany	100	100	100	100	97	97	100	100	100	100	100	100	...	...	...	...	...	...
Greece	84	...	91	...	73	...	...	...	...	...	...	...	...	...	...	...	...	...
Hungary	85	84	92	93	74	67	99	99	100	100	98	98	...	95	100	100	...	85
Iceland	100	100	100	100	100	100	100	100	100	100	100	100	...	...	...	...	...	...
Ireland	91	...	99	99	81	...	...	...	100	100	...	...	...	...	...	...	...	...
Italy	99	99	100	100	96	96	...	...	100	100	...	...	...	...	...	...	...	...
Latvia	...	...	...	93	...	...	...	...	...	...	...	...	...	...	...	...	...	...
Luxembourg	100	100	100	100	98	98	100	100	100	100	100	100	...	...	...	...	...	...
Malta	100	100	100	100	96	96	100	100	100	100	100	100	...	...	100	100	...	...
Monaco	...	...	100	100	...	...	...	...	100	100	...	...	...	...	100	100	...	...
Netherlands	98	98	100	100	95	95	100	100	100	100	99	99	100	100	100	100	100	100
Norway	100	100	100	100	100	100	100	100	100	100	100	100	...	...	...	...	...	...
Poland	78	95	93	99	56	89	...	...	100	100	...	...	...	...	...	...	...	...
Portugal	72	...	97	97	50	...	...	...	...	...	...	...	...	...	...	...	...	...
Republic of Moldova	...	41	...	78	...	9	...	92	97	97	...	88	...	68	...	86	...	52
Romania	...	49	...	79	...	13	...	57	...	91	...	16	...	51	...	86	...	10
Russian Federation	77	81	87	92	49	52	94	96	97	99	86	88	87	87	93	93	70	70
Serbia and Montenegro	82	82	98	98	64	64	93	93	99	99	86	86	87	87	97	97	77	77
Slovakia	...	...	...	80	...	...	100	100	100	100	100	100	100	100	100	100	100	100
Spain	80	...	90	...	50	...	...	...	...	...	...	...	...	...	...	...	...	...
Sweden	100	100	100	100	100	100	100	100	100	100	100	100	100	100	100	100	100	100
Switzerland	100	100	100	100	99	99	100	100	100	100	100	100	100	100	100	100	100	100
Ukraine	...	78	...	93	...	49	...	98	100	100	...	94	99	99	100	100	97	97
United Kingdom	99	...	100	100	92	...	...	...	100	100	...	...	...	...	...	...	...	...
LATIN AMERICA																		
Anguilla	...	45	...	45	...	45	...	60	...	60	...	60	99	99	99	99	99	99
Antigua and Barbuda	...	83	...	90	...	79	...	91	95	95	...	89	...	95	98	98	...	94
Argentina	69	...	76	...	23	...	94	...	97	97	73	...	82	...	87	...	47	...
Aruba	100	100	100	100	100	100	100	100	100	100	100	100	...	...	...	...	...	...
Bahamas	...	70	...	69	...	80	...	97	98	98	...	86	100	100	100	100	100	100
Barbados	...	...	98	100	...	...	100	100	100	100	100	100	100	99	99	99	100	100
Belize	...	80	92	99	...	63	...	91	100	100	...	82	...	47	...	71	...	25
Bolivia	53	75	76	92	23	47	72	85	91	95	48	68	33	45	49	58	13	23
Brazil	74	78	90	91	28	17	83	89	93	96	55	58	70	75	82	83	37	35
British Virgin Islands	97	97	97	97	97	97	98	98	98	98	98	98	100	100	100	100	100	100
Chile	86	92	98	99	25	40	90	95	98	100	49	59	85	92	91	96	52	64
Colombia	78	85	94	96	41	51	92	92	98	99	78	71	82	86	95	96	52	54
Costa Rica	...	92	99	99	...	81	...	97	100	100	...	92	...	92	...	89	97	97
Cuba	65	74	77	82	31	49	...	91	95	95	...	78	98	98	99	99	95	95
Dominica	...	87	98	98	...	58	...	97	100	100	...	90	...	83	...	86	...	75
Dominican Republic	54	35	70	37	35	31	86	93	97	98	72	85	48	57	60	67	33	43
Ecuador	55	59	74	77	32	32	69	86	81	92	54	77	56	72	73	80	36	59
El Salvador	45	60	74	78	16	34	67	82	88	91	47	68	51	63	70	78	33	40
French Guiana	...	79	...	83	...	65	...	84	...	88	...	71	...	78	...	85	...	57
Grenada	...	82	...	93	...	75	...	95	97	97	...	93	97	97	96	96	97	97
Guadeloupe	...	98	98	98	...	75	...	98	98	98	...	93	...	64	...	64	...	61
Guatemala	48	55	67	58	34	53	77	95	88	99	69	92	50	61	71	72	35	52
Guyana	...	53	...	66	...	45	...	83	...	83	...	83	...	70	...	86	...	60
Haiti	10	11	27	24	2	3	53	71	77	91	43	59	15	34	27	52	11	23
Honduras	59	72	82	92	43	55	83	90	89	99	78	82	49	68	77	89	31	52
Jamaica	60	70	87	93	32	45	92	93	97	98	86	87	75	80	85	90	64	68
Mexico	78	89	89	96	50	71	80	91	90	97	54	72	66	77	84	90	20	39
Montserrat	...	...	98	98	...	...	100	100	100	100	100	100	96	96	96	96	96	96
Nicaragua	54	62	89	86	15	31	69	81	92	93	42	65	47	66	64	78	27	51
Panama	...	85	96	96	...	72	...	91	99	99	...	79	...	72	...	89	...	51
Paraguay	30	54	59	82	2	18	62	83	80	100	46	62	58	78	71	94	46	58
Peru	56	72	74	84	16	40	74	81	88	87	42	66	52	62	68	72	15	33
Saint Kitts and Nevis	...	72	...	72	...	72	99	99	99	99	99	99	96	96	96	96	96	96
Saint Lucia	...	75	...	75	...	75	98	98	98	98	98	98	...	89	...	89	...	89
Saint Vincent and the Grenadines	...	...	...	...	...	73	...	...	...	...	...	93	...	...	...	...	96	96
Suriname	...	80	...	91	...	48	...	92	98	98	...	73	...	93	99	99	...	76
Trinidad and Tobago	77	77	81	80	68	67	92	91	93	92	89	88	100	100	100	100	100	100
Turks and Caicos Islands	...	68	...	78	...	60	100	100	100	100	100	100	...	96	98	98	...	94
Uruguay	...	91	95	94	...	56	...	98	98	98	...	93	...	94	95	95	...	85
Venezuela	...	81	79	84	...	61	...	83	...	85	...	70	...	68	...	71	...	48
NORTHERN AMERICA																		
Canada	...	88	100	100	...	...	100	100	100	100	99	99	100	100	100	100	99	99
United States	100	100	100	100	100	100	100	100	100	100	100	100	100	100	100	100	100	100
OCEANIA																		
Australia	...	...	...	...	...	...	100	100	100	100	100	100	100	100	100	100	100	100
Cook Islands	...	...	...	...	...	...	94	95	99	98	87	88	95	100	100	100	88	100
Fiji	...	...	...	...	...	...	...	...	...	...	...	...	98	98	99	99	98	98
French Polynesia	98	98	99	99	96	96	100	100	100	100	100	100	98	98	99	99	97	97
Guam	...	...	...	...	...	...	100	100	100	100	100	100	99	99	99	99	98	98
Kiribati	24	34	46	49	13	22	48	64	76	77	33	53	25	39	33	59	21	22
Marshall Islands	...	...	...	...	...	...	96	85	95	80	97	95	75	82	88	93	51	59

TABLE B.5

continued

	In-house connection						Improved drinking water coverage						Improved sanitation coverage					
	Total (%)		Urban (%)		Rural (%)		Total (%)		Urban (%)		Rural (%)		Total (%)		Urban (%)		Rural (%)	
	1990	2002	1990	2002	1990	2002	1990	2002	1990	2002	1990	2002	1990	2002	1990	2002	1990	2002
Micronesia (Federated State of)	...	...	...	...	...	...	87	94	93	95	85	94	30	28	53	61	21	14
New Zealand	...	...	100	100	...	...	97	...	100	100	82	...	...	...	...	...	88	...
Niue	...	87	100	100	...	80	100	100	100	100	100	100	100	100	100	100	100	100
Northern Mariana Islands	...	...	93	...	...	35	98	98	98	98	100	97	84	94	85	94	78	96
Palau	...	...	...	...	...	10	80	84	71	79	99	94	66	83	72	96	54	52
Papua New Guinea	11	11	61	61	4	4	39	39	88	88	32	32	45	45	67	67	41	41
Samoa	...	57	...	74	...	52	91	88	99	91	89	88	98	100	100	100	98	100
Solomon Islands	11	13	76	76	1	1	...	70	...	94	...	65	...	31	98	98	...	18
Tokelau	...	...	...	...	0	0	...	...	...	...	96	89	...	...	...	...	30	74
Tonga	...	75	...	72	...	76	100	100	100	100	100	100	97	97	98	98	96	96
Tuvalu	...	...	...	...	...	...	91	93	92	94	89	92	78	88	83	92	74	83
Vanuatu	38	38	80	73	28	28	60	60	93	85	53	52	...	50	...	78	...	42

Source: UNICEF and WHO, 2004.

TABLE B.6

Basic Economic Indicators

	PPP Gross national rate		GDP growth rate	Structure of output: Agriculture		Structure of output: Industry		Structure of output: Services		Savings: National Gross	Savings: National Net	Savings: Domestic Gross	Savings: Domestic Net	Development assistance: Aid per capita		Development assistance: Dependency ratio	
	Billions $	$/ capita	(%)	% of GDP		% of GDP		% of GDP		% of GDP		% of GDP		US$		% of GDP	
	2003	2003	2002–2003	1990	2002	1990	2002	1990	2002	2002	2002	2002	2002	1997	2002	1997	2002
AFRICA																	
Algeria	189	5,940	5.2	11	10	48	53	40	37	...	...	27	40	9	12	0.5	0.7
Angola	26	1,890	1.4	18	8	41	68	41	24	23.3	12.9	30	39	31	32	5.5	4.3
Benin	7	1,110	2.9	36	36	13	14	51	50	9.2	1.1	2	6	38	34	10.4	8.3
Botswana	14	7,960	4.0	5	2	57	48	39	50	...	...	43	38	77	22	2.4	0.8
Burkina Faso	14	1,180	4.1	28	32	20	18	52	50	8.0	1.3	5	5	35	40	14.2	15.2
Burundi	4	620	(2.9)	56	49	19	19	25	31	11.0	4.6	(5)	(4)	9	24	6.0	24.2
Cameroon	32	1,980	0.5	25	43	29	20	46	38	...	...	21	18	35	40	5.9	7.3
Central African Republic	4	1,080	(8.8)	48	57	20	22	33	21	...	...	(1)	10	26	16	9.2	5.8
Chad	9	1,100	4.3	29	38	18	17	53	45	...	...	2	6	32	28	14.5	11.8
Congo	3	710	(1.7)	13	6	41	63	46	30	34.6	22.2	24	50	86	115	16.2	19.1
Côte d'Ivoire	23	1,390	(5.6)	32	26	23	20	44	53	20.5	11.3	11	28	30	65	4.1	9.6
Democratic Republic of the Congo	34	640	1.9	30	56	28	19	42	25			9	4	3	16	5.5	14.7
Egypt	266	3,940	1.4	19	17	29	33	52	50	15.1	5.6	16	10	33	19	2.6	1.4
Eritrea	5	1,110	2.8	31	12	12	25	57	63	21.7	16.6	(26)	(30)	33	54	14.3	30.8
Ethiopia	49	710	(5.7)	49	40	13	12	38	48	15.4	9.3	7	2	10	19	8.4	21.7
Gabon	...	...	...	7	8	43	46	50	46	40.7	27.8	37	48	33	55	0.8	1.7
Gambia	...	...	...	29	26	13	14	58	60	...	...	11	4	33	44	9.7	17.3
Ghana	45	2,190	2.5	45	34	17	24	38	42	20.4	13.3	5	7	27	32	7.3	10.8
Guinea	17	2,100	0.0	24	24	33	37	43	39	17.1	9.0	18	11	55	32	10.4	7.9
Guinea-Bissau	...	...	...	61	62	19	13	21	25	...	...	3	(17)	99	41	48.9	30.5
Kenya	33	1,020	(0.7)	29	16	19	19	52	65	13.7	5.7	14	10	16	13	4.3	3.2
Lesotho	6	3,120	20.9	24	16	33	43	43	41	22.0	15.4	(44)	(15)	54	43	6.8	8.7
Liberia	...	...	...	...	...	...	...	...	...	...	...	...	...	26	16	28.8	11.0
Libyan Arab Jamahiriya	...	...	...	...	...	...	...	...	...	...	...	27	26	1	2	...	...
Madagascar	13	800	6.5	29	32	13	13	59	55	8.5	0.6	6	8	59	23	24.1	8.6
Malawi	7	600	3.8	45	37	29	15	26	49	0.8	(6.3)	13	(6)	36	35	13.8	20.2
Mali	11	960	3.5	46	34	16	30	39	36	3.2	(5.2)	6	12	43	42	17.7	15.1
Mauritania	5	2,010	2.9	30	21	29	29	42	50	...	...	5	2	98	128	22.8	45.4
Mauritius	...	...	...	13	7	33	31	54	62	27.7	16.9	23	26	38	20	1.0	0.5
Morocco	119	3,950	3.8	18	16	32	30	50	54	26.1	16.1	19	18	17	21	1.4	1.8
Mozambique	20	1,070	5.0	37	23	18	34	44	43	27.7	19.4	(12)	30	57	112	29.5	60.4
Namibia	13	6,620	(6.7)	12	11	38	31	50	58	39.6	28.1	18	23	96	68	4.1	4.2
Niger	10	820	1.0	35	40	16	17	49	43	...	...	1	4	34	26	18.3	13.8
Nigeria	122	900	8.3	33	37	41	29	26	34	13.1	4.8	29	17	2	2	0.6	0.8
Rwanda	11	1,290	2.1	33	41	25	21	43	37	12.2	4.9	6	1	32	44	12.5	20.8
Senegal	17	1,660	6.0	20	15	19	22	61	63	11.5	3.2	9	10	48	46	9.8	9.2
Sierra Leone	3	530	4.5	32	53	13	32	55	16	...	...	9	(14)	25	68	14.3	47.0
Somalia	...	...	...	65	...	...	...	...	...	...	...	(12)	...	10	21	...	...
South Africa	465	10,270	(2.0)	5	4	40	32	55	64	16.5	3.2	23	19	12	14	0.3	0.6
Sudan	...	...	...	...	39	...	18	...	43	13.1	4.8	...	21	5	11	1.3	2.7
Swaziland	...	...	...	13	16	42	50	45	35	7.2	(1.7)	20	9	29	23	1.8	2.0
Togo	7	1,500	0.9	34	40	23	22	44	38	8.0	0.2	15	5	31	11	8.5	3.8
Tunisia	68	6,840	4.4	16	10	30	29	54	60	22.7	12.6	25	21	21	49	1.1	2.4
Uganda	36	1,440	0.8	57	32	11	22	32	46	15.8	8.2	1	6	38	26	13.0	11.2
United Republic of Tanzania	22	610	3.5	46	44	18	16	36	39	14.5	7.0	1	10	30	35	12.5	13.2
Zambia	9	850	3.5	21	22	51	26	28	52	...	...	17	4	66	63	16.5	18.1
Zimbabwe	28	2,180	(6.7)	16	17	33	24	50	59	...	...	17	11	28	15	4.2	...

ASIA																	
Afghanistan	...	...	...	...	52	...	24	...	24	...	...	...	(16)	10	46	...	...
Armenia	12	3,770	11.9	17	26	52	37	31	37	13.9	5.3	36	3	52	96	9.6	12.0
Azerbaijan	28	3,380	10.5	30	16	33	52	37	32	21.5	6.5	31	25	23	43	4.7	6.1
Bangladesh	258	1,870	3.5	30	23	21	26	48	51	28.5	22.7	10	18	8	7	2.3	1.8
Cambodia	28	2,060	5.8	...	36	...	28	...	36	18.5	11.2	2	14	30	39	10.1	12.7
China	6,435	4,990	8.4	27	15	42	51	31	34	43.7	34.7	38	43	2	1	0.2	0.1
China, Hong Kong SAR	196	28,810	2.9	0	0	25	13	74	87	32.1	19.2	36	32	1	1	0.0	0.0
Democratic People's Rep. of Korea	...	...	...	...	...	...	...	...	...	...	...	...	...	4	12	...	...
Georgia	13	2,540	9.4	32	21	33	23	35	56	15.0	(0.7)	25	9	45	60	6.5	9.2
India	3,068	2,880	6.4	31	23	28	27	41	51	22.3	12.6	23	22	2	1	0.4	0.3
Indonesia	689	3,210	2.8	19	17	39	44	41	38	18.2	12.7	32	21	4	6	0.4	0.8
Iran (Islamic Republic of)	477	7,190	4.4	24	12	29	39	48	49	38.9	29.2	27	37	3	2	0.2	0.1
Iraq	...	...	...	...	...	...	...	...	...	...	...	...	...	10	5	...	...
Israel	128	19,200	(0.8)	...	...	...	...	...	...	13.4	0.2	14	9	205	115	1.2	0.7
Japan	3,641	28,620	2.7	8	2	28	26	64	72	27.2	11.4	34	26	..	..	..	..
Jordan	23	4,290	0.5	...	...	...	...	...	...	26.2	15.6	1	3	104	103	6.6	5.8
Kazakhstan	92	6,170	8.7	27	9	45	39	29	53	25.5	15.5	30	28	9	13	0.6	0.8
Kuwait	42	17,870	(3.3)	1	...	52	...	47	...	19.4	12.7	4	18	0	2	0.0	0.0
Kyrgyzstan	8	1,660	3.9	34	39	36	26	30	35	17.4	9.2	4	15	51	37	14.1	12.0
Lao People's Democratic Republic	10	1,730	2.6	61	51	15	23	24	26	...	...	...	...	67	50	19.3	17.3
Lebanon	22	4,840	1.4	...	12	...	21	...	67	2.1	(8.2)	(64)	(9)	61	103	1.6	2.5
Malaysia	222	8,940	3.2	15	9	42	47	43	44	34.5	22.8	34	42	(11)	4	(0.3)	0.1
Mongolia	4	1,800	3.4	17	30	30	16	52	54	26.7	14.6	9	16	108	85	28.1	18.6
Myanmar	...	...	...	57	57	11	10	32	33	12.4	...	11	12	1	2	...	...
Nepal	35	1,420	0.7	52	41	16	22	32	38	22.1	19.8	7	12	19	15	8.2	6.6
Oman	...	...	...	3	...	58	...	39	...	...	...	35	34	29	16	0.4	0.2
Pakistan	306	2,060	3.3	26	23	25	23	49	53	25.6	17.9	11	14	5	15	1.0	3.6
Philippines	379	4,640	2.5	22	15	34	33	44	53	24.5	16.5	18	19	10	7	0.8	0.7
Republic of Korea	859	17,930	2.4	9	4	43	41	48	55	27.3	15.3	37	27	(3)	(2)	0.0	0.0
Saudi Arabia	281	12,850	(1.8)	6	5	49	51	45	44	28.9	18.9	24	37	1	1	0.0	0.0
Singapore	103	24,180	(1.0)	...	0	...	36	...	64	42.7	28.3	43	45	1	2	0.0	0.0
Sri Lanka	72	3,730	4.3	26	20	26	26	48	54	19.9	14.8	14	14	19	18	2.2	2.1
Syrian Arab Republic	60	3,430	0.0	28	23	24	28	48	49	24.3	13.9	17	30	13	5	1.4	0.4
Tajikistan	7	1,040	7.8	33	24	38	24	29	52	5.0	(2.5)	17	10	14	27	8.0	14.6
Thailand	462	7,450	6.1	12	9	37	43	50	48	30.4	15.5	34	31	11	5	0.4	0.2
Turkey	473	6,690	4.2	18	13	30	27	52	60	16.7	9.8	20	16	0	9	0.0	0.4
Turkmenistan	28	5,840	15.3	32	29	30	51	38	20	36.3	26.6	28	36	3	8	0.4	...
United Arab Emirates	...	...	...	2	...	64	...	35	...	...	...	45	...	1	1	0.0	...
Uzbekistan	44	1,720	3.0	33	35	33	22	34	44	17.2	7.3	13	24	6	7	1.3	2.4
Viet Nam	202	2,490	6.1	39	23	23	39	39	38	33.6	25.4	3	28	13	16	3.8	3.6
Yemen	16	820	0.7	24	15	27	40	49	44	24.1	14.6	9	16	22	31	5.6	6.3
EUROPE																	
Albania	15	4,700	6.9	36	25	48	19	16	56	13.8	4.7	21	(1)	53	101	7.5	6.4
Austria	239	29,610	0.6	4	2	34	32	62	66	21.4	7.0	26	23	..	..	..	..
Belarus	59	6,010	6.1	24	11	47	37	29	52	18.6	9.3	29	18	5	4	0.4	0.3
Belgium	299	28,930	1.0	2	1	33	27	65	72	23.4	8.9	24	23	..	..	..	..
Bosnia and Herzegovina	26	6,320	3.0	...	18	...	37	...	45	7.5	(1.0)	...	(13)	236	143	26.1	10.0
Bulgaria	60	7,610	4.9	17	13	49	28	34	59	15.4	5.1	22	13	26	48	2.2	2.5
Croatia	48	10,710	4.0	10	8	34	30	56	62	21.2	9.7	2	18	9	37	0.2	0.8
Czech Republic	160	15,650	2.9	6	4	49	40	45	57	23.0	10.7	28	26	11	38	0.2	0.6
Denmark	168	31,213	0.2	4	3	27	27	69	71	23.4	8.0	25	26	..	..	..	..
Estonia	17	12,480	5.3	17	5	50	30	34	65	20.2	6.0	22	22	47	51	1.5	1.1
Finland	141	27,100	1.7	6	3	35	33	59	64	27.0	11.0	29	28	..	..	..	..
France	1,640	27,460	(0.3)	4	3	30	25	66	72	21.1	8.7	22	21	..	..	..	..
Germany	2,267	27,460	(0.1)	2	1	39	30	59	69	20.4	5.5	24	22	..	..	..	..
Greece	213	19,920	4.2	11	7	28	22	61	70	19.7	11.0	13	17	..	..	..	..
Hungary	139	13,780	0.7	15	4	39	31	46	65	23.5	11.7	28	22	18	46	0.4	0.7
Ireland	120	30,450	1.1	9	3	35	42	56	54	28.0	15.5	26	38	..	..	..	..
Italy	1,543	26,760	0.4	4	3	34	29	63	69	19.8	6.1	22	21	..	..	..	..
Latvia	24	10,130	8.1	22	5	46	25	32	71	19.6	8.9	39	17	33	37	1.4	1.0
Lithuania	38	11,090	7.0	27	7	31	31	42	62	17.4	7.2	24	17	29	42	1.1	1.1
Netherlands	464	28,600	(0.9)	4	3	30	26	65	71	22.2	7.2	27	26	..	..	..	..
Norway	170	37,300	(0.2)	4	2	36	38	61	60	32.0	16.1	30	33	..	..	..	..
Poland	437	11,450	4.9	8	3	50	30	42	66	16.6	5.4	33	16	22	30	0.6	0.6
Portugal	183	17,980	(0.9)	9	4	32	30	60	66	19.3	4.0	21	18	..	..	..	..
Republic of Moldova	7	1,750	6.5	43	24	33	25	24	51	14.4	7.2	23	(3)	15	33	3.3	8.0
Romania	159	7,140	5.6	24	13	50	38	26	49	19.9	10.0	21	17	10	31	0.6	1.5
Russian Federation	1,279	8,920	7.8	17	6	48	34	35	60	30.6	20.1	30	32	5	9	0.2	0.4
Serbia and Montenegro	...	...	5.5	...	15	...	32	...	53	...	...	...	(7)	9	237	...	12.4
Slovakia	72	13,420	4.8	7	4	59	29	33	67	23.2	12.0	24	24	13	35	0.3	0.8
Slovenia	38	19,240	3.5	6	3	46	36	49	61	25.2	13.5	26	25	50	87	0.5	0.8
Spain	905	22,020	1.9	6	3	35	30	59	66	24.0	11.1	23	24	..	..	..	..
Sweden	238	26,620	1.2	4	2	32	28	64	70	21.4	8.0	25	23	..	..	..	..
Switzerland	235	32,030	(1.2)	...	1	...	27	...	72	26.8	12.0	29	24	..	..	..	..
TFYR Macedonia	14	6,720	2.5	9	12	46	30	46	57	12.9	3.1	9	0	49	136	2.7	7.4
Ukraine	262	5,410	10.2	26	15	45	38	30	47	27.1	8.1	26	24	5	10	0.5	1.2
United Kingdom	1,639	27,650	2.1	2	1	35	26	63	73	14.4	3.1	18	14	..	..	..	..
LATIN AMERICA																	
Argentina	419	10,920	3.3	8	11	36	32	56	57	22.3	11.2	20	27	3	0	0.0	0.0
Bolivia	22	2,450	(0.8)	17	15	39	33	44	52	12.2	3.1	11	10	89	77	9.1	9.0
Brazil	1,322	7,480	(1.4)	8	6	39	21	53	73	19.7	8.9	21	22	2	2	0.0	0.1
Chile	155	9,810	2.0	9	9	41	34	50	57	24.5	14.4	28	27	9	(1)	0.2	0.0
Colombia	290	6,520	2.0	17	14	38	30	45	56	13.7	3.2	24	14	5	10	0.2	0.6
Costa Rica	36	9,040	3.9	18	8	29	29	53	62	15.1	9.2	21	17	(2)	1	(0.1)	0.0
Cuba	...	...	...	...	7	...	46	...	47	...	...	...	7	6	5	0.3	...
Dominican Republic	54	6,210	(2.2)	13	12	31	33	55	55	20.4	15.1	15	15	9	18	0.5	0.8
Ecuador	45	3,440	0.9	13	9	38	28	49	63	...	...	22	20	13	17	0.7	1.0
El Salvador	32	4,890	1.8	17	9	27	30	56	61	14.2	3.8	1	2	47	36	2.5	1.7

TABLE B.6

continued

				Structure of output						Savings				Development assistance			
	PPP Gross national rate		GDP growth rate	Agriculture		Industry		Services		National		Domestic		Aid per capita		Dependency ratio	
										Gross	Net	Gross	Net				
	Billions $	$/ capita	(%)	% of GDP		% of GDP		% of GDP		% of GDP		% of GDP		US$		% of GDP	
	2003	2003	2002–2003	1990	2002	1990	2002	1990	2002	2002	2002	2002	2002	1997	2002	1997	2002
Guatemala	50	4,060	(0.5)	26	22	20	19	54	58	14.8	4.7	10	7	25	21	1.5	1.1
Haiti	14	1,630	(1.8)	...	...	...	...	...	...	...	...	11	(3)	43	19	9.9	4.5
Honduras	18	2,580	(0.5)	22	13	26	31	51	56	23.3	17.7	20	12	50	64	6.6	6.8
Jamaica	10	3,790	1.1	7	6	40	31	52	63	20.7	9.1	22	13	28	9	1.1	0.3
Mexico	915	8,950	(0.1)	8	4	28	27	64	69	18.3	7.8	22	18	1	1	0.0	0.0
Nicaragua	13	2,400	(0.2)	31	18	21	25	48	57	11.2	...	(2)	6	88	97	24.1	13.6
Panama	19	6,310	2.3	9	6	15	14	76	80	24.2	16.6	21	24	17	12	0.5	0.3
Paraguay	27	4,740	(0.3)	28	22	25	29	47	49	14.2	5.2	17	8	22	10	1.1	1.0
Peru	138	5,090	2.4	9	8	27	28	64	64	17.2	6.7	18	18	16	18	0.7	0.9
Puerto Rico	...	...	...	1	1	42	43	57	56	...	...	21	...	...	...	...	...
Trinidad and Tobago	...	...	...	3	2	46	42	51	56	28.9	17.0	29	20	26	(6)	0.6	(0.1)
Uruguay	27	7,980	1.9	9	9	35	27	56	64	13.5	2.4	18	14	11	4	0.2	0.1
Venezuela	121	4,740	(10.9)	5	3	50	43	44	54	26.6	19.2	29	29	0	2	0.0	0.1
NORTHERN AMERICA																	
Canada	941	29,740	0.9	3	...	32	...	65	...	23.2	10.2	21	25	..	..	..	..
United States	10,914	37,500	2.0	2	2	28	23	70	75	14.4	2.6	16	14	..	..	..	..
OCEANIA																	
Australia	563	28,290	1.2	4	4	29	26	67	71	19.7	3.5	22	22	..	..	..	..
New Zealand	85	21,120	0.9	7	...	28	...	65	...	19.4	8.6	20	22	..	..	..	..
Papua New Guinea	12	2,240	0.2	29	27	30	42	41	32	...	...	16	...	73	38	7.4	7.5

Source: World Bank, 2004e.

TABLE B.7

Investment in Infrastructure and Foreign Direct Investment

	Domestic credit to private sector		Investment in infrastructure projects with private participation								Foreign direct investment			
			Telecommunications		Energy		Transport		Water and sanitation		In	Out		
	% of GDP		US$ millions										% of GDP	
	1990	2002	1990–1995	1996–2002	1990–1995	1996–2002	1990–1995	1996–2002	1990–1995	1996–2002	2003	2003	1990	2002
AFRICA														
Algeria	44.4	6.8	...	501.5	2,300.0	...	...	...	...	...	634	14	0.0	1.9
Angola	...	4.7	...	75.3	...	...	...	...	...	...	1,415	...	(3.3)	11.7
Benin	20.3	11.8	...	90.4	...	...	...	...	...	...	51	3	3.4	1.5
Botswana	9.4	18.4	...	80.0	...	...	...	...	...	...	86	40	2.5	0.7
Burkina Faso	16.8	13.5	...	36.6	...	5.6	...	...	...	...	11	...	0.0	0.3
Burundi	12.7	26.1	0.5	15.6	...	...	...	...	...	...	...	...	0.1	0.0
Cameroon	26.7	10.2	...	266.1	...	91.9	30.8	95.0	...	...	215	3	(1.0)	1.0
Central African Republic	7.2	5.7	1.1	...	...	...	...	...	0.7	...	4	...	0.0	0.4
Chad	7.3	4.1	...	13.0	...	...	...	...	...	...	837	...	0.5	45.0
Comoros	...	...	...	...	...	...	...	...	...	...	1	...	...	...
Congo	15.7	2.9	4.6	111.9	...	325.0	...	...	...	...	386	2	0.0	11.0
Côte d'Ivoire	36.5	14.8	...	827.4	147.2	223.0	...	178.0	...	...	389	...	0.4	2.0
Democratic Republic of the Congo	1.8	0.7	...	369.7	...	...	...	...	...	...	158	...	(0.2)	0.6
Djibouti	...	...	...	...	...	...	...	...	...	...	11	1	...	...
Egypt	30.6	60.6	...	2,895.4	...	1,378.0	...	1,057.2	6.0	...	237	14	1.7	0.7
Equatorial Guinea	...	...	...	...	...	...	...	...	...	...	1,431	...	...	
Eritrea	...	32.4	...	40.0	...	...	...	...	...	...	22	...	...	3.3
Ethiopia	19.5	26.7	...	...	...	...	...	...	...	...	60	25	0.1	1.2
Gabon	13.0	12.0	...	35.0	...	624.8	...	46.7	...	...	53	...	1.2	2.5
Gambia	11.0	17.3	...	6.6	...	...	...	...	...	...	60	7	0.0	12.0
Ghana	4.9	12.0	25.0	436.1	...	132.8	...	10.0	...	...	137	55	0.3	0.8
Guinea	3.5	3.8	45.0	75.3	36.4	...	...	...	...	...	8	2	0.6	0.0
Guinea-Bissau	22.0	3.0	...	...	23.2	...	...	...	...	...	2	...	0.8	0.5
Kenya	32.8	23.4	...	107.0	...	171.5	...	53.4	...	...	82	2	0.7	0.4
Lesotho	15.8	14.3	...	33.5	...	...	...	...	...	...	42	...	2.8	11.3
Liberia	30.9	3.2	...	...	...	...	...	...	...	...	-	130	0.0	(11.6)
Libyan Arab Jamahiriya	31.0	18.0	...	...	...	...	...	...	...	...	700	100	...	...
Madagascar	16.9	9.3	5.0	10.1	...	...	...	20.3	...	...	50	...	0.7	0.2
Malawi	10.9	4.1	8.0	25.5	...	...	...	6.0	...	...	23	3	1.2	0.3
Mali	12.8	17.6	...	42.7	0.1	747.0	...	...	...	...	129	13	0.2	3.0
Mauritania	43.5	31.7	...	99.6	...	...	...	...	...	...	214	...	0.7	1.2
Mauritius	35.6	61.3	...	365.6	...	109.3	...	42.6	...	...	70	41	1.7	0.6
Morocco	34.0	54.4	...	3,643.0	2,300.0	4,819.9	...	...	...	1,000.0	2,279	12	0.6	1.2
Mozambique	17.6	2.1	...	44.0	...	1,200.0	...	959.7	...	0.6	337	...	0.4	11.3

Namibia	22.6	48.4	18.0	4.0	...	5.0	...	450.0	...	...	84	(6)	...	...
Niger	12.3	5.0	...	52.7	...	...	...	...	...	4.9	31	(1)	1.6	0.4
Nigeria	9.4	17.8	...	982.7	...	225.0	...	22.8	...	...	1,200	93	2.1	2.9
Rwanda	6.9	10.3	...	15.6	...	...	...	...	...	...	5	...	0.3	0.2
Senegal	26.5	19.6	...	406.8	...	124.0	...	...	...	6.3	78	11	1.0	1.9
Seychelles	...	...	...	...	...	...	...	...	...	...	58	8	...	...
Sierra Leone	3.2	3.5	...	23.5	...	...	...	...	...	...	8	...	5.0	0.6
Somalia	...	...	...	2.0	...	...	...	...	...	...	1	...	0.6	...
South Africa	81.0	131.7	1,072.8	10,654.8	3.0	1,244.3	...	1,874.1	...	212.5	762	720	...	0.7
Sudan	4.8	5.0	...	6.0	...	...	...	...	...	...	1,349	...	0.0	4.7
Swaziland	20.7	14.3	...	33.6	...	...	...	...	...	...	44	...	3.4	3.8
Togo	22.6	13.3	...	5.0	...	...	...	...	...	...	20	(2)	1.1	5.4
Tunisia	66.2	68.6	...	277.0	627.0	265.0	...	...	...	...	584	1	0.6	3.8
Uganda	4.0	6.7	8.8	204.1	...	...	...	...	...	...	283	(15)	0.0	2.6
United Republic of Tanzania	13.9	6.3	30.1	321.0	6.0	490.0	...	23.0	...	...	248	...	0.0	2.6
Zambia	8.9	6.2	...	56.9	...	289.4	...	...	...	...	100	...	6.2	5.3
Zimbabwe	23.0	37.0	...	46.0	...	603.0	18.0	70.0	...	...	20	5	(0.1)	0.3
ASIA														
Afghanistan	...	...	...	70.0	...	...	...	...	...	...	1	...	...	...
Armenia	40.4	6.9	...	468.4	...	12.0	...	50.0	...	...	155	...	...	4.7
Azerbaijan	10.8	5.6	14.0	144.6	...	375.2	...	...	...	...	3,285	933	...	22.9
Bahrain	...	...	...	...	...	...	...	...	...	...	517	741	...	...
Bangladesh	16.7	28.9	146.0	594.4	...	1,040.2	...	25.0	...	...	121	8	0.0	0.1
Brunei Darussalam	...	...	...	...	...	...	...	...	...	...	2,009	5	...	...
Cambodia	...	6.8	31.6	155.7	...	123.2	120.0	72.2	...	...	87	10	0.0	1.3
China	87.7	136.5	...	13,024.7	6,113.5	14,301.6	6,219.8	15,849.8	104.0	1,992.4	53,505	1,800	1.0	3.9
China, Hong Kong SAR	163.7	150.1	...	...	...	...	...	...	...	...	13,561	3,769	...	7.9
China, Macao SAR	...	...	...	...	...	...	...	...	...	...	350	24	...	...
Cyprus	...	...	...	...	...	...	...	...	...	...	830	345	...	...
Democratic People's Republic of Korea	...	...	...	...	...	...	...	...	...	...	-5	...	...	...
Georgia	...	8.1	21.6	43.8	...	36.0	...	...	...	...	338	4	0.0	4.9
India	25.2	32.6	720.5	14,950.0	2,888.5	9,680.5	126.9	1,969.1	...	216.0	4,269	913	0.1	0.6
Indonesia	46.9	22.3	3,549.0	9,215.5	3,202.5	7,534.7	1,204.9	2,314.6	3.8	919.5	-597	130	1.0	(0.9)
Iran (Islamic Republic of)	32.5	34.3	5.0	28.0	...	...	...	...	...	...	120	1,486	(0.3)	0.0
Iraq	...	...	...	...	...	...	...	...	...	...	...	...	...	...
Israel	57.6	97.8	...	...	...	...	...	...	...	...	3,745	1,774	0.3	1.6
Japan	195.1	175.3	...	...	...	...	...	...	...	...	6,324	28,800	0.1	0.2
Jordan	72.3	73.5	43.0	967.9	...	...	...	182.0	...	209.0	379	3	0.9	0.6
Kazakhstan	...	18.6	30.0	1,849.5	...	2,125.0	...	...	...	40.0	2,068	4	0.4	10.5
Kuwait	52.1	73.8	...	...	...	...	...	...	...	...	67	(4,989)	0.0	0.0
Kyrgyzstan	...	4.2	...	94.0	...	...	...	...	...	...	25	5	0.0	0.3
Lao People's Democratic Republic	1.0	8.4	...	185.5	...	535.5	...	100.0	...	...	19	76	0.7	1.5
Lebanon	79.4	90.8	100.0	550.9	...	...	...	200.0	...	...	358	97	0.2	1.5
Malaysia	108.5	146.1	2,630.0	3,241.6	6,909.5	2,131.6	4,657.6	7,919.0	3,986.7	1,105.5	2,474	1,370	5.3	3.4
Maldives	...	...	...	...	...	...	...	...	...	...	12	...	...	...
Mongolia	19.0	18.8	13.1	20.4	...	...	...	...	...	...	132	...	...	7.0
Myanmar	4.7	12.1	4.0	...	394.0	...	...	50.0	...	...	128	...	...	...
Nepal	12.8	30.7	...	45.6	131.4	137.2	...	...	...	...	30	...	0.0	0.2
Oman	22.9	38.6	...	...	204.5	998.3	...	546.1	...	...	138	97	1.4	0.2
Pakistan	27.7	27.9	602.0	343.0	3,417.3	2,519.7	299.6	118.7	...	...	1,405	19	0.6	1.4
Philippines	22.3	36.4	1,279.0	6,700.0	6,831.3	7,013.1	300.0	2,007.5	...	5,867.7	319	158	1.2	1.4
Qatar	...	...	...	...	...	...	...	...	...	...	400	71	...	...
Republic of Korea	65.5	115.6	2,650.0	17,600.0	...	2,690.0	2,280.0	5,950.0	...	...	3,752	3,429	0.3	0.4
Saudi Arabia	54.7	58.2	...	...	...	...	...	...	...	...	208	54	...	...
Singapore	96.8	115.5	...	...	...	...	...	...	...	...	11,409	5,536	15.1	7.0
Sri Lanka	19.6	28.5	43.6	849.6	21.7	286.6	...	240.0	...	...	229	4	0.5	1.5
Syrian Arab Republic	7.5	8.0	...	130.0	...	...	...	...	...	...	150	...	0.6	1.1
Tajikistan	...	18.8	...	1.0	...	...	...	...	...	...	32	...	0.5	0.7
Thailand	83.4	102.5	4,814.0	5,116.2	2,059.6	6,981.0	2,395.9	546.4	153.0	347.5	1,802	557	2.9	0.7
Turkey	16.7	14.9	190.3	7,875.4	2,478.0	5,167.2	...	724.8	...	942.0	575	499	0.5	0.6
Turkmenistan	...	2.3	...	...	...	...	...	...	...	...	100	...	...	1.3
United Arab Emirates	37.4	55.9	...	...	...	...	...	...	...	...	480	992	...	...
Uzbekistan	...	...	2.5	367.4	...	...	...	...	...	...	70	...	0.1	0.8
Viet Nam	2.5	43.1	128.0	18.0	...	2,215.5	10.0	115.0	...	212.8	1,450	...	2.8	4.0
Yemen	6.1	6.2	25.0	340.0	...	...	...	190.0	...	...	-89	...	(2.7)	1.1
EUROPE														
Albania	...	6.8	...	283.2	...	8.0	...	...	...	...	180	3	0.0	2.8
Austria	91.6	106.4	...	...	...	...	...	...	...	...	6,855	7,083	0.4	0.4
Belarus	...	9.1	10.0	180.3	...	500.0	...	...	...	...	171	2	...	1.7
Belgium	37.0	76.3	...	...	...	...	...	...	...	...	29,484	36,646	4.1	...
Bosnia and Herzegovina	...	36.3	...	...	...	...	...	...	...	...	381	...	...	5.2
Bulgaria	7.2	18.4	64.0	547.3	...	...	...	...	...	152.0	1,419	22	0.5	3.9
Croatia	...	51.6	...	1,425.5	...	375.6	...	672.2	...	298.7	1,713	62	...	4.4
Czech Republic	...	33.4	876.0	7,960.9	356.0	4,718.9	263.7	126.7	36.5	314.6	2,583	232	...	13.4
Denmark	52.2	146.4	...	...	...	...	...	...	...	...	2,608	1,158	0.8	3.7
Estonia	20.2	29.2	211.7	629.0	...	26.5	...	299.4	...	81.0	891	148	2.1	4.4
Finland	86.5	60.0	...	...	...	...	...	...	...	...	2,765	(7,370)	0.6	6.2
France	96.1	87.2	...	...	...	...	...	...	...	...	46,981	57,279	1.1	3.6
Germany	90.6	118.9	...	...	...	...	...	...	...	...	12,866	2,560	0.2	1.9
Gibraltar	...	...	...	...	...	...	...	...	...	...	20	...	...	...
Greece	36.3	67.1	...	...	...	...	...	...	...	...	47	586	1.2	0.0
Hungary	46.6	35.3	3,510.9	5,298.9	2,156.7	1,906.1	1,004.0	135.0	10.9	167.6	2,470	1,581	0.9	1.3
Iceland	...	...	...	...	...	...	...	...	...	...	147	168	...	...
Ireland	47.6	110.3	...	...	...	...	...	...	...	...	25,497	1,911	1.3	20.3
Italy	56.5	82.3	...	...	...	...	...	...	...	...	16,421	9,121	0.6	1.2
Latvia	...	29.0	230.0	894.9	...	177.1	...	75.0	...	...	360	32	0.6	4.5
Lithuania	...	14.2	74.0	1,345.0	...	20.0	...	...	...	...	179	37	0.0	5.2
Luxembourg	...	...	...	...	...	...	...	...	...	...	87,557	95,991	...	...
Malta	...	...	...	...	...	...	...	...	...	...	380	24	...	...

TABLE B.7

continued

	Domestic credit to private sector		Investment in infrastructure projects with private participation								Foreign direct investment			
			Telecommunications		Energy		Transport		Water and sanitation		In	Out		
	% of GDP		US$ millions										% of GDP	
	1990	2002	1990–1995	1996–2002	1990–1995	1996–2002	1990–1995	1996–2002	1990–1995	1996–2002	2003	2003	1990	2002
Netherlands	80.0	147.9	...	...	...	...	...	...	...	...	19,674	36,092	3.6	6.8
Norway	81.7	86.3	...	...	...	...	...	...	...	...	2,372	2,176	0.9	0.5
Poland	21.1	28.8	479.0	11,070.3	145.0	2,154.8	3.1	705.9	...	22.1	4,225	386	0.2	2.2
Portugal	49.1	147.9	...	...	...	...	...	...	...	...	962	95	3.7	3.5
Republic of Moldova	5.9	17.6	...	84.6	...	85.3	...	...	...	...	58	-	0.0	6.8
Romania	...	8.3	5.0	2,735.0	...	100.0	...	23.4	...	1,040.0	1,566	56	0.0	2.5
Russian Federation	...	17.6	918.0	6,467.2	1,100.0	2,295.3	...	515.4	...	108.0	1,144	4,133	0.0	0.9
Serbia and Montenegro	...	...	...	1,929.5	...	...	...	...	...	...	1,360	...	...	3.0
Slovakia	...	40.6	118.6	1,754.1	...	3,184.6	...	...	...	...	571	22	...	16.9
Slovenia	34.9	39.2	...	...	...	...	...	...	...	...	181	304	0.9	8.5
Spain	80.2	111.1	...	...	...	...	...	...	...	...	25,625	23,373	2.7	3.3
Sweden	124.4	43.6	...	...	...	...	...	...	...	...	3,296	17,375	0.8	4.9
Switzerland	167.9	159.0	...	...	...	...	...	...	...	...	12,161	10,919	2.6	1.3
TFYR Macedonia	...	17.7	...	607.3	...	...	...	...	...	...	95	-	...	2.0
Ukraine	2.6	18.0	100.6	1,299.9	...	160.0	...	...	...	...	1,424	13	0.3	1.7
United Kingdom	115.8	142.6	...	...	...	...	...	...	...	...	14,515	55,093	3.4	1.8
LATIN AMERICA														
Anguilla	...	...	...	...	...	...	...	...	...	...	28	1	...	...
Antigua and Barbuda	...	...	...	...	...	...	...	...	...	...	57	...	...	...
Argentina	15.6	15.3	11,907.0	13,452.2	12,035.1	13,470.3	5,991.7	8,385.5	5,166.0	3,071.5	478	774	1.3	0.8
Aruba	...	...	...	...	...	...	...	...	...	...	165	12	...	...
Bahamas	...	...	...	...	...	...	...	...	...	...	145	...	...	...
Barbados	...	...	...	...	...	...	...	...	...	...	121	...	...	...
Belize	...	...	...	...	...	...	...	...	...	...	40	2	...	...
Bolivia	24.0	51.4	38.0	808.9	252.4	2,718.2	...	185.3	...	682.0	160	3	0.6	8.7
Brazil	38.9	35.5	...	70,824.6	613.6	48,631.8	1,349.4	19,577.8	155.3	3,019.0	10,144	249	0.2	3.7
British Virgin Islands	...	...	...	...	...	...	...	...	...	...	400	3,088	...	...
Cayman Islands	...	...	...	...	...	...	...	...	...	...	4,600	1,858	...	...
Chile	47.2	68.1	148.9	1,574.8	2,260.0	6,457.3	539.9	6,709.6	67.5	3,886.1	2,982	1,395	2.2	2.7
Colombia	30.8	25.1	1,551.2	1,551.0	1,813.2	5,762.2	1,008.8	1,597.4	...	330.0	1,762	926	1.2	2.5
Costa Rica	15.8	30.1	...	...	76.3	243.1	...	161.0	...	...	587	47	2.8	3.9
Cuba	...	...	371.0	60.0	...	165.0	...	...	...	600.0	3	...	...	...
Dominica	...	...	...	...	...	...	...	...	...	...	17	...	...	...
Dominican Republic	27.5	40.2	10.0	433.2	372.5	1,936.3	...	833.9	...	...	310	...	1.9	4.4
Ecuador	13.6	27.9	51.2	728.8	...	310.0	12.5	886.8	...	550.0	1,555	...	1.2	5.2
El Salvador	...	...	...	...	...	...	...	...	...	...	157	19	...	...
Grenada	...	...	...	...	...	...	...	...	...	...	59	...	...	...
Guatemala	14.2	19.1	20.0	1,673.3	134.8	1,298.4	...	33.8	...	...	104	7	0.6	0.5
Guyana	...	...	...	...	...	...	...	...	...	...	26	...	...	...
Haiti	12.6	18.0	...	19.5	4.7	...	...	...	...	...	8	...	0.0	0.2
Honduras	31.1	40.7	...	71.1	95.3	86.8	...	130.5	...	220.0	198	...	1.4	2.2
Jamaica	36.1	15.7	...	494.0	289.0	201.0	30.0	...	390.0		520	79	3.0	6.1
Mexico	17.5	12.6	18,031.0	17,426.2	1.0	5,759.1	7,910.3	5,432.5	312.1	331.5	10,783	1,390	1.0	2.3
Montserrat	...	...	...	...	...	...	...	...	...	...	2	...	...	...
Netherlands Antilles	...	...	...	...	...	...	...	...	...	...	-81	...	...	...
Nicaragua	112.6	30.8	9.9	162.2	...	347.4	...	104.0	...	...	201	4	0.0	4.3
Panama	46.7	97.6	...	1,429.2	...	1,064.9	409.9	806.0	...	25.0	792	...	2.6	0.5
Paraguay	15.8	24.2	48.1	204.4	...	...	...	58.0	...	...	82	5	1.5	(0.4)
Peru	11.8	23.1	2,568.7	5,412.0	1,207.8	3,095.7	6.6	315.8	...	56.0	1,377	60	0.2	4.2
Puerto Rico	...	...	...	...	...	...	...	...	...	...		975	...	...
Saint Lucia	...	...	...	...	...	...	...	...	...	...	32	...	...	...
Saint Vincent and the Grenadines	...	...	...	...	...	...	...	...	...	...	38	...	...	...
Suriname	...	...	...	...	...	...	...	...	...	...	-92	...	...	...
Trinidad and Tobago	44.7	40.7	47.0	146.7	...	207.0	...	...	...	120.0	616	225	2.2	7.6
Uruguay	32.4	66.4	19.0	57.7	86.0	330.0	96.0	621.2	10.0	351.0	263	3	0.0	1.5
Venezuela	25.4	9.8	4,603.3	6,446.7	...	133.0	100.0	268.0	...	44.0	2,531	1,143	0.9	0.7
NORTHERN AMERICA														
Bermuda	...	...	...	...	...	...	...	...	...	...	8,500	(1,601)	...	...
Canada	75.9	82.2	...	...	...	...	...	...	...	...	6,580	21,542	1.3	2.9
United States	93.5	140.6	...	...	...	...	...	...	...	...	29,772	151,884	0.8	0.4
OCEANIA														
Australia	64.2	89.8	...	...	...	...	...	...	...	...	7,900	15,108	2.6	4.1
Fiji	...	...	...	...	...	...	...	...	...	...	20	25	...	...
Kiribati	...	...	...	...	...	...	...	...	...	...	1	...	...	...
New Caledonia	...	...	...	...	...	...	...	...	...	...	8	...	...	...
New Zealand	76.0	118.1	...	...	...	...	...	...	...	...	2,017	188	4.0	1.4
Papua New Guinea	28.6	13.7	...	...	...	65.0	...	...	...	175.0	101	3	4.8	1.8
Samoa	...	...	...	...	...	...	...	...	...	...	...	...	...	...
Solomon Islands	...	...	...	...	...	...	...	...	...	...	-2	...	...	...
Tonga	...	...	...	...	...	...	...	...	...	...	3	...	...	...
Tuvalu	...	...	...	...	...	...	...	...	...	...	9	...	...	...
Vanuatu	...	...	...	...	...	...	...	...	...	...	19	...	...	...

Source: World Bank, 2004e.

TABLE B.8

Energy and Transport Infrastructure

	Energy production		Energy use per capita			Roads		Motor vehicles				Railways		Fuel prices	
	Total (thousands tn)		Kilogram (oil equivalent)		Rate (%)	Total (kilometre)	Paved (%)	Number per 1000		Number per kilometre		Total kilometre	Electric kilometre	Super US$ per litre	Diesel US$ per litre
	1990	2001	1990	2001	1990–2001	1995–2001	1995–2001	1990	1999–2001	1990	1999–2001	1996–2001	1996–2001	1999–2001	1999–2001
AFRICA															
Algeria	104,559	144,330	956	955	(0.3)	104,000	68.9	...	...	...	...	3,793	283	0.22	0.10
Angola	28,652	43,559	672	663	(0.1)	51,429	10.4	19	...	...	...	...	...	0.19	0.13
Benin	1,774	1,483	356	318	(1.2)	6,787	20.0	3	...	2	...	...	...	0.54	0.41
Botswana	...	...	...	...	...	10,217	55.0	18	69	3	11	...	...	0.41	0.38
Burkina Faso	...	...	...	...	...	12,506	16.0	4	...	3	...	...	...	0.83	0.62
Burundi	...	...	...	...	...	14,480	7.1	...	...	...	...	...	...	0.58	0.54
Cameroon	12,090	12,485	431	417	(0.2)	34,300	12.5	10	...	3	...	1,006	...	0.68	0.57
Central African Republic	...	...	...	...	...	23,810	2.7	1	1	0	0	...	...	1.00	0.87
Chad	...	...	...	...	...	33,400	0.8	2	...	0	...	...	...	0.79	0.77
Congo	9,005	13,668	423	262	(5.8)	12,800	9.7	18	...	3	...	900	...	0.69	0.48
Côte d'Ivoire	3,395	6,177	375	402	1.1	50,400	9.7	24	...	6	...	639	...	0.85	0.60
Democratic Republic of the Congo	12,027	15,707	319	300	(0.5)	157,000	...	...	...	...	...	3,641	858	0.70	0.69
Egypt	54,869	59,301	611	737	1.9	64,000	78.1	29	...	33	...	5,024	59	0.19	0.80
Eritrea	...	...	...	...	...	4,010	21.8	1	...	1	...	...	...	0.36	0.25
Ethiopia	14,158	1,800	296	291	0.1	31,663	12.0	1	2	2	3	781	...	0.52	0.32
Gabon	14,630	14,788	1,350	1,322	(0.4)	8,464	9.9	32	...	4	...	814	...	0.69	0.53
Gambia	...	...	...	...	...	2,700	35.4	13	...	5	...	...	...	0.46	0.40
Ghana	4,392	5,995	349	410	1.6	46,179	18.4	...	...	...	...	953	...	0.28	0.23
Guinea	...	...	...	...	...	30,500	16.5	4	...	1	...	...	...	0.66	0.56
Guinea-Bissau	...	...	...	...	...	4,400	10.3	7	...	2	...	...	...	...	...
Kenya	10,272	12,644	534	500	(0.4)	63,942	12.1	12	11	5	4	2,634	...	0.70	0.56
Lesotho	...	...	...	...	...	5,940	18.3	11	...	4	...	...	...	0.50	0.47
Liberia	...	...	...	...	...	10,600	6.2	14	...	4	...	...	...	...	...
Libyan Arab Jamahiriya	73,173	74,363	2,680	2,994	0.1	83,200	57.2	...	...	...	...	...	...	0.10	0.08
Madagascar	...	...	...	...	...	49,827	11.6	6	...	2	...	...	...	1.08	0.65
Malawi	...	...	...	...	...	28,400	18.5	4	...	4	0	710	...	0.66	0.62
Mali	...	...	...	...	...	15,100	12.1	3	...	2	...	734	...	0.69	0.55
Mauritania	...	...	...	...	...	7,660	11.3	10	...	3	...	...	...	0.63	0.39
Mauritius[1]	...	...	...	...	...	2,000	98.0	59	106	35	64	...	...	...	...
Morocco	773	583	280	377	2.6	57,698	56.0	37	51	15	26	1,907	1,003	0.87	0.55
Mozambique	6,846	7,560	509	425	(2.2)	30,400	18.7	4	...	2	...	...	...	0.46	0.43
Namibia	218	294	445	596	2.5	62,237	12.9	71	82	1	2	2,382	...	0.45	0.43
Niger	...	...	...	...	...	10,100	7.9	6	...	4	...	...	...	0.77	0.55
Nigeria	150,453	207,024	737	735	(0.3)	194,394	30.9	30	...	21	...	3,557	...	0.20	0.19
Rwanda	...	...	...	...	...	12,000	8.3	2	...	1	...	...	...	0.84	0.84
Senegal	1,362	1,765	305	325	0.8	14,576	29.3	11	14	6	2	906	...	0.75	0.53
Sierra Leone	...	...	...	...	...	11,330	7.9	10	0	4	...	...	...	0.51	0.50
Somalia	...	...	...	...	...	22,100	11.8	2	...	1	...	...	...	0.35	0.29
South Africa	114,534	145,287	2,592	2,404	(0.3)	362,099	20.3	139	...	26	...	22,657	10,430	0.43	0.40
Sudan	8,775	21,551	426	421	1.7	11,900	36.3	9	...	22	...	4,599	...	0.30	0.24
Swaziland	...	...	...	...	...	3,107	...	66	71	18	21	...	...	0.47	0.44
Togo	778	1,056	290	305	1.6	7,520	31.6	24	...	11	...	...	...	0.56	0.46
Tunisia	6,127	6,886	679	852	2.3	18,997	65.4	48	79	19	...	2,260	60	0.29	0.19
Uganda	...	...	...	...	...	27,000	6.7	2	...	...	...	261	...	0.83	0.70
United Republic of Tanzania	*9,063*	13,001	385	404	0.4	88,200	4.2	5	...	2	...	2,722	...	0.67	0.61
Zambia	4,923	6,052	703	638	(1.0)	91,440	22.0	14	...	3	...	1,273	...	0.72	0.60
Zimbabwe	8,250	8,531	887	769	(1.3)	18,338	47.4	...	...	...	...	2,759	311	0.85	0.72
ASIA															
Afghanistan	...	...	...	...	...	21,000	13.3	...	...	...	...	...	...	0.34	0.27
Armenia	*263*	602	*1,231*	744	(0.9)	15,918	96.3	5	...	2	...	842	784	0.42	0.29
Azerbaijan	*18,150*	19,581	*2,259*	1,428	(5.0)	25,013	92.3	52	52	7	17	...	...	0.37	0.16
Bangladesh	10,747	16,200	118	153	2.5	207,486	9.5	1	1	0	...	2,768	...	0.52	0.29
Cambodia	...	...	...	...	...	12,323	16.2	1	6	0	49	601	...	0.63	0.44
China	902,689	1,138,617	767	896	1.8	1,698,012	91.0	5	12	4	11	58,656	14,864	0.42	0.37
China, Hong Kong SAR	43	48	1,869	2,421	2.1	1,831	100.0	66	77	253	279	...	...	1.47	0.77
Dem. People's Rep. of Korea	28,725	19,251	1,647	914	(6.1)	31,200	6.4	...	...	...	...	...	...	0.55	0.41
Georgia	*1,470*	1,265	*1,612*	462	(11.4)	20,229	93.5	107	70	27	15	1,562	1,544	0.48	0.41
India	333,978	438,099	427	515	1.8	3,319,644	45.7	4	10	2	...	62,759	14,261	0.66	0.41
Indonesia	161,518	234,314	521	729	2.9	342,700	46.3	16	25	10	...	5,324	131	0.27	0.19
Iran (Islamic Republic of)	179,738	246,644	1,264	1,860	3.6	167,157	56.3	34	...	14	...	6,688	148	0.07	0.02
Iraq	106,715	123,296	1,153	1,202	1.6	45,550	84.3	14	...	6	...	...	...	0.02	0.01
Israel	433	685	2,599	3,291	2.4	16,521	100.0	210	275	74	108	925	...	0.90	0.62
Japan	73,209	104,006	3,534	4,099	1.5	1,166,340	76.6	469	572	52	62	20,165	12,080	0.91	0.66
Jordan	162	280	1,104	1,017	(0.1)	7,245	100.0	60	...	26	...	293	...	0.52	0.17
Kazakhstan	*89,007*	83,752	*4,823*	2,705	(6.6)	82,638	93.9	76	86	8	16	13,545	3,725	0.35	0.29
Kuwait	48,519	108,851	3,959	7,195	6.3	4,450	80.6	...	...	...	...	...	...	0.20	0.18
Kyrgyzstan	1,818	1,353	*1,114*	451	(7.5)	18,500	91.1	44	...	10	...	...	...	0.39	0.25
Lao People's Democratic Republic	...	...	...	...	...	21,716	44.5	9	...	3	...	...	...	0.36	0.30
Lebanon	143	161	635	1,239	6.1	7,300	84.9	321	...	183	...	...	...	0.65	0.25
Malaysia	48,727	77,623	1,234	2,168	4.6	65,877	75.8	124	...	26	...	1,622	152	0.35	0.19
Mongolia	...	...	...	...	...	49,250	3.5	21	31	1	2	1,810	...	0.38	0.37
Myanmar	10,651	15,275	264	252	0.1	28,200	12.2	...	...	...	...	...	...	0.36	0.28
Nepal	5,505	7,338	320	357	0.9	13,223	30.8	...	...	...	...	...	...	0.66	0.34
Occupied Palestinian Territory	...	...	...	...	...	...	...	...	...	...	...	...	...	0.99	0.52
Oman	38,312	64,534	2,804	4,029	1.8	32,800	30.0	130	...	9	...	...	...	0.31	0.26

TABLE B.8

continued

	Energy production		Energy use per capita			Roads		Motor vehicles				Railways		Fuel prices	
	Total (thousands tn)		Kilogram (oil equivalent)		Rate (%)	Total (kilometre)	Paved (%)	Number per 1000		Number per kilometre		Total kilometre	Electric kilometre	Super US$ per litre	Diesel US$ per litre
	1990	2001	1990	2001	1990–2001	1995–2001	1995–2001	1990	1999–2001	1990	1999–2001	1996–2001	1996–2001	1999–2001	1999–2001
Pakistan	34,360	48,606	402	456	1.3	257,683	59.0	6	9	4	5	7,791	293	0.52	0.35
Philippines	15,901	20,006	463	538	1.9	201,994	21.0	10	32	4	12	491	...	0.35	0.27
Republic of Korea	21,908	34,207	2,160	4,114	6.1	86,990	74.5	79	255	60	120	3,123	668	1.09	0.51
Saudi Arabia	368,753	476,831	3,850	5,195	1.6	152,044	29.9	165	...	19	...	1,390	...	0.24	0.10
Singapore	...	64	4,384	7,058	2.8	3,066	100.0	130	168	142	...	...	...	0.85	0.38
Sri Lanka	4,191	4,462	339	423	2.5	11,547	95.0	21	37	4	7	1,447	...	0.54	0.31
Syrian Arab Republic	22,570	34,377	984	841	(0.3)	44,575	21.1	26	29	10	...	1,771	...	0.53	0.18
Tajikistan	*1,553*	1,267	*1,631*	487	(10.1)	27,767	82.7	3	...	1	...	...	...	0.36	0.24
Thailand	25,908	40,059	777	1,235	4.4	57,403	98.5	46	...	36	...	4,044	...	0.36	0.32
Turkey	25,857	26,154	944	1,057	2.0	354,373	35.5	50	85	8	14	8,671	1,752	1.02	0.78
Turkmenistan	*48,822*	50,443	*2,912*	3,244	0.3	24,000	81.2	...	...	...	...	...	...	0.02	0.01
United Arab Emirates	108,472	144,566	9,550	10,860	1.2	1,088	100.0	121	...	52	...	...	...	0.29	0.30
Uzbekistan	*40,461*	55,630	*2,098*	2,029	(0.0)	81,600	87.3	...	...	...	...	...	619	0.38	0.26
Viet Nam	24,988	50,346	373	495	2.8	93,300	25.1	...	...	...	...	3,142	...	0.34	0.27
Yemen	9,792	22,687	221	197	(1.1)	67,000	11.5	34	...	8	...	...	...	0.21	0.10
EUROPE															
Albania	2,449	673	812	548	(1.0)	18,000	39.0	11	66	3	11	440	...	0.80	0.51
Austria	8,080	9,717	3,241	3,825	1.3	200,000	100.0	421	536	30	22	5,780	3,493	0.84	0.73
Belarus	4,103	3,533	3,886	2,449	(3.6)	75,302	89.0	61	112	13	...	5,512	874	0.50	0.36
Belgium	12,490	12,967	4,885	5,735	1.6	149,028	78.3	423	515	30	35	3,471	2,705	1.04	0.80
Bosnia and Herzegovina	*3,642*	3,277	*1,086*	1,074	4.7	21,846	52.3	114	...	24	...	...	...	0.74	0.74
Bulgaria	9,613	10,297	3,306	2,428	(2.0)	37,286	94.0	163	273	39	60	4,290	2,708	0.68	0.59
Croatia	*4,346*	3,720	*1,405*	1,771	3.1	28,275	84.6	...	274	...	44	2,726	983	0.89	0.74
Czech Republic	38,474	30,489	4,574	4,049	(0.9)	127,728	100.0	246	364	46	67	9,365	2,843	0.81	0.71
Denmark	9,835	27,171	3,426	3,692	0.3	71,622	100.0	368	420	27	31	2,047	625	1.09	0.94
Estonia	*4,118*	2,989	*4,091*	3,444	(1.0)	52,038	19.7	211	404	22	11	968	132	0.58	0.56
Finland	12,081	15,156	5,851	6,518	1.3	77,900	64.5	441	461	29	31	5,854	2,372	1.12	0.80
France	111,278	132,709	4,003	4,487	0.8	894,000	100.0	494	575	32	38	32,515	14,104	1.05	0.80
Germany	186,157	133,745	349	410	1.6	230,735	99.1	405	...	53	...	36,652	19,079	1.03	0.82
Greece	9,200	9,965	2,183	2,710	2.1	11,700	91.8	248	328	22	...	2,299	...	0.78	0.68
Hungary	14,239	10,824	2,746	2,487	(0.4)	167,839	43.7	212	271	21	16	7,729	2,628	0.94	0.85
Ireland	3,467	1,729	3,016	3,876	2.7	92,500	94.1	270	408	10	...	1,915	37	0.90	0.80
Italy	25,547	26,264	2,690	2,981	1.0	479,688	100.0	529	606	99	74	16,499	10,937	0.90	0.62
Latvia	*794*	1,717	*2,272*	1,822	(2.2)	69,732	38.6	135	281	6	11	2,331	258	0.70	0.65
Lithuania	*4,189*	4,144	*2,994*	2,304	(1.9)	76,573	91.3	160	345	12	17	1,905	122	0.69	0.59
Netherlands	60,316	60,437	4,447	4,814	0.5	116,500	90.0	405	428	58	58	2,802	2,061	1.12	0.81
Norway	120,304	226,570	5,066	5,896	1.3	91,443	77.0	458	511	22	25	...	...	1.23	1.18
Poland	99,228	79,861	2,619	2,344	(0.8)	364,697	68.3	168	307	18	32	22,560	11,826	0.83	0.68
Portugal	2,805	3,396	1,734	2,435	3.4	68,732	86.0	222	347	34	...	2,814	904	0.97	0.71
Republic of Moldova	*58*	62	*1,582*	735	(8.1)	12,691	86.1	53	82	17	24	...	...	0.45	0.31
Romania	40,834	28,222	2,689	1,644	(3.5)	198,603	49.5	72	160	11	18	11,364	3,929	0.64	0.57
Russian Federation	1,118,707	996,161	5,211	4,293	(2.1)	537,289	67.4	87	176	14	48	86,075	40,962	0.35	0.25
Serbia and Montenegro	11,835	10,774	1,435	1,508	1.6	44,993	62.3	137	163	31	39	4,058	1,103	0.74	0.66
Slovakia	5,273	6,550	4,056	3,480	(1.1)	42,956	87.3	194	266	57	34	3,662	1,536	0.74	0.70
Slovenia	*2,765*	3,161	*2,508*	3,459	3.3	20,236	100.0	306	465	42	46	...	...	0.76	0.67
Spain	34,648	33,022	2,349	3,127	2.7	663,795	99.0	360	467	43	54	13,866	7,523	0.83	0.72
Sweden	29,754	34,377	5,452	5,740	0.4	212,961	78.6	464	494	29	21	10,068	7,405	1.06	0.96
Switzerland	9,831	12,367	3,740	3,875	0.2	71,176	...	491	534	46	54	...	...	0.89	0.93
TFYR Macedonia	...	...	...	...	...	8,684	62.0	132	170	30	27	699	233	0.85	0.63
Ukraine	*110,170*	83,428	*4,187*	2,884	(3.8)	169,630	96.7	63	...	20	...	22,302	9,170	0.47	0.34
United Kingdom	207,007	261,939	3,686	3,982	0.6	371,913	100.0	400	391	64	62	17,067	5,225	1.18	1.20
LATIN AMERICA															
Argentina	47,384	82,862	1,395	1,593	1.6	215,471	29.4	181	181	27	37	28,291	179	0.63	0.46
Bolivia	4,923	6,938	422	496	3.1	53,790	6.5	41	53	6	8	3,163	...	0.69	0.42
Brazil	97,069	145,933	899	1,074	2.1	1,724,929	5.5	88	...	8	...	25,652	1,220	0.55	0.31
Chile	7,641	8,673	1,041	1,545	4.6	79,605	20.2	81	133	13	25	4,814	850	0.58	0.39
Colombia	48,445	73,920	715	680	(0.4)	112,988	14.4	...	51	...	19	3,154	...	0.44	0.24
Costa Rica	1,032	1,733	664	899	2.6	35,881	22.0	87	...	7	13	424	109	0.64	0.44
Cuba	6,271	6,656	1,555	1,216	(1.0)	60,858	49.0	37	32	16	6	4,667	132	0.90	0.45
Dominican Republic	1,031	1,485	586	921	4.7	12,600	49.4	75	...	48	0	...	...	0.49	0.27
Ecuador	16,400	22,872	590	692	1.4	43,197	18.9	35	48	8	14	...	...	0.55	0.27
El Salvador	1,722	2,329	496	677	2.4	10,029	19.8	33	61	14	36	1,202	503	0.46	0.33
Guatemala	3,390	5,230	512	626	2.1	14,118	34.5	...	52	...	119	...	...	0.48	0.32
Haiti	1,253	1,542	245	257	1.3	4,160	24.3	...	...	...	...	...	...	0.54	0.30
Honduras	1,694	1,535	496	488	(0.2)	13,603	20.4	22	60	10	28	...	...	0.63	0.46
Jamaica	485	487	1,231	1,545	2.2	18,700	70.1	...	...	...	...	...	...	0.52	0.44
Mexico	194,454	230,236	1,490	1,532	0.2	329,532	32.8	119	159	41	44	17,697	250	0.62	0.47
Nicaragua	1,495	1,540	554	536	(0.2)	19,032	11.0	19	30	5	8	...	...	0.54	0.41
Panama	612	678	621	1,098	4.3	11,643	34.6	75	...	18	...	...	...	0.51	0.36
Paraguay	4,578	6,077	744	697	0.4	29,500	50.8	...	...	...	...	...	...	0.56	0.34
Peru	10,596	9,363	461	460	0.8	72,900	12.8	...	43	...	13	1,691	...	0.74	0.48
Puerto Rico	...	...	...	...	...	24,023	94.0	...	...	...	...	...	...	...	...
Trinidad and Tobago	12,612	18,385	4,770	6,708	3.2	8,320	51.1	...	...	...	...	...	...	0.40	0.21
Uruguay	1,149	1,211	725	809	1.7	8,983	90.0	138	...	45	...	3,003	...	0.46	0.20
Venezuela	148,854	216,020	2,252	2,227	0.1	96,155	33.6	...	...	...	...	336	...	0.05	0.05

NORTHERN AMERICA															
Canada	273,680	379,207	7,524	7,985	0.8	901,903	35.3	605	580	20	20	39,400	...	0.51	0.43
United States	1,650,408	1,711,814	7,728	7,996	0.4	6,304,193	58.8	758	779	30	34	160,000	484	0.40	0.39
OCEANIA															
Australia	157,712	250,436	5,130	5,956	1.5	811,603	38.7	530	...	11	...	...	...	0.50	0.48
New Zealand	12,256	14,932	4,065	4,714	1.6	92,207	63.1	524	696	19	...	3,913	519	0.55	0.33
Papua New Guinea	...	...	...	...	...	19,600	3.5	...	...	...	...	...	...	0.53	0.34

Notes:

Data are for the most recent year in the indicated intervals. Road and railway data for China include Hong Kong, China SAR.

Source: World Bank, 2004e.

TABLE B.9

Social Indicators

		Inequality	Poverty		Vital data		Health services					Communications				
		Gini index	(below US$/day) US$1	US$2	Life expectancy	Under five mortality	Expenditure	Physicians		Hospital beds		Adult literacy	Radios	TV sets	PC	Mobile phones
			(%)	(%)	(years)	/1000	US$/capita	per 1000		per 1000		(%)	/1000	/1000	/1000	/1000
					2002	2002	2001	1980	1995–2002	1980	1995–2002	2002	2001	2002	2002	2002
AFRICA																
Algeria	1995	35.3	<2	15.1	71	49	73	...	1.0	...	2.1	69	244	114	8	13
Angola		...	...	...	47	260	31	...	0.1	...	...	...	78	52	2	9
Benin		...	...	...	53	151	16	0.1	0.1	1.5	...	40	445	12	2	32
Botswana	1993	63.0	23.5	50.1	38	110	190	0.1	...	2.4	...	79	150	44	41	241
Burkina Faso	1998	48.2	44.9	81.0	43	207	...	0.0	0.0	...	1.4	...	433	79	2	8
Burundi	1998	33.3	58.4	89.2	42	208	4	...	...	...	...	50	220	31	1	7
Cameroon	2001	44.6	17.1	50.6	48	166	20	...	0.1	...	...	68	161	75	6	43
Central African Republic	1993	61.3	66.6	84.0	42	180	12	0.0	0.0	1.6	...	49	80	6	2	3
Chad		...	...	...	48	200	5	...	...	...	...	46	233	2	2	4
Congo		...	...	...	52	108	18	...	0.3	...	...	83	109	13	4	67
Côte d'Ivoire	1998	45.2	15.5	50.4	45	191	41	...	0.1	...	...	...	185	61	9	62
Democratic Republic of the Congo		...	...	...	45	205	5	...	0.1	...	...	...	385	2	...	11
Egypt	1999	34.4	3.1	43.9	69	39	46	1.1	1.6	2.0	2.1	...	339	229	17	67
Eritrea		...	...	...	51	80	10	...	0.0	...	...	...	464	50	3	0
Ethiopia	2000	30.0	26.3	80.7	42	171	3	0.0	...	0.3	...	...	189	6	2	1
Gabon		...	...	...	53	85	127	...	...	...	...	...	488	308	19	215
Gambia	1998	38.0	59.3	82.9	53	126	19	...	0.0	...	...	...	394	15	14	73.
Ghana	1999	30.0	44.8	78.5	55	97	12	...	0.1	...	...	74	695	53	4	21
Guinea	1994	40.3	...	...	46	165	13	...	0.1	...	...	...	52	47	0	12
Guinea-Bissau	1993	47.0	...	...	45	211	8	0.1	0.2	1.9	...	...	178	36	...	0
Kenya	1997	44.5	23.0	58.6	46	122	29	...	0.1	...	...	84	221	26	6	42
Lesotho	1995	63.2	36.4	56.1	38	132	23	...	0.1	...	...	*81*	61	35	...	42
Liberia		...	...	...	47	235	1	...	0.0	...	...	...	274	25	...	1
Libyan Arab Jamahiriya		...	...	...	72	19	143	1.3	1.3	...	4.3	...	273	137	23	13
Madagascar	2001	47.5	49.1	83.3	55	135	6	...	0.1	...	0.4	...	216	25	4	10
Malawi	1997	50.3	41.7	76.1	38	182	13	...	...	...	1.3	62	499	4	1	8
Mali	1994	50.5	72.8	90.6	41	222	11	0.0	0.1	...	0.2	*19*	180	33	1	5
Mauritania	2000	39.0	25.9	63.1	51	183	12	...	0.1	...	...	41	148	99	11	92
Mauritius	1996-97	...	...	...	73	19	128	0.5	0.9	3.1	...	...	379	299	117	289
Morocco	1998-99	39.5	<2	14.3	68	43	59	...	0.5	...	1.0	51	243	167	24	209
Mozambique	1996-97	39.6	37.9	78.4	41	205	11	0.0	...	1.1	...	46	44	14	5	14
Namibia	1993	70.7	34.9	55.8	42	67	110	...	0.3	...	...	83	134	269	71	80
Niger	1995	50.5	61.4	85.3	46	264	6	...	0.0	...	0.1	17	122	10	1	1
Nigeria	1996	50.6	70.2	90.8	45	201	15	0.1	...	0.9	...	67	200	103	7	13
Rwanda	1983-85	28.9	35.7	84.6	40	203	11	0.0	...	1.5	...	69	85	...	...	14
Senegal	1995	41.3	26.3	67.8	52	138	22	...	0.1	...	0.4	39	128	78	20	55
Sierra Leone	1989	62.9	57.0	74.5	37	284	7	0.1	0.1	1.2	...	...	259	13	...	13
Somalia		...	...	...	47	225	6	0.0	0.0	...	...	...	60	14	...	3
South Africa	1995	59.3	7.1	23.8	46	65	222	...	0.6	...	...	86	336	177	73	304
Sudan		...	...	...	58	94	14	0.1	0.1	0.9	...	...	461	386	6	6
Swaziland	1994	60.9	...	...	44	149	41	...	0.2	...	...	...	161	34	24	61
Togo		...	...	...	50	140	8	0.1	0.1	...	...	60	263	123	31	35
Tunisia	2000	39.8	<2	6.6	73	26	134	0.3	0.7	2.1	1.7	73	158	207	31	52
Uganda	1999	43.0	...	...	43	141	14	...	...	...	...	69	122	18	3	16
United Republic of Tanzania	1993	38.2	19.9	59.7	43	165	12	...	0.0	1.4	...	77	406	45	4	19
Zambia	1998	52.6	63.7	87.4	37	182	19	0.1	0.1	...	...	80	179	51	8	13
Zimbabwe	1995	56.8	36.0	64.2	39	123	45	0.2	0.1	3.0	...	90	362	56	52	30
ASIA																
Afghanistan		...	...	...	43	257	8	...	0.1	...	...	...	114	14	...	1
Armenia	1998	37.9	12.8	49.0	75	35	28	3.2	2.9	8.4	4.3	99	264	229	16	19
Azerbaijan	2001	36.5	3.7	9.1	65	96	8	3.4	3.6	9.7	8.5	...	22	332	...	107
Bangladesh	2000	31.8	36.0	82.8	62	73	12	0.1	0.2	0.2	...	41	49	59	3	8
Cambodia	1997	40.4	34.1	77.7	54	138	30	...	0.3	...	...	69	119	8	2	28
China	2001	44.7	16.6	46.7	71	38	49	1.2	1.4	2.2	2.5	*91*	339	350	28	161
China, Hong Kong SAR	1996	43.4	...	...	80	...	...	0.8	1.3	4.0	...	...	686	504	422	942
Dem. People's Rep. of Korea		...	...	...	62	55	22	...	3.0	...	...	...	154	162	...	...
Georgia	2001	36.9	2.7	15.7	73	29	22	4.1	3.9	10.2	4.3	...	568	357	32	102
India	99-2000	32.5	34.7	79.9	63	90	24	0.4	...	0.8	...	*61*	120	83	7	12

TABLE B.9

continued

		Inequality	Poverty		Vital data		Health services					Communications				
		Gini index	(below US$/day) US$1 (%)	US$2 (%)	Life expectancy (years) 2002	Under five mortality /1000 2002	Expenditure US$/capita 2001	Physicians per 1000 1980	Physicians per 1000 1995–2002	Hospital beds per 1000 1980	Hospital beds per 1000 1995–2002	Adult literacy (%) 2002	Radios /1000 2001	TV sets /1000 2002	PC /1000 2002	Mobile phones /1000 2002
Indonesia	2002	34.3	7.5	52.4	67	43	16	...	...	...	...	88	159	153	12	55
Iran (Islamic Republic of)	1998	43.0	<2	7.3	69	41	363	...	0.9	1.5	1.6	77	281	173	75	33
Iraq		...	...	...	63	125	225	0.6	0.6	1.9	1.5		222	83	8	1
Israel	1997	35.5	...	...	79	6	1,641	3.1	3.7	6.8	6.2	95	526	330	243	955
Japan	1993	24.9	...	...	82	5	2,627	1.3	1.9	13.7	16.5	...	956	785	382	637
Jordan	1997	36.4	<2	7.4	72	33	163	0.8	1.7	1.3	1.8	91	372	177	38	229
Kazakhstan	2001	31.3	<2	8.5	62	99	44	3.0	3.6	13.1	7.0	99	411	338	...	64
Kuwait		...	...	...	77	10	630	1.7	1.9	4.1	2.8	83	570	418	121	519
Kyrgyzstan	2001	29.0	<2	27.2	65	61	12	2.6	2.6	12.0	5.5	...	110	49	13	10
Lao People's DemocraticRepublic	1997	37.0	26.3	73.2	55	100	10	...	0.2	...	...	66	148	52	3	10
Lebanon		...	...	...	71	32	...	...	2.1	...	2.7	...	182	357	81	227
Malaysia	1997	49.2	<2	9.3	73	8	143	0.3	0.7	...	2.0	*89*	420	210	147	377
Mongolia	1998	44.0	13.9	50.0	65	71	25	...	2.4	11.2	...	*98*	50	79	28	89
Myanmar		...	...	...	57	108	197	...	0.3	0.9	...	85	66	8	5	1
Nepal	1995-96	36.7	37.7	82.5	60	83	12	0.0	0.0	0.2	0.2	44	39	8	4	1
Oman		...	...	...	74	13	225	0.5	1.3	1.6	2.2	...	621	553	35	171
Pakistan	1998-99	33.0	13.4	65.6	64	101	16	0.3	0.6	0.6	...	...	105	150	4	8
Philippines	2000	46.1	14.6	46.4	70	37	30	0.1	1.2	1.7	...	93	161	182	28	191
Republic of Korea	1998	31.6	<2	<2	74	5	532	...	1.4	1.7	6.1	...	1,034	363	556	679
Saudi Arabia		...	...	...	73	28	375	...	1.7	...	2.3	78	326	265	130	217
Singapore	1998	42.5	...	...	78	4	816	0.9	1.6	4.0	...	93	672	303	622	796
Sri Lanka	1995	34.4	6.6	45.4	74	19	30	0.1	0.4	2.9	...	92	215	117	13	49
Syrian Arab Republic		...	...	...	70	28	65	0.4	1.3	1.1	1.4	83	276	182	19	23
Tajikistan	1998	34.7	10.3	50.8	67	116	6	...	2.1	...	6.4	99	141	357	...	2
Thailand	2000	43.2	<2	32.5	69	28	69	0.1	0.4	1.5	2.0	93	235	300	40	260
Turkey	2000	40.0	<2	10.3	70	41	...	0.6	1.3	2.2	2.6	87	470	423	45	347
Turkmenistan	1998	40.8	12.1	44.0	65	86	57	2.8	3.0	10.5	7.1	...	279	182	...	2
United Arab Emirates		...	...	...	75	9	849	1.1	1.8	2.8	2.6	...	330	252	129	696
Uzbekistan	2000	26.8	21.8	77.5	67	65	17	2.7	2.9	9.2	5.3	99	456	280	...	7
Viet Nam	1998	36.1	17.7	63.7	70	26	21	0.2	0.5	3.5	1.7	...	109	197	10	23
Yemen	1998	33.4	15.7	45.2	57	114	20	...	0.2	...	0.6	49	65	308	7	21
EUROPE																
Albania	2002	28.2	<2	11.8	74	24	48	1.4	1.4	4.3	3.3	99	260	318	12	276
Austria	1997	30.0	...	...	79	5	1,866	1.6	3.2	11.2	8.6	...	763	637	369	786
Belarus	2000	30.4	<2	<2	68	20	68	3.0	4.5	12.5	12.6	100	199	362	...	47
Belgium	1996	25.0	...	...	79	6	1,983	2.3	3.9	9.4	7.3	...	793	541	241	786
Bosnia and Herzegovina	2001	26.2	...	...	74	18	85	1.0	1.4	4.8	3.2	95	243	116	...	196
Bulgaria	2001	31.9	4.7	16.2	72	16	81	2.5	3.4	8.9	7.2	99	543	453	52	333
Croatia	2001	29.0	<2	<2	74	8	394	1.7	2.4	7.2	6.0	*98*	339	293	174	535
Czech Republic	1996	25.4	<2	<2	75	5	407	2.3	3.4	11.3	8.8	...	803	538	177	849
Denmark	1997	24.7	...	...	77	4	2,545	2.2	3.4	8.1	4.5		1,400	859	577	833
Estonia	2000	37.2	<2	5.2	71	12	226	2.9	3.1	12.2	6.7	*100*	1,136	502	210	650
Finland	2000	26.9	...	...	78	5	1,631	1.7	3.1	15.6	7.5	...	1,624	670	442	867
France	1995	32.7	...	...	79	6	2,109	2.0	3.3	11.1	8.2	...	950	632	347	647
Germany	2000	28.3	...	...	78	5	2,412	2.3	3.3	11.5	9.1	...	570	661	431	727
Greece	1998	35.4	...	...	78	5	1,001	2.4	4.4	6.2	4.9	97	478	519	82	845
Hungary	1999	24.4	<2	7.3	72	9	345	2.3	2.9	9.1	8.2	99	690	475	108	676
Ireland	1996	35.9	...	...	77	6	1,711	...	2.4	13.0	9.7	...	695	694	421	763
Italy	2000	36.0	...	...	78	6	1,584	2.6	4.3	9.6	4.9	99	878	494	231	939
Latvia	1998	32.4	<2	8.3	70	21	210	3.6	2.9	13.9	8.2	*100*	700	850	172	394
Lithuania	2000	31.9	<2	13.7	73	9	206	...	4.0	12.1	9.2	*100*	524	487	110	475
Netherlands	1994	32.6	...	...	78	5	2,138	1.9	3.3	12.3	10.8	...	980	648	467	745
Norway	2000	25.8	...	...	79	4	2,981	2.0	3.0	16.5	14.6	...	3,324	884	528	844
Poland	1999	31.6	<2	<2	74	9	289	1.8	2.2	5,6	4.9	...	523	422	106	363
Portugal	1997	38.5	<2	<0.5	76	6	982	2.0	3.2	5.2	4.0	93	301	413	135	825
Republic of Moldova	2001	36.2	22.0	63.7	67	32	18	2.8	2.7	12.1	5.9	99	758	296	18	77
Romania	2000	30.3	2.1	20.5	70	21	117	1.5	1.9	8.8	7.5	97	358	697	69	236
Russian Federation	2000	45.6	6.1	23.8	66	21	115	...	4.2	...	10.8	100	418	538	89	120
Serbia and Montenegro		...	...	...	73	19	103	...	2.1	...	5.3	...	297	282	27	257
Slovakia	1996	25.8	<2	<2.4	73	9	216	...	3.6	...	7.8	100	965	409	180	544
Slovenia	1998-99	28.4	<2	<2	76	5	821	1.8	2.2	7.0	5.2	100	405	366	301	835
Spain	1990	32.5	...	...	78	6	1,088	...	3.3	5.4	4.1	98	330	564	196	824
Sweden	2000	25.0	...	...	80	3	2,150	2.2	3.0	15.1	3.6	...	2,811	965	621	889
Switzerland	1992	33.1	...	...	80	6	3,779	2.4	3.5	...	17.9	...	1,002	552	709	789
TFYR Macedonia	1998	28.2	<2	4.0	73	26	115	1.3	2.2	5.2	4.8	...	205	282	...	177
Ukraine	1999	29.0	2.9	45.7	68	20	33	3.5	3.0	12.1	8.7	100	889	456	19	84
United Kingdom	1999	36.0	...	...	77	7	1,835	1.3	2.0	8.1	4.1	...	1,445	950	406	841
LATIN AMERICA																
Argentina	2001	52.2	3.3	14.3	74	19	679	...	2.7	...	3.3	97	681	326	82	178
Bolivia	1999	44.7	14.4	34.3	64	71	49	...	1.3	...	1.7	*87*	667	121	23	105
Brazil	1998	59.1	8.2	22.4	69	37	222	...	1.3	...	3.1	*86*	433	349	75	201
Chile	2000	57.1	<2	9.6	76	12	296	...	1.1	3.4	2.7	96	759	523	119	428

Colombia	1999	57.6	8.2	22.6	72	23	105	...	1.2	1.6	1.5	92	549	303	49	106
Costa Rica	2000	46.5	2.0	9.5	78	11	293	...	0.9	3.3	1.7	96	816	231	197	111
Cuba		...	...	...	77	9	185	...	5.3	...	5.1	...	185	251	32	2
Dominican Republic	1998	47.4	<2	<2	67	38	153	...	2.2	...	1.5	84	181	...	...	207
Ecuador	1998	43.7	17.7	40.8	70	29	76	...	1.7	1.9	1.6	*91*	422	237	31	121
El Salvador	2000	53.2	31.1	58.0	70	39	174	0.3	1.1	...	1.6	80	481	233	25	138
Guatemala	2000	48.3	16.0	37.4	65	49	86	...	0.9	...	1.0	70	79	145	14	131
Guyana	1999	43.2	<2	6.1	...	...	...	...	...	...	...	...	...	...	...	...
Haiti		...	...	...	52	123	22	...	0.2	0.7	0.7	52	18	6	...	17
Honduras	1999	55.0	23.8	44.4	66	42	59	...	0.8	1.3	1.1	*80*	411	119	14	49
Jamaica	2000	37.9	<2	13.3	76	20	191	...	1.4	...	2.1	88	795	374	54	535
Mexico	2000	54.6	9.9	26.3	74	29	370	...	1.5	0.7	1.1	*91*	330	282	82	255
Nicaragua	2001	55.1	45.1	79.9	69	41	60	0.4	0.9	...	1.5	*77*	270	123	28	38
Panama	2000	56.4	7.2	17.6	75	25	258	...	1.7	...	2.2	92	300	191	38	189
Paraguay	1999	56.8	14.9	30.3	71	30	97	...	1.1	...	1.3	*92*	188	218	35	288
Peru	2000	49.8	18.1	37.7	70	39	97	0.7	0.9	...	1.5	85	269	172	43	86
Puerto Rico		...	...	...	77	...	...	...	1.8	...	3.3	...	761	339	...	316
Saint Lucia	1995	42.6	...	...	...	...	...	...	...	...	...	...	...	...	...	...
Trinidad and Tobago	1992	40.3	12.4	39.0	72	20	279	0.7	0.8	...	5.1	...	534	345	80	278
Uruguay	2000	44.6	<2	3.9	75	15	603	...	3.7	...	4.4	98	603	530	110	193
Venezuela	1998	49.1	15.0	32.0	74	22	307	0.8	2.4	0.3	1.5	93	294	186	61	256
NORTHERN AMERICA																
Canada	1998	33.1	...	...	79	7	2,163	1.8	2.1	6.8	3.9	...	1,047	691	487	377
United States	2000	40.8	...	...	77	8	4,887	2.0	2.7	6.0	3.6	...	2,117	938	659	488
OCEANIA																
Australia	1994	35.2	...	...	79	6	1,741	...	2.5	12.3	7.9	...	1,996	731	565	640
New Zealand	1997	36.2	...	...	78	6	1,073	1.6	2.2	10.2	6.2	...	992	557	414	622
Papua New Guinea	1996	50.9	...	...	57	94	24	0.1	0.1	5.5	...	...	86	21	59	3

Notes: Data are for the most recent year available.

Source: World Bank, 2004e; UNDP, 2004.

TABLE C.1

Urban Agglomerations: Population Size and Rate of Change

		Estimates and Projections (000)						Annual rate of change (%)					Share in urban population (%)	
		1990	1995	2000	2005	2010	2015	1990–1995	1995–2000	2000–2005	2005–2010	2010–2015	2000	2015
AFRICA														
Algeria	Algiers	1,908	2,295	2,761	3,260	3,739	4,165	3.69	3.69	3.32	2.74	2.16	16.0	16.7
Angola	Luanda	1,597	1,958	2,341	2,839	3,487	4,271	4.07	3.58	3.86	4.11	4.05	56.6	49.4
Burkina Faso	Ouagadougou	594	689	764	870	1,038	1,292	2.95	2.06	2.61	3.53	4.38	38.4	30.0
Cameroon	Douala	1,001	1,324	1,663	1,980	2,254	2,481	5.59	4.56	3.49	2.59	1.92	22.5	22.0
Cameroon	Yaoundé	823	1,123	1,438	1,727	1,970	2,171	6.22	4.95	3.66	2.64	1.94	19.4	19.2
Congo	Brazzaville	704	830	980	1,153	1,361	1,609	3.31	3.32	3.25	3.33	3.34	54.4	52.1
Côte d'Ivoire	Abidjan	2,102	2,535	3,057	3,516	3,975	4,432	3.74	3.74	2.80	2.46	2.18	44.3	43.8
Democratic Republic of the Congo	Kinshasa	3,392	4,099	4,745	5,717	7,096	8,686	3.79	2.92	3.73	4.32	4.05	32.2	29.5
Democratic Republic of the Congo	Lubumbashi	660	783	906	1,102	1,384	1,714	3.41	2.91	3.92	4.56	4.28	6.2	5.8
Egypt	Alexandria	3,063	3,277	3,506	3,760	4,074	4,469	1.35	1.35	1.40	1.61	1.85	12.3	11.1
Egypt	Cairo	9,061	9,707	10,398	11,146	12,036	13,123	1.38	1.38	1.39	1.54	1.73	36.4	32.5
Ethiopia	Addis Ababa	1,791	2,157	2,491	2,899	3,429	4,138	3.72	2.88	3.04	3.36	3.76	25.5	22.3
Ghana	Accra	1,197	1,415	1,674	1,970	2,289	2,607	3.35	3.35	3.26	3.00	2.61	19.4	19.3
Ghana	Kumasi	584	664	755	862	986	1,121	2.57	2.57	2.65	2.69	2.56	8.8	8.3
Guinea	Conakry	877	1,041	1,234	1,465	1,769	2,138	3.41	3.41	3.43	3.76	3.79	46.6	43.0
Kenya	Nairobi	1,380	1,755	2,233	2,818	3,443	4,016	4.81	4.81	4.66	4.00	3.08	20.4	21.0
Libyan Arab Jamahiriya	Benghazi	636	800	912	1,033	1,149	1,256	4.58	2.61	2.50	2.12	1.79	20.4	20.5
Libyan Arab Jamahiriya	Tripoli	1,500	1,678	1,877	2,093	2,300	2,497	2.24	2.24	2.18	1.89	1.64	42.0	40.8
Madagascar	Antananarivo	948	1,212	1,494	1,808	2,166	2,598	4.91	4.18	3.82	3.61	3.64	36.0	35.2
Mali	Bamako	737	906	1,114	1,379	1,729	2,178	4.13	4.13	4.28	4.52	4.62	31.0	28.0
Morocco	Casablanca	2,685	2,994	3,344	3,743	4,168	4,579	2.18	2.21	2.25	2.15	1.88	20.7	19.4
Morocco	Fès	684	787	904	1,032	1,165	1,293	2.82	2.76	2.66	2.43	2.08	5.6	5.5
Morocco	Marrakech	580	693	818	951	1,082	1,203	3.54	3.34	3.01	2.58	2.12	5.1	5.1
Morocco	Rabat	1,161	1,374	1,610	1,859	2,102	2,325	3.36	3.17	2.87	2.46	2.02	10.0	9.8
Mozambique	Maputo	776	921	1,094	1,316	1,588	1,880	3.43	3.43	3.71	3.76	3.37	19.1	17.2
Niger	Niamey	447	577	752	997	1,327	1,753	5.11	5.33	5.63	5.71	5.57	34.0	32.3
Nigeria	Benin City	738	824	824	1,022	1,153	1,318	2.22	2.15	2.15	2.41	2.68	1.8	1.5
Nigeria	Ibadan	1,782	1,965	1,965	2,375	2,649	3,001	1.95	1.90	1.90	2.18	2.50	4.3	3.3
Nigeria	Kaduna	961	1,073	1,194	1,329	1,498	1,711	2.21	2.14	2.14	2.39	2.66	2.4	1.9
Nigeria	Kano	2,095	2,337	2,596	2,884	3,242	3,689	2.18	2.10	2.10	2.34	2.58	5.1	4.1
Nigeria	Lagos	4,764	6,434	6,434	11,135	14,037	17,036	6.01	5.95	5.02	4.63	3.87	17.1	19.0
Nigeria	Ogbomosho	623	716	716	959	1,117	1,301	2.78	2.93	2.93	3.03	3.06	1.6	1.4
Nigeria	Port Harcourt	680	760	760	942	1,063	1,216	2.21	2.15	2.15	2.41	2.69	1.7	1.4
Senegal	Dakar	1,461	1,690	1,968	2,313	2,716	3,140	2.90	3.05	3.22	3.21	2.90	44.2	41.2
Sierra Leone	Freetown	581	682	802	1,007	1,202	1,402	3.21	3.25	4.54	3.55	3.07	49.5	46.1
Somalia	Mogadishu	757	896	1,061	1,257	1,488	1,787	3.38	3.38	3.38	3.38	3.65	36.5	27.4
South Africa	Cape Town	2,155	2,394	2,715	3,103	3,205	3,239	2.10	2.52	2.67	0.65	0.21	11.1	11.7
South Africa	Durban	1,673	2,081	2,370	2,643	2,696	2,709	4.36	2.60	2.18	0.40	0.10	9.7	9.8
South Africa	East Rand (Ekurhuleni)	1,531	1,894	2,392	3,043	3,276	3,439	4.26	4.67	4.81	1.47	0.98	9.8	12.4
South Africa	Johannesburg	1,878	2,265	2,732	3,288	3,539	3,666	3.74	3.75	3.70	1.47	0.70	11.2	13.2
South Africa	Port Elizabeth	828	911	958	998	1,018	1,023	1.93	1.00	0.82	0.40	0.10	3.9	3.7
South Africa	Pretoria	911	951	1,084	1,282	1,363	1,405	0.85	2.61	3.36	1.23	0.61	4.4	5.1
South Africa	Vereeniging	743	800	897	1,033	1,075	1,095	1.48	2.30	2.82	0.80	0.37	3.7	3.9
Sudan	Khartoum	2,360	3,242	3,949	4,495	5,044	5,638	6.35	3.95	2.59	2.30	2.23	34.8	27.6
Tunisia	Tunis	1,568	1,722	1,891	2,063	2,215	2,360	1.87	1.87	1.74	1.42	1.27	31.7	31.2
Uganda	Kampala	755	918	1,111	1,345	1,635	2,022	3.91	3.82	3.81	3.91	4.24	39.3	36.2
United Republic of Tanzania	Dar es Salaam	1,316	1,668	2,116	2,683	3,371	4,123	4.75	4.75	4.75	4.56	4.03	18.8	19.2
Zambia	Lusaka	974	1,131	1,307	1,450	1,605	1,792	2.98	2.90	2.07	2.04	2.20	35.7	34.7
Zimbabwe	Harare	1,047	1,257	1,386	1,527	1,670	1,801	3.65	1.95	1.95	1.78	1.52	32.6	33.4
ASIA														
Afghanistan	Kabul	1,565	2,047	2,549	3,288	4,305	5,362	5.37	4.39	5.09	5.39	4.39	54.4	49.5
Armenia	Yerevan	1,173	1,136	1,100	1,066	1,036	1,019	(0.64)	(0.64)	(0.64)	0.56	(0.34)	54.4	53.6
Azerbaijan	Baku	1,733	1,766	1,798	1,830	1,878	1,962	0.37	0.37	0.35	0.52	0.88	43.6	40.4
Bangladesh	Chittagong	2,023	2,565	3,271	4,171	5,168	6,223	4.75	4.86	4.86	4.29	3.71	10.2	11.6
Bangladesh	Dhaka	6,526	8,217	10,159	12,560	15,156	17,907	4.61	4.24	4.24	3.76	3.34	31.8	33.4
Bangladesh	Khulna	900	1,066	1,264	1,497	1,752	2,045	3.40	3.40	3.39	3.14	3.09	3.9	3.8
Cambodia	Phnom Penh	594	836	1,108	1,174	1,292	1,496	6.84	5.63	1.17	1.91	2.93	49.8	31.1
China[1]	Anshan	1,442	1,448	1,453	1,459	1,464	1,499	0.08	0.08	0.08	0.08	0.47	0.3	0.2
China	Anshun	658	720	789	864	947	1,040	1.82	1.82	1.82	1.82	1.88	0.2	0.1
China	Baotou	1,229	1,273	1,319	1,367	1,416	1,488	0.71	0.71	0.71	0.71	0.98	0.3	0.2
China	Beijing	10,819	10,829	10,839	10,849	10,859	11,060	0.02	0.02	0.02	0.02	0.37	2.4	1.6
China	Benxi	938	947	957	967	976	1,005	0.20	0.20	0.20	0.20	0.58	0.2	0.1
China	Changchun	2,192	2,604	2,881	3,092	3,319	3,582	3.44	2.02	1.42	1.42	1.52	0.6	0.5
China	Changde	1,180	1,273	1,374	1,483	1,600	1,735	1.52	1.52	1.52	1.52	1.62	0.3	0.2
China	Changsha	1,329	1,536	1,775	2,051	2,370	2,713	2.89	2.89	2.89	2.89	2.71	0.4	0.4
China	Changzhou	730	804	886	976	1,076	1,187	1.94	1.94	1.94	1.94	1.97	0.2	0.2
China	Chengdu	2,955	3,120	3,294	3,478	3,672	3,910	1.09	1.09	1.09	1.09	1.25	0.7	0.6
China	Chifeng	987	1,036	1,087	1,140	1,196	1,269	0.96	0.96	0.96	0.96	1.18	0.2	0.2
China	Chongqing	3,123	4,073	4,635	4,975	5,340	5,758	5.31	2.59	1.42	1.42	1.51	1.0	0.8
China	Dalian	2,472	2,549	2,628	2,709	2,793	2,918	0.61	0.61	0.61	0.61	0.88	0.6	0.4
China	Daqing	997	1,035	1,076	1,117	1,160	1,221	0.76	0.76	0.76	0.76	1.02	0.2	0.2
China	Datong	1,277	1,220	1,165	1,113	1,062	1,085	(0.92)	(0.92)	(0.92)	(0.92)	0.42	0.3	0.2
China	Dongguan	1,737	1,514	1,319	1,150	1,002	1,023	(2.75)	(2.75)	(2.75)	(2.75)	0.42	0.3	0.1
China	Fushun	1,388	1,400	1,413	1,425	1,438	1,478	0.18	0.18	0.18	0.18	0.55	0.3	0.2
China	Fuxin	743	764	785	807	829	866	0.55	0.55	0.55	0.55	0.86	0.2	0.1
China	Fuyu	945	984	1,025	1,068	1,112	1,173	0.81	0.81	0.81	0.81	1.07	0.2	0.2

China	Fuzhou, Fujian	1,396	1,396	1,397	1,398	1,398	1,428	0.01	0.01	0.01	0.01	0.42	0.3	0.2
China	Guangzhou	3,918	3,906	3,893	3,881	3,868	3,943	(0.06)	(0.06)	(0.06)	(0.06)	0.38	0.9	0.6
China	Guiyang	1,665	2,053	2,298	2,467	2,648	2,858	4.20	2.25	1.42	1.42	1.53	0.5	0.4
China	Handan	1,769	1,879	1,996	2,120	2,251	2,410	1.20	1.20	1.20	1.20	1.36	0.4	0.3
China	Hangzhou	1,476	1,621	1,780	1,955	2,147	2,360	1.87	1.87	1.87	1.87	1.90	0.4	0.3
China	Harbin	2,991	2,959	2,928	2,898	2,867	2,924	(0.21)	(0.21)	(0.21)	(0.21)	0.39	0.6	0.4
China	Hefei	1,100	1,169	1,242	1,320	1,403	1,503	1.22	1.22	1.22	1.22	1.39	0.3	0.2
China	Hengyang	702	749	799	853	910	978	1.29	1.29	1.29	1.29	1.46	0.2	0.1
China	Heze	1,200	1,386	1,600	1,847	2,132	2,439	2.87	2.87	2.87	2.87	2.70	0.4	0.4
China	Huaian	1,113	1,171	1,232	1,297	1,365	1,451	1.02	1.02	1.02	1.02	1.23	0.3	0.2
China	Huainan	1,228	1,289	1,354	1,422	1,493	1,584	0.98	0.98	0.97	0.98	1.19	0.3	0.2
China	Huhehaote	938	958	978	998	1,018	1,057	0.41	0.41	0.41	0.41	0.75	0.2	0.2
China	Hunjiang	722	746	772	798	825	866	0.67	0.67	0.67	0.67	0.96	0.2	0.1
China	Huzhou	1,028	1,052	1,077	1,102	1,128	1,174	0.47	0.47	0.47	0.47	0.79	0.2	0.2
China	Jiamusi	660	759	874	1,006	1,159	1,324	2.82	2.82	2.81	2.82	2.67	0.2	0.2
China	Jiaxing	741	766	791	817	844	885	0.65	0.65	0.65	0.65	0.95	0.2	0.1
China	Jilin	1,320	1,376	1,435	1,496	1,559	1,645	0.83	0.83	0.83	0.83	1.07	0.3	0.2
China	Jinan	2,404	2,484	2,568	2,654	2,742	2,871	0.66	0.66	0.66	0.66	0.92	0.6	0.4
China	Jingmen	1,017	1,083	1,153	1,228	1,307	1,403	1.25	1.25	1.25	1.25	1.42	0.3	0.2
China	Jining, Shandong	871	942	1,019	1,101	1,191	1,294	1.56	1.56	1.56	1.56	1.67	0.2	0.2
China	Jinxi	1,350	1,568	1,723	1,850	1,986	2,144	2.99	1.89	1.42	1.42	1.53	0.4	0.3
China	Jinzhou, Liaoning	736	784	834	888	945	1,015	1.25	1.25	1.25	1.25	1.42	0.2	0.1
China	Jixi	835	890	949	1,012	1,078	1,158	1.27	1.27	1.27	1.27	1.44	0.2	0.2
China	Kaifeng	693	730	769	810	853	908	1.03	1.04	1.03	1.03	1.25	0.2	0.1
China	Kaohsiung	1,380	1,421	1,463	1,506	1,551	1,620	0.58	0.58	0.58	0.58	0.87	0.3	0.2
China	Kunming	1,612	1,656	1,701	1,748	1,795	1,872	0.54	0.54	0.54	0.54	0.84	0.4	0.3
China	Lanzhou	1,618	1,673	1,730	1,788	1,849	1,938	0.67	0.67	0.67	0.67	0.94	0.4	0.3
China	Leshan	1,070	1,103	1,137	1,172	1,208	1,264	0.61	0.61	0.61	0.61	0.90	0.2	0.2
China	Linqing	696	787	891	1,009	1,142	1,288	2.48	2.48	2.48	2.48	2.40	0.2	0.2
China	Linyi	1,740	1,834	1,932	2,035	2,144	2,280	1.04	1.04	1.04	1.04	1.23	0.4	0.3
China	Liuan	1,481	1,641	1,818	2,015	2,233	2,473	2.06	2.06	2.05	2.06	2.04	0.4	0.4
China	Liupanshui	1,844	1,932	2,023	2,118	2,218	2,348	0.92	0.92	0.92	0.92	1.14	0.4	0.3
China	Liuzhou	751	835	928	1,031	1,145	1,272	2.11	2.11	2.11	2.11	2.10	0.2	0.2
China	Luoyang	1,202	1,321	1,451	1,594	1,752	1,927	1.88	1.88	1.88	1.88	1.91	0.3	0.3
China	Mianyang	876	965	1,065	1,174	1,294	1,429	1.95	1.95	1.95	1.95	1.98	0.2	0.2
China	Mudanjiang	751	775	801	827	855	896	0.65	0.65	0.65	0.65	0.94	0.2	0.1
China	Nanchang	1,262	1,474	1,623	1,742	1,870	2,020	3.11	1.93	1.42	1.42	1.54	0.4	0.3
China	Nanchong	619	860	998	1,072	1,150	1,243	6.60	2.97	1.42	1.42	1.55	0.2	0.2
China	Nanjing	2,611	2,674	2,740	2,806	2,875	2,989	0.48	0.48	0.48	0.48	0.78	0.6	0.4
China	Nanning	1,159	1,233	1,311	1,395	1,483	1,591	1.23	1.23	1.23	1.23	1.40	0.3	0.2
China	Neijiang	1,289	1,340	1,393	1,449	1,506	1,586	0.78	0.78	0.78	0.78	1.03	0.3	0.2
China	Ningbo	1,142	1,157	1,173	1,188	1,204	1,242	0.26	0.26	0.26	0.26	0.63	0.3	0.2
China	Pingxiang, Jiangxi	1,388	1,444	1,502	1,562	1,625	1,712	0.79	0.79	0.79	0.79	1.04	0.3	0.2
China	Qingdao	2,102	2,206	2,316	2,431	2,552	2,705	0.97	0.97	0.97	0.97	1.17	0.5	0.4
China	Qiqihar	1,401	1,418	1,435	1,452	1,470	1,515	0.24	0.24	0.24	0.24	0.60	0.3	0.2
China	Shanghai	13,342	13,112	12,887	12,665	12,447	12,666	(0.35)	(0.35)	(0.35)	(0.35)	0.35	2.8	1.8
China	Shantou	885	1,020	1,176	1,356	1,563	1,788	2.85	2.85	2.85	2.85	2.69	0.3	0.3
China	Shenyang	4,655	4,741	4,828	4,916	5,007	5,176	0.36	0.36	0.36	0.36	0.67	1.1	0.7
China	Shenzhen	875	995	1,131	1,285	1,461	1,652	2.56	2.56	2.56	2.56	2.46	0.2	0.2
China	Shijiazhuang	1,372	1,483	1,603	1,733	1,873	2,034	1.56	1.56	1.56	1.56	1.65	0.4	0.3
China	Suining	1,260	1,341	1,428	1,520	1,619	1,737	1.25	1.25	1.25	1.25	1.41	0.3	0.3
China	Suqian	1,061	1,123	1,189	1,258	1,331	1,422	1.14	1.14	1.14	1.14	1.32	0.3	0.2
China	Suzhou, Jiangsu	875	1,017	1,118	1,201	1,289	1,392	3.02	1.90	1.42	1.42	1.55	0.2	0.2
China	Taian	1,413	1,457	1,503	1,550	1,598	1,672	0.62	0.62	0.62	0.62	0.90	0.3	0.2
China	Taichung	754	847	950	1,066	1,197	1,340	2.31	2.31	2.31	2.31	2.26	0.2	0.2
China	Taipei	2,711	2,629	2,550	2,473	2,399	2,447	(0.61)	(0.61)	(0.61)	(0.61)	0.40	0.6	0.4
China	Taiyuan	2,225	2,318	2,415	2,516	2,622	2,763	0.82	0.82	0.82	0.82	1.05	0.5	0.4
China	Tangshan	1,485	1,575	1,671	1,773	1,881	2,012	1.18	1.18	1.18	1.18	1.35	0.4	0.3
China	Tianjin	8,785	8,969	9,156	9,346	9,541	9,874	0.41	0.41	0.41	0.41	0.69	2.0	1.4
China	Tianmen	1,484	1,625	1,779	1,948	2,132	2,339	1.81	1.81	1.81	1.81	1.85	0.4	0.3
China	Tianshui	1,040	1,111	1,187	1,269	1,356	1,460	1.33	1.33	1.33	1.33	1.47	0.3	0.2
China	Tongliao	674	727	785	847	914	993	1.53	1.53	1.53	1.53	1.65	0.2	0.1
China	Wanxian	1,414	1,577	1,759	1,963	2,190	2,438	2.19	2.19	2.19	2.19	2.15	0.4	0.4
China	Weifang	1,152	1,217	1,287	1,360	1,438	1,534	1.11	1.11	1.11	1.11	1.30	0.3	0.2
China	Wenzhou	604	987	1,269	1,475	1,713	1,971	9.80	5.04	3.00	3.00	2.80	0.3	0.3
China	Wuhan	3,833	4,451	5,169	6,003	6,971	8,002	2.99	2.99	2.99	2.99	2.76	1.1	1.2
China	Wulumuqi (Urumqi)	1,161	1,282	1,415	1,562	1,724	1,905	1.98	1.98	1.98	1.98	1.99	0.3	0.3
China	Wuxi	1,009	1,066	1,127	1,192	1,260	1,345	1.11	1.12	1.11	1.11	1.31	0.2	0.2
China	Xian	2,873	2,995	3,123	3,256	3,396	3,580	0.84	0.84	0.84	0.84	1.06	0.7	0.5
China	Xiangxiang	853	880	908	936	966	1,012	0.62	0.62	0.62	0.62	0.92	0.2	0.1
China	Xiantao	1,361	1,482	1,614	1,758	1,914	2,091	1.70	1.70	1.70	1.70	1.77	0.4	0.3
China	Xianyang	737	812	896	988	1,089	1,203	1.95	1.95	1.95	1.95	1.98	0.2	0.2
China	Xiaoshan	1,113	1,119	1,124	1,130	1,136	1,164	0.10	0.10	0.10	0.10	0.50	0.2	0.2
China	Xinghua	1,497	1,526	1,556	1,587	1,618	1,677	0.39	0.39	0.39	0.39	0.72	0.3	0.2
China	Xintai	1,306	1,315	1,325	1,334	1,343	1,378	0.14	0.14	0.14	0.14	0.52	0.3	0.2
China	Xinyi, Jiangsu	884	927	973	1,022	1,072	1,138	0.97	0.97	0.97	0.97	1.19	0.2	0.2
China	Xinyu	608	701	808	932	1,074	1,229	2.84	2.84	2.84	2.84	2.69	0.2	0.2
China	Xuanzhou	769	795	823	851	881	924	0.68	0.68	0.68	0.68	0.97	0.2	0.1
China	Xuzhou	944	1,329	1,548	1,662	1,784	1,926	6.85	3.05	1.42	1.42	1.54	0.3	0.3
China	Yancheng	1,352	1,453	1,562	1,678	1,804	1,950	1.44	1.44	1.44	1.44	1.56	0.3	0.3
China	Yantai	838	1,320	1,590	1,707	1,832	1,978	9.09	3.72	1.42	1.42	1.54	0.3	0.3
China	Yichun, Heilongjiang	882	893	904	916	927	956	0.25	0.25	0.25	0.25	0.62	0.2	0.1
China	Yichun, Jiangxi	836	854	871	890	908	943	0.41	0.41	0.41	0.41	0.75	0.2	0.1
China	Yixing	1,065	1,086	1,108	1,129	1,152	1,195	0.39	0.39	0.39	0.39	0.73	0.2	0.2
China	Yiyang	1,062	1,194	1,343	1,510	1,698	1,903	2.35	2.35	2.35	2.35	2.28	0.3	0.3
China	Yongzhou	946	1,019	1,097	1,182	1,273	1,380	1.49	1.49	1.49	1.49	1.60	0.2	0.2
China	Yueyang	1,078	1,143	1,213	1,286	1,364	1,460	1.18	1.18	1.18	1.18	1.36	0.3	0.2
China	Yulin, Guangxi	1,323	1,436	1,558	1,691	1,835	1,999	1.63	1.63	1.63	1.63	1.71	0.3	0.3
China	Yuyao	794	821	848	876	906	950	0.66	0.66	0.66	0.66	0.95	0.2	0.1

TABLE C.1

continued

		Estimates and Projections (000)						Annual rate of change (%)					Share in urban population (%)	
		1990	1995	2000	2005	2010	2015	1990–1995	1995–2000	2000–2005	2005–2010	2010–2015	2000	2015
China	Yuzhou	1,073	1,122	1,173	1,226	1,282	1,357	0.89	0.89	0.89	0.89	1.13	0.3	0.2
China	Zaoyang	962	1,039	1,121	1,210	1,306	1,418	1.53	1.53	1.53	1.53	1.64	0.2	0.2
China	Zaozhuang	1,793	1,916	2,048	2,189	2,339	2,516	1.33	1.33	1.33	1.33	1.46	0.4	0.4
China	Zhangjiakou	720	796	880	973	1,076	1,191	2.01	2.01	2.01	2.01	2.03	0.2	0.2
China	Zhangjiangang	793	838	886	936	990	1,056	1.11	1.11	1.11	1.11	1.31	0.2	0.2
China	Zhanjiang	1,049	1,198	1,368	1,562	1,783	2,024	2.65	2.66	2.65	2.65	2.53	0.3	0.3
China	Zhaodong	797	824	851	879	908	952	0.65	0.65	0.65	0.65	0.94	0.2	0.1
China	Zhengzhou	1,752	1,905	2,070	2,250	2,445	2,666	1.67	1.67	1.66	1.67	1.73	0.5	0.4
China	Zibo	2,484	2,578	2,675	2,775	2,879	3,024	0.74	0.74	0.74	0.74	0.98	0.6	0.4
China	Zigong	977	1,023	1,072	1,123	1,176	1,246	0.93	0.93	0.92	0.93	1.16	0.2	0.2
China, Hong Kong SAR	Hong Kong[2]	5,677	6,183	6,807	7,182	7,537	7,872	1.71	1.92	1.07	0.97	0.87	100.0	100.0
Democratic People's Republic of Korea	Nampho	580	808	1,022	1,179	1,272	1,329	6.62	4.71	2.85	1.52	0.89	7.6	8.5
Democratic People's Republic of Korea	Pyongyang	2,473	2,865	3,124	3,284	3,399	3,504	2.94	1.73	1.00	0.69	0.61	23.3	22.5
Georgia	Tbilisi	1,227	1,162	1,100	1,042	997	971	(1.09)	(1.09)	(1.09)	(0.87)	(0.52)	39.7	39.8
India	Agra	933	1,095	1,293	1,526	1,758	1,996	3.20	3.32	3.32	2.83	2.54	0.5	0.5
India	Ahmadabad	3,255	3,790	4,427	5,171	5,897	6,632	3.04	3.11	3.11	2.63	2.35	1.6	1.7
India	Allahabad	830	928	1,035	1,153	1,270	1,404	2.23	2.17	2.17	1.92	2.02	0.4	0.3
India	Amritsar	726	844	990	1,162	1,332	1,510	3.00	3.20	3.19	2.74	2.50	0.4	0.4
India	Asansol	727	891	1,065	1,272	1,480	1,691	4.06	3.56	3.56	3.03	2.67	0.4	0.4
India	Aurangabad	568	708	868	1,065	1,265	1,465	4.38	4.09	4.08	3.45	2.94	0.3	0.4
India	Bangalore	4,036	4,744	5,567	6,532	7,474	8,416	3.23	3.20	3.20	2.69	2.38	2.0	2.1
India	Bhopal	1,046	1,228	1,426	1,656	1,884	2,122	3.21	3.00	2.99	2.57	2.38	0.5	0.5
India	Calcutta	10,890	11,924	13,058	14,299	15,462	16,798	1.82	1.82	1.82	1.56	1.66	4.6	4.2
India	Chandigarh	564	658	768	896	1,024	1,159	3.09	3.09	3.09	2.66	2.47	0.3	0.3
India	Chennai (Madras)	5,338	5,836	6,353	6,915	7,450	8,092	1.78	1.70	1.70	1.49	1.65	2.3	2.0
India	Coimbatore	1,088	1,239	1,420	1,628	1,831	2,050	2.60	2.73	2.73	2.36	2.26	0.5	0.5
India	Delhi	8,206	10,092	12,441	15,334	18,226	20,946	4.14	4.18	4.18	3.46	2.78	4.4	5.2
India	Dhanbad	805	915	1,046	1,195	1,342	1,502	2.56	2.67	2.67	2.32	2.25	0.4	0.4
India	Durg-Bhilainagar	670	780	905	1,051	1,195	1,348	3.03	2.98	2.98	2.57	2.41	0.3	0.3
India	Faridabad	593	779	1,018	1,330	1,663	1,983	5.47	5.35	5.35	4.46	3.52	0.4	0.5
India	Ghaziabad	492	675	928	1,277	1,663	2,033	6.30	6.38	6.38	5.28	4.02	0.3	0.5
India	Guwahati	564	675	797	941	1,085	1,234	3.60	3.32	3.32	2.85	2.58	0.3	0.3
India	Gwalior	706	779	855	939	1,022	1,123	1.97	1.88	1.87	1.69	1.89	0.3	0.3
India	Hubli-Dharwad	639	705	776	854	932	1,026	1.95	1.93	1.93	1.73	1.92	0.3	0.3
India	Hyderabad	4,193	4,825	5,445	6,145	6,816	7,536	2.81	2.42	2.42	2.07	2.01	1.9	1.9
India	Indore	1,088	1,314	1,597	1,941	2,289	2,633	3.77	3.91	3.90	3.29	2.80	0.6	0.7
India	Jabalpur	879	981	1,100	1,234	1,364	1,512	2.19	2.29	2.29	2.01	2.06	0.4	0.4
India	Jaipur	1,478	1,826	2,259	2,796	3,341	3,871	4.23	4.26	4.26	3.57	2.95	0.8	1.0
India	Jamshedpur	817	938	1,081	1,246	1,409	1,583	2.75	2.84	2.84	2.46	2.33	0.4	0.4
India	Jodhpur	654	743	842	954	1,065	1,188	2.54	2.51	2.51	2.19	2.19	0.3	0.3
India	Kanpur	2,001	2,294	2,641	3,040	3,429	3,838	2.73	2.82	2.82	2.41	2.25	0.9	1.0
India	Kochi (Cochin)	1,103	1,229	1,340	1,461	1,579	1,726	2.17	1.73	1.72	1.56	1.78	0.5	0.4
India	Kozhikode (Calicut)	781	835	875	917	961	1,033	1.33	0.94	0.94	0.94	1.44	0.3	0.3
India	Lucknow	1,614	1,906	2,221	2,589	2,949	3,322	3.33	3.06	3.06	2.61	2.38	0.8	0.8
India	Ludhiana	1,006	1,183	1,368	1,583	1,794	2,017	3.24	2.91	2.91	2.50	2.34	0.5	0.5
India	Madurai	1,073	1,132	1,187	1,245	1,305	1,402	1.07	0.95	0.95	0.95	1.43	0.4	0.3
India	Meerut	824	975	1,143	1,340	1,535	1,738	3.36	3.18	3.17	2.72	2.48	0.4	0.4
India	Mumbai (Bombay)	12,308	14,111	16,086	18,336	20,468	22,645	2.73	2.62	2.62	2.20	2.02	5.7	5.6
India	Mysore	640	708	776	851	925	1,017	2.01	1.85	1.85	1.67	1.88	0.3	0.3
India	Nagpur	1,637	1,849	2,089	2,359	2,622	2,911	2.44	2.44	2.44	2.11	2.09	0.7	0.7
India	Nashik	700	886	1,117	1,408	1,709	2,003	4.71	4.63	4.63	3.88	3.17	0.4	0.5
India	Patna	1,087	1,331	1,658	2,066	2,484	2,892	4.05	4.40	4.40	3.69	3.04	0.6	0.7
India	Pune (Poona)	2,430	2,978	3,655	4,485	5,321	6,130	4.07	4.09	4.09	3.42	2.83	1.3	1.5
India	Rajkot	638	787	974	1,205	1,442	1,677	4.21	4.26	4.26	3.59	3.01	0.3	0.4
India	Ranchi	607	712	844	999	1,155	1,316	3.21	3.39	3.39	2.90	2.61	0.3	0.3
India	Solapur	613	720	853	1,012	1,171	1,334	3.20	3.41	3.41	2.91	2.62	0.3	0.3
India	Srinagar	730	833	954	1,093	1,230	1,379	2.62	2.72	2.72	2.36	2.28	0.3	0.3
India	Surat	1,468	1,984	2,699	3,671	4,732	5,731	6.01	6.16	6.16	5.08	3.83	1.0	1.4
India	Thiruvananthapuram	801	853	885	918	954	1,021	1.25	0.73	0.73	0.78	1.35	0.3	0.3
India	Tiruchchirapalli	705	768	837	913	989	1,083	1.71	1.74	1.74	1.58	1.83	0.3	0.3
India	Vadodara	1,096	1,273	1,465	1,686	1,903	2,134	2.99	2.81	2.81	2.42	2.29	0.5	0.5
India	Varanasi (Benares)	1,013	1,106	1,199	1,300	1,399	1,526	1.75	1.62	1.62	1.47	1.74	0.4	0.4
India	Vijayawada	821	914	999	1,093	1,184	1,298	2.14	1.79	1.79	1.61	1.83	0.4	0.3
India	Visakhapatnam	1,018	1,168	1,309	1,468	1,624	1,799	2.73	2.29	2.29	2.01	2.05	0.5	0.4
Indonesia	Bandung	2,460	2,896	3,409	4,020	4,687	5,315	3.26	3.26	3.30	3.07	2.51	3.8	3.7
Indonesia	Jakarta	7,650	9,161	11,018	13,194	15,477	17,498	3.60	3.69	3.60	3.19	2.46	12.4	12.1
Indonesia	Malang	620	698	787	898	1,032	1,170	2.40	2.40	2.64	2.77	2.52	0.9	0.8
Indonesia	Medan	1,537	1,699	1,879	2,109	2,392	2,690	2.01	2.01	2.31	2.52	2.35	2.1	1.9
Indonesia	Palembang	1,032	1,212	1,422	1,675	1,957	2,229	3.20	3.20	3.27	3.11	2.60	1.6	1.5
Indonesia	Semarang	804	795	787	816	885	982	(0.21)	(0.21)	0.73	1.62	2.08	0.9	0.7
Indonesia	Surabaja	2,061	2,252	2,461	2,735	3,082	3,453	1.77	1.77	2.11	2.39	2.27	2.8	2.4
Indonesia	Tegal	550	650	762	898	1,052	1,202	3.34	3.19	3.28	3.15	2.67	0.9	0.8
Indonesia	Ujung Pandang	816	926	1,051	1,205	1,387	1,573	2.53	2.53	2.74	2.81	2.51	1.2	1.1
Iran (Islamic Republic of)	Ahvaz	685	784	871	967	1,071	1,183	2.69	2.10	2.10	2.04	1.98	2.0	2.0
Iran (Islamic Republic of)	Esfahan	1,094	1,230	1,381	1,547	1,719	1,898	2.33	2.33	2.26	2.11	1.97	3.2	3.2
Iran (Islamic Republic of)	Karaj	693	903	1,063	1,235	1,405	1,566	5.30	3.25	3.01	2.57	2.17	2.5	2.6

Iran (Islamic Republic of)	Mashhad	1,680	1,854	1,990	2,147	2,331	2,545	1.97	1.41	1.52	1.65	1.76	4.6	4.2
Iran (Islamic Republic of)	Qom	622	744	888	1,045	1,198	1,341	3.56	3.55	3.25	2.73	2.25	2.1	2.2
Iran (Islamic Republic of)	Shiraz	946	1,030	1,124	1,230	1,349	1,483	1.70	1.74	1.80	1.85	1.89	2.6	2.5
Iran (Islamic Republic of)	Tabriz	1,058	1,165	1,274	1,396	1,533	1,684	1.91	1.79	1.84	1.86	1.88	3.0	2.8
Iran (Islamic Republic of)	Tehran	6,365	6,687	6,979	7,352	7,842	8,457	0.99	0.86	1.04	1.29	1.51	16.3	14.1
Iraq	Baghdad	4,092	4,598	5,200	5,910	6,630	7,390	2.34	2.46	2.56	2.30	2.17	33.0	32.3
Iraq	Basra	521	826	1,076	1,187	1,303	1,440	9.21	5.29	1.96	1.87	2.00	6.8	6.3
Iraq	Mosul	736	889	1,056	1,236	1,423	1,618	3.78	3.44	3.15	2.82	2.57	6.7	7.1
Israel	Haifa	435	742	865	948	1,034	1,111	10.66	3.08	1.82	1.75	1.43	15.7	15.5
Israel	Tel Aviv-Jaffa	1,790	2,396	2,752	3,025	3,306	3,542	5.84	2.77	1.89	1.77	1.38	49.8	49.4
Japan	Fukuoka-Kitakyushu	2,487	2,619	2,716	2,815	2,883	2,924	1.04	0.73	0.71	0.48	0.29	3.3	3.4
Japan	Hiroshima	945	968	987	1,005	1,016	1,022	0.48	0.38	0.38	0.21	0.13	1.2	1.2
Japan	Kyoto	1,760	1,804	1,806	1,805	1,797	1,792	0.49	0.02	(0.01)	(0.09)	(0.06)	2.2	2.1
Japan	Nagoya	2,947	3,055	3,122	3,189	3,229	3,253	0.71	0.44	0.42	0.25	0.15	3.8	3.8
Japan	Osaka-Kobe	11,035	11,052	11,165	11,286	11,331	11,359	0.03	0.20	0.22	0.08	0.05	13.5	13.2
Japan	Sapporo	1,561	1,684	1,756	1,828	1,878	1,909	1.52	0.83	0.80	0.55	0.33	2.1	2.2
Japan	Sendai	771	841	890	940	977	1,000	1.73	1.13	1.09	0.78	0.47	1.1	1.2
Japan	Tokyo	32,530	33,587	34,450	35,327	35,879	36,214	0.64	0.51	0.50	0.31	0.19	41.6	42.0
Jordan	Amman	851	987	1,147	1,292	1,421	1,550	2.94	3.02	2.37	1.90	1.74	29.0	27.4
Kazakhstan	Almaty	1,124	1,127	1,130	1,103	1,086	1,095	0.06	0.06	(0.49)	(0.30)	0.17	12.9	12.3
Kuwait	Kuwait City	1,021	873	1,175	1,225	1,297	1,388	(3.13)	5.93	0.84	1.14	1.35	54.5	42.7
Kyrgyzstan	Bishkek	634	698	769	828	887	957	1.93	1.94	1.49	1.37	1.52	45.5	45.5
Lebanon	Beirut	1,153	1,313	1,639	1,875	2,047	2,047	2.61	4.43	2.69	1.76	1.20	54.4	57.4
Malaysia	Kuala Lumpur	1,120	1,209	1,297	1,392	1,506	1,635	1.53	1.40	1.40	1.58	1.65	9.1	7.8
Mongolia	Ulaanbaatar	572	661	764	842	919	919	2.90	2.90	1.95	1.75	1.64	54.0	54.9
Myanmar	Mandalay	631	710	807	927	1,071	1,219	2.36	2.55	2.77	2.89	2.59	6.1	5.8
Myanmar	Yangon	2,893	3,204	3,594	4,082	4,666	5,256	2.05	2.30	2.55	2.67	2.38	27.0	25.1
Pakistan	Faisalabad	1,520	1,804	2,142	2,533	2,985	3,517	3.43	3.43	3.35	3.29	3.28	4.5	4.3
Pakistan	Gujranwala	848	1,019	1,226	1,466	1,742	2,064	3.69	3.69	3.58	3.45	3.40	2.6	2.6
Pakistan	Hyderabad	950	1,077	1,221	1,392	1,609	1,886	2.51	2.51	2.63	2.89	3.18	2.6	2.3
Pakistan	Karachi	7,147	8,467	10,032	11,819	13,837	16,155	3.39	3.39	3.28	3.15	3.10	21.2	20.0
Pakistan	Lahore	3,970	4,653	5,452	6,373	7,440	8,699	3.17	3.17	3.12	3.09	3.13	11.5	10.8
Pakistan	Multan	953	1,097	1,263	1,459	1,698	1,995	2.82	2.82	2.88	3.04	3.23	2.7	2.5
Pakistan	Peshawar	769	905	1,066	1,255	1,477	1,745	3.27	3.28	3.25	3.26	3.33	2.3	2.2
Pakistan	Rawalpindi	1,087	1,286	1,521	1,794	2,113	2,494	3.36	3.36	3.30	3.28	3.31	3.2	3.1
Philippines	Davao	854	1,001	1,152	1,326	1,513	1,694	3.17	2.81	2.81	2.64	2.26	2.6	2.5
Philippines	Metro Manila	7,973	9,401	9,950	10,677	11,610	12,637	3.30	1.13	1.41	1.68	1.69	22.4	19.0
Republic of Korea	Inch'on	1,785	2,271	2,464	2,642	2,732	2,788	4.82	1.62	1.40	0.67	0.40	6.6	6.8
Republic of Korea	Kwangju	1,122	1,249	1,346	1,448	1,503	1,539	2.16	1.49	1.46	0.74	0.48	3.6	3.7
Republic of Korea	Puch'on	651	771	763	745	730	724	3.39	(0.23)	(0.47)	(0.41)	(0.17)	2.0	1.8
Republic of Korea	Pusan	3,778	3,813	3,673	3,527	3,449	3,400	0.18	(0.75)	(0.81)	(0.45)	(0.29)	9.8	8.2
Republic of Korea	Seoul	10,544	10,256	9,917	9,592	9,365	9,215	(0.55)	(0.67)	(0.67)	(0.48)	(0.32)	26.6	22.3
Republic of Korea	Songnam	534	842	911	959	979	993	9.10	1.59	1.02	0.40	0.30	2.4	2.4
Republic of Korea	Suwon	628	748	932	1,168	1,370	1,511	3.50	4.42	4.51	3.19	1.95	2.5	3.7
Republic of Korea	Taegu	2,215	2,434	2,478	2,510	2,480	2,463	1.88	0.36	0.25	(0.24)	(0.14)	6.6	6.0
Republic of Korea	Taejon	1,036	1,256	1,362	1,464	1,519	1,556	3.85	1.62	1.46	0.74	0.47	3.7	3.8
Republic of Korea	Ulsan	673	945	1,011	1,060	1,079	1,093	6.80	1.36	0.95	0.34	0.26	2.7	2.6
Saudi Arabia	Dammam	409	591	759	920	1,075	1,213	7.36	5.00	3.85	3.12	2.42	4.0	4.1
Saudi Arabia	Jidda	1,742	2,494	3,171	3,807	4,406	4,921	7.17	4.81	3.66	2.92	2.21	16.6	16.5
Saudi Arabia	Mecca	856	1,120	1,326	1,529	1,749	1,959	5.37	3.38	2.85	2.68	2.27	6.9	6.6
Saudi Arabia	Medina	529	722	885	1,044	1,206	1,356	6.22	4.08	3.29	2.89	2.36	4.6	4.5
Saudi Arabia	Riyadh	2,325	3,452	4,519	5,514	6,413	7,155	7.91	5.38	3.98	3.02	2.19	23.7	24.0
Singapore	Singapore	3,016	3,478	4,016	4,372	4,574	4,707	2.85	2.88	1.69	0.90	0.57	100.0	100.0
Syrian Arab Republic	Aleppo	1,554	1,869	2,188	2,505	2,818	3,136	3.70	3.15	2.70	2.35	2.14	26.4	26.0
Syrian Arab Republic	Damascus	1,732	1,920	2,105	2,317	2,566	2,849	2.06	1.84	1.92	2.04	2.09	25.4	23.6
Syrian Arab Republic	Homs	565	680	797	915	1,036	1,161	3.69	3.18	2.78	2.47	2.28	9.6	9.6
Thailand	Bangkok	5,888	6,106	6,332	6,604	6,970	7,465	0.73	0.73	0.84	1.08	1.37	33.4	29.2
Turkey	Adana	907	1,011	1,123	1,248	1,353	1,452	2.18	2.10	2.10	1.61	1.41	2.5	2.5
Turkey	Ankara	2,561	2,842	3,179	3,593	3,943	4,250	2.08	2.25	2.45	1.86	1.50	7.2	7.2
Turkey	Bursa	819	988	1,182	1,413	1,625	1,806	3.75	3.59	3.58	2.79	2.11	2.7	3.1
Turkey	Gaziantep	595	710	844	1,004	1,150	1,276	3.54	3.47	3.47	2.71	2.08	1.9	2.2
Turkey	Istanbul	6,552	7,665	8,744	9,760	10,589	11,302	3.14	2.63	2.20	1.63	1.30	19.8	19.1
Turkey	Izmir	1,741	1,966	2,216	2,500	2,741	2,956	2.43	2.39	2.41	1.84	1.51	5.0	5.0
United Arab Emirates	Dubai	473	650	893	1,026	1,137	1,228	6.36	6.36	2.77	2.06	1.54	37.4	39.2
Uzbekistan	Tashkent	2,074	2,111	2,148	2,160	2,211	2,319	0.35	0.35	0.11	0.46	0.96	23.1	20.4
Viet Nam	Hai Phong	1,471	1,570	1,676	1,817	2,019	2,290	1.30	1.30	1.62	2.11	2.52	8.8	7.5
Viet Nam	Hanoi	3,126	3,424	3,751	4,147	4,651	5,276	1.82	1.82	2.01	2.29	2.52	19.7	17.2
Viet Nam	Ho Chi Minh City	3,996	4,296	4,619	5,030	5,587	6,308	1.45	1.45	1.70	2.10	2.43	24.3	20.5
Yemen	Sana'a	677	965	1,264	1,621	2,068	2,658	7.07	5.39	4.98	4.87	5.02	28.4	27.7
EUROPE														
Austria	Vienna	2,096	2,127	2,158	2,190	2,205	2,214	0.29	0.29	0.29	0.14	0.08	40.5	40.9
Belarus	Minsk	1,607	1,649	1,693	1,709	1,718	1,722	0.52	0.52	0.20	0.10	0.04	24.2	24.3
Belgium	Brussels	962	960	962	1,027	1,077	1,106	(0.04)	0.04	1.31	0.95	0.53	9.7	10.8
Bulgaria	Sofia	1,191	1,191	1,133	1,045	1,026	1,009	0.01	(1.00)	(1.62)	(0.37)	(0.34)	20.3	19.0
Czech Republic	Prague	1,210	1,197	1,181	1,164	1,164	1,164	(0.21)	(0.28)	(0.28)	–	(0.01)	15.5	15.3
Denmark	Copenhagen	1,338	1,358	1,079	1,091	1,101	1,107	0.30	(4.61)	0.23	0.18	0.11	23.8	23.4
Finland	Helsinki	872	943	1,019	1,103	1,115	1,119	1.57	1.56	1.58	0.21	0.07	32.2	34.1
France	Bordeaux	699	730	763	794	820	840	0.88	0.88	0.80	0.65	0.48	1.7	1.7
France	Lille	961	984	1,007	1,031	1,053	1,073	0.47	0.47	0.46	0.43	0.37	2.2	2.2
France	Lyon	1,265	1,313	1,362	1,408	1,447	1,475	0.74	0.74	0.67	0.54	0.38	3.0	3.0
France	Marseille-Aix-en-Provence	1,305	1,331	1,357	1,384	1,410	1,432	0.39	0.39	0.39	0.37	0.32	3.0	2.9
France	Nice-Cannes	854	874	894	915	936	954	0.46	0.46	0.46	0.44	0.38	2.0	1.9
France	Paris	9,331	9,510	9,693	9,854	9,963	10,008	0.38	0.38	0.33	0.22	0.09	21.6	20.2
France	Toulouse	654	714	779	839	885	914	1.75	1.75	1.49	1.06	0.64	1.7	1.8
Germany	Aachen	1,001	1,040	1,064	1,073	1,075	1,075	0.77	0.45	0.18	0.04	-	1.5	1.4
Germany	Berlin	3,288	3,317	3,325	3,328	3,329	3,329	0.18	0.05	0.02	0.00	-	4.6	4.5
Germany	Bielefeld	1,201	1,262	1,298	1,312	1,315	1,315	0.98	0.56	0.23	0.05	-	1.8	1.8
Germany	Bremen	840	866	882	889	891	891	0.61	0.36	0.15	0.03	-	1.2	1.2
Germany	Hamburg	2,540	2,624	2,668	2,686	2,690	2,690	0.65	0.33	0.13	0.03	-	3.7	3.6

TABLE C.1

continued

		Estimates and Projections (000)						Annual rate of change (%)					Share in urban population (%)	
		1990	1995	2000	2005	2010	2015	1990–1995	1995–2000	2000–2005	2005–2010	2010–2015	2000	2015
Germany	Hannover	1,230	1,266	1,287	1,296	1,297	1,297	0.58	0.32	0.13	0.03	-	1.8	1.7
Germany	Karlsruhe	912	954	980	990	992	992	0.90	0.53	0.21	0.04	-	1.4	1.3
Germany	Munich	2,134	2,237	2,295	2,318	2,323	2,323	0.94	0.51	0.20	0.04	-	3.2	3.1
Germany	Nuremberg	1,106	1,160	1,193	1,206	1,209	1,209	0.96	0.56	0.22	0.04	-	1.7	1.6
Germany	Rhein-Main[3]	3,456	3,605	3,688	3,721	3,728	3,728	0.85	0.45	0.18	0.04	-	5.1	5.0
Germany	Rhein-Neckar[4]	1,503	1,570	1,609	1,625	1,628	1,628	0.87	0.49	0.19	0.04	-	2.2	2.2
Germany	Rhein-Ruhr Middle[5]	2,699	3,030	3,238	3,325	3,342	3,342	2.31	1.33	0.53	0.11	-	4.5	4.5
Germany	Rhein-Ruhr North[6]	6,353	6,482	6,542	6,566	6,571	6,571	0.40	0.18	0.07	0.01	-	9.1	8.8
Germany	Rhein-Ruhr South[7]	2,854	2,984	3,055	3,084	3,090	3,090	0.88	0.47	0.19	0.04	-	4.2	4.2
Germany	Saarland[8]	878	888	893	896	896	896	0.22	0.13	0.06	0.01	-	1.2	1.2
Germany	Stuttgart	2,484	2,608	2,677	2,705	2,710	2,710	0.97	0.52	0.21	0.04	-	3.7	3.7
Greece	Athens	3,070	3,122	3,179	3,238	3,290	3,330	0.34	0.37	0.37	0.32	0.24	48.5	46.6
Greece	Thessaloniki	746	771	797	824	849	870	0.66	0.67	0.67	0.60	0.49	12.2	12.2
Hungary	Budapest	2,005	1,893	1,787	1,670	1,670	1,670	(1.15)	(1.15)	(1.36)	-	-	27.9	25.6
Ireland	Dublin	916	946	989	1,033	1,082	1,137	0.65	0.87	0.88	0.92	0.99	43.8	40.6
Italy	Genoa	943	893	847	803	801	799	(1.09)	(1.06)	(1.06)	(0.05)	(0.06)	2.2	2.1
Italy	Milan	4,603	4,367	4,183	4,007	3,997	3,985	(1.05)	(0.86)	(0.86)	(0.05)	(0.06)	10.8	10.4
Italy	Naples	3,210	3,087	2,995	2,905	2,898	2,889	(0.78)	(0.61)	(0.61)	(0.05)	(0.06)	7.7	7.5
Italy	Rome	2,965	2,864	2,743	2,628	2,621	2,614	(0.69)	(0.86)	(0.86)	(0.05)	(0.06)	7.1	6.8
Italy	Turin	1,394	1,315	1,247	1,182	1,179	1,176	(1.18)	(1.07)	(1.06)	(0.05)	(0.06)	3.2	3.1
Latvia	Riga	892	833	761	719	688	669	(1.37)	(1.82)	(1.13)	(0.87)	(0.58)	48.0	48.9
Netherlands	Amsterdam	1,053	1,102	1,127	1,157	1,191	1,225	0.90	0.46	0.53	0.57	0.57	11.0	10.2
Netherlands	Rotterdam	1,047	1,078	1,094	1,112	1,136	1,164	0.57	0.29	0.34	0.42	0.48	10.7	9.7
Norway	Oslo	684	729	774	808	839	866	1.28	1.19	0.86	0.77	0.61	22.8	21.2
Poland	Crakow	806	815	818	822	826	828	0.20	0.10	0.10	0.08	0.06	3.4	3.4
Poland	Gdansk	857	858	854	851	851	851	0.02	(0.08)	(0.08)	-	0.01	3.6	3.5
Poland	Katowice	3,357	3,233	3,069	2,914	2,914	2,914	(0.75)	(1.04)	(1.04)	-	-	12.9	11.9
Poland	Lodz	1,030	1,006	974	943	943	944	(0.47)	(0.64)	(0.64)	-	0.00	4.1	3.9
Poland	Warsaw	2,165	2,183	2,194	2,204	2,212	2,217	0.17	0.09	0.09	0.07	0.04	9.2	9.1
Portugal	Lisbon	1,830	1,908	1,942	1,977	2,016	2,057	0.83	0.35	0.35	0.39	0.39	36.6	33.7
Portugal	Porto	1,101	1,206	1,254	1,303	1,352	1,395	1.84	0.77	0.77	0.74	0.63	23.6	22.8
Romania	Bucharest	2,040	2,054	2,009	1,764	1,764	1,764	0.14	(0.44)	(2.60)	-	0.00	16.4	14.4
Russian Federation	Chelyabinsk	1,130	1,109	1,088	1,067	1,023	988	(0.38)	(0.38)	(0.38)	(0.85)	(0.70)	1.0	1.0
Russian Federation	Ekaterinburg	1,350	1,326	1,303	1,281	1,227	1,185	(0.35)	(0.35)	(0.35)	(0.85)	(0.70)	1.2	1.2
Russian Federation	Kazan	1,094	1,099	1,103	1,108	1,086	1,064	0.08	0.08	0.08	(0.39)	(0.42)	1.0	1.1
Russian Federation	Krasnoyarsk	910	911	911	912	892	872	0.02	0.02	0.02	(0.45)	(0.45)	0.9	0.9
Russian Federation	Moscow	9,053	9,563	10,103	10,672	10,898	10,934	1.10	1.10	1.10	0.42	0.07	9.5	11.0
Russian Federation	Nizhni Novgorod	1,420	1,375	1,331	1,288	1,235	1,192	(0.65)	(0.65)	(0.65)	(0.85)	(0.70)	1.2	1.2
Russian Federation	Novosibirsk	1,430	1,428	1,426	1,425	1,365	1,319	(0.03)	(0.03)	(0.03)	(0.85)	(0.70)	1.3	1.3
Russian Federation	Omsk	1,144	1,140	1,136	1,132	1,085	1,047	(0.07)	(0.07)	(0.07)	(0.85)	(0.70)	1.1	1.1
Russian Federation	Perm	1,076	1,044	1,014	984	943	911	(0.59)	(0.59)	(0.59)	(0.85)	(0.70)	0.9	0.9
Russian Federation	Rostov-on-Don	1,022	1,041	1,061	1,081	1,073	1,058	0.38	0.38	0.38	(0.16)	(0.28)	1.0	1.1
Russian Federation	Saint Petersburg	5,019	5,116	5,214	5,315	5,274	5,202	0.38	0.38	0.38	(0.15)	(0.28)	4.9	5.2
Russian Federation	Samara	1,244	1,208	1,173	1,140	1,092	1,055	(0.58)	(0.58)	(0.58)	(0.85)	(0.70)	1.1	1.1
Russian Federation	Saratov	901	890	878	868	831	803	(0.25)	(0.25)	(0.25)	(0.85)	(0.70)	0.8	0.8
Russian Federation	Ufa	1,078	1,063	1,049	1,035	992	958	(0.27)	(0.27)	(0.27)	(0.85)	(0.70)	1.0	1.0
Russian Federation	Volgograd	999	1,005	1,010	1,016	997	977	0.11	0.11	0.11	(0.37)	(0.41)	0.9	1.0
Russian Federation	Voronezh	880	867	854	842	807	779	(0.30)	(0.30)	(0.30)	(0.85)	(0.70)	0.8	0.8
Serbia and Montenegro	Belgrade	1,127	1,126	1,121	1,116	1,103	1,101	(0.02)	(0.09)	(0.09)	(0.22)	(0.05)	20.6	19.0
Spain	Barcelona	4,201	4,332	4,378	4,424	4,452	4,468	0.62	0.21	0.21	0.12	0.07	14.1	13.9
Spain	Madrid	4,805	4,929	5,036	5,145	5,223	5,269	0.51	0.43	0.43	0.30	0.18	16.2	16.4
Sweden	Göteborg	729	758	792	829	846	856	0.77	0.89	0.89	0.42	0.22	10.7	11.3
Sweden	Stockholm	1,487	1,557	1,641	1,729	1,777	1,803	0.92	1.05	1.04	0.54	0.30	22.2	23.8
Switzerland	Zürich	834	926	955	984	997	1,003	2.10	0.61	0.61	0.26	0.12	19.7	20.8
Ukraine	Dnepropetrovsk	1,162	1,119	1,077	1,036	1,004	979	(0.77)	(0.77)	(0.77)	(0.64)	(0.49)	3.2	3.2
Ukraine	Donetsk	1,097	1,061	1,026	992	961	937	(0.67)	(0.67)	(0.67)	(0.64)	(0.49)	3.1	3.1
Ukraine	Kharkov	1,586	1,534	1,484	1,436	1,391	1,357	(0.66)	(0.66)	(0.66)	(0.64)	(0.49)	4.4	4.4
Ukraine	Kiev	2,574	2,590	2,606	2,623	2,612	2,591	0.13	0.13	0.13	(0.08)	(0.16)	7.8	8.5
Ukraine	Odessa	1,092	1,064	1,037	1,010	978	955	(0.52)	(0.52)	(0.52)	(0.64)	(0.49)	3.1	3.1
Ukraine	Zaporozhye	873	847	822	798	773	754	(0.60)	(0.60)	(0.60)	(0.64)	(0.49)	2.5	2.5
United Kingdom	Birmingham	2,301	2,272	2,243	2,215	2,215	2,215	(0.25)	(0.25)	(0.25)	–	0.01	4.3	4.0
United Kingdom	Leeds	1,449	1,433	1,417	1,402	1,402	1,404	(0.22)	(0.22)	(0.22)	0.01	0.04	2.7	2.5
United Kingdom	Liverpool	831	876	924	975	1,018	1,047	1.06	1.06	1.06	0.87	0.57	1.8	1.9
United Kingdom	London	7,654	7,641	7,628	7,615	7,615	7,615	(0.03)	(0.03)	(0.03)	-	-	14.6	13.8
United Kingdom	Manchester	2,282	2,252	2,223	2,193	2,193	2,194	(0.26)	(0.26)	(0.26)	-	0.01	4.3	4.0
United Kingdom	Tyneside (Newcastle)	877	933	993	1,056	1,111	1,147	1.24	1.24	1.24	1.00	0.65	1.9	2.1
LATIN AMERICA														
Argentina	Buenos Aires	11,180	11,861	12,583	13,349	14,017	14,563	1.18	1.18	1.18	0.98	0.76	37.9	36.4
Argentina	Córdoba	1,188	1,310	1,444	1,592	1,729	1,844	1.95	1.95	1.95	1.65	1.29	4.4	4.6
Argentina	Mendoza	758	851	955	1,072	1,182	1,273	2.31	2.31	2.31	1.95	1.49	2.9	3.2
Argentina	Rosario	1,084	1,155	1,231	1,312	1,387	1,457	1.27	1.27	1.27	1.12	0.98	3.7	3.6
Argentina	San Miguel de Tucumán	611	679	754	837	916	983	2.10	2.10	2.10	1.79	1.41	2.3	2.5
Bolivia	La Paz	1,062	1,267	1,394	1,533	1,668	1,817	3.53	1.91	1.91	1.68	1.71	27.1	24.3
Bolivia	Santa Cruz	616	833	1,061	1,352	1,653	1,932	6.04	4.84	4.84	4.03	3.12	20.6	25.8
Brazil	Baixada Santista (Santos)	1,184	1,319	1,468	1,634	1,775	1,890	2.15	2.14	2.14	1.65	1.26	1.1	1.1
Brazil	Belém	1,214	1,459	1,749	2,097	2,416	2,663	3.68	3.63	3.63	2.83	1.95	1.3	1.5
Brazil	Belo Horizonte	3,548	4,093	4,659	5,304	5,855	6,275	2.86	2.59	2.59	1.98	1.39	3.3	3.5
Brazil	Brasília	1,863	2,257	2,746	3,341	3,891	4,312	3.84	3.92	3.92	3.05	2.05	2.0	2.4

Brazil	Campinas	1,693	1,954	2,264	2,640	2,974	3,233	2.86	2.94	3.07	2.38	1.67	1.6	1.8
Brazil	Curitiba	1,829	2,156	2,494	2,871	3,200	3,456	3.28	2.92	2.81	2.17	1.54	1.8	1.9
Brazil	Fortaleza	2,226	2,542	2,875	3,261	3,591	3,849	2.66	2.46	2.52	1.93	1.39	2.1	2.2
Brazil	Goiânia	1,132	1,369	1,609	1,878	2,119	2,308	3.80	3.22	3.10	2.41	1.71	1.2	1.3
Brazil	Grande São Luís	672	778	876	982	1,074	1,150	2.93	2.36	2.30	1.79	1.37	0.6	0.6
Brazil	Grande Vitória	1,052	1,221	1,398	1,602	1,781	1,923	2.97	2.72	2.72	2.11	1.54	1.0	1.1
Brazil	João Pessoa	652	737	827	931	1,022	1,096	2.44	2.31	2.37	1.85	1.41	0.6	0.6
Brazil	Maceió	660	798	952	1,137	1,307	1,441	3.77	3.55	3.54	2.78	1.96	0.7	0.8
Brazil	Manaus	955	1,159	1,392	1,673	1,932	2,134	3.87	3.68	3.67	2.88	1.99	1.0	1.2
Brazil	Natal	692	793	909	1,049	1,172	1,272	2.72	2.74	2.85	2.23	1.63	0.7	0.7
Brazil	Norte/Nordeste Catarinense	603	709	815	936	1,044	1,131	3.22	2.78	2.78	2.18	1.61	0.6	0.6
Brazil	Pôrto Alegre	2,934	3,236	3,505	3,795	4,027	4,220	1.96	1.59	1.59	1.19	0.93	2.5	2.4
Brazil	Recife	2,690	2,958	3,230	3,527	3,768	3,965	1.90	1.76	1.76	1.32	1.02	2.3	2.2
Brazil	Rio de Janeiro	9,595	10,174	10,803	11,469	11,961	12,364	1.17	1.20	1.20	0.84	0.66	7.7	6.9
Brazil	Salvador	2,331	2,644	2,968	3,331	3,638	3,880	2.53	2.31	2.31	1.76	1.29	2.1	2.2
Brazil	São Paulo	14,776	15,948	17,099	18,333	19,256	19,963	1.53	1.39	1.39	0.98	0.72	12.3	11.2
Brazil	Teresina	614	699	789	895	989	1,065	2.58	2.42	2.54	1.98	1.49	0.6	0.6
Chile	Santiago	4,571	4,931	5,266	5,623	5,979	6,297	1.52	1.31	1.31	1.23	1.03	40.2	38.7
Colombia	Barranquilla	1,244	1,396	1,683	1,918	2,125	2,305	2.29	3.74	2.62	2.05	1.62	5.3	5.4
Colombia	Bucaramanga	648	776	937	1,069	1,187	1,292	3.61	3.75	2.64	2.10	1.69	3.0	3.0
Colombia	Cali	1,591	1,818	2,233	2,583	2,884	3,134	2.67	4.11	2.91	2.21	1.66	7.1	7.4
Colombia	Cartagena	576	667	845	1,002	1,140	1,252	2.96	4.72	3.42	2.57	1.88	2.7	3.0
Colombia	Cucuta	520	637	772	883	983	1,072	4.07	3.82	2.70	2.15	1.73	2.4	2.5
Colombia	Medellín	2,147	2,403	2,866	3,236	3,561	3,842	2.25	3.53	2.43	1.91	1.52	9.1	9.1
Colombia	Santa Fé de Bogotá	4,970	5,716	6,771	7,594	8,301	8,900	2.80	3.39	2.30	1.78	1.39	21.5	21.0
Costa Rica	San José	737	867	998	1,145	1,299	1,441	3.25	2.80	2.75	2.51	2.09	43.1	42.9
Cuba	Havana	2,108	2,183	2,187	2,192	2,197	2,200	0.69	0.04	0.05	0.05	0.03	26.0	24.4
Dominica	Santo Domingo	1,522	1,653	1,781	1,920	2,049	2,185	1.65	1.50	1.50	1.30	1.28	36.6	33.4
Ecuador	Guayaquil	1,572	1,808	2,077	2,387	2,679	2,953	2.80	2.78	2.78	2.31	1.95	27.7	28.8
Ecuador	Quito	1,088	1,217	1,357	1,514	1,660	1,806	2.25	2.18	2.18	1.84	1.70	18.1	17.6
El Salvador	San Salvador	970	1,140	1,339	1,472	1,596	1,718	3.24	3.21	1.90	1.61	1.47	36.9	35.4
Guatemala	Guatemala City	803	839	908	982	1,077	1,204	0.89	1.57	1.57	1.85	2.23	17.6	14.3
Haiti	Port-au-Prince	1,134	1,427	1,767	2,090	2,427	2,765	4.60	4.27	3.36	2.99	2.60	62.0	62.7
Honduras	Tegucigalpa	710	812	928	1,061	1,199	1,349	2.68	2.68	2.68	2.45	2.35	32.4	30.0
Mexico	Ciudad Juárez	809	997	1,239	1,469	1,659	1,800	4.19	4.34	3.40	2.44	1.63	1.7	1.9
Mexico	Culiacán	606	690	750	799	849	901	2.60	1.67	1.28	1.20	1.19	1.0	1.0
Mexico	Guadalajara	3,011	3,431	3,697	3,905	4,105	4,309	2.61	1.50	1.09	1.00	0.97	5.0	4.6
Mexico	León	961	1,127	1,293	1,438	1,564	1,671	3.19	2.75	2.13	1.68	1.33	1.7	1.8
Mexico	Mérida	664	765	849	919	985	1,048	2.83	2.07	1.60	1.39	1.25	1.1	1.1
Mexico	Mexicali	607	690	771	840	904	964	2.57	2.22	1.72	1.46	1.29	1.0	1.0
Mexico	Mexico City	15,311	16,790	18,066	19,013	19,854	20,647	1.84	1.47	1.02	0.87	0.78	24.4	21.9
Mexico	Monterrey	2,594	2,961	3,267	3,517	3,741	3,947	2.65	1.97	1.47	1.23	1.07	4.4	4.2
Mexico	Puebla	1,699	1,932	1,888	1,880	1,911	1,987	2.57	(0.46)	(0.09)	0.34	0.77	2.6	2.1
Mexico	Querétaro	561	671	798	913	1,011	1,090	3.58	3.45	2.70	2.05	1.51	1.1	1.2
Mexico	San Luis Potosí	665	774	857	927	993	1,057	3.04	2.05	1.58	1.37	1.24	1.2	1.1
Mexico	Tijuana	760	1,017	1,297	1,570	1,796	1,957	5.82	4.86	3.82	2.69	1.72	1.8	2.1
Mexico	Toluca	835	981	1,455	1,987	2,442	2,735	3.22	7.89	6.23	4.12	2.27	2.0	2.9
Mexico	Torreón	882	954	1,012	1,057	1,108	1,169	1.55	1.18	0.88	0.95	1.06	1.4	1.2
Nicaragua	Managua	735	870	1,009	1,159	1,323	1,497	3.37	2.98	2.77	2.65	2.47	35.4	33.9
Panama	Panama City	845	875	905	950	1,019	1,109	0.68	0.68	0.97	1.40	1.69	54.6	47.4
Paraguay	Asunción	928	1,140	1,457	1,750	2,002	2,290	4.12	4.92	3.66	2.70	2.68	48.2	46.5
Peru	Lima	5,825	6,667	7,454	8,180	8,822	9,365	2.70	2.23	1.86	1.51	1.20	39.5	37.5
Puerto Rico	San Juan	1,539	1,855	2,237	2,357	2,386	2,398	3.74	3.74	1.04	0.25	0.10	62.0	59.9
Uruguay	Montevideo	1,274	1,299	1,324	1,353	1,384	1,413	0.38	0.38	0.43	0.46	0.41	43.1	40.6
Venezuela	Barquisimeto	742	828	923	1,009	1,094	1,178	2.18	2.18	1.78	1.61	1.48	4.4	4.2
Venezuela	Caracas	2,867	3,007	3,153	3,276	3,432	3,628	0.95	0.95	0.77	0.93	1.11	14.9	12.9
Venezuela	Maracaibo	1,351	1,603	1,901	2,182	2,429	2,634	3.41	3.42	2.75	2.15	1.62	9.0	9.4
Venezuela	Maracay	766	881	1,015	1,138	1,252	1,355	2.82	2.82	2.29	1.91	1.58	4.8	4.8
Venezuela	Valencia	1,129	1,462	1,893	2,330	2,705	2,982	5.17	5.17	4.15	2.99	1.95	9.0	10.6
NORTHERN AMERICA														
Canada	Calgary	738	809	927	1,074	1,211	1,319	1.84	2.72	2.93	2.41	1.70	3.8	4.6
Canada	Edmonton	831	859	924	1,005	1,078	1,139	0.67	1.47	1.67	1.40	1.11	3.8	4.0
Canada	Montréal	3,154	3,305	3,409	3,511	3,600	3,691	0.94	0.62	0.59	0.50	0.50	14.0	12.9
Canada	Ottawa	918	988	1,052	1,120	1,182	1,236	1.48	1.25	1.26	1.07	0.90	4.3	4.3
Canada	Toronto	3,807	4,197	4,607	5,060	5,458	5,762	1.95	1.86	1.87	1.52	1.08	18.9	20.1
Canada	Vancouver	1,559	1,789	1,959	2,125	2,273	2,393	2.75	1.81	1.63	1.34	1.03	8.0	8.3
United States	Atlanta	2,184	2,781	3,542	4,284	4,883	5,260	4.84	4.84	3.80	2.62	1.48	1.6	1.9
United States	Austin	569	720	913	1,101	1,258	1,365	4.73	4.73	3.76	2.67	1.62	0.4	0.5
United States	Baltimore	1,849	1,962	2,083	2,178	2,281	2,382	1.19	1.19	0.90	0.92	0.87	0.9	0.9
United States	Boston	3,428	3,726	4,049	4,313	4,555	4,760	1.66	1.66	1.26	1.09	0.88	1.8	1.7
United States	Bridgeport-Stamford	714	799	894	977	1,052	1,115	2.25	2.25	1.77	1.49	1.16	0.4	0.4
United States	Buffalo	955	966	977	985	1,011	1,051	0.23	0.23	0.16	0.52	0.78	0.4	0.4
United States	Charlotte	461	596	769	942	1,086	1,183	5.10	5.10	4.06	2.86	1.71	0.3	0.4
United States	Chicago	7,374	7,839	8,333	8,711	9,080	9,411	1.22	1.22	0.89	0.83	0.72	3.7	3.4
United States	Cincinnati	1,335	1,419	1,508	1,580	1,657	1,734	1.22	1.22	0.93	0.95	0.91	0.7	0.6
United States	Cleveland	1,680	1,734	1,789	1,831	1,892	1,968	0.63	0.63	0.46	0.66	0.78	0.8	0.7
United States	Columbus, Ohio	950	1,040	1,138	1,222	1,301	1,372	1.81	1.81	1.42	1.26	1.06	0.5	0.5
United States	Dallas-Fort Worth	3,219	3,665	4,172	4,612	4,981	5,249	2.59	2.59	2.00	1.54	1.05	1.9	1.9
United States	Denver-Aurora	1,528	1,747	1,998	2,219	2,408	2,550	2.68	2.68	2.10	1.63	1.15	0.9	0.9
United States	Detroit	3,703	3,804	3,909	3,980	4,094	4,234	0.54	0.54	0.36	0.56	0.68	1.7	1.5
United States	Hartford	783	818	853	882	919	962	0.86	0.86	0.66	0.82	0.91	0.4	0.3
United States	Houston	2,922	3,353	3,849	4,283	4,644	4,904	2.76	2.76	2.14	1.62	1.09	1.7	1.8
United States	Indianapolis	921	1,063	1,228	1,375	1,501	1,597	2.87	2.87	2.26	1.76	1.24	0.5	0.6
United States	Jacksonville, Florida	742	811	886	950	1,012	1,068	1.78	1.78	1.40	1.26	1.08	0.4	0.4
United States	Kansas City	1,233	1,297	1,365	1,419	1,482	1,549	1.02	1.02	0.78	0.87	0.89	0.6	0.6
United States	Las Vegas	708	973	1,335	1,717	2,036	2,237	6.34	6.34	5.03	3.41	1.88	0.6	0.8
United States	Los Angeles-Long Beach Santa Ana	10,883	11,339	11,814	12,146	12,522	12,904	0.82	0.82	0.55	0.61	0.60	5.2	4.7
United States	Louisville	757	810	866	913	963	1,012	1.34	1.34	1.05	1.06	1.00	0.4	0.4

TABLE C.1

continued

		Estimates and Projections (000)						Annual rate of change (%)					Share in urban population (%)	
		1990	1995	2000	2005	2010	2015	1990–1995	1995–2000	2000–2005	2005–2010	2010–2015	2000	2015
United States	Memphis	829	899	976	1,041	1,104	1,163	1.64	1.64	1.28	1.19	1.04	0.4	0.4
United States	Miami	3,969	4,431	4,946	5,380	5,752	6,034	2.20	2.20	1.68	1.33	0.96	2.2	2.2
United States	Milwaukee	1,228	1,269	1,311	1,343	1,391	1,449	0.65	0.65	0.48	0.69	0.82	0.6	0.5
United States	Minneapolis-St. Paul	2,087	2,236	2,397	2,526	2,656	2,777	1.38	1.39	1.05	1.00	0.89	1.1	1.0
United States	Nashville-Davidson	577	660	755	840	915	974	2.69	2.69	2.13	1.71	1.26	0.3	0.4
United States	New Orleans	1,039	1,024	1,009	1,007	1,027	1,066	(0.30)	(0.30)	(0.03)	0.40	0.73	0.4	0.4
United States	New York-Newark	16,086	16,943	17,846	18,498	19,142	19,717	1.04	1.04	0.72	0.68	0.59	7.9	7.2
United States	Orlando	893	1,020	1,165	1,294	1,406	1,493	2.66	2.66	2.09	1.66	1.21	0.5	0.5
United States	Philadelphia	4,725	4,938	5,160	5,325	5,515	5,714	0.88	0.88	0.63	0.70	0.71	2.3	2.1
United States	Phoenix-Mesa	2,025	2,437	2,934	3,393	3,767	4,020	3.71	3.71	2.91	2.09	1.30	1.3	1.5
United States	Pittsburgh	1,681	1,717	1,755	1,782	1,833	1,903	0.43	0.43	0.30	0.57	0.75	0.8	0.7
United States	Portland	1,181	1,372	1,595	1,795	1,964	2,090	3.01	3.01	2.36	1.80	1.24	0.7	0.8
United States	Providence	1,047	1,111	1,178	1,233	1,293	1,355	1.18	1.18	0.91	0.95	0.93	0.5	0.5
United States	Richmond	696	757	822	878	932	983	1.66	1.66	1.30	1.21	1.06	0.4	0.4
United States	Riverside-San Bernardino	1,178	1,336	1,516	1,674	1,812	1,920	2.53	2.53	1.98	1.58	1.15	0.7	0.7
United States	Sacramento	1,104	1,244	1,402	1,540	1,661	1,759	2.39	2.39	1.87	1.52	1.14	0.6	0.6
United States	Salt Lake City	792	840	890	932	978	1,027	1.17	1.17	0.91	0.97	0.97	0.4	0.4
United States	San Antonio	1,134	1,229	1,333	1,419	1,504	1,581	1.62	1.62	1.26	1.16	1.00	0.6	0.6
United States	San Diego	2,356	2,514	2,683	2,818	2,955	3,085	1.30	1.30	0.98	0.95	0.86	1.2	1.1
United States	San Francisco-Oakland	2,961	3,095	3,236	3,342	3,468	3,603	0.89	0.89	0.65	0.74	0.76	1.4	1.3
United States	San Jose	1,376	1,457	1,543	1,611	1,687	1,764	1.14	1.14	0.87	0.92	0.90	0.7	0.6
United States	Seattle	2,206	2,453	2,727	2,959	3,164	3,328	2.12	2.12	1.64	1.34	1.01	1.2	1.2
United States	St. Louis	1,950	2,014	2,081	2,131	2,202	2,288	0.65	0.65	0.47	0.66	0.77	0.9	0.8
United States	Tampa-St. Petersburg	1,717	1,886	2,072	2,228	2,372	2,493	1.88	1.88	1.45	1.25	1.00	0.9	0.9
United States	Virginia Beach	1,286	1,341	1,397	1,441	1,498	1,563	0.83	0.83	0.62	0.77	0.85	0.6	0.6
United States	Washington, DC	3,376	3,651	3,949	4,190	4,416	4,611	1.57	1.57	1.18	1.05	0.87	1.8	1.7
OCEANIA														
Australia	Adelaide	1,046	1,074	1,104	1,137	1,166	1,199	0.53	0.55	0.59	0.51	0.56	6.4	5.8
Australia	Brisbane	1,329	1,486	1,626	1,769	1,894	1,996	2.24	1.80	1.68	1.37	1.05	9.4	9.7
Australia	Melbourne	3,118	3,258	3,447	3,663	3,846	3,996	0.88	1.13	1.21	0.98	0.77	19.8	19.4
Australia	Perth	1,160	1,273	1,376	1,484	1,580	1,659	1.87	1.56	1.52	1.24	0.98	7.9	8.0
Australia	Sydney	3,632	3,839	4,099	4,388	4,633	4,829	1.11	1.31	1.36	1.09	0.83	23.6	23.4
New Zealand	Auckland	870	976	1,063	1,152	1,220	1,272	2.30	1.71	1.60	1.16	0.83	32.8	35.1

Notes:

1 For statistical purposes, the data for China do not include Hong Kong and Macao Special Administrative Regions (SAR) of China.

2 As of 1 July 1997, Hong Kong became a Special Administrative Region (SAR) of China.

3 Including Darmstadt, Frankfurt am Main, Offenbach am Main and Wiesbaden.

4 Including Ludwigshafen am Rhein, Heidelberg, Mannheim, Frankenthal (Pfalz), Neustadt an der Weinstrasse and Speyer.

5 Including Düsseldorf, Mönchengladbach, Remscheid, Solingen and Wuppertal.

6 Including Duisburg, Essen, Krefeld, Mühlheim an der Ruhr, Oberhausen, Bottrop, Gelsenkirchen, Bochum, Dortmund, Hagen, Hamm and Herne.

7 Including Bonn, Cologne and Leverkusen.

8 Including Neunkirchen, Saarbrücken and Saarlouis.

TABLE C.2

Housing and Basic Services, Selected Cities

			Compliance with requirements		Access to			In-house connections		
			Building material (%)	Sufficient living area (%)	Improved water (%)	Improved sanitation (%)	Piped water (%)	Sewerage (%)	Electricity (%)	Telephone (%)
AFRICA										
Angola	Luanda	2000	51.6	62.9	51.9	59.5	13.1	20.4	36.2	...
Benin	Djougou	2001	79.3	81.0	82.9	31.1	43.0	0.5	40.9	3.6
Benin	Porto-Novo	2001	87.0	80.2	72.5	50.0	54.0	8.4	58.1	13.6
Burkina Faso	Ouagadougou	2003	96.5	85.1	98.3	49.8	36.4	14.7	56.7	25.1
Cameroon	Yaounde	1998	92.6	90.2	84.5	81.2	34.2	24.2	94.9	9.4
Cote d'Ivoire	Abidjan	1999	98.9	74.9	99.7	78.3	70.9	34.4	90.6	13.2
Democratic Republic of the Congo	Butembo	2001	21.6	55.7	70.1	82.5	14.4	0.0	100.0	6.2
Democratic Republic of the Congo	Kinshasa	2001	86.9	46.5	85.5	78.2	64.0	6.7	100.0	11.2
Egypt	Alexandria	2003	98.5	98.3	99.8	99.9	99.5	87.2	99.8	65.7
Egypt	Assyut	2003	94.2	95.6	100.0	97.8	97.8	29.2	99.3	44.5
Egypt	Aswan	2003	83.1	96.9	100.0	98.8	98.5	30.0	100.0	56.9
Egypt	Beni Suef	2003	80.6	98.6	100.0	100.0	91.7	52.8	100.0	56.9
Egypt	Cairo	2003	98.9	96.2	99.9	100.0	99.2	75.8	99.9	73.4
Egypt	Port Said	2003	99.3	98.9	100.0	100.0	100.0	89.9	100.0	78.3
Egypt	Suez	2003	99.7	99.7	100.0	99.7	99.1	81.2	99.7	66.6
Ethiopia	Addis Ababa	2000	66.7	64.5	98.4	48.1	60.8	4.2	97.1	20.6

Ethiopia	Nazret	2000	22.7	61.2	85.7	34.9	16.0	0.3	79.7	5.3
Gambia	Banjul	2000	...	...	100.0	96.0	45.4	30.5	...	...
Ghana	Accra	2003	98.8	80.5	97.1	81.5	51.6	41.5	84.3	31.9
Guinea	Conakry	1999	98.7	72.4	93.7	42.5	39.2	11.2	71.4	7.2
Lesotho	Maseru	2000	85.4	90.2	90.3	45.2	42.0	5.5	18.1	...
Mali	Bamako	2001	74.1	77.1	89.4	43.6	39.9	22.0	55.8	15.7
Morocco	Casablanca	1995	99.6	74.7	99.8	91.1	81.9	78.6	87.0	44.7
Morocco	Fes	1995	98.1	73.1	98.9	98.1	89.6	86.5	93.4	34.9
Morocco	Marrakech	1995	98.1	73.1	98.9	98.1	89.6	86.5	93.4	34.9
Morocco	Meknès	1995	98.4	68.3	95.4	95.4	86.8	88.2	92.7	26.0
Morocco	Rabat	1995	99.6	74.7	99.8	91.1	81.9	78.6	87.0	44.7
Morocco	Tangier	1995	98.4	68.3	95.4	95.4	86.8	88.2	92.7	26.0
Mozambique	Maputo	1997	83.2	81.7	96.7	46.3	65.4	22.1	39.2	6.9
Nigeria	Akure	2003	100.0	75.1	84.5	51.1	13.8	10.8	95.5	8.3
Nigeria	Ibadan	2003	96.9	69.9	62.6	67.3	3.0	38.0	98.9	14.8
Nigeria	Lagos	2003	99.8	61.2	88.5	74.8	9.0	49.2	99.8	31.8
Nigeria	Ogbomosho	2003	94.4	84.9	73.0	37.5	2.8	19.7	94.4	7.7
Nigeria	Zaria	2003	98.7	68.3	100.0	57.9	58.6	15.8	100.0	12.4
Rwanda	Kigali	2000	71.6	86.7	81.8	72.1	33.4	4.5	44.4	8.6
Senegal	Dakar	1997	99.8	70.1	94.7	70.6	77.8	27.2	80.2	...
South Africa	Cape Town	1999	97.2	85.7	98.8	94.7	95.7	93.8	92.0	45.2
South Africa	Durban	1999	78.5	85.1	72.3	42.2	44.8	37.9	58.5	24.5
South Africa	Johannesburg	1999	99.0	90.9	98.3	90.5	87.1	87.5	84.9	47.7
South Africa	Port Elizabeth	1999	57.8	79.9	61.4	35.8	36.9	28.4	38.2	17.6
South Africa	Pretoria	1999	99.0	90.9	98.3	90.5	87.1	87.5	84.9	47.7
South Africa	West Rand	1999	98.4	81.9	98.4	83.4	84.5	78.8	78.2	41.5
Sudan	Juba	2000	19.6	58.7	90.7	15.0	10.9	0.0	30.0	...
Sudan	Kassala	2000	8.4	43.4	75.0	23.0	47.4	0.0	39.4	...
Sudan	Khartoum	2000	25.9	54.9	96.0	18.0	63.6	1.0	54.2	...
Sudan	Nyala	2000	16.0	57.3	69.9	14.5	25.7	0.0	26.5	...
Sudan	Port Sudan	2000	28.7	54.9	96.2	32.9	30.9	0.0	35.1	...
Sudan	Wad Medani	2000	19.2	63.6	89.7	17.0	81.0	0.0	73.1	...
Sudan	Waw	2000	16.1	59.7	69.1	16.3	0.0	0.0	6.3	...
Uganda	Kampala	2001	86.3	62.7	93.1	60.7	14.6	11.9	55.2	20.3
United Republic of Tanzania	Arusha	1999	51.5	78.3	97.8	51.1	23.7	0.0	32.6	100.0
United Republic of Tanzania	Dar es Salaam	1999	86.5	84.5	85.9	52.0	78.8	3.2	46.9	100.0
Zambia	Chingola	2002	92.6	79.7	89.1	92.0	74.3	84.8	75.7	3.0
Zambia	Ndola	2002	83.5	76.2	88.0	83.4	66.1	71.2	52.8	16.8
Zimbabwe	Harare	1999	96.4	85.0	98.7	97.1	92.1	90.9	81.9	20.9
ASIA										
Armenia	Yerevan	2000	98.9		99.4	93.6	99.2	93.0	99.1	81.6
Azerbaijan	Baku	2000	99.4	88.2	91.6	85.3	81.6	64.8	96.0	
Bangladesh	Dhaka	1999	71.0	60.2	99.5	90.4	52.0	60.1	88.2	0.0
Bangladesh	Rajshahi	1999	42.9	55.5	99.1	73.8	3.9	38.9	57.8	0.0
Cambodia	Phnom Penh	2000	96.9	...	81.2	95.4	76.4	81.1	97.6	39.9
Cambodia	Siem Reab	2000	100.0	...	57.9	45.8		29.0	55.7	16.8
China	Anqing	2000	...	92.3	...	...	21.7	10.5	...	...
China	Beijing	2000	...	92.3	...	...	97.7	47.6	...	...
China	Changzhi	2000	...	92.4	...	...	49.3	12.6	...	...
China	Chifeng	2000	...	92.2	...	...	33.4	10.3	...	...
China	Dandong	2000	...	92.2	...	...	51.3	25.6	...	...
China	Datong	2000	...	92.3	...	...	63.3	22.7	...	...
China	Dezhou	2000	...	92.4	...	...	20.6	7.2	...	...
China	Guangzhou	2000	...	92.2	...	...	86.3	45.5	...	...
China	Harbin	2000	...	92.2	...	...	65.9	31.7	...	...
China	Hegang	2000	...	92.2	...	...	71.3	18.5	...	...
China	Huaibei	2000	...	92.5	...	...	30.7	12.7	...	...
China	Lanzhou	2000	...	92.4	...	...	69.1	44.3	...	...
China	Leshan	2000	...	92.3	...	...	31.5	13.0	...	...
China	Shanghai	2000	...	92.3	...	...	99.3	66.2	...	...
China	Shaoguan	2000	...	92.3	...	...	52.4	10.8	...	...
China	Xuzhou	2000	...	92.3	...	...	34.6	12.4	...	...
China	Yiyang	2000	...	92.3	...	...	23.8	9.8	...	...
China	Yongzhou	2000	...	92.3	...	...	20.4	6.7	...	...
China	Yueyang	2000	...	92.3	...	...	30.5	16.5	...	...
China	Yulin	2000	...	92.3	...	...	17.3	9.6	...	...
China	Zhengzhou	2000	...	92.3	...	...	66.8	32.6	...	...
India	Agartala	1999	...	72.0	97.0	83.0	32.7	65.6	81.5	18.9
India	Akola	1999	...	65.8	93.1	72.0	73.2	46.2	95.5	19.6
India	Amritsar	1999	...	71.1	100.0	97.2	85.1	87.2	100.0	39.0
India	Coimbatore	1999	...	78.6	97.0	90.1	36.0	50.3	89.6	19.1
India	Delhi	1999	...	73.3	99.2	95.4	80.8	77.9	97.6	45.4
India	Gadag-Betigeri	1999	...	74.9	95.4	73.9	46.2	44.9	89.6	17.6
India	Hisar	1999	...	69.5	99.7	78.5	71.6	74.5	97.7	35.7
India	Hyderabad	1999	...	78.9	100.0	90.6	87.5	51.5	96.1	29.7
India	Jaipur	1999	...	78.5	100.0	93.0	83.7	66.6	98.0	28.5
India	Jalna	1999	...	94.8	99.6	95.4	25.1	44.6	90.4	25.9
India	Jodhpur	1999	...	77.9	98.6	91.3	81.9	75.2	97.3	19.6
India	Kanpur	1999	...	64.8	100.0	84.8	48.2	31.8	93.9	18.9
India	Karnal	1999	...	82.9	99.8	87.4	72.9	62.1	95.5	34.0
India	Kharagpur	1999	...	68.2	96.7	92.8	40.4	68.8	82.6	15.0
India	Kochi (Cochin)	1999	...	93.5	96.1	98.0	27.5	27.5	87.3	35.3

TABLE C.2

continued

			Compliance with requirements		Access to			In-house connections		
			Building material (%)	Sufficient living area (%)	Improved water (%)	Improved sanitation (%)	Piped water (%)	Sewerage (%)	Electricity (%)	Telephone (%)
India	Kolkota	1999	...	73.0	98.6	94.8	35.1	43.5	93.8	25.6
India	Krishnanagar	1999	...	73.3	96.7	79.0	51.6	47.6	91.3	20.1
India	Mumbai	1999	...	59.0	99.7	97.9	76.7	36.9	99.0	31.6
India	Pune (Poona)	1999	...	68.9	98.4	76.8	55.2	27.1	92.3	9.0
India	Rajahmundry	1999	...	80.2	96.4	56.9	35.9	39.5	87.0	13.0
India	Srinagar	1999	...	77.1	98.1	86.0	87.9	66.7	99.3	20.3
India	Vijayawada	1999	...	80.5	97.8	75.5	39.2	49.3	96.8	13.2
India	Yamunanagar	1999	...	74.2	100.0	83.0	59.7	67.2	98.3	27.0
Indonesia	Bandung	2002	99.1	...	98.6	90.5	42.9	51.2	99.4	...
Indonesia	Bitung	2002	95.1	...	98.9	88.5	52.4	63.7	96.3	...
Indonesia	Bogor	2002	98.0	...	99.2	83.6	11.9	48.1	98.6	...
Indonesia	Denpasar	2002	100.0	...	100.0	100.0	53.6	92.1	100.0	...
Indonesia	Dumai	2002	99.1	...	97.7	86.1	17.2	38.6	85.8	...
Indonesia	Jakarta	2002	99.5	...	100.0	96.7	35.6	59.5	99.9	...
Indonesia	Jambi	2002	99.4	...	100.0	99.4	53.0	80.9	98.7	...
Indonesia	Jaya Pura	2002	96.3	...	94.1	88.4	61.1	59.2	88.0	...
Indonesia	Kediri	2002	88.6	...	100.0	61.6	17.9	38.1	98.6	...
Indonesia	Medan	2002	99.6	...	100.0	98.8	68.0	81.4	92.5	...
Indonesia	Palembang	2002	99.6	...	100.0	98.7	81.2	79.0	100.0	...
Indonesia	Palu	2002	97.1	...	100.0	83.2	39.7	47.9	92.1	...
Indonesia	Pekan Baru	2002	100.0	...	100.0	99.1	51.8	68.1	97.9	...
Indonesia	Purwokerto	2002	81.7	...	95.2	71.4	21.3	51.1	95.1	...
Indonesia	Surabaja	2002	99.0	...	100.0	100.0	71.0	56.3	100.0	...
Indonesia	Surakarta	2002	93.4	...	100.0	100.0	48.6	63.9	98.7	...
Indonesia	Ujung Pandang	2002	98.0	...	100.0	98.6	36.3	79.7	98.4	...
Iraq	Amara	2000	...	88.8	93.1	88.8	88.3	75.0	...	...
Iraq	Baghdad	2000	...	93.3	99.4	98.1	97.2	96.7	...	...
Iraq	Mosul	2000	...	87.8	99.8	98.0	99.6	95.1	...	...
Kazakhstan	Chimkent	1999	37.4	...	82.2	80.2	76.9	60.9	99.6	44.8
Kazakhstan	Dzhezkazgan	1999	43.0	...	100.0	99.8	100.0	99.5	100.0	69.3
Mongolia	Ulaanbaatar	2000	98.4	44.1	97.0	75.3	49.4	49.1	99.0	...
Myanmar	Yangon	2000	93.0	44.8	95.3	81.4	36.8	31.3	...	...
Pakistan	Faisalabad	1991	98.6	39.5	98.1	87.2	78.1	87.2	98.7	...
Pakistan	Islamabad	1991	98.9	49.1	94.1	70.3	80.3	70.3	97.8	...
Pakistan	Karachi	1991	99.6	42.3	96.6	90.0	77.4	90.0	96.8	...
Philippines	Bacolod	1998	57.9	71.3	92.7	75.0	31.1	62.2	78.7	12.8
Philippines	Cagayan de Oro	1998	63.2	68.4	86.8	97.4	28.9	78.9	86.8	7.9
Philippines	Cebu	1998	62.7	76.0	88.0	88.4	42.1	52.4	85.6	21.6
Philippines	Metro Manila	1998	84.7	73.2	91.0	97.0	65.9	72.5	98.7	45.7
Syrian Arab Republic	Damascus	2000	...	...	99.7	99.1	...	...	...	...
Tajikistan	Dushanbe	2000	94.2	90.4	99.7	89.1	93.3	69.6	99.0	...
Turkey	Adana	1998	99.0	88.7	100.0	98.0	100.0	83.3	...	71.6
Turkey	Aksaray	1998	50.0	76.2	97.6	70.2	40.5	21.4	...	69.0
Turkey	Ankara	1998	96.3	97.4	97.4	99.5	96.1	99.0	...	90.3
Turkey	Antakya	1998	74.0	94.8	92.7	90.6	87.0	19.3	...	83.3
Turkey	Bursa	1998	89.5	96.3	92.0	99.1	91.4	88.3	...	82.7
Turkey	Gaziantep	1998	100.0	64.7	96.8	90.4	94.9	89.1	...	73.1
Turkey	Istanbul	1998	94.9	95.1	90.0	99.3	55.8	98.7	...	79.9
Turkey	Izmir	1998	85.6	95.2	100.0	100.0	95.8	98.1	...	84.0
Uzbekistan	Tashkent	1996	99.7	97.1	100.0	90.7	98.7	79.4	...	64.5
Viet Nam	Da Nang	2002	100.0	70.9	99.0	100.0	88.8	98.5	100.0	80.0
Viet Nam	Ha Noi	2002	98.5	80.0	100.0	97.9	74.1	88.3	100.0	72.9
Viet Nam	Hai Phong	2002	97.8	92.0	100.0	95.5	95.5	88.0	100.0	39.0
Viet Nam	Ho Chi Minh City	2002	99.4	75.1	98.7	98.1	88.8	94.7	99.8	74.5
Yemen	Aden	1997	87.6	56.7	97.0	93.6	93.3	83.1	95.6	...
Yemen	Sana'a	1997	91.0	65.9	93.9	77.9	78.7	24.8	98.8	...
Yemen	Taiz	1997	91.5	58.0	85.6	77.1	84.0	39.9	95.2	...
LATIN AMERICA										
Brazil	Belo Horizonte	1996	97.6	91.2	94.1	98.6	84.4	78.9	100.0	...
Brazil	Brasilia	1996	99.6	88.7	94.2	86.4	89.8	69.0	99.6	...
Brazil	Curitiba	1996	96.8	96.1	97.3	95.9	84.2	55.4	100.0	...
Brazil	Fortaleza	1996	95.3	90.5	88.6	80.2	76.8	19.8	97.2	...
Brazil	Goiânia	1996	99.1	92.0	97.8	89.2	93.4	73.8	98.3	...
Brazil	Rio de Janeiro	1996	99.6	89.7	97.1	98.0	88.5	63.3	99.6	...
Brazil	Sao Paolo	1996	99.6	83.3	99.2	99.4	93.8	79.9	99.6	...
Brazil	Vitoria	1996	97.1	87.9	96.2	95.4	90.4	82.1	99.2	...
Colombia	Bogotá	2000	95.5	90.8	100.0	100.0	100.0	100.0	99.8	100.0
Colombia	Medellín	2000	99.9	93.8	100.0	99.7	100.0	99.5	99.9	100.0
Colombia	Neiva	2000	96.9	91.2	100.0	99.5	100.0	95.4	98.7	100.0
Colombia	Valledupar	2000	99.6	82.0	99.6	99.8	99.6	98.7	99.6	100.0
Guatemala	Guatemala City	2000	80.0	71.6	97.4	73.0	52.7	65.3	91.0	31.9

Source: UN-Habitat, Urban Indicators Programme III: Preliminary results, 2005.

TABLE C.3

Urban Transport and Environment, Selected Cities

		Urban transport					Urban environment			
			Transport used for work trips							
		Travel time Per work trip (minutes)	Car (%)	Train (%)	Bus (%)	Other (%)	City population (000) 2000	Particulate matter (milligrams per cubic metre) 1999	Sulphur dioxide (milligrams per cubic metre) 1995–2001	Nitrogen dioxide (milligrams per cubic metre) 1995–2001
AFRICA										
Benin	Cotonou	...	90.0	-	-	10.0	...	...	...	...
Benin	Parakou	45	80.0	-	-	20.0	...	...	...	...
Benin	Porto-Novo	50	83.0	-	-	17.0	...	...	...	...
Burkina Faso	Ouagadougou	...	63.4	-	2.2	34.4	...	...	...	...
Burundi	Bujumbura	25	12.4	-	48.2	39.4	...	...	...	...
Cameroon	Yaounde	45	30.0	-	42.3	27.7	...	...	...	...
Central African Republic	Bangui	60	3.7	-	66.3	30.0	...	...	...	...
Chad	N'Djamena	...	17.0	-	35.0	48.0	...	...	...	...
Congo	Brazzaville	20	19.0	-	55.0	26.0	...	...	...	...
Congo	Pointe-Noire	30	8.0	-	55.0	37.0	...	...	...	...
Democratic Republic of Congo	Kinshasa	57	13.0	42.0	30.0	15.0	...	...	...	...
Egypt	Cairo	...	...	...	...	...	7,941	178	69	...
Ethiopia	Addis Ababa	...	4.2	-	12.6	83.3	...	...	...	...
Gabon	Libreville	30	-	55.0	25.0	20.0	...	...	...	...
Gambia	Banjul	22	19.5	-	54.9	25.6	...	...	...	...
Ghana	Accra	21	34.7	4.0	50.0	11.3	1,938	31	...	...
Ghana	Kumasi	21	22.2	0.6	50.0	27.2	...	...	...	...
Guinea	Conakry	45	22.0	-	25.5	52.5	...	...	...	...
Kenya	Kisumu	24	21.1	-	43.5	35.5	...	...	...	...
Kenya	Mombasa	20	2.1	-	47.0	50.9	...	...	...	...
Kenya	Nairobi	57	6.0	1.0	70.0	23.0	2,383	49	...	...
Lesotho	Maseru	15	3.0	-	47.0	50.0	...	...	...	...
Liberia	Monrovia	60	10.0	-	80.0	10.0	...	...	...	...
Libyan Arab Jamahiriya	Tripoli	20	81.0	-	18.0	1.0	...	...	...	...
Madagascar	Antananarivo	60	7.0	-	60.0	33.0	...	...	...	...
Malawi	Lilongwe	5	6.0	-	27.0	67.0	...	...	...	...
Mali	Bamako	30	24.9	-	12.2	62.9	...	...	...	...
Mauritania	Nouakchott	50	16.5	-	45.0	38.5	...	...	...	...
Morocco	Rabat	20	40.0	-	40.0	20.0	...	...	...	...
Mozambique	Maputo	60	6.5	-	80.0	13.5	...	...	...	...
Nigeria	Ibadan	45	45.0	0.5	45.0	9.5	...	...	...	...
Nigeria	Lagos	60	51.0	2.5	45.5	...	...	...	...	...
Rwanda	Kigali	45	12.0	-	32.0	56.0	...	...	...	...
Senegal	Bignona	10	1.7	-	-	98.3	...	...	...	...
Senegal	Dakar	30	8.1	1.3	77.2	13.4	...	...	...	...
Senegal	Thies	12	18.2	-	59.3	22.6	...	...	...	...
South Africa	Cape Town	...	...	...	...	...	2,942	15	21	72
South Africa	Durban	...	...	...	...	...	1,364	29	31	..
South Africa	Johannesburg	...	...	...	...	...	2,344	30	19	31
South Africa	Port Elizabeth	35	52.4	1.8	45.8	-	...	...	...	...
Togo	Lome	30	45.0	-	40.0	15.0	...	...	...	...
Togo	Sokode	15	60.0	-	10.0	30.0	...	...	...	...
Uganda	Entebbe	20	35.0	-	65.0	-	...	...	...	...
Uganda	Jinja	12	18.0	-	49.0	33.0	...	...	...	...
Zimbabwe	Bulawayo	15	22.8	-	74.9	2.3	...	...	...	...
Zimbabwe	Chegutu	22	19.0	-	20.0	61.0	...	...	...	...
Zimbabwe	Gweru	15	...	...	...	...	...	...	...	...
Zimbabwe	Harare	45	18.0	-	32.0	50.0	...	...	...	...
Zimbabwe	Mutare	20	12.0	-	70.0	18.0	...	...	...	...
ASIA										
Armenia	Yerevan	30	2.0	11.5	72.5	14.0	...	...	...	...
Bangladesh	Chittagong	45	4.0	1.0	25.0	70.0	...	...	...	...
Bangladesh	Dhaka	45	4.6	0.0	9.2	86.2	...	...	...	...
Bangladesh	Sylhet	50	1.3	-	10.0	88.7	...	...	...	...
Cambodia	Phnom Penh	45	87.3	-	0.2	12.5	...	...	...	...
China	Anshan	...	...	...	...	...	3,132	99	115	88
China	Beijing	...	...	...	...	...	9,302	106	90	122
China	Changchun	...	...	...	...	...	3,766	88	21	64
China	Chengdu	...	...	...	...	...	4,401	103	77	74
China	Chongquing	...	...	...	...	...	3,945	147	340	70
China	Dalian	...	...	...	...	...	4,389	60	61	100
China	Guangzhu	...	...	...	...	...	495	74	57	136
China	Guiyang	...	...	...	...	...	2,103	84	424	53
China	Harbin	...	...	...	...	...	4,545	91	23	30
China	Jinan	...	...	...	...	...	3,037	112	132	45
China	Kunming	...	...	...	...	...	2,037	84	19	33
China	Lanzhou	...	...	...	...	...	2,044	109	102	104
China	Liupanshui	...	...	...	...	...	2,330	70	102	..
China	Nanchang	...	...	...	...	...	1,594	94	69	29
China	Pinxiang	...	...	...	...	...	1,754	80	75	..
China	Quingdao	...	...	...	...	...	2,316	..	190	64
China	Shanghai	...	...	...	...	...	10,367	87	53	73
China	Shenyang	...	...	...	...	...	5,881	120	99	73
China	Taiyuan	...	...	...	...	...	2,811	105	211	55

TABLE C.3

continued

		Urban transport					Urban environment			
			Transport used for work trips							
		Travel time Per work trip (minutes)	Car (%)	Train (%)	Bus (%)	Other (%)	City population (000) 2000	Particulate matter (milligrams per cubic metre) 1999	Sulphur dioxide (milligrams per cubic metre) 1995–2001	Nitrogen dioxide (milligrams per cubic metre) 1995–2001
China	Tianjin	...	...	...	...	...	7,333	149	82	50
China	Urumqi	...	...	...	...	...	1,467	61	60	70
China	Wuhan	...	...	...	...	...	4,842	94	40	43
China	Zhengzhou	...	...	...	...	...	2,214	116	63	95
China	Zibo	...	...	...	...	...	3,139	88	198	43
India	Ahmedabad	...	...	...	...	...	4,154	104	30	21
India	Bangalore	30	39.6	-	35.7	24.7	5,180	56	..	..
India	Calcutta	...	...	...	...	...	13,822	153	49	34
India	Chennai	23	42.0	11.0	25.0	22.0	6,002	..	15	17
India	Delhi	..	24.6	0.4	62.0	13.0	10,558	187	24	41
India	Hyderabad	...	...	...	...	...	5,448	51	12	17
India	Kanpur	...	...	...	...	...	2,546	136	15	14
India	Lucknow	...	...	...	...	...	2,093	136	26	25
India	Mumbai	...	...	...	...	...	15,797	79	33	39
India	Mysore	20	39.1	-	0.1	60.8	...	...	...	...
India	Nagpur	...	...	...	...	...	2,087	69	6	13
India	Pune	...	...	...	...	...	3,128	58	...	...
Indonesia	Jakarta	...	...	...	...	...	10,845	103	...	...
Indonesia	Surabaya	35	80.0	-	17.8	2.2	...	...	...	...
Iran (Islamic Republic of)	Tehran	...	...	...	...	...	7,689	71	209	...
Japan	Osaka	...	...	...	...	...	2,626	39	19	63
Japan	Tokyo	45	...	...	...	...	12,483	43	18	68
Japan	Yokohama	...	...	...	...	...	3,366	32	100	13
Jordan	Amman	25	51.0	-	21.0	28.0	...	...	...	...
Kazakhstan	Astana	27	30.0	28.0	34.0	8.0	...	...	...	...
Kuwait	Kuwait	10	68.0	-	21.0	11.0	...	...	...	...
Kyrghyzstan	Bishkek	35	5.0	35.4	59.6	0.0	...	...	...	...
Lao PDR	Vientiane	27	41.8	-	2.1	56.1	...	...	...	...
Lebanon	Sin El Fil	10	25.0	-	50.0	25.0	...	...	...	...
Malaysia	Kuala Lumpur	...	...	...	...	...	1,530	24	24	...
Malaysia	Penang	40	42.0	-	55.0	3.0	...	...	...	...
Mongolia	Ulaanbaatar	30	10.0	21.0	59.0	10.0	...	...	...	...
Myanmar	Yangon	45	16.7	3.7	65.0	14.7	...	...	...	...
Nepal	Butwal	15	10.0	-	15.0	75.0	...	...	...	...
Nepal	Pokhara	20	11.0	-	14.0	75.0	...	...	...	...
Oman	Muscat	20	..	..	..	..	...	...	...	...
Pakistan	Karachi	..	16.5	-	41.0	39.5	...	...	...	...
Philippines	Cebu	35	..	..	..	..	...	...	...	...
Philippines	Manila	...	...	...	...	...	10,432	60	33	..
Republic of Korea	Pusan	42	37.1	6.6	32.5	23.8	4,075	43	60	51
Republic of Korea	Seoul	60	20.1	32.3	38.8	8.8	11,548	45	44	60
Republic of Korea	Taegu	...	...	...	...	...	2,417	49	81	62
Singapore	Singapore	30	25.1	14.5	38.7	21.7	3,163	41	20	30
Sri Lanka	Colombo	25	23.7	8.1	65.0	3.2	...	...	...	...
Syrian Arab Rep.	Damascus	40	15.0	-	32.6	52.4	...	...	...	...
Thailand	Bangkok	60	58.7	1.0	27.0	13.3	7,296	82	11	23
Thailand	Chiang Mai	30	94.1	-	5.0	0.9	...	...	...	...
Turkey	Ankara	32	20.0	6.3	..	15.9	...	...	...	...
Turkey	Istanbul	...	...	...	...	...	9,286	62	120	...
Viet Nam	Hanoi	30	64.4	-	2.0	33.6	...	...	...	...
Viet Nam	Ho Chi Minh	25	74.0	-	2.0	24.0	...	...	...	...
Yemen	Sana'a	20	20.0	-	78.0	2.0	...	...	...	...
EUROPE										
Albania	Tirana	25	...	...	...	...	...	...	...	...
Austria	Vienna	...	...	...	...	...	1,904	39	14	42
Belgium	Brussels	...	...	...	...	...	983	31	20	48
Bosnia and Herzegovina	Sarajevo	12	..	57.0	43.0	..	...	...	...	...
Bulgaria	Bourgas	32	6.0	0.1	61.0	33.0	...	...	...	...
Bulgaria	Sofia	32	21.0	26.0	53.0	-	1,177	83	39	122
Bulgaria	Troyan	22	18.0	-	44.0	38.0	...	...	...	...
Bulgaria	Veliko Tarnovo	30	2.4	-	45.8	51.8	...	...	...	...
Croatia	Zagreb	31	37.5	35.9	20.4	6.2	908	39	31	...
Czech Republic	Brno	25	25.0	29.0	21.0	25.0	...	...	...	...
Czech Republic	Prague	22	33.0	-	54.5	12.5	1,211	27	14	33
Finland	Helsinki	...	...	...	...	...	1,095	22	4	35
France	Paris	...	...	...	...	...	9,851	15	14	57
Germany	Berlin	...	...	...	...	...	3,555	25	18	26
Germany	Frankfurt	...	...	...	...	...	668	22	11	45
Germany	Munich	...	...	...	...	...	1,275	22	8	53
Greece	Athens	...	...	...	...	...	3,229	50	34	64
Hungary	Budapest	...	...	...	...	...	1,958	26	39	51
Iceland	Reykjavik	...	...	...	...	...	164	21	5	42
Ireland	Dublin	...	...	...	...	...	991	23	20	...
Italy	Milan	...	...	...	...	...	1,381	36	31	248
Italy	Rome	...	...	...	...	...	2,713	35	...	...

Italy	Torino	...	...	...	...	...	969	53	...	...
Lithuania	Vilnius	37	22.3	29.1	23.2	25.5	...	...	...	...
Netherlands	Amsterdam	...	...	...	...	...	1,131	37	10	58
Norway	Oslo	...	...	...	...	...	805	23	8	43
Poland	Bydgoszcz	18	42.5	10.5	24.0	..	...	...	...	...
Poland	Gdansk	20	43.0	32.9	23.4	0.7	...	...	...	...
Poland	Katowice	36	46.2	9.4	19.9	24.6	...	...	...	...
Poland	Lodz	...	...	...	...	...	873	45	21	43
Poland	Poznan	25	33.0	30.0	21.0	16.0	...	...	...	...
Poland	Warsaw	...	...	...	...	...	1,716	49	16	32
Portugal	Lisbon	...	...	...	...	...	3,318	30	8	52
Republi of Moldova	Chisinau	23	15.0	-	80.0	5.0	...	...	...	...
Romania	Bucharest	...	...	...	...	...	2,070	25	10	71
Russian Federation	Astrakhan	35	16.0	31.0	35.0	18.0	...	...	...	...
Russian Federation	Kostroma	20	5.0	19.5	48.0	27.5	...	...	...	...
Russian Federation	Moscow	62	15.0	63.7	21.0	0.3	8,811	27	109	...
Russian Federation	Nizhny Novgorod	35	17.0	37.3	41.7	4.0	...	...	...	...
Russian Federation	Novomoscowsk	25	5.0	22.5	38.9	33.6	...	...	...	...
Russian Federation	Omsk	43	9.5	16.5	69.0	5.0	1,206	28	20	34
Russian Federation	Pushkin	15	6.0	-	60.2	33.8	...	...	...	...
Russian Federation	Surgut	57	1.5	-	81.0	17.5	...	...	...	...
Russian Federation	Veliky Novgorod	30	9.5	-	75.0	15.5	...	...	...	...
Serbia and Montenegro	Belgrade	40	12.5	18.8	53.0	...	...	...	...	...
Slovakia	Bratislava	...	...	...	...	...	456	22	21	27
Slovenia	Ljubljana	30	43.0	0.1	20.0	36.9	...	...	...	...
Spain	Barcelona						1,645	43	11	43
Spain	Madrid	32	60.0	-	16.0	24.0	3,068	37	24	66
Sweden	Stockholm	28	35.1	34.5	13.8	16.6	916	15	3	20
Sweden	Umea	16	...	...	...	...	...	...	...	...
Switzerland	Zurich	...	...	...	...	...	980	24	11	39
Ukraine	Kiev	...	...	...	...	...	2,622	45	14	51
United Kingdom	Birmingham	20	73.9	1.4	9.1	15.6	2,344	17	9	45
United Kingdom	Cardiff	20	81.0	0.3	5.7	13.0	...	...	...	...
United Kingdom	Edinburgh	20	69.9	2.4	13.0	14.7	...	...	...	...
United Kingdom	London	24	...	...	...	...	7,812	23	25	77
United Kingdom	Manchester	19	71.8	1.9	8.1	18.0	2,325	19	26	49

LATIN AMERICA AND CARIBBEAN

Argentina	Buenos Aires	42	33.5	16.4	42.2	...	...	...	...	...
Argentina	Comodoro Rivadavia	29	44.0	-	36.0	20.0	...	...	...	...
Argentina	Córdoba	32	26.5	2.9	40.9	...	1,370	52	...	97
Brazil	Icapui	30	6.0	...	1.0	93.0	...	...	...	...
Brazil	Maranguape	20	5.0	-	30.0	..	...	...	...	...
Brazil	Recife	35	28.6	1.8	44.2	25.4	...	...	...	...
Brazil	Rio de Janeiro	...	...	...	...	...	5,902	40	129	...
Brazil	São Paulo	40	42.0	6.0	37.0	15.0	9,984	46	43	83
Chile	Gran Concepcion	35	19.6	-	56.5	23.9	...	...	...	...
Chile	Santiago de Chile	38	14.1	4.0	55.8	26.2	4,522	73	29	81
Chile	Valparaiso	..	42.0	19.0	36.0	3.0	...	...	...	...
Colombia	Armenia	60	31.0	-	41.9	27.2	...	...	...	...
Colombia	Bogotá	...	...	...	...	...	5,442	33	...	...
Colombia	Marinilla	15	14.3	-	18.4	67.3	...	...	...	...
Colombia	Medellín	35	21.9	4.8	33.1	40.2	...	...	...	...
Cuba	Camaguey	60	2.5	-	2.1	95.4	...	...	...	...
Cuba	Havana		6.5	1.0	57.1	35.4	2,270	28	1	5
Cuba	Santa Clara	48	30.3	3.2	4.1	62.4	...	...	...	...
Ecuador	Cuenca	25	..	..	..	..	...	...	...	...
Ecuador	Guayaquil	45	10.7	-	89.3	-	2,120	26	15	...
Ecuador	Manta	30	..	..	..	..	...	...	...	...
Ecuador	Puyo	15	..	..	..	..	...	...	...	...
Ecuador	Quito	33	..	..	..	..	1,598	34	22	...
El Salvador	San Salvador	..	29.0	..	..	2.0	...	...	...	...
Mexico	Ciudad Juarez	23	51.3	-	23.7	25.0	...	...	...	...
Mexico	Mexico City	...	...	...	...	...	18,017	69	74	130
Nicaragua	Leon	15	..	..	56.0	..	...	...	...	...
Panama	Colon	15	...	...	...	...	...	...	...	...
Paraguay	Asuncion	25	49.8	...	..	..	...	...	...	...
Peru	Cajamarca	20	22.0	...	20.0	58.0	...	...	...	...
Peru	Huanuco	20	17.5	...	45.0	..	...	...	...	...
Peru	Huaras	15	...	...	...	...	...	...	...	...
Peru	Iquitos	10	35.0	-	25.0	40.0	...	...	...	...
Peru	Lima	...	16.9	-	82.2	0.9	...	...	...	...
Peru	Tacna	25	37.5	...	66.0	1.0	...	...	...	...
Peru	Tumbes	20	25.0	...	..	5.0	...	...	...	...
Trinidad and Tobago	Port of Spain	...	56.2	-	43.8	-	...	...	...	...
Uruguay	Montevideo	45	26.9	-	59.6	13.5	...	...	...	...
Venezuela	Caracas	...	...	...	...	...	3,488	18	33	57

NORTHERN AMERICA

Canada	Hull	...	73.3	-	16.3	10.4	...	...	...	...
Canada	Montreal	...	...	...	...	...	3,519	22	10	42
Canada	Toronto	...	...	...	...	...	4,535	26	17	43
Canada	Vancouver	...	...	...	...	...	1,880	15	14	37
United States	Atlanta	26	...	...	...	...	...	...	...	...
United States	Birmingham-US	23	...	...	...	...	...	...	...	...
United States	Boston	25	...	...	...	...	...	...	...	...
United States	Chicago	...	...	...	...	...	9,024	27	14	57
United States	Des Moines	18	...	...	...	...	...	...	...	...
United States	Hartford	21	...	...	...	...	...	...	...	...
United States	Los Angeles	...	...	...	...	...	16,195	38	9	74

TABLE C.3

continued

		Urban transport					Urban environment			
			Transport used for work trips							
		Travel time Per work trip (minutes)	Car (%)	Train (%)	Bus (%)	Other (%)	City population (000) 2000	Particulate matter (milligrams per cubic metre) 1999	Sulphur dioxide (milligrams per cubic metre) 1995–2001	Nitrogen dioxide (milligrams per cubic metre) 1995–2001
United States	Minneapolis-St. Paul	21	...	...	...	...	...	...	...	...
United States	New York	35	...	...	...	...	20,951	23	26	79
United States	Providence	19	...	...	...	...	...	...	...	...
United States	Salt Lake	20	...	...	...	...	...	...	...	...
United States	San Jose	23	...	...	...	...	...	...	...	...
United States	Seattle	24	...	...	...	...	...	...	...	...
United States	Tampa	22	...	...	...	...	...	...	...	...
United States	Washington, DC	30	...	...	...	...	...	...	...	...
OCEANIA										
Australia	Melbourne	...	...	...	...	...	3,293	15	...	30
Australia	Perth	...	...	...	...	...	1,245	15	5	19
Australia	Sydney	...	...	...	...	...	3,855	22	28	81
New Zealand	Auckland	...	...	...	...	...	989	15	3	20

Source: UN-Habitat, 2002; World Bank, 2005.

TABLE C.4

Social indicators, selected cities

			Life expectancy			Gross school enrolment ratio				Literacy rate	
						Primary		Secondary			
		Households in poverty (%)	Female (years)	Male (years)	Under five mortality rate	Female (%)	Male (%)	Female (%)	Male (%)	Female (%)	Male (%)
AFRICA											
Algeria	Algiers	...	71.0	68.0	4.0	...	...	...	...	76.3	86.4
Benin	Cotonou	35.0	60.6	55.9	8.2	74.3	78.3	27.7	39.2	70.0	94.0
Benin	Parakou	35.0	62.2	58.0	10.1	74.3	120.3	26.5	39.3	54.0	79.0
Benin	Porto-Novo	22.0	59.5	54.6	12.0	...	...	37.1	49.8	75.0	90.0
Botswana	Gaborone	54.1	67.1	63.1	10.5	49.7	50.3	52.6	47.4	66.9	70.3
Burkina Faso	Bobo-Dioulasso	12.2	...	...	21.0	...	...	...	...	...	...
Burkina Faso	Koudougou	23.1	...	...	21.0	...	...	...	...	...	...
Burkina Faso	Ouagadougou	12.2	...	...	21.0	...	...	...	...	...	...
Burundi	Bujumbura	66.5	53.7	52.3	...	81.5	81.6	43.3	44.0	64.2	80.1
Cameroon	Douala	19.7	...	...	15.0	...	...	...	...	...	...
Cameroon	Yaounde	30.0	...	...	15.0	...	...	...	...	...	...
Central African Republic	Bangui	49.0	...	...	16.2	50.0	...	27.0	...	...	...
Chad	N'Djamena	...	50.0	48.0	17.2	64.4	45.6	16.5	8.0	...	...
Congo	Brazzaville	21.7	56.0	52.0	12.2	36.0	41.8	6.8	8.2	12.0	31.0
Congo	Pointe-Noire	25.0	56.0	52.0	14.3	26.4	26.6	28.1	23.8	15.0	28.0
Côte d'Ivoire	Abidjan	...	60.0	55.0	9.0	61.7	81.7	14.8	29.8	36.8	63.3
Côte d'Ivoire	Yamoussoukro	...	60.0	65.0	...	34.5	45.0	7.0	18.1	36.8	63.3
Democratic Republic of Congo	Kinshasa	22.9	51.0	50.0	14.1	36.0	48.7	9.2	21.9	...	...
Egypt	Ismailia	9.7	67.7	66.6	3.6	47.6	52.4	49.2	50.8	78.1	89.6
Egypt	Tanta	...	...	...	5.6	48.5	51.5	51.0	49.0	...	...
Ethiopia	Addis Ababa	...	61.5	57.8	17.1	83.5	86.1	44.1	53.0	...	...
Gabon	Libreville	30.0	56.5	53.3	14.4	72.9	86.0	72.9	86.0	60.5	80.3
Gabon	Port-Gentil	30.0	56.5	53.3	14.0	...	...	...	...	60.5	80.3
Gambia	Banjul	40.0	57.0	54.0	...	56.3	64.2	...	...	37.0	63.0
Ghana	Accra	...	69.0	66.2	9.6	...	...	...	...	74.5	87.3
Ghana	Kumasi	26.0	69.0	66.2	9.6	...	...	...	...	74.5	87.3
Guinea	Conakry	9.0	41.0	46.0	...	63.8	82.3	...	...	...	...
Kenya	Kisumu	58.2	66.3	62.8	12.4	...	...	...	...	81.4	91.7
Kenya	Mombasa	33.5	...	...	12.4	...	...	...	...	...	...
Kenya	Nairobi	46.6	60.9	57.6	12.4	...	...	...	...	...	...
Lesotho	Maseru	...	52.3	47.7	...	76.0	67.0	76.0	70.0	...	...
Liberia	Monrovia	...	53.0	50.0	...	72.5	72.9	...	...	26.0	40.0
Libyan Arab Jamahiriya	Tripoli	...	71.0	69.0	2.7	...	...	...	...	72.8	89.6
Madagascar	Antananarivo	54.2	0.6	0.6	13.9	64.0	67.0	...	...	...	...
Malawi	Lilongwe	...	44.6	41.4	22.9	...	...	...	...	31.0	52.0
Mali	Bamako	16.2	58.7	55.3	...	41.0	59.0	35.0	65.0	71.2	71.2
Mauritanie	Nouakchott	25.0	54.3	52.3	14.8	83.5	87.6	14.2	19.2	...	...
Morocco	Casablanca	11.9	74.4	70.1	6.1	...	...	...	...	...	...
Morocco	Rabat	11.7	74.0	70.0	6.1	...	...	...	...	...	...
Mozambique	Maputo	47.8	61.7	54.6	...	132.8	136.7	26.2	27.0	77.4	92.9
Namibia	Windhoek	...	...	...	6.5	52.0	48.0	52.5	47.5	67.0	66.0
Niger	Maradi	...	56.0	55.0	25.0	...	...	...	...	...	...
Niger	Niamey	...	56.0	55.0	25.0	...	...	...	...	53.0	67.0
Nigeria	Ibadan	53.0	55.5	52.0	11.9	...	...	...	...	13.1	17.2
Nigeria	Lagos	53.0	55.5	52.0	11.9	...	...	...	...	13.1	17.2

Rwanda	Kigali	65.0	50.0	47.0	...	50.0	71.0	...	...	45.0	57.0
Senegal	Bignona	65.0	58.2	60.2	...	92.0	105.6	...	...	23.7	44.7
Senegal	Dakar	38.2	58.2	60.2	...	86.0	88.9	...	...	47.7	74.7
Senegal	Thies	48.7	58.2	60.2	...	59.4	78.8	...	...	23.7	44.7
South Africa	Durban	...	...	...	...	...	...	...	...	...	...
South Africa	East Rand	...	...	...	...	...	...	...	...	...	...
South Africa	Port Elizabeth	...	...	...	3.7	...	...	...	...	...	...
Togo	Lome	20.0	60.0	54.0	14.4	52.0	55.0	...	...	75.0	94.0
Togo	Sokode	33.0	53.0	51.0	9.5	75.9	90.3	...	...	50.0	74.0
Tunisia	Tunis	...	74.2	70.6	3.2	47.2	52.8	50.2	49.8	59.2	80.0
Uganda	Entebbe	...	...	...	17.0	43.0	53.0	53.0	45.0	93.6	98.0
Uganda	Jinja	...	51.0	47.0	17.0	94.0	95.0	51.0	76.0	53.0	77.0
Zimbabwe	Bulawayo	...	...	...	12.5	...	...	...	...	...	...
Zimbabwe	Chegutu	...	...	...	12.5	...	...	...	...	...	...
Zimbabwe	Gweru	...	...	...	12.5	...	...	...	...	...	...
Zimbabwe	Harare	...	...	...	12.5	...	...	48.6	54.4	...	...
Zimbabwe	Mutare	...	...	...	12.5	...	...	...	...	...	...
ASIA											
Armenia	Yerevan	58.2	76.2	69.3	1.5	...	...	...	...	100.0	100.0
Bangladesh	Chittagong	...	...	...	9.6	93.0	94.0	...	...	...	...
Bangladesh	Dhaka	44.3	60.9	61.7	9.6	77.9	80.4	62.3	65.9	60.3	60.3
Bangladesh	Sylhet	...	...	...	9.6	93.6	86.9	...	...	...	...
Bangladesh	Tangail	50.0	...	...	9.6	...	...	...	...	...	...
Cambodia	Phnom Penh	16.4	69.0	64.0	11.5	74.1	82.2	8.3	12.7	57.0	79.5
Georgia	Tbilisi	54.7	76.8	68.5	...	...	...	...	...	99.0	99.0
India	Alwar	...	...	...	...	...	...	...	...	...	...
India	Bangalore	18.6	...	...	4.9	...	...	...	...	...	...
India	Chennai	20.5	68.5	65.0	3.7	49.5	50.5	50.7	49.3	69.0	72.0
India	Delhi	16.0	...	...	2.6	...	...	...	...	76.0	91.0
India	Mysore	18.8	...	...	...	96.1	93.6	69.7	74.3	...	...
Indonesia	Bandung	2.0	...	...	4.0	...	...	...	...	...	...
Indonesia	Jakarta	6.6	...	...	2.4	97.6	98.9	95.7	...	97.3	99.2
Indonesia	Semarang	24.8	...	...	3.9	98.1	97.7	92.9	...	91.4	97.5
Indonesia	Surabaya	0.9	...	...	3.9	...	...	...	...	...	...
Iraq	Baghdad	...	...	...	12.5	...	...	...	...	...	...
Japan	Tokyo	0.0	84.1	77.5	3.9	100.0	100.0	100.0	100.0	100.0	100.0
Jordan	Amman	17.7	71.3	68.6	2.9	91.2	91.7	63.4	62.4	86.9	95.5
Kazakhstan	Astana	18.8	74.0	63.0	0.5	...	...	89.0	94.0	100.0	100.0
Kuwait	Kuwait	6.9	72.0	70.0	1.3	...	...	...	...	78.6	85.4
Kyrghyzstan	Bishkek	51.0	71.2	63.1	4.4	...	...	...	...	96.2	98.4
Lao PDR	Vientiane	19.0	...	...	7.5	52.7	47.4	54.9	45.2	78.9	92.2
Lebanon	Sin El Fil	...	...	...	3.2	...	...	...	...	...	...
Malaysia	Penang	6.1	74.6	69.6	0.7	...	...	...	...	82.0	91.0
Mongolia	Ulaanbaatar	30.0	63.9	59.7	4.3	100.0	100.0	74.2	64.7	97.1	99.1
Myanmar	Yangon	...	64.6	60.6	7.2	99.8	92.2	57.7	53.3	88.7	90.6
Nepal	Butwal	...	57.8	60.5	...	49.7	53.7	85.3	74.3	25.6	58.8
Nepal	Pokhara	20.0	50.0	55.0	2.1	88.0	83.3	35.4	26.6	42.0	66.2
Occupied Palestine Territory	Gaza	38.0	73.1	69.9	...	21.5	24.4	22.1	21.8	76.9	90.4
Oman	Muscat	...	72.0	70.0	2.5	...	...	...	...	...	...
Pakistan	Karachi	35.0	65.0	63.0	12.0	58.7	60.9	67.3	70.6	64.2	72.0
Pakistan	Lahore	28.0	65.0	63.0	6.3	66.2	68.5	73.3	71.9	65.1	72.7
Philippines	Cebu	...	71.6	67.6	3.8	...	...	...	...	...	...
Qatar	Doha	...	...	...	...	...	...	...	...	...	...
Republic of Korea	Hanam	1.5	65.9	77.7	0.2	98.8	97.9	99.9	99.9	...	...
Republic of Korea	Pusan	2.1	65.9	77.7	0.8	95.9	94.9	99.7	99.8	...	...
Republic of Korea	Seoul	1.1	65.9	77.7	0.2	98.8	97.9	99.9	99.9	...	...
Singapore	Singapore	4.0	79.2	75.0	...	93.0	100.0	100.0	100.0	89.2	96.8
Sri Lanka	Colombo	18.0	...	...	...	...	...	...	...	...	...
Syrian Arab Republic	Damascus	...	...	...	3.2	46.0	62.0	...	...	89.0	96.0
Thailand	Bangkok	15.9	79.0	76.0	3.3	...	...	...	...	95.1	98.4
Thailand	Chiang Mai	9.7	71.0	66.0	3.3	...	...	...	...	90.0	93.0
Turkey	Ankara	14.9	...	...	4.2	...	...	...	...	...	...
Vietnam	Hanoi	2.1	69.6	64.9	4.2	...	...	...	...	89.0	95.1
Vietnam	Ho Chi Minh	10.6	69.6	64.9	4.2	...	...	...	...	89.5	95.1
Yemen	Sana'a	...	...	...	9.6	...	...	...	...	...	...
EUROPE											
Albania	Tirana	18.7	76.0	70.0	...	48.4	51.6	48.0	52.0	50.1	49.9
Belarus	Minsk	17.9	76.0	65.1	1.0	...	...	...	...	...	...
Bosnia and Herzegovina	Sarajevo	...	...	...	1.4	...	...	...	...	...	...
Bulgaria	Bourgas	...	74.8	67.9	1.0	...	...	...	...	99.0	99.0
Bulgaria	Sofia	55.0	74.3	67.1	1.3	...	...	...	...	99.5	99.8
Bulgaria	Troyan	6.4	74.5	67.6	0.5	100.0	100.0	100.0	100.0	99.8	...
Bulgaria	Veliko Tarnovo	...	74.3	67.1	1.5	...	...	...	...	...	...
Croatia	Zagreb	2.5	77.0	68.0	...	...	...	...	...	99.5	99.9
Czech Republic	Brno	11.0	77.6	70.8	0.6	...	...	...	...	100.0	100.0
Czech Republic	Prague	1.1	78.1	71.1	0.6	100.0	100.0	96.7	99.5	99.7	99.7
Estonia	Riik	3.6	76.0	64.7	...	100.0	100.0	100.0	100.0	100.0	100.0
Estonia	Tallin	1.9	73.8	62.5	...	100.0	100.0	100.0	100.0	100.0	100.0
Germany	Berlin	15.8	...	...	0.1	78.4	87.7	...	...	...	...
Germany	Cologne	11.2	...	...	0.1	80.6	87.9	...	...	...	...
Germany	Duisburg	11.2	...	...	0.1	69.9	85.6	...	...	...	...
Germany	Erfurt	6.8	...	...	0.3	...	...	88.9	88.3	...	...
Germany	Freiburg	8.5	...	...	0.1	...	...	95.2	96.5	...	...
Germany	Leipzig	11.2	...	...	0.1	69.9	85.6	...	...	...	...
Germany	Wiesbaden	6.3	...	...	0.1	...	...	81.2	89.0	...	...
Hungary	Budapest	...	75.5	67.9	0.9	...	...	...	...	...	...
Italy	Aversa	14.2	...	...	0.6	...	...	...	...	...	...
Latvia	Riga	...	75.9	65.2	1.4	...	...	...	...	99.7	100.0
Lithuania	Vilnius	16.0	76.9	66.5	1.1	...	...	...	...	...	...

TABLE C.4

continued

		Households in poverty (%)	Life expectancy: Female (years)	Life expectancy: Male (years)	Under five mortality rate	Gross school enrolment ratio: Primary: Female (%)	Gross school enrolment ratio: Primary: Male (%)	Gross school enrolment ratio: Secondary: Female (%)	Gross school enrolment ratio: Secondary: Male (%)	Literacy rate: Female (%)	Literacy rate: Male (%)
Netherlands	Amsterdam	...	...	...	1.0	...	...	...	...	100.0	100.0
Netherlands	Eindhoven	...	...	...	...	...	...	...	...	100.0	100.0
Netherlands	Meppel	...	...	...	...	...	...	...	...	100.0	100.0
Poland	Bydgoszcz	8.0	76.5	68.8	1.4	98.0	98.8	91.0	90.0	99.0	99.0
Poland	Gdansk	4.9	77.0	69.0	0.6	99.4	99.4	100.0	100.0	99.9	99.9
Poland	Katowice	3.6	76.6	67.8	1.2	100.0	100.0	100.0	87.7	99.5	98.5
Poland	Poznan	5.9	76.7	69.3	0.8	99.7	99.3	96.3	97.8	99.9	99.9
Republi of Moldova	Chisinau	...	...	...	2.2	...	...	...	...	...	...
Russian Federation	Astrakhan	34.4	72.6	60.0	2.6	100.0	99.0	98.0	93.0	97.4	99.6
Russian Federation	Belgorod	19.9	75.4	64.5	1.5	99.0	99.0	100.0	100.0	97.9	99.8
Russian Federation	Kostroma	26.7	73.0	61.5	2.0	100.0	98.0	100.0	100.0	98.8	99.8
Russian Federation	Moscow	17.6	73.8	62.8	1.6	100.0	100.0	100.0	100.0	97.6	99.7
Russian Federation	Nizhny Novgorod	21.5	73.7	61.4	1.6	100.0	99.0	100.0	100.0	98.2	99.8
Russian Federation	Novomoscowsk	23.0	71.2	58.1	1.9	100.0	100.0	100.0	100.0	96.7	99.4
Russian Federation	Omsk	25.2	73.7	63.0	1.8	100.0	100.0	100.0	100.0	97.6	99.7
Russian Federation	Pushkin	27.2	74.4	63.8	1.4	100.0	100.0	100.0	100.0	99.4	99.9
Russian Federation	Surgut	15.3	74.3	63.4	1.5	100.0	99.0	100.0	98.0	97.3	99.5
Russian Federation	Veliky Novgorod	18.8	71.9	57.9	1.4	100.0	100.0	100.0	100.0	98.9	99.9
Serbia and Montenegro	Belgrade	48.0	74.5	68.8	1.3	98.7	97.5	94.0	89.0	97.9	99.6
Slovenia	Ljubljana	5.5	78.0	71.0	0.7	94.7	94.6	94.0	89.5	100.0	100.0
Spain	Madrid	9.9	82.7	75.2	0.6	100.0	100.0	98.3	98.1	98.1	99.3
Spain	Pamplona	3.9	...	...	0.7	100.0	100.0	87.4	88.1	99.3	99.6
Sweden	Amal	3.4	81.2	75.5	0.5	100.0	100.0	...	...	...	...
Sweden	Stockholm	5.6	75.8	81.4	0.5	100.0	100.0	...	...	...	...
Sweden	Umea	4.6	81.5	76.7	0.5	100.0	100.0	...	...	...	...
Switzerland	Basel	7.1	82.5	76.5	...	...	...	...	...	...	...
United Kingdom	Belfast	...	...	...	0.5	100.0	100.0	100.0	100.0	...	...
United Kingdom	Birmingham	...	...	...	0.9	100.0	100.0	100.0	100.0	78.0	80.0
United Kingdom	Cardiff	...	...	...	0.8	100.0	100.0	100.0	100.0	77.0	75.0
United Kingdom	Edinburgh	...	...	...	0.7	100.0	100.0	100.0	100.0	78.0	76.0
United Kingdom	London	...	...	...	0.7	100.0	100.0	100.0	100.0	78.0	80.0
United Kingdom	Manchester	...	...	...	0.8	100.0	100.0	100.0	100.0	78.0	80.0
LATIN AMERICA AND CARIBBEAN											
Argentina	Buenos Aires	4.4	...	...	4.2	...	...	...	...	...	...
Argentina	Comodoro Rivadavia	17.6	74.0	67.3	...	...	...	...	...	97.8	98.4
Argentina	Córdoba	26.8	78.7	71.6	4.0	...	...	...	...	...	...
Argentina	Rosario	27.2	75.7	71.7	0.3	98.8	99.1	...	...	98.0	98.0
Barbados	Bridgetown	9.0	...	...	...	...	...	...	...	...	...
Belize	Belize City	18.8	71.8	68.2	3.2	69.9	79.2	67.9	58.8	75.0	75.0
Bolivia	Santa Cruz de la Sierra	40.1	67.7	64.2	7.8	86.8	92.0	51.0	52.5	...	...
Brazil	Belém	...	...	...	4.0	...	...	...	...	...	...
Brazil	Icapui	...	...	...	4.0	30.2	27.9	4.9	2.9	12.0	9.8
Brazil	Maranguape	40.5	...	...	4.0	...	...	...	...	...	...
Brazil	Porto Alegre	...	76.2	66.2	4.0	92.3	93.0	57.4	51.0	...	...
Brazil	Recife	44.4	...	...	5.8	...	...	...	...	86.7	89.6
Brazil	Rio de Janeiro	17.0	...	...	4.0	...	...	...	...	...	...
Brazil	São Paulo	6.5	76.2	67.3	2.0	...	...	...	...	92.2	94.7
Chile	Gran Concepcion	19.8	78.4	72.4	1.4	...	...	...	...	...	...
Chile	Santiago de Chile	4.7	...	...	...	...	...	...	...	...	...
Chile	Tome	16.9	...	...	1.2	...	...	...	...	...	...
Chile	Valparaiso	18.2	...	...	...	49.6	51.0	51.3	47.2	...	...
Chile	Vina del mar	11.6	...	...	...	...	...	...	...	...	...
Colombia	Armenia	17.9	65.4	72.6	3.2	47.3	52.7	46.4	53.6	8.0	12.0
Colombia	Marinilla	31.3	71.3	64.0	2.8	41.8	43.3	35.9	31.2	81.0	77.0
Colombia	Medellín	...	72.5	62.5	...	95.9	94.0	98.0	85.8	...	...
Cuba	Baracoa	...	...	...	0.9	...	...	...	...	...	...
Cuba	Camaguey	...	...	...	0.9	...	...	...	...	...	...
Cuba	Cienfuegos	...	...	...	0.9	...	...	...	...	...	...
Cuba	Havana	...	...	...	0.9	...	...	...	...	...	...
Cuba	Pinar Del Rio	...	78.0	74.0	6.5	...	...	...	...	...	...
Cuba	Santa Clara	...	...	...	0.9	...	...	...	...	...	...
Dominican Republic	Santiago de los Caballeros	40.0	...	...	6.1	...	...	...	...	...	...
Ecuador	Ambato	...	...	...	3.7	...	...	...	...	...	...
Ecuador	Cuenca	...	75.0	66.1	...	94.6	97.5	64.5	67.7	93.2	97.5
Ecuador	Guayaquil	48.0	71.2	67.4	3.7	98.8	98.9	75.3	68.6	97.8	98.2
Ecuador	Manta	25.0	68.0	64.0	4.3	...	...	...	...	...	...
Ecuador	Puyo	...	50.3	61.0	3.7	...	...	...	...	...	...
Ecuador	Quito	11.5	77.1	71.7	3.7	100.0	100.0	94.2	97.3	95.6	...
Ecuador	Tena	...	64.8	56.6	3.7	...	...	...	...	...	...
El Salvador	San Salvador	27.4	74.7	70.1	3.2	...	...	...	...	...	...
Guatemala	Quetzaltenango	...	67.2	62.9	4.6	...	...	...	...	...	...
Jamaica	Kingston	10.1	...	...	2.4	...	...	...	...	...	...
Jamaica	Montego Bay	13.4	...	...	2.4	...	...	...	...	...	...
Mexico	Ciudad Juarez	70.0	75.0	70.0	4.9	...	...	...	...	...	...
Nicaragua	Leon	28.3	...	...	3.5	...	...	...	...	...	...
Panama	Colon	21.3	75.0	69.6	2.5	...	...	...	...	...	...
Paraguay	Asuncion	9.8	72.0	67.5	2.6	...	...	...	...	89.3	93.0

Peru	Cajamarca	60.0	68.0	70.0	5.0	...	...	...	...	...	...
Peru	Huanuco	...	...	...	5.5	...	...	...	...	...	...
Peru	Huaras	...	82.0	75.0	4.7	...	...	...	...	...	...
Peru	Iquitos	46.3	67.5	62.4	5.0	39.7	36.0	37.0	41.0	41.1	48.4
Peru	Lima	...	80.0	74.0	4.7	...	...	...	...	...	...
Peru	Tacna	14.7	70.9	65.9	...	49.0	51.1	49.8	50.2	92.0	92.0
Peru	Tumbes	26.0	75.0	80.0	3.7	...	...	...	...	...	...
Trinidad and Tobago	Port of Spain	...	...	...	2.8	...	...	...	...	89.8	85.8
Uruguay	Montevideo	15.4	76.1	68.6	1.9	100.0	100.0	100.0	93.9	98.3	98.6
NORTHERN AMERICA											
Canada	Hull	...	81.4	75.7	0.1	...	...	...	...	...	...
United States	Atlanta	11.0	...	...	0.2	...	...	...	...	...	...
United States	Birmingham-US	13.2	...	...	0.3	...	...	...	...	...	...
United States	Boston	9.3	...	...	0.1	...	...	...	...	...	...
United States	Des Moines	8.2	...	...	0.2	...	...	...	...	...	...
United States	Hartford	9.3	...	...	0.2	...	...	...	...	...	...
United States	Minneapolis-St. Paul	7.7	...	...	0.2	...	...	...	...	...	...
United States	New York	20.4	...	...	0.2	...	...	...	...	...	...
United States	Providence	11.5	...	...	0.2	...	...	...	...	...	...
United States	Salt Lake	8.9	...	...	0.2	...	...	...	...	...	...
United States	San Jose	9.0	...	...	0.1	...	...	...	...	...	...
United States	Seattle	7.8	...	...	0.1	...	...	...	...	...	...
United States	Tampa	13.6	...	...	0.2	...	...	...	...	...	...
United States	Washington, DC	8.2	...	...	0.2	...	...	...	...	...	...
OCEANIA											
Samoa	Apia	38.9	71.9	65.4	1.9	92.7	95.5	89.6	76.0	98.9	99.1

Source: UN-Habitat, 2002.

REFERENCES

Abrams, C. (1964) *Man's Struggle for Shelter in an Urbanizing World*. MIT Press, Cambridge, MA

ACHR (Asian Coalition for Housing Rights) (2002) *ACHR Newsletter*, Special Issue on Community Development Funds, **14**, February, Bangkok

ACHR (2004) 'Negotiating the right to stay in the city' *Environment and Urbanization* **16**(1): 9–25

ACHR, CODI (Community Organization Development Institute) and IIED (International Institute for Environment and Development) (2004) 'Catalysing pro-poor development: The role of savings and savings organizations', Key issues arising from an International Workshop on Housing Finance and Poverty, Bangkok, June, International Institute for Environment and Development, London

Ahn, H. H. (2002) '"Global capitalism" and the transition in South Korean housing finance' in G. Dymski and D. Isenberg (eds) *Seeking Shelter on the Pacific Rim: Financial Globalization, Social Change and the Housing Market*. M.E. Sharpe, London and New York

Albee, A. and N. Gamage (1996) *Our Money, Our Movement*. Intermediate Technology Publications, London.

Alimuddin, S., A. Hasan and A. Sadiq (2004) 'The work of the Anjuman Samaji Behbood in Faisalabad' in D. Mitlin and D. Satterthwaite (eds) *Empowering Squatter Citizen*. Earthscan, London, pp139–161

Alm, J., J. A. Holman and R. M. Neumann (2002) *Globalization and State/Local Government Finances*. World Bank, Washington, DC

Al-Mansoori, M. A. J. (1997) 'Government low-cost housing in the United Arab Emirates: The Example of the Federal Government Low-Cost Housing Programme' PhD thesis, University of Newcastle upon Tyne, Newcastle upon Tyne, UK

Angel, S. (2002) *Housing Policy Matters*. Oxford University Press, London and New York

Anzonera, J., J. Bolnick, S. Boonyabancha, Y. Cabannes, A. Hardoy, A. Hassan, C. Levy, D. Mitlin et al (1998) 'Reducing urban poverty: Some lessons from experience' *Environment and Urbanization* **10**(1): 167–186

Aphimeteetamrong, V. and B. Kritayanavaj (1998) 'Integrating housing finance and capital markets in Thailand' in M. Watanabe (ed) *New Directions in Asian Housing Finance*. International Finance Corporation, Washington, DC, pp221–235

Arimah, B. C. (2000) 'Housing sector performance in global perspective: A cross-city investigation' *Urban Studies* **37**(13): 2551–2579

Arrossi, S., F. Bombarolo, J. Hardoy, D. Mitlin, L. P. Coscio and D. Satterthwaite (1994) *Funding Community Initiatives*. Earthscan, London

Ashworth, A. (1993) 'How life cycle costing can improve existing costing' in J. W. Bull (ed) *Life Cycle Costing for Construction*. Blackie Academic and Professional, Glasgow

Avault, J., Consalvo, R. and Lewis, G. (2000) *Survey of Linkage Programs in Other U.S. Cities with Comparisons to Boston*. Boston Redevelopment Authority, Boston

Baëta Ansah, S. (2002) 'Financing adequate shelter for all in Africa' in UN-Habitat (ed) *Financing Adequate Shelter for All: Addressing the Housing Finance Problem in Development Countries*. UN-Habitat, Nairobi, pp55–61

Baken, R.-J. and P. Smets (1999) 'Better a "hut" on the ground than a castle in the air: Formal and informal housing finance for the urban poor in India' in K. Datta and G. Jones (eds) *Housing Finance in Developing Countries*. Routledge, London, pp101–118

Ballesteros, M. M.(2002) 'Rethinking institutional reforms in the Philippine housing sector' *Discussion Paper Series* No 2002–16, Philippine Institute for Development Studies (PIDS)

Ballesteros, M. M. and D. C. Vertido (2004) 'Can group credit work for housing loans? Some evidence from the CMP' *Policy Notes* No 2004–05, Philippine Institute for Development Studies (PIDS)

Bamberger, M., B. Sanyal and N. Valverde (1982) *Evaluation of Sites and Services Projects: The Experience from Lusaka, Zambia*. World Bank, Washington, DC

Basu, A., R. Blavy and M.Yulek (2004) 'Microfinance in Africa: Experience and lessons from selected African countries' *IMF Working Paper* No WP/04/174

Batley, R. (1996) 'Public–private relationships and performance in service provision' *Urban Studies* **33**(4–5): 723–752

Baumann, T. (2003) 'Housing policy and poverty in South Africa' in F. Khan and P. Thring (eds) *Housing Policy and Practice in Post-apartheid South Africa*. Heinemann, Johannesburg

Baumann, T. (2004) *Housing Finance in South Africa*, mimeo

Baumann, T. and J. Bolnick (2001) 'Out of the frying pan into the fire; the limits of loan finance in a capital subsidy context' *Environment and Urbanization* **13**(2): 103–116

Baumann, T., J. Bolnick and D. Mitlin (2004) 'The age of cities and organizations of the urban poor: The work of the South African Homeless People's Organization' in D. Mitlin and D. Satterthwaite (eds)

Empowering Squatter Citizen. Earthscan, London, pp193–215

Baumann, T. and D. Mitlin (2003) 'The South African Homeless People's Federation: Investing in the poor' *Small Enterprise Development* **14**(1): 32–41

Beier, G., A. Churchill, M. Cohen and B. Renaud (1976) 'The task ahead facing developing countries: 1975–2000' *World Development* **4** (5): 314–332

Bird, R. and E. Slack (2003) *Fiscal Aspects of Metropolitan Governance*. Inter-American Development Bank, Washington, DC

Birdsall, N. (2001) 'Why inequality matters: Some economic issues' *Ethics and International Affairs* **15**(2):3–28

Biswas, S. (2003), 'Housing is a productive asset – housing finance for self-employed women in India' *Small Enterprise Development* **14**(1):49–55

Boonyabancha, S. (2004) 'A decade of change: From the Urban Community Development Office to the Community Organization Development Institute in Thailand' in D. Mitlin and D. Satterthwaite (eds) *Empowering Squatter Citizen*. Earthscan, London, pp25–53

Boston Housing Authority (2000) *Leading the Way – A Report on Boston's Housing Strategy FY 2001–FY2003.* Boston Redevelopment Authority, Boston

Boston Housing Authority (2002) *Leading the Way – A Report on Boston's Housing Strategy FY 2001-FY2003-A Midpoint Progress Report.* Boston Redevelopment Authority, Boston

Boston Housing Authority (2004) *Leading the Way 11 – A Report on Boston's Housing Strategy FY 2004–FY2007.* Boston Redevelopment Authority, Boston

Boston Municipal Research Bureau (1998) *Boston's Linkage Program: A New Approach to Managing Linkage Funds for Housing and Job Training.* City of Boston, Boston

Brakarz, J. (2003) *La convergencia de los fondos de crédito municipal y de inversión social: El caso de Bolivia*. Banco Interamericano de Desarrollo, Washington, DC

Buckey, R. (1996) *Housing Finance in Developing Countries*. MacMillan Press Ltd., London

Buckley, R. M. (1999) 'Housing finance in developing countries: A review of the World Bank's experience' in K. Datta and G. Jones (eds) *Housing and Finance in Developing Countries*. Routledge, London

Buckley, B. and J. Kalarickal (2004) 'Shelter strategies for the urban poor: Idiosyncratic and successful but hard mysterious', *World Bank Policy Research Working Paper 3427*, World Bank, Washington, DC

Buckley, R. and S. Mayo (1989) 'Housing policy in developing economies: Evaluating the macro-economic impacts' *Review of Urban and Regional Development Studies* **2**: 27–46

Buechler, S. (2000) 'The growth of the informal sector in São Paulo, Brazil' Paper prepared for National Academy of Sciences Panel on Urban Population Dynamics, New York

Bugie, S. (2004) 'The key to the development of mortgage funding in emerging markets' in *Introducing the Issues: 16 Expert Views.* Presented at International Union of Housing Finance 25th World Congress, June 2004, pp32–33

Burgess, R. (1982) 'Self-help housing advocacy: A curious form of radicalism – a critique of the work of John F. C. Turner' in P. M. Ward (ed) *Self-help Housing: A Critique*. Mansell, London.

Burgess, R. (1985) 'The limits of self-help housing' *Development and Change* **16**(2): 271–312

Cabannes, Y. (2002) 'Overview of community finance in Latin America' *HiFi News* **10**: 6–7

Cabannes, Y. (2004) 'Participatory budgeting: A significant contribution to participatory democracy' *Environment and Urbanization* **16**(1): 27–46

Calderón, J. (2004) 'The formalisation of property in Peru 2001–2002: The case of Lima' *Habitat International* **28**: 289–300

Carmon, N. (1992) 'Housing renovations in moderately deteriorated neighbourhoods: Public–individual partnership in Israel and its lessons' *Housing Studies* **7**(1): 56–73

Carney, D. (1998) 'Implementing the sustainable rural livelihoods approach' in D. Carney (ed) *Sustainable Rural Livelihoods: What Contribution Can We Make?* Department for International Development, London, pp3–23

Carolini, G. Y. (2004) *As Good As It Gets? A Survey of the US Housing Finance System and its Clientele*, mimeo

Cavalcanti, D., O. Marques and T. H. Costa (2004) 'Municipal programme for the report and extension of homes: Casa Melhor/PAAC Cearah Periferia, Brazil' in D. Mitlin and D. Satterthwaite (eds) *Empowering Squatter Citizen*. Earthscan, London, pp165–192

Center for Urban Development Studies (2000) *Housing Microfinance Initiatives*. Center for Urban Development Studies, University of Harvard Graduate School of Design, Harvard

CGAP (Consultative Group to Assist the Poor) (2004) *Housing Microfinance*, Donor Brief No 20. CGAP, Washington, DC

Chernyavsky, A. V. (undated) *Review of the Municipal Finance Development in Russia in 1992-2002.* Institute for Urban Economics, Washington DC

Chi-Man Hui, E. and B. Seabrooke (2000) 'The housing allowance scheme in Guangzhou' *Habitat International* **24**: 19–29

Chin Beng, Y. (2002) 'The experience of Singapore in financing housing for the middle and low-income groups', International Conference on Social Housing, United Nations Human Settlements Programme, Ministry of Construction of People's Republic of China and Baotou Municipal Government, Baotou, People's Republic of China

Chiquier, L., O. Hassler and M. Lea (2004) 'Mortgage securities in emerging markets', *World Bank Policy Research Working Paper 3370*. World Bank, Washington, DC

Christen, R. P. (2004) 'Foreward' in F. Daphnis and B. Ferguson (eds) *Housing Micro-finance: A Guide to Practice*. Kumarian Press Ltd., Bloomfield, US, ppix–xiv

Cities Alliance (2000) 'Cities Alliance: Cities without slums', www.citiesalliance.org/citiesalliancehomepage.nsf/, accessed 30 November 2004

Cities Alliance (2002) 'Sewa Bank's housing microfinance program in India' *Shelter Finance for the Poor Series*. Cities Alliance, Washington, DC

Cleaver, F. (2004) 'The social embeddedness of agency and decision-making' in S. Hickey and G. Mohan (eds) *Participation: From Tyranny to Transformation*. Zed Books, London, 271–276

CMP (Community Mortgage Programme) Bulletin (2004) 'National Congress of CMP Originators and Social Development Organizations for Low-income Housing', January

CODI (Community Organization Development Institute) (2004) *Codi Update* **4** (June)

Cohen, M. (1987) 'Macroeconomic adjustment and the city' *Cities* **7**(1): 49–59

Cohen, M. A. (1998) 'Stock and flow in metropolitan investment' *Brookings Review* **16**(4): 37–39

Cohen, M. A. and D. Debowicz (2004) 'The five cities of Buenos Aires: Poverty and inequality' in S. Sassen (ed) *UNESCO Encyclopedia of Sustainable Development*. UNESCO, Paris

Collyns C. and A. Senhadji (2002) 'Lending booms, real estate bubbles and the Asian Crisis' *IMF Working Paper WP/02/20*. International Monetary Fund, Washington, DC

Connolly, P. (2004a) 'The Mexican National Popular Housing Fund' in D. Mitlin and D. Satterthwaite (eds) *Empowering Squatter Citizen*. Earthscan, London, pp82–111

Connolly, P. (2004b) *Housing Finance in Mexico*, mimeo

Co-operative Housing Foundation (1993) 'Supporting shelter and community improvements for low-income families in Central America' *Environment and Urbanization* **5**(1): 38–51

Coovadia, C. (2004) 'Housing finance in Africa' in *Introducing the Issues: 16 Expert Views*. Presented at International Union of Housing Finance 25th World Congress, June 2004, pp10–11

Costa, R. (2002) 'Hogar de Cristo – Ecuador: 30 Years!' *SELAVIP Newsletter* (2002) April: 39–40

Cotton, A. P., M. Souhail and W. K. Taylor (1998) *Community Initiatives in Urban Infrastructure*. Water, Engineering and Development Centre, University of Loughborough, Loughborough, UK

Counts, A. (1996). *Give Us Credit: How Muhammad Yunus's Micro Lending Revolution Is Empowering Women from Bangladesh to Chicago*. Random House, New York

Cummings, J. and D. Di Pasquale (1997) *The Spatial Implications of Housing Policy in Chile*, mimeo. City Research, Boston

D'Arista, A. (1998) 'Comment on "Housing finance in the age of globalization: From social housing to life-cycle risk"' in D. Baker, G. Epstein and R. Pollin (eds) *Globalization and Progressive Economic Policy*. Cambridge University Press, Cambridge

D'Cruz, C. (2004a) 'Securitization of mortgage portfolios in Latin America: The Chilean case' *Housing Finance International* March: 15–20

D'Cruz, C. (2004b) *Slum Dwellers International: Local Voices, Global Goals*, mimeo. Yale University, US

D'Cruz C. and D. Mitlin (2005) 'Shack/Slum Dwellers International: One experience of the contribution of membership organizations to pro-poor urban development', Paper presented to the conference on Membership Bases Organizations of the Poor: Theory, Experience and Policy, 17–21 January 2005, Ahmedabad, India

Dale-Johnson, D. and G. Towle (2002) 'The Mexican mortgage market: Has the ship come in?' *Housing Finance International* June, **19**(2): 19–32

Daphnis, F. (2004a) 'Housing micro-finance: Toward a definition' in F. Daphnis and B. Ferguson (eds) *Housing Micro-finance: A Guide to Practice*. Kumarian Press Ltd., Bloomfield, pp1–14

Daphnis, F. (2004b) 'Elements of product design for housing micro-finance' in F. Daphnis and B. Ferguson (eds) *Housing Micro-finance: A Guide to Practice*. Kumarian Press Ltd., Bloomfield, pp85–114

Daphnis, F. and B. Ferguson, (2004) (eds) *Housing Micro-finance: A Guide to Practice*. Kumarian Press Ltd., Bloomfield, US

Datta, K. (1999), 'A gendered perspective on formal and informal housing finance in Botswana' in G. Jones and K. Datta (eds) *Housing and Finance in Developing Countries*. Routledge, London, pp192–212

David, P. (2004) 'Public mortgage experience: The Canadian experience' in *Introducing the Issues: 16 Expert Views*. Presented at International Union of Housing Finance 25th World Congress, June 2004, pp26–27

Davies, G. and E. Mahony (2001) *Housing Microfinance: Building the Assets of the Poor, One Room at a Time*. John F Kennedy School of Government, Harvard University, US

De Soto, H. (2002) *The Mystery of Capital: Why Capitalism Triumphs in the West and Fails Everywhere Else*. Basic Books, New York

Department of Housing (2003) *A Social Housing Policy for South Africa*, www.housing.gov.za/Content/legislation_policies/Social%20Housing%20Policy.pdf

DFID (UK Department for International Development) (2004a) *Financial Sector Development: A Prerequisite for Growth and Poverty Reduction?*, www.dfid.gov.uk/pubs/files/fsdbriefingnote.pdf, accessed 2 September 2004

DFID (2004b) *Poverty Reduction Support: A DFID Policy Paper*. Department for International Development, London

Diko, J. and A. G. Tipple (1992) 'Migrants build at home: Long distance housing development by Ghanaians in London' *Cities* **9** (4): 288–294

Dillinger, W. et al (1994) *Study on Ciudad*

Juarez. World Bank, Washington, DC

Douglass, M. (1997) 'Structural change and urbanization in Indonesia: From the "Old" to the "New" international division of labour' in G. W. Jones and P. Visara (eds) *Urbanization in Large Developing Countries: China, Indonesia, Brazil, and India*. Clarendon Press, Oxford

Dübel, A. (2004) 'Capital market funding for mortgages: Where do we stand, where do we go?' in *Introducing the Issues: 16 Expert Views*. Presented at International Union of Housing Finance 25th World Congress, June 2004: 28–29

Dymski, G. and D. Isenberg (1998) 'Housing finance in the age of globalization: From social housing to life-cycle risk' in D. Baker, G. Epstein and R. Pollin (eds) *Globalization and Progressive Economic Policy*. Cambridge University Press, Cambridge

Dymski, G. and D. Isenberg (eds) (2002) *Seeking Shelter on the Pacific Rim: Financial Globalization, Social Change and the Housing Market*. M.E. Sharpe, London and New York

Earley, F. (2004a) 'Challenges in the European housing markets' in *Introducing the Issues: 16 Expert Views*. Presented at International Union of Housing Finance 25th World Congress, June 2004, pp14–15

Earley, F. (2004b) 'The housing and mortgage markets in 2003' in European Mortgage Federation (ed) *Hypostat 2003: European Housing Finance Review*. European Mortgage Federation, Brussels, pp4–13

ECLAC (Economic Commission for Latin America and the Caribbean) (2003) *Statistical Yearbook*. ECLAC, Santiago

The Economist (2004) 'The global housing market: Flimsy foundations' *The Economist*, 11 December, pp77–78

Edwards, M. (1995) 'Public/private sector partnerships in housing provision: What are the Possibilities?' *Habitat Debate* **1**(4): 5

Environment and Urbanization (1993) Special issue on 'Funding community level initiatives: The role of NGOs and other intermediary institutions in funding and supporting low-income households to improve shelter, infrastructure and services' April **5** (1)

Environment and Urbanization (2001) Special issue on 'Civil society in action – transforming opportunities for the urban poor' October: **13** (2)

Escalante, C. (2004) 'Towards decentralised housing improvements policies in Peru' *Journal of Low-income Housing in Asia and the World*, April: 56–60

ESCAP (Economic and Social Commission for Asia and the Pacific) (1991), *Guidelines on Community Based Housing Finance and Innovative Credit Systems for Low-income Households*. United Nations, Bangkok

Escobar, A. (undated) *Part 1. Microfinance of Housing: State of the Practice*, mimeo

Escobar, A. and S. R. Merrill (2004) 'Housing micro-finance: The state of the practice' in F. Daphnis and B. Ferguson (eds) *Housing Micro-finance: A Guide to Practice*, Kumarian Press Ltd., Bloomfield, US, pp33–68

EMF (European Mortgage Federation) (2004) *Hypostat 2003: European Housing Finance Review*. EMF, Brussels

Farha, L. and R. Goba (2003) 'Access denied: Canada's housing crisis' *Journal of Low-income Housing in Asia and the World* October: 21–23

Ferguson, B. (1999) 'Micro-finance of housing: A key to housing the low or moderate income majority?' *Environment and Urbanization* **11**(1): 185–200

Ferguson, B. (2002) 'A housing paradigm and new programmes for development countries: The Latin America case' in UN-Habitat (ed) *Financing Adequate Shelter for All: Addressing the Housing Finance Problem in Development Countries*. UN-Habitat, pp165–170

Ferguson, B. (2003) 'Housing microfinance – a key to improving habitat and the sustainability of microfinance institutions' *Small Enterprise Development* **14**(1): 21–31

Ferguson, B. (2004a) 'The key importance of housing micro-finance' in F. Daphnis and B. Ferguson (eds) *Housing Micro-finance: A Guide to Practice*. Kumarian Press Ltd., Bloomfield, US, pp15–32

Ferguson, B. (2004b) 'Scaling up housing micro-finance: A guide to practice' *Housing Finance International*, September: 3–13

Ferguson, B. and J. Navarrete (2003) 'A financial framework for reducing slums: Lessons from experience in Latin America' *Environment and Urbanization* **15**(2): 201–216

Fernandez, V. (2004) *Housing Finance – the Case of Chile*, mimeo

Flood, J. (2004) *Cost Estimate for Millennium Development Goal 7, Target 11 on Slums*, Background Report prepared for UN Millennium Project Task Force 8 and UN-Habitat, available at www.unmillennium project.org

Forero, E. (2004) 'Evolution of the mortgage system in Colombia: From the UPAC to the UVR system' *Housing Finance International*, March: 32–41.

Forrest, R., P. Kennett and M. Izuhara (2003) 'Home ownership and economic change in Japan' *Housing Studies* **18**(3): 277–293

Frank, D. (2004) 'A market-based housing improvement system for low-income families – the Housing Incentive System (SIV) in Ecuador' *Environment and Urbanization* **16**(1): 171–184

Freedom to Build (2004) 'Freedom to Build' *Journal of Low-income Housing in Asia and the World* April: 75–78

Freire, M. and M. Polese (2003) *Connecting Cities with Macro-economic Concerns: The Missing Link*. World Bank, Washington, DC

Freire, M. et al (2004) *Sub-sovereign Credit Access and Infrastructure Financing in Four East Asian Countries: China, Philippines, Indonesia, and Vietnam – Phase One: A Reconnaissance*. World Bank, Washington, DC

Fruet, G. M. (2005) 'The low-income housing cooperatives in Porto Alegre, Brazil: A state/community partnership' *Habitat International* **29**: 303–324

Fry, M. and Drew, J. (1964) *Tropical Architecture in a Humid Zone*. Batsford, London

Fujita, K. (2000) 'Asian crisis, financial systems and urban development' *Urban Studies* **37**(12): 2197–2216

Gadzama, H. M. (2002) 'Experiences of housing finance operations in Nigeria and lessons to be learnt from these experiences' in UN-Habitat (ed) *Financing Adequate Shelter for All: Addressing the Housing Finance Problem in Development Countries*. UN-Habitat, Nairobi: 68–82

Gallarado, J. (1998) 'Rationalising housing finance and developing capital markets in the Philippines' in M. Watanabe (ed) *New Directions in Asian Housing Finance*. International Finance Corporation, Washington, DC: 199–221

Gaye, M. and F. Diallo (1997) 'Community participation in the management of the urban environment in Rufisque' *Environment and Urbanization* **9**(1): 9–30

Ghouri, N. S. and H. Nihal (1993) 'The housing loan programme of the Catholic Social Services in Karachi' *Environment and Urbanization* **5**(1): 18–25

Gibb, K. (2002) 'Trends and change in social housing finance and provision within the European Union' *Housing Studies* **17**(2): 325–336

Gilbert, A. (1999) 'A home is for ever? Residential mobility and home ownership in self-help settlements', *Environment and Planning* **A**: 1073–1091

Gilbert, A. (2000) 'What might South Africa have learned about housing subsidies from Chile?' *South African Geographical Journal* **82** (1): 21–29

Gilbert, A. (2002a) 'Power, ideology and the Washington Consensus: The development and spread of Chilean housing policy' *Housing Studies* **17**(2): 305–324

Gilbert, A. (2002b) 'On the mystery of capital and the myths of Hernando de Soto' *International Development Planning Review* **24**(1): 1–19

Gilbert, A. (2004) 'Helping the poor through housing subsidies: Lessons from Chile, Colombia and South Africa' *Habitat International* **28**: 13–40

Gitau, S. (2004) *Part C: Housing Finance Conditions and Trends in Africa*, mimeo

Goetz, M. and R. Sen Gupta (1996) 'Who takes the credit? Gender power and control over loan use in rural credit programs in Bangladesh' *World Development* **24** (1): 45–64

Gold, J., A. Muller and D. Mitlin (2002) 'The principles of Local Agenda 21in Windhoek: Collective action and the urban poor', *Working Paper on Local Agenda 21s and Urban Environmental Action Plans* No 9. International Institute for Environment and Development, London

Gonzáles de Kauffman, M. and H. Rincón (2004) 'Information on micro-credit experience: Programma Ciudadanía Plena, Maracaibo, Venezuela', Presentation to an International Workshop on Housing Finance and poverty, June 2004, Bangkok

Gordon, A. (1999) 'Informal finance and women's survival strategies: Case studies from Cameroon and Zambia' in G. Jones and K. Datta (eds) *Housing and Finance in Developing Countries*. Routledge, London: 181–191

Gough, K. (1999), 'Affording a home: The strategies of self-help builders in Colombia' in G. Jones and K. Datta (eds) *Housing and Finance in Developing Countries*. Routledge, London: 119–135

Government of Tanzania and UN-Habitat (United Nations Human Settlements Programme) (2003) *Re-establishing Effective Housing Finance Mechanisms in Tanzania: The Potentials and the Bottlenecks*. UN-Habitat, Nairobi

Graham, S. and S. Marvin (2001) *Splintering Urbanism: Networked Infrastructures, Technological Mobilities and the Urban Condition*. Routledge, London

Grameen Bank (2004) *Newsletter* July, www.grameen-info.org

Groves, R. (2004) 'Challenges facing the provision of affordable housing in African cities' *Housing Finance International* June: 26–31

Gulyani, S. and G. Connors (2002) 'Urban upgrading in Africa: A summary of rapid assessment in ten countries', available at http://web.mit.edu/urbanupgrading/upgrading/case-examples/overview-africa/country-assessments/index.html

Guttentag, J. (2004) 'Protection of the mortgage borrowers in the US' in *Introducing the Issues: 16 Expert Views*. Presented at International Union of Housing Finance 25th World Congress, June 2004, p17

Ha, S. (2002a) 'The evolving role of the Korean government in low-income housing' in G. Dymski and D. Isenberg (eds) *Seeking Shelter on the Pacific Rim: Financial Globalization, Social Change and the Housing Market*. M.E. Sharpe, London and New York

Ha, S. (2002b) 'The urban poor, rental accommodations and housing policy in Korea' *Cities* **19**(3): 195–203

Hanchett, S., S. Akhter and M. Hoque Khan (2003) 'Water, sanitation and hygiene in Bangladesh slums: An evaluation of the WaterAid–Bangladesh urban programme' *Environment and Urbanization* **15**(2): 43–56

Hardoy, J. and D. Satterthwaite (1989) *Squatter Citizen*. Earthscan Publications, London

Harris, J. R. and M. P. Todaro (1970) 'Migration, unemployment and development: A two-sector analysis' *American Economic Review* **60**:126–142

Harris, R. and G. Arku (2004) *Housing and Economic Development: The History of an Idea*. School of Geography and Geology, McMaster University, Hamilton, Ontario

Hart, K. (1973) 'Informal income opportunities and urban employment in Ghana' *Journal of African Studies* March: 151–164

Hegedüs, J. (2002) *Housing Finance in South-eastern Europe*. Metropolitan Research Institute, Budapest.

Hegedüs, J. (2004) 'Social housing experiences in East European transition countries', Paper presented at the EHNR (European Network for Housing Research) International Housing Conference, 2–4 July, Cambridge, UK

Hegedüs, J. and N. Teller (2003) 'Management of the housing stock in south-eastern Europe', Paper prepared for the joint programme of the Council of Europe–Council of Europe Development Bank to the preparation of a high-level conference on housing in Southern Europe, mimeo

Helao, A. N. (2004) 'Ministry regional and local government and housing: The Build Together program', Presentation to an International Workshop on Housing Finance and Poverty, June, Bangkok

HiFi News (2002) Issue no 9, International Institute for Environment and Development, London

Ho, M. H. C. (2004) 'Privatisation of public housing in Hong Kong: A genuine agenda or propaganda' *Habitat International* **28**: 481–494

Hoek-Smit, M. (1998) 'Housing finance in Bangladesh: Improving access to housing finance by middle and lower income groups', Prepared for the Government of Bangladesh (Ministry of Local Government, Rural Development and Cooperatives) and UNDP/UNCHS (Habitat), Nairobi

Hoek-Smit, M. C. and D. B. Diamond (2003) 'Subsidies for housing finance' *Housing Finance International* **17**(3): 3–13

Hogar de Cristo (undated) *Our Mission*, www.hogardecristo.com/navegacion/home.asp, accessed 10 February 2005

Huchzermeyer, M. (2003) 'A legacy of control: The capital subsidy for housing and informal settlement intervention in South Africa' *International Journal of Urban and Regional Research* **27**(3): 591–612

Hulme, D. (2000) 'Is microdebt good for poor people? A note on the dark side of microfinance' *Small Enterprise Development* **11**(1): 26–28

IADB (Inter-American Development Bank) (1998) *Facing Up to Inequality in Latin America*. IADB, Washington, DC

IADB (2003) *Colombia: Urban Social Housing Program – Loan Proposal*. IADB, Washington, DC

ILO (International Labour Organization) (1972). *Employment, Income and Equality: A Strategy for Increasing Productive Employment in Kenya*. ILO, Geneva

IMF (International Monetary Fund) (2004) *World Economic Outlook*. IMF, Washington, DC

IMF and IDA (International Development Association) (2004) 'Debt sustainability in low-income countries: Proposal for an operational framework and policy implications', 3 February, IMF and IDA, Washington, DC

Itoh, M. (2002) 'Housing finance in Japanese financial instability' in G. Dymski and D. Isenberg (eds) *Seeking Shelter on the Pacific Rim: Financial Globalization, Social Change and the Housing Market*. M.E. Sharpe, London and New York: 150–168

Jacobs, M. and W. D. Savedoff (1999) 'There's more than one way to get a house: Housing strategies in Panama', *Working Paper No 392*. Inter-American Development Bank, Washington, DC

Jain, A. K. (2003) 'Actioning new partnerships for Indian cities', *Cities* **20**: 353–359

Jiminez, E. (1982) 'The economics of self help housing: Theory and some evidence from a developing country', *Journal of Urban Economics* **2**: 205–228

Jiron, M. P. and G. Fadda (2003) 'A quality of life assessment to improve urban and housing policies in Chile', Paper presented to the World Bank Urban Research Symposium, December 2003, Washington, DC

Joint Center for Housing Studies at the University of Harvard (2004) *The State of Mexico's Housing Finance*. Joint Center for Housing Studies at the University of Harvard, Harvard, US

Jones, G. and K. Datta (eds) (1999) *Housing and Finance in Developing Countries*. Routledge, London: 26–43

Jones, G. and D. Mitlin (1999) 'Housing finance and non–governmental organizations in developing countries' in G Jones and K. Datta (eds) *Housing and Finance in Developing Countries* Routledge. London: 26–43.

Jones, G. A. and R. A. Pisa (2000) 'Public–private partnerships for urban land development in Mexico: A victory for hope versus expectation? Charting changes in governance in the Mexican municipality' *Habitat International* **24**(1): 1–18

Kabir, A. H. M. (2002) 'Development and human rights: Litigating the right to adequate housing' *Asia–Pacific Journal on Human Rights and the Law* **1**: 97–119

Karley, N. K. (2002) 'Alternative options to mortgages in Ghana' *Housing Finance International* **17**(2): 26–30

Karley, N. K. and Whitehead, C. (2002) 'The mortgage-based securities market in the UK: Developments over the last few years' *Housing Finance International* December: 31–36

Kamete, A. Y. (2000) 'The practice of cost recovery in urban low-income housing: A discourse with experiences from Zimbabwe' *Habitat International* **24**: 241–260

Karnad, R. S. (2004) 'Housing finance and the economy: Regional trends, South Asia perspectives', Presentation to the 25th World Congress, International Union for Housing Finance, June

Kasongo, B. A. and A. G. Tipple (1990) 'An analysis of policy towards squatters in Kitwe, Zambia', *Third World Planning Review* **12** (1): 27–46

Keare, D. H. (1983) 'Assessing project impacts' in Y. M. Yeung (ed) *A Place to Live: More Effective Low-cost Housing in Asia*. Ottawa, IDRC

Keare, D. H. and S. Parris (1982) *Evaluation of Shelter Programs for the Urban Poor: Principal Findings*. World Bank, Washington, DC

Keivani, R. and E. Werna (2001) 'Refocusing the housing debate in developing countries from a pluralistic perspective' *Habitat International* **25**(2): 191–208

Kessides, C. (1997) 'World Bank experience with the provision of infrastructure services for the urban poor: Preliminary identification and review of best practices', www.worldbank.org/urban/publicat/alpha.html, accessed 10 September 2004

Kevane, M. and B. Wydick (2001) 'Microenterprise lending to female entrepreneurs: Sacrificing economic growth for poverty alleviation?' *World Development* **29**(7): 1225–1236

Kim, K.-H. (1997) 'Improving local government finance in a changing environment', *Habitat International* **21**(1): 17–28

Kim, S. H. and H. H. Ahn (2002) 'The peculiar "publicness" of housing in South Korea' in G. Dymski and D. Isenberg (eds) *Seeking Shelter on the Pacific Rim: Financial Globalization, Social Change and the Housing Market*. M.E. Sharpe, London and New York

Klaassen, L. H., J. G. D. Hoogland and M. J. van Pelt (1987) 'Economic impact and implications of shelter investments' in L. Rodwin (ed) *Shelter, Settlement and Development*. Allen and Unwin, Boston

Klopfer, E. (2004) 'Two cheers for private mortgage insurance' in *Introducing the Issues: 16 Expert Views*. Presented at International Union of Housing Finance 25th World Congress, June 2004: 24–25

Koenigsberger, O. (1973) *Manual of Tropical Housing and Building*. Longmans, London

Kosareva, N. and A. Puzanov (2000) *The Implications of Globalization and Privatization for the Provision of and Access to Housing and Urban Development in Transition Economies: Poverty, Inequity, Polarization*. Report prepared for UN–Habitat, Nairobi

Kritayanavaj, B. (2002) 'Financing affordable homeownership in Thailand: Roles of the government housing bank since the economic crisis (1997–2002)' *Housing Finance International* **17**(2): 15–25

Kumar Garg, Y. (1998) 'New directions in housing finance in India' in M. Watanabe (ed) *New Directions in Asian Housing Finance*. International Finance Corporation, Washington, DC: 83–112

La Grange, A. and N. Nam Jung (2004) 'The commodification of land and housing: The case of South Korea' *Housing Studies* **19**(4): 557–580

Lai, O.-K. (1998) 'Governance and the housing question in a transitional economy: The political economy of housing policy in China reconsidered' *Habitat International* **22**(3): 231–243

Lall, S. and V. D Lall (2003) 'ITDG integrated urban housing strategy experiences of a secondary town – Alwar', Paper presented to the International Workshop on Integrated Housing Development, 16–18 March 2003, Rugby, UK

Lambert, A. (2004) 'Consumer protection in the European Union' in *Introducing the Issues: 16 Expert Views*. Presented at International Union of Housing Finance 25th World Congress, June 2004: 18–19

Lamoreaux, P. (1998) 'Housing finance and capital markets: The Hong Kong experience' in M. Watanabe (ed) *New Directions in Asian Housing Finance*. International Finance Corporation, Washington, DC: 50–82

Laquian, A. A. (1983a) *Basic Housing: Policies for Urban Sites, Services and Shelter in Developing Countries*. International Development Research Centre, Ottawa, Canada

Laquian, A. A. (1983b) 'Sites, services and shelter – an evaluation' *Habitat International* **7**(5/6): 291–301

Lea, M. (2000) 'The role of the primary mortgage market in the development of a successful secondary mortgage market', *Sustainable Development Department Technical Papers Series*, Inter-American Development Bank, Washington, DC

Lea, M. (2004a) 'The US mortgage market, progress and prospects' in *Introducing the Issues: 16 Expert Views*. Presented at International Union of Housing Finance 25th World Congress, June 2004: 12–14

Lea, M. (2004b) 'Housing finance in the accession countries' in European Mortgage Federation (ed) *Hypostat 2003: European Housing Finance Review*. European Mortgage Federation, Brussels: 21–24

Lee, J. (2003) 'Mortgage securitization in Korea' *Housing Finance International* March: 24–30

Lee, J. and S. Lee (1998) 'Restructuring the housing finance system and broadening the linkage with capital markets in the Republic of Korea' in M. Watanabe (ed) *New Directions in Asian Housing Finance*. International Finance Corporation, Washington, DC: 157–183

Lee, K. S., A. Anas and G. T. Oh (1999) 'Costs of infrastructure deficiencies in manufacturing in Indonesia, Nigeria and Thailand' *Urban Studies* **36**(12): 2135–2149

Lewis, B. D. and Chakeri, J. (2004) 'Decentralized Local Government Budgets in Indonesia: What Explains the Large Stock of Reserves?' Unpublished manuscript, World Bank, Jakarta

Lincoln Institute of Land Policy (2002) *Access to Land by the Urban Poor*. Lincoln Institute of Land Policy, Cambridge, Massachusetts, US

Litvack, J., J. Ahmad and R. Bird (1998) 'Rethinking decentralization in developing countries', *Sector Studies Series*, World Bank, Washington, DC

Lohse, U. H. (2002) 'Housing finance – overview' in UN-Habitat (ed) *Financing Adequate Shelter for All: Addressing the Housing Finance Problem in Development Countries*. UN-Habitat, Nairobi: 41–47

Lykova, T., E. Petrova, S. Sivaev and R. Struyk (2004) 'Participation in a decentralised housing allowance programme in a transition economy' *Housing Studies* **19**(4): 617–634

Mahanga, M. M. (2002) 'Legislative and regulatory roadblocks to the effective and sustainable functioning of the housing finance system in African countries: The case of Tanzania', International Conference on Social Housing, United Nations Human Settlements Programme, Ministry of Construction of People's Republic of China and Baotou

Municipal Government, Baotou, People's Republic of China

Malhotra, M. (2003) 'Financing her home, one wall at a time' *Environment and Urbanization* **15**(2): 217–228

Malpezzi, S. and G. Ball (1991) *Rent Control in Developing Countries*. World Bank, Washington, DC

Malpezzi, S. J., A. G. Tipple and K. G. Willis (1990) *Costs and Benefits of Rent Control: A Case Study in Kumasi, Ghana*. World Bank, Washington, DC

Martin, R. (1983) 'Upgrading' in R. J. Skinner and M. J. Rodell (eds) *People, Poverty and Shelter: Problems of Self-help Housing in the Third World*. Methuen, London

Mathur, O. P. and Thakur, S. (2004) *India's Municipal Sector. A study for the 12th Finance Commission (TFC)*. National Institute of Public Finance and Policy, New Delhi

Mayo, S. (1999) 'Subsidies in housing', *Sustainable Development Department Technical Papers Series*, Inter-American Development Bank, Washington, DC

Mayo, S. K. and D. Gross (1987) 'Sites and services – and subsidies: The economics of low-cost housing in developing countries' *The World Bank Economic Review* **1** (2): 305–335

McAuslan, P. (1997) 'The making of the Urban Management Programme: Memoirs of a mendicant bureaucrat' *Urban Studies* **34**(10): 1705–1727

McLeod, R. (2002) 'Experiences of linking community-based housing finance in formal finance mechanisms' in UN-Habitat (ed) *Financing Adequate Shelter for All: Addressing the Housing Finance Problem in Development Countries*. UN–Habitat, Nairobi: 190–221

Meier, G. M. and J. E. Stiglitz (2000) *Frontiers of Development Economics*. World Bank and Oxford University Press, New York

Menon, B. et al (2003) *Cities in Transition: An Urban Sector Review of Indonesia*. Mimeo

Merrill, S. and D. Whiteley (2003) 'Establishing a mortgage guarantee insurance in transition and emerging markets: A case study of Kazakhstan' *Housing Finance International* September: 10–19

Mersmann, H. (2004) 'Mortgage guarantee systems around the world' in *Introducing the Issues: 16 Expert Views*. Presented at International Union of Housing Finance 25th World Congress, June 2004: 22–23

Milbert, I. and V. Peat (1999) *What Future for Urban Cooperation?* Swiss Agency for Development and Cooperation, Bern

Ministry of Regional, Local Government and Housing (2003) *Build Together National Housing Programme Implementation Programme, Third Revision*. Ministry for Regional, Local Government and Housing, Windhoek, Namibia

Mintz, G. (2003) 'Mortgage financing in developing countries', Paper presented to the Annual Meeting of the Association of Development Financing Institutions in Asia and the Pacific, www.citysailor.com/talks/Mortgage1.htm

Mitlin, D. (1997) 'Building with credit: housing finance for low-income households', *Third World Planning Review*, **19**(1), February: 21–50

Mitlin, D. (2003) 'Finance for shelter: Recent history, future perspectives' *Small Enterprise Development* **14**(1): 11–20

Mitlin, D. and A. Muller (2004) 'Windhoek, Namibia – towards progressive urban land policies in Southern Africa' *International Development Policy Review* **26**(2): 167–186

Mitlin, D. and S. Patel (2005) 'Reinterpreting the rights based approach – a grassroots perspective on rights and development', Paper presented at the Winners and Losers from Rights-based Approaches to Development, Manchester University, Manchester, UK, 21–22 February

Mitlin, D. and D. Satterthwaite (2004a) (eds) *Empowering Squatter Citizen*. Earthscan, London

Mitlin, D, and D, Satterthwaite (2004b) 'Introduction' in D. Mitlin and D. Satterthwaite (eds) *Empowering Squatter Citizen*. Earthscan, London: 3–24

Mohamed, S.-I. (1997) 'Tenants and tenure in Durban' *Environment and Urbanization* **9**(2): 101–118

Montgomery, M. R., Stren, R., Cohen, B. and Reed, H. E. (2004) *Cities Transformed: Demographic Changes and Its Implications in the Developing World*. Earthscan, London

Mosha, A. C. (2004) 'The challenges of city financing: The Botswana experience', Paper presented at the panel on Cities: Cross Roads of Culture, Inclusiveness and Integration in the Second World Urban Forum, Barcelona, Spain, 13–17 September 2004

Mosley, P. and D. Hulme (1998) 'Microenterprise finance: Is there a conflict between growth and poverty alleviation?' *World Development* **26**(5): 783–790

Moss, V. (2001) 'The state of housing finance in South Africa' *Housing Finance International*, **11**: 30–35

Moss, V. (2003) 'Understanding the reasons to the causes of defaults in the social housing sector of South Africa' *Housing Finance International* September: 20–26

Mukhija, V. (2004a) 'The contradictions in enabling private developers of affordable housing: A cautionary case from Ahmedabad, India' *Urban Studies* **41**(11): 2231–2244

Mukhija, V. (2004b) 'How is housing financed? The case of a group of tenants who became property developers in Mumbai, India' *International Development Planning Review* **26**(3): 287–304

Mulenga, C. (2003) *Responding to the Housing Problems of the Urban Poor in Zambia*. MA thesis, University of Manchester, Manchester, UK

Murcia de López, E. and L. Castillo (1997) 'El Salvador: A case of urban renovation and rehabilitation of *mesones*' *Environment and Urbanization* **9**(2): 161–179

Mutagwaba, H. C. (2002) 'The challenges of re-starting a market-based housing finance system in Tanzania: Constraints, lessons and the way forward' in UN-Habitat (ed)

Financing Adequate Shelter for All: Addressing the Housing Finance Problem in Development Countries. UN-Habitat, Nairobi: 83–92

Mutua, K., P. Nataradol, M. Otero and B. R. Chung (1996) 'The view from the field: Perspectives from managers of microfinance institutions' *Journal of International Development* **8**(2): 179–194

Napier, M., A. G. Tipple, N. Majija, R. Beän and K. Wall (2003) *Urban Sector Network Phase II Mid-term Evaluation Report: Global Report for the Period January 2000–December 2002. Mid-term Evaluation of Financing Agreement (SA/73200–99/20) between the European Union and the Urban Sector Network*. Council for Scientific and Industrial Research and University of Newcastle upon Tyne, Pretoria

National Academy of Science (2004) *Proceedings of the National Academy of Sciences*. National Academics Press, Washington, DC

National Research Council (2003) *Cities Transformed*. National Academy of Science Press, Washington, DC

Nell, M., R. Gordon and A. Bertoldi (2004) *Final Report: Findings, Conclusions and Implications. Workings of the Township Residential Property Market Project*. Rosebank, South Africa, Shisaka Development Management Services (Pty) Ltd. for FinMark Trust, Ford Foundation, Micro Finance Regulatory Council/ USAID, South African National Treasury and the National Housing Finance Corporation, South Africa

Ng'ayu, M. (2003) 'Integrated urban housing project (IUHP), Nakuru, Kenya: Project impact assessment', Paper presented to the International Workshop on Integrated Housing Development, Rugby, UK, 16–18 March 2003

Nozdrina, N. and G. Sternik (1999) 'Housing markets and migration in cities of Russia'. *Executive Reports* No 6, Moscow Carnegie Center, Moscow

Nuri Erbas, S. and F. E Nothaft (2002) 'Improving living standards and stimulating growth: A survey of MENA countries' *IMF Working Paper* No WP/02/17, International Monetary Fund, Washington, DC

ODPM (Office of the Deputy Prime Minister) (2003) 'The mortgage backed securities market in the UK: Overview and prospects' *Housing Research Summary* No 201, ODPM, London

OECD (Organisation for Economic Co-operation and Development) (1992) *Cities and New Technologies*. OECD, Paris

OECD (2002) *Reporting Directives for the Creditor Reporting System*, www.oecd.org/ dataoecd/16/53/ 1948102.pdf, accessed 14 March 2005

OECD (2003) *Ageing, Housing and Urban Development*. OECD, Paris

OECD (2004) 'Final ODA data for 2003', www.oecd.org/ dataoecd/19/52/ 34352584.pdf, accessed 9 March 2005

Ogu, V. I. and J. E. Ogbuozobe (2001) 'Housing policy in Nigeria: Towards enablement of private housing development' *Habitat International* **25**: 473–492

Oizumi, E. (2002) 'Housing provision and marketization in 1980s and 1990s Japan: A new stage of the affordability problem?' in G. Dymski and D. Isenberg (eds) *Seeking Shelter on the Pacific Rim: Financial Globalization, Social Change and the Housing Market*. M.E. Sharpe, London and New York

Okonkwo, O. (2002) 'Financing of housing for low and middle income groups in Africa: The role of government', Paper presented at the International Conference on Social Housing, United Nations Human Settlements Programme, Ministry of Construction of People's Republic of China and Baotou Municipal Government, Baotou, People's Republic of China

Okpala, D. (1994) 'Financing housing in developing countries: A review of the pitfalls and potentials in the development of formal housing finance systems' *Urban Studies* **31**(9): 1571–1586

Okwir, N. J. (2002) 'Lessons learnt so far from housing finance operations experiences in Uganda: What these experiences portend for the realisation of adequate shelter for all' in UN-Habitat (ed) *Financing Adequate Shelter for All: Addressing the Housing Finance Problem in Development Countries,* UN-Habitat, Nairobi: 93–98

Pacheco, M. F. (2003) 'Co-financed housing improvement program' SELAVIP *Journal of Low-income Housing in Asia and the World*, October: 40–44

Pardo, C. A. (2000) 'Housing finance in Chile: The experience in primary and secondary mortgage financing', *Sustainable Development Department Technical Papers Series*, Inter-American Development Bank, Washington, DC

Patel, S. and C. D'Cruz (1993) 'The *Mahila Milan* crisis credit scheme: From a seed to a tree' *Environment and Urbanization* **5**(1): 9–17

Patel, S., C. D'Cruz and S. Barra (2002) 'Beyond evictions in a global city: People-managed resettlement in Mumbai' *Environment and Urbanization* **14**(1): 159–172

Patel, S. and D. Mitlin (2004) 'Grassroots-driven development: The alliance of SPARC, the National Slum Dwellers Federation and *Mahila Milan*' in D. Mitlin and D. Satterthwaite (eds) *Empowering Squatter Citizen*. Earthscan, London: 216–244

Payne, G. and M. Majale (2004) *The Urban Housing Manual: Making Regulatory Frameworks Work for the Poor*. Earthscan, London

PDM (Programme de Développement Municipal) (1998) 'L'équilibre financier des collectivités locales', Observatoire des Finances Locales, Cotonou, Benin, 16p

PDM (1999a) 'Regard sur les finances locales dans les pays de l'UEMOA' Programme 1999, Cotonou, Benin, p19

PDM (1999b) 'L'équilibre financier des collectivités locales', mimeo,16p.

PDM (2000) 'L'équilibre' financier des collectivités locales, Observatoire des Finances Locales, Cotonou, 2000, p16

PDM (2001a) *Gérer l'économie localement en Afrique – Evaluation et prospective de l'économie locale*. Manuel, Tome 1, p64

PDM (2001b) 'Regard sur les économies locales, Une approche renouvelée sur les stratégies de développement en Afrique de l'ouest' *Les Cahiers du PDM*, No. 3 Avril

Pettis, M. (2001) *The Volatility Machine*. Oxford University Press, New York

Pickering, N. (2000), *The SOFOLES: Niche Lending or New Leaders in the Mexican Mortgage Market?* Joint Center for Housing Studies at the University of Harvard, Harvard, US

Pitt, M. and S. Khandker (1998) 'The impact of group-based credit programs on poor households in Bangladesh: Does the gender of participant matter?' *Journal of Political Economy* **106**(5): 958–995

Porio, E. (1998) *Reexamining Partnerships in Social Housing: State–Civil Society Dynamics in Southeast Asia*. Proceedings of the International Conference on the Occasion of the First General Assembly of the Forum of Research on Human Settlements, Geneva, 6–8 July, www.gruppo–cerfe.org /pdf/porio.pdf

Porio, E. with C. S. Crisol, N. F. Magno, D. Cid and E. N. Paul (2004) 'The Community Mortgage Programme: An innovative social housing programme in the Philippines and its outcomes' in D. Mitlin and D. Satterthwaite (eds) *Empowering Squatter Citizen*. Earthscan, London: 54–81

Priemus, H. and F. Dieleman (2002) 'Social housing policy in the European Union: Past, present and perspectives' *Urban Studies* **39**(2): 191–200

PRODEL (Programa de Desarollo Local) (2002) *Newsletter: Improving Livelihoods*, PRODEL, Managua

PRODEL (2004) *Newsletter* April, PRODEL, Managua

Proxenos, S. (2002) 'Homeownership rates: A global perspective' *Housing Finance International* **17**(December): 3–7

Prugl, E. (1996) 'Biases in labour law: A critique from the standpoint of home-based workers' in E. Boris and E. Prugl (eds) *Homeworkers in Global Perspective: Invisible No More*. Routledge, New York and London: 203–217

Pugh, C. (1994) 'Development of housing finance and the global strategy for shelter' *Cities* **11**(6): 384–392

Pugh, C. (1995) 'The role of the World Bank in housing' in B. C. Aldrich and R. S. Sandhu (eds) *Housing the Urban Poor: Policy and Practice in Developing Countries*. Zed Books, London

Pugh, C. (1997) 'Poverty and progress? Reflections on housing and urban policy in developing countries' *Urban Studies* **34**(10): 1547–1595

Pugh, C. (2001) 'The theory and practice of housing sector development for developing countries, 1950–1999' *Housing Studies* **16**(4): 399–423

Rahman, A. (1999) 'Micro-credit Initiatives for equitable and sustainable development: Who pays?' *World Development* **27**(1): 67–82

Rakodi, C. and T. Lloyd-Jones (eds) (2002) *Urban Livelihoods: A People-centred Approach to Reducing Poverty*. Earthscan, London

Ratha, D. (2003) *Workers' Remittances: An Important and Stable Source of External Development Finance*. World Bank, Washington, DC

Rees, W. (1992) 'Ecological footprints and appropriated carrying capacities: What urban economics leaves out' *Environment and Urbanization* **4**(2): 121–130

Renaud, B. (1984) 'Housing and financial instruments in developing countries: An overview', *World Bank Staff Working Papers No 658*, World Bank, Washington DC

Renaud, B. (1999) 'The financing of social housing in integrating financial markets: A view from developing countries' *Urban Studies* **36**(4): 755–773

Republic of South Africa (1996) *The Constitution of the Republic of South Africa*. Republic of South Africa, available at www.acts.co.za/ constitution/

Roberts, B. and M. A. Cohen (2002) 'Enhancing sustainable development by triple value adding to the core business of government' *Economic Development Quarterly* **16**(2): 127–137

Roberts, J. (2005) 'Millenium Development Goals: Are international targets now more credible?' *Journal of International Development* **17**(1): 113–129

Robinson, K. (2001) 'Big players jockey for position in microlending market' *The Banker* **151**(903): 80

Rodwin, L. and B. Sanyal (1987) 'Shelter, settlement and development: An overview' in L. Rodwin (ed) *Shelter, Settlement and Development*. Allen and Unwin, Boston

Rogaly, B. (1996) 'Micro-finance evangelism, "destitute women" and the hard selling of a new anti-poverty formula' *Development in Practice* **6**(2): 100–112

Rojas, E. (2004) 'Housing finance in Latin America', Presentation to the 25th World Congress, International Union for Housing Finance, Brussels, June

Rome, A (2001) *The Bulldozer in the Countryside: Suburban Sprawl and the Rise of American Environmentalism*. Cambridge University Press, New York

Rubenstein, J. (2002) 'Regional overview of Latin America' in UN-Habitat (ed) *Financing Adequate Shelter for All: Addressing the Housing Finance Problem in Development Countries*. UN-Habitat, Nairobi: 15–16, 141–146

Sahn, D. E. and D. C. Stifel (2003) 'Progress towards the Millennium Development Goals in Africa' *World Development* **31** (1): 23–53

Sánchez-Campos, T. (2004) *Revolving Fund for the Promotion of Small Hydro Electric Schemes: A Public Private Investment Model*, mimeo, ITDG, Los Angelos

Sassen, S. (2001) *The Global City*. Princeton University Press, Princeton

Sassen, S. (ed) (2002) *Global Networks, Linked Cities*. Routledge, for the United Nations University and Institute for Advanced Studies, New York

Satterthwaite, D. (2000) 'The roles of donors and developing agencies in combating poverty, inequity and polarization in a globalizing world', Background paper prepared for the 2001 Global Report on Human Settlements

Satterthwaite, D. (2004a) 'The Millennium Development Goals and poverty reduction' in D. Satterthwaite (ed) *The Millennium Development Goals and Local Processes: Hitting the Target or Missing the Point?* IIED, London

Satterthwaite, D. (2004b) 'The under-estimation of urban poverty in low and middle-income nations', *Poverty Reduction in Urban Areas Series Working Paper 14*, IIED, London

Scanlon, K. and C. Whitehead (2004) 'Cross country trends in tenure and finance' in European Mortgage Federation (ed) *Hypostat 2003: European Housing Finance Review*. European Mortgage Federation, Brussels: 14–20

Schlyter, A. (2003) 'Multi-habitation: Urban housing and everyday life in Chitungwiza, Zimbabwe', *Research Report No 123*, Nordiska Afrikainstitutet, Uppsala

Schumacher, E. F. (1973) *Small Is Beautiful: A Study of Economics as if People Mattered.* Harper and Row, New York

Seki. M. and M. Watanabe (1998) 'Housing finance and capital markets in Indonesia' in M. Watanabe (ed) *New Directions in Asian Housing Finance*. International Finance Corporation, Washington, DC: 113–126

SELAVIP (Servicio Latinamericano y Asiatico de Vivienda Popular) (2003) *Journal of Low-income Housing in Asia and the World*, October

SELAVIP (2004) 'The Gungano Fund reconsidered' *Journal of Low-income Housing in Asia and the World*, April: 129–134.

Septanti, D. (2004) 'Micro-credit system for housing finance in comprehensive KIP and social rehabilitation on slums area program in Surabaya', Paper prepared for an International Workshop on Housing Finance, ACHR/IIED/CODI, Bangkok, June

Serageldin, M. (1990) *The Impact of Investments in Urban Infrastructure on Municipal Revenues and the Integration of Informal Sector Activities*, report prepared for The Office of Housing and Urban Programs US Agency for International Development. Cambridge, MA

Serageldin, M. et al (2003a) 'Assessment of Participatory Budgeting in Brazil'. Paper prepared for the Inter-American Development Bank, Cambridge, MA

Serageldin, M. et al (2003b) 'Local Authority Driven Interventions and Processes'. Paper prepared for the UN Millennium Project Task Force 8 on Improving the Lives of Slum Dwellers, Cambridge, MA

Serageldin M. (team leader), Jones, D., Vigier, F. and Solloso, E. with the assistance of S. Bassett, B. Menon and L. Valenzuela (2004) *Municipal Finance Conditions and Trends.* Background paper for the 2005 Global Report. Center for Urban Development Studies. Harvard School of Design, Cambridge, MA

Shah, A. and T. Thompson (2004) *Implementing Decentralized Local Governance: A Treacherous Road with Potholes, Detours and Road Closures*. Policy Research Working Paper Series 3353, World Bank, Washington, DC

Sharma, N. (2005) 'British tech to help DJB stem huge losses', www.timesofindia.indiatimes.com/articleshow/990046.cms, accessed 14 February 2005

Shelter Afrique (2002) 'Housing finance operations in the Africa region: Lessons learnt and prospects for the realisation of the goal of adequate shelter for all' in UN-Habitat (ed) *Financing Adequate Shelter for All: Addressing the Housing Finance Problem in Development Countries*. UN-Habitat, Nairobi: 49–54

Shukla, V (1996) *Urbanization and Economic Growth.* Oxford University Press, New Delhi

Silas, J. (2004) 'Housing finance and the KIP model', Paper prepared for an International Workshop on Housing Finance, ACHR/IIED/CODI, Bangkok, June

Singh Maini, T. (2004) 'Tamil Nadu Urban Development Fund' *IADF Bulletin*, **1**(1), March: available at www.developmentfunds.org/news.htm

Skinner, R. J. and M. J. Rodell (1983) *People, Poverty and Shelter*. Methuen, London

Smets, P. (2002) *Housing Finance and the Urban Poor: Building and Financing Low-income Housing in Hyderabad, India*. Vrije University, India

Solis, E. and E. Ortiz (2002) 'Cities and social housing development and management: Successful models, Mexico City's housing policy – new focuses' in UN-Habitat (ed) *Financing Adequate Shelter for All: Addressing the Housing Finance Problem in Development Countries,* UN-Habitat, Nairobi: 155–164

Sood, R. (2003) 'A New Delhi slum resident works to improve her neighbourhood' *Habitat Debate*, **9**(1), April:14–15

Speak, S. and G. Tipple (2004) 'Housing and homelessness in developing countries' in D. Levinson (ed) *Encyclopedia of Homelessness*. Sage Publications, Thousand Oaks, California, and London: 270–277

Steffensen, J. and P. Tidemand (2004) *A Comparative Analysis of Decentralisation in Kenya, Tanzania and Uganda: Final Synthesis Report*. Report prepared for the World Bank, Washington, DC

Stein, A. (2004) 'Participation and sustainability in social projects: The experience of the Local Development Programme in Nicaragua' in D. Mitlin and D. Satterthwaite (eds) *Empowering Squatter Citizen*. Earthscan, London: 112–138

Stein, A. with L. Castillo (2005) 'Innovative financing for low-income housing improvement: Lessons from programmes in Central America, *Environment and Urbanization* **17**(1): 25–39

Stephens, M. (2002) 'International models of housing finance: Housing systems in Western and Transition Economies' in *Housing Finance in Transition Economies*. OECD, Paris: 175–182

Stephens, M. (2003) 'Globalisation and

housing finance systems in advanced and transition economies' *Urban Studies* **40**(5–6): 1011–1026

Stephens, M. (2004) *Housing Finance, 'Reach' and Access to Owner-Occupation in Western Europe*, mimeo, York

Struyk, R. (ed) (1997) *Restructuring Russia's Housing Sector: 1991–1997*. The Urban Institute, Washington, DC

Stuart, I., B. Badcock, A. Clapham and R. Fitzgerald (2004) 'Changing tenure: Housing trends, financial deregulation and housing policy in New Zealand since 1990' *Housing Finance International* June: 3–10

Suresh, V. (2002) 'Strategies for financing housing for low-income groups and the poor: Experiences from Asian countries' in UN-Habitat (ed) *Financing Adequate Shelter for All: Addressing the Housing Finance Problem in Development Countries*, UN-Habitat, Nairobi: 107–135

Susilastuti, D. H. (1996) 'Home-based work as a rural survival strategy: A central Javanese perspective' in E. Boris and E. Prugl (ed) *Homeworkers in Global Perspective: Invisible No More*. Routledge, New York and London: 129–141

Tacoli, C. (1998). 'Bridging the divide: Rural–urban interactions and livelihood strategies' *London, Gatekeeper Series, No 77*, IIED Sustainable Agriculture and Rural Livelihoods Programme, International Institute for Environment and Development, London

Taylor-Hayford, K. (2002) 'Funding mechanisms for low income housing in the United States of America', Paper presented at the International Conference on Social Housing, United Nations Human Settlements Programme, Ministry of Construction of People's Republic of China and Baotou Municipal Government, Baotou, People's Republic of China

Thorp, R., F. Stewart and A. Heyer (2005) 'When and how far is group formation a route out of chronic poverty?' *World Development* **33**(6): 907–920

Tipple, A. G. (1988) *The History and Practice of Rent Controls in Kumasi, Ghana*. World Bank, Washington, DC

Tipple, A. G. (1994) 'A matter of interface: The need for a shift in targeting housing interventions' *Habitat International* **18**(4): 1–15

Tipple, A. G. (1995) 'Dear Mr President, housing is good for development' *Norsk Geografisk Tidsschrift* **49**(4): 175–186

Tipple, A. G. (2000) *Extending Themselves: User Initiated Transformations of Government Built Housing in Developing Countries*. Liverpool University Press, Liverpool, UK

Tipple, A. G. (2005) 'The place of home-based enterprises in the informal sector: Evidence from Cochabamba, New Delhi, Surabaya and Pretoria' *Urban Studies* April: **42**(4): 1–15

Tipple, A. G. and D. Korboe (1998) 'Housing policy in Ghana: Towards a supply-oriented approach' *Habitat International* **22**(3): 245–257

Tipple, A. G., D. Korboe, G. Garrod and K. Willis (1999) 'Housing supply in Ghana: A study of Accra, Kumasi and Berekum' *Progress in Planning D* **51**: 324

Tipple, A. G. and K. G. Willis (1991) 'Tenure choice in a West African city' *Third World Planning Review* **13**(1): 27–45

Tjonneland, E. N., H. Harboe, A. M. Jerve and N. Kanji (1998) *The World Bank and Poverty in Sub-Saharan Africa: A Study of Operationalizing Policies for Poverty Reduction*. Chr Michelsen Institute in cooperation with CROP, Bergen

Tomlinson, M. R. (2001) 'New housing delivery model: The presidential job summit housing pilot project' *Housing Finance International* December: 24–29

Tucker, R. and M. Tomlinson (2000) *The Implications of Globalisation on Housing Finance for Low-income Households in South Africa*. Report prepared for UNCHS (Habitat), Nairobi

Turner, B. (ed) (1988) *Building Community: A Third World Casebook*. Habitat International Coalition, London

Turner, B. and C. Whitehead (2002) 'Reducing housing subsidy: International lessons from the experience of Sweden' in UN-Habitat (ed) *Financing Adequate Shelter for All: Addressing the Housing Finance Problem in Development Countries*, UN-Habitat, Nairobi: 171–189

Turner, J. F. C. (1967) 'Barriers and channels for housing development in modernizing countries' *Journal of the American Institute of Planners* May: 167–181

Turner, J. F. C. (1968) 'Housing priorities, settlement patterns and urban development in modernising countries' *Journal of the American Institute of Planners* November: 354–363

Turner, J. F. C. (1972) 'Housing issues and the standards problems' *Ekistics* **196**: 152–158

Turner, J. F. C. (1976) *Housing by People: Towards Autonomy in Building Environments. Ideas in Progress*. Marion Boyars, London

Turner, J. F. C. and R. Fichter (eds) (1972) *Freedom to Build*. Macmillan, London

UN (United Nations) (1948) *Universal Declaration of Human Rights*. United Nations, New York

UN (1966) *International Covenant on Economic, Social and Cultural Rights*. United Nations Committee on Economic, Social and Cultural Rights, General Assembly Resolution 2200A (XXI) of 16 December, New York

UN (1976) *Report of Habitat: United Nations Conference on Human Settlements*. United Nations, New York

UN (1987) *Realization of the Right to Adequate Housing: Resolution 42/146*. United Nations General Assembly, New York, 7 December.

UN (1992) *Rio Declaration*. United Nations Conference on Environment and Development (UNCED), Rio de Janeiro, Brazil, 3–14 June

UN (1993) *Vienna Declaration*. World Conference on Human Rights, Vienna, Austria, 14–25 June

UN (1995a) *Beijing Declaration*. Fourth World Conference on Women, Beijing, Peoples Republic of China, 4–15 September

UN (1995b) *Programme of Action of the World Summit on Social Development*. World Summit for Social Development, Copenhagen, Denmark, 6–12 March

UN (1996a) *Report of the United Nations Conference on Human Settlements (Habitat II)*. United Nations Sales publication, Sales No E.97.IV.6, New York

UN (1996b) *Habitat Agenda and Istanbul Declaration*. Second United Nations Conference on Human Settlements (Habitat II), Istanbul, Turkey, 3–14 June

UN (2000) *United Nations Millennium Declaration*. A/55/L.2 adopted at 55th session under agenda item 61(b) called 'The Millennium Assembly of the United Nations'

UN (2001a) *Durban Declaration on Racism, Racial Discrimination, Xenophobia and Related Intolerance*. World Conference against Racism, Racial Discrimination, Xenophobia and Related Intolerance, Durban, South Africa, 31 August–8 September

UN (2001b) *Declaration on Cities and Other Human Settlements in the New Millennium*, available at www.unhabitat.org/istanbul+5/declaration_cities.htm

UN (2002) *Financing for Development: Building on Monterey*. United Nations, New York

UN (United Nations) Millennium Project (2003) 'Background paper of the Task Force on Improving the Lives of Slum Dwellers', April 18

UN Millennium Project (2005a) *Task Force 8 Report: A Home in the City*. UNDP, New York

UN Millennium Project (2005b) *Investing in Development: A Practical Plan to Achieve the Millennium Development Goals. Overview*. UNDP, New York

UN Millennium Report (2000) *We the Peoples: The Role of the United Nations in the 21st Century*. Report of the Secretary-General of the United Nations, available at www.un.org/millennium/sg/report/

UN Population Division (2004) *World Urbanization Prospects: The 2003 Revision*. United Nations, New York

UNCED (United Nations Conference on Environment and Development) (1992) *Agenda 21*, 'Chapter 7: Promoting sustainable human settlement development'. UNCED, Rio de Janeiro, 14 June

UNCHS (United Nations Conference on Human Settlements) (1976) *The Vancouver Declaration on Human Settlements and the Vancouver Action Plan*. UNCHS (Habitat), Nairobi

UNCHS (1987) *Global Report on Human Settlements 1986*. Oxford University Press for UNCHS (Habitat), Oxford

UNCHS (1990a) *The Global Strategy for Shelter to the Year 2000*. UNCHS (Habitat), Nairobi

UNCHS (1990b) *Shelter for All: The Global Strategy for Shelter to the Year 2000*, UNCHS (Habitat), Nairobi

UNCHS (1993a) *Public/Private Partnerships in Enabling Shelter Strategies*. UNCHS (Habitat), Nairobi, www.hq.unhabitat.org/programmes/housing policy/publications.asp

UNCHS (1993b) *Shelter Sector Performance Indicators*. UNCHS (Habitat), Nairobi

UNCHS (1994) *Sustainable Human Settlements Development: Implementing Agenda 21*. Report prepared for the Commission on Sustainable Development, UNCHS (Habitat), Nairobi

UNCHS (1996) *An Urbanising World: Global Report on Human Settlements 1996*. Oxford University Press, Oxford

UNCHS (1997) *Shelter for All: The Potential of Housing Policy in the Implementation of the Habitat Agenda*, UNCHS (Habitat), Nairobi, www.unhabitat.org/programmes/housing policy/publications.asp

UNCHS (1998a) *Implementation of the Habitat Agenda: Guidelines for the United Nations Resident Coordinator System*. UNCHS (Habitat), Nairobi, www.unchs.org/unchs/english/hagenda/guide1/contents.htm

UNCHS (1998b) *Financing Cities for Sustainable Development: With Specific Reference to East Africa*. UNCHS, Nairobi

UNCHS (2001) *Cities in a Globalising World: Global Report on Human Settlements, 2001*. UNHCS/Earthscan, London

UNCHS/ILO (International Labour Organization) (1995) *Shelter Provision and Employment Generation*. United Nations Centre for Human Settlements (Habitat), Nairobi; International Labour Office, Geneva

UNCTAD (United Nations Conference on Trade and Development) (2003) *Trade and Development Report*. United Nations, New York and Geneva

UNCTAD (2004) *Trade and Development Report*. United Nations, New York and Geneva

UNDP (United Nations Development Programme) (1991) *Cities, Poverty and People: Urban Development Cooperation for the 1990s*. UNDP, New York

UNDP (2004) *Human Development Report*. UNDP/Oxford University Press, New York

UNDP (undated) *Global Learning Network*, www.undp.org/pppue/gln/, accessed on 11 December 2004

UN-Habitat (2002) *Housing Rights Legislation: Review of International and National Legal Instruments*. UN-Habitat and Office of the High Commissioner for Human Rights, Nairobi

UN-Habitat (2003a) *The Challenge of Slums: Global Report on Human Settlements*. Earthscan/UN-Habitat, London

UN-Habitat (2003b) *Slums of the World: The Face of Urban Poverty in the New Millennium*. UN-Habitat, Nairobi

UN-Habitat (2003c) *Rental Housing: An Essential Option for the Urban Poor in Developing Countries*. UN-Habitat, Nairobi

UN-Habitat (2004) *State of the World's Cities: Globalization and Urban Culture*. Earthscan/UN-Habitat, London

United Nations Handbook 2003 (2003) New Zealand Ministry of Foreign Affairs and Trade, Wellington

USAID (US Agency for International Development) (1996) *The Housing Indicators Program: Regional Housing Indicators Database in the Transitional Countries of Central and Eastern Europe*. USAID, Washington, DC

Van der Rest, J. (2003) 'The poor first dwell, then build' *SELAVIP Newsletter, Journal of Low-income Housing in Asia and the World*, **10**: 5–8

Van Order, R. (2001) 'The structure and evolution of American secondary mortgage markets, with some implications for developing markets' *Housing Finance International* September: 16–31

Van Rooyan, O. (2004) *The Kuyasa Fund*, mimeo

Vance, I. (2004) 'Land and collateral issues: The asset dimension of housing micro-finance' in F. Daphnis and B. Ferguson (eds) *Housing Micro-finance: A Guide to Practice*. Kumarian Press Ltd., Bloomfield, US: 123–150

Wahba, S. (2001) 'From land redistribution to integrated development: The evolution and impact of shelter and poverty alleviation strategies in marginalized settlements in Nouakchott, Mauritania', Paper presented to the Third Annual Global Development Network Conference, Brazil 9–12 December

Ward, P. M. (ed) (1982) *Self–help Housing: a Critique*. Mansell, London

Watanabe, M. (ed) (1998) *New Directions in Asian Housing Finance*. International Finance Corporation, Washington, DC

WCED (World Commission on Environment and Development) (1987) *Our Common Future*. Oxford University Press, Oxford

Weru, J. (2004) 'Community federations and city upgrading: The work of Pamoja Trust and Muungano in Kenya' *Environment and Urbanization* **16**(1): 47–62

Whitehead, C. M. E. (2003) 'Financing social housing in Europe' *Housing Finance International* June: 3–8

Whittington, D., D. T. Lauria and X. Mu (1990) *Paying for Urban Services: A Study of Water Vending and Willingness to Pay for Water in Onitsha, Nigeria*. World Bank, Washington, DC

Williams, P. (2004) 'The challenges of affordable housing' in *Introducing the Issues: 16 Expert Views*. Presented at International Union of Housing Finance 25th World Congress, June 2004: 20–21

Willis, K. G. and A. G. Tipple (1991) 'Economics of multihabitation: Housing conditions, household occupancy and household structure under rent control, inflation and nonmarketability of ownership rights' *World Development* **19**(12): 1705–1720

World Bank (1980) *Shelter, Poverty and Basic Needs*. World Bank, Washington, DC

World Bank (1983) *Learning by Doing*. World Bank, Washington, DC

World Bank (1989) *Financial Systems and Development*. Oxford University Press for the World Bank, Oxford

World Bank (1991) *Urban Policy and Economic Development: An Agenda for the 1990s*. World Bank, Washington, DC

World Bank (1992) *World Development Report*. Oxford University Press, New York

World Bank (1993) *Housing: Enabling Markets to Work.* World Bank Policy Paper, World Bank, Washington, DC

World Bank (1994) *World Development Report*. Oxford University Press, New York

World Bank (1999) 'New study confirms benefits of Bangladesh's microcredit programs', www.worldbank.org/html/extdr/extme/2063.htm, accessed on 2 May 2002

World Bank (2003a) *Sub-Sovereign Credit Access and Infrastructure Financing In Four East Asian Countries: China, Philippines, Indonesia, and Vietnam – Phase One: A Reconnaissance*. World Bank, Washington, DC

World Bank (2003b) 'Tamil Nadu Urban Development Fund (TNUDF)', Power point presentation graciously contributed by program officers, March 2003

World Bank (2004a) *IBRD Program Document for a Proposed Programmatic Loan to the Amount of US$100 Million to the United Mexican States for Affordable Housing and Urban Poverty Sector Adjustment Loan*, Report no 27627–MX. World Bank, Washington, DC

World Bank (2004b) *Project Information Document, Concept Stage – Pakistan Housing Finance Project*. World Bank, Washington, DC

World Bank (2004c) 'Total GDP 2003', www.worldbank.org/data/databytopic/GDP.pdf, accessed 8 March 2005

World Bank (2004d) *Concept Memoranda (CM) Proposed Repeater Project, Third Tamil Nadu Urban Development Project (TNUDP III)*. World Bank, Washington, DC, 7 May 2004

World Bank (2004e) *World Development Indicators 2004.* World Bank, Washington, DC

World Bank (2005) *Global Economic Prospects 2005*. World Bank, Washington, DC

Yasui, T. (2002a) 'Summary of the meeting' in *Housing Finance in Transition Economies*. OECD, Paris: 7–16

Yasui, T. (2002b) 'Housing finance in transition economies' in *Housing Finance in Transition Economies*, OECD, Paris: 17–36

Yunus, M. (1997) 'The Grameen Bank story: Rural credit in Bangladesh' in A. Krishna, N. Uphoff and M. J. Esman (ed) *Reasons for Hope: Instructive Experiences in Rural Development.* Kumarian Press, London: 9–24

Zaltzman, M. (2003) 'Mexican mortgage market – access to housing' *Housing Finance International* December: 21–24

Zaman, H. (2004) 'The scaling up of micro-finance in Bangladesh: Determinants, impacts and lessons', *World Bank Policy Research Working Paper 3398*, World Bank, Washington, DC

Zehnder, A. (2004) 'Savings mobilization through contractual savings schemes for housing' in *Introducing the Issues: 16 Expert Views*. Presented at International Union of Housing Finance 25th World Congress, June 2004: 30–31

Zhao, Y. and S. C. Bourassa (2003) 'China's urban housing reform: recent achievements and new inequities' *Housing Studies* **10**(5): 721–744

INDEX

Note: Prefix letters before page numbers 186 to 227 refer to detailed tables in the Statistical Annex.